Language and Culture in Eighteenth-Century Russia

Studies in Russian and Slavic Literatures,
Cultures and History

Series Editor — *Lazar Fleishman* (Stanford University)

Victor Zhivov

Language and Culture in Eighteenth-Century Russia

Boston

2009

Library of Congress Cataloging-in-Publication Data

Zhivov, V. M.

[IAzyk i kul'tura v Rossii XVIII veka. English]
Language and culture in eighteenth-century Russia / by Victor Zhivov; translated by Marcus Levitt.
    p. cm. — (Studies in Russian and Slavic literatures, cultures and history)
Includes bibliographical references and index.

ISBN 978-1-61811-807-3

   1. Russian language—18th century—History. 2. Russia—Civilization—18th century. 3. Russian language—Style. 4. Language and culture—Russia—History—18th century. I. Levitt, Marcus C., 1954 — II. Title. III. Title: Language and culture in 18th century Russia.

PG2075.Z4813 2009

491.709'033—dc22

    2009020250

The book is supported by Mikhail Prokhorov Foundation (translation program TRANSCRIPT).

Copyright © 2009 Academic Studies Press

Cover design by Samuel Volchek

Published by Academic Studies Press
28 Montfern Avenue
Brighton, MA 02135, USA
www.academicstudiespress.com

Translator's Introduction

Victor Zhivov's magisterial *Language and Culture in Eighteenth-Century Russia* tells the story of what was arguably Russia's most important and long-lasting achievement of the century, on a par with its extraordinary military successes, territorial expansion, development of the arts or reorganization of the state mechanism into a modern empire. In the eighteenth century, Russia created a new vernacular Russian literary language, the primary vehicle for Russia's modernization and entry into the Western European cultural sphere that also made possible her extraordinary literary outpouring of creativity in the following century. With remarkable clarity, Zhivov demonstrates how during this period "the establishment of the new type of literary language continually intersected with struggles between tradition and reform, secular versus religious culture, western orientation versus indigenous traditions. This imparted an especially intense semiotic significance to the history of the literary language .., [permitting] us to glimpse the dynamics of the most important social and cultural processes through the prism of linguistic development, as the problem of power in language was invested in exceedingly concrete forms, down to polemics over particular morphological indicators." As Zhivov shows, the uniqueness of this process—its "especially intense semiotic significance" — makes the history of the literary language not only of technical interest for linguists but a chronicle of the most vital cultural, social, and political concerns of the era. It offers a fundamentally new perspective on the development of eighteenth and early nineteenth-century Russian culture, as well as precise way of defining the progressive stages of its development—far more cogent and convincing than, for example, attempts to describe it by political reigns or by period labels such as the Baroque, Classicism and Sentimentalism.

Language and Culture is remarkable both for its methodology and for the many ways in which it revises our understanding of eighteenth century culture. In this short introduction I can only point to a few of those things that I consider important, although no doubt historians, linguists, and other students of literary, religious, and cultural life will find many other challenging issues raised by the author's rich study. The most obvious methodological strength of the book is the way it brings together linguistic and cultural analysis, based on a thorough consideration of how Western European linguistic theory was applied to the very different linguistic situation in Russia. In particular, Zhivov considers Claude Favre de Vaugelas' (1585–1650) doctrine of linguistic "purism," the starting point for ideas about language throughout the early modern world. As Zhivov emphasizes, this process of cultural transplantation and application was "an experiment in accommodation and invention that was full of creative potential and unexpected, sometimes contradictory, meanings." Part of the challenge in deciphering these meanings comes from the fact the very same terms and concepts (e.g., the things that qualified as "pure" or "impure" usage) took on far different valence when applied to Russian linguistic material. Just as today, when terms like "democracy," "capitalism," and political "right" and "left" take on almost unrecognizable contours when used in the post-Soviet Russian context, it requires an intimate knowledge of both the donor culture and the soil into which the transplantation occurs to uncover the genuine, deeper significance of the cultural processes taking place.

Language and Culture thus offers a brilliant example of the methodology of the Tartu-Moscow semiotic school, offering a new reading of the complex transition to a "modern" literary language of a new type. Zhivov revises the work of his predecessors (foremost of whom include Viktor Vinogradov, Iurii Lotman and Boris Uspenskii) in various ways,[1] from his overarching insistence on a functional approach to linguistic change to his rejection of the notion of Church Slavonic — Russian "diglossia" (the dualism between the "church language" and the "language of daily life," a linguistic situation he prefers to describe in terms of the various "registers" of the written language). Zhivov convincingly refutes traditional attempts to differentiate "Church Slavonic" from "Russian" on purely genetic grounds, demonstrating how these categories have significantly changed from period to period, rendering genetic classifications anachronistic and essentially meaningless. Rather, as he argues, one must understand how the linguistic consciousness of the specific historical moment defines the linguistic elements in question. The very tradition he examines and defines — including what

---

[1] On his revision of Vinogradov, see also V. M. Zhivov, "Literaturnyi iazyk i iazyk literatury v Rossii XVIII veka," *Russian Literature*, 52 (2002), Special Issue on Eighteenth Century Russian Literature, 1–53.

he calls the "Slaveno-Russian" linguistic synthesis — illustrates the radical relativism of defining not only particular linguistic elements as "Russian" or "Slavonic" but of the character of the language itself (e.g., Russian perceived as sharply opposed to Slavonic, as in the Petrine era, versus "Russian" as a synthesis — "of a single nature" — with Slavonic, as seen at mid-century).

Furthermore, the late seventeenth-century and Petrine Russian cultural soil that was to receive transplanted French linguistic doctrine emerges in Zhivov's account not as barren ground of decay and disorder (one of the retrospective myths fostered by Peter's cultural revolution) but as a field of creative experimentation, of attempts (by such writers as Simeon Polotskii and Feofan Prokopovich) to modernize the language by "Russifying" Slavonic (a formation Zhivov defines as "hybrid Slavonic"). Peter the Great's subsequent wholesale rejection of Slavonic as *Old Church* Slavonic" (i.e., an outdated clerical language unfit for modern communication) demanded a new literary language in the vulgar tongue. However, given the fact that no viable tradition of written Russian existed that could serve as a model, in many respects this new language had to be created *ex nihilo,* in a virtual vacuum, so that it was perhaps inevitable that (to borrow Boris Unbegaun's formula) "Russified Slavonic" by mid-century came to be replaced by "Slavonicized Russian." That is, the earlier literary tradition made itself felt willy nilly, despite contemporaries' explicit assertions to the contrary. The contradiction between purist theory and literary practice (purist strictures had no linguistic material to which they could be applied!) led to what Zhivov describes as a new "Slaveno-Russian synthesis" that defined mid-century Russian language and culture. The final declaration of a literary language in the vulgar tongue did not come until the end of the century as Karamzin rejected the earlier "slavonicization" and oriented the literary language on modern European vernaculars (especially French), although as Zhivov rightly shows, both Karamzin's "innovators" and Shishkov's "archaists" (those who defended the "Slaveno-Russian" legacy) functioned within the very same framework of linguistic purism that had been assimilated with the Petrine reforms.

As is well known, the rejection of the eighteenth-century cultural tradition was particularly vehement in later Russia, first by the "Karamzinian reform," and even more definitively by the subsequent Decembrist generation. Zhivov's notion of the "Slaveno-Russian cultural synthesis" resurrects a central formation of eighteenth-century culture that was at the center of the first flowerings of modern Russian literature from Lomonosov, Trediakovskii and Sumarokov to Fonvizin, Radishchev and Derzhavin. This new cultural formation that in linguistic terms represented a synthesis of Slavonic and Russian also signaled a validation of "church books" and the

Orthodox literary tradition (albeit within certain limits), a reversal of the sharp Petrine distinction between the "secular" and "religious." Among other things, *Language and Culture* reintegrates the contribution of religious writing (dukhovnaia literatura) into Russian linguistic and literary history, a tradition that has been totally ignored (not even acknowledged) in our received view of modern Russian literature. In particular, Zhivov traces the history of the sermon, revived as a genre in the later seventeenth century, and often written in hybrid Slavonic, to its adoption of "Slaveno-Russian" by Russian Enlightenment clergymen, and to the subsequent defense of this linguistic tradition in the first half of the nineteenth century, which he sees as the last echo of eighteenth-century linguistic and cultural debates.

The development of the literary language as described in *Language and Culture* has important ramifications for our understanding of Russia's entry into the modern European orbit and of the special nature of her "early modern" national consciousness. As opposed to other nations on what Martin Malia has described as the "West-East cultural gradient" that characterized eighteenth-century Europe, Russia, as the farthest eastern point on the Enlightenment spectrum,[2] retained certain political and cultural features of a pre-modern system. Zhivov's study fully validates Harvey Goldblatt's revisionist suggestion that the Petrine revolution signaled not the rejection but "the survival and resystematization of the Orthodox Slavic tradition..., a premodern type of supranational spiritual solidarity... based on the common Orthodox Slavic heritage" (which Goldblatt also relates to the "language question," suggesting that linguistic self-definition in the Slavic world offers a paradigm for the development of national consciousness).[3] The eighteenth-century tradition, in these terms, represents an attempt to synthesize modern Enlightenment culture with the older religious and linguistic heritage, with the real break in continuity (the segregation of religious and secular traditions, both cultural and linguistic) actually coming in the first half of the nineteenth-century.

However we see this, a basic challenge that *Language and Culture in Eighteenth-Century Russia* poses is to reintegrate (or, to better integrate) the eighteenth-century tradition into Russian cultural history as a whole, which all too often is seen as beginning *ab ovo* from Pushkin. It is fully obvious that

---

[2] Martin Malia, *Russia Under Western Eyes: From the Bronze Horseman to the Lenin Mausoleum* (Cambridge, MA : The Belknap Press of Harvard University Press, 1999), chap. 1.
[3] Harvey Goldblatt, "Orthodox Slavic Heritage and National Consciousness: Aspects of theEast Slavic and South Slavic National Revivals," *Harvard Ukrainian Studies* 10, nos. 3–4 (December 1986): 347and 353.

the unique nature of the "classics" of Russian culture, starting with Pushkin,[4] as well as subsequent Russian history and culture as a whole, with its crises and discontinuities, were profoundly shaped by the earlier, formative period that Zhivov's study brilliantly illuminates.

* * *

My thanks to those who provided help and advice at various stages of this translation, especially to Irina Luchko, Lada Panova, Lev Berdnikov, Thomas Seifrid, Alik Zholkovsky, and Pani Norindr; and to the College of Letters of Arts and Letters at the University of Southern California, who aided in this publication with a subvention. Thanks also to Igor Nemirovsky who made this publication possible. And of course, it could never have come to pass at all without the generous help and support of Victor Markovich himself.

* * *

Note on the Text

The translation that follows is aimed at as general an audience as possible. The Library of Congress transliteration system has been followed. Limited cuts have been made in the text, mostly in illustrative examples and extended linguistic analysis (it is assumed that linguists will want to consult the Russian text); all deletions are marked by an ellipsis surrounded by square brackets ([…]). References within the text refer to the Introduction (§ 0) and chapters 1–4 (§ 1, §2, etc.) followed by section and subsection (thus § 2–2.1 refers to Chapter 2, section 2, subsection 1).

M. Levitt
Los Angeles

---

[4] In recent years have increasingly come to connect Pushkin's art with the eighteenth-century tradition. See, for example, B.M. Gasparov, *Poeticheskii iazyk Pushkina kak fakt istorii russkogo literaturnogo iazyka*. Wiener slawistischer Alamanch, Sonderband 27 (Vienna: Gesellschaft zur Föderung slawistischer Studien, 1992); Iu. V. Stennik, *Pushkin i russkaia literatura XVIII veka* (Saint Petersburg: Nauka, 1995); David M. Bethea, *Realizing Metaphors: Alexander Pushkin and the Life of the Poet* (Madison: University of Wisconsin Press, 1998); Andrew Kahn, *Pushkin's Lyric Intelligence* (New York: Oxford University Press, 2008). As Zhivov's study itself indicates (§ 4–1.1), Pushkin's mature linguistic position both incorporates the "Slavonic" and "Russian" heritages and transcends them, in the sense that genetic requirements give way to generic and stylistic ones.

Preface to the English Edition

Of course, the title of this book — "Language and Culture" — describes its subject. However, if I were to try to formulate its main theme, by which I connect the history of language and of culture in eighteenth century Russia, it could be described as "language and power." From this point of view language is not merely a system of signs that makes communication possible but an instrument of human ambitions, desires and passions. I would actually assert that language is not even a single instrument, but a set of instruments that conform to the various situations in which it is used; the nature of these situations is changeable and defines the most vital cultural parameters.

For example, there were scarcely any spoken sermons in Russia before the second half of the seventeenth century. When sermons began to be given, a particular communicative space was formed whose characteristics were defined by the authoritative task that the sermon set itself. Sermons were delivered by the educated clergy, and their very nature, including their language, asserted the power of education over tradition; Baroque erudition claimed the right to interpret Holy Writ and thus to determine who of the Orthodox flock believed correctly and who was a heretic and should be driven from the church. Both the syntax and vocabulary of the sermon bear the stamp of this task and it is appropriate to study them primarily from this perspective rather than from that of some abstract semiotic system. More than a century later the sentimental tale, so different in appearance from the sermon, in essence realized the very same mechanism: in writing "Poor Liza" Karamzin not only introduced a new discursive practice but positioned himself as master of sentiment and mentor of emotional experience.

Language, as they said in the Age of Enlightenment, was determined by a people's customs and mores. As these changed, so too did language, and vice versa: changing the language led to changes in manners. It wasn't clear which came first, but it was perfectly apparent that they were interconnected, and Russia, like other countries, had no dearth of historical figures who strove to make use of this interconnection for their own ends. In periods of change such attempts are particularly common and intensive. In this book this kind of cultural and political effort is evident with particular clarity in Peter the Great's reforms. Peter loved to do everything himself, from building ships to pulling the teeth of his subordinates. He himself also gave orders about changes to the language, created the new civil script, made demands on the language of translations, and in general, wanted to create a new literary language for everyday use. His heirs did not attempt such an all-embracing task themselves, although this merely meant that the relationship between the literary language and politics became more mediated. The imperial court had its agents in the sphere of linguistic politics (such as Mikhail Lomonosov), and their choices represented the tastes and preferences of the ruling elite. Like imperial architectural projects, the construction of a new literary language demanded powerful support for its realization.

The Russian eighteenth century was a time of Europeanization and modernization. Starting with Peter, Russian monarchs strove to make Russia a European power, to transfer Europe to the banks of the Neva, so to speak. This newly created Europe was not very similar to the original, but this merely increased the importance of the very process of recreation, which, given the dissimilarity to the original, became an experiment in accommodation and invention that was full of creative potential and unexpected, sometimes contradictory, meanings. Until almost the end of the century the monarchy was the supreme authority that guided this process of recreating Europe, which even in this case could pursue different, competing projects and ends. It was the monarch who decided how much of the European and how much of the Russian was to constitute the "Russian European," and the dominating formula changed from reign to reign and from decade to decade.

Thus in Catherine the Great's journal *Odds and Ends* (*Vsiakaia vsiachina*) in 1769 there was a debate over the relative value of French (i.e., European) versus Russian (i.e., traditional) clothing, and a rather vague compromise was suggested as something desirable: "It is incontestable that Russian dress is more compatible with our cold climate; but that any long clothing decreases one's maneuverability and ability to move quickly is also incontestable. But if we add a caftan to French dress, which it lacks, and subtract from Russian what is excessive, could we not come up with clothing that is compatible with the climate as well as with common sense?"[1]

---

[1] *Vsiakaia vsiachina*, 1769, p. 203. Mention of the climate is not accidental. The issue is not only about common sense, but refers to the currently fashionable European discussions of

This Catherinean program, proposing a union of European and Russian, was polemically directed against the Petrine project (Peter, as is well known, made Russian nobles reject their own clothing for "German" dress), and represented a symbolic rejection of Peter's radical violation of national traditions, offering instead a new conceptualization of the national past.

Competing projects of cultural importation defined both the development of the language and of literature. Characteristically, for example, the fashion of using borrowed foreign words that dominated in the Petrine period and gave the language social and cultural prestige was replaced in a few decades by "purist" moderation in using this kind of language. The mockery of the language of "petimetry" (from the French, "petits-maîtres," dandies) that began in Elizabeth's reign (e.g., by Elagin and Sumarokov) and continued in the age of Catherine by Novikov, Fonvizin and many of their contemporaries, did not mean, of course, that an orientation toward the West (first of all, France) was being rejected, but indicated the limits that were to be observed in reshaping oneself into a Frenchman. In debates over "foppish language" the issue was thrashed out concerning how to accommodate Europeanism and still preserve national identity.

Just such instances of rethinking the materials of language became part of the field of cultural and political contention that shaped the development of the Russian literary language, to which this book is dedicated. Naturally, in order to appreciate the specific nature of what was happening in Russia, it is necessary to understand the European background (first of all the French); only by comparison do the peculiarities of the Russian reception of European literary and linguistic practices stand out in relief. Therefore, I have paid significant attention to the French models on which Russian Europeans could orient themselves. It seems to me that work with linguistic materials may be extremely productive insofar as the historical practices that are reflected in language may be determined with much greater precision than ideological or literary processes. One might say that language limits the arbitrariness of interpretation, setting limitations for the researcher that are so sorely needed in this heyday of postmodern voluntarism.

The Russian edition of this book came out more than ten years ago. However, having finished it, I did not cease working on either problems of the literary language or on the Russian eighteenth century. Insofar as I

---

the Russian national character in whose formation climate was held to be a defining factor. See the interesting recent work by Ingrid Shirle, "Uchenie o dukhe i kharaktere narodov v russkoi kul'ture XVIII v." in *"Vvodia nravy i obychai Evropeiskie v Evropeiskom narode": K probleme adaptatsii zapadnykh idei i praktik v Rossiiskoi imperii*, ed. A.V. Doronin (Moscow: ROSSPEN, 2008), 119–137.

have continued to consider various issues touched on in the book, I could have added to or altered what I had written earlier. However, it would be regrettable to have my own books become inseparable life companions, as I would prefer to write new things rather than rewrite old ones. For this reason, here I will stand by the principle "What I have written I have written." Nevertheless, I will note two issues that would have marked a "revised and expanded" version.

This book is dedicated to the formation of the Russian literary language. "Literary language" is understood (according to the definitions of the Prague linguistic circle) as an idiom possessing polyfunctionalism, general acceptance, codification and stylistic differentiation. This is the definition followed in this book, and it determined the interpretation of the main processes that are analyzed: the history of codification, how the need for a polyfunctional linguistic standard came to be realized, and how that standard was modified to meet the needs of the situation (the formation of the "Slavenorossiiskii" language). It seems to me now that this history lacks an institutional component whose theoretical importance I have tried to outline in another recent study.[2]

If one is to write a history of the literary language as the history of its basic features (listed above), then a necessary component must also be a history of the institutions that guarantee the integrity of these features. This I have partially done for the first half of the eighteenth century, when I describe the Academy codification of the Russian language. Right up until the 1760's the Academy of Sciences itself was the institution responsible for codifying the literary standard and for guaranteeing (or rather, for wanting to guarantee) the general acceptance of the standard they were codifying. The basis for this assertion is the fact that until the end of the 1750's the Academy ran the single typography publishing books in civil type. Hence the norms that were applied in Academy publications were established as the standard for the language in this period.

The situation changed in Catherine II's reign as the reading public expanded and the book market became more diverse. In this period, the general acceptance of the standard that had been introduced and the value of the Academic prescriptions were called into question and aristocratic literary men like A. P. Sumarokov began to express skepticism toward Academic prescriptions. At this time the norms of the literary language were being developed not so much as a reaction against Academic regularization as

---

[2] V. M. Zhivov, "Literaturnyi iazyk i iazyk literatury v Rossii XVIII veka," *Russian Literature*, 52 (2002), Special Issue on Eighteenth Century Russian Literature, 1–53.

much as at the expense of literary practice, which for all its diversity was nevertheless working out certain practices for public written speech. This change and its social parameters deserve more attention than that given in this book.

The establishment of popular schools (narodnye uchilishcha) in the 1780's, when the Russian language became part of public education, had primary importance for establishing a literary standard and realizing its general acceptance. From this time the ability to write in Russian as part of elementary school education came to characterize the majority of the literate population. Obviously, after this the general acceptance of the language was ensured by the institutions of elementary education. To trace how this worked is not always easy, but one may point to specific indicators. For example, I have studied the language of the sermons by the Moscow Metropolitan Platon Levshin, published over many years (from 1779 to 1806) and making up twenty volumes. Going from volume to volume, one may clearly observe the gradual transition from a specific type of religious language (analyzed in detail in this book) to a more generally accepted linguistic standard. This generally accepted standard, connected to the school reform, undoubtedly played no small role here.

Unfortunately, the influence of the school on the development of the literary language is virtually unstudied, and this important issue is hardly touched upon in this book. At the same time, it seems to me that many of the issues involved in the dynamic working out of the linguistic standard could be significantly clarified if we had more information about the social parameters of elementary education, about the principles for creating textbooks and readers, and about the choice of examples from "classic" authors used in grammar and spelling exercises. When the native tongue is taught, model authors are those who have made their way into textbooks and passages from which are used in exercises and reproduced in expositions and dictations. It seems to me that is precisely through this means that literary syntax — very poorly described in school grammars and at the same time radically different from spoken speech—is established. It would be worth considering whether Pushkin's role as creator of the Russian literary language grew out of such textbooks and readers. I hope that some future researcher will take up this set of issues.

A more particular question that it seems to me I could now present with greater fullness and clarity than in the book is that of the "simple language" of the Petrine era. I continue to hold that this language was formed by eliminating markers of bookishness from the traditional written language. However, study of the morphology of texts from that time has led me to the idea that the composition of the simple language, shorn of markers of bookishness, could vary according to the writing habits of authors of different texts.[3] These writing habits could derive from various written traditions (which in the book I refer to as "registers"), for example, the hybrid register or that of business or everyday writing. This explains the variety of texts in the simple language, which brought together what earlier had been dispersed among different registers of the written language. This chaotic development I call the "Petrine pool" and suggest that its lack of correspondence to European notions of a refined language was a fundamental stimulus to the normalizing activity that began in the Academy in the late 1720's. While this notion is not crucial, it would bring more precision to the picture proposed in the book and permit us to explain a series of phenomena connected to the history of the linguistic standard (for example, the elimination of non-bookish syntactic constructions, similar to those in contemporary spoken Russian) which did not make their way into it.

In conclusion, I wish to thank my colleague and friend Marcus Levitt, who took on the none too easy task of translating this book, and to the publisher Igor Nemirovsky, who has graciously agreed to see it into print.

Victor Zhivov

Moscow
December, 2008

---

[3] See my book *Ocherki istoricheskoi morfologii russkogo iazyka XVII–XVIII vekov* (Moscow: Iazyki slavianskoi kul'tury, 2004).

Contents

Translator's Introduction..v
Preface to the English Edition..x

Introduction. Problems in the Prehistory of the New Type of Russian Literary Language..1

  1. The Literary Language of the New Type as an Object of
     Social and Cultural History..1
  2. The Functional Reconceptualization of Genetically Heterogeneous
     Elements in the History of Russian Writing..7
  3. The Main Registers of the Bookish Language and the
     Processes of Their Formation..16
  4. The Reconceptualization of the Varieties of the Bookish Language.........25
  5. Linguistic "Simplicity" and the Means of its Realization 34
  6. The Secularization of Culture, Its Specifics in Russia, and
     Its Significance for Rethinking Linguistic Usage....................................41

Chapter 1. The Petrine Language Reform; The Linguistic and Cultural Situation of the Petrine Era...49

  1. Tasks of the Language Reform and the Nature of its Realization............49
     1.1 The Reform of the Alphabet as the Prototype of Language Reform....53
     1.2 Petrine Linguistic Directives...65
     1.3 From Hybrid Church Slavonic to the "Simple" Russian Language.....73
     1.4 Innovation and Continuity in the New Literary Language..................83

  2. Language Policy and the Conflict of Cultures...94
     2.1 Language Reform and Political-Ecclesiastical Conflicts.....................95
     2.2 "Simplicity" and the Semiotic Functions of Civil Speech.................108

Chapter 2. The Start of Normalization of the New Literary Language; The Formulation of Linguistic Theories and Literary Practice.................118

  1. The Formation of Petersburg Culture and the New Conception of
     the Literary Language..118
     1.1 The Linguistic Program of the First Codifiers: New Issues..............124
     1.2 Classicist Purism and Its Initial Reception..132
     1.3 The Actualization of Genetic Parameters: Slavonicisms..................143
     1.4 Normalization in Morphology and the Use of Genetic Parameters...153

2. The Conflict Between Linguistic Theory and Actual Practice;
   The Concept of a Poetic Language..167
   2.1 Poetic License and the Church Slavonic Literary and
   Linguistic Tradition...171
   2.2 The Language of the Ode and Church Slavonic Panegyric Poetry............189

**Chapter 3. The Changed Conception of the Literary Language;
The "Slavenorossiiskii Language" and the Synthesis of Cultural and
Linguistic Traditions**..210

  1. The New Nature of the Russian Literary Language and the Emergence of
     Slavonicizing Purism..210
     1.1 The Polyfunctionism of the New Literary Language...............215
     1.2. The Single Nature of Russian and Church Slavonic.................221
     1.3 The New Interpretation of Purist Categories...........................232
  2. Rationalist Purism and the Richness of the Slavenorossiiskii Language........248
     2.1 The Richness and "Antiquity" of Russian.................................249
     2.2 The New Stylistic Normalization..266
     2.3 Rationalist Purism and Its Russian Metamorphosis..................286
  3. The Synthesis of Cultural and Linguistic Traditions:
     The Slavenorossiiskii Language and Its Functioning......................301
     3.1 The Evolution of the Language of Religious Literature............309
     3.2 The Unified Language of a Unified Culture..............................332

**Chapter 4. The New Cultural Differentiation; Linguistic Purity as
an Ideological Category**..346

  1. The Emancipation of Culture and the Polemic Between
     Archaists and Innovators..346
     1.1 The Collapse of the Cultural-Linguistic Synthesis and
     the Karamzinian Program...356
     1.2 The Polemic over Language and Problems of Cultural
     Self-Consciousness..367
  2. Slavonicizing Purism and Its Reconceptualization in Religious Literature.....381
     2.1 The Understanding of Purist Rubrics.......................................394
     2.2 The Attitude Toward the Linguistic Sign..................................407
     2.3 The Secularization of Slavonicisms and the Juxtaposition of
     Religious and Secular Traditions..417

Works Cited..430

Index...473

Introduction

Problems in the Prehistory of the New Type of Russian Literary Language

1. The Literary Language of the New Type as an Object of Social and Cultural History

The eighteenth century witnessed a radical transformation of the Russian linguistic situation that encompassed all levels of the Russian language and all of the spheres in which it functioned. In this period a new type of literary language came into existence, a national literary language, and the process of its formation marks one of the most important aspects of the modernization and rationalization of Russian society and culture. This process not only reflected the social and cultural changes taking place, but helped to create the very conditions for them to occur, insofar as it was precisely a unified literary language that served as the basis for the new state discourse. The unification and universalizing of the new literary tongue not only caused it to absorb the new configurations of power but also imprinted these new relations onto society, asserting the exclusive primacy of the reigning culture. It is precisely for this reason that the frequent changes occurring in the literary language may be directly or indirectly seen as reflecting the socio-cultural dynamics of Russian social consciousness.

Down through the mid-seventeenth century Russian society remained relatively weakly stratified and relatively mobile socially. Subsequently stratification increased sharply, reaching an apogee in the Petrine period, when on the ruins of medieval society a social structure based on estates (castes) came into being that secured a place for every individual in the new state mechanism (cf. Hellie 1978; Hellie 1982). Toward the end of the Petrine transformation the tax reform definitively divided the population of the empire into classes and introduced a system of control over the size and membership of each one (cf. Anisimov 1982). This pseudo-Hobbseian mechanism was put into practice and supported by a state elite which defined itself as the center which guaranteed the unity of all of the state's component parts. The unity of culture and of language emerged as necessary attributes of the imperial Russian leviathan, and this determined the cultural and linguistic policies of the ruling elite. At the height of French absolutism, Charles Perrot wrote: "In France there is nothing but pure French, or to put it better, nothing but the language of the court that can be used in a serious work, because in a kingdom language is like money: to be put into circulation both of them must bear the mark of a prince" (Perrot 1964, 312). Perrot thus equated the unity of the literary language in a properly maintained monarchy with the emission of monetary signs. However utopian such a state unity may have been (and in Russia even more so than in France), it was precisely this notion that transformed the linguistic situation and conditioned the development of the new type of literary language.

The attributes of modern literary languages are well known. According to the definition of the Prague theses, literary languages represent "the monopoly and characteristic feature of the dominant class" (Vachek 1964, 45), and are defined by their polyfunctionalism, universal comprehensibility, codified nature and differentiation of stylistic means. These are precisely the features that the new Russian literary language acquired in the eighteenth and early nineteenth century. Not one of the varieties of written language of pre-Petrine Russia possessed all of these things together, so that the very question whether or not a literary language existed in old Rus' remains problematic. We may recall that A. V. Isachenko considered that "a Russian literary language in the modern meaning of the term… only came into being during the eighteenth century" (Isachenko 1976, 297), while V. V. Vinogradov argued, to the contrary, that "the Russian literary language of the medieval period was Church Slavonic" (Vinogradov 1938, 5), and it is precisely the latter view that underlies the conception of Church Slavonic — Russian diglossia developed by B. A. Uspenskii (Uspenskii 1987; Uspenskii 1994).

Whether or not Church Slavonic was the Russian literary language remains predominantly a question of terminology, and may therefore not detain us here. What is significant for us is that Church Slavonic, however we define it and whichever works we connect with the sphere of its functionality, was neither polyfunctional nor codified. The written language of ancient Russia was not unitary; together with standard Church Slavonic, represented primarily by the texts of Holy Writ and liturgy, there was another variant of the bookish (Church Slavonic) language which one could call hybrid (on this, see below), as well as a non-bookish language, which itself was not

§0–1. The Literary Language of the New Type

without variants. Apart from the question whether we call these "languages" or "registers" (the term I prefer), they do not comprise the kind of unitary system which defines a modern literary language. One may say that the written language of ancient Russia was fragmentary, and that its separate fragments (registers) had different functions (that is, none of them were polyfunctional), and were only normalized to varying degrees (that is, even speaking of codification in the broadest terms one can't say that the language as a whole was codified).

A prehistory of the Russian literary language of the new type (or in other terms, a history of the Russian literary language during the medieval period) must include a consideration of the development of these traits —polyfunctionalism, universality, codification and stylistic differentiation— that define modern literary languages (see Keipert 1988b, 315–6). Obviously, these qualities did not appear instantaneously, or at least in some cases we should speak of their gradual growth. As regards polyfunctionalism, one could mention: the broadening of the repertoire of genres of texts in the bookish language in the sixteenth and seventeenth centuries; the new arenas in which the bookish language was used in parallel with the non-bookish (for example, in active jurisprudence; cf. Zhivov 1988b, 74); the appearance of texts in the non-bookish business language (the official or *prikaznoi iazyk*), but that was not used for business per se (e.g., the translation "Doctrine and Craft of Military Building for the Infantry" of 1647 or the work by Kotoshikhin — see Stang 1952; Pennington 1980). For the development of codification the emergence of the grammatical approach to the bookish language in the sixteenth century was significant (cf. Zhivov 1993a) as was the appearance of grammars of the bookish tongue, which in many ways influenced the codification of the literary language of the new type.

Nonetheless, radical changes only came during the Petrine epoch. It was just at this time that in various spheres of writing and pursuant to a conscious linguistic policy the new literary language was established and the old registers of the written language were reduced to the periphery of discourse, marking the start of their gradual demise, for some complete (as in the case of official and hybrid Church Slavonic), and for others partial (in the case of standard Church Slavonic, which remained in use only as the liturgical tongue). As a result of this process, the new literary language acquired polyfunctionality and universal comprehensibility. Codification of this new literary language began in the 1730's, when material from the disappearing written traditions was selectively chosen, systematized, and formulated into a single norm. The literary material that remained outside the bounds of this norm in many cases was not completely excluded from usage, but was kept in reserve as an alternative; these alternative variants could take on stylistic value, as a rule reflecting the written tradition from which they derived. Thus the new literary language acquired stylistic differentiation.

These processes of unification and stylistic adjustment are not in any way specific to the Russian cultural and linguistic situation, but find numerous analogies in the development of other literary languages. The special nature and substantial differences in the Russian situation emerge from the different starting point and setting in which these processes took place, and the main features of their dynamics were determined precisely by these initial parameters. One of these parameters was the complex interrelationship between Russian (Eastern Slavic) and Church Slavonic in the history of Russian letters. Another related feature was the varying cultural significance given to genetically Church Slavonic and Eastern Slavic linguistic media in the functioning of the registers of the written language.

The traditional bookish language, Church Slavonic, was directly related to traditional religious values, and for this reason its being pushed to the periphery of language usage reflected a radical transformation of cultural space. For its entire development, through the early nineteenth century, the establishment of the new type of literary language continually intersected with struggles between tradition and reform, secular versus religious culture, western orientation versus indigenous traditions. This imparted an especially intense semiotic significance to the history of the literary language in this period, making it quite unusual in the typological sense. It permits us to glimpse the dynamics of the most important social and cultural processes through the prism of linguistic development, as the problem of power in language was invested in exceedingly concrete forms, down to polemics over particular morphological indicators.

That the history of language becomes involved in social and cultural processes occurs owing to the fact that in the consciousness of speakers and writers linguistic elements exist not as abstract means of communication but as indicators of social and cultural positions. Linguistic activity is inseparable from its interpretation, and the symbolic (culturological) dimension of language is created by the hermeneutic strata that accumulate over the course of its history (see Riker 1995). In the creation of a literary language of the new type the hermeneutic aspect plays an especially large role, insofar as it is precisely the symbolic connotations of linguistic elements that determine their fate during the process of purposeful choice and classification by means of which the unified norm of the new language is defined. Because of this, in analyzing this process we need to reconstruct the interpretations that guided those who established the new literary language and this in turn requires that we reconstruct the various hermeneutic strata that were actualized in those interpretations. The need for this reconstruction leads us to the prehistory of the new language which is what defines the field of signification on which the redivision of cultural space takes place.

An example: In the 1750's Trediakovskii accused Sumarokov several times of using vulgar (*ploshchadnye*) expressions and forms characteristic of "coarse village" language or the language of "street venders." In particular, Trediakovskii ascribes masc. sg. nom.-acc. adjectival forms ending in -*ой* (e.g., злой rather than злый, чермной rather than чермный—see § III–1.3) to this group. If we accept Trediakovskii's opinion literally, that is, without considering the symbolic dimension of its prehistory, then we might assume his position to be the following: that the norms of the literary language must reflect the usage of the social elite, which use the -*ый* ending rather than -*ой*, used by social inferiors. Such socio-linguistic criteria appear very plausible, and direct parallels may be seen in the history of the French literary language, which was undoubtedly familiar to Trediakovskii and which served as a model.

This interpretation, however, is by no means correct. Trediakovskii's socio-linguistic criteria had no real relation to actual social and linguistic differentiation. What was central for him at this moment was the opposition between the "pure" tongue, based on grammatical "reason" (according to a particular literary and linguistic tradition), as opposed to "impure" language that was relatively open to the influence of living speech. Trediakovskii's main conception was that of rationalist purism, and socio-linguistic criteria served only as familiar labels that had been adopted from French debates over language. The issue boiled down to a convenient (conventional) way of describing anything that Trediakovskii considered a deviation from the norms of the unified literary language that he was asserting. In the last analysis, the development of rationalist purism itself was conditioned by the desire to harmonize general European linguistic principles with national literary and linguistic traditions. (See the examination of Trediakovskii's views in § III–2.3.)

Analysis of this prehistory demonstrates that the ending -*ый* in no way characterized usage of the Russian social elite; it derived from the written rather than spoken tradition. The ending -*ой* was characteristic of the spoken language, and it is that which underlay Trediakovskii's criticism of Sumarokov; in attacking his "street usage" Trediakovskii was rejecting that conception of the literary norm that took general conversational usage as its basic criterion. Sumarokov, however, in using the -*ой* ending might well have been basing himself not on spoken speech but on the very same written tradition, which permitted this as well as the -*ый* ending (this was characteristic for both hybrid Slavonic texts of the seventeenth century and for texts in the "simple" tongue of the Petrine era and the 1730's—see Zhivov 1988a, 36). Thus Trediakovskii's accusations in no way describe Sumarokov's linguistic position, but were determined by the dynamic of Trediakovskii's own views, and they characterize his reformist position relative both to his own linguistic conception of the 1730's and also to his radical revision of traditional practices as a whole. The choice of the *-ыŭ* ending represented an attempt at normalization based on model Church Slavonic texts (not hybrid ones), on the grammatical tradition, and on ideas concerning the genetic character of grammatical elements. This choice presupposed a rethinking of the variant *-oŭ* and *-ыŭ* endings as an instance of the opposition between Russian and Church Slavonic (something which had not been juxtaposed earlier) and an orientation of literary norms on the national literary and linguistic tradition, in this case the Church Slavonic tradition. Trediakovskii's normalization put emphasis on his own academic expertise and historical knowledge that corresponded to the social position to which he aspired.

In rejecting Trediakovskii's criteria for normalization, Sumarokov juxtaposed aristocratic taste to that of educated reason, and he refused to cede the task of enlightening the new elite to déclassé academics (§ III–2.2). Teaching noble sentiments and behavior (including linguistic) should be done by those who themselves have received a noble upbringing, those who belong to that select part of society that Sumarokov, somewhat anachronistically, conceptualizes in terms of West European knighthood, picturing Russia as a "feudal utopia" (Gukovskii 1941, 359). It is precisely this position that Trediakovskii tries to discredit, alleging Sumarokov's numerous linguistic blunders. At first glance this might seem to be the senseless criticism of a pedant, posing no substantive issues. However, Trediakovskii's myriad petty criticisms allow him to conclude that Sumarokov "did not receive… the necessary university education in grammar, rhetoric, poetry, philosophy, history, chronology and geography, without which it is impossible to be a mediocre poet, not to speak of a great one" (Kunik 1865, 496)—and hence unfit for the role of enlightener. Thus the crucial condition for creating a new literary language is revealed as learning, and it is scholars who should be given control over it. The two authors' linguistic opinions also correspond to their overall literary positions and that complex of aesthetic, historical, cultural, discursive and stylistic notions that are made up of particular oppositions such as these that serve as ground for struggle over the reigning discourse, a struggle that acquired unprecedented intensity following the Petrine transformation.

In the pre-Petrine period the repertoire of registers of the written language had been realized primarily by the varying combination of genetically Church Slavonic and East Slavic elements. Accordingly, it was just these elements, relating to different spheres of social consciousness, that made up the linguistic material on which the symbolic dimension of language was constructed. The elements' provenance did not in and of itself define their social and cultural connotations—it was not their provenance itself that was important, but their role in the linguistic consciousness of their carriers, that is, not their genetic but their functional parameters. As comparative historical analysis shows, particular elements took on the role of symbolic indicators of either traditional religious culture or of secular innovation not because of their origin (East Slavic, South Slavic or other), but because their carriers (who had no inkling of comparative historical issues!) perceived them as characteristic of particular linguistic registers, i.e., as bookish or non-bookish, normative or non-normative, and so on. In order to reveal how language participates in social and cultural processes, its prehistory must reveal not the etymological but the functional role of linguistic elements, their hermeneutic status in the linguistic consciousness of speakers and writers. Hence in examining that prehistory, we seek traces of how their functional relationships developed out of the diversity of linguistic elements of various origins, and how the functional particular acquired particular symbolic meanings.

2. The Functional Reconceptualization of Genetically Heterogeneous Elements in the History of Russian Writing

The function of Church Slavonic in the world of *Slavia Orthodoxa* is often juxtaposed to the functioning of Latin in Catholic countries (on the history of such juxtapositions and their parameters, see Keipert 1987). However, the relationship between autochthonous and imported linguistic means in the two situations is completely dissimilar. In the last analysis, the dissimilarity may be explained by the different ways the languages were taught: Latin was assimilated via grammar and with a dictionary, while Church Slavonic via the Psalter and prayer book, which were learned by heart (see Tolstoi 1963, 259–64; Tolstoi 1976, 178–9). Learning Latin in medieval Germany or Ireland is typologically similar to learning language in school today. Learning Church Slavonic in Slavic lands was a fundamentally different experience, at least through the seventeenth century: pupils learned to read by rote (*po skladam*), reading and repeating texts and comprehending them through the resources of their native tongue. The nature of the acquisition of the written language also defined the place which these memorized elements of the bookish language occupied in the pupils' linguistic experience, the basis for which served the spoken language that they had assimilated with their mother's milk.

The surviving information about learning the bookish language in ancient Rus' is scarce and fragmentary, and for the eleventh and twelfth centuries direct evidence is completely lacking. Nevertheless one may reconstruct the corresponding phenomena with some degree of certainty, relying on comparative material and on later evidence. The basic means of learning language was reading by "po skladam" ("by syllables"). The procedure was strictly regimented and was considered sacred.[1] It began and ended with prayer and was seen as a kind of introduction to Christian life. The special importance of correct and comprehensible reading was conditioned by the fact that the failure to follow the rules of reading could, from the point of view of Eastern Slavic bookmen, lead to heretical error. (See the "Instructions for Teachers How to Teach Children Literacy and How Children Can Learn Holy Writ and Understanding," foreword to the *Psalter*, Moscow, 1645; [...] Buslaev 1861, col. 1087–8).

By the early thirteenth century learning literacy *po skladam* may be considered generally accepted, as is evidenced by the writings (gramoty) of the boy Onfim (NBG, no. 199–210). The birchbark gramoty no.'s 199, 201, 204 and 206 belong to this period and include notations of sklady that correspond to what we find in later primers, and so may be taken as indication of an established system of primary education based on reading and memorizing them. After learning to read syllables came learning texts by heart, first prayers and then the Psalter. The first witness of this order of learning is those same gramoty of Onfim of the early thirteenth century. Thus, as N. A. Meshcherskii determined, one may make out several fragments of psalms on NGB no. 207 (Meshcherskii 1962, 108; cf. Zalizniak 1995, 387). As Zalizniak recently reported (in an oral communication), Onfim was also responsible for birchbark gramota no. 331, that also contains phrases from the psalms. These jottings indicate that the Psalter was used as a textbook for teaching basic literacy. The order of texts that were used is also indicated in the "Instructions for Teachers" of 1645 cited above ("in the beginning the letters, that is, the alphabet, then the prayerbook and the Psalter and other

---

[1] A good description of the Russian method is found in a later but fully trustworthy source, a treatise by Epifanii Slavinstskii. [...] (NRB, Sof. 1208, l.52–52 verso; cited in Uspenskii 1970, 82).

divine books"), and a century and a half earlier in the epistle of Archbishop Gennadii to Metropolitan Simon (AI, I, no. 104, 148; cf. Upotreblenie knigi Psaltyr' 1857, 816–7).

As far as one can judge, elementary education culminated with learning the Psalter by heart. Indeed, we have no information at all that any grammar books, dictionaries or texts on rhetoric were used in language learning; in the oldest period of the Eastern Slavic literary tradition such texts were also completely absent. Methods of teaching including the use of grammar appeared in Muscovite Russia no earlier than the seventeenth century, and even at the start of the eighteenth were perceived as a novelty. In his edition of Smotritskii's grammar of 1721 F. Polikarpov wrote:

> …from ancient times it was (and still is) the custom for Russian educators of children and teachers to start with the primer, then [go to] the breviary and Psalter, and also to write using them, [and] some also teach reading the apostle. For the older ones they also have them read the Holy Bible and gospel and apostolic sermons and discuss the lofty ideas in these books. But that true instrument for understanding (that is, a grammar book) they do not show them, [a tool] with which to analyze every phrase and period and every word, and [to understand] how to put them in proper order, and which makes it possible to discuss the power of reason concealed in them. (Smotritskii 1721, Foreword, l. 2 verso)

The traditional type of teaching clearly doesn't satisfy Polikarpov insofar as it doesn't include a mechanism for analyzing the memorized texts. This is what grammar supplies, and it is the desire to incorporate it into education that motivates Polikarpov to publish this edition. In the same foreword it also says that "after studying the breviary and Psalter (without which they [students] do not know how to learn the bookish language) this grammar with commentary (that is, with examples and explanation of its contents) should start [to be used]" (ibid, Foreword, l. 5).

In this system of learning, new texts are acquired by means of the experience gained by reading previous works, that is, in the final analysis-- when this experience is derived from the initial assimilation of bookish texts—based on the resources of the living language. On the basis of the habits developed in the process of reading, original texts are created. When we analyze these habits and see them as active mechanisms that ensure the understanding and the production of new texts, we need to emphasize two relatively autonomous processes: a) the mechanism of markers of bookishness or the mechanism of retabulation (*pereschet*), and b) the mechanism of orientation on texts.

The mechanism of markers of bookishness is based on the fact that individual elements of a bookish text are understood by relating them to elements of the living language. It is natural to conclude that for understanding a bookish text the pupil does not need to comprehend all of the connections among the various elements that are absent in his oral usage, since many are more or less synonymous to elements of that usage, although for many of them (for example, abstract lexicon) this kind of connection cannot be drawn. Relating the oral and written is needed only for those frequently repeating elements that form the structural basis of the statement. The established relationships may not form one-to-one correspondences, as in those cases when the set of categories of the living language differs from that of the bookish tongue. In these cases the grammatical semantics of the living language may be superimposed on the formal oppositions that are present in the bookish language.

In active mastery (that is, the production of texts) this mechanism will condition the reverse substitution of bookish forms for non-bookish ones, for example, simple preterits in the place of л-forms. Understandably, this mechanism will operate mostly when the author has something new to say, i.e, something he has not read many times, in this or another form. In this case, of course, the mechanism of retabulation will only involve particular elements, the ones with which difficulties arise and which can be easily retabulated, i.e., that have a formal correlation to elements of the non-bookish tongue. Such a correlation may be established between preterit forms of the bookish and non-bookish languages, between bookish participles functioning as secondary predicate and non-bookish gerunds, etc.

The mechanism of orientation on texts is clearly even more significant than that of retabulation. It conditions the reproduction of ready-made fragments of text, forms and constructions that the writer knows from the corpus of texts he has learned by heart. One must think that when someone has memorized a large corpus of texts (for example, the Psalter) that this significantly influences his cultural and linguistic consciousness, so different from ours in the modern age, and that this directly affects the character of his use of language. This person may automatically reproduce ready-made blocks of description (of situations, actions, feelings) following the pattern of bookish narration when writing about that which in one way or another has been processed in the texts he has memorized. In this instance the power of form-creating institutions that exist above individual discourse, and that will influence a person his whole life, is realized in a most explicit way; in this process individual consciousness is absorbed by the dominating mental tradition.

The given process may be seen as significant from a religious and cultural perspective, as it turns becoming literate into full-fledged indoctrination. This character of learning the bookish language as forming one's consciousness, and connected with learning a corpus of religious texts by heart, was amply clear to contemporaries, at least in the period when alternatives to this educational system began to arise. Thus the project for establishing schools that was proposed by the Catherinean Commission for Composing a New Law Code in the late 1760's suggested that elementary education be changed so that literacy be taught "both by church books and by civil laws." It presumed studying the civil alphabet together with the traditional Slavonic one. During the course of the entire eighteenth century people became literate using the church alphabet, while the civic was supplementary and only learned by small social groups (§ IV–2.2). The cited project (that was not put into practice) was an attempt to change this. In supporting the advisability of teaching "by civil laws" the authors of the project recalled that due to having learned the Psalter by heart "it happens that during normal conversations we approve or disapprove of things with whole verses from the psalmist; hence it will occur that we immediately see the consequences of any action [in terms of the Psalter]" (Sukhomlinov, I, 78). It was thus proposed to unite legal with religious indoctrination; according to the authors of the project, a person who been educated in this system would recall the laws punishing transgression just as automatically as they remembered formulations from the Psalter when evaluating life situations. The secularized power was trying to create a new state discourse parallel to the religious, making use of its mechanisms, which as we see were fully understood.

With this kind of education, a person's memory can evidently generate not only fragments of text describing a particular situation but also smaller textual elements, down to individual forms and constructions. Texts that have been learned by heart create a stock of images that may be reproduced when they are for some reason activated (usually connected with the imagery of the created text). The two mechanisms we have described, the mechanisms of retabulation and of orientation on texts, coexist and act simultaneously in creating new texts. Understandably, the mechanisms of retabulation will function in cases when for some reason memorized images are not activated. The simplest reason for this is the case when an author can't find material from this ready linguistic stock for a phrase that he wants to create, for example, because the content of this phrase goes beyond the subject matter represented there.

The differences in relating the mechanism of orientation on models and the mechanism of retabulation allow us to explain the genesis of various registers of the bookish language. If only the mechanism of orientation on texts is used, the product will be a standard Church Slavonic text that does not differ significantly from the texts of Holy Writ and the liturgy (i.e., the basic corps of bookish texts) that are being reproduced. We find this kind of language, for example, in Metropolitan Ilarion's "Sermon on Law and Grace" or in Russian supplements to service menalogia. Texts of this kind create their own tradition in whose framework new texts appear that have a similar function in the system of bookish literature. If the mechanism of retabulation is dominant, the result is a hybrid Church Slavonic text (see Zhivov 1988, 54–63), also oriented on the basic corpus of bookish texts but differing from it in a series of linguistic features. This kind of text also creates its tradition which in time gathers more and more new texts. Insofar as the intensive use of the mechanism of retabulation is caused by non-standard content (from the point of view of religious literature), the appearance of this tradition is evidently connected to the development of writing chronicles.

The action of these mechanisms determined the functional differences between registers of the bookish and non-bookish languages, i.e., in traditional terms, between the Church Slavonic and Russian languages. These two languages differentiate that which draws the main attention of users, those areas of difficulty that cause the problematic correlation of the bookish and conversational languages. This limited set of elements, requiring special analysis, are markers of bookishness in linguistic consciousness (as opposed to other elements of language that are not relevant). For example, the agreement of active participles that are absent in the non-bookish language may run into problems, both when the text is copied, when the copyist doesn't know if the form was used correctly, and when a new text is created and the author isn't sure what form to use. At the same time, other issues are unimportant, for example, pleophonic or non-pleophonic forms that don't require verification when being copied, and in creating a new text the choice of forms depends on a multitude of individual factors that have no relation to the bookish — non-bookish opposition.

Genetic heterogeneity that arose due to the assimilation of bookish material from other Slavic traditions served as the initial basis for the functional differentiation of linguistic elements. The fate of various elements that were categorized by the genetic opposition of "Eastern Slavic" versus "other Slavic" could be quite different. In some cases adaptation took place, that is, the assimilation of an Eastern Slavic element (an element of one of the East Slavic dialects) to the norm of the Russian recension of Church Slavonic and the simultaneous rejection of the corresponding element of other Slavic origin. In other cases the result could be the creation of a marker of bookishness, when the other Slavic element was preserved as part of the norm of the Russian recension and reconceptualized as a specific marker of the bookish character of the text. Finally, in still other cases, the opposition of Eastern and other Slavic became the source of variability: the opposition was neutralized and both elements became acceptable variants of the East Slavonic bookish language.

Adaptation took place primarily in orthography and inflexions. It was precisely orthographic and morphological norms that most clearly differentiated the various local recensions of Church Slavonic, while in the area of lexicon and syntax the notion of the normative was eroded; here the habits of bookish exposition that were basically similar for all recensions and not related to conversational usage were operative. Orthographic and morphological adaptation and the local norms that followed from it were motivated precisely on these levels by the very spread of literacy. Manuscripts traveled from one Slavic area to another and were copied and edited. Coexistence of manuscripts of various recensions and mistrust of the originals created the stimulus for each local tradition to unify orthographic and morphological features. The basis for this unification were rules that produced the "correct" form using linguistic information available to the copyist. This information derived from bookish pronunciation that had been established as a result of the church service's use of assimilated texts and as a rule excluding sounds and sound combinations that were alien to conversational pronunciation, as well as from aspects of the living language that could serve to verify bookish forms (see: Durnovo 1933; Lant 1950; Zhivov 1984; Zhivov 1986a). The very use of rules of this type conditioned the adaptation of Church Slavonic, making bookish forms dependent on those of the living language and assimilating them to local usage; traditional forms deriving from other Slavic literatures were accepted only in those cases when they coincided with local ones or could be correlated to them with the help of simple rules.

The functional reconceptualization of genetically heterogeneous elements was also accomplished thanks to the mechanism of retabulation, as the opposition of East and other Slavic elements was transformed into the juxtaposition of bookish and non-bookish elements, with the bookish ones no longer perceived as foreign. This perception reflected the way bookish elements were used in implementing the mechanism of retabulation; it not only juxtaposed the bookish and non-bookish languages but also correlated them. Actually, the grammatical semantics of the bookish language as fixed in the corpus of basic texts that were recopied and continually read was not unambiguously related to the grammatical semantics of the living language in any of the Slavic regions; and to the degree that the living languages developed this lack of correspondence only increased. Therefore the production of bookish texts on the basis of the mechanism of retabulation did not lead to the creation of texts whose grammatical system was fully analogous to that of the basic corpus. Their degree of closeness depended on the expertise of individual bookmen (in particular, their mastery of the basic corpus of texts), but was never absolute. As a result, original bookish texts to a greater or lesser extent reflected the grammatical semantics of the living language.[2]

Those processes of rethinking the genetically heterogeneous elements discussed above were connected to correlating the features of the two initial linguistic systems. The difference consisted in the fact that in the case of adaptation the genetically East Slavic elements displaced other Slavic ones as the norm of the East Slavic recension, while in the cases where the mechanism of retabulation came into play genetically non-East Slavic elements were preserved, serving as the bookish equivalent of certain forms or constructions of the bookish language. Such a direct correlation was possible or available, however, only in some cases. In cases where there was no direct correlation, genetically heterogeneous elements functioned as acceptable variants in the bookish language, and in this instance genetic characteristics lost their meaning, having been functionally reconceptualized in terms of variability.

A direct correlation may be established, as noted, with the help of general rules. In places where general rules were not formulated, there were no grounds for eliminating one of the elements (genetically Eastern Slavic or other). Moreover, the normal historical phonetic correlation could not serve as basis for formulating a general rule either. For the old Russian bookman these correlations were not a conscious factor, as they involved the linguistic material of their native language, for example, when there was a combination of /ro/ or /lo/ at the start of a word, but whether this was there "*in place of the*" proto-Slavic **or,* *ol he waz incapable of figuring out. In some cases these combinations correlated to the initial *pa-* or *ла-* in bookish texts that were familiar to him, while in other cases the very same consistencies in the living language turned out to be related to the bookish *po-* and *ло-* (cf. *родити, роса, лобъзати, ловити*). Therefore in his arsenal there could not be a rule of the

---

[2] Thus, for example, after the imperfect disappeared from living East Slavic dialects the imperfect form in the bookish language could be related to the forms of the non-bookish language, and the result of this correlation was reflected in the character of its usage in original East Slavic texts that deviated from the main corpus (Holy Writ and the liturgy), and especially in relatively late texts (e.g., saints lives or chronicles of the fifteenth-sixteenth centuries) (cf. Zhivov 1986, 102–11).

type: "where in the conversational language one hears /ro/, /lo/ at the start of a word the bookish language has *ра-*. *ла-*." The lack of a rule meant the lack of a clear norm, and therefore *работа* and *робота* or *лакъть* and *локъть* were permissible coexisting variants. Nothing in essence differentiates these cases from the situation with pleophonic and non-pleophonic lexemes. The writer was dealing with a colloquial combination of the /oro/ type, which in some cases was linked to the bookish *ра-* (*порогъ* — *прагъ*) but in others not (for example, *порокъ* [vitium, fault] but not **пракъ*). And in this case the natural consequence of the lack of a general rule was the variability of pleophonic and non-pleophonic forms. In monuments that were copied variability of this kind would only occur occasionally. In creating original texts the lack of a general rule relating bookish and non-bookish elements was much more consequential, since variability became a constituent feature of the texts that made up the hybrid register of the bookish language.

Thus the reconceptualization of genetically heterogeneous elements took place in tandem with the development of the bookish tradition. In the composition of the Eastern Slavic recension of Church Slavonic these elements formed a unique mixture whose constituent parts were not juxtaposed as "ours" and "theirs" but led to a diversity of linguistic usages out of which later developed various written traditions. In some cases Eastern Slavic elements supplanted other Slavic ones in the bookish norm, and in others they were correlated with them, creating an opposition of bookish and non-bookish forms, and in a third instance both Eastern and other Slavic elements became acceptable variants. In all of these cases genetic categories were replaced by functional ones. This same mechanism also worked later on, when due to the development of the living language there appeared new differences between bookish and non-bookish usage.[3] They also stimulate the process of adaptation (for example, accommodating bookish usage to the results of the fall and vocalization of reduced vowels — see Zalizniak 1986, 100; Zhivov 1984, 262–3) or are reconceptualized as markers of bookishness (for example, forms of the dual number) or as acceptable variants (for example, the gen. sg. masc. and neut. endings *-аго/-ого* in the declension of full-form adjectives).

---

[3] New oppositions formed with special intensity after the final disintegration of Slavic linguistic unity in the late twelfth century (see Durnovo 1931). The active changes in the living language during this period led to a significant dissimilation (raspodoblenie) of the bookish and living languages and called forth a new series of functional reconceptualizations that marked a new period in the history of the bookish language. At the same time, the new oppositions broadened the diapason of choices available to East Slavic bookmen, and with this the possibility of separating out the various relatively independent written traditions expanded; some of them (for example, hymnology) could resist changes in usage more strongly than others (for example, hagiography).

The reconceptualization of genetically heterogeneous elements in functional categories also influenced the character of linguistic consciousness. The bookish language was perceived not as an alien tongue that existed independently of the native language (in contrast to Latin) but as a cultivated variety of it. The mastery of the bookish language was superimposed onto native linguistic ways and united with them, forming the complex conglomerate of the speech habits of the written language whose concrete content depended both on the social and cultural status of the writer as well as on the type of written texts that he usually produced (these are understandably connected). Differing writing habits that primarily come from reading create different written traditions that have dissimilar cultural (and religious) importance. Linguistic phenomena that are characteristic of each of the written traditions (registers) acquire the same cultural weight as the tradition as a whole, and this significantly defines their role in the creation of the new type of literary language.

3. The Main Registers of the Bookish Language and the Processes of Their Formation

The main division in the written language of medieval Rus' was into bookish and non-bookish texts. Bookish texts were characterized primarily by their logically ordered and rhetorically organized syntax and their use of markers of bookishness (for example, forms of the imperfect or gerunds in agreement with their subjects). The syntax of non-bookish texts was oriented on the communicative situation (on what the addressee knows or doesn't know), so that the pragmatic structure plays a significantly greater role than logical organization, and markers of bookishness are not used (except for isolated cases and clichéd formulas). However, the division into bookish and non-bookish languages alone is not sufficient for describing the linguistic situation of medieval Rus' insofar as the linguistic features of both kinds of text are too heterogeneous to see them as opposing unities. This is one of the issues that prevents us from defining the linguistic situation of the Eastern Slavs as diglossia, as it does, for example, the coexistence of classical Arabic and modern Arabic languages.[4]

---

[4] However, it seems that in the case of Arabic as well the division into "high" and "low" languages is not as unambiguous as one might conclude from classical descriptions of Arabic diglossia (see Ferguson 1959). Here too there are texts that significantly diverge from the bookish standard (Talmoudi 1984), but it is not clear if they form a discrete tradition.

§0–3. The Main Registers of the Bookish Language

Within the framework of the bookish language at least two registers stand out, one of which may be called standard and the other hybrid. The standard register is realized primarily in texts of the main corpus, i.e., Holy Writ and liturgy; from among these the texts that were learned by heart had the greatest impact. A significant part of the standard bookish texts were non-Eastern Slavic in origin, including texts of the main corpus, on which the entire given written tradition was directly based. Texts from other Slavic traditions were adapted on Eastern Slavic soil on the orthographic and morphological levels, but their syntactic construction and grammatical structure did not experience any major influence of the non-bookish language of the Eastern Slavs. Those original Eastern Slavic works that were created primarily via the mechanism of orientation on texts also belong to this register. The clearest illustration of this is the already mentioned Eastern Slavic additions to the service menalogia whose language does not differ from that of the basic text that came from the South Slavs.

The hybrid register was realized in original Eastern Slavic texts (that is, texts created by Eastern Slavic bookmen; naturally, these could also be translations from Greek, Latin or some other language). If works in the standard register were created primarily by the mechanism of orientation on texts, the main role in creating texts in the hybrid register was played by the mechanism of retabulation. The mechanism of retabulation created the possibility of the writer's special linguistic stance in which the goal was not the maximal convergence of the language of the new texts with that of the corpus of basic texts but the relative similarity of these languages according to a series of formal markers. Understandably, given this stance the set of relevant formal markers only has relative significance and may be reduced to a minimum, including primarily those features that most clearly differentiate the bookish language from the non-bookish. The choice of markers that are involved with the retabulation is limited and selective. Together with this, the use of the formal markers that belong to the set is also selective; insofar as these markers primarily function as indicators of the bookish nature of the text, they may be used inconsistently and infrequently, as their very presence serves as the indicator, while the degree of their use depends on various particular factors.

Insofar as the use of markers of bookishness in such texts takes on the character of a signal, extensive influence of the non-bookish language on the bookish becomes possible. The identification of especially bookish elements in linguistic consciousness acquires a completely functional character as the process of functional reconceptualization of genetic heterogeneity is brought to its logical limit. Without the direct orientation on the texts of the basic corpus and grammatical codification variability increases greatly and elements of non-bookish origin freely make their way into new texts. Thus in this register of the bookish language bookish and non-bookish elements are synthesized into a single system, so that the very question of the linguistic basis of the corresponding texts as traditionally bookish or as popular and conversational (that has been debated many times without any notable results — cf. Vinogradov 1958; Vinogradov 1978, 65–151) turns out to be without any basis. Either of these two aspects may be seen in isolation but the functioning of this type of text can only be understood in terms of their combination and interaction. It is for this very reason that we find it appropriate to label this register of the bookish language hybrid.

In the context of the hybrid register usage fundamentally depends on the correlation of the bookish and non-bookish languages, insofar as the markers of bookishness are what distinguish them in the linguistic consciousness of users. Due to the fact that the standard of the bookish language was based on model Church Slavonic texts and remained largely unchanged over the course of centuries, the set of the markers of bookishness and changes in this set were conditioned by features of the non-bookish language. Thus in the Russian tradition as represented by texts of the fifteenth through seventeenth century, the markers of bookishness include: simple preterits, active participles and, in general, participles as gerunds in agreement with their subjects, forms of the dual number, the dative absolute, etc. Changes in the non-bookish language influenced the make-up of the hybrid register. The dual number, for example, acquired the status of a marker of bookishness, naturally, only after it disappeared from the non-bookish language.[5]

However, this fundamental dependence only determined the basic contours, not the details. The details were worked out with reference to the

---

[5] The hybrid register, as a natural consequence of the functioning of the mechanism of retabulation, was characteristic not only of the written language of the Eastern Slavs but also of the Southern Slavs (analogous phenomena may also certainly be seen in other language groups, but this is another topic). The set of markers of bookishness, however, is specific in each case, and it is precisely these specifics that clearly display the dependence of what constitutes the hybrid register on the special features of the non-bookish language. Naturally, Bulgarians did not perceive the forms of the simple preterits as specific to the bookish language, so they did not become markers of bookishness in the framework of the Bulgarian tradition. For the Bulgarian tradition markers of bookishness included: noun and adjective case forms, the absence of articles, infinitives in -*mu*, the simple future, synthetic forms of the comparative degree, etc. This set of markers came into being by virtue of the fact that they became alien to living Bulgarian idioms. As one can see, similar mechanisms of producing bookish texts in differing Slavic traditions give significantly different results, which is ultimately attributable to the differences among the living languages.

continuity of usage, and the fact that in creating a hybrid text a bookman directly turns not to his conversational tongue but to the sum total of his linguistic experience in which reading (i.e., the assimilation of written texts) plays no less a role than spontaneous speech. Slavic scholars ignored hybrid languages for a long time precisely because all of their attention was focused on the correlation between the bookish and spoken language, while they only ascribed an organic systematic character to the latter. The absolutized dichotomy of nature and culture that became a basic myth of the Neogrammmarians and that has survived as an article of faith practically until the present day thanks to structuralism and structuralist semiotics led to the rejection of any "natural" aspects of written language which was seen as a cultural phenomenon *par excellence.* This dichotomy also defined the history of Church Slavonic, on the one hand as a completely artificial language (with emphasis given to the standard register), and on the other as contrasted to the completely natural living language. Between these two poles was chaos that scholars simply did not wish to deal with, as hybrid texts were seen as conglomerations of heterogeneous material. However, if we ascribe to written usage the same natural continuity that oral usage has (realized in the transfer of reading habits into habits of writing), then the hybrid register appears (in the words of R. Mathiesen) not as "a mere conglomerate of heterogeneous elements, but [as] a secondary linguistic system in its own right" (Mathiesen 1984, 47).[6]

The continuity of writing habits explains how the relatively stable and relatively autonomous use of the hybrid register developed. It was not only the selection of relevant markers of bookishness and the consideration of differences between the standard bookish and non-bookish languages that were the individual decision of each author but the way in which particular elements were used that gave continuity to the language of successive generations of bookmen, a language which underwent changes that were gradual and "organic" (even from the point of view of the nature-culture dichotomy that we have rejected). Analysis of the heterogeneous language of hybrid texts (primarily chronicles) shows that the sections bookmen reproduced based on chronologically distant sources and those which they wrote themselves are connected by an uninterrupted chain of links that demonstrates the gradual nature of the evolution of usage (cf. Zhivov 1995a; Petrukhin 1996).

---

[6] Furthermore, in my opinion the epithet "secondary" is completely superfluous here and is a concession to the reigning line of linguistic thought that leads from the Neogrammarians to the Structuralists, for which writing is always secondary, artificial, and therefore requiring the exclusion of phenomena connected with it from properly linguistic investigation (cf. Derrida 1967; Derrida 1968).

This evolution proceeded thanks to constant semantic reinterpretation. Because the assimilation of the earlier bookish tradition took place without the aid of grammars and dictionaries, reading presupposed the interpretation of the linguistic material in those semantic categories which were within the reach of the author (first of all from linguistic experience connected to colloquial usage). Trying to preserve the formal elements that were characteristic of the existing written corpus, the author did this to the extent that he could, making use of these elements as he understood them in the context of the material that he had assimilated. Understandably, this usage could significantly differ from the original structure of the assimilated texts. The degree of difference evidently depended on two things: in the first place, the extent to which the language of these texts differed from the spoken language of the author (in terms of some concrete feature), and in the second place, the author's individual situation, that is, his education, his feel for language, and his desire to reproduce the language of his predecessors (either in a general way or in all things). The manner of transmission of linguistic habits from generation to generation does not differ here in its structure from that observed in the oral (living) language and functions as the standard of "naturalness" for the study of language oriented on "nature."

The evolution of the use of the perfect in the Laurentian Chronicle, brilliantly analyzed in the recent work of E. Klenin (1993), may serve as a good illustration of this. According to her observations, the perfect and aorist gradually redistribute their functions. Initially the perfect is used in the resultative meaning (which may refer both to the present and the past) and the aorist is used as the basic narrative tense. In the oldest part of the chronicle (the "Primary Chronicle" [Povest' vremennykh let]), there are already rare examples (precisely, two) where the perfect is used in narrative fragments, although in both cases not for presenting successive actions but for designating isolated events. In the section from the twelfth century this last usage becomes more widespread, and the perfect is used in fragments of commentary when indicating isolated actions or when there are gaps in narrative continuity. Isolated examples of the perfect in describing continuous action only occur in the last part of the chronicle (π-forms alternate with the aorist that is more usual in the given context).

Insofar as this evolution seems "natural," Klenin interprets this data as evidence of changes in the living language in which the functions of the perfect are expanding, gradually displacing use of the aorist, one function at a time. This interpretation corresponds to traditional views that "naturalness" and a systematic quality exclusively belong to the living language, while any changes in the bookish language, if they are not merely completely artificial, are of a "secondary" character. One may conclude with equal success that the expansion of the perfect's sphere of use takes place due to reinterpretation, when each successive chronicler builds upon the precedents left to him by his predecessor, assigning them more general significance; the resultative is perceived to be any non-narrative usage, non-narrative usage is then understood as a category applicable to any action mentioned outside of strict narrative order, and so on. The stimulus to such an interpretation indeed apparently comes from the conversational language, in which the use of the perfect differs (say, in the fourteenth century) from that which the later chronicler finds in his earlier sources, although the influence here is of a mediated character and may by no means be reduced to processes in the non-bookish language being reflected in the bookish language.[7]

The differences in the evolution of the bookish language compared with those of the spoken tongue arose by force of the fact its starting point was not the speech of the older generation, as is the case with the oral language, but the corpus of texts for reading, created at various times; this corpus functioned as the sum of the linguistic practices of many generations and conditioned the conservatism of bookish usage in comparison with oral. At the same time the correlation with such a broad and chronologically disparate body of texts made the hybrid language rather heterogeneous, in any case according to the standard of homogeneity that literary languages of the new type have made us expect. The bookman could to a greater or lesser extent adapt the usage he

---

[7] Understandably, reinterpretation may change the status of the variants involved, gradually turning occasional deviations into stable features of usage. Thus, for example, F. Otten, analyzing the *Stepennaia kniga* (Otten 1973), demonstrates that inconsistency in forming the imperfect from verbs of the fourth class (with l-epenthenticum or without it) are met significantly more often in the last two parts of the chronicle than in the beginning. One may hypothesize that the occasional variants in ancient chronicle collections (on which see Khaburgaev 1991) are interpreted by the fourteenth-century author as precedents that justify a usage that he finds more convenient, with which he can create an imperfect from the familiar л-form without thinking. We find an eloquent example of the way in which the reinterpretation of a precedent was used by a chronicler in order to avoid difficulties in creating various forms in the *Tsarstvennaia kniga* [*Royal Book*] of the late sixteenth century (PSRL, XIII, 506). In the description of the siege of Kazan', the newest layer of the chronicle, we read: "И много розни въ городѣ сотвориша: овїи хотяху за неизможенїе бити челомъ государю нашему; инїи измѣннки воду начаша копати и не обрѣтоша, но токмо малъ потокъ докопашася смраденъ, и до взятїя взимаху воду с нужею, от тое же воды болѣзнь бяше въ нихъ, пухли и умираху съ нее." The chronicler evidently had difficulty creating the imperfect form from the verb пухнути, which he clearly could not derive from the written tradition. He therefore preferred using a combination of the л-form and the imperfect in the capacity of coordinated elements (пухли and умираху). This freedom was the result of reinterpreting the written tradition, in which this kind of word combination could sometimes be met. It was just this sort of reinterpretation and the use of the forms it produced that contributed to the evolution of the written tradition.

had assimilated to his own spoken practices or could orient the text he was creating on more or less archaic layers of the corpus, whether or not he was following a particular archaizing or modernizing agenda. Because of this state of affairs, some texts in the hybrid register could radically differ from standard bookish ones while others could be very similar in many of their linguistic characteristics.

As we have suggested, the fundamental difference between standard and hybrid registers depended on their relation to the mechanism of orientation on models and the mechanism of retabulation. Understandably, the border between the two registers remained imprecise, especially in the earlier period when the distance between the bookish and non-bookish language had not yet become such that many markers of bookishness acquired unconditional status. Insofar as continuity in the bookish language was realized as a transformation of the habits of reading into the habits of writing, its concrete parameters depended not only on linguistic but also literary history. The immediate guide for a bookman and the source of his templates was not so much the whole corpus of literature that he had read as the texts of that "genre" to which the text he was creating belonged. Therefore chronicles were situated in the line of succession of chronicles, hymnographical works in the line of hymnographical works, and so on.[8] And of course in literary history the mechanism of reconceptualization is also at work, so that chronicles may be seen not only as annalistic works but as narratives in the broader sense, so that they may serve as a model not only for other chronicles, but for any narrative (for example, saints lives, or in the seventeenth century, romances). This sort of branching out of textual continuity was conditioned by the course of the literary process, so that in this respect the history of the bookish language was connected in the most intimate way with the history of literature, and, in particular, with its social aspect.

In the course of centuries the conditions of literary activity significantly changed, and although the social composition, size, and occupations of that small portion of medieval society that one can see as analogue of the modern literary public (creators and consumers of books) have been insufficiently studied, primarily because of the lack of evidence,

---

[8] On the notion of templates and their role in a person's reinterpretation of linguistic experience, see: Nichols and Timberlake 1991; Timberlake 1996. On the qualifications necessary to apply the notion of "genre" in the history of Eastern Slavic writing, see: Lenhoff 1984; Seeman 1987; Marti 1989. On the "generic" factor in the history of Slavic literary languages, see Tolstoi 1978; Alekseev 1987a, 44–5.

these factors clearly did not remain unchanged from the eleventh through the seventeenth centuries (and equally so, say from the thirteenth though sixteenth). In sixteenth century Muscovy there could hardly have existed someone like the thirteenth-century Novgorodian sexton Timofei who copied church books, kept chronicles, and compiled treaties (see Gippius 1992). In the sixteenth century literary activity clearly became more differentiated, so that each of these activities was associated (even if not unambiguously) with a particular circle of people with more or less professional preparation (of course, not in the modern sense). Given such differentiation, potential authors' circle of reading also separates out, as well as the scope and character of their linguistic experience acquired in assimilating the particular corpus of texts.

This differentiation should have led to the consolidation of the various registers of the written language. Understandably, we are dealing here with a long term, gradual process that makes precise dating, and indeed any dating at all, fairly conditional. One may say definitely that in the sixteenth-seventeenth centuries a special type (register) of the bookish language came into being that manifested its writers' particular linguistic position and which formed its own tradition. A monk who was composing the canon of a newly glorified saint clearly felt himself in a different literary and linguistic tradition than a worker in the patriarchal chronicle scriptorium (like Isidor Skazkin, compiler of the Mazurinskii chronicle — see Koretskii 1968), and the latter did not feel at home in the language that a clerk preparing responses to petitions had assimilated. As a result of the consolidation of written traditions they could function as relatively autonomous systems so that it becomes possible to remake a text from one register into another. The revision of the Life of Mikhail Klopskii, carried out by Vasilii Tuchkov in Moscow in the first half of the sixteenth century, may serve as an example of this. We may surmise that Tuchkov felt that the hybrid language of the first draft was more fitting for a chronicle than for a saint's life so that he tried to rework the text to conform to the demands of the standard register (see Dmitriev 1958; Zhivov 1992a, 262–3). By the end of the seventeenth century the autonomy of the hybrid register was felt so strongly that it could be considered as a special "simple" tongue into which texts could be translated that previously existed only in standard Church Slavonic (I have in mind Firsov's 1683 translation of the Psalter — see below).

Moreover, the reconceptualization of the hybrid language as "simple" relates to the period that immediately preceded the Petrine linguistic reform and represents one of the reinterpretations of the entire medieval heritage that took place on the threshold of the new era. In the earlier period one could hardly speak of the special culturological (or symbolic) significance of the hybrid register or of its being associated with a particular value system. Although particular traditions of writing appeared and gradually crystallized within the bookish tradition there was no corresponding differentiation of cultural space. One cannot say, for example, that the standard register was associated with religious values and the hybrid with secular culture or that the standard register belonged to highbrow culture and hybrid to the lowbrow. The sphere of bookish culture continued to be concentrated around a single center, which was embodied (in terms of texts) in Holy Writ and liturgical books (cf. Edlichka 1976; Alekseev 1987a). In the hierarchical edifice of Eastern Slavic medieval literature these texts served as the absolute, ontological cornerstone, the ideal and model for the entire cultural space (cf. Picchio 1973; Alekseev and Likhachev 1987, 69).

This applies in the most direct way to texts in standard Church Slavonic, which were immediately connected to religious life, and for which the basic corpus of texts (Holy Writ and liturgy) served as the direct model — ideological, literary, and linguistic. However, hybrid texts were not separated from this core of texts by any clearly recognized and formulated differences. As noted in regard to their language, these may significantly differ from the standard Church Slavonic and in the strength of these differences form their own separate tradition, i.e., they were not oriented on this central core directly but via the key monuments of some particular "genre." Nonetheless these differences were evidently perceived as acceptable departures, used out of weakness rather than design, a kind of poetic license. Thus the benchmark for the "correct" and hybrid written languages remained the texts of the main corpus, and hybrid texts were still considered part of Christian culture rather than some something standing apart. This is seen most clearly in the example of chronicles.

In his day I. P. Eremin wrote quite extensively about the significance of chronicles as a unique part of religious literature that depicts God's providence working itself out in human history (Eremin 1966, 64–71). Their main idea therefore remained religious — to show the achievements and sufferings of humankind (or a small part of it) on its path to salvation and to derive spiritual lessons from them. For this view of history the fundamental religious texts remained the central and most important source, apart from the question of how many times the chronicler cites the Bible or some other chronicle. At the same time, the interconnection of one chronicle with another was just as natural. They do not so much continue the record of events begun by their predecessors as document new stages revealing the divine plan for humanity. This view of chronicle writing may not only be reconstructed from the way historical events are presented in them but is also very explicitly expressed by the Eastern Slavic annalists themselves.[9]

It is understandable that if this religious understanding is characteristic of chronicle writing, it is no less central to other hybrid texts, for example, saints lives written in this register. Furthermore, this common understanding made possible the mutual interaction of various types of text, for example, using fragments from chronicles in hagiography or incorporating saints lives, patericons, and tales of miraculous icons into collections of chronicles, in whole or in part. United by a common religious understanding, these texts did not form precise generic groups and redistributed textual material in a relatively free fashion. Given this historical and literary background the borders between registers of the bookish language were not particularly precise, and in any case were not perceived as manifestations of cultural differentiation.

4. The Reconceptualization of the Varieties of the Bookish Language

The process of culturological reconceptualization of the varieties of the bookish language began within bookish culture and its starting impulses may be glimpsed in its own dynamic development rather than in external stimuli. The processes of functional reconceptualization of genetically heterogeneous elements discussed earlier was the result of the interaction of the bookish and non-bookish languages and may be seen as the accommodation of the bookish language to local conditions. From a certain point of view, however, such accommodation represents corruption (cf. the perception of colloquial Greek by Byzantine connoisseurs of classical culture or the Humanists' view of medieval Latin), and this idea, that is potentially present in the conception of any bookish language, only awaits the appropriate cultural conditions to become an active factor in its transformation. In Muscovite Rus' such conditions occurred in the late fourteenth century, when the unification of the Orthodox world became the common concern of Constantinople and the Slavic lands, and they put into motion the process that is traditionally called the "Second South Slavic influence," although a more fitting label should have been found long ago.

---

[9] See, for example, the end of the Rogozhskii chronicle […] (PSRL, XV, col. 185).

A defining moment of the Second South Slavic influence was the reevaluation of the relations between bookish and spoken usage, while the external influence (the influence of the South Slavic bookish tradition) remained secondary, conditioned by the search for a new model that had not been subject to "corruption" (cf. Worth 1983b, 354; Uspenskii 1983, 55). The turn to South Slavic models was motivated by the desire to purify and systematize the basic corpus of texts (Holy Writ and liturgy); in this period South Slavic book culture was perceived as more "correct" and cultured, i.e., as a fitting tool to resolve questions that had arisen on Eastern Slavic soil. The posing of these questions was of primary importance. It indicated the development of linguistic self-awareness the result of which was a new perception of the previous literary tradition, not as something usual and given but as an object to be reformed. As for the Humanists in the West, this moment signified, at least potentially, "the end of any *scriptum est* or *ipse dixit*, truths established once and for all" (Picchio 1975, 170). It was precisely from this new perspective that the previous evolution of the bookish language began to be seen as corrupt. Accordingly, Russian bookmen faced the task of "purifying" the bookish language, and the natural means for this was separating bookish from conversational usage. South Slavic texts assumed the role of the model insofar as their linguistic characteristics were clearly opposed to the natural speech habits of Russian writers.[10]

Initially the new relationship to the text was realized in the sphere of textual reproduction. i.e., of those texts that were copied, edited, revised, but not created from scratch. The basic corpus of texts belonged precisely to this sphere whose reformation as basis for the entire culture was the

---

[10] In his well-known report at the Fourth International Congress of Slavists, D. S. Likhachev juxtaposed the Second South Slavic influence on the Eastern Slavs to the cultural phenomena that were characteristic for Western Europe on the eve of the Renaissance (Likhachev 1958). In general, this conception is not justifiable because the Second South Slavic influence has no relation to the Byzantine or Western European humanist tradition at all. Still, particular analogies in the sphere of relations to texts and to problems of their transmission, preservation and correction may be brought to light (see Picchio 1975). Nevertheless, there is no basis for speaking of a single Byzantine source of Western humanism and the processes connected to the Slavs' correcting of books; here, in my opinion, R. Picchio's proposed picture of development also somewhat simplifies the actual situation. The most significant thing differentiating Eastern Slavic from Western European development was the content of the basic corpus of texts on which their cultures were based, which also shaped their literary activity, in particular, the development of normative narrative structures, the norm of the written language, etc. In the world of Slavia orthodoxa this corpus included only religious texts (Holy Writ and liturgy), while for Western Europe and Byzantium classical authors were also included. As a result for the Eastern Slavs the connection between literary tasks and religious values was primary, linking linguistic and confessional purity, which did not exist in such a direct way even in Erasmus, not to speak of other Humanists.

§0–4. The Reconceptualization of the Varieties of the Bookish Language

mission that led to interest in South Slavic sources. However, the changes could not stop here insofar as the new principles inevitably affected aspects of original literary production. The principle of distancing oneself from the living language made appeal to the bookman's natural linguistic experience illegitimate, as a result of which a different kind of regimentation became necessary that was based not on this experience but on a system of abstract rules. The appearance of these rules signified the development of a grammatical approach to the bookish language, and the Second South Slavic influence acted as a stimulus in this process.

The need for grammatical regimentation brought about the appearance of a variety of grammatical guides. At first they came from the Southern Slavs (the treatise "Concerning the Eight Parts of Speech" [O osmi chastekh slova] — Iagich 1896, 38f; Worth 1983a, 14–21; the orthographic treatise of Konstantin Kostechenskii — Iagich 1896, 247f; Goldblatt 1987; and possibly other works — cf. Sobolevskii 1903, 34–6). These materials were assimilated into Russia, where they were taken up and developed, creating the basis for contacts with the Western European (primarily German) philological tradition. Overlooking a series of short articles concerning grammar, it is sufficient to point to Dmitrii Gerasimov's *Donatus* (Iagich 1896, 524f; cf. Worth 1983a, 76–165; Mechkovskaia 1984, 38–40; Zhivov 1986, 93–107; Keipert 1989; Zakhar'in 1991), completed in 1522 (or perhaps somewhat earlier — Mechkovskaia 1984, 39), which contained "a certain semantic systematization of linguistic forms" (Mechkovskaia, ibid). With Maksim Grek's arrival in Moscow in 1518 the study of grammar received further stimulus and was conceived as "the beginning and end of every philosophy (liubomudrie)" and "guide to divine vision (bogovidnomu smotreniiu) and to the most glorious and inaccessible theology" (Iagich 1896, 333). Moreover the cultivation of grammar was tied to the values of the bookish language, and grammar became the most important criteria for determining textual correctness.

This new attitude toward grammar radically changed the correlation between model texts and grammatical prescriptions. Model texts ceased to be the ultimate arbiter and could themselves be corrected in connection with newly developed grammatical rules. The correction of books based on grammar began precisely with Maksim Grek. I will illustrate the main lines of this development by describing how verbal forms were changed. The first step toward grammatical normalization was organizing the paradigms. Compiling verbal paradigms of past tenses, Russian grammarians confronted the problem of homonymic forms of the second and third pers. sg. of the type глагола — глагола or глаголаше — глаголаше. This arrangement of the paradigm contradicted models they knew (in Greek and Latin) and apparently also their notions of correct grammar. Therefore in the paradigm of past tenses in the second or second and third pers. *л*-forms were introduced, which resolved the problem of homonymns and created an acceptable paradigm according to grammatical ideas of the time. This is exactly how Dmitrii Gerasimov proceeds in his *Donatus* (Iagich 1896, 566–5, 572, 575, 578, 583), and this solution is accepted by all subsequent Eastern Slavic grammars of the bookish language (Zhivov and Uspenskii 1986, 261).

In the corrections that Maksim Grek introduced (together with the same Dmitrii Gerasimov) into his edited versions of the *Explanatory Psalter (Tolkovyi Psaltyr')* and the *Festal Triodion (Tsvetnoi Triod')* this normalization became the basis for book editing. Thus in the editing of the *Explanatory Psalter* of 1521–22 there are replacements of the type *призва — призвал еси, услыша — услышал еси, сотвори — сотворил еси*, and so on (Kovtun et al, 1973, 108). Maksim continued with this editing even later, despite persecution by proponents of the traditional forms ((Kovtun et al, 1973; Zhivov and Uspenskii 1986, 259–60). Responding to his opponents' charge that these changes altered the basic meaning of the texts, Maksim said that "there is no difference here, or just something momentary and transitory" (Pokrovskii 1971, 90; cf. 109, 126, 140, 158, 160). This answer eloquently testifies that for Maksim and his pupils the correctness of his changes were exclusively connected to grammatical considerations; what was important was that forms belonged to a uniform grammatical category (which could, understandably, be rather artificial), while their dissimilarity to traditional usage was no longer an area of concern.

As we know, Maksim was condemned twice (in 1525 and 1531) and among the charges against him figured purely linguistic ones. Maksim's corrections were rejected, although editing based on textological considerations alone (finding the most ancient and linguistically least corrupted copies and basing corrections on them) had not had much success, as the evidence was contradictory and they couldn't establish criteria for determining the most correct (or oldest) copies. In these conditions appeal to grammatical criteria became inevitable, and the history of book correcting in the seventeenth century shows that editors of various tendencies all referred to them, to a greater or lesser extent. Maksim's principles and concrete paradigms were taken up and continued by Nikonian and post-Nikonian text editors (spravshchiki). However, grammatical criteria also played a role in pre-Nikonian editing, as one may see in the polemics of Moscow editors (Ivan Nasedka and the hegumen Il'ia) with Lavrentii Zizanii in 1627 (see Preniia 1859, 95; cf. Zhivov 1993a, 110–10). The grammatical approach

§0–4. The Reconceptualization of the Varieties of the Bookish Language

thus became firmly established in Russian book culture and isolated protests against particular of its applications remained of secondary importance in the larger development.

The development of the grammatical approach changed both the correlation and interpretation of registers of the bookish language. It is important to note that the grammatical approach by no means applied to all book culture, and clearly — both in the seventeenth, and even more in the sixteenth century — was practiced by a limited group of bookmen, while the majority of those involved with book production not only did not master this branch of learning but apparently were not even familiar with the grammatical treatises. Due to this hybrid texts were untouched as a rule by the new development and the hybrid register continued to function without significant changes. It was not its functioning that changed but its perception. Those authors who assimilated the grammatical approach evidently saw these texts as "semi-literate," created by ignorant people who didn't bother with grammatical teachings. The philippics of the elder Evdokim, author of the *Prostoslovie,* one of the late sixteenth century grammatical tracts, were directed against just this kind of bookman [...] (Iagich 1896, 633–4). Evdokim criticizes those who learn by rote (starting with the Psalter) and who undertake to write without first receiving elementary grammatical training, creating hybrid texts as a result.[11]

If from the new perspective the hybrid register was seen as the language of ignoramuses, the language that adhered to grammatical normalization was the language of the educated, which could not help but influence the way it was elaborated as well as its social functioning. Its elaboration turned into a scholarly project whose degree of complexity was established by Greek, a knowledge of which — from the point of view of Maksim's pupils and those who continued his tradition — was necessary to adequately translate Greek texts. This scholarly elaboration brought home the importance of normative regularization of the bookish language and opened the way for normalization that was completely artificial in character. The verbal system as presented in Smotritskii's grammar may serve as an eloquent illustration of this. As N. B.

---

[11] In the foreword to the *Prostoslovie* Evdokim writes that "A person who does not understand simplicity cannot be wise. A person who attends to simplicity can acquire even greater wisdom." By "simplicity" Evdokim evidently means elementary knowledge of grammar which is presented (at least in part) in his treatise. "For those seeking understanding and wisdom I have presented a non-bookish teaching about grammar in brief. I have made it intelligible for quick learning and [to give] the greatest skill in books" (Iagich 1896, 629–30). "Non-bookish teaching about grammar" apparently means the collection of rules that Evdokim is contrasting to memorization. This elementary knowledge is the necessary condition for the further mastery of "the greatest skill in books."

Mechkovskaia justly notes, in Smotritskii's work "the system of past tenses cannot be equated to the system of the imperfect, perfect, pluperfect, or aorist of Old Slavic" (1984. 90). The scheme of four past tenses is taken from Greek grammars (although the larger structure comes from Latin ones — see Kociuba 1975), and in order to fill in the missing links Smotritskii creates completely artificial analogous forms (e.g., л-forms with double vowel in the 2nd pers. suffix, like читаалъ).

This artificial normalization was but one of the particular results of learned authors' new view of the bookish language as their own domain. Their appropriation of the bookish language was reflected in the fact that it was not seen so much as the language of tradition as the language of their own learning. For this reason they strove to use it in all of those cases when other "scholarly languages" were used (i.e., Greek and Latin). It could be used as the language for teaching, for scholarly discussion and correspondence, etc. These processes occurred both in Ukraine and in Muscovite Rus'. An example of such usage is the record of a discussion among Simeon Polotskii, Epifanii Slavinetskii and Paisii Ligarid with Nikolai Spafarii that took place in Moscow in 1671 (see the publication — Golubev 1971; cf. Uspenskii 1983, 87–9). No less indicative is the note of the Chudov monk Evfimii on the translation of an explanation of the liturgy that was in pure Church Slavonic: "I paid for the translation myself" (Sobolevskii 1903, 340).[12]

Insofar as the standard bookish language was interpreted here as a scholarly tongue, its "correctness" was tied not to its age or sacred status but with its learned cultivation. Traditional standard works that had not been subject to grammatical revision were now considered substandard due to past ignorance, and this was also considered true, in principle, of the texts of Holy Writ and liturgy, that had formerly served as the uncontested model for all book culture. A critical attitude toward the legacy of Cyril and Methodius may even be found in Maksim Grek, who wrote in defense of his corrections to the books they edited that "I correct them, for they have mistakes either from an uneducated copyist, unskilled and unknowledgeable in grammar, or from the very fathers of blessed memory who first made written translations, and let the truth be said, nowhere was there a full comprehension of the Greek language, and for this reason they fell far from the truth" (Maksim Grek, III, 62; cf. Iagich 1896, 301). These words were apparently not characteristic of the first half of the sixteenth century; this was the position of

---

[12] As an example from the early eighteenth century, see the "Kalendar' ili mesiatseslov" for 1721 which contains diary entries in Church Slavonic by F. Polikarpov (RGADA, f. 1251, no. 271/z). [...]

a Greek man of letters, hardly shared by his Russian colleagues. But with the spread of the grammatical approach a similar attitude toward old translations became widespread. Thus Afanasii Kholomogorskii, polemicizing with the Old Believers, repeated Maksim's comments about the complexity of Greek and the difficulty of translation almost word for word. This difficulty could only be overcome gradually, by many generations of bookmen, who have to "correct [the books] better. For when there are more reasonable people, they understand more than a single person... And besides the wise men of old and their translations, Holy Scripture says that a multitude of wise men is the salvation of the world" [Wisdom 6: 24; in the Slavonic Bible 6: 26] (RGADA, f. 381, no., 413, l. 82–82 verso; Afanasii Kholmogorskii 1682, l. 262 verso). Referring to the imperfection of earlier translations, Afanasii wrote: "However, from the original image [i.e, text] many can do better, but they are not given praise for the first attempt, because the first is hardest of all, and they [who attempted it first] should not be blamed for not doing better. But the more is done the better for a most excellent and honest cause" (l. 82)

In the framework of the standard register a special, grammatically refined version of the bookish language developed. This serves as the scholarly bookish language and in this capacity may be juxtaposed to the traditional bookish language, which, not having been revised, is now considered coarse and ignorant like the hybrid language. The task of revising the bookish language and the correction of the texts written in it, requiring broad philological knowledge. is assumed by learned bookmen. In this respect Church Slavonic is likened to Greek, which, in the words of Maksim Grek, became "quite dense and incomprehensible [to the ignorant] due to the skill of ancient men who were outstanding in rhetorical ability" (Maksim Grek, II, 312; cf. Iagich 1896, 297–304; Ikonnikov 1915, 178–80). As in the case with Greek, expertise in Slavonic is now seen as dependent on mastering a whole complex of disciplines in the humanities, insofar as "if someone is not sufficiently and fully trained in grammar and poetics and rhetoric and philosophy itself, he cannot directly and completely either understand what is written nor transpose it into his own language" (Maksim Grek, III, 62; cf. Iagich 1896, 301). This new view of the bookish language was fully manifested in the polemics between defenders of Nikon's book correction and the Old Believers, in the course of which the bookmen of the reformist camp accused their opponents of ignorance of grammar, rhetoric and philosophy, rendering them incapable of judging the accuracy of church books.

As noted, the number of these learned bookmen was very small and for many of those who were occupied with book culture the presumption of these innovators that they had a monopoly over the correct bookish language was strange, and at times simply unacceptable. However, insofar as they denied this presumption, they were also obliged to develop their own somewhat new conception of the bookish language. It seems likely that it was these circumstances that triggered the idea of the holiness of Church Slavonic, according to which its correctness was ensured not by the scholarly efforts of connoisseurs of grammar and philosophy but by its essentially sacred quality that was due to the fact that it was created by holy men and even by God Himself. Statements about the holiness of Church Slavonic may be met even earlier, but mostly in polemical works that were defending its status as no less of an autonomous holy language than Greek or Latin. It is precisely in this context that its divine origin is argued in the "Skazanie o russkoi gramote" (Tale of Russian Letters) (see Zhivov 1992), and its holiness claimed in juxtaposition to the "profane" Greek language in the writings of the monk Khrabr and the tradition he began ("Slavonic letters are more honest and holy because a holy man created them, whereas Greek letters [were created] by the pagan Hellenes" — Iagich 1896, 11; Kuev 1967, 190–1; on this tradition, see Uspenskii 1987, 232–4). This interpretation remained on the periphery of Eastern Slavic cultural consciousness until the sixteenth century.[13]

Despite all objections, the grammatical approach undermined the notion of the holiness of ancient translations. The new consciousness made possible the scholarly upgrading of the basic corpus of texts, i.e., Holy Writ and liturgical books, and made philological interpretation and critical analysis inevitable. These tasks were realizable with the aid of knowledge that was not directly dependent on faith, that is, that was secular in character. The value of this knowledge did not rely on the confessional purity of its source, so that the new perception created the preconditions for turning to European scholarship and European educational models. For traditional Orthodoxy this was an extreme innovation and evoked profound opposition.

---

[13] B. A. Uspenskii (1984) is hardly justified in stating that the notion of Church Slavonic as an "icon of Orthodoxy" was a constant of linguistic consciousness from ancient times through the seventeenth century and in connecting this to the situation of linguistic diglossia. This ignores the dynamics of the symbolic level in the history of the bookish language, so that the views of specific periods (e.g., the seventeenth century) are extrapolated for the entire middle ages as a whole (to cite just one example, the notion of the substantial unity of Church Slavonic and Greek among a series of late sixteenth century Ukrainian writers and among Muscovite Grecophiles of the late seventeenth century, which Uspenskii practically attributes to the earliest period of Eastern Slavic literature — Uspenskii 1987, 33–5); this creates a misleading picture of continuity existing over the course of six centuries. It also allows Uspenskii to assert the existence of diglossia throughout the middle ages, as he refers to phenomena separated in time that there is no basis for synchronizing.

§0–4. The Reconceptualization of the Varieties of the Bookish Language

It is indicative that the proponents of the traditional approach to the bookish language who saw it as something sacred and inviolable and who objected to any reworking of sacred texts rejected the entire learned tradition that underpinned such reworking, that is, they rejected the very idea of Church Slavonic as a language of learning. Such a reaction occurred both in Ukraine and in Muscovite Rus', and the schism caused by Nikon's reforms was from this perspective simply a particular instance of it. Thus Archpriest Avvakum wrote: "Do not strive after rhetoric and philosophy or eloquence, but live, following the [dictates of] the healthy, genuine word (glagol)... For a rhetorician and philosopher cannot be a Christian... And all of the saints teach us that rhetoric and philosophy — is external delusion, worthy of the inextinguishable fires" (RIB, XXXIX, col. 547–8). One may find similar statements by other Old Believer writers as well as by zealots of Orthodoxy in South Western Rus' of the late sixteenth — early seventeenth century, who—for all their cultural differences — ran into similar problems (see, for example, Ivan Vishenskii — Ivan Vishenskii 1955, 23, 162–3, 175–6, 194).[14] These authors write about the holiness of Church Slavonic.

Whatever the actual social limits of the spread of the grammatical approach, it was rich soil for rethinking all aspects of literary activities, and as we have seen, it also had an influence on those bookmen to whom it remained alien or who were hostile to it. Although the issue concerned forming the norms of the bookish language (based on texts or on grammatical rules), that is, a rather abstract problem, a social dimension formerly absent or insignificant now played a role in the functioning of the bookish language. The very possibility of being educated in grammar acted as a social differentiator. If earlier various levels of mastery of the bookish language formed a continuum, now there was a clear-cut separation between the learned elite who knew "grammar and poetics and rhetoric and philosophy itself" and the rest of the reading and writing public. This differentiation made it possible to address texts to different audiences; some could be meant for learned colleagues and others for the uneducated. Insofar as choice of addressee was connected with choice of linguistic register, these variants of the bookish language could be reconceptualized as neutral, simple, rhetorically refined, and so on.[15] As a

---

[14] B. A. Uspenskii cites a large collection of examples of protests against grammar and other philological pursuits from works by Ukrainian as well as Muscovite authors (Uspenskii 1987, 257–8). On Ivan Vishenskii's possible influence on Old Believer writers, see Goldblatt 1991.

[15] Earlier the role of the audience in book culture had been secondary. One may point to rare instances when the choice of addressee was significant. For example, Kliment Smoliatich, responding to the priest Foma, noted of the epistle to which Foma had objected that "I wrote it not to you but to the prince" (Nikol'skii 1892, 103–4). Of course, in many works the

result, first in Ukraine and then in Muscovite Rus' the conditions arose for the assimilation and development of the notion of a "simple tongue," which was of extraordinary importance for the history of Slavic literary culture.

5. Linguistic "Simplicity" and the Means of Its Realization

Traditional Slavic book culture confronted the idea of linguistic "simplicity" in the sixteenth century. Although the issue of the comprehensibility of bookish texts could have been posed earlier it was in this century that it acquired fundamental importance and became a motivating factor in linguistic change in the framework of *Slavia Orthodoxa*. It entered into complex interaction with other factors in creating a new attitude both toward the traditional bookish language and toward the learned linguistic tradition, provoking changes in the functioning of particular variants of the bookish language and, ultimately, the rejection of traditional bookishness as the principal medium for the expression of cultural values.

The transformation of linguistic thought was common throughout Europe, although in various regions it proceeded differently, at different speeds, influenced by the specifics of national traditions and their starting points, and produced diverse, at times dissimilar, results. The cause of this transformative process was religious conflict, which gripped all of Europe to a greater or lesser extent and radically altered the traditional social organization of religious life; if earlier continuity of religious convictions from generation to generation had been the norm, now to a significant extent they were a

---

addressee may be discerned with greater or lesser clarity: the "Merilo Pravednoe" (Scale of Righteousness) was meant for rulers and judges while collections of ascetic works were for monks. However, the differentiation of addressees remained rudimentary and imprecise, as the free transfer of texts from one collection to another — say, from the "Merilo Pravednoe" into compilations of ascetic texts—testifies. The usual addressee remained the Christian people as a whole, without any further specification. As regards the most important texts — the liturgical ones - social characteristics of the addressee did not exist at all, as they were addressed to God and not to men. This is seen most clearly in liturgical polyphony (mnogoglasie), when various parts of the service are performed simultaneously by various clergymen and church servitors in order to fulfill the instructions of the typicon and not to leave out any part of the service. This turns the texts that are read and sung simultaneously into an undifferentiated hubbub as far as the congregants are concerned, but not for God, who is believed to be able to comprehend any number of texts at one time. It is indicative that in the middle of the seventeenth century sequential performance (edinoglasie) was introduced, that is, reading all parts of the service in order (cf. Zen'kovskii 1970, 112–8). This makes it comprehensible to the listener, i.e., it presumes a certain attention to the audience, and is clearly connected to the process of differentiation of addressees in bookish culture of the time.

§0–5. Linguistic "Simplicity" and the Means of Its Realization

matter of personal involvement and individual choice. This process began in the framework of the Reformation in its various manifestations and was not extinguished by the Counter-Reformation, which gave it new stimuli. Each person's convictions became the target of opposing religious doctrines so that religious polemics and doctrinal apologetics were addressed to an ever wider audience.

Orthodox Slavdom did not remain apart from this process. The rethinking of linguistic ideas overtook Lithuanian Rus' first of all because it was directly touched by Reformation and Counter-Reformation trends. Evidence of this are the bible translations of Fransiscus Skorina, who published them so that "not only doctors and educated people will understand them but any simple and common person reading or listening can understand what is needed for his spiritual salvation" (Karskii 1921, 24). This development further led to the formation of the "simple" or "Russian tongue" (ruskaia mova) as the literary language of South-Western Rus', functioning alongside Church Slavonic (see Tolstoi 1963; Uspenskii 1983, 64f). In the seventeenth century appear the new Bulgarian translations of the "damaskins," whose language reflected the linguistic position of Damaskin Studite, who wrote in the *koine glosse* (common tongue), hoping to bring spiritual enlightenment to the broad masses (Dell'Agata 1984, 15–89; Demina, III, 18–9). This century also witnessed the turn to the "simple tongue" in Serbia.

As far as Muscovite Rus', the corresponding processes were more complex and less obvious. Here in the first half of the seventeenth century the idea of necessary universal religious enlightenment developed within the context of attempts at the "ecclesiasticization" ("otserkovlenie") of Russian life, the establishment of religious discipline (blagochinie) and religious statues as the norm for everyday life of the entire population (cf. Zen'kovskii 1970, 59-90). These efforts that were characteristic of the Bogoliubtsy or Zealots of Piety demanded active propaganda and intensive religious education for the masses. Such activity naturally presupposed the use of language that would be comprehensible to a wide audience. What this language was, we don't know exactly, but individual texts by Avvakum and Nasedka can give some sense of them. In the supplement to the Life of Dionisii Zobninovskii, written by Nasedka, and the Life of Avvakum significant fragments are written in a language that is almost completely devoid of specifically bookish features; the literary character of the text is signaled by the rare use of markers of bookishness. In this case the choice of the hybrid register is intentional and reflects the authors' individual polemical position (see below).

At the same time we may presume that these linguistic efforts were connected to a certain religious tradition whose general program included the regularization of Russian ecclesiastical culture and hanges in church customs aimed at expanding the influence of church teaching on all aspects of the people's life. Nasedka's activities may thus be connected to traditions going back to Dionisii Zobninovskii and Arsenii Glukhoi (see Jaksche 1985; Skvortsov 1890), and from them to Maksim Grek and his pupils. This tradition had to have a philological aspect, and in this connection we cannot fail to mention the evaluation of Maksim Grek's linguistic practice that is given in the works of Maksim's pupil Zinovii Otenskii. Otenskii wrote: "Maksim… thought … that after bookish speech we have common speech. [But] I think it is an evil idea of heretics or the ignorant to liken and degrade the bookish language to [the level of] common popular speech… Maksim cannot be blamed because he did not know the Russian language thoroughly" (Zinovii Otenskii 1863, 967). Paradoxically, Maksim appears here to be initiator of the rapprochement between bookish and popular languages, although he was unquestionably far from an orientation on colloquial speech. However, in advancing the grammatical approach Maksim did not strive for the maximal distancing of the written language from the conversational. For him grammatical education that (as noted above) presumed varying levels of knowledge was primary. An uneducated person needed a "simple" text, which led to the idea of a "simple language," and this connected Maksim to the Bogoliubtsy. In the context of active religious and educational policies these potential aspects of linguistic thought were actualized, and conditioned the unique manifestation of the idea of linguistic "simplicity" in Muscovite Rus'.

The spread of the idea of linguistic "simplicity" in Slavic lands differed from the similar process in Western Europe because of differences in their initial situations. In France, England, and Germany the national languages had existed as the languages of culture long before the spread of ideas of linguistic simplicity. Latin was clearly juxtaposed to the national tongues in linguistic consciousness, and ideas of linguistic simplicity were manifested in the shifting borders of the cultural territory to which each of them was assigned. In Muscovite Rus', as for other Orthodox Slavs, Church Slavonic alone functioned as the language of culture. Therefore the idea of linguistic simplicity could not be realized by redistribution of the functions of Church Slavonic and some other language. In these conditions one of two possible developmental schemes was possible: either the functions of the separate registers of the bookish language could be redefined, with one singled out as "simple," or a new "simple" language could be created that was juxtaposed to Church Slavonic. In both instances, the creation of works in the "simple tongue" ran into significantly greater difficulties and was subject to greater restrictions than in the Western European case.

These difficulties were conditioned by the inner contradiction that the notion of a "simple" language introduced into the Orthodox tradition. Indeed, this idea demanded the comprehensibility and accessibility of religious texts. This demand could be fulfilled fairly easily in the case of newly created texts, as they could be fashioned on the basis of some new "simple" language. But transferring this language into all spheres of cultural activity would mean a rejection of the whole earlier tradition, the entire corpus of Church Slavonic texts that had been compiled over centuries and that made up the core of Orthodox culture. If religious and cultural needs could have been satisfied by literature in the new language, the use of literature in the traditional bookish tongue would become the affair of a small number of aficionados; it would threaten its existence as a living tradition: comprehensibility of the new ran counter to the comprehensibility of the old. This conflict led to attempts to seek a compromise between tradition and the comprehensibility of the "simple" language. In different situations the result could be closer to one or the other pole, to tradition or comprehensibility; the compromise itself, however, was in all cases reflected in the functioning of the "simple" texts, limiting the polyfunctionalism of the new means of expression and superimposing a certain imprint on the structure of the "simple" language (for all the diversity of the linguistic manifestations of this simplicity).

In Muscovite Rus', that was not seriously threatened by Catholic or Protestant proselytism (which stimulated the creation of literature in the "simple" tongue, for example, in Ukraine), the need for the "simple" language was not so pressing as in Kiev, L'vov or Vilnius. Here there was no basis even for a partial rejection of the Church Slavonic tradition, and compromise clearly tended toward the pole of traditionalism. And here in the second half of the seventeenth century appeared a series of monuments that their authors considered written in the simple language. On closer inspection, however, it turns out that most of these were written in standard Church Slavonic, and the declarations about "simplicity" were purely for show. They only indicate that the authors' concern about their addressees was limited (voluntarily or due to their lack of knowledge) to the rejection of grammatical refinement, that is, the issue boiled down to the opposition between "learned" and "simple" writing that arose consequent to the spread of the grammatical approach to the bookish language (discussed above).[16]

---

[16] Simeon Polotskii's Obed dushevnyi and the book called Statir, written by an unknown clergyman from the Perm diocese (Alekseev 1965; Uspenskii 1994, 196-9; Zhivov 1991; on Statir's language, see § III–3.1) are examples of this kind of "simple" language. Polotskii's linguistic practice is especially instructive. Very familiar with the Ukrainian variant of the "simple" language, in the context of Muscovy he chose a traditional variant of Church

Still, there were individual texts that were declared to be "simple" that were written in a language different from standard Church Slavonic, and whose choice of register was clearly connected to the writer's reformist position. The clearest monument of this type is the 1683 Psalter of Avraamii Firsov that was translated "for easiest understanding" (udobneishego radi razuma) into "our simple Slavonic tongue... without any ornamentation" (Tselunova 1989, 28). The inconsistent use of the perfect with auxiliary verb, aorist and imperfect, gerunds in *-ще*, etc. (Tselunova 1985; Tselunova 1988), testify to the hybrid nature of this translation. Understandably, the choice of the hybrid language in this case was purposeful and represents a reforming innovation insofar as this was an extremely important book for Orthodox piety and universally known in its traditional form (i.e., as a text in standard Church Slavonic). The new version was juxtaposed to the old as comprehensible to incomprehensible or as "simple" to complex. It is telling that Firsov's translation was banned by Patriarch Ioakim, who presumably saw it as a threat to the Orthodox tradition. From his point of view the balance between traditionalism and comprehensibility was evidently violated in favor of comprehensibility, which quite clearly describes the specific character of the problem of the "simple" tongue in Muscovite Rus'.

Another stimulus for the choice of nonstandard register evidently also existed. When a work was of polemical character and had to convey the authors' personal convictions and the pathos of his individual achievement, the standard bookish language, which could be perceived as the means for conveying the single and supra-personal truth (see Upsenskii 1983, 49–50), was inappropriate.[17] However, the majority of polemical tracts of the seventeenth century were written in the traditional bookish language; see if only the "Objection or the Ruin of Humble Nikon, by God's Grace the Patriarch. Against the Questions of Boyar Simeon Streshnev" [Vozrazhenie ili razorenie smirenago Nikona, Bozheiu milostiiu pariarkha. Protivo voprosov boiarina Simeona Streshneva] (RGADA, f. 27, no. 140, ch. III), Simeon Polotskii's *Zhezl pravleniia* [*Crozier Staff of Rule*] (1667) or Afanasii Kholmogorskii's *Uvet dukhovnyi* [*Spiritial Admonition*] (1682).

Slavonic as its equivalent, clearly preferring tradition to comprehensibility, at the same time presumably counting on Moscow's relatively high level of Church Slavonic culture.

[17] The action of this stimulus is quite visible in the confessional polemics in Ukraine in the late sixteenth-early seventeenth century. Thus Ivan Vishenskii, asserting the unchanging importance of the Church Slavonic language, its holiness and the need to study it, writes about this in the "simple tongue" (prostaia mova -on Vishenskii's ideas about language see Gröschel 1972, 10–14, 18–26). A hundred years later Mikhailo Andrella follows the same pattern (Petrov 1921, 241).

§0–5. Linguistic "Simplicity" and the Means of Its Realization

These treatises were conceived not as defenses of individual points of view but as exposing the obvious incompatibility of the opponent's perspective with supra-personal and generally understood dogma. However, in those cases when the author's goal was to convey personal, subjective conviction, the rejection of standard Church Slavonic was nevertheless appropriate. This may have been the situation with the sermons of Ioanna Neronov[18] and Avvakum and partially with the latter's other writings, and this factor could later influence Old Believer polemical literature.

Given the necessity to compromise between traditionalism and "simplicity"' the hybrid register offered an ideal solution that combined both of these features. The move from the standard to hybrid register was understandably perceived as a simplification. As has been noted, in the linguistic consciousness of Slavic bookmen the bookish language was connected to a limited set of markers of bookishness. Their consistent and regularized use, characteristic of the standard register, indicated mastery of the bookish language and linguistic refinement, while the use of the hybrid language indicated common, unskilled proficiency, characteristic of someone who was not very well versed in book culture. "Not learned in grammatical reason, but being a simple man I wrote with my own hand," explained the elder Avramii in his notebooks of 1696 (Baklanova 1951, 150), and these notebooks offer a typical example of the hybrid language. Given this attitude, the change from the first to the second type of using markers of bookishness was definitely supposed to be perceived as simplifying the language, as a step toward greater comprehensibility. At the same time, insofar as the language preserved markers of bookishness, this change did not take linguistic usage beyond the bounds of Church Slavonic and did not signify a break with tradition.

In these conditions it is natural that in the history of all literary languages of *Slavia Orthodoxa* the early stages of the movement toward a "simple" language are characterized by the use of the hybrid language in this capacity (cf. Zhivov 1988, 77–8). As we have seen in the case of Avraamii Firsov's translation of the Psalter, Muscovite Rus' was no exception. The hybrid register was used in the Life of Archpriest Avvakum (see the materials characterizing his language: Cocron 1962; Chernov 1977; Chernov 1984; Timberlake 1995), which was undoubtedly connected to the author's

---

[18] See the description of Neronov's preaching in the "Zhitie Ioanna Neronova" […] (Materialy, I, 257). We cannot judge the concrete linguistic parameters of Neronov's sermon, but it clearly reflected a new linguistic consciousness that was undoubtedly tied to his religious stance; notably, Ioann not only preaches himself but also calls his flock to universal preaching, which clearly fits into the reformist paradigm.

reformist attitude toward his audience. The consistency of using hybrid variants in the capacity of a "simple" or "comprehensible" written language was directly related to the strong desire of the given social group to retain ties to traditional culture. It was precisely the determination not to break with centuries'-old cultural and linguistic tradition that imposed limitations on the development of literary languages of the new type; "simple" languages were either compromises in terms of their structural organization (hybrid languages seen as "simple") or they remained secondary citizens in the functional regard. In order to change this situation, a culturological stimulus was needed — the decision to create a new culture of the secular type that would radically break with the past and allot traditional literature a markedly subordinate place in socio-cultural development.

The historical-cultural and cultural-linguistic development connected with ideas about the "simplicity" of the written language created the prerequisites for a radical break of this type, although it by no means pre-ordained it. Indeed, the conscious use of a variety of "simple" languages and the correlation between varieties of the bookish language with various degrees of grammatical proficiency were what formed linguistic consciousness. These processes, however limited they may have been in social terms, made it possible to look at the traditional bookish language from a new perspective. In opposition to the "simple" tongue, this language became "not simple," in opposition to grammatically elementary language it was seen as not elementary, and the striving of the "simple" language to be comprehensible pigeonholed it as "incomprehensible." For centuries Church Slavonic had been seen as a universal literary language that served needs of culture as a whole. With the appearance of "simple" variants the significance of the traditional Church Slavonic language within the cultural and linguistic value system was asserted primarily on the basis of its ecclesiastic and religious usage and its learned grammatical cultivation. In this context the complete rejection of Church Slavonic was associated with the rejection of Orthodoxy and its grammatical educational system that functioned completely within the framework or religious culture. From a certain perspective this could assign Church Slavonic the attribute of clericalism and lead to its rejection as a "clerical" language. However, the appearance of such a perspective presupposes the secularization of culture. And indeed the cultural and linguistic situation described above "began to experience shocks only when secular literature began to lay claim to the role of supreme literature" (Vinokur 1983, 258). At the same time the very character of the new cultural and linguistic situation was dependent on the nature of the secularizing process, for which reason the specifics of its introduction into Russia were a significant influence on the way the literary language of the new type came into being.

6. The Secularization of Culture, Its Specifics in Russia, and Its Significance for Rethinking Linguistic Usage

The process of cultural secularization was begun in Europe during the Renaissance, not because there was no secular culture before the Renaissance, but because until that time it had not presumed an independent role. This was a revolutionary moment, although it had organic roots in the past, first of all in the system of secular education that medieval Europe inherited from the Roman Empire; however weak this may have become, and however much an accessory to religious education, it remained capable of regeneration, and became organic soil for secularization. The Renaissance's continuity in this area was clearly marked, for example, in the character of its assimilation of the classical rhetorical tradition and of classical mythology (see Seznec 1961; Zhivov and Uspenskii 1984). A particular instance of this continuity is the fact that secular culture was by no means alien to connections with the Latin linguistic tradition; in this respect it wasn't opposed to religious culture. For this reason the process of secularization did not have a direct connection to the question of language. Secularization, of course, could serve as one of the factors influencing the redistribution of spheres of usage between Latin and the new national literary tongues, but the conception of a particular subject as specifically religious or secular by no means predetermined the language in which that subject was described. The democratizing of education significantly influenced the new distribution, but at least up to the eighteenth century democratization was more characteristic of religious than secular culture.

The starting points for the Eastern Slavs as a whole and Muscovite Rus' in particular were completely different. Here secular culture had no organic roots at all, and in this Russia differed not only from the West, but also from Byzantium. The issue then was not the specifics of Eastern Christianity, as is sometimes asserted (e.g. Trubetskoi 1973, 19–28), but in the special nature of the reception of Christian culture by the Eastern Slavs. It would be a mistaken exaggeration to assert that *all* spiritual interests of medieval Russian society were exclusively religious, that the life of the court or the patrimony of a boyar were but light-weight versions of monastic customs, and that rituals sanctioned by the church consumed all spiritual interests beyond its pale. Nevertheless, no institutionalized forms of secular culture existed in medieval Rus'. Here, unlike Byzantium, there was no tradition of secular education stretching back uninterruptedly to ancient times, there were no universities with schools of law and medicine, as in Western Europe, there were no juridical corporations, and, finally, there was no tradition of chivalric love and the literary and social practices connected with it. Those little beginnings of secular culture that researchers have sought out, and that were peripheral phenomena relative to the main lines of cultural development (like the "Song of Igor's Campaign," for example), may only be interpreted as such with significant qualifications, and though they may somewhat spoil the clarity of the historical picture, and make it impossible to speak in unambiguous structuralist terms, they nevertheless provide no basis for speaking of a special tradition; if there were such sprouts, they produced no fruit.

With this in mind, there are no grounds to speak of the secular culture of Kievan or Muscovite Russia, as is often done. It is unjustified to consider the chronicles as monuments of secular literature, and the same goes for the so-called military tales. One can certainly examine various lines of literary continuity from monument to monument, but these do not form any kind of special secular tradition. Most indicative in this case is the fact that during the entire medieval period there was an unceasing exchange of textual material and narrative models among works of religious literature and those monuments which from a modern point of view may be called secular (for example, between chronicles and hagiographical works). Unlike Byzantine or West European literatures, there were no boundaries between genres that could be seen to correspond to such differentiation of cultural traditions, and this absence of rhetorical organization is connected with the fact that in the last analysis the fundamental text that served as the standard for all written works without regard for their individual features was Holy Writ. The presence of this single supra-model relativizes the significance of isolated individual models that may form textual groups. As R. Picchio writes, "Imitation of the Bible resulted in a structural conception of each literary work as a component of a larger whole" (Picchio 1973, 447). As stated, this situation affected the development of the literary language in a fundamental way, insofar as its registers were not separated from each other by any kind of fixed border. For all of the importance of the religious tradition in Byzantium, no such single supra-model existed there. As I. Shevchenko remarks, "In Christian Byzantium the Scriptures never became a predominant model of style at any level, except, and there rarely, for the lowest forms of hagiography" (Shevchenko 1981, 209). To some extent this also applies to the medieval period in Western Europe, where the imitation of classical authors remained a required part of rhetoric. Considering these profound differences, the process of secularization, for all its universal importance in creating modern society, could not have proceeded in Russia according to that well-studied scheme that we observe in Western Europe.

In Russia, secular culture as an autonomous phenomenon only declared its existence in the seventeenth century. Whether this was because of typologically universal social processes on the cusp of the new era, or whether it was due to such special circumstances as contact with Polish court practices during the reign of the False Dmitri, need not concern us here. More crucial is the fact that new forms of cultural exchange come into being in the first half of the century, forms like the writing of poetry, so important for cultural self-identity. Insofar as (as we have argued) there was no basis for secular culture in Russia, its place was taken by imported elements. Before original secular tales like the Tale of Savva Grudtsyn or Frol Skobeev appeared, translated chivalric novels had to be circulated, and it was just such borrowed productions that formed the kernel of a secular tradition, at first quite restricted. However limited it was in terms of its content and in terms of its audience, it acquired a certain autonomy, and it is this that signals its most important innovation. In the 1630's polemic tract "On the Visible Image Of God," Ivan Begichev accuses his opponents of theological ignorance, and declares that they are familiar not with religious works but with "incredible tales" (basnoslovnye povesti), among which he names "the one about Bova Korolevich [prince Bovain]"; he thus makes the opposition between religious and secular literary traditions very clear [...] (Begichev 1898, 4).

As soon as a kernel of secular culture is formed, it begins to accumulate new material, not necessarily taken from without. Choices begin to become available, as older texts or other cultural artifacts are reconceptualized to fit new models and are included into paradigms to which they had no relation earlier. Thus the chronicles could now be taken as a simple telling of past events that could be regarded as parallel to western historical works and taken as part of a common secular tradition. For example, Andrei Lyzlov's *Scythian History,* written in the last decade of the seventeenth century, is a combination of fragments taken from various borrowed sources which taken together form a fully secular narrative, with no religious underpinning. Notably, Lyzlov defined his sources as "history books," including in their number as equals *The Book of Degrees* (*Stepennaia kniga*) and old Russian chronographs, on the one hand, and the histories of Baronius, Pliny, Martin Kromer and Alexander Guanini on the other (Lyzlov 1990, 7).

However significant these accumulations, the kernel itself remained borrowed, and this determined the main semiotic characteristics of the new secular tradition. At its origin lay the mechanism by which heterogeneous cultures act on each other, stimulated by the change of context, that is, the mechanism of inadequate translation from one language to another, whose very inadequacy fuels creative development (see Lotman, I, 34–5; Klein 1990). Cultural borrowing, including the secularizing and Europeanizing of Russian culture in the seventeenth and eighteenth centuries, is expressed first of all in the assimilation of a series of external forms of behavior, daily life, literature, etc. These external elements play a historically defined role in the donating culture's cultural paradigm; they conform to a given set of values, life style, and way of thinking, and are that culture's organic expression. On transplantation into foreign soil, they lose their context, and, liberated from their original content, assume a heretofore nonexistent creative power; from external forms of expression they become generators of content.

Thus in Europe the German clothing which Peter I made state servitors assume there only fulfilled the simple function of clothing—to cover nakedness, defend from frost and heat, and adorn the wearer in accordance with his or her notions of elegance and fashion. However, transferred to Russia, a German caftan became an engine for enlightenment and an incarnation of Petrine absolutism, acquired didactic significance and as a symbol of the new culture served to differentiate the enlightened from those sunk in ignorance, the adherents of the past from the voluntary or involuntary supporters of change. State institutions and literary genres, philosophical doctrines and aesthetic conceptions all functioned in this same way. When we discover, for example, that Feofan Prokopovich's *Rhetoric* was almost completely based on analogous European moderate Baroque treatises (those of Nicolaus Caussinus and Melchior Junius — Lachmann 1982; Kibal'nik 1983), we naturally want to place it in this same series and to ascribe to it the same functions as its European models. The similarity, however, is deceptive. In Europe rhetorical manuals regulated already existing oral practice, helping the reader to combine certain rhetorical strategies with available rhetorical means. But in Russia the very same manual created new practices, and prescribed rather than recommended how to perform on occasions analogous to those in Europe. For all the external similarity of the rules, they took on a different meaning, and rhetoric turned into rules that governed the entire range of socially significant behavior ("Decorum-Rhetorik" as R. Lachmann calls them; Lachman 1982, lxi ff; Zhivov 1985a).

This metamorphosis of secular discourse was not very apparent in the seventeenth century insofar as secular culture was limited to a very small

§0–6. The Secularization of Culture

and rather closed social group. Practically it did not extend father than the court, and moreover was meant for internal consumption. At the court of Aleksei Mikhailovich a theater was set up, but only those close to the person of the tsar attended, and these innovations were not evidently perceived as a cultural reform but only as just another change in court life, bringing things up to date with other European court practices. And insofar as even earlier the inner life of the court stood somewhat apart in the cultural tradition, the tension between traditional and Europeanized culture was of limited, isolated importance. The supreme power reserved this culture for itself and did not try and spread it among its subjects, so that the cultural conflict and clash of paradigms it stimulated only existed in embryonic form and did not affect the main cultural categories. That which began to percolate out of palace halls could provoke negative reactions, but these were fully subsumed into religious discourse, related for example to the schism in the church, that is, a conflict between religious movements and not between secular and religious culture.[19]

In the Petrine epoch this esoteric culture went out into the streets. This is especially evident in what happened with that very same theater. As E. V. Petukhov writes (1916, 375), "From the very start, Peter looked at the theater not as a court amusement but as a social issue. The Boyar F. A. Golovin was commanded by the tsar to build "a hall for comedy" (komediinaia khoromina) on Red Square, right by the Kremlin, and it is quite typical that this order was opposed by the clerks of the foreign office, who found this a very questionable enterprise; however the hall was completed in December, and by Yule 1702–03 performances had probably already begun." Having become public, secular culture took on a completely new role: it no longer entertained the few but now educated society as a whole, or at least, that part of society that came within the grasp of the authority's new cultural paradigm. Assimilation of the new secular discourse became a criterion of loyalty (§ I-1), and this was a basic change. Insofar as assimilating the new discourse became a life problem, people occupied in completely different spheres of activity began to adapt this imposed language to their own situatians, habits, and preexisting notions. This adaptation brought into play the mechanism of transformation that brought new content to the adopted forms of European

---

[19] There exist several testimonies of how Old Believers perceived the theatrical presentations at the court of Aleksei Mikhailovich. [...] (Bubnov and Demkova 1981, 143). They were seen as a sign that the tsar had lost his faith and were considered of a piece with his innovations in church ritual. One can find this view in Avvakum's own Book of Interpretations and Admonitions (RIB, XXXIX, col. 466) and in his "Advice to the Sainted Holy Fathers" (Avvakum 1960, 255).

culture described earlier. This was particularly complex and confused due to the fact that from the very start of its public existence the new system of values was sharply antagonistic toward traditional culture, which made it impossible to reconcile the old and new directly and openly and led to multiple ambiguities.

It is within the framework of this new value system that the Russian literary language of the new type was created, cutting all ties—at least in theory—with the entire previous written tradition. This new literary language was part of the new secular culture, and therefore the struggle for its dominance became an element of state policy that asserted the undivided authority of secular power. Thus from the very start, Russia's historical, cultural and linguistic development, inspired by Europeanization, gave rise to phenomena quite far from those European models on which it was oriented. One may say that imitation and borrowing took place only on an external level. The Europeanization of Russian culture turns out to be not so much a transfer as much as a reconceptualizing of European models, during the course of which the basic structures and categories of European thought acquired different meanings. The process of borrowing formed but a superficial layer; an examination of the actual functioning of the cultural system, and of those cultural conflicts that arose during that functioning, demonstrates what a profound transformation borrowed phenomena undergo, and in what complex relations they engage with traditional culture.

This transformation was manifested most significantly in the change in linguistic consciousness. In Peter's cultural program, what was European was perceived as new and progressive, and his cultural reforms aimed to introduce them onto Russian soil. One result of this program was the literary language of the new type. From the start, however, this result radically differed from its European correlatives. The differences were embedded in their very connection to the cultural politics of secularization. The opposing of the traditional written language and a literary language of the new type (the "simple language" of the Petrine era) was directly linked with the contrast between traditional versus secular cultures; and this connection was a specific peculiarity of the Russian linguistic situation that had no parallel in Europe. This connection also conditioned many special features of the new literary language that had an important influence on its development. If the notion of "simplicity" lay at the origin of the new language, then during its formation it became secondary to another cultural imperative, opposition to the traditional written language. This imperative derived from the correlation between the formation of the new language and the new system of values. The new literary language became a sign of the new secular culture, and this

§0–6. The Secularization of Culture

semiotic imperative defined both its structural characteristics as well as its functioning.

Thus secularization, in creating the possibility of a radical break with the Church Slavonic written tradition and a realization of the notion of a "simple tongue," at the same time led to the formation of a literary language for which the idea of simplicity had only secondary importance, while the main requirement was the connection to the new secular culture (§ I–2.2). While this connection retained its force the new literary language could not acquire polyfunctionality, a basic attribute of European literary languages (§ III–1.1). Limited in its functional sphere, it could not embody and impose on society the principle of the undivided authority of secular power, which was after all a basic reason for its creation. Because of this the broadening of the new language's functions combined with the problem of asserting the new imperial discourse and reflected all of those equivocations by means of which the Russian autocracy assumed the guise of enlightened absolutism, striving for the general good (§ IV–1).

No less paradoxical and far from European models was the new literary language's pretension to universality. The estate and caste stratification of society, strengthened by the Petrine reforms and restricting social mobility to an extreme, insofar as this was within the power of the not especially numerous and poorly educated bureaucracy, led not only to the growth of social tensions but to unprecedented cultural divisions within society. Various social groups assimilated (or failed to assimilate at all) the reigning Europeanized culture in various ways, and were loyal to traditional culture in varying degrees, so that each developed its own cultural language which was passed down to its children (insofar as children almost always inherited the profession and social status of their parents). Together with this inherited language children remained isolated from the values and views of other social groups, a lack of understanding that in time became an established tradition and social norm. As Isabella de Madariaga comments, "with the introduction of Western secular ideas, the different classes lived at a different tempo, according to how much or how little of the new ways they adopted, and the unifying principle was greatly weakened" (Madariaga 1982, 111).

In different social groups different sets of texts had currency, and in different ways combined elements from a corpus including traditional religious texts, translated entertainment literature (like *Bova* or *Peter of the Golden Keys*), as well as the new Europeanized literature (cf. Rothe 1984). Because of this different social groups had different linguistic experiences that they related to their own cultural principles and transformed into new practices that in turn defined the language of texts they themselves created. One mission of the new literary language was to be universally comprehensible, but in practice its formation led to a new differentiation of written traditions that in addition took on a socially motivated character. If we can permit a simplified illustration, one might say that while an Old Believer continued to read the "Prologue" and write in hybrid Church Slavonic, an archimandrite of the church might imitate Prokopovich's rhetoric, a clerk could read *Bova* and write tales like the "History of Korolevich Arkhilabon" (cf. Sipovskii 1905; Berkov 1949), while a Sumarokov or Kheraskov would browse French and German journals, understanding at the same time that "the people can't understand my creations" — and each one of them scorning, and in part even hating, the others. In this way the universalism of the new language turned into a fiction, and its penetration into society functioned together with the propagation of the other political and cultural fictions that was a major component of government policy in eighteenth century Russia.

In light of these factors, the analysis of "language and culture" in Russia during this period is justified not only by the existence of a symbolic level in the language, a universal factor in all languages, but due to the special intensity of its formation, transformation, and dissemination into cultural consciousness. Language not only responded to and recorded in itself the stages of cultural evolution, but also served as one of the principle means of inculcating the reigning culture, and as such became one of the main elements of government policy. The establishment of the new type of literary language and its acquisition of the above-mentioned characteristics (polyfunctionalism, universal comprehensibility, codification, and differentiation of stylistic means) took place in direct and unusually expressive connection with the assertion of new cultural, religious, and political values, so that the development of the language serves not only as a mirror but as a magnifying glass, allowing us to view all of the complexity and contradictions in the genesis of modern Russian culture.

Chapter 1

The Petrine Language Reform; The Linguistic and Cultural Situation of the Petrine Era

1. Tasks of the Language Reform and the Nature of its Realization

The goal of the Petrine transformation was not only to create a new army and navy, a new governmental system and new industry, but the creation of a new culture as well, and among Peter's activities cultural reform occupied no less of a place than those of a more pragmatic nature. The change in dress, shaving of beards, renaming of state posts, the introduction of "assemblies," the regular organization of triumphal public processions, masquerades, and parodic and blasphemous spectacles (such as the wedding of a prince-pope, the funeral of a dwarf, a false fire alarm on April 1st, etc.—see, among others, Bergholts IV, 13–14, 91) were not accidental attributes of the age of reform but substantive elements of state policy whose aim was to reeducate society and to impress upon it a new conception of state power. It was not without reason that Feofan Prokopovich wrote in *The Right of a Monarch's Will* (*Pravda voli monarshei*)—an apology for Petrine absolutism and the Petrine reforms — that

> A sovereign monarch can lawfully command of the people not only whatever is necessary for the obvious good of his country, but indeed whatever he pleases, provided that it is not harmful to the people and not contrary to the will of God. The foundation of this power, as stated above, is the fact that the people has renounced in his favor its right to decide the common weal, and has conferred on him all power over itself: this includes civil and ecclesiastical ordinances of every kind, changes in customs and dress, house-building, procedures and ceremonies at feasts, weddings, funerals, etc., etc., etc. (PSZ, VII, no. 4870, p. 628; translation from Lentin, 1996, 223)

In presenting this theory of the social contract and the police state, based on Hobbes and Pufendorf (cf. Gurevich 1915), Prokopovich especially singled out the monarch's right to introduce cultural (semiotic) innovations; the need for such declarations did not arise in European treatises on absolutism, and a comparison with them shows that there were no direct analogues for the special nature of Peter's cultural reform in Europe.

There are many contemporary testimonies to Peter's cultural revolution. In an extensive speech of 1725 "in praise of Peter the Great," Prokopovich wrote: "He would never have considered something his own individual good, if he had not communicated its advantage to his entire fatherland... And was what he achieved with his efforts little? Whatever there is flourishing now that was previously unknown to us, is it not it all his undertaking ? If we look at the littlest thing, [and see] that is honorable and necessary, and then at the best ordered things, I say, at clothing and friendly social commerce, at eating and celebrating and other beneficial customs, will we not admit that Peter has taught us these as well? And we are now ashamed of what we praised before" (Feofan Prokopovich, II, 148–9). In a dispatch of March 14, 1721, the French envoy Campredon commented that "This prince... has taken it into his head to completely change black into white, as well as the genius, the mores and customs of his nation" (SRIO, XL, 180).[1]

One may presume that Peter saw a definite guarantee of the stability of the new order precisely in his transformation of culture. The new order was antagonistically opposed to the old. From Peter's point of view, the old culture stood for ignorance, barbarism, even "idolatry" (idolatstvo) (see Peter's foreword to the Maritime Regulations [Ustrialov II, 397]; cf. also Prokopovich's foreword to Apollodorus's *Library* [Apollod 1725, foreword, 13–15]). From the point of view of that culture, the new order appeared demonic, the kingdom of the Antichrist, and this perception was well known to the reformers (see Uspenskii 1976, Zhivov and Uspenskii 1984, 216–21). In these conditions the choice between old and new culture represented a kind of religious decision that bound a person for his or her whole life. The transition to the new culture turned out to be a magical rite marked by the

---

[1] It is indicative that in Karamzin's *Memoir on Ancient and Modern Russia* it is Peter's cultural policies that provoke his doubts and condemnation; while accepting the Europeanization of Russia, Karamzin sees the reform of culture and daily life as something profoundly non-European, contradicting both European theories of absolutism as well as the general European view of the relation between politics and individual life, public and private spheres. [...] For Karamzin, as for the whole later historiographical tradition, the Petrine reform of culture and everyday life was an anomaly that was at odds with both common sense and the proper natural development of the state.

1. Tasks of the Language Reform and the Nature of its Realization

renunciation of old values and acceptance of new antithetical ones. That is precisely how I. I. Khovanskii saw his induction into Peter's "All-Jesting Council" (Vseshuteishii sobor):

> They took me to Preobrazhenskoe and in the main yard Nikita Zotov pretended to make me a metropolitan and gave me a document (stolbets) [to sign] for my renunciation, and by this writing I destroyed myself, but at the renunciation, instead of "Do you believe?" they asked "Do you drink?" and by my renunciation I condemned myself in the worst way, because I did not argue, and it would have been better to accept a crown of martyrdom than to have made such a renunciation. (Solov'ev, VIII, 101).

Acceptance of Peter's cultural innovations took the form of entering a new faith and required endorsing the whole complex of his reforms — from the cult of Peter himself to the reorganization of the state apparatus. This original conversion to the "Petrine faith" was the basis for all of imperial culture and defined its understanding of the relationship between society and political power, irrespective of whether this understanding was of a revolutionary or conservative nature. To what extent the "semiotic" cultural reforms were conditioned by faith in Peter's mission was vividly expressed by the historian M. P. Pogodin, unable to deny this more than a century and a half after the tsar's death. After becoming acquainted with the materials concerning the killing of Peter's son Aleksei published by N. G. Ustrialov, and admitting that both the entire trial and Aleksei's attempted escape had been a set up by his father, Pogodin nevertheless could not condemn Peter: "What verdict may we come to about Peter, and his treatment of his son?... We are speaking in an academy that Peter the Great founded!... The city in which this academy has been laboring for 150 years got its name from him, and at every step, each stone seems to proclaim his memory, in every wave of the Neva we hear his name. No, ladies and gentlemen, our tongue cannot bring itself to pronounce judgment on him..." (Pogodin 1860, Pogodin, II, 375–6).[2] Accepting Petrine culture thus became a guarantee of one's loyalty

---

[2] Cf. another of his well-known statements about Peter: "We wake up. What day is it today? January 1, 1841 — Peter the Great ordered us to count the years from Christ's birth. Peter the Great ordered us to count the months starting with January. It is time to get dressed — our clothing is cut to the fashion Peter I gave us, the uniform he devised... Our glance falls on a book — Peter the Great ordered this script, and carved the letters himself. You start to read it — this language became written, literary under Peter I, having replaced the church language. They bring newspapers — Peter the Great founded them... After dinner you go visiting — Peter the Great's assemblies. You meet ladies here — they were allowed to join male company on Peter's order... You are given a rank — according to the Table of Ranks Peter the Great established. Your rank confers nobility — as Peter the Great instituted. I need to file a complaint — Peter the Great defined its form. It is accepted — in front of Peter

to the entire new reformed order, something like that "spilt blood" with which Peter Verkhovenskii bound his revolutionary cell in Dostoevskii's *Devils*. It is indicative that, according to P. J. von Strahlenberg's testimony (1730, 232), adherents of the old ways considered Peter's blasphemous entertainments on an equal level with his crimes, like killing Aleksei or establishing the Secret Chancellery (see Golikov's rebuttal: Golikov 1788, 14–5; and also Panchenko 1984, 116f).

In this context all spheres of semiotic behavior acquired fundamental political and ideological significance, and the sphere of semioticized behavior itself was greatly expanded (cf. Lotman 1976, 294–5). Behavior was split into two, and in each area an opposition arose between new and old, European and traditional, secular and clerical. Whatever a person did, a known given set of signs immediately defined his behavior in terms of this dualism (dikhtomiia) — he was either friend or foe of the Petrine cause. Insofar as everything had significance, it was impossible to hide one's position or to decline to take sides, taking a neutral stance. One's loyalty was constantly being tested, and the arena for such testing was constantly being widened to include even those things which from our remote perspective might seem trivial and unworthy of attention.

Peter's linguistic policy was an organic part of this process of demarcation, as language was completely defined by the new attitudes toward power. "The fledglings of Peter's nest" could repeat word for word what Dominique Bouhours wrote about Louis XIV: "Kings should learn how to rule from him, but people should learn how to speak from him. If under him the French language was what Latin was under Augustus [Caesar], he himself is for his age what Augustus was in his" (Bouhours, 1671, 169). This role of transformer of the language was equally clear to opponents of Peter's regime. Thus in the treatises against Peter which the clerk Larion Dokukin wanted to post on the Church of the Trinity in Petersburg in 1714–18 it said that: "They have changed the words and names of our Slavonic language and our clothing, shaved heads and beards and abusively dishonored their persons; we no longer look different or have moral distinction from people of other faiths" (Esipov I, 183). Changes in language are here specifically connected with other "semiotic" reforms. In the process of the reforms, the traditional written language was defined as an attribute of the old culture, and was tarred

---

the Great's the mirror [of justice]. They debate it — according to his General Regulation… Whatever we think, or speak, or do, everything, harder or easier, nearer or farther, I repeat, may be accounted for by Peter the Great. He is the key and the lock" (Pogodin, I, 341–3; Rubinshtein 1941, 270–1).

with the same negative features that were assigned to that culture by Petrine enlightenment. The new culture had to create a new language for itself which differed from the old. Hence from the point of view of the reformers, the old written language was labeled barbarous, clerical, and ignorant, while the new language was destined to become European, secular and enlightened. The linguistic policy of the Petrine period embodied this clear-cut social imperative.

1.1 The Reform of the Alphabet as the Prototype of Language Reform

This social mission was most visibly reflected in the reform of the alphabet, that is, the creation of the Russian civil script. The division of the alphabet into church and civic variants superimposed the opposition of secular and religious onto all printed texts, and this opposition created a new conceptual scheme for juxtaposing Russian and Church Slavonic. The opposition of other linguistic characteristics flowed from this basic graphic juxtaposition. In this sense the reform of the alphabet contained all of the basic features of Petrine linguistic policy in schematic form.

The initiative for introducing the civil script itself belonged to Peter, and he directly supervised all of the preparations for the undertaking.[3] Peter himself also sketched out the sphere in which the new alphabet was to be used, which was something like his own personal realm in which the new culture was to reign. On the first edition of the *Azbuka (Primer)* on Jan. 29, 1710, Peter wrote in his own hand: "Historical and manufacturing books must be printed with these letters. And those that are underlined [that is, the Cyrillic letters that Peter had crossed out] are not to be used in these books" (PiB, X, 27, cf. 476–77; see also Shitsgal 1959, 265; Shitsgal 1974, 36). This command may apparently be taken as the final formulation of a previous decision. Indeed, already on Jan. 1, 1708, Peter had ordered that "the geometry book in Russian should be printed in the [new] alphabet which was sent from the military campaign and the other secular books should be printed with the very same letters" (Brailovskii 1894, no. 10, 254; Shitsgal

---

[3] See Peter's correspondence about this with M. P. Gagarin and I. A. Musin-Pushkin (PiB, VII, 158–159; PiB, VII, 2, 731–733, 815; PiB, VIII, 1, 289, 303–304; PiB, VIII, 2, 937–938, 952–955; PiB, IX, 1, 12–13, 31–32, 49, 50–51, 370; PiB, IX, 2, 541–543, 626–627, 628, 1228–1229; Zhivov 1986c, 64–65).

1959, 259; Proskurnin 1959, 378f). It was thus presumed, apparently, that secular books were to be written in Russian and printed in civil script, while books of religious content be written in Church Slavonic and printed in church script.

Despite the order of Jan. 1, 1708, it remains unclear whether or not this distribution of functions had been foreseen from the very start of work on the new alphabet. On the one hand, books of secular and religious content were clearly considered as two different types of publication, with different functions and addressees, and from this perspective the idea of formatting them differently seems natural. A precedent for such a division may already be seen in the privilege given to Ian Tessing in February, 1700. In it it says that Peter I

> ordered him in the city of Amsterdam to print pictures and plans of Europe, Asia and America, of land and sea, as well as all kinds of printed sheets and portraits, and of army and navy people, books on mathematics, architecture, city-planning, as well as other arts, in Slavonic and Dutch together, as well as separately in Slavonic and Dutch, in the original size and together with explanatory information, but not [to print] church books in the Slavonic Greek language, because Slavonic Greek church books for the celebration of the entire Orthodox order [of divine service] of the Eastern church, are printed in our reigning city of Moscow. (PiB, 1, no. 291, 329; Bykova and Gurevich, 1958, 321).

On the other hand, in Peter's letters of 1708 concerning the alphabet reform he suggests several times that as a trial "some prayer of other" should be printed (PiB, VIII, 1, p. 303), "some prayer or other... if only the 'Our Father'"(ibid 289). These may indicate that at first Peter had in mind converting all publications into the new script, and that the ecclesiastical sphere would be subject to the same transformation as the secular. Preserving *kirillitsa* (the Church script) in Church books represents Peter's accommodation of traditional religious culture, as the change of scripts in liturgy books could not help but have been taken as a denial of traditional Orthodox Slavonic-Greek piety. In any case, Fedor Polikarpov declared that in the reformed alphabet, lacking the letters ѡ, ѱ, ѯ, etc., it was "impossible to print church books" (RGADA, f. 381, no. 423, l. 43), and his opinion was apparently brought to the tsar's attention. Insofar as a radical reform of religion (as opposed to reform of church administration) was not part of Peter's plans, he left church books to the clerics, who as a rule did not share his ideas about enlightenment. Consequently, the old alphabet became semioticized as the sign of an ecclesiastical culture that hung onto the past, while the new one symbolized change. The relationship between old and new scripts also modeled the relationship between the old and new literary languages.

1. Tasks of the Language Reform and the Nature of its Realization

It seems probable that the connection between the Church Slavonic language and church books established in this way, on the one hand, and that between the Russian ("simple") language and civic books, on the other, was what Peter had in mind when on June 9, 1710, he wrote to I. A. Musin-Pushkin about supplying books to create libraries in St. Petersburg: "Send all the books there are in Slavonic and Russian, church and civil books" (PiB, X, 182, cf. 615).[4] Thus the thematic division of subject matter prescribed by Peter corresponded to the separation between old and new culture (to the extent that it was accepted in the new society); Church Slavonic and the church script served the old culture while Russian and the civil script served the new secularized state culture.

In the reform of the alphabet both the changed form of the letters was significant as well as the alteration of its composition. In the last analysis, the change of the alphabet's content came down to the exclusion of the letters ѿ, ѡ, ѱ and the elimination of superscript marks. However, this was the result of a compromise. At first Peter had ordered that an alphabet be made without superscript marks and excluding nine letters of the Slavonic alphabet: "These excluded letters included six that duplicated the same sound ('izhe,' 'zemlia,' 'omega,' 'uk,' 'fert,' 'izhitsa') , the Greek combination letters 'ksi,' 'psi,' and also the ligature 'ot'" (Shitsgal 1959, 81; Shitsgal 1974, 38). It was this very version of the alphabet that was used in Mikhail Efremov's test primer (1707) and also for the first book set in civil type — the *Геометріа славенскі землемѣріе* (1708).

Such a radical reduction in the alphabet was apparently met with skepticism by Peter's advisors. On May 8, 1708, Peter wrote to Musin-Pushkin that "in books of the new print we should place marks and stresses (tochki i sily) as in previous printing" (PiB, VII, 1, 159), and in July-August of 1708 he ordered those who were casting the type in Moscow and Amsterdam to make letters that had earlier been excluded (Shitsgal 1959, 81). However, this was not the final decision. In January, 1709, Peter again returned to his

---

[4] In other cases Peter could naturally relate the opposition between Church Slavonic and Russian not with the civic — church split but with the opposition between written and oral. Thus in the letter to P. M. Apraksin of July 31, 1709, Peter gave instructions for the education of the court jester named Vymeni, French by birth, who had come to Moscow from Poland and who received the nickname "Prince of the Samoyeds": he "ordered that they teach the Samoyed prince… to speak Russian and also to read and write Slavonic little by little" (PiB, IX, 329–30). This last association was not necessarily significant insofar as it was a concession to tradition, to the previous epoch's usual scheme of linguistic consciousness, as in Ludolf's well-known comment "And among them it has long been said, Russian is spoken and Slavonic is written" (Adeoque apud illos dicitur, loquendum est Russice & scribendum est Slavonice) (Ludol'f 1696, Preface, A/2).

Chapter 1. The Petrine Language Reform

original version and ordered they print "without using the newly corrected letters and stresses, but only the Amsterdam print, as it was imported" (letters to M. P. Gagarin of January 25, 1709 and to I. A. Musin-Pushkin on the same day — PiB, IX, 1, 50). Although this order referred to just one book, it was responding to Musin-Pushkin's inquiry of a more general character. Musin-Pushkin had written to Peter on January 16, 1709: "And I ordered one page of Rimpler's book printed with the Amsterdam letters without accent marks and without the newly-corrected letters… But from now on whether we should publish using accents and the newly revised letters, I await your tsarist majesty's order" (PiB, IX, 2, 542–3). Judging by the fact that further books in the new print were published without superscript marks, Peter's decision concerning the one book was extended to typographical practice for the use of civil script as a whole.[5] As far as the composition of the alphabet, a certain compromise was reached. The final form of the civil script was established by the primer Peter corrected in 1710 which preserved the letters и, з, ѵ, ѧ, ѵ, ѯ; and in which he crossed out the letters ѡ, щ, and ѱ (PiB, X, inset before p. 27).

Whatever the vacillations, it is very clear that the change in the composition of the alphabet led to the separating out of the Slavonic (Russian) and Greek alphabets; kirillitsa widely used the letters щ, ѵ, ѱ, ѧ, and superscript marks that had been developed during the Second South Slavic influence following Greek usage (Talev 1973, 61–2; Worth 1983b, 352–3; Uspenskii 1987, 203, 209). In this way the change expressed the new cultural orientation of Petrine culture in opposition to the Hellenizing tendency that had been characteristic of the previous period of Orthodox enlightenment. The changed composition of the alphabet could thus be tied to Peter's rejection of Orthodox "Slaveno-Greek" piety.

In this context it becomes clear why Musin-Pushkin was disturbed to receive Peter's orders, and after the tsar's letter of January 25, 1709, he immediately consulted with F. Polikarpov, the direct implementer of the alphabet reform and at the same time a leading representative of traditional educated culture. He wrote to Polikarpov three times (February 25, March 9 and 31), asking him to explain the significance of using the letters и, з, ѧ, ѱ

---

[5] Peter clearly experimented with superscript marks. As noted, on May 8, 1708, he wrote to Musin-Pushkin that "In books with the new print they should use marks and stresses as in previous publications" (PiB, VII, 1, 159). After six months the tsar changed his mind, and wrote to the same Musin-Pushkin (in regard to the newly revised [novoperepravlennye] letters): "I only ordered them to be made, but did not order that they print with them, I only wrote that they should include stress marks, but now you should order [that they] not put in stresses" (PiB, IX, 1, 50).

1. Tasks of the Language Reform and the Nature of its Realization

and "upper prosody" (i.e., the use of accent marks).[6] I have not been able to locate Polikarpov's answer, but his argumentation may be reconstructed from the preface to the 1701 *Primer* (*Bukvar'*) he published in which he specially reviewed the question of superscript marks. The basic argument is precisely that these marks are necessary in correct (bookish) writing, owing to their connection to Greek and the need to differentiate meanings, that is, he appealed to those artificial orthographic prescriptions that had become widespread after the Second South Slavic influence and which were connected to the grammatical approach to the bookish language (see Zhivov 1993).

In the "Correct Learning of Orderly Reading and Writing" that prefaced the *Primer*, Polikarpov defended the use of stress marks to differentiate doublets (such as мукà [flour] — мýка [torment]) as well as letters of Greek origin for words and names of Greek derivation (such as ψаломь [psalm] and not псаломъ) [...] (Polikarpov 1701, 1. 6–7). The principle of differentiating Greek names via spelling was even more sharply formulated in Polikarpov's grammatical treatise of 1724, which evidently defended the same point of view as he had once presented to Musin-Pushkin. [...] (RGADA, f. 201, no. 6, l. 62–3). The same arguments are also made in the *Tekhnologiia* of 1725, which asks, "Are Ф and Ѳ the same in meaning and pronunciation? They are not same in either meaning or pronunciation, but very different, however, not in Slavonic but in Greek words, which is why these letters are called foreign among Slavs, as Феодоръ written with Ф is construed as 'snake's gift,'... [while] Ѳеодоръ written with an Ѳ is translated as 'God's gift'" (RNG, NCRK, F 1921, 26).

As is clear from the history of post-Nikonian book editing, fidelity to Greek forms in language was seen as a sign of loyalty to Eastern Orthodox belief. Peter and his followers, interpreting this Grecophile orientation in Western terms, took it as a mark of clerical opposition. The alphabet reform was one of the first manifestations of this cultural antagonism, as "clerical" letters were banished from the secular alphabet and relegated to those who, in Trediakovskii's phrase, "have long been grecianizing in Slavonic or rather slavonicizing in Greek" (Trediakovskii 1748, 69 / III, 44).

---

[6] The views of Bishop Afanasi of Kholmogorsk, very reminiscent of Polikarpov's, that took shape in the framework of traditional Church Slavonic education, may help to characterize the attitude toward the orthographic features we are considering here. In polemics with the Old Believers and insisting on the grammatical approach to the bookish language, Afanasii rejected the authority of ancient manuscripts whose spelling hadn't been influenced by Greek, asserting that "Spelling and superscript marks and prosody and points did not exist anywhere at all [previously], whereas through them the light of Holy Writ is revealed" (Afanasii Kholmogorskii 1682, l. 261 verso).

Chapter 1. The Petrine Language Reform

The Grecophile orientation of ecclesiastical culture was juxtaposed to the pro-Latin tendency of Peter and his followers, possibly reflecting in part the cultural dominant of an earlier epoch (that of the court of Fedor Alekeseevich and Tsarevna Sofia), but primarily expressing an antagonism toward traditional culture and a pro-Western position. The change in form of the civil alphabet's letters directly reflected the new importance of the Latin model. "The Latin 'antiqua' script... was definitely a basis for the civil script" (Shitsgal 1959, 84; cf. 10714; cf. also Kal'dor 1969–70; Shitsgal 1974, 39–46). It was the orientation on the Latin script that led Peter to choose the letters that corresponded to Latin when confronted with homophonic pairs in his initial shortening of the alphabet (*i* and not *u*, *s* and not з). This was why the type-maker Mikhail Efremov referred to the examples of the civil alphabet Peter had sent "from on campaign" as "Russian with Latin handwriting" (Dvukhsotletie... 1908, 11).

The connection between the civil script and Latin was obvious to contemporaries and perceived precisely as the borrowing of a foreign model and a break with learned orthography that, in the framework of traditional Church Slavonic literary culture, was oriented on the Greek model and reflected the grammatical approach. In Polikarpov's grammatical treatise from the early 1720's cited earlier he referred to both of these, the Latin model and the rejection of traditional norms (first of all superscript signs [verkhstrochnye prosodii]) (cf. Sobolevskii 1908, II; Babaeva 1989). The new orthography is here called "foreign looking" (strannoobraznyi) and the foreign lands that produced it are referred to as "Latin." The grammar is written in the form of a dialogue and contains the following conversation between a teacher and pupil:

> Does the writing of the Slavs all look the same? No, the writing—that is, printed writing and manuscript writing—are different, and moreover, foreign-looking writing is used in civil books... How many of these foreign-looking letters are there and what do they look like? There is the same number as ours, and you may see how they are written in the book called *The Honest Mirror of Youth* (*Iunosti chestnoe zertsalo*), and writing them is very easy. Why are they called foreign-looking? Because foreign countries use this way of writing. Which ones? Latin ones; their writing looks just the same. Do words in the foreign-looking writing preserve the same spelling? No, because the foreign way of writing does not use superscript prosody, only interlinear punctuation, but it does preserve the differences between the letters *e*, ѣ, *u*, ɩ. And in proper names they also preserve the spelling, and the [word] division is the same as in our own. (RGADA, f. 201, no. 6, l. 34 verso — 36).

Later, Trediakovskii — for whom the question of the cultural — semiotic interpretation of the alphabet reform was no less important than for Polikarpov —

made much the same argument: "The very first and most important reason for inventing today's beautiful civil type was the desire that our letters be as much as possible similar to today's Latin (not Gothic) type... This is clear, and their modern form is the strongest evidence of this, as they are as close to Latin letters as possible, and far from the Greek style in which the entire old alphabet is composed, and today only used in church printing" (Trediakovskii 1748, 120–22 / III, 76–67; cf. also 1748, 256 / III, 170).[7] There is no question that contemporaries perceived this connection to the Latin tradition not only as a formal likeness but as a direct manifestation of Peter's cultural program, his "westernism" and antagonism to native tradition.

The Latin subtext of the culture Peter was creating linked the new Russia not so much with Christian as with imperial Rome (see Lotman and Uspenskii 1982). In his "Short Introduction and Historical Exploration of the Origin... of All of the Names of the Letters of the Alphabet." A. I. Bogdanov reported that "When Peter the Great..., being then in the midst of a difficult war, with God's grace accomplished many victories, great and extremely glorious triumphs were organized for his entry into Moscow, and for these most glorious entrances a great many richly magnificent triumphal gates were built on which were depicted historical and hieroglyphic symbols and emblems [...], under which were placed inscriptions of Russian words whose lettering looked like Latin..." (Koblents 1958, 149). This concerns Peter's triumphal entry into Moscow of November 9, 1703 (Pekarskii, NL, II, 75; Shitsgal 1959, 23). Bogdanov's report was based on the testimony "of older students from the Spasskii schools who were there and wrote about it" (Koblents 1858, 149).

The official description of the triumph has survived (see Torzhestvennaia vrata... 1703), and it also testifies that Peter's celebration was modeled on ancient Roman pagan triumphs and that this choice of a model was fully intentional. Both its general idea and various details make this clear. For example, "on the capitols on both sides facing the entryway four angels were [depicted] strewing flowers, an ancient image of celebration like

---

[7] The question of the initial model for the alphabet was still an issue in the second half of the eighteenth century. In his article "On Spelling," Sumarokov wrote: "Mr. Trediakovskii rejected the letter з and introduced s, basing this on the Primer published under Emperor Peter I, but although typographies followed this Primer, which was based on the contours of Latin letters, they departed imperceptibly from these alien Latin shapes and adhered to our own, given to us by the Greeks (and from which the Romans also took the form of their letters), and we stuck to what was genuine, distancing ourselves from the transformed copy." And further: "In the Primer issued during the reform of Russia, and perhaps printed in Amsterdam, we learned to write like this: 'Пріімі sа Імѣніе sлата' instead of 'прими за именіе злата.' The entire design [of the letters] followed the Latin Alphabet, [and] in a word, we sought beautification in deformity and in what was odious to our writing" (Sumarokov, X, 9–10).

that on the Apian Way leading to the Capitoline..." (Grebeniuk 1979, 142). Peter was compared to Julius Caesar [...] (ibid, 147–8). More than that, like a Roman emperor, Peter's arrival was depicted like an epiphany of Jupiter [...]) (ibid, 139). Above Peter in the image of Jupiter there was a biblical saying (Psalm 76: 8; Slavonic 75:8), and significantly, an image of this type, typical of European Baroque, mixing the Christian and the classical pagan, had never been seen before in Russia. This marked the emergence of a single, syncretic Christian-pagan deity, a thunder-god (cf. on the European tradition Ebert, I, 144f) which combined Jupiter the thunder-god, often mentioned in the description of the triumph (Grebeniuk 1979, 143, 145) and "the God of glory who thunders on many waters..." (ibid, 145; a paraphrase of Psalm 29: 3 [Slavonic Psalm 28: 3]; on the mixing of Christian and pagan terminology, see Zhivov and Uspenskii 1984). No less indicative was Peter's titulature, echoing that of ancient Rome and prefiguring the tsar's official titles of the 1720's:

> On the pedestal is written: pio fel. sereniss, potent, inuicussimo que monar Petro Alexiewicz rosso imp. monocrat, patri patriae, triumph, suec, rest, plus quam qo annis inique detentae haered, fulmini tiuon... That is: "To the most pious, most fortunate, most brilliant, greatly powerful and unconquerable monarch, great sovereign tsar and grand prince Peter Alekseevich, commander and autocrat of Great and Little and White Russia, father of the fatherland, triumph–bearer, re-conqueror of the territory unjustly held by Sweden for over ninety ears, blasting Livonia with thunderbolts..." (Grebeniuk 1979, 148–09)

True, Peter is only called emperor in the Latin inscription, but "father of the fatherland" does make it into the Slavonic translation. The Latin form of the Slavonic letters corresponded to the Roman design of the larger celebration. Thus the known connection between the civil script and Latin 'antiqua' was actualized on the occasion of its first use, realizing the correspondence between new Russia and imperial Rome.

Bogdanov's report permits us to consider the alphabet reform as a constituent element in the creation of a special civic cult that was formed on an ancient model and that placed imperial (tsarist) power higher than any social institution (see Zhivov and Uspenskii 1987; Zhivov 1989; on the specific classical elements of the cult, see Zhivov and Uspenskii 1984, 221f). The Petrine triumphs were important rituals of this new civic cult. On the occasion of the triumph of 1704, the prefect of the Moscow Slaviano-Greco-Latino Academy Iosif Turoboiskii explained the significance of this kind of ceremony to the uninformed observer:

> I believe that the Orthodox reader will be surprised that we purposefully depict on the triumphal entryway, as in previous years, not things from holy writings but from secular history, not saintly subjects, but things related either

by historians or figures invented by poets, and likenesses of beasts, reptiles, birds, trees and other such things. You should know first of all that this is not a temple or church, created to honor one of the saints, but something social (politicheskaia), that is, civic praise for those who toil to keep the fatherland whole with their works, aided by God, defeating their enemies since times of old (as Tsar Constantine defeated Maxentius in Rome), [praise] that has been established by all cultured (politicheskikh) and not barbarous peoples... For this reason in these times in all Christian countries free of the barbarian yoke it is customary for grateful subjects... to compose wreaths of praise for glorious victors when they return in triumph out of two [kinds of] writing. Each victor should be rendered fitting and proper honor with godly writings in churches... and with writings from secular histories in ceremonies, in the streets, and in other appropriate places for everyone to see... In an open and universally publicized location with triumphal arches [decorated with writing] from secular and civil histories as well as with victorious wreaths [of praise], these most precious verbal wells, and with the help of God who bestows upon the fatherland joy, health, freedom and glory from the living water of his sweat, we venerate... his tsarist most radiant majesty and all of his victorious champions *in the manner and image of the ancient Romans*... (Grebeniuk 1979, 154; italics added)

Peter thus emerged as a half Christian and half pagan deity, the new Russia as the inheritor of imperial Rome, and the newly instituted "Russian civic speech" as the language of new imperial culture, which, together with those of Europe, derived from ancient civilization and rejected the barbarous religiosity of the "dark ages." It was precisely this reformist scheme that was applied to medieval Russian culture.[8]

The Latin subtext of the official secular culture created by Peter related the new imperial discourse to the introduction of the civil script, and the script itself became a symbol of Petrine secular enlightenment. Traditional culture became associated with clericalism and was displaced to the periphery together with the old alphabet. As noted, this could be seen as a compromise, and Fedor Polikarpov's position may serve as a good example of the way this was realized. Peter made active use of Polikarpov in his cultural undertakings despite the fact that Polikarpov was alien and antagonistic to this new culture. However, in fulfilling the tsar's commissions, Polikarpov (like many others in his position) negotiated for himself the possibility of

---

[8] On the process of sacralizing the monarch in eighteenth-century Russia, see Uspenskii and Zhivov 1983, 30f; Zhivov and Uspenskii 1987; Wortman 1995, 42f. In this regard Prokopovich's "Rozysk o pontifekse" (Investigation of the Pontifex) is particularly indicative, as among other things it shows the reasonableness of applying the title of bishop to a monarch. As a result the emperor (Peter) is seen as head of two sacred hierarchies, the Christian and pagan. Thus divine attributes accrue to the tsar both as the heir to the Roman emperors who were recipients of divine honors and as to Christ's deputy on earth. On Petrine Russia as heir to imperial Rome, see esp. Lotman and Uspenskii 1982.

Chapter 1. The Petrine Language Reform

continuing to function within the framework of traditional culture, even if this had been relegated to a very secondary socio-cultural position. In this negotiation the opposition of Greek and Latin subtexts and their associated cultural systems was one of the factors.

In his *Trilingual Primer* Polikarpov directly juxtaposes secular and church culture, secular and church books, leaving no doubt about which tradition he prefers.

> You will see not printed here in the typography Aesop the Phrygian's laughable fables, but you will acquire for yourself a path up to heaven, precisely, the *Stoglav* (*Hundred Chapters*) of Patriarch Gennadius that could be justly considered a guide (vozvozhdenie) to piety, just like Jacob's ladder, and it perhaps would not be a sin against the truth [to call it a work] leading to the celestial Zion. (Polikarpov 1701, l. 5 — 5 verso)

The work of Patriarch Gennadius published in the *Primer* is juxtaposed here to the publication a year earlier in Amsterdam of Aesop's fables by Jan Tessing (Aesop 1700). This very juxtaposition clearly speaks to the rejection of Peter's cultural innovations and adherence to the church tradition. Such was Polikarpov's initial position. Subsequently, however, he did not make such direct attacks on Peter's undertakings. We may conclude that he recognized autonomous secular culture, even if against his will, and only strove to prevent its contamination of church culture, i.e., to guarantee if only the relative autonomy of church culture. This was the compromise by which Peter was able to work with his opponents.

Indeed, in the foreword to the *Trilingual Lexicon* of 1704 Polikarpov tried to isolate secular and church culture from one another, defining their different initial sources — Latin culture and language used primarily "in civil and school matters," for secular culture, and Greek culture and language, the language of Holy Writ, for church culture. On Greek it says that "our Orthodox faith grew out of Greek piety, and our entire [Divine] law, the prophets, and our divinely inspired books by the holy fathers, radiant with wisdom and virtue were translated from the Greek language at various times and places. To this day the Russian people preserve their sayings unchanged, as well as the holy books and church rituals" (Polikarpov 1704, l. 6). On Latin it says that "Latin has been included as a third language because today this language is used around the world more than others in civil and educational matters. The same [is true] for all kinds of sciences and arts that are necessary for human society. A great many books have been translated [into Latin] from other languages, and many are still composed in this language. To sum up, there is no one who can do without it, who would not desire to have it available for his needs, whether an artist or a soldier skilful in military

1. Tasks of the Language Reform and the Nature of its Realization

matters" (ibid, l. 6 verso; cf. Pekarskii, NL, I, 191). He thus described different spheres for the use of Latin and Greek that corresponded to the split between secular and religious culture which was the basis forPetrine linguistic policy.[9] Significantly, by 1704 Polikarpov's program somewhat changed: he was no longer speaking about a struggle with secular culture but about defending the independence of the church tradition which did not accept Europeanizing changes as a matter of principle. His assertion about the impossibility of using the new alphabet for church books cited above directly relates to this latter program.

We need to keep still one more issue in mind. The use of the Roman imperial example, the turn to classical culture, and, more broadly, to European models in general, were all superimposed onto cultural paradigms of the previous era. These could be interpreted by contemporaries as invocations of the "impure" and "demonic" (Lotman and Uspenskii 1977). The German clothing in which Peter dressed Russian nobles was not new — demons had been depicted in this guise long before Peter (Uspenskii 1976). Similarly, the Junos, Minervas, and Herculeses that populated Petrine triumphs were familiar figures of Hellenic idolatry, equated in Russia with worshipping unclean powers (Zhivov and Uspenskii 1984). The same duality applied to the civil script: on the one hand, it was related to Latin and European models, and on the other could be seen as a variation of *skoropis'*.[10]

Indeed, the shape of the letters of the civil alphabet, especially its earlier variants, in many cases derived directly from skoropis', which some

---

[9] I cannot agree with G. Keipert's objections to this view ("This interpretation is doubtful if only because civilian affairs and the educational system which are here connected with Latin are not the only areas of its application nor can they be considered the epitome of secular culture" — Keipert 1988, xvi). In reality, of course, the sphere of using Latin in the Petrine era was not limited to those Polikarpov indicated, as already in the 1700's Latin was established as the medium for religious education, and in this respect the Moscow Slaviano-Greko-Latino Academy duplicated the Kievan Academy. We do not know exactly how Polikarpov felt about this. As a Grecophile, he may have considered the expansion of Latin unjustified and not have included religious education in the category of "school matters." However, he may also have approved of Latin in this area as an auxiliary language. Nonetheless, according to Polikarpov, Latin is needed primarily for uses that are not connected to faith or the salvation of the soul but "for all arts and sciences" as well as "for civil and school matters." Whether he considered these embodiments of secular culture isn't clear, as Polikarpov does not operate with this notion. In any case, he relates the two languages, Greek and Latin, to different cultural spheres, and that ascribed to Latin relates to the secular pursuits introduced by the Petrine cultural reform of the 1700s. However artificial this may have been, Polikarpov was negotiating for the autonomy of church culture which demanded Greek and traditional educational methods. Significantly, this compromise position was upheld over the course of the Petrine cultural transformation.

[10] Skoropis' — a simplified cursive form of writing Church Slavonic that developed in the late fourteenth century, and used mostly for bureaucratic and private uses. (Translator's note)

scholars see as "the fundamental basis of the civil script" (Shitsgal 1974, 39; Shitsgal 1959, 82–114). This connection was obvious for contemporaries, as it was for the very person who created the new alphabet. In a letter to M. P. Gagarin of November 8, 1708, Peter ordered: "Print the entire alphabet in which all of the letters were made in Moscow, not [the ones from] Amsterdam, but if letters are missing take them from the Amsterdam ones. Only [the letters] 'dobro,' 'tverdo' print the ones that are closer to print, and not to skoropis', that look like this: 'Д,' 'Т'" (PiB, VIII, 1, 289). Thus in the case of these two letters they were to follow the traditional form of kirillitsa, and not skoropis'; the similarity of the other letters to skoropis' was implied. The continuity between the civil alphabet and skoropis' led Polikarpov to note in his grammar that in texts printed in this script spelling "is not maintained.., although the use of these letters — є, ѣ, и, ι — is preserved" (RGADA, f. 201, no. 6, l. 36). Indeed, from the point of view of bookmen there were no orthographic norms in skoropis' at all, in particular the bookish rule for using the letters *u* and *ï* (*ï* before a vowel, *u* in other cases) was not observed, and *e* and *ѣ* were used interchangeably. This is why Polikarpov asserts that texts in the new script follow the spelling of skoropis' texts, except that use of the letters *ѣ, e, ï,* and *u* observes the norm of bookish writing.

The juxtaposition of "ustav"[11] writing (and the corresponding print) to skoropis' could be connected to the opposition between semantic spheres, between the sacred and the profane, church and secular, cultural and non-cultural (Uspenskii 1983, 60–4). Thus contrasting two types of writing for a series of letters in the foreword to his conversational manual of 1607 Tönnies Fenne asserted that one is used when writing "about divine, tsarist or seigniorial things" and the other for writing "about infernal and base things" (Fenne, I, 23; II, 17); it is hard to say whether this is an adequate representation of Russian cultural consciousness of the time, but it undoubtedly reflects some kind of connection between paleographic differences and basic cultural oppositions. This connection was part of the prehistory of the juxtaposition between church and civil scripts that underwent semiotic reconceptualization; something emphatically profane, secular, and without cultural value from the traditional point of view now enters the sphere of culture and cult. In this context European forms function as transformations of elements that already existed in the Russian cultural heritage; traditional elements did not disappear, but took on new semiotic functions.

And so the devising of a new literary language began with the creation of a civil script, and orthography served as the mirror of culture.

---

[11] "Ustav" — the oldest form of the Slavonic alphabet (kirillitsa), originally modeled on Greek uncial script of the ninth-eleventh century. (Translator's note)

1. Tasks of the Language Reform and the Nature of its Realization

The juxtaposition of new and old alphabets helped establish the demarcation of cultural spheres and played a role in the functional differentiation of the traditional (Church Slavonic) and new ("simple") literary language. The opposition of the two languages was part of a single complex that included the opposition of church and civil scripts and was related to a whole sequence of interrelated cultural conflicts, including "Helleno-Slavic" learning versus the "Slaveno-Latin schools" (one of the names for the Moscow Academy in documents of Peter's day [Smirnov 1855, 82]); traditions of the Church Fathers and Hellenic learning; Greek-Russian Orthodoxy and Roman-European Enlightenment, church and secular culture, priesthood and bureaucracy, Church and Empire.

1.2 Petrine Linguistic Directives

The goals and results of the Petrine reform of the alphabet are more or less obvious: we know what tradition was being overthrown and we can see the significance of the new phenomenon that was being created. But when we turn to the reform of the language, its tasks and results are not nearly as self-evident.

It is usually said that during the Petrine era Church Slavonic was rejected (or, definitively rejected) as the literary language, and that the Russian language took its place (e.g., Larin 1975, 275). But insofar as these labels are genetic rather than functional, as we argued earlier (§ 0–2), they are poorly fitted for describing the processes by which the literary language was transformed. It turns out that, on the one hand, the use of Church Slavonic was limited, but on the other, that Church Slavonic "elements" were widely employed. To the extent that the significance of these elements remains unexplained, the composition of the new literary language and its differences from the traditional written language also remain unclear. V. V. Vinogradov can even assert that "the literary style of the Petrine epoch, despite its mixed character, does not cease being and being called 'Slavonic'" (Vinogradov 1938, 75).

The consequence of this approach is the conclusion that Peter's cultural and linguistic policies for all their radicalism did not find consistent expression in linguistic practice; if it produced certain results, they may only be characterized as a chaotic mixture of heterogeneous features that do not lend themselves to any kind of systematization. This was, in the words of N. A. Meshcherskii, "a bizarre combination of the basic linguistic elements out of which the Russian literary language had historically come together by this time. On the one hand, these were words, expressions and grammatical forms of traditional, Church Slavonic derivation; on the other, words and word forms of a popular, even dialectical character; and in the third place, these were foreign speech elements, frequently poorly assimilated by Russian in the phonetic, morphological and semantic aspect" (Meshcherskii 1981, 150; cf. Levin 1972, 216–8).

The reasoning here is quite clear. Insofar as genetic parameters are taken as the starting point, the only conclusion to be drawn when analyzing the linguistic material is that it is genetically heterogeneous. Genetic heterogeneity is taken as the basic feature of the Petrine literary language, and according to this parameter all of its component parts fall into three groups, Church Slavonic elements, Russian elements, and borrowed elements. Insofar as it is hard to imagine any linguistic elements that would not be covered by these categories, this categorization seems rather banal. More than that, it is not very clear what the innovation of the Petrine epoch actually was. Indeed, as we have seen, the mixing of genetically Russian and genetically Church Slavonic elements was also characteristic of the written language of the earlier period (§ 0–2, § 0–3); this language also had a certain quantity of borrowings (among them poorly assimilated ones). This is what led Vinogradov to conclude that the literary language of the Petrine period remained Church Slavonic.

As far as genetic parameters are concerned, the main difference between the Petrine literary language and the earlier tradition was purely quantitative — a greater number of borrowings. It is for this reason that historians of the literary language of this period have focused their attention on them (cf. Sobolevskii 1980; Vinogradov 1938, 59–62; Meshcherskii 1981, 143–50; Isaatschenko 1983, 545–8). It is obvious, however, that borrowings is a special issue that does not help in defining a language's status; no matter how many borrowings from Dutch or German during the period in question, Russian neither became Dutch or German nor even became similar to them. If the basic innovation of the Petrine period was borrowings, then there was nothing essentially new in its language, and it does not differ fundamentally from the language of traditional book culture. The logical conclusion of this line of reasoning is that drawn by A. V. Isachenko, who speaks of "the helplessness, the chaos, the mangling of the current (tragbar) linguistic conception of the Petrine period" (Isachenko 1983, 532).

Nevertheless, Peter had a rather definite conception of the language. His many statements about language that reveal the basic planks of his

1. Tasks of the Language Reform and the Nature of its Realization

linguistic program testify to this. Peter demanded certain changes in the language and certain changes were effected, so one can't say that the tsar's ideas were not put into linguistic practice. However, to clarify these changes and to define their significance demands an adequate methodology, both in order to choose the relevant material for analysis and to specify the functional categories that are necessary to describe it.

Naturally, we should not expect that the changes caused by Peter's linguistic policies extended to all linguistic practice; the old does not disappear instantaneously, but continues to exist in parallel to the new for a rather long time (even in Lomonosov's era stories continued to be copied and composed in a language close to that of *Gesta Romanorum, Acts of the Romans* [*Rimskie deianiia*] and the *Tale of Peter of the Golden Keys* that were written in hybrid Church Slavonic). Texts were created in the traditional bookish language and business documents written in the non-bookish tongue that differed little from those of previous century. Of course, such texts tell us nothing about the changes taking place in the Petrine era. The significant texts were those created in accordance with Peter's direct instructions, or those of his closest associates. It is the language of these texts that should be studied first of all, and the new features they reveal should be compared to those of other texts, including later ones (for example, of the mid-eighteenth century), that unquestionably represent examples of the new literary language. It will then become clear which features of the Petrine language were ephemeral and which [91] were definitely assimilated by the new literary language. In this manner it may be determined what was new in Peter's linguistic policies and to what extent the realization of Peter's linguistic views may be seen as the basis for the Russian literary language of the new type, as opposed to Church Slavonic.

Hence the issue concerns the interpretation of Peters' linguistic views with the help of those texts in which it was immediately realized. Without doubt, this interpretation requires the application not of genetic, but of functional criteria. Neither Peter nor his associates were concerned with etymology or with historical grammar, so that in calling this or that element "Slavonic," "Russian," or "the language of the foreign office (posol'skii prikaz)," they had in mind not their derivation but their function. The content of these labels was defined by the linguistic consciousness of the given era, which needs to be understood in terms of the functional categories that take into account the frequent reconceptualization of genetically heterogeneous elements during the long process of interactions between the registers of the written language during the previous period. Consequently, the analysis of the cultural and linguistic innovations of the Petrine era divide into two parts.

Chapter 1. The Petrine Language Reform

In the first place, Peter's linguistic positions must be defined as they were articulated by the tsar and his associates. Secondly, they must be examined as expressed in the texts that attempted to put them into practice.

Peter's linguistic declarations are rather numerous and clearly testify to the tsar's intention to exclude the traditional bookish language from the secular cultural sphere. Extremely significant in this context is the history of translating Bernhard Varenius' *General Geography* (see Lukicheva 1974; Uspenskii 1983, 96–99; Zhivov 1986b). This history clearly reveals all of the basic facets of Peter's linguistic position.

In early 1715 Peter ordered the translation of Varenius' book which contained the sum of contemporary knowledge of the natural sciences; it was needed to combat what Peter saw as the prejudices and superstitions of medieval culture. By October of 1716 the translation of this extensive work was finished and the text recopied. The book was translated into Church Slavonic, and in his foreword Fedor Polikarpov wrote:

> As regards the translation of this book, duty bound me to follow both the author's sense and the text, and to translate it not into the common Russian language (obshchenarodnym dialektom Rossiiskim) but to preserve as far as possible the rules of grammatical order (reguly china grammaticheskogo), so as to make clear the loftiness and beauty of the author's words and style. (BAN, Petrovskaia gallereia, no. 72, l. 9, quoted from: Uspenskii 1983, 98)

The translation (whose manuscript is preserved in BAN) was sent to Peter for his approval, but he did not like it, and on the tsar's orders I. A. Musin-Pushkin informed Polikarpov on June 2, 1717:

> ...I am sending you the translation of your Geography as well, which for lack of skill or some other [reason] was translated very poorly; so you should correct it, not using high Slavonic words but the simple Russian language... Labor with all diligence, and you need not use high Slavonic words; use the language of the Foreign Office (Posol'skii prikaz) instead. (Cherty iz istorii 1868, col. 1054–55).

A new version of the translation was prepared taking the tsar's instructions into consideration and was published in Moscow in 1718. In the new foreword Polikarpov wrote in the name of "the group of people who labored on this task" that: "It is my duty to announce that I translated it not into the most high Slavonic language, that would correspond to the author's [language], and following the rules of grammar; but rather I used the average civil speech (mnozhae grazhdanskogo posredstvennago upotrebliakh narechiia), preserving the sense and the words (sens i rechi) of the foreign original" (Varenii 1718, foreword, l. 17 verso). The new version satisfied the

1. Tasks of the Language Reform and the Nature of its Realization

tsar, and Musin-Pushkin informed Polikarpov on August 25, 1718, "that the geography... was accepted and pleasing to his majesty" (RGADA, f. 381, no. 423, l. 317).

This episode represents, in essence, the collision of two antagonistic linguistic positions. Polikarpov translated the *General Geography* into Church Slavonic, and anticipating Peter's objections defended his choice of language by saying that "the generally used Russian language" was not capable of conveying the "loftiness and beauty" of the original, that only Church Slavonic was able to do so (on Polikarpov's position, see above, § I–1.1). Peter rejected this, referring to the poor quality of the translation, and demanded that it be translated into "the simple Russian language." He thus insisted on Russian's essential dignity and assigned it the role of language for the new culture. Polikarpov refers to this as "average civil speech," at the same time noting the impossibility of "following the rules of grammar."

In the development of this conflict, it was apparent that Polikarpov did not want to take on the task of reworking the text himself, which would have led in his opinion to the absurd destruction of the "rules of grammatical order." He assigned the unpleasant task to his former teacher Sofronii Likhud, with whom his relations at this particular time were rather strained.[12] Sofronii would seem to have been a good choice insofar as he was, in distinction to the other Moscow bookmen, hardly one of those proponents of Church Slavonic who disallowed the use of any other language as a cultural vehicle. His linguistic views have yet to be studied in full. He had arrived in Moscow in 1685 where he occupied a position teaching Greek, Latin, and Italian; he was one of the founders of the Novgorod school, established by Metropolitan Job, and together with his brother worked on translations into Slavonic (including Athanasius Kirchner's *Sphinx* and *Mantle of Roman Virtues of Aeneas that Are in Virgil* [*Riza rimskikh dobrodetelei Eneia, izhe v Virgile*], from Latin, and *Sigismond Albert on Artillery and on the Means to Defeat the Turks* from Italian — Smentsovskii 1899, 349). He also took part in the commission to review and correct the Slavonic bible. Thus Sofronii was a representative of not only Greek but Slavonic literary culture. His linguistic views were probably formed in the Helleno-Slavic tradition as were those of Evfimii, Patriarch Ioakim and others (in the late 1680's the Likhud brothers allied with them against the Latinophiles), and his pupils (Polikarpov, Nikolai Semenov, and F. Maksimov — cf. Ialamas 1988). This movement was characterized by an insistence on the grammatical norms of Church

---

[12] On their difficult relations, see the letter of Musin-Pushkin to Polikarpov of May 6, 1715 […] (RGADA, f. 381, no. 423, l. 249–249 verso).

Slavonic, desire for its improvement and codification, and a perception of the language as a polyfunctional literary language analogous to Latin and Greek. Unlike Evfimii, however, the Likhuds apparently did not see Church Slavonic as the same as Greek in its structure, and did not consider that this structure itself was of sacred character. Evidence of this, in particular, is the limited "Grecianization" of the Slavonic texts in the books of the bible that Sofronii edited (see Bobrik 1988); the grammatical tradition of the Likhud brothers evidently paid significant attention to the differences between Greek and Church Slavonic (as the grammatical works of Polikarpov and F. Maksimov indicate; the Likhuds' influence on them requires special analysis).

For Sofronii Likhud, as for his pupils, the model for conceptualizing the relationship between Church Slavonic and the "simple" tongue was the relationship between bookish Greek and demotic ("simple") Greek that was oriented on modern Greek dialects (cf. Uspenskii 1983, 106; Strakhova 1986, 67–8). Significantly, Russian sources of the late seventeenth and early eighteenth century may refer to demotic Greek as "the simple" or "common Greek language" (cf. for example Gorskii and Nevostuev, II, 2, 657; Gorskii and Nevostuev, II, 3, 293; Sobolevskii 1903, 336; Sobolevskii 1980, 43–4), in the same way, mutatis mutandis, as the "simple" language of the Petrine era (cf. Uspenskii 1983, 65). This label for demotic Greek is also found in the Likhuds' writing (see below). The task of revising texts from Church Slavonic into the "simple" tongue could not help but be associated with the known precedent of translations (as it says in one manuscript) from "the old Greek language which today's Greeks do not understand" into the "commonly used (obshchii) Greek language" (Sobolevskii 1903, 356). For the post-Byzantine period this was a widespread practice and the Likhud brothers taught it to their students. In their petition of 1687 they wrote: "our great work is known to all through the success of our students who learned Greek and Latin grammar, poetics, and some rhetoric, and to speak our simple language and Greek and Latin well and correctly" (RGADA, f. 159, op. 2, gg. 1685/99, no. 2991, l. 231; thanks to D. Ialamas for showing me this manuscript). Their educational program included translations of bookish Greek to demotic and vice versa (Ialamas 1992). Polikarpov could hardly have found someone more appropriate to revise from bookish Slavonic into the "simple" tongue than Sofronni Likhud, who was so well versed in the Greek practice.

That the second version of the translation did belong to Sofronii is evidenced by the edited manuscript of the *Geography*, whose basis was the first draft, while the original typeset version of 1718 represents the corrected text (RGADA, f. 381, no. 1008). [...] Sofronii Likhud was responsible for

1. Tasks of the Language Reform and the Nature of its Realization

the final edition of the text as published in 1718, i.e., it was he who fulfilled Peter's demand that the traditional bookish language be replaced by "the simple Russian language." This signaled the victory of Peter's linguistic program over that of Polikarpov and the other traditionalists. The "high Slavonic style" was thus opposed to "average civil speech," and Peter's desire was precisely that civil books be written in this civil language, just as they would be printed in civil script. The same linguistic ideas are reflected in Peter's other pronouncements.

Thus the tsar's instructions to Feofilakt Lopatinski, rector of the Moscow Slaveno-Greco-Latin Academy, were expressed in the same terms as those in Musin-Pushkin's letter on the *General Geography:*

> By personal order of his royal highness, in the two lexicons which his highness sent, one from Latin into French, the other from Latin into Dutch, it is ordered to replace the Latin with Slavonic words... And upon finishing this matter, from these same lexicons be pleased to make lexicons from Slavonic into Latin, but in all of them do not be pleased to use lofty Slavonic words, but rather the simple Russian language (letter of June 2, 1717 — Cherty iz istorii 1868, 1053–54; an analogous statement is made about the dictionaries in a letter to Polikarpov, ibid, col. 1054; cf. Pekarskii, NL. I, 411)

Musin-Pushkin also gave similar instructions to Gavriil Buzhinskii, prefect of the Moscow Academy, about which he informed Peter in a letter of December 10, 1716: "Your majesty's letter about Erasmus' book, that the translation did not correspond to the Dutch, and that this be rectified, and that a written [notification] be sent to your majesty, I received on the third of this month... I ordered the prefect to correct it and to use some expressions from the Russian everyday language (russkim obkhoditel'nym iazykom)" (Pekarskii, NL, II, 368). He was talking about the book *Friendly Conversations. By Desiderius Erasmus* (Erasmus 1716). Here too Musin-Pushkin's comments clearly reflect Peter's opinion.

Peter's later instructions concerning the Russian translation of Apollodorus' *Library*, which Peter thought of as kind of guide to anti-clerical enlightenment, also indicate the consistency of his position. The spread of knowledge of classical mythology as represented in this book became a part of state policy directed toward Europeanizing the country. It does not seem fortuitous that Peter commissioned the Synod with the translation. This was calculated to counter those conservative clerics concerned with the purity of the faith who considered ancient mythology to be demonic, and was part of the state's ecclesiastical policy in which the Synod, as a state department, was obliged to participate. If the old (patriarchal) church organization was, in Peter's view, a breeding-ground of ignorance, the new (Synodal) administration was called on to promote enlightenment and to eradicate ignorance; accordingly, popularizing mythology was part of the Synod's responsibility.[13] Peter ordered that this book be translated into Russian, the language of the new enlightenment, in opposition to Church Slavonic as the language of old ignorance. Indeed, in the "preliminary admonition (pred"uveshchanie) from the translator of this book" (A. K. Barsov) included in the edition, it is pointed out that

> In the month of December of last year, 1722, His Most Royal Highness the Most Powerful Peter the Great, Emperor and Autocrat of All the Russias, Father of the Fatherland, upon his successful return to Moscow..., when he was pleased to grace the Most Holy Governing Synod with his Royal person, presented a book by Apollodorus the Athenian Grammarian, published in the Greek and Latin languages, to the Most Holy Governing Synod, ordering that it also be translated into the common Russian tongue. (Apollodor 1725, foreword, p. 19)

The publishing of Apollodorus was a major undertaking of Petrine cultural policy, so the linguistic demands made on it were especially significant.

A similar instruction of Peter's is described in the foreword to the *System of Mohammedan Religion* compiled in 1722 by D. Kantemir (and translated by I. Il'inskii): "His Royal highness was pleased to charge me, his loyal slave, with the publication [of this book] about the Mohammedan religion and about the form of Mohammedan government in the low style and simple language (nizhnim stilem i prostorechiem)" (RGADA f 381, no.1035, l. 13 — thanks to N. N. Zapol'skaia for pointing out this manuscript). Finally, on April 19, 1724, Peter wrote an order for the Synod to compose short sermons, commanding that they "write simply so that even a countryman (poselianin) can understand, or in two [versions], simple for countrymen and more ornate for the pleasure of listeners in the city, as it seems fitting to you" (PSZ, VII, no. 4493, p. 278; Pekarskii NL I, 181 — there are errors in Pekarskii's citation). It seems that here Peter is also calling for a break with traditional linguistic behavior by providing for definite variations in language depending on the text's audience. Moreover, the impression is created that marked elements of Church Slavonic are perceived as rhetorical

---

[13] In his foreword to Apollodorus' book Feofan Prokopovich particularly emphasized that paganism was "obriadoverie" ("faith in rites"); this view was explicitly opposed to traditional ideology. [...] (Apollodor 1725, foreword). The book embodied the ideas of rationalist Enlightenment that Peter used as a weapon in the struggle against religious and cultural traditionalism, and use of the "commonly used Russian language" (as opposed to Church Slavonic) was prescribed in accordance with this ideological task.

embellishment, allowed to satisfy the taste and habits of the urban population, creating a dependence of linguistic code on the socio-cultural task which was evident, for example, in Feofam Prokopovich's linguistic practice (cf. Zhivov 1985, 78–81; Zhivov 1985a, 276–7; see also § III–2.1).

1.3 From Hybrid Church Slavonic to the "Simple" Russian Language

The statements analyzed above allow us to envisage Peter's linguistic views rather clearly. It is obvious that Peter's instructions about the use of a "simple," "average," "common" language were directed against the earlier linguistic tradition in which Church Slavonic served as the universal language of culture. Its place, at least in the sphere of the new culture, was to be taken by another language defined by the above epithets. In principle, these could be applied to a wide spectrum of linguistic phenomena with very diverse structural characteristics (§ 0–5). The question therefore arises what exactly was this "simple" language that Peter imagined. The clearest answer to this question, as noted above, may be found in those texts that were edited to satisfy the linguistic demands of the new cultural policy.

The *General Geography* was perhaps the most important of such texts. We know of Peter's negative attitude toward the first version of the translation and his approval of the final edition. Accordingly, the almost 900 folia of the corrected manuscript on which we can trace the changes from one version to the next may be seen as a direct realization of Peter's linguistic position. Obviously, the "high Slavonic words" are what were being eliminated from the text, and "the simple Russian language" is the language of the final version. The nature of the corrections made by Sofronii Likhud undeniably reveals that the issue was not about stylistic editing but about changing the language itself: Church Slavonic is to be replaced by non-Church Slavonic. How was this replacement expressed? Naturally, it had to do not with the markers that connect the opposition between Church Slavonic and Russian texts for a researcher of today but with those things that distinguished the traditional bookish language from the non-bookish in the linguistic consciousness of the Petrine epoch. It was these precise elements that were subject to elimination, and as we will see, Sofronii's work for the most part embodied the imperatives of this linguistic consciousness rather than his individual bias as an editor.

Chapter 1. The Petrine Language Reform

The corrections which Sofronii Likhud made only related to a limited set of features, primarily of a morphological and syntactic character. To the morphological belong: replacing the aorist and imperfect with forms of the unbookish past tense (*л*-form without auxiliary verb); omission of the auxiliary verb in the perfect; replacing the athematic conjugation with analogous word formations; substituting infinitives in -*ти* with -*ть*, the second pers. sg. ending -*ши* by -*шь*, dual forms with plurals, adverbs in -*ѣ* with those in -*о*; the elimination of the superlative form with the suffix -*айш*/ -*ѣйш* and the comparative with the suffix -*ш*-. To the syntactic belong: replacing participles as gerunds in agreement with the subjects by forms without agreement; omission of the dative absolute and the construction *еже* + infinitive; replacing phrases in *да* + the present tense by an infinitive or subordinate clause with the conjunction *дабы*; the elimination of inversions; substituting double for single negations; and replacing constructions with nouns in the genitive by constructions with possessive or relative adjectives. As far as lexical editing is concerned (if we disregard editing whose goal was finding the optimal Russian variant for the corresponding Latin term), it almost exclusively concerned function words (pronouns, conjunctions, particles, individual adverbs); content words played practically no role in the opposition of the bookish and "simple" language. Hence changing the language of the initial translation of the *General Geography* consisted in eliminating the markers of bookishness in the text (as they were perceived in the late seventeenth — early eighteenth century), i.e., those elements that in the previous tradition indicated the bookish nature of the text (§ 0–2, § 0–3). The "simple" tongue was defined not in its own terms as an independent norm, but only negatively, in relation to the traditional (Church Slavonic) bookish language (for a detailed analysis of Likhud's editing, see Zhivov 1986a).

The fact that when making substitutions of a particular marker Sofronii could ignore all others testifies to this negative dependence of the "simple" tongue on the traditional bookish language. Thus on fol. 96 Sofronii makes the following corrections (here and below corner brackets indicate things crossed out, while italics indicate additions:

...<что> понеже егда вавѵлѡнъ ѿ алеѯандра пл<е>ѣненъ былъ, обрѣтены тамѡ <сѹть> помраченїя затменїя сл҃нца напнсан<н>ы<е> и ичисле<н>ы<е> за лѣта многа прежде Рж҇ства Хр҇стова, еже без познанїя се<й>я земли фїгѹры <познанїя> быти немо<жаше>гло бы.

The original word order was: "без се<й>я земли фїгѹры познанїя";

1. Tasks of the Language Reform and the Nature of its Realization

Sofronii changes it to "бєз познанїѧ фі́гу́ры се‹й›ѧ земли." In this passage Sofronii also eliminates the imperfect and the inversion; he crosses out the auxiliary verb in the predicate, and replaces full participles with short ones in predicative use; these corrections are found throughout the text of the *Geography*. At the same time Sofronii preserves: the construction with *еже*, which he usually replaces with a *который* clause; the form *лѣта многа* despite the usual replacement of short adjectives by long ones in the attributive function; the nom.-acc. neut. pl. ending *а/ая* to *и/ие*; and the infinitive in *-ти*, often replaced by the form with *-ть*. The incomplete and nature of the replacements is characteristic of the entire manuscript and can't be explained by the proofreader's carelessness. We may suggest that this situation is due to the fact that the "simple" tongue is only defined negatively in relation to the traditional bookish language, and not as an independent norm. The markers juxtaposing the traditional bookish and "simple" languages allow us to understand how the Church Slavonic text could be simplified; actually' the editing is not a translation from one language to another, but Church Slavonic's movement in the direction of a "simple" text. If a certain number of corrections are made, this minimal task has been fulfilled, even if the editing hasn't touched all of the relevant markers. The norm of the "simple" language is the ideal result of all corresponding corrections, and is only partially realized in concrete texts.

In general, one is led to conclude that for Likhud, as for his contemporaries, there is no clear sense of what a bookish (cultured) text should be in the Russian ("simple") language, and that there is only a notion of the markers that distinguish the bookish and non-bookish language that was worked out by the linguistic consciousness of previous epochs. This notion conditioned his understanding of Peter's orders that demanded a rejection of the language of traditional book culture. That we are dealing here with the linguistic consciousness of the period rather than Likhud's individual understanding is indicated by the fact that the set of elements subject to correction is almost identical in other manuscripts. We may include in this group Feofan Prokopovich's *History of Peter the Great* with Feofan's own corrections (RGADA, f. 9, op. 1, no. 1) and A. K. Barsov's translation of Apollodorus' *Library* (the printer's proofs with corrections by Krechetovskii and Maksimovich, correctors [spravshchiki] of the Synodal press, are preserved in RGADA, f. 381, no. 1015; a colophon by the correctors is on fol. 9). Although compared with the *General Geography* the material in these manuscripts is relatively little, it does permit us to conclude that the notion of the "simple" language as a definite transformation of the old literary language (a bookish language minus marks of bookishness) was quite widespread among a broad circle of authors (bookmen). The acceptance of this transformation as the language of the new culture may be seen as the realization of Peter's linguistic program, expressing the goal of his reform and revealing the actual significance of the ideas he was promoting.

Feofan Prokopovich's work as editor is especially significant insofar as he was one of the main exponents of Peter's cultural policy; his activities during 1717–26 were just as important an example of this policy as the activities of the tsar himself. His *History of Peter the Great* has come down to us in the copyist's version, written in one hand (for the edition with extensive linguistic corrections by M. Shcherbatov see Feofan Prokopovich 1773). This work's narrative of events begins with 1672, and down through 1696 (the death of Ioann Alekseevich) it is told in hybrid Church Slavonic. This part of the book is a compilation (see Shmurlo 1912, notes 16–18; Peshtich, I, 142–3), and it is precisely here, on fol. 3–17, that Feofan's linguistic editing is concentrated. His corrections also have as their goal changing the character of the language, i.e., "simple" Russian is to replace Church Slavonic. The following forms were involved in the revision: the forms of aorist and imperfect were replaced by forms of the non-bookish past tense; participles as gerunds in agreement with the subjects were replaced by forms without agreement ; infinitives ending in *-mu* were replaced by those in *-mь*; dual forms were replaced by plurals; phrases using the dative aabsolute were replaced by temporal subordinate clauses; and a series of function words were also changed (*когда* took the place of *егда*, *однакожь* the place of *обаче*, *а хотя* instead of *аще же*, and so on) (for a detailed analysis of the editing, see Zhivov 1988a).

No less indicative was the editing of the manuscript of Apollodorus' *Library*. As we noted above, this book was ordered to be translated into the "simple Russian language." Unlike Polikarpov, its translator A. K. Barsov followed the orders of the tsar from the start. For him, however, it was natural to write a bookish text in the traditional bookish language (cf. in particular the "Preliminary Admonition [Preduveshchanie]," written in Church Slavonic), and writing in the "common Russian tongue" was an artificial task, so from time to time he stumbled back into using more familiar Slavonic forms. It was precisely these missteps that the Synodal correctors who prepared the text for publication rectified. Their editing once again concerned those very elements which had been significant in revising the *General Geography*. We find here the forms of the aorist replaced by forms of the non-bookish past tense; infinitives in *-mu* replaced by *-mь*; use of possessive adjectives instead of the genitive of possession; expressions using the dative absolute and "accusativus cum infinitivo" replaced by subordinate clauses; the conjunction что instead of яко; and the omission of the particle убо.

Of course, the editing of the three works we have examined is not fully identical. This is conditioned first of all by the scope of the changes. The fifteen sheets corrected by Feofan or the individual lapses corrected by Krechetovskii and Maksimovich do not offer as diverse material as the almost thousand folia edited by Likhud. Differences in the editing are directly connected to the character of the initial text. As concerns Apollodorus' *Library,* Barsov's text was already written in the "simple" tongue, and it was only his individual "errors" that followed no system that were subjected to correction. By habit, Barsov sometimes used simple preterits and did not avoid single negatives, and this defined the range of the corrections. There were also differences in the initial language of the *General Geography* and the *History of Peter the Great*; the *General Geography* was written in a significantly more refined bookish language. As opposed to the *General Geography,* the *History* lacked perfects with auxiliary verb, forms of athematic conjugation, "еже + infinitive" and "да + present tense" constructions, the relative pronouns иже, еже, юже, яже, etc. (so of course there were no corrections of these forms). Apart from these differences, dependent on the basic material, the divergence between Feofan's and Likhud's corrections comes down to details. For example, Likhud does not correct reflexive forms (-ся into -сь) that occurs twice in Feofan's text, and Feofan doesn't change adverbs in -ѣ to ones in -о. Unlike Likhud, Feofan also does not change forms of the comparative and superlative degrees, although the starting text has only minimal basis for such editing. These individual differences take second place in comparison to the far reaching similarities that may extend to details (e.g., обаче replaced by однакожь, аще by хотя, the elimination of убо).

And so we see that in all three of these cases, despite individual differences, the editing was basically identical, and this is certainly a very significant fact. Feofan Prokopovich and Sofronii Likhud belonged to completely different circles and were adherents of different, in many cases, opposed, cultural, political, literary and linguistic traditions, so that the similarity of their editing cannot be explained by external factors (for example, common education or the continuity of editing practices, and so on; nothing is known about the views of Krechetkovskii and Maksimovich). The similarity was based on the fact that they shared the same linguistic consciousness and on the fact that all of those who took part in the process understood which markers defined the bookish language (the markers of bookishness) and which, consequently, needed to be eliminated in order to turn it into the "simple" tongue. A common (written) literary and linguistic tradition underlay this identity, a tradition of texts whose bookish character was defined by precisely this set of specifically bookish linguistic features. It is natural to see this tradition as that of the hybrid register of Church Slavonic; in this case we should connect the formation of the literary language of the new type with changes in this literary and linguistic tradition (§ 0–3).

Evidence of this understanding of the correlation between the traditional bookish language and the "simple" tongue may be found in several works on grammar that appeared during the Petrine era. Thus Polikarpov's *Tekhnologiia* of 1725 (RNB, NSRK, F 1921.60; cf. Babaeva 1989) describes a series of differences between "Slavonic" and "Great Russian" grammar. These include the presence or absence of simple preterits, the vocative form, the dual number, and the analytical or suffixed formation of comparatives and superlatives (Uspenskii 1994, 110–1). As Boris Uspenskii writes, "one can't help but note that the codification of differences between Russian and Church Slavonic is based on the same oppositions used in transforming a Church Slavonic text into the simple tongue… At issue here was the very same system of juxtapositions, which in one case was defined in a grammatical description, and in the other realized in linguistic editing. In both cases the 'simple' Russian language is juxtaposed to Church Slavonic via a limited number of markers, as a result of which it becomes possible to more or less automatically transform a Church Slavonic text into Russian and vice versa" (Uspenskii 1987, 343).

One may presume that Polikarpov did not approve of establishing the "simple" tongue as the literary language (see above), although as concerns the differences that separate the traditional bookish and "simple" languages his understanding did not diverge from that of other authors. It should be noted, however, that among the differences between "Slavonic" and the "Great Russian" language Polikarpov also included the presence/absence of the alternation of velars and sibilants in noun declensions, the use of the second genitive, the potential (precisely the potential) coincidence of gen. sg. fem. and dat. sg. fem. adjectives (that is, the use of the *-ой* ending in the gen. sg. fem.), as well as the use of the "plural nominative… in *a* or in *я*" with the numerals *два, три, четыре* (RNB, NSRK, F 1921.60, 96–7). These things do not correspond to the corrected texts we have analyzed, and we may conclude that they were actualized by the specifics of the task of codification itself, its artificiality (for example, the perception of grammatical homonymy as an anomaly that "correct" grammar must eliminate). In these cases the grammarian proceeds not on the basis of linguistic practice but in order to work out his grammatical system in the greatest possible detail. In Polikarpov's case the tendency to see variability in existing written traditions

1. Tasks of the Language Reform and the Nature of its Realization

as genetically motivated (see below § II–1.4) also evidently played a role; this tendency was characteristic precisely of normative grammarians, but did not find full expression in linguistic practice, in particular, in the corrections made to the texts in the Petrine era. Nonetheless, even in this case the similarity of basic principles dominates over particular differences.

The continuity of the "simple" language of the Petrine period in relation to the language of the previous literary and linguistic tradition, and in particular to the tradition of hybrid Church Slavonic, may be seen in the way the edited texts treated elements that did not accord to the opposition between bookish and non-bookish languages in this period's linguistic consciousness. The variability of such elements in hybrid Church Slavonic transfers in one way or another to the new "simple" language, a process which is clearly reflected in the edited texts, although its concrete realization may vary.

In Feofan Prokopovich's *History of Peter the Great* these features remained untouched in the editorial revisions. It follows that they did not correlate to the opposition between languages, and for this reason the free variability of the original text did not change in the text Feofan edited. The elements of this type in the given manuscript include, in nouns: *-омъ/-амъ* in the dat. pl., *-ы/-ами* in the instr. pl., *-ѣхъ/-ахъ* in prep. pl.; and in adjectival inflexions, *-ый/-ой* in nom-acc. sg. masc., *-аго/-ого* in gen.-acc. sg. masc. and neut., *-ыя/-ой* in gen. sg. fem., *-ыи/-ые/-ыя/-ая* in nom.-acc. pl (all genders). The variability of lexemes with the prefixes *раз-* and *роз-* and pleophonic and non-pleophonic forms remained unchanged. In both the original and the text corrected by Feofan bookish and non-bookish lexicon also combined freely, for example, *лютость, вопль* and *махая шапками* (fol. 4 verso — 5); *молвотворенія, позоръ правды* and *навѣтовать во взяткахъ, сыскъ, посылки, править (деньги)* (fol. 7 verso — 8), etc.

In Apollodorus' *Library* and the *General Geography* things were somewhat different. In Apollodorus' *Library* this kind of variability was significantly limited. The original text was normalized in regard to these markers, and the character of this normalization to a great degree corresponds to the prescriptions of the normative grammars of the traditional bookish language (for example, the 1721 edition of Smotritskii's grammar). Thus in this manuscript endings in *-ый/-ій* in nom.-acc. sg. masc., *-аго/-яго* in gen-acc. sg. masc. and neut., *-ыя/-ия* in gen. sg. fem. were all used with basic consistency. Insofar as these endings were used regularly in a text that was declared to be in "the common Russian language," which was edited without regard to a series of other markers relevant for juxtaposing bookish and non-bookish texts in the traditional bookish language, it is obvious that the endings *-ый, -аго,* and *-ыя* were not perceived as special markers of this language. Their use was determined not by choice of linguistic code but independent of that code, by the orthographic norm of the written (printed) text.

This same general picture also holds for the *General Geography*. The original text only allows a limited number of variations here, and in many ways follows the norm codified by the Slavonic grammarians (isolated discrepancies are probably due not only to Polikarpov's own practice, oriented as expected on the written tradition of hybrid Church Slavonic, but also to the carelessness of the copyists). Varying elements may occasionally be subject to correction. In some cases traditional variants are chosen, for example, endings in *-ый, -аго*, and *-ыя* (Sofronii Likhud changed *-ой* to *-ый* in nom.-acc. sg. masc., *-ого* to *-аго* in gen.-acc. sg. masc., *-ой* to *-ыя* in gen. sg. fem.see — Zhivov 1986b, 257), which clearly shows the influence of the grammatical norm of the old bookish language. In other cases, however, only the intention to normalize the text is evident, while the principles of normalization remain unclear and the attempts at normalization themselves tend in different directions. This is the case, for example, with prep. pl. noun endings; in three cases the old ending is replaced by the new (*островѣх, брезѣхъ, днехъ* are changed to *островах, брегахъ, дняхъ* — 423 verso, 360, 587), and in one case the new by the old (*мѣстахъ* by *мѣстѣхъ* — 93 verso). Analogously, in some cases the alternation of velars and sibilants was eliminated (replacing *книзѣ* by *книгѣ* [64], *Америцѣ* by *Америкѣ* [147 verso, 148], *на воздусѣ* to *на воздухѣ* [502 verso], *мнози* to *многи* [428], etc.), and in others restored (*пресѣкатель* by *пресѣцатель* [74], *книгѣ* by *книзѣ* [80], *брегу* by *брезѣ* [288], etc.). In precisely the same way non-pleophonic forms could be replaced with pleophonic ones (*во градѣ* by *в городѣ* [186, 712 verso], *два прага* by *два порога* [382 verso]) and vice versa (*переходимъ* by *преходимъ* [154], *солоности* by *сланости* [255 verso], *болота* by *блата* [438]). Such attempts at normalization did not eliminate grammatical and lexical variability, and this kind of inconsistency that is not generally typical of the work of the correctors (spravshchiki) was evidently caused by the unusual task of having to normalize a text "in the simple Russian language." Particular criteria for such normalization had not yet been worked out, and Likhud mostly followed the traditional norms of the bookish language, although the peculiar result reflected in irregular and contradictory editing puts the justification for this procedure in doubt.

The disconnect between this kind of normalization and the problem of changing languages follows from the fact that it could be carried out in texts that were from the beginning written in the "simple" language and even meant as models of this language. Normalizing editing of this kind was carried out, for example, on the proofs of *Honest Mirror of Youth* (*Iunosti chestnoe zertsalo*) (RGADA, f. 381, no. 1021). One may take this book as an example of the standard usage of the civil script and of the orthographic practice of newly printed books (see Polikarpov's comment in his grammatical work of 1724, cited above — § I–1.1, RGADA, f. 201, no. 6, l. 35 verso). The nature of the orthographic normalization here is manifested in such changes as *другова* replaced by *другого* (14 verso), *ево* by *его* (17 verso; bis), *в страхе* by *въ страсѣ* (21 verso and 23 verso), *должны* by *должни* in the nom. pl. (fol. 1). As in other texts that were edited by the typography's correctors, the problem of normalization was resolved by affirming traditional bookish usage.

If in regard to markers of bookishness the editing of Prokopovich, the typography's correctors and Likhud display almost complete [108] similarity, they treated linguistic features that were not associated with differentiating linguistic codes. In particular, Feofan left all of these elements as they were, while Sofronii's editing did involve them, although these changes were of a fundamentally different nature than those involving markers of bookishness. In the first case the elimination of specifically bookish elements was meant to change the language itself. As regards features that did not involve the opposition between linguistic codes, the goal of the editing was to normalize the language within the parameters permitted by variability.

However, these differences were not of fundamental importance, but the fact that for Prokopovich, the typography's correctors and for Likhud the range of features not involving the opposition of linguistic codes itself largely coincided; this was noun declensions, adjectival declensions, and lexical variants. Prokopovich preserves the variability while Likhud tries to eliminate it. Likhud's conduct would seem to be due to the fact that the *General Geography* was being prepared for typesetting; his normalizing corrections very much recall those of a typography corrector who is trying to get rid of errors in the copyist's text. The only difference is that correctors usually worked with traditional bookish texts, while Likhud was correcting a text in the "simple" language. However, it was precisely for the range of features not involving the opposition of linguistic codes that this difference was irrelevant and made it possible for the direct continuity of normalizing activity (which is what we observe in Apollodorus' *Library* and the *Honest Mirror of Youth*).

The similarity of Likhud's normalizing editing with the usual activity of correctors who prepared manuscripts for typesetting is underscored by the fact that during the course of his corrections Sofronii eliminated orthographic mistakes and typos [...]. Sofronii also normalized the spelling of borrowed words, orienting himself on Greek etymology, something typical of learned Church Slavonic orthography. In a series of cases he changes spelling reflecting Latin models (for instance: Гомеръ > Омир, fol. 424 verso), although his normalization was not reduced to this. […] His corrections fully support G. O. Vinokur's statement that in the Petrine era "in printed books orthography remained correct and etymological, i.e., as before it corresponded to the Church Slavonic grammatical tradition" (Vinokur 1959, 115).

We should keep in mind that there was no clear border between orthographic corrections and the normalization of variable elements. Indeed, when Sofronii corrected *озеро* to *езеро* (317 verso), it is impossible to say whether this was the normalization of variable lexical elements or correcting an accidental slip by a copyist (notably, the regular form used in the *Geography* was precisely *е* — e.g., *езеро, есень, единъ*, etc.). The interpretation depends on one's perspective, on how one understands the reasons for the initial spelling. It is obvious that when the original text has multiple words with the prefix *роз-* and they are consistently changed to *раз-* (cf. Zhivov 1986b), one may speak of normalizing variable elements. It is just as obvious, however, that when teachers of today correct *робота* to *работа* in their pupils' notebooks they perceive an error in writing an unstressed vowel and their correction is purely a question of spelling. For texts of the Petrine period this kind of dilemma is often fundamentally irresolvable.

Thus Likhud was concerned with normalizing the language, while Feofan Prokopovich, who did not have the job of preparing texts for print, did not, and therefore did not pay attention to linguistic variability. Beyond this external difference, however, there was a deeper similarity in their positions. As shown above, the juxtaposition between the traditional bookish and new "simple" language was defined for various authors by the same aggregate of markers. The data cited allows us to conclude that for these authors the variations of forms and lexemes which do not correlate with this opposition are also the very same ones. In this case as well, the commonality of linguistic views leads back to the literary and linguistic (written) tradition, in particular, the tradition of hybrid Church Slavonic, as we have suggested. This tradition provided both the very principle of division by markers that distinguished linguistic codes as well as the variant forms that were not involved in this division. The group of markers of bookishness that were eliminated as well as the set that was not subject to elimination coincided with the same ones that were relevant for the hybrid register.

In hybrid texts the markers that distinguish linguistic codes function not as a systematic means of expression, motivated by a system of differences on the level of content, but as de-semanticized elements that serve as a semiotic indicator of the bookish character of the text. In their turn, these markers are superimposed onto an undifferentiated background (undifferentiated in terms of bookish versus non-bookish), which permits a wide span of variations of genetically heterogeneous elements. In the Petrine period this principle took on new significance, as markers of bookishness were eliminated (which had been made possible by their de-semanticization in the framework of hybrid Slavonic) and the undifferentiated background material (undifferentiated in terms of the opposition of languages) took on the status of a new literary language. The concrete nature of the variations in this language point to its genesis from hybrid Church Slavonic (cf., for example, the "simple" language's forms of gen. sg. fem. adjectives with variant endings in -ыя /-ой, present in the hybrid language, and the absence of -ые endings, widespread in administrative writing), as well as the particular aspects of the semantic differentiation of lexical variants (for example, pleophonic and non-pleophonic forms).

1.4 Innovation and Continuity in the New Literary Language

The data analyzed above allows us to answer the question how innovation and continuity came together during the initial period of the new literary language's formation. As we have seen, the novelty of the "simple" language of the Petrine era and its break with tradition consisted in rejecting markers of bookishness that indicated the value (the literary character) of the language. In edited texts this rejection was clearly expressed by the elimination of the corresponding elements; in texts that were created in the "simple" tongue from the start (like the *Honest Mirror of Youth* [*Iunosti chestnoe zertsalo*, 1717] and *History of the Swedish War* [*Gistoriia Sveiskoi voiny*] — (Peshtich, I, 154–76), this innovation was manifested in the lack of this kind of element. Given this development, the literariness of a text was inevitably connected to its cultural function rather than to its formal adherence to one of the bookish written traditions; it was no longer defined by grammatical features that established an identity with model Church Slavonic texts. On the one hand, this signified a radical break from the former situation, and on the other, it created the basis for the expansion of the new type of literary language, insofar as the language was no longer tied to the particular type of cultural situation.

At the same time, rejection does not exclude continuity. The new norm differed from the old in a limited set of markers, and outside of these there was nothing to prevent the re-use of traditional material. The very notion of continuity implies continuity in relation to a certain linguistic tradition, which in the given case was, in my opinion, hybrid Church Slavonic. This development seems perfectly natural insofar as the sphere of using hybrid Church Slavonic was very close to that which, according to Peter, the "simple" language was to serve; it was in hybrid Church Slavonic that historical works were composed, for the most part, and it also served as the language into which a variety of professional texts had been translated in the second half of the seventeenth century. It was precisely the hybrid language that functional analysis (understanding how and why genetically heterogeneous elements were mixed) reveals as the source of the linguistic material reproduced in the "simple" tongue. Justifying these criteria, and more broadly, the issue of linguistic continuity, leads us to the problem of defining the origins of the modern Russian literary language.

Debates over this issue have continued over many decades (see the surveys in: Vinograodov 1969; Isachenko 1975; Filin 1981; which include bibliography). In this debate one side insisted that the modern Russian language derived directly from Church Slavonic (this position was formulated most consistently in the works of B. O. Unbegaun: Unbegaun 1965; Unbegaun 1970; Unbegaun 1971). The opposite view was that modern Russian is rooted in vernacular Russian, with "Church Slavonicisms" considered alien elements assimilated under the influence of Church Slavonic. Both sides argued their case on the basis of the percentages of "Church Slavonic" and "Russian" elements in the modern language, and for their calculations they naturally used genetic rather than functional criteria. Indeed, the functional approach would not allow this kind of calculation insofar as functional characteristics are changeable over time and may be different at different stages in the history of the written language for one and the same material element. Because of this, data collected from the modern language cannot be extrapolated back to previous periods, and thus can tell us nothing about derivation or continuity. For example, the difference between the markers of high style in the modern literary language and those of the mid-eighteenth century literary language can only inform us about the processes of stylistic change, but can give us no clue for judging continuity or rupture. Genetic characteristics are no more significant, and tell us no more either about the question of continuity or about the linguistic status of a particular text (§ 0–2).

Indeed, the very diversity of opinions testifies to the senselessness of calculations based on genetic features. The categories that this research is based on are indefinite, as words with a "Church Slavonic" root form and "Russian" affix or "Russian" root form and "Church Slavonic" affix may be arbitrarily assigned to this or that group. This lack of clarity is something fundamental, and in the last analysis reflects the fact that the researchers are operating with oppositions that are alien to the linguistic consciousness of the periods under study, so that in periods when the question of continuity represented a vital problem of language-building they may be ascribing significance to things that had none.

As stated, continuity means a connection to some definite literary and linguistic tradition. However, genetic calculations (for example, of pleophonic and non-pleophonic lexicon) tell us nothing about such traditions. Is it worth asking the question from where words with the root *врем-* or *здрав-* or those with the prefix *пере-* came into the literary language when these elements may be found in any of the registers of the medieval written language? What relation can neologisms like *вратарь* or *млекопитающее* — that have been the subject of discussion on this issue — have to the question of continuity? It is obvious that the genetic (or pseudo-genetic) features of particular elements can contribute nothing to the solution of the problem.

These features contribute nothing primarily because the mixing of genetically heterogeneous elements may be observed in all monuments of ancient Russian writing — both in those that strictly follow the norm of the Russian recension of Church Slavonic and in business and everyday documents written in the non-bookish tongue. It is not possible to judge the connection of the literary language of the new type to any one of these traditions on the basis of the presence or absence of individual elements, but only on the basis of the very character of the mixing — one must determine what the particular nature of the mixture of genetically heterogeneous elements is in the new literary language and with what tradition (what register of the written language) these particular features may be connected. For this reason, analysis of the question of the derivation of the Russian literary language of the new type demands as a prerequisite the reconstruction of the functional relations (differentiation of languages, variability, the semantic differentiation of variants) in the registers of the literary language of the previous period. The formation of the new type of Russian literary language was without question connected to the radical reconceptualization of these relations, although even in this reconceptualized aspect there must still remain traces of the initial linguistic system.

What then are the levels of the linguistic system that must be analyzed in order to resolve this problem? In the genetic approach the basic objects for analysis are lexicon and phraseology, and this choice is reasonable. Indeed, Church Slavonic and Russian are interpreted from this perspective as two genetically heterogeneous languages. Accordingly, Slavonicisms

Chapter 1. The Petrine Language Reform

in the Russian literary language of the new type are seen as a particular type of borrowing. Understandably, the question of borrowing is primarily a problem of lexicon (insofar as — at least for the everyday language of communication on which the genetic approach is oriented — the borrowing of morphological or syntactic constructions are anomalous), and therefore the main attention of research is focused on this. For this reason the problem of the Russian literary language's derivation and the nature of its continuity is seen first of all as one of vocabulary, and vocabulary is precisely the object of those calculations whose futility we discussed above.

In contrast, with the functional approach the main attention is paid to grammar. Indeed, the differences in literary and linguistic traditions were connected in linguistic consciousness with grammatical parameters (cf. Khaburgaev and Riumina 1971, 65–7; Hüttl-Folter 1978; see also Hüttl-Folter 1984–5). Grammatical parameters clearly reveal the variability that is most important for linguistic consciousness; in the absence of stylistic normalization (in the Petrine period that laid the basis for the new literary language this still hadn't begun), lexical variability was only recognized in those cases where it was marked by the formal similarity of the variants (for example, lexemes with the prefixes *раз-* and *роз-*). As G. O. Vinokur wrote, "it seems that the line between 'Slavonic' and 'simple Russian' was most evidently revealed in the area of morphology. For Russians of the first half of the eighteenth century, simple past tenses..., participial forms in nominative singular masculine without the suffix sound *щ* in the present and *ш* in the past of the type *даяй, давый* expressed a much stronger connection to olden times and church language than Church Slavonic *words,* many of which had already become completely usual, and, most important, might not even have Russian equivalents in the everyday language" (Vinokur 1959, 126).

Curiously, perhaps the first suggestion of taking a functional approach occurred in Unbegaun's work of 1935, although this was not followed up in his further writings. He wrote:

> ...one is somewhat at a loss to trace a line of demarcation between Russified Slavonic and Slavonicized Russian. However, it is evident that in this matter vocabulary cannot serve as the decisive criterion and only grammatical structure is significant... Conjugation... offers two grammatical categories that are essentially Slavonic and inconceivable in spoken Russian, from which they had died out many centuries before: the aorist and imperfect. Thus we may consider a text to be Slavonic if it regularly uses these two verbal forms... To these two morphological categories we may add two syntactic locutions which indicate the same association with Slavonic: the dative absolute and infinities with еже (еже сотворити). As far as vocabulary, it is not abstract words that clearly suggest Slavonic because such words were freely admitted into Russian

literature, but primarily particles, conjunctions and adverbs, all of those [words like] абїе, аще, убо, обаче, зане, яко, точїю, паки, сирѣчь, сѣмо, which were totally alien in Russian literature. (Unbegaun1935, 32)

As we see, Unbegaun identifies those very markers of bookishness that were eliminated in the corrected texts of the Petrine era; he asserts the importance of grammatical parameters and the irrelevance of lexicon. It would be logically consistent to see the creation of the Russian literary language of the new type as a change from "Russified Slavonic" to "Slavonicized Russian", as expressed in the rejection of the noted features, and not involving vocabulary (apart from functional words). In his later works, however, Unbegaun asserts the continuous development from Church Slavonic to the Russian literary language of the new type and defends this position by reference to the ration of "Russicisms" and "Slavonicisms" in the lexicon.

Insofar as Peter's language policy was embodied in those changes that were dictated by the linguistic consciousness of his era, the formation of the literary language of the new type (the "simple" language) needs to be described in functional categories that reflect this consciousness. The same corrected texts that we used to reconstruct the basic features of this development may also provide evidence of the place that lexicon occupied in the process. In all of the corrected texts except the *General Geography* lexical corrections are virtually absent, and this testifies to the fact that they were irrelevant for the formation of the "simple" language. In the *General Geography*, lexical changes are numerous, but for the most part they are not connected to the task of turning "Slavonic" into "simple Russian." Most of the lexical changes are purely editorial — the desire for the best equivalent of a Latin term — and have no connection to the change of languages.[14]

Only a very limited number of lexical corrections may be connected in one way or another to the issue of changing linguistic codes, such as

---

[14] For example, among these changes we find тѣлесные → корпоралные (392 verso), Імпеть → устремленїе (502, 503), обсервацїи → усмотренїи (509), индеѕь → указатель (583 verso), дифференцїа → разность (773), разстоянїе → дистанцїа (865), поверхности → суперфицїи (874), etc. None of these, obviously, may be seen as an opposition between "Slavonic" and "Russian" or "bookish" and "non-bookish." In many cases, Sofronii's editing involved putting Polikarpov's marginal glosses into the text. For example, on l. 73 the word "четверогранный" was glossed as "квадратный"; Sofronii crossed out the first word and substituted the second; analogously, on l. 71 in place of the term аркусь the gloss дуга was substituted. This type of correction could serve as interesting material for the history of scientific terminology in Russia (and in this respect the *General Geography* was a very important text — cf. Kutina 1966, 10), although it has no relevance for the question of the choice of language.

истинѣподобнѡ → достовѣрно [483 verso]. [A list of examples is omitted.] What was the nature of these changes? Obviously, they do not involve the opposition of Church Slavonic and Russian, but that of specifically bookish and neutral lexicon (that was formed as a result of the Second South Slavic influence, the separating of bookish written traditions from the non-bookish, and the development of the grammatical approach, which reconceptualized the bookish language as a scholarly language).

It is curious that Likhud's corrections include replacements in those very lexical pairs whose stylistic differentiation was directly connected to the division between the "simple" and refined bookish language (§ II–1.3; see also Uspenskii 1987, 192–6). [...] This kind of editing seems to be connected to the general orientation on linguistic "simplicity" (§ 0–5) and not on any specific linguistic type that embodies this. It is indicative that the majority of lexemes that Sofronii uses for substitution may often be met in the initial draft of the translation. This suggests that on the lexical level the juxtaposition of the traditional bookish and new literary languages had still not taken shape in the Petrine era, that this opposition did not exist in the initial stage of the new literary language at the start of the eighteenth century, but only arose later as the result of a long process of lexical stylistic regularization. In the initial stage of the process lexical markers do not play any role in opposing linguistic codes, which rely almost exclusively on grammatical markers, that accordingly serve as the basis for defining the linguistic character of a text.[15]

Attention to grammatical markers leads directly to the conclusion that the special nature of the mixing of genetically heterogeneous elements in the "simple" language of the Petrine era derives from hybrid Church Slavonic. This conclusion relies not on genetic but on functional criteria, on analysis of the choice and correlation of variant forms that were allowed in the hybrid language and which were transferred from here into the "simple" language. The issue becomes not what may be defined as a genetic Russicism or Slavonicism but which Russicisms and Slavonicisms (and in what relation) could make their way from the old language into the new. The nature of this transfer from one language to the other is of critical importance. The transfer should also be defined in functional terms, as the elimination of markers

---

[15] The material we have analyzed leads us to disagree with the interpretation of E. V. Lukicheva, who examined the corrections to the first edition of the *General Geography* (comparing the manuscript in BAN and the printed text). She came to the conclusion that here "bookish lexicon" was replaced by "lexicon from the business (delovoi) and conversational language" (Lukicheva 1974, 293). This does not accord with the actual material and is ultimately conditioned by the genetic approach that focuses primarily on lexicon arbitrarily divided into "Slavonicisms" and "Russicisms."

of bookishness that were important for Petrine linguistic consciousness and whose functional role is revealed primarily in the hybrid language; from this perspective, the fact that genetically these markers may to a significant extent be characterized as Slavonicisms is only of secondary interest.

The genetic approach does not make it possible to see hybrid Church Slavonic as a special linguistic system, and consequently, to adequately reconstruct the prehistory of the literary language of the new type (§ 0–3). For this reason the reconstruction of the genesis of this language, the "simple" language of the Petrine period, is also impossible. In fact, the mixing of genetically heterogeneous elements in the hybrid language is of primary importance. Using the genetic approach hybrid texts are not seen as constituting an independent literary and linguistic tradition but are ascribed to various languages, depending on which features are chosen as the basis of the classification. In any case, these texts are relegated to the periphery of the basic corpus and the special mechanism of their creation remains undisclosed. Hence the nature of the change from the old literary language to the new also remains unidentified.

Without defining the precise nature of their continuity, the correlation of the new Russian literary language to previous traditions is arbitrary. One result of this arbitrariness is the repeated assertion in the scholarly literature that the Russian literary language of the new type depended directly on the administrative language (prikaznoi iazyk) of Muscovite Rus'. There is no real evidence for this view, and moreover, many facts bear witness that there was no connection between them. For example, as already stated, in the "simple" language of the Petrine period (as well as in the entire later literary language that developed on its basis) there were almost no examples of the widespread gen. sg. fem ending. in *-ые/-ие,* while the variant endings *-ыя/-ие* and *-ой/-ей* were common in the hybrid language; such a difference would hardly have been possible had there been continuity between the two languages (on the administrative language, cf. Unbegaun 1935a, 323–5; Chernykh 1953, 306–7; Pennington 1980, 252). In the same way the parameters of *a*-expansion in plural dat., instr. and prep. endings indicate continuity with hybrid Church Slavonic and not the administrative tongue; for example, in masc. *o*-declension nouns (the main type), prep. pl. was the most advanced in regard to *a*-expansion in texts in the "simple" language of the Petrine era, and these texts are similar precisely to seventeenth-century hybrid texts, where as in administrative texts the instr. pl. *a*-expansion was most advanced (see Zhivov 1993). In this instance examination of grammatical parameters clearly demonstrates the scheme of development, while analysis of lexicon can give no results, if only because it is difficult to determine the lexical

Chapter 1. The Petrine Language Reform

material that was specific to the administrative language.[16]

The single significant similarity which one may see in comparing the "simple" language of the Petrine period and the administrative language of Muscovite Rus' is the absence of markers of bookishness. In this sense the administrative language may be seen as a precedent, but its significance is limited to this. Moreover, the Ukrainian "prosta mova" (simple tongue) may also be seen as a precedent, or even the linguistic situation in other language collectives (for example, writing in bookish Greek versus demotic). Whether writers in the "simple" language needed a precedent or whether they ever looked to the administrative language as one remains doubtful in view of the complete absence of supporting evidence. In sum, there is no basis to speak of the administrative language of Muscovite Rus' as precursor to the Russian literary language of the new type.

It seems likely that the basis for this misunderstanding was Peter's order to Polikarpov cited earlier in which he said that "you need not use high Slavonic words; use the language (words) of the Foreign Office (Posol'skii prikaz) instead" (Cherty iz istorii... 1968, col. 1055). What Peter had in mind as "the language of the Foreign Office" is unclear;[17] the Foreign Office

---

[16] It is extremely indicative that even such a connoisseur of the history of the Russian literary language as Vinokur could write of "bureaucratic words like *аз, понеже, точию*, etc." (Vinokur 1959, 123). All three of these lexemes were extremely uncharacteristic of administrative language, but very common in traditional bookish texts. The usual form of the 1st pers. sg. pronoun in business documents was *я* (in the sixteenth century together with *язъ* — Unbegaun 1935a, 354–5; Cocron 1962, 134; Pennington 1980, 244). An exception is the opening formula of certain documents "се азъ...", established in ancient times (on its derivation, see Zoltan 1984, 6–8; Zoltan 1987; Zoltan 1987a, 9–13) and preserved down through Petrine times (cf. the description of deeds which "began *се азом* according to ancient practice" in Peter's ukaz of January 30, 1701 — PSZ, IV, no. 1833, 138); it was this formula that evidently misled Vinokur. For administrative language of the seventeenth century, the usual conjunctions were *потому что* and *для того что* (Pennington 1980, 363–4, 385), while *понеже* was a secondary form of expression; its association with the language of clerks arose artificially in the mid-eighteenth century (see below, § III-1.3) and does not indicate its bureaucratic derivation at all. The particle *точию*, usual in Church Slavonic texts, was also extremely rare in bureaucratic documents, where as a rule *только* and (more rarely) *токмо* were used (cf. Pennington 1980, 710; Vesti-kuranty 1983, 271; Kotkov, Astakhina et al. 1984, 351). [...]

[17] In one of my earlier works (Zhivov and Upenskii 1983, 158; see the same hypothesis in Uspenskii 1983, 97–8), I suggested that "the words of the Foreign Office" were interpreted in light of the translation of the *General Geography* as Polonisms, which served as a means of making the spoken language bookish and which connected the "simple" Russian language being created with the "simple tongue" of South-Western Rus', via the mediation of the linguistic traditions of the Foreign Office (cf. on them Zoltan 1984). Analysis of Likhud's corrections contradicts this idea. The Polonisms (mostly lexical) seen in the final edition of the *Geography* were already present in the initial text, and Likhud did not introduce anything new. As a result of his editing, several new Polonisms appeared in the text [...], but these do

made various translations from foreign languages, although there was no uniformity in the practice of its various translators; in any case, there is no indication what Peter meant.

Nevertheless, much was read into Peter's words, and on this flimsy basis a whole theory developed about the development of the literary language. Thus E. Budde wrote:

> Peter the Great widely expanded translating activity and took direct part in it to see that the newly translated books in various branches of science were easily comprehensible, and he himself supervised the translation of books into Russian, issuing orders about the language of the new compositions. Through Peter's personal involvement the administrative language of literate Muscovites (gramoteev) was put into use, and if we examine the works of Russian literature since Peter we will see how this bureaucratic language with all of its syntactic turns, words and forms penetrated into them, in particular, into dramas, interludes, novels, tales, and other works which were all fundamentally connected to the bureaucratic language. (Budde 1908, 47).

While any concrete analysis of the kinds of literature Budde lists is enough to put his argument in doubt, this became a commonplace in descriptions of the language of the Petrine era and has made its way more or less openly from one scholarly work to another (e.g., Smolina 1981, 37; Chaikina 1991, 14, etc.).

Still, there is one more important thing that connects the Russian literary language of the new type to the administrative language of Muscovite Rus': with the appearance of the former the latter gradually fell out of use. Of course, this gives no logical basis to the argument about continuity between them, which would be a typical example of *post hoc, ergo propter hoc,* however the very mechanism of this change deserves attention and is an important aspect of the Petrine linguistic situation. The supplanting of the administrative language began precisely during the Petrine era (see Unbegaun 1965a) and the language of many legislative acts of the time significantly differed from the previous model both in terms of its syntactical structure as well as its terminology (cf. Zhivov 1988b). Naturally, in day to day business the bureaucratic language continued to hold on for many more decades, so that it fully died out only in the second half of the eighteenth century. For that period it is indicative that Fonvizin, parodying the language of a bureaucrat

---

not represent a "Polonization" of the text, but a result of editing for precise meaning. [...] Thus the Polonisms in the text characterize not the "simple" language but the Church Slavonic of the original draft. They indicate the interesting and little studied process of Polonisms' incorporation into Muscovite Church Slavonic of the late seventeenth-early eighteenth century.

in "The Brigadier," filled the Councilor's lines with Slavonicisms rather than any kind of specific administrative language (§ III–1.3; moreover cf. Strycek 1976, 164–5); linguistic consciousness no longer perceived administrative language as a particular linguistic tradition. Lawgiving and administrative language were gradually assimilated into the sphere of the new literary language.

In my opinion, what was happening here was that the separate existence of an administrative language came into conflict with the formation of the literary language of the new type. In the linguistic situation of the previous period the use of the bookish language was based on the mechanism of retabulation, oriented on markers of bookishness which indicated the cultural status of the text as related to written bookish traditions (§ 0–2, § 0–3). The action of the mechanism of retabulation was directly conditioned by the cultural mission at hand. Bureaucratic language had no such cultural mission, and it was just this that made a special business language necessary — this was a normalized written language in which the mechanism of retabulation did not function (cf. Alekseev 1987a, 42). This language created its own tradition, worked out special linguistic norms and was maintained by the writing habits of state servitors for whom linguistic parameters were untied with diplomatic ones (the reproduction of documents, the use of fixed formulas, etc.). Outside of properly office business, the use of these habits was if not completely unthinkable for other uses (cf. Kotoshikhin's work, written in the administrative language), it would demand radical experimentation on the part of the writer.

The formation of the literary language of the new type begins, as we have seen, with the elimination of markers of bookishness, that is, the destruction of the mechanism of retabulation. Accordingly, the correlation of the administrative language to the new literary language is deprived of any basis. On the contrary, it comes into direct conflict with the new literary language's pretensions to polyfunctionalism and universality. If earlier the administrative language, in opposition to Church Slavonic, was a second level of linguistic usage, separated from the bookish language by its unique means of creating texts, it now moves to the periphery. It is no longer maintained by the larger system of linguistic behavior and can only be preserved by force of conservative habits of the bureaucratic milieu, preserved, naturally, in those specific texts (official correspondence) in the framework of which its corresponding speech habits have been developed.

At the same time in the new conditions the literariness of a text ceases to be connected with markers of bookishness and becomes wholly defined by its cultural functions, i.e., by extra-literary parameters. This creates the possibility for non-literary texts to exist in the literary language. This possibility removes all potential obstacles to extrapolating the norms of the new literary language to any sphere of use, independent of its cultural status—that is, obstacles to acquiring the attribute of polyfunctionalism. The process of extrapolating the new literary language into all spheres of use independent of their cultural status occurs simultaneously with the complementary process of semiotization, that is, the assimilation into culture of those areas of behavior that had earlier had no cultural status. In particular, jurisprudence and administration were being brought into the cultural sphere (a process begun even earlier, under Aleksei Mikhailovich), which in the area of law led to changes in administrative practice as well as juridical terminology (its Slavonicization) (see Zhivov 1988b). Naturally, this complementary process facilitated the expansion of the functional sphere of the new type of literary language.

It is curious to note that as in the case of linguistic reform (e.g. the transformation of the alphabet), the administrative reform (its assimilation of new semiotic functions) began with changes that were completely of an external character. Administrative reform began with decrees requiring that business be recorded not in scrolls but in folded sheets (PSZ, IV, no. 1803 of July 2, 1700, cf. also no.'s 1797, 1817, 1901). This formal change not only corresponded to European models but also gave business documents the same form as book texts. It thus eliminated the external difference between book and business writing. At the same time, the new forms of doing business transformed the habits of state servitors: new ways of preparing the external look of documents opened the way to transforming the linguistic dimension of these same practices.

Thus the use of the new literary language was extrapolated into areas that had initially been outside its functional purview. One of these areas was religious literature, in which the new literary language gradually displaced Church Slavonic, whose function was limited to serving as the sacred language of liturgy (§ III–2.2). Another was jurisprudence and administration. As the bureaucratic apparatus was modernized the habits of the old administrative language disappeared and the language of the new literary language gradually took its place, with time assimilating individual specific features of it ("chancellerisms"), which were as a rule in no way connected with the earlier administrative tradition.

And so, Peter's language policy radically changed the Russian linguistic situation. It was precisely at this time that the new literary language arose, in opposition to Church Slavonic; Peter's idea was that it would serve as the new means of communication for the new secular culture, that was breaking with traditional cultural values (into which category Church Slavonic was relegated). The formation of a literary language of the new type came into being by eliminating the use of markers of bookishness, those things which in the linguistic consciousness of the era were connected with the notion of the correct bookish language. Markers of bookishness as the main indicators of the linguistic norm were characteristic first of all of the hybrid language. The appearance of the new language radically transformed the linguistic situation and gave new meaning to the very notion of "literariness," which was now defined in terms of cultural function and not by markers of bookishness. As a result, the assertion of the "simple" language of the Petrine era as literary led to the expansion of its usage in regard to previous literary traditions. The new literary language displaced the administrative language and entered into competition with the traditional written language (Church Slavonic). This competition was directly tied to the clash of cultures and ideologies that played out in the first decades of the eighteenth century, and represented in essence one of the most eloquent expressions of these conflicts. The further developments in the new literary language were to a significant degree conditioned by this connection, which thus deserves our special attention.

2. Language Policy and the Conflict of Cultures

Peter's reform of the alphabet and his oft-repeated demand for writing "simply" had one and the same goal: to give the new culture a new means of expression. As a result of this linguistic policy, the opposition of languages — of Church Slavonic and "simple" Russian — became connected with the opposition between cultures. In the context of this cultural conflict, Church Slavonic and Russian were juxtaposed antagonistically; they no longer complemented one another, but engaged in a dispute over supremacy. During this conflict, a reevaluation of Church Slavonic took place: if the new literary language was defined as *civic* (as in the "average civic speech" of Polikarpov's introduction to the *General Geography*, § I–1.2), then the old inevitably acquired the attribute of an *ecclesiastic* language. It is no accident that it was just at this time that the label "Church Slavonic" itself came into being; earlier no one referred to "Slavonic" in this way. Indeed, Gavrill Buzhinskii, who completely accepted the Petrine linguistic program, in a letter of May, 1726, to Thomas Consett, praised his addressee because he, alone among other foreigners, had learned not only the conversational tongue (vernaculum nostrum) but also "the Church Slavonic style" (Ecclesiasticum Slavonicum Stylum) (Cracraft 1982, 369).

Hence in the framework of Petrine cultural policy, Church Slavonic began to be perceived as a specifically religious, clerical language, as opposed to the Russian literary language as the language of new secular education. Language behavior was thus directly tied to cultural and political programs, and this connection defined both the new status of the traditional bookish language and the character of the new type of literary language being formulated. Secularization became the driving force of linguistic dynamics, and this constituted a radical difference between the linguistic situation in "Europeanized" Russia and that in Western Europe (cf. § 0–6). This cultural selectivity was a given for the new literary language, but it contradicted its pretensions to polyfunctionalism, that could not help but lead to conflict in the future between two incompatible characteristics, polyfunctionalism and secularism. At the same time, the secular dominant so clearly connected the new language with a certain set of cultural values that it gave it a symbolic significance that overshadowed other features basic to a polyfunctional language, first of all, its universality, that is, accessibility to all of educated society. As a result, Peter's linguistic brainchild was born into a singularly complex cultural situation, laden with cultural tensions, which would have significance for its entire further development.

2.1 Language Reform and Political-Ecclesiastical Conflicts

No direct statements by Peter containing his opinion of Church Slavonic have come down to us, yet his linguistic policy as a whole, and, more indirectly, his parodic use of the language in texts that were blasphemous in content and anticlerical in function, testify to his view of the language as specifically connected to the church. These parodic texts include references to Church Slavonic within the context of Peter's struggle against the Orthodox tradition. Peter's blasphemous pageants focused precisely on those elements of tradition that provoked his greatest hostility and that were isolated as the primary targets of criticism; the use of Church Slavonic in these pageants (as a language of culture) classified it as one of them.

The rules and acts of the All-Jesting and All-Drunken Council (Vseshuteishii i vsep'ianeishii sobor) are among the main parodic Church Slavonic texts that issued from Peter's pen. The tsar founded this sacrilegious society no later than 1692 (according to Gordon — see Gordon, II, 360; cf.

Bogloslovskii, I, 131, 136f; Wittram, I, 106f), and it continued to exist until his death; it was thus the longest-lasting of all the institutions he established. Its main goal was to discredit the patriarchate and, more broadly, the idea of priesthood and tsardom coexisting as two equally important principles within the state (cf. Uspenskii 1982, 212; Zhivov and Uspenskii 1987, 94–5). Modeling the institutions of the past in caricature, the Most Comical Council anticipated the future order of things, and thus served as a kind of testing ground for the changes being contemplated. In particular, as it was founded during the reign of the last patriarch, it prepared the way for the abolition of the patriarchate and assertion of single absolute rule.

All of Peter's parodic and blasphemous activities were evidently meant to model his coming reforms. Thus the Poteshnyi ("amusing") Regiments and the Kozhukhovskii campaign may be seen as rehearsals for Peter's later military undertakings. Significantly, in the Kozhukhovskii campaign of 1694 the Poteshnyi Regiments were put under the command of the parodic king-caesar F. Iu. Rodomanovskii while the strel'tsy regiments (musketeers) were led by the "Polish king" I. I. Buturlin. Of course, the result of these maneuvers was preordained, as the Polish king and the strel'tsy regiments were to be defeated. The defeat of the strel'tsy served as augury of their further sad fate; here too parodic performance anticipated Peter's actual reforms. That Church Slavonic was included in this parodic context suggests that its exile from the sphere of the new culture was an organic part of Peter's cultural and religious program.

The rules of election and ordination of the prince-pope (the parodic patriarch) were written by Peter himself as a parody of the Orthodox ritual of ordination (chirotony) of a bishop, and he worked on this document very meticulously, covering several copyists' versions with corrections (see Peter's autographs: RGADA, f. 9, otd. II, no. 67, ll. 5–7, 20–1, which includes the corrected copies; see the rather imprecise publication in Semevskii 1885). Church Slavonic was not only used in the texts that directly parodied the church service but also in the correspondence concerning the Most Comical Council. [Several examples are omitted.]

Insofar as in this framework Church Slavonic was connected to the old culture, for Peter and his followers it automatically assumed those characteristics which they assigned to that culture as a whole, that is, Church Slavonic began to be thought of as a backwards language which was an obstacle to enlightenment, a language of false learning which stood in the way of the true, an obscure language which hindered understanding. Such an evaluation was implicit (although not expressed directly) in the *Spiritual Regulation*, written by Feofan Prokopovich in 1718 and edited by Peter.

2. Language Policy and the Conflict of Cultures

Speaking of the necessity "of having some short and clear little books (knizhitsy) which could be understood by simple people and which would include everything needed for popular edification," Feofan declared that the existing Church Slavonic catechisms were incomprehensible and unsuited for teaching "the simple folk." He wrote: "the Orthodox confessional book is not small, and so is not convenient for memorization by the simple folk, and not very comprehensible to them because it is not written in the common language. The same goes for the books of the great teachers: Chrysostom, Feofilakt and others, written in the Hellenic tongue, and only clear in that language; their Slavonic translation has become obscure (temen), and can be understood even by the learned only with difficulty, but are by no means accessible to the simple and ignorant" (Verkhovskoi II, 32, second pagination; Dukhovnyi Reglament 1904, 25–6). The same idea is repeated in the foreword to the *First Lesson to Youth* (*Pervoe uchenie otrokom*), in which Feofan declares that "the general need arose to compose a little book with commentary on the Ten Commandments, given us by God. But this was not enough. For there were such books in Russia, but because they were written in the high Slavonic language and not in the simple tongue they could not serve to teach the young, who thus up to now have been deprived of a proper appropriate education" (Feofan Prokopovich 1790, l. 6).

Feofan was speaking here of widely disseminated editions which reflected the standard Church Slavonic of the late seventeenth and early eighteenth centuries. Translations of John Chrysostom's *Homilies* were published several times during the seventeenth century, and Feofilakt of Bulgaria's commentary on the Gospels was reprinted in Moscow in 1698. Peter Mohyla's *Catechesis or Confession of the Orthodox Faith* was published several times during this period (in 1696, 1712, and 1717). In Patriarch Adrian's foreword to this book it was specially noted that it was being published "for the sake of teaching priests and the simple folk (narodnye liudi)" (Petr Mogila 1696, l. 7), that is, it was aimed not at a scholarly audience but at an average reader. This orientation on accessibility was carried over from the Greek edition that had come out in the "simple" tongue. In the epistle from Nectarius, patriarch of Jerusalem, that was also taken from the Greek edition, it said: "If this is published in a simple language (so that it will be easily understood not only by wise men but by the many), one should not be surprised, for every reasonable person [should strive] not for the beauty of words but for the truth of what is said" (Petr Mogila 1696, l. 13). The sharp contrast between "the beauty of words" and "ease of understanding" must have suggested a certain linguistic program for Slavonic translators. Of course, these categories meant something different when

Chapter 1. The Petrine Language Reform

applied to Slavonic material. Apparently, they were related to the opposition in the Russian tradition between rhetorically adorned learned speech and the elementary, grammatically correct, bookish language which had arisen when Church Slavonic was reconceptualized as a scholarly language. The standard version of Church Slavonic, not laden with complex syntactic constructions or rhetorical periods, is seen here as generally accessible, and consequently as a logical analogue of simple Greek (cf. on the significance of "simple" Greek in Russian linguistic thought, § I–1.2). Indeed the *Catechesis* could be used as a textbook. Thus an ukaz of 1700 ordered that there be built in Tobol'sk "a school for priests', deacons', and [other] church children, to teach them reading and writing, and then Slavonic grammar and other books and the catechesis of the Orthodox faith in Slavonic" (Znamenskii 1881, 24).

It was the ordinary bookish language that Feofan declared to be obscure and incomprehensible. This view, having been set forth in the *Spiritual Regulation*, became one of the official planks of the Petrine ecclesiastical reform, and was clearly directed polemically against traditional views. Feofan ascribed the traditional view of Church Slavonic as the natural language for education to the whole complex of "unenlightened" and "clerical" ideas which were attributed to opponents of Peter's church policy. Although formally Feofan's statements are not very different from the usual calls for linguistic "simplicity" (§ 0–5), they presume a much more radical rejection of traditional linguistic ideology than these do. Feofan was criticizing a linguistic tradition that itself laid claim to "simplicity," and his demands for comprehensibility and accessibility acquired a new polemical force. Even more, the attribute of "incomprehensibility" essentially lost its concrete content and was subordinated to the attribute of "clericalism"—traditional Church Slavonic is seen as incomprehensible not because it causes difficulties for understanding but because it is the tool of clerics who purposefully hold the people in ignorance.

The polemical orientation of Feofan's insistence on "comprehensibility" is fully evident in his opinion of August 10, 1736, on correcting the translation of the Bible:

> ...the decrepit grammatical doctrine (uchenie) of the Slavonic language is extremely coarse, [as it is reflected] both in many expressions and in its stylistic make-up. One comes across defunct phrases which have long become worn out like rags wrapped around bast shoes (onuchi), and poorly understood by the reader as well, for example, words like елма, колма, вресноту, убо, непщую, потщаваю, плищ, щуди, голимый, etc., and turns of phrase (sklady) are often perverted, especially the [use of] Hellenisms, that is, expressions which are devised according to the nature of Greek rather than Slavonic, for example,

2. Language Policy and the Conflict of Cultures

учуся грамоте instead of грамоты, because the Hellenic σπουδέω, учуся, is used with the dative case; similar to this are the following: прииде, во еже освятити (why not прииде освятити? the во еже is superfluous and only makes for confusion); надеюся быти прошению (but wouldn't надеюся, яко будет прощение be better?), etc. etc. But people who are not skilled and do not understand the power of language will come upon this sort of willfulness and corruption in the lexicon and think that they have found wisdom, and use them to impress people, and because of the swaggering of these most senseless bookworms (bezumnye knigochii) which is only worthy of laughter. (ODDS, III; appendix, col. xxiii–xxvi).

Feofan was evaluating the Bible translation composed in Moscow in response to Peter's order of November 14, 1712. Its revision, which in the words of the ukaz was supposed to "make [the translation] agree... in chapter, verse and in words with the grammatical order of the Greek Bible," was entrusted to Sofronii Likhud, Feofilakt Lopatinskii, Fedor Polikarpov and the correctors of the Moscow typography, while Stefan Iavorskii was to supervise the task. Hence the translation which Feofan condemned was the work of his political opponents, opponents to a significant degree of the very principles behind the Petrine cultural transformation, although they were opponents who had come to a compromise with Peter. The compromise consisted in allowing church culture to remain traditional (see the discussion of Polikarpov's position, § I–1.1). Feofan did not accept this compromise (evidently also true of Peter at the end of his reign) and maintained the necessity of reforming church culture, declaring the quite moderate traditionalism of his opponents to be obscurantism. What were the linguistic views of the "bible workers" (bibliotrudniki) and how did they accord with those which Feofan ascribed to them?

The basic linguistic position of the Bible editors was the grammatical approach to Church Slavonic (§ 0–4). This approach presumed the perfecting of Church Slavonic through grammatical normalization that took into consideration actual linguistic practice within the framework of the correct bookish language. Thus in republishing Smotritskii's grammar in 1721 Polikarpov explained the corrections he had made to it:

As far as our Slavonic language, with God's help, has with time become more and more rich and purified, and in just a hundred years has attained better quality, because of this, judging by its state today, some new little rules are added to this ancient grammar and some other old ones are now deleted for lack of use. (RGADA, f. 381, no. 1241, l. 11–11 verso)

When Polikarpov speaks here about a hundred years of perfecting Church Slavonic, he is obviously suggesting that this began with the first

Chapter 1. The Petrine Language Reform

publication of Smotritskii's grammar of 1619. According to this scheme, grammatical normalization leads to the "purification" of the language, which is manifested in particular by the fact that individual normalized elements become fixed in usage, while others that exist only due to tradition fade away (he has in mind written, bookish usage, of course). In the same document, Polikarpov cites as an example "the dual number in nouns, verbs, and in pronouns, whose place is taken by plurals" (RGADA, f. 381, no. 1241, l. 11 verso). In the grammar itself elements that are "today uncommon" or "today unused" are the nom. pl. *ти*, forms of the aorist in -*тъ* (like *зачатъ*), forms of the "transitional" (prekhodiashchee) tense with linking verb (like *чли есмы*), etc. (Smotritskii 1721, l. 97, 117, 118 verso; cf. Gorbach 1964, 56; Uspenskii 1987, 328). The grammatical perfecting of Church Slavonic thus presumes the displacing of "archaic" elements to the periphery, elements which have been preserved only due to tradition and that are not important for actual practice. It was precisely this modernized Church Slavonic that in Polikarpov's opinion was destined for unlimited and continually expanding functioning, that is, for use as a polyfunctional, standard (literary) language. Polikarpov's ideas were a continuation and natural development of the thinking of those sixteenth and seventeenth-century bookmen who adhered to the grammatical approach to the bookish language (§ 0–4). And it was just this approach that provoked Feofan Prokopovich's protest against the "coarseness" of the "decrepit grammatical doctrine" of the Slavonic language.

Indeed, Polikarpov and his allies were also reformers, but their reform was conceived as a development of and supplement to traditional bookish culture, not as a break with it. In his edition of Smotritskii's grammar of 1721, Polikarpov says that the traditional type of education does not include the study of grammar, does not make it possible to analyze a text, and hence to understand and interpret it correctly (Smotritskii 1721, foreword, l. 2 verso — see the quotation in § 0–2). In Polikarpov's opinion, the traditional type of education needs to be supplemented by the study of grammar that includes methods for understanding the texts that have been committed to memory. As shown in the Introduction, this approach significantly changes the parameters of the linguistic situation, although the proposed innovation is not seen as a denial of the past.

Their attitude toward the grammatical approach determined Polikarpov and his associates' view of the relationship between Church Slavonic and Greek. To them, Church Slavonic, which they felt was equal in merit to Greek (cf. Polikarpov 1704, l. 5 verso–6), had to be normalized, grammatically refined, and comprehensible, just as Greek was. For them the grammatical structures of Greek and Church Slavonic were not the same, but were juxtaposed, with differences pointed out and correlations between Greek and Slavonic constructions outlined. This was Meletii Smotritskii's approach as well, and Polikarpov preserved it with his republication of the Slavonic grammar. Polikarpov consciously retreated from the tradition of equating Slavonic grammatical structures to Greek and of transferring lots of Greek constructions into Slavonic, practices which had been promoted by Epifanii Slavinetskii and the Chudov monk Evfimii (cf. Strakhova 1990). Indicative in this respect is Polikarpov's review of Slavinetskii's patristic translations (cf. Rotar 1901, 62–5) that were published in Moscow in 1665. In this review, presented to the Synod in 1723, it said that: "the book of Gregory of Nazianzus the Theologian [and other writings in the same book]... are translated using an unusual amount of Slavonicizing (slavianshchizna), and even more Hellenizing, so that many are confused and avoid it. But this may be translated again, more comprehensibly, and the impassible paths made smooth" (Brailovskii 1894, no. 9, 31).

It seems likely that these views of Polikarpov also generally reflect those of the bookmen working on editing the Bible during the Petrine period. The corrections that they made to the Bible of 1663 were oriented on grammatical normalization and on standardizing correlations between Greek and Slavonic constructions (see Bobrik 1988). They did not introduce "hard to understand" archaisms and did not use calques from Greek with the single-minded insistence of Slavinetskii and Evfimii. This relative freedom from the Greek original is clearly seen when comparing the editing of the 1710's with that of 1741–2, carried out by Kirill Florinskii and Faddei Kakailovich; a principle method of the latter editing was indeed using Greek calques, and this motivated many of the changes they made to the previously edited text.[18]

Characteristically, Feofan's critical comments about constructions with *еже* also probably go back to Meletii Smotritskii [...] (Smotritskii 1619, l. Щ/2; Smotritskii 1648, l. 310 verso), who describes this as a Grecianism and points to its optional use in Slavonic. Polikarpov assimilated this view (cf. Smotritskii 1721), and in many cases he could note the differences between

---

[18] Furthermore, the editing done after that of Florinskii and Kakailovich reversed directions again, and the rejection of Greek calques led to restoring many of the variants that the Petrine editors had suggested. This is the case with the editing conducted by the Synod in 1743 and with that done by Varlaam Liashchevskii... and Gedeon Slonimskii in preparing the Elizabethan Bible in 1751 (Bobrik 1988). The Synod's corrections of 1743 include the elimination of such Grecianisms as phrases with *еже* + infinitive, constructions with adverbs of time and infinitive (like *дондеже изглаголати ми, внегда благословляти его*, etc.), and the genitive of possession (replaced by an adjective, as in replacing *в стран ѣ Халдеовъ* with *в стран ѣ Халденст ѣй*) (RGADA, f. 381, no. 1053, lo. 10, 17, 22 verso, 28 verso etc.).

Greek and Slavonic, following Smotritskii's first edition and not the revised Moscow version (see Gorbach, 1964, 61). Understandably, Feofan was not interested in such subtleties.

Thus a comparison of the view of the Petrine editors with Feofan Prokopovich's evaluation of their work clearly reveals how tendentious his opinion was. Feofan equates the linguistic position of the Bible editors to those of the Grecophiles of the previous century (Patriarch Ioakim, Epifanii Slavinetskii, Evfimii). This tendentious identification of linguistic positions was likely due to equating their broader cultural and political positions. Indeed in the late seventeenth century the Grecophile tendency could be associated with that trend in the church which wanted to model Russian church life on that of Byzantium, to recreate on Russian soil the "symphonic" relationship between sacred and secular power. Peter and his followers (Feofan in the first place) looked on this as clerical reaction that wanted the clergy to gain independence from the state and to revive Patriarch Nikon's "ambitions" that Peter so detested (cf. Verkhovskoi, II, 32, first pagination / Dukhovnyi reglament 1904, 17; see also Zhivov and Uspenskii 1987, 93f). The linguistic signs of this tendency were, on the one hand, Hellenized orthography (§ I–1.1), and on the other, Grecianized syntax and the predilection for specifically bookish lexicon, in particular, for artificial constructions modeled on Greek (see below, § II–1.3). Ascribing these features to his opponents, Feofan fuses their linguistic and cultural-political views into one: he discloses the vicious roots of their ideology (from the perspective of the new state) and at the same time demonstrates what "unenlightened" practice results from the "clericalism" of his opponents.

For Feofan these Grecianized forms and constructions as well as specifically bookish lexicon indicated the pseudo-scholarship of his opponents, which they assumed "to impress people" and which masked the false and potentially treasonous opinions of the clerical party in the guise of profound learning. To the category of pseudo-scholarship Feofan also assigned the entire "decrepit Slavonic grammatical doctrine." Feofan saw grammatically refined Church Slavonic as a kind of clerical deception, predicated on an ignorant audience; for these people "who are not skilled and do not understand the power of language" the prestige of educated Church Slavonic sanctified the entirety of traditional views and traditional piety. The perfecting and modernization of Church Slavonic as well as extending the sphere of its use from this point of view would only lead to the strengthening of this tendency, so noxious to the tradition of Petrine enlightenment. Hence Feofan defines the intentions of his opponents as pseudo-enlightenment, in that the instruments they proposed to use merely create the appearance of enlightenment, but in fact enhance ignorance.

Feofan's goal, apparently, was to destroy the very basis of traditional Church Slavonic education. It was this aim, most likely, that inspired replacing the traditional method of teaching literacy. As discussed above (§ 0–2), this system was based on the general knowledge of the bookish language, and acquainted the student with the basic elements of the Christian faith. Polikarpov, as we have seen, strove to supplement this traditional system by including the study of grammar. Feofan wanted to break with the old system even more radically. The publication of the *First Lesson to Youth* as the basic textbook destroyed this tradition, as it ended the requirement to read and memorize the fundamental texts, Psalter and prayerbook.

It was just this destructive impact that D. Kantemir ascribed to this innovation, as he made a special protest against the new textbook, arguing that it would demolish a system that had developed over centuries and which had been maintained "throughout the entire Eastern Orthodox Church" (Chistovich 1968, 51–2). [...] Kantemir considered the rejection of the traditional way of education to be the first step toward destroying the Orthodox tradition as a whole (ibid, 52). It was no coincidence that Kantemir took note of other passages from the *First Lesson to Youth* in which a Protestant type of rationalized religion contradicted traditional Orthodox piety, in particular, the question of venerating relics and icons (ibid, 52–4). According to Kantemir, the Orthodox tradition presupposed knowledge of the Greek, and he charged Prokopovich with incorrect and distorted translations of Greek concepts, such as when he relates the Greek είδολον not to the traditional *кумир*, but to *образишко,* and the Greek λατρεία to *служение*. This translation could give the reader, especially the unsophisticated one, the idea that icon veneration is seen as idolatry, and therefore, in Kantemir's opinion, "it would be better to leave Greek words (символ, λατρία, δουλία, υπερδουλία, προσκίνησιϚ) without translation, because in several theological expressions the Slavonic language is deficient and sins, while in Greek they are clear and simple" (Ibid, 54). Prokopovich responds that "this entire objection rests on two errors, one grammatical and the other theological" (ibid, 57), thus tying the linguistic conflict to the ideological.

For Feofan, Helleno-Slavic erudition is a precise analogue for Catholic (especially Jesuit) scholasticism. Even during his Kievan period, Prokopovich had been critical of Jesuit scholarship and its characteristic forms of education and religious propaganda, including sermons and its method of interpreting Holy Writ (see Cracraft 1978, 48–9; and also: Stupperich 1940, 87–102; Tetzner 1958; Vinter 1966). Prokopovich applies the scheme that European rationalism had worked out for doing battle with the Jesuit educational system to the Russian material, assigning the role of Jesuits to the proponents of Helleno-Slavic education and lumping all adherents of the traditional bookish language and traditional culture in the same pot without distinction.

Essentially, Feofan condemns Hellenized Church Slavonic on the same basis on which he mocks the Baroque subtleties of the sermons of T. Młodzianowski and other Polish Jesuit preachers (see his *Rhetoric* — Lachmann 1982, 39–5). Intricate exegetical devices and play with language Prokopovich stigmatizes as a lure for ignoramuses ("apud imperitos et idiotas") , with the aid of which advocates of clerical scholastics ("rabula," as Feofan characterizes them) spread prejudices that contradict reason (Feofan Prokopovich 1782, 131–2). In Prokopovich's view, this same role is played by the learned words, Grecianized constructions, etc., of "Russian clerics (klerikaly)." Rational, universally accessible study of the catechesis that is also beneficial to the state is juxtaposed both to obscure Church Slavonic doctrine as well as to unnatural Baroque sermons (cf. in the *Spiritual Regulation* — Verkhovskoi, II, 64–5 first pagination; Dukhovnyi reglament 1904, 69–70); both are defined as a clerical device for opposing enlightenment.[19]

This kind of lumping together of two significantly different, dissimilar traditions—Church Slavonic and Jesuit Baroque educational systems—is far from accidental. For Feofan they were united by one single negative quality, their opposition to Petrine religious and cultural policies; however, this quality was vital and had defining significance. Indeed, the polemical battles between Grecophiles and Latinophiles which blazed during the 1680's,

---

[19] Ideological oppositions extended to the most diverse cultural spheres, for example, to the conception of academic educational disciplines, poetics in particular. Prokopovich's course in poetics which he gave at the Kievan Academy in 1705 (see Feofan Prokopovich 1961) was founded on the same principles of rationalism and enlightenment that are characteristic of his other philological works (cf. Smirnov 1971). This course was clearly conceived to oppose the tradition of Jesuit poetics (with its characteristic attention to word play, figural poetry, *carmina curiosa* and other aspects of Baroque poetics). Here Prokopovich's principles may be connected to his Enlightenment, anti-clerical, and reformist position (see Uhlenbruch 1985, xciv–xcvii). Propkopovich's later pedagogical activity was presumably based on these same principles (ibid). In the context of fierce religious and political struggle these principles were sharply opposed to the eclectic approach (with noticeable dependence on Jesuit traditions) that reigned in the teaching of the liberal arts , including rhetoric, at the Moscow-Slaviano-Greco-Latino Academy (as well as in the Kievan Academy — cf. Levin 1972). Uhlenbruch's suggestion that this kind of eclecticism in poetics was a stable attribute of Russian church culture is hardly just (cf. Zhivov 1988c, 98). Rather, Prokopovich's poetic doctrine could be seen as a component of a new world view that was opposed to traditional culture in all ways. This evidently motivated the great influence that Feofan exercised upon the new Russian literature (Kantemir, Trediakovskii, etc); here the disdain for Jesuit Baroque poetics could be connected with rejecting the literary traditions of ecclesiastical education..

and whose echoes could still be felt at the start of the eighteenth century in the debate between Hierodeacon Damaskin and Gavriil Dometskii (see Iakhontov 1883), had lost their relevance by the 1710's. In particular, Stefan Iavorskii, who had been received by the Great Russian church leaders with extreme mistrust (cf. Shevelov 1951; see also Ternovskii 1864; Ternovskii 1879), became closely associated with them in the 1710's (especially as a result of the Tveritinov affair). Their opposition to Peter's anticlerical policy and their desire to preserve the church's independence united them, and this political unity was reflected in a certain rapprochement of their cultural positions (cf. Morozov 1880, 176). Feofan equated the cultural and linguistic positions of both parties, applying anti-Jesuit rationalist arguments to the proponents of Church Slavonic education. This identification was connected to the application of another far more politically serious one, as the struggle for church autonomy was described as a form of papism. Church Slavonic education was equated to Hellenophilism and Hellenophilism with Jesuit opposition to Enlightenment, and this allowed Feofan to charge the whole tendency with papism and to associate it with Patriarch Nikon's policy; for him the Byzantine model in its Slavic reception was fundamentally indistinguishable from the Roman Catholic one.

The identification of Byzantium and Rome as negative models juxtaposed to properly ordered states in which the monarch's power was unlimited was clearly outlined in the *Spiritual Regulation:*

> And we are not only capable of making this Conjecture in our Thoughts, which God inspires us with; but it has very often been demonstrated in fact in many Countries, and is particularly manifested in the History of Constantinople down from the Reign of Justinian to this time. And the Pope effected so great things by this Means, he did not only overthrow the Roman Empire, and grasp a great part of it himself, but more than once has almost shaken the Power of Other Dominions, and threatened them with the last Destruction. To say nothing of the like Contentions that have been amongst us. (Verkhovskoi, II, 32, first pagination; Dukhovnyi reglament 1904, 17; translation modernized from Cracraft 1982, 10)

Cf. the similar identification in Feofan's "Declaration When and for What Reason the Monastic Order Began":

> When several German emperors, forsaking their rank, began to play the hypocrite, and their wives even more, then several rogues came to them and asked permission to build monasteries not in the wilderness but in the cities themselves, and demanded financial help for their pseudo-shrines; and what is even worse, they wanted to be fed not by their own labors but for free, by the labors of others; the emperors, forsaking their duty, supported this pseudo-

holiness, whether deceived by these people or were motivated themselves by some sort of infatuation, and [they brought] great ruination onto themselves and onto their people... This gangrene was also very widespread in our country under the protection of those who [supported] the church's absolute rule (edinovlastnikov tsertkovnykh), like the Romans; but the Lord God did not deprive our former rulers of his grace, as he did the Greeks... (PSZ, VII, no. 4450; cf. Chistovich 1868, 709–18)[20]

The opposition of Prokopovich and Peter's cultural position, on the one hand, and that of Stefan Iavorskii, Feofilakt Lopatinskii (and in the same category, Fedor Polikarpov), on the other, correlates in certain ways with orientations on Protestant and Catholic doctrine. The connection between Petrine cultural and religious struggles with Protestantism and Catholicism is well known; Peter's party charged its opponents with papism, while Stefan Iavorskii and his confederates saw the religious and political ideas of the reformers in theological terms as a Protestant heresy (recall that Stefan died under investigation for having called Peter an "iconoclast" [ikonoborets] — Runkevich 1900, 169; Cracraft 1971, 164). It was charges of Protestantism that were raised against Prokopovich by Iavorskii, Lopatinskii and Vishnevskii when they objected to his being made bishop in 1718 (Titlinov 1913, 458).

---

[20]   The association of Hellenophilism and papism and its correlation with opposition to Peter's church reform was clearly manifested in the polemic of 1721 between Feofan and Stefan Iavorskii over the commemoration of the names of the eastern patriarchs (see Feofan Prokopovich 1721a; Stefan Iavorskii. Apologiia... — GIM, Uvar. 1728 / 378 / 588; cf. Zhivov 1987a; it is published in Zhivov 2004). In this polemic the issue was over the commemoration of their names during the liturgy which had been established in Russian church practice after the death of Patriarch Adrian and suspended right after the establishment of the Synod. Commemoration of the names of the patriarchs in the liturgy signaled a certain kind of canonical subordination, and there is reason to think that in the opinion of church leaders during the very prolonged period of going without a patriarch the church had been transferred to the jurisdiction of the eastern patriarchs; they served as a kind of temporary collective substitute for the Moscow patriarch. Justifying the necessary end to the practice, Feofan noted that "many... hearing the consecrated patriarchal name think that the Ruling Synod is subordinate to the patriarchs or to a patriarch" (Feofan Prokopovich 1721a, l. 11 verso). Subordination to the eastern patriarchs, even symbolic, was seen by Feofan as an analogue to subordination to the pope. The Byzantine model is thus combined with the Roman Catholic, and to these is juxtaposed the principle of the church's territorial autonomy as part of the state and sharing its interests. Iavorskii, on the contrary, passionately defended the symbolic leadership of the eastern patriarchs, and his Latinophile past in no way hindered this. Recall that in 1703 the Jersualem Patriarch Dositheos had sent Iavorskii a special epistle criticizing him for being pro-Latin and anti-Greek (Kapterev 1914, 541–6). Obviously, by the time of the "Apologiia" (1721) this conflict had completely played itself out. [...] Thus even for Iavorskii Byzantine and Roman Catholic models had become associated, so that the very character of the polemic between him and Feofan unquestionably demonstrates that the opposition of Hellenophilism and Latinophilism had become a matter of the past and no longer had any significance for the cultural process.

2. Language Policy and the Conflict of Cultures

The question of Protestantism was raised in a very sharp way in the Tveritinov affair that grew into one of the main ideological conflicts of Peter's reign. Stefan Iavorskii's struggle to condemn Tveritinov and his adherents, who had spread Protestant doctrine in Moscow and who enjoyed the support of several Petrine grandees as well as Feodosii Ianovskii, archimandrite of the Alexander Nevskii Lavra (before Feofan Prokopovich's arrival in Petersburg Peter's main agent in the Church administration), grew into a battle for the independence of the church and the ecclesiastical court. In 1714 Peter published an order to free Tveritinov and his followers. Stefan, however, ordered the investigation to continue and on October 24, 1714, convened a council in Moscow which on the basis of new materials anathematized Tveritinov and forbade Feodosii Ianovskii, who had given him communion, from holding mass. In terms of the opposing groups in the cultural conflicts that concern us here, it is significant that Polikarpov took a direct role in attacking Tveritinov (see Tikhonravov, II, 192f), serving as an intermediary between Iavorskii and Tsarevich Aleksei (ibid, 260–1).

The correlation of cultural positions with Catholicism or Protestantism could not help but have definite linguistic consequences. While there were no strictly linguistic points of conflict in Prokopovich's clash with Iavorskii, their varying attitudes toward the comprehensibility of the Bible is significant. Feofan held that the text of the Bible should be accessible and comprehensible to everyone, and that therefore Holy Writ should in principle be translated into national languages (cf. his course of theology, Feofan Prokopovich1782, 236–61); here Feofan concurs with Protestant theology and uses the same arguments that Protestants directed against Catholic doctrine. In his *Rock of Faith*, which was directed against Protestant views, Iavorskii, on the contrary, expressly cites "the reasons why there should be obscurity and unfathomable profundity in Holy Writ." Among these reasons the following is singled out: "many, looking at the [Bible's] impenetrable mysteries and thinking them easily comprehensible, have exalted themselves, trusting in the natural quickness of [their] intellect" (Stefan Iavorskii 1841–2, III, 102, 105–6). Iavorskii's thesis accords with Catholic doctrine and he uses arguments developed in Catholic literature (cf. Morev 1904; cf. the views of Stanisław Hosius whose works may have been known to Iavorskii — Frick 1989, 36–44). Although Iavorskii says nothing about language, it is obvious that Feofan's demand for simplicity and comprehensibility as applied to the text of the Bible (and at the basis of his condemnation of the "Hellenophilic" version of the translation) had no place in his thinking.

It is quite indicative in this context that in his criticism of the Bible translation cited above Feofan calls his opponents "senseless bookworms" (bezumnye knigochii). This appellation may derive from the fragment about the "senseless bookworm" well known in Russia and attributed to Cyril the Philosopher (GIM, Sin. 569, l.142–142 verso; cf. Gorskii and Nevostruev II, 3, 637). In this fragment it says that "if [people] do not read them with attention and intelligence, they will not be able to understand anything that books say." The mention of Cyril connects this passage to the argument of St. Cyril-Constantine from the sixteenth chapter of his Slavonic "Life," where he challenges the trilingualists, citing Jesus' words [from Mat. 23, 13–29, passim; Lk. 11,24]: "Woe unto you, scribes [bookworms] (knigchie) and Pharisees, hypocrites!" (Kliment Okhridskii III, 106; cf. Skazaniia…, 1981, 89). It seems likely that Feofan is simultaneously equating the adherents of "obscure" (temnyi) Church Slavonic both to the trilingualists and to the scribes and Pharisees who opposed Christ's teaching. In this case Feofan again makes use of anti-Catholic Protestant polemics against his own opponents.[21]

In this way the question of the "obscurity" of the traditional written language was posed within the context of religious and political struggles, and under its influence properly linguistic issues were transformed into a debate over the symbolic attributes of the "true" or "false" faith. The issue was not about comprehensibility per se or about the most rational ways to structure education (in particular, religious education) but concerned the choice of culturological reference points and the negation or assertion of Orthodox tradition, its correlation to Catholicism or Protestantism, and about juxtaposing Petrine Enlightenment to enlightenment of the preceding period. In this context linguistic behavior became directly linked to the entire range of semiotic parameters that marked the political and cultural struggles of the Petrine era.

2.2 "Simplicity" and the Semiotic Functions of Civil Speech

And so the new literary language, created in association with Peter's cultural program, was supposed to contrast to the traditional language as

---

[21] Curiously, such reuse of St. Constantine's argument with the trilingualists as part of anti-Catholic polemics had taken place long before Prokopovich. This episode from the sixteenth chapter of the lengthy "Life" had been excerpted in the "Prenie Konstantina Filosofa s zhidy" (Debate of Constantine the Philosopher with the Jews) that was included in the *Khronograficheskaia Paleia* and a series of other collections (cf. Franko 1896, I, lv–lxii; Kliment Okhridskii, III, 51–7). This compilation was evidently created no later than the thirteenth century and has a clear anti-Catholic bias; it probably belongs to the corpus of anti-Latin literature written in the twelfth — thirteenth centuries. It is possible that Feofan was familiar with this material and borrowed if not its arguments than phraseology that would have been familiar to his audience.

one that was comprehensible rather than "obscure"; at the same time, it was to serve as the "civil language," i.e., the language of secular culture, thus transforming the traditional written language into the expression of a specifically clerical culture. As has been stated, this meant that the literary language created under Peter was not thought of as polyfunctional. In this sense the linguistic program of Prokopovich and his group remained Baroque; for all of his radical reformism, Prokopovich here followed the pattern dictated by his Ukrainian experience rather than the latest European models. While for Prokopovich the "simple" language was to serve as the new literary language, a principle shared by Peter that lay at the basis of the language reform, the later tradition's very significant demand for polyfunctionalism was foreign to him (cf. a different point of view in Uspenskii 1985, 126). As opposed to later authors (§ II–1.2), Feofan did not experience the influence of Classicist linguistic and stylistic theories and the Baroque principle of linguistic diversity remained wholly acceptable to him. Prokopovich had defended the principle of functional multilingualism as early as his *Rhetoric* of 1706 (Lachmann 1982, xxix–xxxii; Zhivov 1985a, 277) and it subsequently became the basis for his reform activity. His linguistic views were formed within the framework of multilingual practice that included Latin, Church Slavonic, Polish, and the "simple" tongue (in Ukrainian and Great Russian variants). The choice of concrete language (or register) for a particular text depended on its communicative goals, which led to the generic and functional distribution of languages. Prokopovich's pragmatism in this area contrasted both to the Jesuits' universal use of Latin and the "universalizing" of Church Slavonic promoted by Russian adherents of "Helleno-Slavonic" learning.

In this context the evolution of Feofan's homiletic language is extremely indicative (see Kutina 1981; Kutina 1982), as standard Church Slavonic was progressively replaced by the hybrid language (§ III–3.1; cf. Zhivov 1985). This change was obviously conscious; it would have been impossible had Prokopovich not believed that Church Slavonic could be preserved as an active, functioning language. It was precisely preserving Church Slavonic in this capacity that made the task of simplifying it, applying the demands for simplicity and comprehensibility, so necessary and immediate. These demands, applied to texts with various functional purposes, produced varied results; for the Bible text meant for reading this apparently entailed only a moderate modernization of standard Church Slavonic from which "decrepit" (archaic) words and Hellenisms would be eliminated, while in sermons the changes would be more profound, as "simplicity" was embodied in a hybrid type of language.

Chapter 1. The Petrine Language Reform

This kind of functional differentiation dictated the use of the "simple" language together with the hybrid. A conscious functional differentiation between the "simple" and hybrid language is quite clear in comparing analogous passages from the *History of Peter the Great* (whose "simple" language was discussed above, § I–1.3) and the "Sermon (Slovo) in Praise of the Battle of Poltava" of 1717, written in Church Slavonic—that is, between a secular work of history and a work of homiletics (cf. Levin 1972, 219). [...] [There follow several long passages.] Such examples clearly demonstrate that Feofan's choice of linguistic register was functionally motivated, that is, that the characteristics of his language depended on the functional purpose of the text. Understandably, this dependency could subsequently be rethought in stylistic terms.

Insofar as polyfunctionalism was not demanded of the new literary language, it remained optional in the cultural regard and was therefore connected with a set of defined (reformist) cultural values. This connection was conditioned by the symbolic significance of the new language, which acted not only as means of expression for the new culture but also as its symbolic embodiment. This semiotic function of the new literary language could come into conflict with the demand for comprehensibility and accessibility that had been put forward as the main reason for its creation. This contradiction was manifested with special expressiveness in the wide use of unassimilated or poorly assimilated borrowings in texts of the Petrine period that were written in the new "civic language." Borrowings from Western European languages were assimilated in extremely large quantity during the Petrine period, and their history has been described in the scholarly literature many times (Christiani 1906; Smirnov 1910; Birzhakova, Voinova, Kutina 1972; Otten 1985). This process was so intensive that it has often been seen as the main feature of linguistic development of this period. We have written above about the error of this view (§ I–1.2), but this does not free us of the need to provide an adequate interpretation of what was happening.

The broad assimilation of borrowings in the Petrine era was almost always connected to intensive developments in the various spheres of science, industry, military and state organization, and culture; the impression is created that these lexical imports were motivated for the most part by importations of new things and ideas. This pragmatic factor certainly played a role in the process of borrowing, but it was not the only one, and perhaps not the most important. Borrowings served first of all as markers of the new cultural orientation—that is, not primarily a pragmatic but a semiotic function. Their use indicated adherence to the new Petrine culture, the assimilation of a new

2. Language Policy and the Conflict of Cultures

system of values and at the same time the rejection of traditional notions. The intensity of using borrowings was conditioned by this particular role, so that words arrived not following things and ideas but anticipated them or without being correlated with them.

This semiotic function of borrowings is fully visible in those cases where textual borrowings are accompanied by glosses that give lexical equivalents in common terms that the reader will understand. Thus in a declaration (ob"iavlenie) to the Senate of June 13, 1718, Peter writes: "But so as not to err in this, however, I thus beg of you, that this affair be judged in truth, in accordance with what [Tsarevich Aleksei] deserves, without flattering (or complimenting) me… (не флатируя [или не похлѣбуя] мне)" (Ustrialov, VI, 516). Obviously, using the borrowing (*флатировать*) that was hardly familiar to most of the senators together with its precise Russian equivalent (*похлѣбить*) was not needed for any communicative reason but served as a conventional sign of Peter's Europeanism. A similar practice, fulfilling the same semiotic function, is characteristic of Peter's associates (cf. for example, of Prokopovich in *The Right of a Monarch's Will*: *презервтива, или предохранительное врачество; резонами или доводами; резоны или доводы; экземпли или примѣры*, etc. — PSZ, VII, no. 4870, 606, 607, 634), and may be cited as a characteristic feature of that "civic" literature that Peter initiated (cf. Vasilevskaia 1967; Birzhakova, Voinova, Kutina 1972, 63; see also the many examples of similar glosses in the list of borrowings given in the last work under the heading "glosses," ibid, 101–70).

Such glosses are especially common in the legal monuments of the Petrine period, which may be directly connected to the fact that these played the role not only of juridical documents but no less as didactic works (cf. Morozov 1880, 254–5; Zhivov 1988b). The use of glosses in Petrine juridical monuments serve the same didactic function as the monuments as a whole. Borrowing plus gloss as if reenact the clash of the old and new state order and serve as a guide to a citizen's correct behavior. In essence they create a normative dictionary for the new state servitor whose very speech signals the acceptance of the new political ideas. The glosses unequivocally demonstrate the combination of borrowings' symbolic function and their communicative redundancy. Here are some additional examples from the *General Regulation or Charter* of 1720: *Генеральныя инструкция* is glossed as *наказ, дирекция* as *управление, ваканции* as *упалые места, реляции* as *отписки, квитанцыная книга* as *расписки, генеральные формуляры* as *образцовыя письма, акциденции* as *доходы, ландкарты* as *чертежи, рапорт* as *доношение*, etc. (PSZ, VI, no. 3534, 141–60). It is also indicative that an "Interpretation of Foreign Expressions" is appended to the *General Regulation* that serves to instruct state employees in use of the new language.²²

Glosses within a text testify to the process of renaming, by which old things receive new names (cf. Birzhakova, Voinova, Kutina 1972, 289–90). The cultural importance of this process is obvious; constructing the new culture is here reflected in purposeful mythologizing activity that symbolically makes short shrift of the past and just as symbolically establishes the new. As in other analogous situations, new names are signs of a new cosmos, and renaming reveals the enduring presence of an archaic, mythologizing layer of consciousness; the connection between name and denotatum (signifier and signified) is perceived as something absolute and non-conventional, so that the new name transforms the old thing and places it within a new cosmic social order.

Thus borrowings fulfilled primarily a semiotic function, seen most obviously in glosses. However, glossing did not solve the problem of comprehensibility insofar as for all its intensive use it was only used occasionally and many new borrowings remained unexplained. The common use of borrowings made texts in the new civic language poorly comprehensible to a significant part of the audience to which they were addressed. Cases of misunderstanding due to the use of borrowings and leading to anecdotal results are described in contemporary sources (see Pekarskii, IA, II, 53; Tatishchev 1990, 227–30; Obnorskii and Barkhudarov, II, 2, 90–1). This polyglossia — speaking in different languages — which directly contradicted the demand for comprehensibility became a fact of the linguistic and cultural consciousness of the time, so that there even appeared texts parodying the situation (see Zapiski OR GBL, XVII, 153). The problem of polyglossia, manifested in the lack of mutual understanding, was the most extreme example of the new literary language's struggle for universality that came into conflict with the growing differentiation of linguistic practices on the part of various social groups (cf. § 0–6).²³

---

22   Many similar examples may be seen in the "Artikul voinskii" (Military Code) of 1715 […] (PZ, IV, 329–63) and in the "Kratkoe isobrazhenie protsessov ili sudebnykh tiazheb" (Short Description of Trials or Judicial Litigation), which together with the "Artikul voinskii" was part of the "Voinskii ustav" (Military Code) of 1716 (PSX, V, no. 3006, 203–453); here the gloss is even included in the work's title!

23   In the later eighteenth century polyglossia leading to misunderstanding became a staple theme of Russian comedies, in which linguistic confusion always illustrates the clash of opposing cultural traditions and thus also the cultural heterogeneity of the society created by the Petrine reforms. Thus in Gorodchaninov's comedy "Mitrofanushka in Retirement" (Mitrofanushka v otstavke) we find the following dialogue: "*Zasluzhenov*: So this bride won't be to your taste. *Domosedova*: Hey, father! What taste does she have? After all she's not mutton. *Zasluzhenov*: (suppresses his laughter). *Mitrofanushka*: Oh how you babble, mother. As if we were talking

2. Language Policy and the Conflict of Cultures

The fact that borrowings were used extensively in juridical monuments is especially significant, in that their inaccessibility coexists with the implicit requirement that they be understood and carried out independent of one's knowledge of foreign languages. Complaints about the incomprehensibility of the laws became a regular feature of Russian social development in the eighteenth century, and this offers a certain perspective on the Petrine linguistic policy as a whole. The intensive use of borrowings in juridical monuments may be illustrated with an example from the already-cited Military Code of 1716. Apart from the borrowings that were glossed one meets a whole series of similar lexical elements which readers had to figure out on their own, for example: *патент, офицер, кавалерия, инфантерия, арест, пас, президент, фискал, штраф, артикул, шпицрутен, гарнизон, регимент, профос, маркитентер, гевальдигер, банкет, регулы, меланхолия, магазейн, цейхгауз, процесс, кригрехт, эксекуция,*[24] etc. Significantly, many borrowings appeared in juridical acts for the first time. For this reason, many, understandably, remained incomprehensible.[25]

The comprehensibility and accessibility of the new language that the reformers proclaimed were standard European linguistic slogans (primarily Protestant ones, although the idea of linguistic "simplicity" was by no means bound by confessional limits, cf. § 0–5), and in Russian conditions they carried more a polemical than actual weight. The new literary language was

---

about mutton" (Gorodchaninov 1800, 87). The misunderstanding arises from the clash between the literal meaning of "taste" and its figurative meaning that was a semantic calque of the French "goût." Sumarokov plays on a similar kind of same misunderstanding in this dialogue between Arlikin and Diulizh: "*Diulizh*: So tell me, is your young lady visible? *Arlikin*: Well she's not a spirit that's impossible to see, she has arms as well as legs, and everything that her other sisters have" (Sumarokov, V, 265). Diulizh is confused by the French semantic calque "to be visible" (*être visible,* быть видимым, in the sense of "to be ready to receive visits or guests"). Thus misunderstanding as an instance of the opposition of cultures arises as a result of Western European influence on the language of a certain part of society (see also § IV–2.3).

[24] *patent, ofitser, kavaleriia, infanteriia, arest, pas, prezident, fiskal, shtraf, artikul, shpitsruten, garnizon, regiment, profos, markitenter, geval'diger, banket, reguly, melankholiia, magazein, tseikhgauz, protsess, krigrekht, eksekutsiia.*

[25] Because of this throughout the eighteenth century there appeared declarations (made for an effect rather than for practical ends) about the necessity of making the laws clear and accessible. Thus in 1736 V. N. Tatishchev wrote that "It is necessary that the law be written clearly and accessibly in the language used by those governed by it, so that the least educated (prosteishii) person can correctly understand the law and the will of the lawgiver." Therefore, "no foreign word or rhetorical composition may be used" in the legal language (Obnorskii and Barkhudarov, II, 2, 89–90; Tatishchev 1990, 224, 227). See also Tatishchev's notes on the instructions for the new census (novaia reviziia) of 1743 [...] (Tatishchev 1979, 361) and the chapter "On the Composition and Style of Laws" in the *Nakaz* [...] (Ekaterina 1770, 294–8), which is echoed by M. M. Shcherbatov (Shcherbatov, I, col. 371). The connection between lawgiving and the Petrine policy of social differentiation was so profound, however, that attempts to bring the language of the laws closer to that of the majority of the population, educated in traditional culture, had no success (cf. Zhivov 1988b).

more than anything else an expression of the new culture. It shared with this culture both its European goals, its polemical orientation against national tradition, and its lack of familiarity for an audience brought up in that tradition.

In this way language differentiation (the new literary language versus the language of traditional written, bookish culture) represented one aspect of the differentiation of cultures and worldviews. From the 1710's the question of one's attitude toward Church Slavonic and the new literary language entered into the complex of religious, political, historical and cultural as well as literary and linguistic views which separated the era's two basic factions, that which included Feofan, Peter, Gavriil Buzinskii, and Ia. Dolgurukii, on the one hand, and that of Tsarevich Aleksei, Stefan Iavorskii, Feofilakt Lopatinskii, and Fedor Polikarpov, on the other. The complex of reformist views formed under the influence of Peter's policies was extremely powerful and fully carried over to following generations. It served as the common platform of the "learned guard" (uchenaia druzhina) which formed around Feofan at the end of the 1720's (see Pumpianskii, 1941a, 178–84), that included A. D. Kantemir and V. N. Tatishchev. The combination of political, cultural and linguistic secularism that was characteristic of these latter figures directly derived from the cultural confrontations of the Petrine epoch. This complex of views was further transmitted (with some modifications) from the "learned guard" to Adodurov and Trediakovskii (see below), and permits us to speak of a continuity of cultural and linguistic trends in the first half of the eighteenth century.

In the post-Petrine era Fedor Polikarpov came to personify opposition to Peter's reforms in the cultural and linguistic sphere. He became a common target for charges of pseudo-scholarship, senseless Hellenophilism, and clerical bias in favor of Church Slavonic. The cultural and linguistic aspect of the anti-Petrine tradition came to be just as identified with Polikarpov as its political program was with Tsarevich Aleksei and its ecclesiastic and ideological agenda with Stefan Iavorskii. The specific content of attacks on Polikarpov was diverse. Kantemir, for example, made fun of him as a bad versifier (Kantemir, I, 284; cf. Pumpianskii 1941a, 178; the fact that Kantemir grouped Polikarpov the Hellenophile together with the Latinophile Sil'vestr Medvedev again indicates how insignificant the cultural and ideological oppositions of the end of the seventeenth century had become for the later period). Adodurov and Trediakovskii rejected the spelling of Grecianisms which Polikarpov had codified in his *Primer* of 1701 as a matter of principle (see Uspenskii 1975, 61).

It is noteworthy that at the same time Trediakovskii tried to discredit the very idea of turning to Greek as a model for Russian or Church Slavonic. Appealing to the authority of Greek came to signify the entire Helleno-Slavonic educational tradition; by ridiculing this linguistic phenomenon, Trediakovskii was demonstrating the falsity of the given world-view as a whole, just as Prokopovich had done somewhat earlier. He wrote: "Russian orthography does not have the slightest need to resemble any foreign one whose practice is not in accord with our own" (1748, 165 / III, 107). He rejected the distinction in meaning in Greek between the writing of "Theodore" and "Feodor" (Ѳеодоръ vs. Феодоръ) made by Polikarpov (Polikarpov 1701, l.7; cf. Gorskii and Nevostruev, II, 2, 10; Sobolevskii 1903, 310; § I–1.1; Trediakovskii specifically cites the *Primer*), adding: "let these names be different in meaning in Greek, but how does this concern us?" (1748, 187 / III, 123) […].

At the same time Trediakovskii subjected Polikarpov's entire cultural and linguistic program to ridicule: "Farewell to you, Theodore with a 'Th' (Ѳ)! I used to think that you, who stood at the beginning of the syllables embodied some secret power, but it was only imaginary, not to say empty. In vain do many place their hopes on you even today. And truly, if I were to lead you out onto the field of battle against the more powerful and dignified warrior Feopomp [with an "Ф"], I would still have to beat a retreat. Before Feopomp you are just plain Fediusha" (ibid, 191 / 125–6; for more criticism of Polikarpov's spelling, see ibid, 1748, 359 / III, 245–6, notes).[26]

Polikarpov's lexical preferences evoked a similarly negative response. Thus Trediakovskii in the foreword to *Voyage to the Island of Love* begged for pardon that formerly he had spoken in Church Slavonic, and noted that "I with my foolish Slavonic wordplay (gluposloviem slavenskim) wanted to display myself as a *scribolocutor (rechetochets)*" (Trediakovskii 1730, foreword, l. 7; III, 650). The word Trediakovskii emphasized apparently refers to Polikarpov's *Trilingual Lexicon*, which in fact contains this artificial form (Polikarpov 1704, l. 83, third pag.; see Uspenskii 1985, 75). It is possible that Trediakovskii's neologism "gluposlovie" was also a parody of the many compound words which Polikarpov created; "gluposlovie slavenskoe" correlates to the phrase "glubokoslovnaia slavenshchizna" (Slavonicizing

---

[26] Trediakovskii returns to Polikarpov's orthographic practice in another passage in the *Conversation About Orthography*: "In 1718, Fedor Polikarpov published, on order, in Moscow, Varenius' *General Geography*, which he translated from Latin; and so that his patronimic would be written correctly using our letters, that is, so that our orthography would be similar with the Greek, he also introduced into print [the letter] (ѵ)" (Trediakovskii 1748, 359 / III, 245–6, note). Indeed, in the signature to the *General Geography*'s foreword, "Polikarpov" is written with a "ѵ" (cf. Varenii 1718, foreword, l. 17 verso).

Chapter 1. The Petrine Language Reform

pomposity) used in the same foreword which served as another mockery of Church Slavonic erudition (see Uspenskii 1985, 74–5). Here Trediakovskii's ideological position may also be connected with that of the "learned guard." It is indicative that Tatishchev's pupil and follower P. I. Rychkov, who compiled a Russo-Tatar-Kalmyk lexicon at Tatishchev's request, wrote to him in March, 1741, that "as concerns the Russian in it, although it was taken from Polikarpov's lexicon, the Greek macaronisms (mokoronizmy) and unusual Slavonic words (slovenskiia zvaniia) have been thrown out, and on the contrary, much that could be called to mind was explained in simple language..." (Pekarskii 1867, 11–12; Aver'ianova 1950, 52). These words clearly demonstrate that Tatishchev's circle connected Polikarpov with Hellenizing and a partiality for specifically bookish expressions, as opposed to "simple language." These two issues served as the basis for condemning the given type of education, and the "learned guard" thus functioned as a connecting link between Prokopovich and Trediakovskii.

And so the change in attitude toward Church Slavonic may be seen as a significant indicator of the general cultural transformation of the Petrine era. The new critical attitude toward the language developed during the course of a bitter struggle over politics, religion and culture, and emerged as an indispensable part of the ideology of those who supported the Petrine reforms. Church Slavonic became associated with the old culture and the old state order; the Russian literary language of the new type was juxtaposed to it, and so by association became the symbol of the new cultural and governmental system. This specific interconnection between cultural, historical, and linguistic issues defined the reevaluation of Church Slavonic that is evident from the material that we have cited.

Indeed, the Petrine reforms created not only the image of a new Russia, but its polar opposite, the image of old Russia. In a sermon of 1716 Prokopovich asked:

> What opinion and estimation did foreign peoples formerly hold of us? The politically [advanced] considered us as barbarians, the proud and imposing ones — saw us as contemptible, the learned ones — as ignorant, the predatory ones — as desirable prey, in the opinion of all — as inferior, and disrespected by all... Today, however,... those who disdained us as coarse now zealously seek our friendship, those who dishonored us now glorify us, those who threatened us, fear and tremble before us, and those who despised us are not ashamed to serve us. (Feofan Prokopovich, I, 114–5)

And in the speech given in church when Peter was awarded the title "Father of the Fatherland" it was said that "By means of your unceasing labors and leadership, we, your loyal subjects, have been brought out of the darkness of ignorance and into the whole world's theater of fame, and, so to speak, brought forth from non-existence into being and incorporated into the society of cultured (politicheskikh) peoples" (ODDS, I, appendix, col. cccclviii — cccclix; cf. also Lotman and Uspenskii 1982, 244–5).

This historiographical scheme was created with Peter's direct influence (see for example his comments recorded by Berkhgol'ts, II, 57). The juxtaposition of old and new Russia was constructed upon a set of mutually exclusive traits, and left no room for any kind of historical continuity, so that Peter was envisaged as a creator as if *ex nihilo*, a demiurge giving birth to a new people and a new kingdom. Therefore in ascribing enlightenment to the new Russia, the old Russia was defined as ignorant, and in endowing the new Russia with wealth and grandeur, poverty and destitution fell to the lot of the old. In pursuit of propagandistic and didactic goals, the new Russia made something of a caricature of the old, as it took its own idealized image (which was equally far from reality) and turned it inside out. This mechanism also operated in the linguistic sphere. Therefore, in defining the new culture as secular, the old was classified as clerical. Language followed culture: the traditional written language was transformed into a clerical language, attractive only to the ignorant folk and to pseudo-scholarly bookworms "who do not understand the power of language." As with most Petrine historiographical schemes, this conception became firmly rooted in the cultural consciousness of following epochs and has survived almost completely intact even down to the present day. Many notions about the written language of medieval Russia also derived from this framework, as well as a series of ideas about the literary language of the new type. These were of fundamental importance for the formation of the literary language in the post-Petrine period.

Chapter 2

The Start of Normalization of the New Literary Language; The Formulation of Linguistic Theories and Literary Practice

1. The Formation of Petersburg Culture and the New Conception of the Literary Language

And so, Peter's cultural policies led to a radical change in the linguistic situation. Speaking of the Petrine era, the historian M. P. Pogodin rightly asked, "did not precisely the same revolution take place in language as in the state?" Characterizing the state of the literary language as "chaotic" as a result of the Petrine revolution, he posed the question: "How could our glorious literature have arisen and blossomed from out of this chaotic jumble?" (Pogodin, I, 349). As noted already, the idea that the language of the Petrine era had been in a state of chaos became firmly rooted in later linguistic thought. This notion was based on later conceptions of linguistic norms, with their corresponding criteria for linguo-stylistic analysis. It was based on the hidden conviction that these norms were universally valid, and the variability that was characteristic of Petrine era usage was considered incompatible with normativeness. Thus the very notion of the language's "chaotic state" was itself a result of a new stage of Russian linguistic consciousness, a product of the transformation which the literary language underwent in the eighteenth and early nineteenth centuries.

Indeed in the texts of Peter's time elements of Church Slavonic, Russian, and new borrowed elements freely mingled in unrestricted and disorderly fashion. These texts are characterized by "the variability of words and forms together with the absence of clear principles of stylistic distinction among the variants" (Levin 1972: 216). In the context of Petrine linguistic policy the very rejection of the old literary language was normative, while the heterogeneity of the elements comprising the new language was of no interest to the reformers. In such conditions there were virtually no formal criteria that would have allowed for distinguishing literary from non-literary texts. It is this very fact that modern linguistic consciousness has perceived as evidence of the language's chaotic state. The rejection of the traditional literary norm and the traditional system of registers that correlated the type of text with the type of language led to a situation in which–within the parameters of the "simple" language — there was no distinct dividing line between texts of different types. "Literary" works like Apollodorus' *Library* or the *General Geography*, historical and documentary works like the *History of the Swedish War* or Feofan Prokopovich's *History of Peter the Great*, juridical acts, diaries, personal correspondence (which could traditionally be of a non-literary character), and so on — constituted a continuous spectrum of idioms which did not lend itself to unambiguous categorization. Between this situation and the established norm of the mid-nineteenth-century literary language (which is still valid today, with a few minor changes) lay a hundred and fifty years of experimentation, and it is these attempts and experiments which make up the history of the Russian literary language of the new type. Normalization and codification of the new literary language reflect its aspiration for universal applicability, which in turn indicates the new role of the new literary language as a realization of Petersburg culture's hegemonic status in the system of imperial power.

As has been discussed (§ I–1.4), in the beginning of the linguistic reform the "literariness" of a text was connected to its cultural function rather than to its formal characteristics. Such a situation was anomalous both from the point of view of the traditional conception of the literary language and from the point of view of European notions then being adopted. A text's "literariness" had to be marked formally, and its cultural function correlated to its particular idiom. In the traditional literary language this marking had been realized with indicators of bookishness. One of the consequences of their removal was the appearance of new parameters that marked a polished idiom. These new parameters had to do with regulating and unifying linguistic variants, so that the creation of the new norm was put into practice first of all by eliminating the unmotivated variability which the "simple" language had inherited from the hybrid.

The variability of the "simple" language which directly derived from hybrid Church Slavonic not only indicates their continuity but also determined the new language's further course of development towards normalization. It should be kept in mind that variability is a fundamental characteristic of the "simple" language and not merely a characteristic of certain hybrid texts that have been corrected so as to become "simple." Indeed, such variability can be also found in texts that were originally written in the "simple" language. As examples, we can cite the great linguistic similarity between the *History of Peter the Great* as corrected by Feofan Prokopovich (§ I–1.3) and Fontenelle's *Conversations About the Plurality of Worlds* (*Entretiens sur la pluralité des mondes*) as translated by Kantemir in the early 1730's.

Iu. Sorokin, analyzing the language of Kantemir's translation, notes that in it "the old simple forms of verbal tenses (aorist and imperfect) and forms of the perfect with auxiliary verb are completely absent... The old system of participles is totally transformed... only in the function of gerunds appear short forms in *-а, -я, -ая, -яя,* ... and in *-ши, -вши*... The old forms of the infinitive with *-ти* in the unstressed position are also absent" (Sorokin 1982, 64). In this text "also missing are... a series of conjunctions usual for another type of writing: *аки (акибы), аще, внегда, воеже, егда, еже*" (ibid, 70). Thus as in the *History of Peter the Great* the basic indicators of bookishness have been eliminated from this text.

At the same time, in both works occurs variability in those categories that were unconnected with the opposition of bookish and non-bookish language. In Kantemir occur the following noun endings: gen. sg. masc. forms in *-у* and *-а,* the endings *-амъ, -ами, -ахъ* in dat. and instr., and prep. pl. on a par with the variant endings -омъ, -ы, -ѣхъ (ibid, 64–5). In adjectival declensions in nom.-acc. sg. masc. occur the variant endings *-ой/-ей* and *-ый/-ий,* the gen. sg. fem. endings *-ыя/-ия* and *-ой/-ей* (the latter predominate, as in the *History* — ibid, 74–5). In the sphere of pleophonic and non-pleophonic vocabulary are observed both the free variability of a series of lexemes as well as the semantic differentiation of variants, moreover in specific details the type of differentiation coincides with that observed in the *History.* Thus the prefix *пере-* is used primarily in the meaning of spacial displacement, while *пре-* occurs in abstract meanings (ibid, 72–3).[1]

---

[1] One may note a further series of similarities in the language of the *History of Peter the Great* and *Conversations About the Plurality of Worlds*. In *Conversations* the prefix предъ is only met (with one special exception) in the non-pleophonic form (Sorokin 1982, 74), and the same is true of the *History*. In *Conversations* the alternation of жд/ж in the root нужд- occurs with the ж variant appearing before the adjectival suffix -н- (нужда/нужный — Sorokin 1982, 74). The same alternation occurs in the *History*: нужду (5 verso), принужден (5 verso), нуждею (8 verso), нужда (10 verso), нуждою (15 verso, 16 r verso), понужденъ (19 verso), however — нужнѣйшихъ (8 verso). (On the fact that this distribution is not automatic, see, for example, V. N. Tatishchev, who uses the root нужд- in all cases.) These particular phenomena are evidently the legacy of hybrid Church Slavonic.

1. The Formation of Petersburg Culture and the New Conception

One may observe a similar pattern in a series of other texts from the 1710's–1730's. In essence, analogous features may also be seen in Trediakovskii's *Voyage to the Island of Love*, where in adjectival declensions the following endings alternate: *-ой/-ый* in nom.-acc. sg. masc., *-ой/-ыя* in gen. sg. fem., *-аго/-ого /-ова* in gen.-acc. sg. masc. and neut., etc. There is also variability of pleophonic and non-pleophonic forms and forms with the prefixes *роз-* and *раз-* (cf. Sorokin 1976, 48–51; Alekseev 1982, 88–9). True, in plural noun declensions the endings *-амъ/-ами/-ахъ* occur consistently, which evidently indicates the first steps being taken toward normalizing the new literary language. However, the connection to the variability of Petrine era language is still very clearly felt, so that the features we have noted may be seen as standard features of the initial stage of forming a literary language of the new type.

Hence, the "simple" language of the Petrine era was characterized by variability, and this variability required normalization. The first steps in this process were taken fully within the limits of traditional ideas about regulating the literary language. This is the type of normalization we find in the *General Geography* corrected by Sofronii Likhud and in Apollodorus's *Library* translated by A. K. Barsov. Despite a certain fluctuation due to the novelty of the task (normalization of a language which by traditionall standards was non-bookish), regularizing these texts was part of the traditional duties of the typographical corrector (spravshchik) who was responsible for editing texts published in Church Slavonic (see above). Since the task was new and the principles not yet clear this regulation was incomplete and inconsistent.

Subsequent generations of Russian philologists faced the same problem of normalization. Its solution, however, was based on new principles, whose development was one of the main factors stimulating the creation of the Russian literary language. Within the larger context of eighteenth-century cultural evolution, it is no surprise that the main point of reference for establishing the literary language was European experience. The early stages of normalization are closely connected to the activities of the Academy of Sciences, and in particular to its *Notes to the Gazette* (*Primechanii k vedomostiam*). The *Notes* were translated from German (V. E. Adodurov and M. Shvanvits being among the translators) and had clear Enlightenment goals — to introduce European life and ideas to the Russian reader (Berkov 1952, 64f). Comparison of issues over several years reveals a gradual process of normalization, and also indicates that the assimilation of European concepts included ideas about language. It is interesting that on many issues the editors of *Notes* were in line with Feofan Prokopovich's "learned brigade" (uchenaia druzhina) (Berkov 1950, 24).

The ways of making use of European experience were various. They included studying the grammar of European languages, which gave an idea about how literary norms were established and their relationship both to the grammatical tradition and to spoken usage. We may assume that preparations to teach Russian grammar, requiring some codification of new literary norms, was also of great importance. V. E. Adodurov, author of the first textbook on Russian orthography for Russians (Uspenskii 1975; Baumann 1980; Keipert 1988a), describes his linguistic schooling: "I learned Latin, German and French at the Academy of Sciences and so was able to see some of my own shortcomings in correct usage of my own native language, and as far as I could, to correct them" (Pekarskii, IA, I, 511). It is clear that correcting Russian with the help of knowledge gained from learning other European languages meant transferring European principles of normalization and grammatical codification onto Russian. The development of Russian grammatical terminology, especially in the 1730's, is particular evidence of this, as are the descriptive schemes that Adodurov applied to his linguistic material; the main sources were textbooks in Latin and German (Alvar's *Institutio grammatica, Lateinischen Grammatica Marchica*, M. Shvanvits' *Teutsche Grammatica*, etc.), which were used in academic teaching (Keipert 1983; Keipert 1984; Keipert 1986; Keipert 1987a, Keipert 1989a).

The teaching of Russian as the native language evidently only began in the late 1730's, although courses of Russian for foreigners preceded courses for Russians, so that the principles of grammatical normalization could be adopted from the former and transferred to grammar textbooks for native Russian speakers. Systematic teaching of Russian as a foreign language had begun in 1703 with the establishment of Pastor Glück's school in Moscow (Belokurov and Zertsalov 1907), and it is not impossible that certain principles of grammatically describing the Russian language that remained valid for the later period came from the grammar that Glück composed (Keipert, Uspenskii, Zhivov 1994). Glück's grammar was followed by an extensive *Slavono-Russian Grammar*, written by Glück's closest associate, J. W. Paus, in 1729, which was a predecessor to Shvanvits' grammar of 1730 (Keipert 1992) and to Adodurov's essay on grammar of 1731 (Adodurov 1731; see below § II–1.4). All of these grammars were meant to teach Russian to foreigners and all of them began to work out new principles of normalization that were based on European models. Even at this early stage the principles used by the various authors did not coincide, and the differences between them depended on their varying cultural orientations. These anticipated later linguistic debates.

This attempt at codification thus links the process of normalizing the new literary language with foreign descriptions of Russian. Certain elements of normalization already present in these descriptions (perhaps due to the fact that for early eighteenth-century linguistic thought grammatical description without elements of normalization was something unusual and unfamiliar) could be assimilated by the later Russian grammatical tradition. Thus, for example, in Sohier's grammar we find the normalized distribution of nom. pl. endings which was later required by the Academy typography (Sohier, I, xii). Turning to European models shaped the new conception of a "correctly organized" literary language, and new criteria for choosing from among variants were developed with this in mind.

European models led to a break with the traditional Slavic grammatical tradition, but this break was neither full nor consistent. In practice there was a certain synthesis of the new principles with the older grammatical tradition, most clearly evidenced in the continued use of Smotritskii's grammar in creating grammars for the new literary language; even Lomonosov did not avoid its influence, which speaks to the continuity between the new philology and the former grammatical tradition. The character of this synthesis was not uniform, and could differ from author to author and period to period. As L. Ďurovič and A. Sjöberg write (1987, 266), in the early period it was by no means clear "where between the poles of Church Slavonic and conversational Russian the new literary language that was taking shape should lie." This or that combination was defined by the general linguistic program and changed as the program changed. A given form was related to an orientation on conversational usage or on literary tradition and defined in relation to the understanding of "rules" and "reason" in the given program. One or the other interpretation of particular criteria were reflected in specific and concrete normalizing decisions.

These decisions testify precisely to the process of normalization, rather than to the Russification or Slavonicizing of the literary language. Comparing the language of a series of eighteenth-century texts in which the nom.-acc. masc. sg. adjective ending is *-ой/-ей*, and the masc. and neut. gen. sg. is in *-аго/-яго* with contemporary Russian usage, where in the corresponding places we have *-ый/-ий* (in unstressed position) and *-ого/-его*, one can't help but conclude that the notions of Russification or Slavonicizing have nothing to do with the evolution of the new type of literary language, and that the choice of ending reflects a process of continual rethinking of linguistic material which, in the form of the "simple language," lay at the origin of this process.

As the result of this process the variability characteristic of the "simple tongue" was consistently eliminated from the literary language – either due to stylistic differentiation of variants, to getting rid of one of them, or, finally, due to establishing a complementary distribution. In defending these decisions one could speak of the "Slavonic" or "popular" character of a given variant. However, it is important to keep in mind that this or that characteristic was not a given which the normalizers of the language derived from earlier linguistic consciousness. Rather, in every case this was a discovery, a novelty, revealing linguistic issues that no one had paid attention to before and which became relevant due to the linguistic program at hand. Furthermore, the choice of which characteristics were relevant also depended on the linguistic (and, more broadly, cultural) position of the author. If oriented on conversational usage the variants being discarded could be defined as "Slavonic," while an orientation on the literary tradition could use "popular" as a similar discrediting label.

Two significant issues arise here. First, in this process the notions of "Slavonic" and "popular" took on a functional character (non-bookish, non-conversational, obsolete, little used, inconsistent with the rules, etc.) and lost their genetic significance (although references to this may indicate the codifiers' etymological interests). It is therefore a mistake to equate them with the categories of "Slavonicisms" and "Russicisms" as used by contemporary linguists. Second, the classification and normalization of variants was an extended process in which certain grammatical and lexical elements could be involved only partially, while the very criteria employed by no means remained unchanged. At the same time, certain normalized forms could be passed on from period to period, becoming part of a tradition, while others could be reconsidered as linguistic programs underwent change.

Hence the development of the literary language in the eighteenth century materialized as a process of repeatedly rethinking and reevaluating the variability that was characteristic of the "simple tongue" of the Petrine era, the legacy of hybrid Church Slavonic. Moreover, working out the principles of the literary language of the new type emerged as part of the new cultural development, as the criteria for normalization themselves reflected larger cultural concerns. Because of this the history of the creation of literary norms represents a kind of intermediate stage between the history of culture and the history of linguistic phenomena per se.

1.1 The Linguistic Program of the First Codifiers: New Issues

New principles of normalization of the literary language that differed from those developed in the course of typographical practices were developed in the 1730's. The linguistic program that served as their

1. The Formation of Petersburg Culture and the New Conception

basis was by no means the simple result of Peter's language reform and the natural realization of the challenges that had carried over from the past. The conscious posing of the challenge to normalize the new literary language itself marked a new period and gave new impetus to its development. This impetus was generated by the new cultural self-consciousness which lay at the heart of Petersburg culture as a whole.

To understand this new self-consciousness we must, in the words of L. V. Pumpianskii,

> imagine that first moment when rapture over the West suddenly, in an outburst, became rapture over Russia as a Western nation. This was the second revelation in the new history of the Russian people: the first was that Europe exists, and that its grandeur was incontestable, like the sun; the second was that Russia also had grandeur, and of the same quality. Consequently, one could confess to a single rapture over both Europe and Russia. This we may refer to as the 'post-Petrine revelation' — the 'second revelation' — of the Russian people. It is precisely this, the rapturous confession of faith in one self, that is connected to the awakening of rhythm in linguistic consciousness. (Pumpianskii 1983a,: 310)

The new linguistic consciousness demanded order, organization, and harmony in the new literary language — precisely those things which the "simple" language of the Petrine era lacked. It was not merely necessary to reject the former Church Slavonic tradition, but to create a language that measured up to European standards; it had to be not only not Church Slavonic, but to be European, to take its place among the literary languages of Europe.

For this reason, the program of the new codifiers went further and manifested qualitatively new phenomena than the Petrine agenda. In the foreword to *Voyage to the Island of Love* Trediakovskii wrote:

> Do not, I humbly beg you, be angry with me, (even if you are still devotees of profoundly-worded Slavonic pomposity [glubokoslovnyia derzhites' slavenshchizny]), that I did not translate this book into Slavonic, but merely into the simplest Russian, that is, the kind we speak among ourselves. This I did for the following reasons. First, the Slavonic language is our church language, and this book is worldly. Second, in the present day the Slavonic language is very obscure (temen) to us, and many of us are not able to understand it when reading . But this book is about *sweet love*, and so must be comprehensible to everyone. Third — which might seem the most frivolous to you, but which for me is the most serious — is that the Slavonic language now sounds harsh to my ears, although formerly I not only used to write in it, but also conversed with everybody in it. But I hereby ask pardon of all those in whose presence I used to present myself as a special *wordifier* (rechetochets) with my foolish bandying of Slavonic (s gluposloviem moim slavenskim). (Trediakovskii 1730, foreword, l. 6 verso — 7; III, 649–50)

In these often-cited words the imprint of the Petrine linguistic program is fully visible. Slavonic is seen as the language of traditional ecclesiastical culture, unsuitable for expressing modern values. Using the language outside of its traditional cultural frame of reference is declared a "foolish bandying" of words, proceeding from the absurd desire to pass as "a special *wordifier* (rechetochets)," a formula which corresponds to Prokopovich's attack on the "arrogance of senseless bookworms (scribes)" who try and use Church Slavonic "to amaze the people" (§ I–1.2). The notion of Slavonic as obscure and inaccessible to many readers also derives from Prokopovich (cf. Uspenskii 1985, 124). The language for the new culture is proclaimed to be "the simplest Russian" (samoe prostoe Ruskoe slovo).

At the same time we may observe fundamentally new ideas here which were outside the purview of Peter and his entourage. In the first place, the opposition between Church Slavonic and Russian is evaluated primarily in aesthetic categories, as an aesthetic criterion is put forward as the main reason for switching to Russian. In this Trediakovskii's statement coincides exactly with that of Adodurov. Like Trediakovskii, Adodurov speaks about the "harshness" (or "hardness," zhestkost') of Church Slavonic (Adodurov 1731, 26; cf. Unbegaun 1958, 110; Uspenskii 1975, 65); in comparison Russian is valued as "refined" (iziashchnyi, zierlich) (Uspenskii 1975, 66–7; Uspenskii 1985, 80–88). The aesthetic evaluation of linguistic material was common to all of the early … codifiers. Secondly, the new literary language was oriented on spoken usage, on the language that "we speak among ourselves." This theoretical tenet was also new; Peter had spoken about the "words of the Foreign Office," i.e., he had a written tradition rather than the spoken language in mind as a model. This tenet was also common to Trediakovskii and Adodurov (see Uspenskii 1975, 55–57). As will become apparent, both of these principles were to play a most substantive role in the development of the literary language. Aesthetic criteria entailed not only the rejection of the earlier bookish tradition, which was not new, but elaborating the new literary language that resulted from that rejection; spoken usage was put forward as the principle to guide this task.

And so, Russian, that very language spoken in the newly created capital of St. Petersburg, turned out to be better than Church Slavonic; this was the chosen language, the "gentle" language that was to express the new culture. A few years would pass and Trediakovskii would set out to demonstrate, with great conviction, that "true eloquence can be achieved using our everyday language alone, without making use of seemingly lofty Slavonic composition" (Pekarskii IA II: 104). For all the utopianism of this assertion, it clearly reveals the Europeanizing pathos which inspired all of the early codifiers — that Russia had a Russian literary language just like any of the European ones, no less rich or full of potential. In Trediakovskii's imagination, Petersburg was transformed into Paris, and the linguistic situation of Russia into that of France, model of enlightenment and refinement. "It is true that Russian (Rossiiskii iazyk) is entirely based upon Slavonic," wrote Trediakovskii in 1737, "however, as one can justly say that French, or better Italian, is not the same as Latin, although it comes from Latin, so one can legitimately assert that Russian is not Slavonic; for just as an Italian does not understand when they speak Latin, so neither will a Slav (Slavianin) when they speak Russian, or a Russian (Rossianin) when they speak Slavonic" (Trediakovskii 1737: 16). The classical scheme of the European "Questione della lingua" with its opposition of dead Latin to living European tongues was thus transferred to Russia, with Church Slavonic the analogue for Latin, and Russian the analogue for the vulgar, national spoken languages (cf. § 0–6). Applying this scheme to the Russian situation introduced the issue of genetic differences between Russian and Church Slavonic into the equation; these, as noted, poorly corresponded to the nature of the opposition between the bookish and non-bookish languages of the pre-Petrine period, and were equally problematic for describing the differences between the traditional and new literary languages. The new conception inevitably provoked the rethinking of many very diverse features of language and new ways of reworking it to correspond to the new understanding.

    The European ideal defined the conception of the new literary language and prescribed its road to perfection. Naturally, declarations alone were insufficient. If the new literary language was declared to be just as good as the languages of France and Italy, it had to acquire (in opposition to the "hard" church language) those qualities of polish and harmony, which, according to the opinion of the day, all properly organized modern literary languages possessed. These qualities presupposed, first of all, the normalization of literary usage at all levels. Attempts at such regularization began in the 1730's, and the early stage of the process was marked by special intensity. The work was centered primarily in the Academy of Sciences, in the Academy's gymnasium and typography, which connects it to the introduction of Russian as a subject of instruction and the publication of books in the new "civic" tongue . Here a series of philologists — Adodurov, Shvanvits, Trediakovskii, Taubert, and later V. Lebedev, generally united by common ideas, strove to establish norms (primarily orthographic and morphological) for the new language. To a significant degree the work was collective; one may presume, for example, that the materials they used for teaching were shared, revised and augmented among them, so that the authorship of particular documents is sometimes hard to determine. Following L. Ďurovič

(1992), it seems appropriate to speak here of the "grammar of the Academic gymnasium" as an aggregate of texts that comprised a single tradition that culminated in Lomonosov's *Russian Grammar.*

The process of normalization is manifested with great clarity in the transformations of orthography, which reflected the self-consciousness of the literary language in the most immediate way. In his grammatical outline of 1731, Adodurov already proposed certain orthographic innovations (e.g., he indicated that the certain letters were superfluous; Adodurov 1731, 4–6). Evidence of intensive work in this area is also evident in Adodurov's editing of the Russian text of M. Shvanvits' *German Grammar.* The first edition of this work came out in 1730 (Shvanvits 1730) and on the whole represents the state of the language before the start of the attempts at normalization; the Russian texts of its further two editions (1734 and 1745) were corrected by Adodurov and Ia. Shtelin (Bauman 1969; Keipert 1983; Riazanskaia 1988). These corrections, to which we will often refer, are extremely valuable evidence of the dynamism of changing literary norms. The orthographic changes in the 1734 edition indicate the normalization of a series of phenomena, for example, the distribution of *и* and *i* (*i* before a vowel and *и* in other cases; spelling according to etymology in borrowed words); ѧ and ѡ (according to etymology), etc. (Riazanskaia 1988). In 1735 the Russian Assembly (on this see below) decided to exclude the letters ѵ, ѕ, ѯ from the civil script, and this reformed alphabet was accepted by the Academy typography (Trediakovskii 1748, 360; Pekarskii, IA, I, 639–40). Further work in this direction was connected with the ideas Adodurov presented in his note about use of the letters (1737) and in his course on Russian grammar (or orthography only?) which he read in the Academy gymnasium in 1738–40 (see Uspenskii 1975). The active efforts of the 1730's created the basis for all further discussions about Russian orthography (see especially Trediakovskii's *Conversation About Orthography*, 1748; see also Vinokur 1948; Uspenskii 1975).

The process of normalizing morphology was no less active. Scrutiny of the evolution of Trediakovskii's linguistic practice indicates that the variability characteristic of *Voyage to the Island of Love* significantly decreased in the "Ode" of 1734 and the *New and Short Guide* of 1735. The gen. masc. and neut. sg. of adjectives consistently ends in *-аго,* and in nom.-acc. pl. endings it is asserted (and in almost all cases actually practiced) that *-ue* is used in the masc. and *-ия* for fem. and neut. With somewhat less consistency *-ия/-ыя* are used in gen. fem. sg. and *-ый/-ий* in nom.-acc. masc. sg.

We may assume that Trediakovskii followed those norms which Adodurov presented in his *Short Grammar* of 1731 (cf. here *-ий/-ый* is the single variant for nom. and acc. masc. sg. and *-ия/-ыя* for gen. fem. sg.; see Adodurov 1731, 29–30). However, Trediakovskii's normalization in the works cited goes farther than Adodurov and encompasses new areas; for the gen. masc. and neut. sg. Adodurov still gives the variants *-аго/-ова* and the nom. and acc. pl. are not regularized at all (Adodurov 1731, 30). The normalization of nom. and acc. pl. endings may be traced to the rule adopted by the Academy typography in 1733, according to which masc. adjectives end in *-ие/-ые*, and fem. and neut. adjectives in *-ия/-ыя*. Although it remains unclear who was the author of this reform, it was undoubtedly connected with the work of Trediakovskii, Adodurov or Taubert. About the reform Trediakovskii reported that "In 1733 the masculine ending was permanently established, though even today it is not used regularly anywhere except in the Academy" (Lomonosov, IV, notes, 21). The same information can be found in the *Conversation about Orthography*: "today and since 1733 we write and print *-е* for masc. nom. pl. adjectives and *-я,* for fem. and neut... they were always and still are indistinguishable according to the common and simplest usage " (Trediakovskii 1748, 97 and 291; III, 62 and 197).

The innovations in Trediakovskii's practice, as suggested, were intimately related to Adodurov's efforts at normalization, and this gives us cause to consider them indicators of the normalization undertaken by the Academy's philologists. Adodurov's corrections to the *German Grammar* of 1734 are extremely revealing. The use of variant adjectival endings in the 1730 edition was in general chaotic, and Adodurov introduced rather strict order. Thus in the nom.-acc. sg. masc. *-ой* is systematically changed to *-ый* (except when stressed after consonants without soft-hard counterparts; here *-ой* is used consistently). In gen. sg. fem. *-ой* is changed to *-ыя/-ия*. In these cases Adodurov followed the rules he had formulated in his 1731 essay on grammar. (This is also true of his editing of infinitives. Here he changed *-ти* to *-ть;* cf. G. Bauman's note on the normalizing of infinitives in *-ть* in the 1731 essay, contrasted to the use of *-ти* in Weismann's lexicon to which the essay was appended — Baumann 1969, 3.) Adodurov normalized the nom.-acc. pl. in accord with the rule of 1733 (the 1730 edition had *-ые/-ие* in all three genders). For the gen. sg. masc. and neut. Adodurov eliminated the variation between *-аго* and *-ого*, keeping only the former variant (Riazanskaia 1988).

Looking at these changes as a group suggests that the goal was doing away with unmotivated variations. Insofar as variability was not perceived in terms of the opposition between Russian and Church Slavonic, the reformers could select the traditional bookish variant as attested in the Slavonic grammatical tradition. But this, however, was secondary. As the normalization of the nom.-acc. pl. ending, which was not connected with the Slavonic tradition, demonstrates, normalization itself was of importance, while its sources were evidently of lesser concern. What was important was that "the general and simplest usage" be replaced by more refined practice.

However, these were only the first steps toward solving the larger problem of normalization, regularizing particular cases that could be solved *ad hoc* and *ad interim* without working out general principles. The larger problem demanded the elimination of all stylistically unmotivated variability and not only in morphology and orthography, where one could get along with arbitrary prescriptions, but also in syntax and vocabulary, areas in which norms had to arise practically in a vacuum, insofar as linguistic practice as it had developed here was almost completely without order. It was therefore impossible to proceed without guiding principles. Furthermore, asserting such principles meant reconsideration of the entire language, and this could not help but stimulate repeated reconsideration of decisions that had already been made.

Semantics presented no fewer complex problems. The task of sorting through existing linguistic material combined with that of enriching the language's lexicon, as the new culture was creating new objects that needed new names. (Strictly speaking, it was the new names that were to demonstrate the new culture, as the newness of the objects might only be illusory.) This issue was significant for the entire formation of Europeanized Russian culture, starting with the Petrine era (§ I–2.2). In the 1730's this took on a new dimension, connected with the creation of new cultural values, in light of which a romance novel could become a textbook for life, both in terms of behavior and in terms of language (cf. Karlinsky 1963; Lotman 1985). The new secular culture demanded new "secular" names, that is, words not tainted by traditions of church usage that to some degree implied an ideological judgment and which were associated with traditional religious discourse. From the point of view of secular culture the connotations of traditional religious usage were unacceptable. The ecstasy that female beauty inspired of course had its nomenclature in the "church" language, but there it was called lust or lewdness; the usual context in which these words were used clearly indicated that one was dealing with a reprehensible and immoral feeling.

The significance of such connotations had been clearly explained by seventeenth-century linguists. A. Arnauld, whose works were evidently known to Trediakovskii (on his ties with Jansenism, see Uspenskii, 1985,

1. The Formation of Petersburg Culture and the New Conception

131–2; Uspenskii and Shishkin, 1990), wrote in his *Language, or the Art of Thinking* that:

> ...philosophers have not paid enough attention to the incidental ideas which the mind connects to the principal ideas of things. As a result, the same thing can be expressed decently by one sound and indecently by another, if one of these sounds is connected to some other idea that conceals the shame, and if the other, by contrast, presents it to the mind in an immodest manner. Hence the words "adultery," "incest," and "abominable sin" are not shameful, although they represent extremely shameful actions, because they only represent them as covered by a veil of horror which causes them to be viewed simply as crimes. On the other hand, certain words express these actions without the sense of horror, being somewhat pleasant rather than criminal, and even join to them an idea of immodesty and effrontery. These are shameful and indecent words. (Arnault 1668, 131; translation from Arnauld 1996, 69).

Understandably, a book concerning "sweet love" such as Trediakovskii's required just such potentially "shameful and indecent" words, but not those which presumed that the corresponding actions were criminal. True, the young Trediakovskii made an attempt to demonstratively reject the traditional connotations of the word *похоть* ("lust") when he wrote, for example:

> Тамо все то что небо, воздух, земля, воды
> Произвели лучшее людеи для породы.
> В чювствителнои похоти весело играет,
> И в руках любящаго с любовью вздыхает.
>
> (Trediakovskii 1730, 72; cf. also 104, 113 etc.)

(There all that the sky, air, land and water brought forth was the best for the race of men [There one] gaily plays in tender lust and lovingly sighs in the arms of the beloved.)

There is a similar usage in Lomonsosov's first verses. In his translation of Fénélon's ode "Montagnes de qui l'audace," done in 1738–39, he writes:

> О мои коль могут кусты
> Хладны, тихи, дать и густы
> Похоти предел моей.
>
> (Lomonosov, I, 11)

(O how may my bushes, cold, quiet, and thick, put a limit to my lust.)

The phrase in Fénélon is completely neutral: "Bornent mieux tous mes desires" (They better limit all my desires). However, as the further history of the word, in part, shows, this rather shocking approach did not resolve the problem of creating a new literary vocabulary.² The "civil" tongue needed a decisive revitalization and enrichment with new terms for "sweet love," as it did for other spheres of behavior that were alien cultural phenomena in regard to traditional Russian society (later the eighteenth century saw great success in secularizing Slavonicisms — see § IV–2.3). Accordingly, the "civic" tongue, in contrast to "perfectly complete" Western languages, was in the eyes of the Russian European "not only not complete, but to this day not even begun to be enlarged" (Trediakovskii, 1735a, 8; 1935, 328).

The task which lay ahead was titanic, and demanded the combined efforts of many champions of the native word. Addressing the members of the Russian Assembly in 1735, Trediakovskii said:

> However useful this [task may be] for the Russian people, that is, the possible elevation of [our] language, its purity and beauty, and however desirable its perfection; however hard it may seem, it does not frighten me — nor I trust, you, Gentlemen — with its difficulty and burdensomeness. We do not speak here only about the precise translation of recognized authors, new and old... but also about [creating] a good and correct Grammar, in agreement with the usage of the wise and based on their usage. In this [task] I see just as much need as difficulty [of achievement]... [Creating] a complete and sufficient dictionary demands of you, who are capable of laboring, even more strength than that of the legendary Sisyphus... (Trediakovskii 1735a, 6–7; 1935, 327–8).

For all the extreme complexity of fulfilling these tasks (with which the Russian Assembly of course could in no way cope), they were precisely the ones which the new culture proclaimed as crucial, and eighteenth-century linguistic consciousness developed by continually measuring itself against them.

1.2 Classicist Purism and Its Initial Reception

And so the Russian literary language was to become pure and perfected. The questions naturally arose, what is purity and what is perfection? To refine the entire new literary language required clarification of the basic principles of linguistic and stylistic theory. In the mid-eighteenth century the dominant European linguistic doctrine was that of French Classicism, and it was to this that Russian authors turned. Petersburg culture was declaratively

---

² In modern Russian, the word похоть maintained its negative connotations (of lust, carnality, lewdness). (Translator's note)

European, and the new conception of linguistic correctness also necessarily had to be European. In trying to create a European type of literature in Russia, Trediakovskii also tried to create a European literary language, and in both cases French literary and linguistic theory served as the model (cf. Achinger 1970, 16–29). Just as the leading light in literature was Boileau (Pumpianskii 1937, Pumpianskii 1983), so in creating a literary language the guiding influence proved to be the theories of C. F. de Vaugelas and his followers and interpreters (which included the purists of the Académie française; for surveys of these theories, see: Brunot III: 1–65, 152–227; Brunot IV: 2–77; Brunot 1969; Gukovskaia 1957).

The linguistic views of the French Academy had made their way successfully across all of Europe, and the "Russian Europeans" felt obliged to assume the French yoke as well, however onerous it may have been. "More than that," declared Trediakovskii in the Russian Assembly,

> are we the first in Europe to whom this [task] seemed not only difficult but well neigh impossible? There were, there were such [peoples before us], who were not afraid, but thinking of future profit went to work, continued to work, and some of whom finished the task successfully. For example: was it not difficult for the Florentine Academy to conceive the task of purifying their language? Yet they conceived it. It must also have been frightening for the French Academy to undertake the same thing, to make the qualities of their dialect most perfect; yet they undertook it. It must also have seemed impossible, I imagine, for the Leipzig Association to effectively emulate the aforesaid academies, which having begun, achieved success; yet they did emulate them, and have done so successfully. (Trediakovskii 1735a, 12; 1935, 330–1)

Classical and French authors were to serve as the immediate model: "A great number of Roman writers… will help us, in particular Mark Tulius Cicero, clever and sweet with words. And the French Balzacs, Costars, Patrus and many others" (Trediakovskii 1735a: 14; 1935: 331).

Trediakovskii's German colleagues who heard his speech must have found his program understandable and familiar. Societies for improving the language (Sprachgesellschaften) had played a significant role in seventeenth-century German cultural life (Bircher and Ingen 1978) and served as the natural framework within which German members of the Academy perceived the problem of creating a literary language in Russia. Although German literary politics was somewhat different than the French (more stress was put on enriching the lexicon than on stylistic clarity—see Blume 1978), in the first decades of the eighteenth century they came a bit closer, with the rise of the so called "school of reason." In particular, Juncker belonged to this school, and in many respects served as a model for

Trediakovskii, and the president of the Academy, I. A. Korf, who had invited Juncker to Petersburg, also possibly shared its views (see Pumpianskii 1937, Pumpianskii 1983, Keil 1965). The program presented in Trediakovskii's speech to the Russian Assembly was formulated in rather general terms, and in no way contradicted the German precedent (see, for example, the passage cited above about "enlarging" the language, which recalled the German even more than French linguistic programs). In essence, Trediakovskii merely Russianized the scheme for defining good taste in language that Juncker's teacher F.R.L. Canitz had sketched out in his 1727 *Investigation of Good Taste in Poetry and Prose* (*Untersuchung von dem guten Geschmack in der Dicht- und Rede- Kunst*; Pumpianskii 1937, 173), written in the same year that Gottsched founded the "German Assembly" that Trediakovskii cited as a model. Thus there was an example of how to create a literary language close at hand, and there was every reason to expect the support and encouragement of colleagues and administration. The conflicts connected to the role of Russian in the life of the Academy began later, in the 1740's (Bak 1984), but at the founding of the Russian Assembly there was no opposition as regards the language issue.

Nevertheless, the main model remained the French. The plan drawn up for the Russian Academy by Trediakovskii precisely recalled that of the Académie française. As outlined in his speech, the Russian Assembly was to concern itself with creating "a good and correct Grammar, in agreement with the usage of the wise," "a complete and satisfactory dictionary," and "a Rhetoric and Science of Versification" (1735a, 6–7; 1935, 327–28). This was an exact copy of the statues of the Académie française, whose twenty-sixth point declared, "A dictionary, a grammar, a rhetoric and a poetics will be composed under Academy supervision" (Livet, I, 493; Caput, 1, 206).[3]

One needs to keep in mind that the Russian reception of Western linguistic theories in this period was synthetic. In particular, when asserting that the young Trediakovskii assimilated Vaugelas' views, this does not mean that all of his positions precisely conformed to Vaugelas' scheme, or to those of his many followers. The mission of the Russian Europeans was to bring to Petersburg Europe as a whole rather than some particular tendency of European thought. The views of the Russian reformers were thus of necessity eclectic (see Pumpianskii 1941a, 184). One may even suggest that, even within the work of one single author, there could occur a conscious attempt to reproduce opposing positions in order to transfer onto Russian soil the full

---

[3] A formulation close to Trediakovskii's may also be found in Chapelain's project that could have been known to Trediakovskii via Pellison's *History of the French Academy* (Pellison, 1, 35–6).

1. The Formation of Petersburg Culture and the New Conception

breadth of European diversity (cf. Lotman 1985). Hence the issue of whether all of the opinions adopted derived from one specific source or conception did not arise; it was overshadowed by the far more difficult and important question of how to reconcile borrowed ideas with the Russian linguistic and cultural situation, which in many respects were products of a development different from the European.

This aspect of Russia's reception of European linguistic theories is evident in the young Trediakovskii's attitude toward the "Quarrel Between Ancients and Moderns," whose basic issues were undoubtedly familiar to him. This dispute was the main cultural and ideological conflict of Classicist France, and its implications went far beyond the question of the attitude toward the classics and defined the far greater problem of relating reason and tradition, the historical (or pseudo-historical) heritage versus modern reality as the basis for one's perception and worldview (cf. Hazard, 1961, 26–47). Obviously, the dilemmas as formulated in this debate could have direct influence on Russian self-consciousness, including the choice of paths for language-building; debates over criteria for the new language (such as the importance of tradition or the artificiality of normalization) could, in principle, be played out in its terms.

L. B. Pumpianskii suggested that the young Trediakovskii adhered to the position of the moderns, citing both his literary practice and his direct declaration in the "Epistle from Russian Poetry to Apollo" (Pumpianskii 1937, 157–9; 1941b, 217). There Trediakovskii lists the main achievements of French Classicism and proclaims:

> Песен их что может быть лучше и складняе?
> Ей! ни Греция, ни в том мог быть Рим умняе.
> Славны и еще они, но по правде славны,
> Что жены, тот красный пол, были в том исправны,
> Са́пфоб б греческа была в зависти великой,
> Смысл девины Скудери́ есть в стихе коликой;
> Горько плачущей Стихом нежной дела Сю́зы
> Сладостнее никогда быть не может му́зы.

(Trediakovskii 1735, 39; 1963, 392).

(What could be better and better-made than their songs?/Hey! Neither Greece nor Rome could be cleverer in anything./They were also glorious, indeed truly glorious,/That [their] women, the beautiful sex, were practiced in this;/The Greek Sappho would be greatly envious./There is so much sense in the maid Scudery's verse;/ De la Suze, bitterly crying in tender verse,/Could never have a rival for sweetness.)

This directly asserts the superiority of contemporary French poetry over classical, which was, of course, the position of the "moderns."

However, we get another picture if we consider the "Discourse on the Ode in General" that was published in 1734 as an appendix to the "Ode on the Taking of the City of Gdansk"— just a year before the *New and Short Guide* which included the "Epistle to Apollo." The "Discourse" was a reworked version of Boileau's "Discourse on the Ode" (1693), that was directed against Pierrot's "Parallel Between Ancients and Moderns" (cf. Peskov, 1989, 20–21). The very fact that Trediakovskii chose to emulate Boileau's defense of the "ancients" itself puts his adherence to the doctrine of the "moderns" in doubt, and the direct condemnation of the moderns in Trediakovskii's treatise cannot be reconciled with such a position. Indeed, Trediakovskii writes:

> In truth, although some people without taste have disagreed, Pindar, lyric poet in the Greek language, and Horace, of a similar trade in Latin, wrote Odes of such perfection that those desirous of being skillful in this today cannot fail to follow their lead. They alone were able to write so marvelously, that when in order to express their idea as if from without, they purposefully interrupted the continuity of their speech, and in order to enter into an idea (if one may say so, following Boileau), departed from it, with great effort distancing themselves from precise, properly connected sense, in order to squeeze out all of the flavor, all of the juice, or better, the very soul of lyric poetry. (Trediakovskii 1734, l.13 verso)

The latter portion of this passage is a direct translation of Boileau (see Boileau, II, 201–2), while the first part belongs to Trediakovskii himself and consequently expresses his own opinion—condemning the moderns as "people without taste" (in the edition of 1752 these words are eliminated; Trediakovskii 1752, II, 21–2).

Thus Trediakovskii's position on the Quarrel between Ancients and Moderns turns out to be completely contradictory; in one place he is pro moderns, in another pro ancients, and he apparently feels no qualms about this inconsistency. The struggle of opinions going on in the West apparently does not concern him, as European culture appears in some sort of synthetic aspect that eliminates or generalizes the oppositions that are crucially important in the European context. Thus while Boileau juxtaposes Pindar and Horace, connecting them to two different types of poetic speech, in Trediakovskii the opposition disappears and Horace is equivalent to Pindar as model of odic poetry. Boileau consciously juxtaposes the poetics of his "Ode in the Taking of Namur" — as an experiment — to "the prudent enthusiasms (aux sages emportements) of Malherbe" (Boileau, II, 203); Trediakovskii chooses

1. The Formation of Petersburg Culture and the New Conception

Boileau as a model, repeating his statements about poetic ecstasy and describing his poetics, but also states that "There is no little *enthusiasm* in the odes of Mr. *Malherbe*, the great French lyric poet" (Trediakovskii 1734, l. 13 verso). If we assume that the details of the French literary dispute were well known to Trediakovskii, we cannot help but see the conscious choice of a synthesizing approach (see also Zhivov and Uspenskii, 1984, 271–3).

It is appropriate that the same synthesizing approach that we see in the young Trediakovskii and in other contemporary Russian authors was also applied to other European literary and linguistic theories.[4] Questions like the role of scholars ("all reasonable people") in determining "proper usage," the admissibility of borrowings and neologisms, the allowable differences between the poetic language and the "pure" speech of the court (see below § III–2.3), the relative degree of stylistic normalization, syntax and the enrichment of vocabulary were all resolved by Russian authors relative to the linguistic situation and to literary tradition, and moreover, they could employ arguments and formulations from the most varied of Western authorities, often ignoring the polemical context of the given statements. Moreover, we may note that if in the mature period Trediakovskii oriented himself on the rationalist version of French purism (§ III–2.3), this was also not connected to the victory of one group of French authorities over another but to the way in which Western concepts were applied to the needs of the Russian literary and linguistic process.

For all the variety of European theories assimilated to Russia they shared a series of generally accepted principles that were taken for granted, but which were not characteristic of the previous Russian linguistic tradition. As noted earlier, these European ideas created a series of problems for Russian language building. Among these was applying aesthetic criteria to language. It was characteristic that defining Church Slavonic as "hard" and the new literary language as "tender" derived directly from the French opposition between the old, unpolished language of the Baroque and the new French literary language; the Russian "zhestkii" was a calque for the French "dur," the word which French critics used to condemn the outmoded tongue, while "nezhnyi" corresponded primarily to the French "délicat," which defined the

---

[4] One might point to the remarkable fact that, as L. V. Pumpianskii (1937) convincingly demonstrated, in Trediakovskii's "Epistle from Russian Poetry to Apollo" he followed the so-called German "school of reason," both in the choice of authors and in a series of theoretical statements. However, the genres Trediakovskii cites and for which he provides examples (the rondo, sonnet, madrigal) are not characteristic for the "school of reason" but for the very Silesian school which it opposed (see: Freidank 1985, 39). The same eclectic approach marks Sumarokov's "Epistle on Poetry" (Klein 1990, 260–264).

character of the new style (Uspenskii 1985: 80–88).⁵

From France also came the new orientation of the literary language on the conversational usage of the cultural elite. Vaugelas based "good usage" upon "the fashion of speaking by the healthiest part of the Court that conforms to the way of writing of the healthiest writers of the day" (Vaugelas 1647: l.a1 verso). His disciple Buffier preferred to speak of "the most numerous party" (Buffier 1741: 21), and this formula was interpreted with varying nuances by Bouhours, Racan, T. Corneille, and many others (see § III–2.3). However, whatever the variations, the basic notion came from Vaugelas, and it was this idea that Trediakovskii and Adodurov adopted. Concerning the language "which we speak among ourselves" Trediakovskii had written in the foreword to the *Voyage to the Island of Love*. In his speech of 1735 he formulated this directive more specifically, orienting the literary language on "Her Majesty's court, in speech most courteous..., [on] Her most prudent Ministers, and most wise Church Leaders..., [on] the most illustrious and masterful nobility," and, finally, on "our own reasoning concerning it [language], and the accepted usage of all intelligent people" (Trediakovskii 1735: 13; 1935: 331). In 1736 he repeated the French formulation almost word for word in his "Letter of a Certain Russian," where he proposed that grammar be based "on the best usage of the court and clever people" (Trediakovskii 1849: 105; cf. Tomashevskii 1959: 44–5; Uspenskii 1985: 131–34; Signorini 1988. 519–21). In this way the French conception of linguistic purity defined the general direction for normalizing the grammar of the new Russian literary language. It was to be oriented on spoken usage, which could in principle lead to rethinking individual grammatical elements which had earlier been perceived as neutral as far as the opposition between the bookish and non-literary languages.

As far as grammatical normalization, French could give no concrete course of action, only a general orientation. The French model was significantly more influential concerning lexical norms. Indeed, Classicist

---

⁵ The French "doux" (soft, sweet) could also be adduced as source of the Russian "nezhnyi." Thus Théophile de Viau speaks of the "douceur de Malherbe," describing the style of the founder of French Classicism (Viau, II, 12, 39). Desmarets writes of the women of fashion and their "delicate ears, accustomed to the sweetest terms (les plus doux)" serving as "the main authority for usage" (Desmarets 1657, l.e1 verso). Finally, Boileau writes of "these terms... so noble and sweet to the ear" in rejecting Pierrot's criticism of the coarseness and baseness of Homer and Virgil's words (Boileau II, 442).

On the use of "dur" as an epithet characterizing Baroque and its excesses, see Balzac on Heinsius (Balzac 1658, 114); Boileau on Chapelain (Boileau II, 265, 272, 340; III, 219); and Nicole on Ronsard (Nicole 1720, 177, 194). Ronsard himself uses this term to characterize the style of his follower du Monin, speaking about his stylistic excesses (see Brunot 1969, 179–80).

linguistic doctrine put a premium on proper vocabulary; primary attention to lexicon and phraseology and to problems of stylistics was natural in France, where by the middle of the seventeenth century normalization of grammar had been basically achieved. But in Russia, as has been noted, this area was still terra incognita; the brief history of the new literary tongue in the Petrine period had neither put the question on the main agenda nor created the conditions in which it could be solved. Thus it was precisely the adoption of the Classicist doctrine of linguistic purism that gave the primary impetus to normalize lexical and phraseological practice. From the middle of the century these issues increasingly became areas of scholarly interest and served as subjects of constant debate among would-be literary legislators.

In the lexical sphere, Classicist doctrine (purism) based the literary language on the idealized speech of the court: the vocabulary of a work of literature was to emulate the natural quality, lack of constraint, lightness and polish of speech at court. Accordingly, the "pure" language had to be free of dialect (the sign of provincialism), archaisms (the sign of one who is out of fashion), scholarly speech (Latinisms), legal speech ("the language of the courtroom [Palais]"), and low or vulgar words (which would offend against "good taste" and "decorum"). Neither was there place in the "pure" tongue for borrowings or neologisms, which according to the prevailing view hampered ease of perception and introduced barbaric disharmony into perfect French. (The attitude toward borrowings or neologisms could be less harsh, but they could only be permitted in a very limited quantity.) As Nicolas Faret stated in his speech at the Academy, it was necessary to "cleanse the language of the trash that it had accumulated, whether from the mouth of the people, or from the rabble of the courthouse and the impurities of the bar (or lawyers), or from the bad usage of ignorant courtiers, or from the mistreatment by those who corrupt it when writing…" (Caput I, 203). Within the framework of "pure" vocabulary, one could distinguish words of high, middle, and low style (see § III–2.2). Classicist doctrine thus supplied a ready system of rubrics which could separate "pure" from "impure" vocabulary. Russian Europeans merely had to apply this system to the lexical material of their own native tongue.

However, the linguistic situation in Russia at the start of the eighteenth century was radically different from that of France in the mid-seventeenth: in Russia there was neither a tradition of spoken usage at court nor a generally accepted literary tradition, those cardinal supports on which the entire French purist doctrine rested (cf. Martel 1933: 34–5). Fitting the Russian material into the French rubrics was therefore quite an original, creative endeavor, which demanded a radical reworking of the very categories of French theory. Although for the first stage in which the new literary language was being worked out — until the mid-1740's — almost no testimony has been preserved concerning the nature of this process, the fact that the purist system was accepted is quite clear. Its main elements may be reconstructed by means of indirect evidence.

The notion of ***archaisms*** presumes that there is a literary tradition within which definite elements serve to mark "old" works. In the absence (or rejection) of such a tradition, archaisms cannot but be a fiction, since the very institution that defines the aging and obsolescence of words is missing. Nonetheless Trediakovskii speaks of archaisms, indicating that they may only be used in limited situations: "The words *рыцерь, ратоборец, рать, витязь, всадник, богатырь* and the like, which are not nowadays used in prose, may remain in verse" (Trediakovskii 1735, 18; 1963: 379). The words cited themselves testify to the artificial construction of this category: these are not so much outdated vocabulary as outdated medieval historical realia.

A negative attitude toward elements of ***dialect*** may be seen in the criticism of those poets who allow themselves "the great license (vol'nost') which is harmful to our language of using, for example, instead of *из глубины души — з глубины души, мею способ* instead of *имею способ*" (ibid, 20; 380); these constructions are obviously considered ukrainianisms, unacceptable in the new literary language (on Trediakovskii and Adodurov's negative attitude toward Ukrainian bookish pronunciation, see Uspenskii 1975, 83, 90–91).

A negative attitude toward linguistic ***borrowings*** is evidenced by the fact that although contemporary narrative literature used borrowed words extensively (they commonly served as markers of the new cultural orientation), in *Voyage to the Island of Love* "the number of direct lexical barbarisms, Gallicisms in particular, is extremely limited (37 words in all, which include words which were not new even in Petrine times)" (Sorokin 1976, 47; cf. Alekseev 1982, 89, 96–7). In this connection one may also cite Kantemir's "Foreword to the Translation of Justinian's History" (written after 1738), in which he says that he tried to translate "without using foreign words (rechei), which I attempted to avoid as far as possible" (Druzhinin 1887, 198; cf. Veselitskii 1974, 39–42). In his 1736 letter to Trediakovskii, V. V. Tatishchev declared himself against "foreign" (chuzhestrannye) words; curiously, in his opinion, these words are used by "the most self-important secretaries and clerks who know no languages, who take their extreme stupidity as great cleverness and who praise what they should be ashamed of" (Tatishchev 1990, 224). The use of borrowings changes from being something elite and prestigious into something worthy of scorn, according to Tatishchev, characterizing the lowest levels of educated society; this sudden

1. The Formation of Petersburg Culture and the New Conception

change of assessment is an undoubted result of assimilating Classicist purism.

It would seem that for Russian linguistic thought of this period it would be natural to associate the French "la langue du Palais" (language of the law courts) with the **bureaucratic tongue** (prikaznoi iazyk), that would lead to attacks on official words and phrases. However there are no such criticisms, either in Trediakovskii or in other writers of the 1730's, while Tatishchev, as we have seen, accuses them not of employing their own special language but of using borrowed words. This indicates that bureaucratic language did not exist as a discrete norm in the cultural and linguistic consciousness of the period. It is additional evidence that bureaucratic language played no part in the formation of the new literary language, that it had been gradually displaced from its functional sphere by the new literary language and that it had ceased to be felt as a separate tradition (§ I–1.4). This displacement took place as administrative and juridical practice assumed the character of culture building. It thus turned out that the bureaucratic tradition played no role within the new culture, so that there was no correlative to the French language of the courts (which, for all of the negative assessments, still nevertheless had cultural significance).[6]

We should also note that in Trediakosvkii and Adodurov's early works there is no indication of their attitude toward "low," "coarse," or "popular" words. True, in his sketch on orthography of 1738–40, Adodurov describes "folk usage" as a negative characteristic (Uspenskii 1975, 97; cf. 56–7), but he is concerned with spelling and does not connect any concrete linguistic elements with this category. We may conclude that in general the lexical rubric of "popular speech" was not relevant for the work of the first reformers of the Russian language (Trediakovskii, Adodurov, Kantemir). Indeed in the first decades of the eighteenth century, bookish and

---

[6] Notably, nowhere in *Voyage to the Island of Love* does the hero in love use language like "humbly submit" (бить челом) – a phrase that was very clearly connected to bureaucratic practice and fully acceptable in the secular tales that were widespread in the late seventeenth and early eighteenth century (for example, in the "Povest' o Petre Zlatykh Kliuchei [Tale of Peter of the Golden Keys]" — Kuz'mina 1964, 278, 288, 295, 299, and passim). In an analogous way the specifically bureaucratic construction (from the language of the Foreign Office [Posol'skii prikaz]) of a passive participle made from a reflexive verb, like *договоренось*, which was a Polonism (see Isachenko 1975a, 160–1; Zhivov and Uspenskii 1983, 158) appeared in early issues of the academic *Notes to the Gazette* (*Primechanii k vedomostiam*) [...] (e.g., Primechaniia 1728, 8, 10, 12), although it disappeared in later years. In principle, this could be seen as a rejection of the bureaucratic tradition. It seems more likely, however, that the new literature was almost completely isolated from those sources that derived from the language of "popular literature" of the earlier period. This was still another aspect of the opposition between pre- and post-Petrine literary and linguistic development.

Chapter 2. The Start of Normalization of the New Literary Language

popular were relative, mutually supplementary categories, with no neutral space between them (cf. § II–1). In rejecting the bookish tradition, i.e., the Church Slavonic linguistic legacy, the reformers did not leave themselves the possibility of defining any kind of element of the new literary language as popular. Therefore, scholars' references to the abundance of popular or vulgar lexicon in Kantemir's satires, in the *Voyage to the Island of Love* or in Trediakovskii's translations of Italian plays (see Vinogradov 1938, 70–1; Alekseev 1982, 89, 95) suffer from anachronism, as categories are applied to the early eighteenth-century language that only became relevant much later (cf. Kniaz'kova 1974, 20–4).

In the unique cases when these labels were nevertheless used, and not in the sense of "not bookish," "not Church Slavonic," they clearly carried different meanings from those which they bore later, underscoring the impropriety of using the above-mentioned anachronistic categories. Thus Kantemir, in the note to lines 31–2 of the Second Satire («И не сильно принест и мне ни какой польги./Знатны уж предки мои были в царство Ольги»), writes: "*Ни какой польги.* It would have been better to write *ни какой пользи,* but the need for the rhyme persuaded me to use the popular word instead of the pure Russian" (Kantemir, I, 34, 51). "Popular" is actually juxtaposed here not to "Slavonic" but to "the pure Russian," although the "popular" word is in fact a marked dialecticism.

In his "Discourse on the Ode in General," Trediakovskii also tries to transfer to Russian soil the rhetorical scheme of dividing lexical material by high, middle and low styles, corresponding to various literary genres. In Western Europe one of the basic ways in which national literary languages achieved parity with classical languages was by subordinating themselves to this rhetorical scheme (for example, the Ciceronianism of the Venetian Academy in the sixteenth century). Trediakovskii shared this assumption, a case in which direct Western influence could complement that which came indirectly through school rhetorical treatises of Russian origin (see Vomperskii 1970; Lachmann 1982, 53–4; Zhivov 1988c; Vomperskii 1988). According to Trediakovskii's scheme the ode and epic verse are to be written "in speech most extremely poetic, and very high [in style]," love songs were assigned "a speech... often vain and jocular, not rarely peasant or childish," while "stansy" (stanzas) are to be presented "in middle speech, that is, neither very high nor too low, but better taking something from the high than from the low" (Trediakovskii 1734, l.S/4 verso). These stylistic prescriptions have a declarative character, however; what precise lexical parameters Trediakovskii places at the basis of his classification remains unclear, and it is unclear in general whether this scheme is meant to be realized in actual practice. In distinction to Lomonosov's later proposal, this classification is not connected with the juxtaposition of particular lexemes (or, as with the French, with a stable stylistic tradition). Be that as it may, the first Russian treatise on poetry assigns the new literary language the capacity to rhetorically differentiate between styles — that very differentiation which the Academy Dictionary defined for the French language. Defining perfection in terms of the European model emerges as a program for perfecting one's own native tongue.

Thus Russia assimilated the linguistic and stylistic conception of Classicist purism. As a result, linguistic material began to be viewed through the prism of purist prohibitions. This is reflected most obviously in new evaluations of lexicon and phraseology. It undoubtedly also influenced both the stylistic reassessment of syntactic constructions and the normalization of morphology, although on these different linguistic levels the process could not be fully analogous. In particular, if lexical normalization developed almost in a vacuum, the normalization of morphology involved a clash of the new conceptions with a rather well developed grammatical tradition. However, in order to trace these differences we must keep in mind still another aspect of this development and that is the new understanding of the relationship between Church Slavonic and Russian, the language of traditional bookishness and the literary language of the new type.

1.3 The Actualization of Genetic Parameters: Slavonicisms

The assimilation of French linguistic and stylistic conceptions presumed that the Russian linguistic situation was analogous to the French. As seen in Trediakovskii's commentaries to *The Military State of the Ottoman Empire* (see the quotation above, § II–1.1), this presumption was indeed accepted in Russian linguistic thinking (cf. Uspenskii 1985, 105–120). The significance of this juxtaposition was not only that it enabled seeing the new literary language as alive, as opposed to "dead" Church Slavonic, and hence to transfer onto Russian those stylistic principles applied to European (living) literary languages, but also that the basic perception of linguistic material changed. Insofar as the opposition between old and new languages was likened to the relationship of Latin and French (or Italian), the evaluation of linguistic elements came to depend on genetic parameters of the kind with which Latinisms were culled from French or Italian.

In this respect it is indicative that Adodurov and Trediakovskii could apparently identify Church Slavonic as ancestor of the South Slavic languages (see Uspenskii 1985, 105–108). In Trediakovskii's opinion, "The Russian language is not Slavonic: because just as an Italian does not understand when they speak Latin, so too a Slav (Slavianin) when they speak Russian, or a Russian when they speak Slavonic" (Trediakovskii 1737, 16). "Slav" here, by all appearances, signifies one of the southern Slavs, and Trediakovskii, in assigning to them a native (natural) understanding of Church Slavonic, equates the relationship between Church Slavonic and the South Slavic languages to the relationship between two developmental stages of one language (say, English and Old English; an Englishman appears then as one with a "natural understanding" of Old English). This conception may derive from older notions about contrasting recensions of Slavonic, defined in ethnic terms (cf. Tolstoi 1976; Dell'Agata 1986). However, what was earlier seen as local deviation was now perceived as a genetic feature. In these terms, the opposition of Russian and Church Slavonic is fully equated with the opposition between Latin and French; the supranational bookish language is understood as the archaic form of one of its cognate languages.

The perception of Church Slavonic elements in the new literary language followed from this conception. Elements of the language of traditional bookishness now appear as analogues to Latinisms in the French literary tongue. In this way they easily fit into the ready Classicist theoretical rubric of "learned words" and as a result take on stylistic significance (negative, of course). It is precisely in the framework of the purist conception that Slavonicisms assume the status of a special stylistic category, i.e., the genetic characteristic of a linguistic element begins to be seen as a factor that defines its stylistic parameters.

This fundamental change of perspective should be emphasized, as it may be somewhat obscured in our perception by the surface terminological continuity: the bookmen of the sixteenth and seventeenth centuries called the bookish language "Slavonic," Peter spoke of "high Slavonic words," and these same phrases were used by the first codifiers of the new literary language. When in the Petrine period "Slavonic" was used to differentiate it from "the simple" language, this terminological difference referred to a rather concrete linguistic correlative. However, as shown above (§ I–1.3), this juxtaposition was made on the basis of a limited set of markers, and elements not included in this set had no relation to the opposition. The lexical level, as well as a whole series of morphological elements allowed for broad variability that had nothing to do with the opposition of bookish and non-bookish languages. The use of this or that variant was not differentiated, and in particular, did not carry fixed stylistic significance. Therefore, before the 1730's Slavonicisms as a stylistic category did not exist, and its appearance

1. The Formation of Petersburg Culture and the New Conception

as one was a radical theoretical innovation. This relates especially to the level of lexicon.

This does not mean that before the Russians adopted French theories there had not existed any stylistic differentiation of lexicon. Peter's demand that "high Slavonic words" be eliminated and that one use "sayings from the everyday Russian language" (§ I–1.2) referred to definite stylistic and lexical groupings or to the lexical composition of various linguistic registers that to a greater or lesser extent did not coincide. However, as the linguistic practice of those who tried to fulfill Peter's orders unmistakably demonstrates, these groupings did not at all coincide with a division into genetic Russicisms and Slavonicisms. We may assume that for Peter and his contemporaries a different lexical opposition was in effect, not genetic but of a purely functional kind. There existed a distinction between specifically bookish and neutral lexicon that had formed after the Second South Slavic influence as a result of the attempt to differentiate the literary (bookish) language from the spoken (see § 0–4), and served as one of the markers separating the two registers of the bookish tongue, the common and refined variants.

The moving away from the spoken tongue during the period of the Second South Slavic influence had led to the hierarchical organization of the bookish language's registers and to the rethinking of linguistic elements as characteristic of particular registers. Not only grammatical but also lexical elements underwent this stratification. For example, such varying lexemes as чаяти and ждати, успение and смерть could be reconceptualized in terms of an opposition between the specifically bookish and the neutral (cf. Zinovii Otenskii 1863, 961–7; Kovtun 1975, 37; Uspenskii 1987, 192–6). Stylistic oppositions arose in which neutral lexical material was juxtaposed to specifically bookish vocabulary, on the one hand, and specifically non-bookish lexicon, on the other.[7] The formation of a class of specifically bookish

---

[7] As a result of these processes it became possible to carry out stylistic lexical corrections whose goal was making the text more bookish (cf. the editing of a series of sources for inclusion in the *Stepennaia kniga*, for example, the "Ustav" of Prince Vladimir and the "Tale of the Novgorodians' Betrayal" ('Povest' ob izmene novgorodtsev'), listed in chronicles under 1474 — Shchapov 1976, 22–4, 82–4; PSRL, XXI, 530–1; cf. Uspenskii 1987, 248–50). This is the process that F. P. Filin, examining the lexical changes in the language of the chronicles, incorrectly called "Churchslavonicization" (Filin 1949, 28–37), trying to define in genetic terms something that had a purely functional character. These processes became especially marked during "unifying undertakings" of the sixteenth century (the compilation of the *Great Menalogions for Reading*, the *Stepennaia kniga*, etc.) that were connected with the reevaluation of the corpus of traditional bookishness, including its language (cf. Kovtun 1989, 122–3). These things led to an increase in lexicographical work and the appearance of dictionaries which interpreted not only borrowings but also generally accepted bookish words (Kovtun 1963, 216–317; cf. Uspenskii 1987, 56–7). Obviously, the goal of these dictionaries was not only to explain unknown words but also to designate stylistic correlatives, as the translating

vocabulary together with the spread of the grammatical approach were clearly connected to the grammatically refined and normativized bookish language that was forming at this time. While part of its linguistic ideology, this normalizing tendency was reflected in linguistic practice with varying fullness and consistency. Although the goal was differentiating the refined bookish language from Church Slavonic "popular speech," in lexicon this opposition only extended to a limited number of elements which could act in a text as signals of its special bookish status. The lexical opposition formed in this way preserved its importance through the start of the eighteenth century. The rejection of the specifically bookish language and the desire to replace it with the "simple" tongue was realized in the lexical sphere by using neutral rather than specifically bookish elements.

Genetic Slavonicisms belonged to both neutral and specifically bookish vocabulary. Insofar as this was a functional differentiation, the border between them was changeable. As a matter of fact, that which one period could see as specifically literary might be felt by another as neutral, and vice versa. For example, the words *суевѣрь* and *суевѣріе* which as V. V. Vinogradov suggested (1958, 109) came into the literary language with the Second South Slavic influence, by the eighteenth century were apparently no longer perceived as specifically bookish. This changeability of perception led to periodic attempts to recreate specifically bookish vocabulary; new forms to serve as a sign of literary artistry and erudition had to be created to replace old neologisms and borrowings that had already been assimilated by linguistic consciousness.

Attempts of this kind did not arise arbitrarily of themselves but demanded a specific cultural and historical stimulus which emphasized the importance of a particular bookish culture, as opposed to mere elementary literacy. In part, they were a natural consequence of the Grecophile orientation, and a legacy of the period when the problem of finding precise and adequate equivalents with which to translate the well-developed language of Greek patristics had been acute, and had sanctioned the unlimited expansion of specifically bookish lexicon. It was natural then that specifically bookish words came to be associated with a definite cultural position and would take on the role of semiotic markers. The significance of "high Slavonic words" in the battle between adherents of a secular state culture and those who in their eyes were clerics and papists was defined by their connection with this

---

or interpretive purpose of the dictionaries gave way in part to a normalizing function. As L. Kovtun formulates it, the given lexicographical practice reflects the change "from the stage of the functional usage of two languages (Russian and Church Slavonic) to the creation of a system of functional styles for the Russian literary language" (Kovtun 1989, 15).

1. The Formation of Petersburg Culture and the New Conception

cultural stance — with the position of those who defended Orthodox piety and the Helleno-Slavonic school tradition (§ I–2.1). Polikarpov's frequent neologisms of the type *воспутеводствитися* or *проюдолити* (Polikarpov 1701, l. 5) or compound words like *хвалебночинонебесноземнотрїсвятов оспѣваемый* which he proposed in his *Tekhnologiia* of 1725 (GPB, NSRK, F 1921.60, 9) functioned as the same kind of unmistakable semiotic markers of "clerical" sympathies as the "Greek" letters of the Cyrillic alphabet (§ I–1.1). Here too Polikarpov carried on the traditions of the linguistic Grecophilism of Epifanii Slavinetskii and the Chudov monk Evfimii (cf. Strakhova 1986; Strakhova 1988; Strakhova 1990), and this strongly linked refined bookish vocabulary with the cultural and historical position of the clergy in the latter half of the seventeenth century. To the degree that "high Slavonic words" mentioned by Peter related to lexical elements, their removal from the new secular literature became part of the Petrine language policy.

As stated (§ I–1.3), the lexical correction that Sofronii Likhud made to the *General Geography* was based on the opposition between specifically bookish and neutral elements. Especially indicative in this regard are such replacements as *истинѣподобно* → *достовѣрно* (l. 438 verso), *въ мѣстѣхъ блгоразтворенныхъ* → *умѣренныхъ* (l. 647 verso), *общенародство* → *простыи народъ* (l. 821). The editing of those lexical pairs whose stylistic differentiation was specifically connected to the work of the bookmen of the sixteenth and seventeenth centuries (e.g., *истинна* → *правда* [381], *чаютъ* → *ѡжидают* [506]) is also of interest.[8] At the same time one should keep

---

[8] The pair *чаютъ* → *ѡжидают* deserves special commentary. Likhud writes: "Чесо [changed to: чего] ради плаватєлїє [changed to: навигаторы] от присмотренаго облака наипаче, которын влѣднаго нан пречернаго вида єсть, вѣтра от тоя страны себѣ чаютъ [changed to: ѡжидаютъ]" (l. 506). At one time, *чаяти* had been changed to *ждати* by Maksim Grek in the last part of the "Simvol Very" (the creed), which had been criticized by Zinovii Otenskii, who asserted that "Maksim Grek does not know the Russian language well" and that "to put the verb *жду* instead of *чаю* is not [correct] according to bookish speech" (Zinovii Otenskii 1863, 964, 967). Subsequently, Maksim's correction came to be perceived as setting the norm, as he gained the reputation of creator of the bookish language who developed the grammatical approach and who corrected books according to the Greek model. Hence the Grecophiles of the late seventeenth century also accepted it, ignoring the stylistic associations cited by the bookmen of the sixteenth century. Cf. the "Uveshchanie" (Admonition) in the name of Patriarch Adrian, appendix to the "Orthodox Confession of Faith" of 1696, in which Maksim, together with Metropolitan Aleskei and Epifanii Slavinsteskii, is included in the group of "marvelous wise men" who corrected books "according to the character of both languages, Slavonic... and Greek" (Gorskii and Nevostruev, II, 2, 598). Thus Epifanii Slavinsteskii writes in his translation of the Simvol Very: "ѡжидаю востанїѧ мертвыхъ" (Gezen 1884, 126). Even more significant, in the manuscript "Sobor Nikeiskii pervyi vselenskii na chetyri knigi razdelennyi chrez Al'fonsa Pizana" (The First Universal Nicene Council Divided into Four Books by Alphonsus Pisanus), corrected by the monk Evfimii of the Chudov Monastery, we

in mind that the original text did not offer Likhud much material for this kind of correction; in translating the *General Geography,* Polikarpov had only used specifically bookish lexicon occasionally, unlike in his translations of patristic texts or, for example, in his foreword to the *Primer* (Bukvar') of 1701. So the individual cases that were nonetheless subject to correction were all the more significant. Understandably, in texts that were originally written in "simple" tongue specifically bookish language was practically not encountered, which allows us to consider the elimination of this stylistic category of words one of the attendant aspects of rejecting the traditional bookish language.

Thus for the Petrine era the opposition between specifically bookish and neutral lexicon was important — specifically bookish words were precisely those "subtleties of insane bookworms " (premudrosti bezumnykh knigochii) that were to be eliminated by adherents of the new culture. Distinguishing between genetically Russian and Church Slavonic elements had nothing to do with this, as genetic Slavonicisms were an organic part of "simple" lexicon and made up an inseparable part of the legacy which this language inherited from hybrid Church Slavonic (which of course does not eliminate the possibility that some Slavonicisms could also make their way into the spoken language). The very notion of genetic Slavonicisms as a special lexical element arose as result of the search for normalizing criteria for the new literary language, and the application of Classicist purist linguistic categories to Russian material. Slavonicisms were defined as analogous to Latinisms, although their stylistic appraisal did not only reproduce the negative connotations which Latinisms did for French but also absorbed the negative assessment which specifically bookish lexicon had acquired in the framework of Petrine linguistic policy. In this way the negative attitude to the traditional bookish language (Church Slavonic) was transferred onto the lexical level, that is, genetic Slavonicisms had in principle to take the place of specifically bookish words; the opposition between Church Slavonic and Russian is superimposed onto that of bookish and neutral. This led to a series of theoretical and practical difficulties that became a major stimulus to the new literary language's development.

Indeed, before one could struggle against Slavonicisms, one had to define what they were. The Latin-French model inevitably led to the idea of

---

find not only "ѹжидаю востанїѧ мертвыхъ" in the "Simvol Very" but also the correction of чающе to ожидаю in another fragment (GIM, Sin. 544, 1. 7 verso, 86). In Sofronii Likhud's correction the given tradition apparently combines with the task of eliminating specifically bookish lexicon.

1. The Formation of Petersburg Culture and the New Conception

composing parallel dictionaries. However, while Latin-French dictionaries actually did exist, ones that systematically related bookish and non-bookish lexicon did not, and the very idea of its creation was fundamentally alien to the Great Russian linguistic situation as well as unrealizable in practical terms due to the character of specifically bookish lexicon. Here, as noted (see note 7), there only existed dictionaries of specifically bookish lexicon (of "words difficult to comprehend") whose commentaries served more for stylistic purposes than to translate.[9] Translating dictionaries presume that the words of one language may be given the full range of correspondences in the other, but between Church Slavonic and Russian lexicon no such relations had been established. Beyond the issue of the limited number of correlative pairs based on morphonological indicators or those based on word formation, only isolated correlations could be uncovered (of the type глаз — око), while the great mass of lexical material was common to both languages and did not lend itself to division. Nevertheless, attempts to demarcate the class of lexical Slavonicisms and limit their usage were undertaken, clearly testifying to the strong imperative posed by the newly adopted theory.

And so, speaking about poetic license, Trediakovskii defines as such a series of lexical elements which apparently may be generally represented by non-pleophonic forms. He writes: "Poetic liberties (vol'nosti) should be such that, in general, the locution presented as license is quite recognizable as truly Russian, and even more, that it even be one that is sometimes used. For example: one may write брегу instead of берегу; брежно instead of бережно; стрегу instead of стерегу; but to putострожно instead of осторожно is

---

[9] Parallel Church Slavonic — Russian dictionaries existed in Southwestern Russia, whose linguistic situation was fundamentally different from that in Great Russia. Such dictionaries included Zizanii and Berynda's lexicon and, in part, Kopievskii's *Nomenklator*. These dictionaries established a correspondence between Church Slavonic words and those of the "simple tongue" (prostaia mova), and were compiled primarily for translation (although all of them manifest a certain inconsistency and the differentiation of vocabulary is by no means complete). The way these dictionaries were perceived in Great Russia is very revealing. As is well known, Kopievskii's *Nomenklator* was the direct source for the "Short Collection of Nouns" that was part of the *Primer* Polikarpov published in 1701 (see Pekarskii, NL, I, 19–20; Berezina 1980). However, while making use of the *Nomenklator*, Polikarpov changed its function and made a normative and stylistic dictionary out of one designed for translation. Indeed, in Polikarpov neutral elements took the place of "simple" lexemes, and the place of Church Slavonic words were taken by specifically bookish ones [...] (Berezina 1980, 18–9). Thus the differences between the linguistic situations in Great Russia and Southwestern Rus' in the late seventeenth — early eighteenth century determined the dissimilarity of the dictionaries created here. In the Southwest these were dictionaries for translation while in Great Russia, where Church Slavonic education had not declined and there was no need for translations, dictionaries functioned to normalize style. In the Petrine period the basis for this normalization was not the opposition of Church Slavonic and Russian but that between neutral and specifically bookish lexicon.

impossible" (Trediakovskii 1735, 20; 1963, 380). This proviso must have seemed rather strange to an older reader, who (like Trediakovskii himself) had been used to using non-pleophonic forms without thinking, while in the examples cited saw an incomprehensible mix of familiar and unfamiliar forms. This was evidently meant as a kind of declaration, as it embodied for the first time the idea that genetic Russicisms alone were proper for the new literary language, juxtaposing them to genetic Slavonicisms, whose use had to be reserved for special occasions. However distant this declaration was from an actual differentiation of words based on genetic criteria, it presumed the basic possibility of parallel vocabularies possessing different stylistic values.

The presumption may be seen even more clearly in the dictionaries that V. N. Tatishchev compiled. The attempt to juxtapose Slavonicisms and Russicisms led, as one would expect, first of all, to emphasizing well-known morphophonemic and morphological markers which genetically distinguish Russian and Church Slavonic, such as pleophonic versus non-pleophonic forms, *ж/жд* for **dj*, *ч/щ* for **tj*, *o/e* at the start of words, *-ть/-ти* in infinitives, prefixes *-роз-/-раз*, *вы-/из-*, *в-/во-*, etc. Tatishchev demarcated the two forms with the either the label "r." (for Russian) or "sl." (for Slavonic), but even within this framework the juxtaposition was not carried out consistently. Hence while pleophony was often noted, and even artificial oppositions created (of the type *короче/* sl. *краче, оперетися/* sl. *опретися*), we also find *перегородка* opposed to sl. *переделъ* (Aver'ianova 1957, 63, 77, 80; Aver'ianova 1964, 242). Tatishchev was even less consistent in treating other markers. For example, while he distinguishes such pairs as *знать — знати, есть/* sl. *ясти, лить/* sl. *лити*, and so on, infinitives are usually given in the *-ти* form, a form which, moreover, he sometimes gives as being explicitly Russian, as in *греяти/* r. *грети, даяти/* r. *давати, обладѣти/*r. *овладѣти*, and so on (Aver'ianova 1957, 55, 59, 66, 50, 51, 74; Aver'ianova 1964, 102, 123, 166, 80, 84, 223). Together with pairs juxtaposing the prefixes *вы-/из-* we find *изгнанїе/* r. *изгонъ* (Aver'ianova 1957, 59); together with pairs juxtaposing *роз-/раз-* we find *разглагольствовасти/* r. *разговаривати, раздражение/*r. *раздражнение, размерити/* r. *размерять* (Aver'ianova 1964, 338, 340, 343).

These examples lead us to conclude that what was important for Tatishchev was primarily the need to separate Slavonicisms and Russicisms, but that the concrete markers which signaled the opposition did not have independent significance for him. Therefore, when he had succeeded in juxtaposing two lexemes according to one marker or another, all other markers then seemed irrelevant. As a rule, Tatishchev gave prominence to Church Slavonic rather than Russian markers; this indicates that Tatishchev was most likely more accustomed to Church Slavonic, and that he defined Russian forms negatively, as being unlike familiar Slavonic ones. This was in essence the same approach that Likhud had taken in correcting the *General Geography* (§ I–1.3); Tatishchev includes new markers indicating the opposition of Russian and Church Slavonic, but the basic forms for him, as for Likhud, remain those of the bookish language; this indicates the deeper identity between the two men's linguistic conceptions and their common genesis.

The demand to consistently oppose the two languages is also apparent in the fact that Tatishchev tried to interpret all formal linguistic oppositions in terms of Russian versus Church Slavonic without concern either for consistency or for the stylistic uniformity of his directives. Hence, for example, forms with the suffixes *-анie* and *-енie* were often juxtaposed (as Church Slavonic to Russian) to forms with zero suffixes, the suffix *-к-* or *-ота-*, this opposition is treated cf.: *изгнанïе/* r. *изгонъ*; *иканïе*/r. *икота*; *лганïе*/r. *ложь*; *напускъ/* sl. *напусченie*; *плясанïе/* r. *пляска*; *превезенïе/* r. *перевозка*; *раздаянiе/* r. *раздача* (Aver'ianova 1957, 59, 60, 65,71, 81; Aver'ianova 1964, 132, 162, 197, 275, 304, 340). In other instances this marker turns out to be irrelevant as in: *введенïе/* sl. *воведенïе*; *выбиранïе/* sl. *избиранïе; кропленïе/* r. *брызганïе*; *обниманïе/* sl. *объятïе*; *плаканïе/* sl. *плачь*, and so on (Aver'ianova 1957, 44, 47, 64, 74, 81; Aver'ianova 1964, 51, 68, 155, 224, 272). The arbitrariness of Tatishchev's classifications is especially clear in such cases as *здe/* r. *здеся*; *леность/* r. *лень*; *оконце*/r. *окошечко*; *певчïи/* sl. *певецъ*; *пенисто/* r. *пенно*; *превелïй*/r. *превеликий* (Aver'ianova 1957, 58, 66, 76, 80; Aver'ianova 1964, 119, 164, 238, 265, 266, 304). It is clear that while Tatishchev sets out to separate Russian and Church Slavonic lexemes, he is unable to draw any kind of clear dividing line between them.

In this context, even the actual lexical correlatives which Tatishchev puts forward must be seen as an individual attempt to distinguish Slavonicisms and Russicisms in which the lexical material is divided up arbitrarily and inconsistently. The author's labels testify to his complete confusion before the task he had set himself. He relies at times on "etymological" facts (in large part apparently fantastic), at others on individual stylistic notions, and in consequence this results in a collection of heterogeneous oppositions. Indeed it is impossible to see a single principle at work in such pairs as *глазъ/* sl. *око*; *глиста/* sl. *червь*; *длина/* sl. *долгота*; *доброта/* sl. *благость*; *драка/* sl. *битва*; *зола/* sl. *пепелъ*; *мокрота/* sl. *влажность*; *одежда/* r. *риза*; *одолети/* r. *осилети*; and so on (Aver'ianova 1957, 48, 52, 54, 59, 69, 76; Aver'ianova 1964, 73, 89, 95, 124, 181, 235).

Chapter 2. The Start of Normalization of the New Literary Language

Tatishchev's dictionaries eloquently demonstrate how the practical attempt to realize the idea of separating Russian and Church Slavonic vocabulary only produced a conglomerate of heterogeneous pairs which were unable to resolve any questions of literary stylistics.[10] Beneath the newly formulated opposition of Russian and Church Slavonic clearly shows through the traditional oppositions between specifically bookish and neutral vocabulary, on the one hand, and between neutral and specifically unliterary vocabulary, on the other. In deciding on his labels, Tatishchev in some cases substituted the former opposition for the one he wanted, as in the pairs *глупый/* sl. *буй, лакомитися/* sl. *сластолюбствовати, левая/* sl. *шуяя, ножны/* sl. *ножевлагалище, однакожъ/*sl. *обаче* (Aver'ianova 1957, 48, 65, 73, 76); and in other cases the latter one (in this case the unliterary may merge with the dialectal: cf. *доколе/* г. *покуль, ватага/* sl. *обсчество, лазунчик/* sl. *соглядатель, спіонъ* (op. cit., 53, 43, 65). It is quite clear here that the new theoretical directive came into conflict with older linguistic consciousness. The new theory demanded the elimination of Slavonicisms, but what those were remained unclear.

---

[10] A. P. Aver'ianova interprets the label "r." to indicate stylistic neutrality, and "sl." high style, and on this basis concludes that Tatishchev oriented himself on a "neutral style" or "on the speech practice of his contemporaries" and refers to his "sense for language that helped him almost without error to delineate spheres of lexical usage" (Aver'ianova 1964, 12, 16, 18, 19). The material cited above gives no basis for such conclusions (cf. Zamkova 1975, 18–19), and may be completely explained by the irrational bias that publishers feel for the authors they publish. Tatishchev's dictionaries testify precisely to the fact that there existed no stable literary practice on which he could base his work. Literary and linguistic practice preserved the variability that came from hybrid Church Slavonic and attempts to connect the new theoretical principles with this practice ran into the resistance of traditional linguistic consciousness and led to artificial constructions that were marked by the individual thinking of their authors.

In Tatishchev's case, his individual constructions were also influenced by his etymological research which was inspired by the same desire to describe variability in genetic terms (as well as by his historical interests, of course). The creation of lexical pairs connected with the opposition of "Slavonic" and "Russian" were explained by the fact that Russian had assimilated a series of Varangian and Tatar borrowings that took the place of ancient "Slavonic" words preserved in Church Slavonic. Naturally, this kind of etymological consideration only increased the arbitrariness of ascribing lexemes to this or that category, as we find in his dictionaries. [...] For a typical example of his thinking on these issues, see Tatishchev 1979, 96.

1.4 Normalization in Morphology and the Use of Genetic Parameters

An analogous situation existed with grammatical forms, although here the starting situation significantly differed from that with lexicon. If there was practically no experience in normalizing vocabulary, there did exist a distinct tradition of grammatical normalization. The creators of the new literary language could refer, on the one hand, to the Church Slavonic grammatical tradition and the tradition of book editing connected with it; and on the other, to the grammatical descriptions of Russian that were either the fruit of foreigners' curiosity (Ludolf's grammar) or of the first attempts at teaching Russian to foreign pupils (Pastor Glück's grammar, and in part that of Paus).

The Church Slavonic grammatical tradition played a dual role. In the first place, it fixed the grammatical norm of the bookish language and in doing so could serve as starting point for norms of the new literary language; the task of repudiating the traditional bookish language demanded some sense of what was to be repudiated, and Church Slavonic grammars presented this in systematic form. At the same time, and in direct contradiction to this first role, the very same grammatical tradition reflected bookish (literate) practices that did not correspond to the opposition of linguistic codes (cf. § I–1.3), and because of this were carried over into the new type of literary language.

It would seem that the task of repudiation would be very simple in morphology; one could take Smotritskii's grammar, match it up against the Russian spoken language (which corresponded to the orientation on spoken usage) and replace the forms that didn't correspond with those from oral practice. However, this was easier said than done. As is well known, actual spoken language can only be set aside by a native speaker with great difficulty. Those differences between the traditional bookish language and the spoken tongue which were obvious to linguistic consciousness constituted a set of markers of bookishness that had already been rejected in forming the "simple language" of the Petrine era. In actualizing genetic parameters in the 1730's these rejected elements were reconceptualized as "Slavonicisms," but defining them as a special category did not resolve any problems of normalization (insofar as these elements were already gone). If these elements did play any role in the given process, it was very limited. In seeking a genetic differentiation of the new and traditional literary languages, they appeared as a kind of center of gravity for those grammatical "Slavonicisms" which it still remained to locate. To simplify, one could say that in rethinking some particular form as "Slavonic," the creators of the new language assigned it the same status, say, as the forms of the aorist tense that had already been eliminated from it.

But what had to be rethought in this way was not at all obvious. As we have seen, written usage was characterized by broad variability, and separating these variants into "Slavonic" and "Russian" ran into significant difficulties. In orientation on spoken usage the formal problem was defining the correspondence between oral speech and its written form, which led to a heightened interest in spelling and the desire to bring it closer to orthography based on phonetics (see Adodurov's works on orthography — Uspenskii 1975). Significant complexity arose as a result of the fact that the variants of oral origin came into conflict with practices of literate writing, that is, they were mostly perceived not as "Russian" but as "illiterate." In these conditions dividing variants by genetic criterion was at odds with ingrained linguistic thinking.

In this context a second source of normalizing innovations proved to be extremely important for academic philology, and that was the grammatical descriptions of the Russian language compiled by foreigners. The task they set themselves was to describe the language in accord with observed usage. Naturally, they could understand usage in different ways, taking into consideration oral practices and unbookish written texts to various degrees. They could and did make use of Church Slavonic grammars (e.g., that of Smotritskii) as a model. For all this, however, foreign authors did not have the same difficulties in separating Russian and Church Slavonic as did native speakers, with their traditional ways of linguistic thinking. Due to this they were able to qualify a rather large quantity of known variants as Russian or Church Slavonic, which provided the basis for debating various normalizing choices in the 1730's.[11]

Ludolf's grammar, which was available in St. Petersburg (see Winter

---

[11] Features defining the differences between Russian and Church Slavonic could also be defined in terms of the Slavonic grammatical tradition. I have in mind F. Polikarpov's *Tekhnologiia* of 1725, in which are listed the traits that distinguish the "Great Russian dialect" from the "Slavonic" language (RNB, NRSK, F 1921.60; cf. Uspenskii 1994, 110–11). As already stated (§ I–1.3), such traits included first of all markers of bookishness (simple preterits, the vocative, dual numbers), but also features that did not correspond to the traditional bookish-nonbookish opposition, as, for example, the alternation of velars with sibilants in the declension of nouns, the use of second genitive, and the use of the ending –*oŭ* in nom. sg. fem. adjectives. Apparently, academic philologists of the 1730's were not familiar with Polikarpov's work and so did not experience its influence. Whether foreign descriptions of Russian (like Ludolf's grammar) were known to and influenced Polikarpov remains an open question.

1. The Formation of Petersburg Culture and the New Conception

1958, 758–62) and most likely known to the academic philologists (Shvanvits, Adodurov, Trediakovskii), presented an extensive list of differences between Russian and Church Slavonic. Although Ludolf did not intend on giving an exhaustive description of differences, his list is rather far-reaching and includes the forms of the preterit tense, differences in nominal inflexion (the alternation of velars and sibilants in Slavonic as opposed to in Russian, *-го/-во* in gen. sg. masc. and neut.), lexical and morphological characteristics (pleophony, *ч* instead of *щ*, *о* instead of *е* at the start of words), and a series of strictly lexical oppositions, cf.:

> An "a" in Slavonic following two consonants changes into two "o's." Slav. *глава*, head, Russian *голова*... A Slavonic "e" always becomes "o" in Russian. Slav. *единъ,* one, Russ. *одинъ*... In Slavonic declensions the consonant of the nominative case changes in several cases, but in Russian remains, for example, *рука*, hand, in dat. and prep. sg. becomes *руцѣ*, in Russian *рукѣ*. Similarly, in Slavonic declension of nouns *з* sometimes changes to *з* and *ж*, *х* to *с*. correctThe Slavonic *щ* often changes to *ч* in Russian, Slav., *нощь*, Rus. *ночь*. In Slavonic adjectives the genitive singular masculine and neuter is *-го* but *–во* in Russian. In Slavonic verbs the past tense ends in *х* while Russian verbs end in *л*, *любихъ*, I loved, *любилъ*. Sometimes the words are entirely different, Slav. *глаголю, реклъ, днѧсъ, выну, истина, туне*... Russ. *говорю, сказалъ, севодни, всегда, вселди, правда, даромъ.* (Ludolf 1696, 4–5).

Ludolf's list was exactly reproduced in Sohier in a section on differences between Russian and Church Slavonic (Sohier, I, 30–3), although in the text of Sohier's grammar one more difference was added concerning infinitive endings in *-ти* versus *-ть*. However, this innovation is not significant for us, insofar as Sohier's work was not known in Petersburg and so could not have influenced the academic tradition there. That is not the case with Pastor Glück's grammar of 1704 (see the edition of 1994, Glück 1994). It is not very probable that the academic philologists knew of it, but J. W. Paus unquestionably did, and his work served as connection between them and Glück. In his description of the Russian language, Glück used Smotritskii's grammar, in a series of cases revising him, but in others following his lead (Gliuk 1994, 54–61, 77–86), but at the same time ignoring Ludolf, if he knew of his work at all. As a rule, Glück eliminated marked Slavonicisms (marks of bookishness) from his grammatical materials, and in many cases offered normalizing choices that contrast the Russian norm to the Church Slavonic (for example, for nouns in plural oblique cases the endings *-ам, -ами, -ахъ* are unified [loc. cit., 74–6]), although one cannot discern any consistent juxtaposition of the two languages. The differences between them are explicitly mentioned in three cases. It is mentioned that the dual number is more used in Slavonic than Russian (loc. cit., 238), and the Russian and Slavonic forms of acc. sg. and nom. pl. fem. are juxtaposed «нш҃и» Sl. «н҃шга» (ibid, 252 and 261). Glück's grammar was meant for use in teaching Russian in the school he organized and thus had a "synthetic" character, combining material from the traditional bookish and non-bookish languages. In this his grammar radically differed from that of Ludolf.

Indeed, Ludolf, describing the Russian language and the Russian linguistic situation from the position of an external observer, and in no way trying to resolve problems of normalization (which in his time had not yet begun to be formulated), distinguished between Russian and Church Slavonic in a rather consistent manner, proceeding from what was a natural model for him of bilingualism, and based on spoken usage and on written texts such as the Law Code (Ulozhenie) of 1649 (although in his opinion, in this work "some constructions follow Slavonic grammar rather than the common way of speaking" [constructiones nonnullae Slavonicam Grammaticam potius quam communem modum loquendi sequantur] — Ludolf 1696, A2). At the same time Ludolf considered that in Russians' opinion, "Russian is the spoken language and Slavonic the written" (loquendum est Russice & scribendum est Slavonice)" (ibid). Glück intended his description of Russian to help students master it in its various manifestations, and at the same time, like any author of a language textbook who presumes his description has a normative character, proceeded from a different conception of usage and grammatical description. He evidently connected the use of Russian with a significantly larger circle of texts than Ludolf, and derived his normative observations from this view of polyfunctional usage (he evidently made use here of the experience he gained in translating the Bible into Russian; this translation has not survived, but undoubtedly a significant number of "Slavonic" elements were present there). Hence arose a certain synthesis of Slavonic and Russian material. Given this framework, the genetic differentiation of Russian and Church Slavonic elements was not very relevant, and not presented with the kind of consistency that may be seen in Ludolf and Sohier.[12]

---

[12] To this synthesizing trend in the grammatical tradition also belong the anonymous grammar tables printed in Kopievich's script (Ďurovič and Sjöberg 1987). In the opinion of their publishers, these tables appeared in 1706–7 and contain many remarkable innovations that were assimilated by the later grammatical tradition; their language "offers a synthesis of some elements of Church Slavonic... and several elements described by Ludolf" (ibid, 266). According to Ďurovič, this synthesizing attempt at codification served as the basis for I. S. Gorlitskii and his *Grammaire Francoise et Russe* of 1730 (Ďurovič 1995), for Adodurov's *Anfangs-Gründe der Rußischen Sprache* of 1731(Ďurovič and Sjöberg 1987; Ďurovič 1992), and defined all further work by Russian philologists, as well as J. C. Stahl's *Rudimente Linguae Russicae* of 1745. The proposed dating raises major doubts insofar as the compiler of the tables could not be Kopievich himself and no other possible candidates seem to be available

1. The Formation of Petersburg Culture and the New Conception

The project begun by Glück was continued, with significant innovations, by his colleague in the Moscow school, J. W. Paus. Like Glück, Paus made use of a broad spectrum of texts, both traditional bookish and non-bookish ones. It was just this broad conception of usage that inspired his synthetic view of Russian and Church Slavonic that was reflected in the title of his textbook — *Grammatica Slavono-Russica* (cf. Winter 1958, 758).[13] Paus suggested that Slavonic and Russian form a unique unity, so that "the two languages may well be considered brother and sister languages" (Biblioteka Akademii nauk, Sobr. Inostrannykh rukopisei, Q 192, l. 3 verso). His grammar, finished in 1729, was meant to teach both languages simultaneously. In his "Observations," sent to the Academy of Sciences in 1732, he wrote: "The two languages, Slavonic and Russian, the first of which has dominated religious and church topics from time immemorial, and the other now in our times used in state and military affairs for secular and public purposes,... live together in peace like brother and sister in this small book [i.e., his grammar]" (Winter 1858, 759). He based his view that Slavonic had to be studied together with Russian on the idea that without it church books would remain incomprehensible as well as texts dealing with "high and spiritual questions" and scholarly and historical works (BAN, Q 192, l. 3). On the same note Paus remarks that in the "Slaviano-Russian" language

---

at that time. There are no traces of this work in Paus' grammar, although he would have been familiar with it had it been available in Petersburg. B. A. Uspenskii's hypothesis seems more probable, that the tables which L. Ďurovič and A. Sjöberg found were printed in Halle (where Kopievich's type was ultimately available) not long before Stahl's grammar appeared, that is, in the early 1740's (Uspenskii's proposal that Shtal was the author seems difficult to prove). In this case, the relationship between the anonymous tables and the grammars of Gorlitskii and Adodurov is reversed: the tables were compiled on the basis of Adodurov's work of 1731, possibly with some additional material from Gorlitskii. These could then have been reworked by Stahl in his *Rudimenta*, for which he again employed Adodurov as a guide. Curiously, Stahl's work, like that of Glück, was connected with the task of translating the Bible "into the popular Russian language in its civic dialect" (lingua Russica populari, dialect quidem civili, Ďurovič 1994, 193), which could have motivated the use of Church Slavonic elements.

[13] Paus' grammar remained unpublished. Paus submitted it to the Academy of Sciences on Dec. 10, 1729, with a request to copy it and return the original (Materialy AN, I, 592). It is not clear if a full clean copy was made; the Archive of the Academy of Sciences contains only the first pages of the clean copy (Razriad III, no. 332), but the Academy refused to publish the grammar. After Paus' death in 1735 a draft manuscript of the grammar ended up in the Academy library, where it still remains (Biblioteka Akademii Nauk, Sobranie inostrannykh rukopisei, Q 192). D. E. Mikhal'chi undertook publication of this manuscript in the 1960's but this did not take place. He produced a series of articles on it (Mikhal'chi 1964; Mikhal'chi 1968; Mikhal'chi 1969) and his doctoral dissertation, "Slaviano-russkaia grammatika Ioganna Vernera Pause" (Mikhal'chi 1969a). Paus' manuscript is very hard to read, and so Mikhal'chi's publications contain numerous indecipherable words, incorrect readings, and misplaced additions and notes. Nevertheless, all of my citations of Paus' text are to this manuscript, as reproduced in Mikhal'chi's publications.

Chapter 2. The Start of Normalization of the New Literary Language

people speak, read and write books, manuscript compositions and laws. The simple folk use many religious formulas in their speech that derive from the Bible, and therefore are in Slavonic (ibid, l. 5).

For Paus, unlike Glück, the synthetic approach made it important to find those markers which distinguished the two languages insofar as the descriptive model that he chose presupposed determining a common basis for Russian and Slavonic, supplemented by indicating all of the differences between the two languages. Because of this genetic characteristics acquired primary importance for him and he collected all of the relevant information that he could. He reiterated Ludolf's data with numerous additions and some corrections (ibid, l. 22 verso — 24), and at the end of his list notes that the differences of Russian and Church Slavonic in the "accidents" (i.e., in grammatical markers) are seen in the examination of the parts of speech. And indeed, differences between Russian and Church Slavonic are regularly mentioned in every section of his morphological description of the "Slaviano-Russian" language. Thus in describing the categories of nouns it says that Slavonic constantly uses the dual form whereas in Russian its use is limited to word combinations in which the noun agrees with the numerals *два, двѣ* (l. 42, 44) as well as *три, четыре;* Paus follows Ludolf here (Ludol'f 1696, 12–3). The formation of the superlative degree in Slavonic is described as adding *ѣй* or *ай* to the comparative (both the idea and the example coincide with Ludolf — 1969, 20); while Russian instead uses the "pronoun" *само,* the word *всѣхъ,* or the diminutive.

In describing noun declensions Paus makes many comments on the differences between Slavonic and Russian. Following Ludolf he shows that in Russian as opposed to Slavonic the vocative coincides with the nominative, not only in the plural but in the singular, apart from the words *Господи, Боже* and other "sacred" (sacris) names, connected with religion (ll. 44, 45 verso, 48 verso). It is noted that for animate masc. nouns the accusative and genitive are the same, and that while for the singular this is the general norm, this is not always the case for Slavonic in the plural (l. 48). It says (again following Ludolf) that in Slavonic, as opposed to Russian, in nouns ending in *г, к,* and *х* in many cases (prep. sg., nom., voc., prep pl.) these letters change into *з, ц,* and *с* (l. 48 verso). In certain paradigms (both Russian and Slavonic) a whole series of concrete inflexions are juxtaposed. In particular, these include several endings in the paradigm of the word *судія* (in Russian, -ѣ in the dat. sg.,, as opposed to -*и* in the Slavonic — l. 47), the ending -*амъ* in the dat. pl. *o*-declension in masc. nouns, as opposed to the Slavonic -*омъ,* the ending -*ахъ* in prep. pl. as opposed to the Slavonic -*ехъ* and -*ѣхъ* (l. 49), the Slavonic gen. sg. -*e* and nom. pl. -*ie* (*дне, днie*) as opposed to the Russian -*я, -и* (*дня, дни*) in masc. *i*-declension nouns (l. 55). It is stated that in Slavonic the collective *господіе* from *господинъ* is in Russian *господи* or (according to usage) *господа* (l. 56), and Paus adds that "in Slav[onic] *господь* can be said also about people, see John 12: 21" (ibid). As equivalent of the Slavonic forms *вравіи* (sic) and *мравіи* Paus offers the Russian *воровей* and *моравей* (l. 57); the latter example is evidently from Ludolf (1696, 18) but the opposition belongs to Paus. The Slavonic declension of paradigms in -*ер*- (*матерь, мати, дщи*) is juxtaposed to the Russian *мать, дочь,* and in these nouns where the Slavonic gen. sg. ending is -*е*, the Russian often has -*u*, while where the Slavonic dat. sg. has -*u* the Russian has -*ѣ* (l. 59).

Differences in adjective declensions are defined no less carefully, although it is noted that despite them the similarities are quite numerous, so that it is possible to mark the Slavonic variants by the letter *S* and the Russian variants by *R* in the framework of one paradigm (l. 60). For adjectives the marker of presence/absence of the alternation of velars with sibilants and hushers is also indicated (l. 60). An alternation with sibilants is also noted in prep. sg., nom., voc. and prep. pl. of masc. adjectives, in prep. sg. of fem. and neut. adjectives; and in voc. masc. sg. velars alternate with sibilants. Endings that distinguish Russian and Slavonic include: gen. and acc. sg. masc. (and neut.) in *огw, ово, ова* (л. 60) versus the Slavonic -*аго* (l. 61); the gen. sg. fem. -*ой, -ей* as well as -*ые*, which is juxtaposed to the Slavonic -*ыя/-ия*. It is noted that in Russian in the nom.-acc. pl. neut. the ending -*ие* or -*ые* is often used (l. 60 verso), while in the paradigm of the adjective *добрый* the ending -*ая* is cited (l. 61–61 verso). In the paradigm of the adjective *добрый* the ending -*ой* is given for the nom. sg. masc. with the note "R" (Russian), and "S" (Slavonic) for the ending -*ый*. For the majority of these variants Paus defines the genetic oppositions for the first time; in certain cases he may have arrived at his conclusions by juxtaposing the paradigms in Smotritskii and Glück, although many of his interpretations are completely original.

A large number of oppositions are also cited: for numerals (for example, in the paradigm of *единъ* both full and short forms are given in oblique cases, while for *одинъ* only full forms [l. 62 verso]); for pronouns, moreover both in listing the basic forms (*азъ — я, кто — хто, той — тотъ, кій — кой, иже — которои, чій — чей, кіиждо — каждой* — l. 91–91 verso, 94 verso) and in inflexional paradigms (for example, the Slavonic enclitic forms *ми, мя, ти, тя, си, ся* are opposed to the Russian *мнѣ, меня, тебѣ, тебя, себѣ, себя*); in the paradigm of the pronoun *той* the nom. pl. for the three genders of the Slavonic are given as *тіи* and *ти, тія* and *ти, тая* and *та,* which are juxtaposed to the Russian *тѣ* for all three (l. 94); for adverbs (here Russian adverbs in *о* are juxtaposed to Slavonic ones in ѣ — l. 143; several dozen lexical pairs are cited; and for conjunctions and prepositions several oppositions are also noted (l. 148–50).

Naturally, the greatest contrast between Slavonic and Russian is seen in describing verbs, in whose paradigms are concentrated the basic markers of bookishness. In the "Observations" of 1732 Paus had even written that "one must omit the endings of Slavonic preterits and indefinites so that there is less difference between the two" (Winter 1958, 759). Paus indicates that in the preterit "the Slav[onic] *x* changes to лъ, fem. ла, neut. ло, which applies to all persons" (l. 104). In a special annotation (l. 104), it is noted that in the present and future tenses the Slavonic 2nd pers. sg. endings *-еши, -иши* correspond to the Russian *-ешь, -ишь*, and that the same change (*и* to *ь*) occurs in the infinitive. Following Ludolf, Paus introduces into the Russian verbal paradigm the compound future with the auxiliary verbs *стану* or *буду,* and like Glück (and unlike Ludolf) it appears together with the simple future (formed by means of "addition" or augmentation — l. 103 verso).

Paus' innovations played a very significant role in normalizing morphological variants and in establishing the repertoire of Russian — Slavonic oppositions for the academic tradition of the 1730's. His grammar was known to Shvanvits and Adodurov, probably to Trediakovskii, and perhaps also to Lomonosov (Zhivov and Keipert 1996).

Although Adodurov as well as Shvanvits did not get along with Paus, they made use of his work in many ways. Their enmity was not only due to personal issues, but also to divergent theoretical orientations. Paus, as we have seen, regarded Russian and Church Slavonic as a unique unity, while Shvanvits and Adodurov adhered to the Petrine cultural doctrine that saw them as different, demanded their partition, and declared Russian self-sufficient. Paus' synthetic approach freed him in defining as Slavonic quite divergent morphological elements, a characterization that allowed him to create a certain systematization of variants within the Slaveno-Russian language. Adodurov's position was much more difficult. In his short grammatical treatise of 1731 he formulated the principle according to which all Slavonic forms (actually, he was only speaking of declensions) had to be eliminated from the new literary language and replaced by "natural" elements. Speaking of the groundless partiality of "lovers of Slavonic expressions" (in whose number he probably included Paus), Adodurov formulated his position:

> Now modern people exclude all Slavonicisms from the Russian language, [Slavonic] declensional forms first of all, the sound of which is perceived as detestable, so that they cannot be blamed if they prefer to follow the natural way of declining. (Adodurov 1731, 26; cf. § II–1.1)

1. The Formation of Petersburg Culture and the New Conception

Therefore, having qualified this or that element as Slavonic, Adodurov had to prohibit its presence in the new literary language. Because of this he had to balance between the desire to differentiate between Church Slavonic and Russian, on the one hand, and the acceptability of breaking with accepted literate practices that this might cause on the other.

The need to compromise led to Adodurov defining as Slavonicisms a significantly smaller number of elements than Paus, including in this group primarily those forms that he had no regrets about eliminating. His dependence on Paus, however, is quite distinct. The most indicative of this are those passages in which Adodurov discusses the Russian — Church Slavonic opposition, whether or not he agrees with Paus' interpretation. Notably, Adodurov was definitely familiar with Ludolf's grammar, but it is not likely that he had access to Glück's, and there is no evidence that Polikarpov's list of differences between "Slavonic" and "the Great Russian dialect" served as a source for either of them. Hence the tradition that Adodurov was responding to was that of Ludolf and Paus. We should keep in mind that in describing Russian grammar there was no need to mention the Church Slavonic nature of this or that element, and one could simply have said nothing about this issue. This is the case with Groening's grammar, whose section on morphology is a reworking of Adodurov's treatise (or of Shvanvits' grammar; on the relation between them, see Unbegaun 1969, XII–XIV; Uspenskii 1975, 27–44; Baumann 1980; Keipert 1988a; Zhivov 1992a, 266–7), and which omits any discussion of this opposition (Groening 1750, 77, 80, 82.)

[A detailed analysis of Adodurov's views of Slavonicisms, with reference to what he took or modified from Paus, is omitted.] Many elements that had been marked as Slavonic by Paus made their way into Adodurov's grammar without any special mention. However, Adodurov was unable to follow Paus all the way because in that case he would have had to get rid of elements that he considered normative, obligatory for the new literary language if the notion of literacy was to preserve any meaning. Thus in the declension of adjectives the variants *добраго* and *доброво* are given for the gen.-acc. sg. masc. and neut. (Brien 1983, 30), i.e., the ending *-аго* is not interpreted as a Slavonicism as it is by Paus. In the gen. sg. fem. Adodurov gives the ending *-ыя* which Paus defines as Slavonic. In the nom. sg. masc. Adodurov has the form *добрый*, while Paus gives *доброи* as the specially Russian variant. Adodurov indicates that in place of the numeral *одинъ*, *единъ* is also used, and in oblique cases is declined like adjectives in *-ый* (ibid, 32); Adodurov thus refuses to juxtapose *одинъ* and *единъ* as Russian and Slavonic, but at the same time follows Paus, for whom the short forms of the numeral *единъ* in oblique cases are a peculiarity of Slavonic. For the numerals *семь* and *восемь* Adodurov also makes provisions for the variants *седмь* and *осмь*, which he, unlike Paus, does not distinguish by language (Russian and Slavonic). In the section on pronouns, Adodurov excludes the form *хто* which Paus gives as the Russian correlate of the Slavonic *кто*. We may conclude that in all of these cases Adodurov decided to ignore the Russian-Slavonic opposition and to normalize the forms that correspond to the written, bookish tradition.

And so the academic philologists of the 1730's proceeded from a starting point that differed from Paus and demanded the purist elimination of Slavonic elements from what they asserted was "self-sufficient" Russian. Their stance actualized the genetic parameters that distinguished Russian from Church Slavonic and determined their sharply negative view of Paus' synthetic approach. At the same time, the tasks of normalization of the new literary language limited the possibilities of "cleansing" "hard" Slavinicisms from it. As a result Adodurov produced a very heterogeneous inventory of Slavonicisms, another indication that the theoretical task which the author posed for himself created a conflict between the material analyzed and established linguistic consciousness.

In his list appear first of all a series of elements which are very familiar from the evidence of those corrected texts that revised hybrid Church Slavonic into the "simple" language (§ I–1.3). The old markers of bookishness were defined as Slavonicisms, that is, genetic differentiation here simply followed the traditional functional one. This is the case with comparatives, dual number, and vocative. The connection between genetic differentiation and traditional markers of bookishness is quite clear here, and is underscored by the already noted circumstance that in describing Russian grammar there was no need to pay attention to things that had nothing to do with Russian per se

The unrealizability of the purist program is also seen in the fact that while particular elements were defined as "Slavonic" there was nevertheless no question of getting rid of them. These include "irregular" word forms based on *матер-* and *дочер-* (Adodurov 1731, 23) as well as forms of the singular like *Господь*; they were preserved apparently because there was nothing to replace them with, and attempts to make exceptions contradicted blanket declarations about the exclusion of all Slavonicisms [...]. Adodurov excluded 2nd pers. sg. present and future forms in *-ши* and infinitives in *-ти,* but then almost immediately, as if fearing excess scruple, declares that occasionally they may be allowed, as in verse. [...] No less telling is the explanation that accompanies the codification of the pair *одинъ — единъ:*

1. The Formation of Petersburg Culture and the New Conception

"*Единъ, едина, едино* is used instead of *одинъ* and in oblique cases is declined like adjectives in *ый*" (Adodurov 1731, 32; the same formula is repeated in Groening's grammar — Groening 1750, 114).

And so, as before, multiple linguistic variants persisted, and the introduction of genetic parameters didn't lead to stylistic differentiation. The unregulated intermingling of variants remained a characteristic feature of the new literary language, and this allowed for continuity with the older grammatical tradition, insofar as removal of its forms (like the nom. sg. ending -*ый* or the gen.-acc. sg.-*аго*) would have necessarily led to a sharp break. The issue of genetic parameters acquired more of a symbolic than practical character.

It appears that the same thing is true of Trediakovskii's classification of grammatical elements in the *New and Short Guide*. If we accept that in granting exceptions for poetic license Trediakovskii was legitimizing Slavonicisms in the poetic language that remained beyond the norm in his general theoretical framework (see below, § II–2.1; and Uspenskii 1985, 89–90), then in this case as well the procedure also appears arbitrary and does not solve the problem of stylistic differentiation. It appears that at this time Trediakovskii and Adodurov were working on their theories in close cooperation, and that Trediakovskii's indication of grammatical elements needing special defense is but a repetition of Adodurov's provisions as applied to the needs of versification (see above on the exclusion of infinitives and 2nd pers. sg. present and future forms).

Later, however, in the 1740's, genetic parameters were applied to morphological elements with much greater consistency, so that the oppositions of Paus' inventory that had been ignored by Adodurov again became relevant. In this were possibly felt those attempts to differentiate Russian from Church Slavonic that related to the lexical level. The search for oppositions that drove Tatishchev to see a combination of Russian and Slavonic in almost every related pair had to lead on the morphological level to the genetic juxtaposition of coexisting variants, with "Slavonic" applied to the one that earlier had remained outside of the norm. We should note, however, that these attempts were not part of a complete codification of the literary language and therefore permitted a freer attitude toward the grammatical tradition. In this process the extension of genetic oppositions to the variability of adjectival declension was a fundamental innovation. Adjectival declension was a morphological subsystem whose variability permeated the "simple" language and appeared as a constant, not occasional, feature of written texts in this language; at the same time, in this subsystem the grammatical tradition was clearly established in opposition to variants based on spoken usage. It was precisely this, as we have seen, that motivated Adodurov to retain traditional forms in his grammatical treatise. Insofar as potential Slavonicisms were supported here by the grammatical tradition, applying genetic parameters to this material ran into significant difficulties, and this was an important aspect of the innovation.

For the first time after Paus and most likely independent of him this innovation reappeared in Antiokh Kantemir's "Letter of Khariton Makentin" (in the chapter on poetic license—see below, § II–2.1). This special point is entitled "Slavonic endings are permitted in adjectives," and states that "With no less confidence one should use all of the Slavonic endings of adjectives in place of the Russian ones; thus *сладкій* is a good replacement for *сладкой* and *изрядный* for *изрядной*" (Kantemir 1744, 22/II, 18–19). Characterizing the ending *-ій/-ый* as "Slavonic" and *-ой* as "Russian," Kantemir at the same time speaks of "all" the variant inflexions of the adjectival paradigm, that is, the differentiation he offers is presented as a general principle. At the same time, according to his overall theoretical position in the given period the "Russian" variant is basic and the "Slavonic" the supplemental one, permissible in poetic speech. Insofar as such an interpretation contradicted both the grammatical tradition and linguistic practice that had become established by that time, it led to reconsideration of previously established norms.

Lomonosov followed in Kantemir's footsteps. In his comments on Trediakovskii's treatise on plural adjective endings (1746), he writes: "The Slavonic language differs from the Great Russian in nothing so much as grammatical endings. For example, in Slavonic, singular adjectives masculine nominative cases are in *ый* and *ій*, [as in] *богатый, старшій, синій*; while in Great Russian they end in *ой* and *ей*, [as in] *богатой, старшей, синей*. In Slavonic, *сыновóмъ, дѣлóмъ, рýцѣ, менé, пихомъ, кланяхуся;* in Great Russian *сыновьямъ, дѣламъ, рýки, меня, (мы) пили, (они) кланялись*. In the same way Slavonic masculine plural adjectives in the nominative case differ from the Great Russian" (Lomonosov IV, 1; VII², 83). Especially noteworthy in this passage is the fact that within the framework of a single genetic opposition of "Slavonic" and "Great Russian" are also considered those markers which in the previous system signaled bookishness (simple preterites) as well as those variants which did not correlate to the bookish — non-bookish opposition, and moreover among the latter group there was no distinction between those which the contemporary norm confidently accepted as the "Russian" variant (*дѣламъ* rather than *дѣлóмъ*) and those where variability remained or the choice was made in favor of the traditional grammatical norm (the endings of nom. sg. masc.).[14] Thus here genetic differentiation was carried out in a most radical fashion (on the young Lomonsosov's radicalism, see Uspenskii 1985, 88–9). For Lomonosov, all "Slavonic" endings were united in their divergence from spoken usage, the criterion which emerges as the single important one. In principle such a radical differentiation should have required a sharp change in language practice as well: if all "Slavonic" endings were just as foreign to the new literary language as the forms of the imperfect that had been eliminated from the very beginning, then they too all had to share the same fate and be purged.

Such radical changes do not occur, either in the literary language in general, or in Lomonosov's own language (see below, § II–1.2). However, the juxtaposition of morphological elements according to genetic parameters does not turn out to be a mere fancy, one that plays lip service to European linguistic theories but does not influence actual practice. The new understanding of relations between morphological elements did not inevitably lead to the abolition of the "Slavonic", although in one way or another it did help legitimize the "Russian" variant, and moreover, this legitimization could take place in opposition to that normalizing tendency that derived from the grammatical tradition, and that was still very actual in the 1730's (§ II–1.1). It is indicative in this case that in the 1745 edition of Shvanvits' *German Grammar* in nom. sg. masc. adjectival endings in *-ый/-ий* are corrected to *-ой* in many cases, where in the edition of 1734 the opposite case was true (Riazanskaia 1988). This reevaluation was apparently conditioned by the fact that many contemporary Russian authors preserved the *-ой* variant.

Thus the introduction of genetic parameters into Russian linguistic and stylistic theory, based on Classicist purist principles, led to a new understanding of the variant forms that coexisted in the language on various linguistic levels. The first attempts to apply these parameters to the concrete material of the language within the framework of the theory did not lead to a consistent classification of variants either in lexicon or morphology and had more of a symbolic than practical significance. These attempts clearly demonstrate Russian authors' assimilation of European theories, but that correlation between genetic and stylistic features that was obvious in the

---

[14] In juxtaposing Russian and Church Slavonic Lomonosov thus once again put into play the whole repertoire of oppositions that Paus had outlined. It is as if Lomonosov had returned to Paus' scheme, skipping over Adodurov. Although similar minor similarities of interpretation do not of themselves prove the influence of Paus' grammar on Lomonosov, his familiarity with it seems probable, so that there certainly might have been continuity, whether conscious or unconscious. […]

French or German linguistic context ran into significant obstacles in the Russian situation. In the area of lexicon, these obstacles arose from the fact that both linguistic practice and linguistic consciousness formed over the centuries were built upon the unity of vocabulary of the bookish tradition and spoken tongue and upon the functional reconceptualization of variants in which word provenance played but a tertiary role. In morphology the basic source of difficulty was the contradiction between genetic (or quasi-genetic) characteristics and the grammatical tradition, thanks to which the use of a series of morphological elements was associated not with an opposition between language types but with literacy as such. It is obvious at the same time that however different these difficulties, the process of reconceptualizing variants in lexicon and morphology could not be completely independent; they could apparently mutually stimulate each other, but also be a restraining force, as the task of regulating variability accumulated problems, different for various linguistic levels.

Nonetheless, a definite reevaluation was taking place and had an influence, if quite limited, on linguistic practice. This was a consequence of ideas about linguistic purity that had been assimilated that demanded the purging of all alien elements from the literary norm, or at least severely limited their use. Insofar as in the framework of Petrine linguistic policy "Slavonic" had been perceived by the codifiers of the new literary language as an alien phenomenon, this attribute was now transferred onto elements of that language and now sought out within the new language. Thus the struggle with Church Slavonic that Peter began was now carried over onto the level of specific elements of the language. Classes of language elements united by genetic attributes now acquired new significance, and however changeable their evaluation, Slavonicisms became and remained a fundamental stylistic category.

Naturally, this category also acquired culturological importance. The multifaceted connections that developed between Church Slavonic and various aspects of Russian history and culture (cf. § I–2.1) also became associated with particular linguistic elements that genetically derived from Church Slavonic. This created a new association between normalization (the choice and differentiation of variants) and historical-cultural positions, as certain linguistic trends became correlated with antiquity, national traditions, religious values, and so on.

Still another important consequence of the attempt to delineate Slavonicisms as a stylistically significant category was the gradual recognition of the specific nature of the Russian linguistic situation. As has been shown, early efforts proved unable to define genetic Slavonicisms consistently, and ran into various difficulties. These difficulties did not have analogies in the history of European language-building, and this could not help but perplex those who strove to create a new literary language on the European model. The inadequacy of applying genetic parameters demonstrated that the very character of Russian linguistic material was somehow different from that of other European languages. For this reason the attempts described above formed the potential basis for new theoretical inquiries. True, these inquiries did not begin at once. They were preceded by attempts to find a compromise solution based on things that, in one way or another, European theory did provide for.

2. The Conflict Between Linguistic Theory and Actual Practice. The Concept of a Poetic Language

The new European power, in transforming the swampy shores of the Neva into a European capital with amazing speed, cut its clothes according to European fashion and was attentive to Parisian styles. European ideas about elegance, and about language and literature, were tried on incessantly and without discrimination. The background of national tradition appeared to be just so much yielding material to which a gifted sculptor could give European form. The new literature, which assimilated the prescriptions of Boileau and Vaugelas, was European in its very conception, and the tradition of Church Slavonic literature easily substituted for those French Baroque authors condemned by Classicism. Similar censure fell to the lot of poets "of the Spasskii Bridge"[15] (see Trediakovskii 1730: foreword, l. 7 verso; III: 650) as that which Boileau had showered upon Ronsard and Saint-Amant, or, with similar success, upon "les chansons du Pont-Neuf" (Boileau II: 299; cf. Zhivov 1988c, 94). The plot of historical and cultural development was borrowed from Europe, and the old Russian cast of characters was rechristened with European names. In precisely the same way, the plan for the new literary language was also imported from Europe, first of all the names and categories with whose help a language's purity was judged at the time.

However, as we have already seen in part, it was not always easy to find objects that fit the new categories; the starting point from which Classicist

---

[15] A bridge off Red Square in Moscow, known as a marketplace for *lubki* (popular prints) and cheap popular literature (and hence analogous to the Pont Neuf in Paris). (Translator's note)

normalization of language proceeded in France was fundamentally different from the situation that the first codifiers of Russian faced. As we have noted, in Russia there was no normalized spoken language (like the well developed language of the court or of the salon which served as models for French theoreticians), nor was there an accepted literary tradition which could define the diversity and permissible limits of lexical and grammatical elements in literary speech. Both Vaugelas and the Académie française based their normalizing efforts upon the spoken "usage of the court" as well as on that of "the best writers" (Livet I, 102–3; Vaugelas 1647, l. a2, o3–o3 verso). These two sources complemented one another, and Vaugelas explicitly asserted that only their mutual accord could establish proper usage (Vaugelas 1647, l. a2). For Chapelain and his project for an academic dictionary the nature of this accord was somewhat different: academicians would choose from among the best writers what seemed to them to correspond to proper (spoken) usage, supplementing this with words which had no literary precedent (Livet I: 103). Be that as it may, the two given sources were mutually correcting, and the result was to be that ideal literature which *un gallant homme* could read with ease and pleasure.

Nothing comparable to these two ingredients could be found in the Russian linguistic situation at the start of the eighteenth century. The existing Church Slavonic literary tradition in no way accorded with spoken usage of the court, which apparently differed from the speech of the other layers of society not by its normalization but by the frequency of its foreign borrowings. Hence the desired "pure" language could not be attained by straining the literary tradition through the filter of exemplary spoken usage. The impossibility of applying these borrowed notions to the linguistic material at hand was predetermined from the start by the contradiction between the theory and actual linguistic practice. In particular, appeals to the two sources of linguistic normalization were a mere fiction. Insofar as the Church Slavonic heritage was rejected, the literary tradition was beyond the pale; and insofar as the spoken language was not normalized, references to it were merely verbal homage to unquestioned European authority (cf. Lehfeldt 1992).

"Foppish speech" (shchegolskoe narechie) could hardly serve as a substitute for the language of the court, as B. A. Uspenskii has suggested, noting that "the transfer of Vaugelas' scheme onto Russian soil naturally suggested a reliance on foppish speech, that is, on the elite speech of the socially privileged" (Uspenskii 1985, 139). It is quite unclear how developed and self-conscious was the linguistic practice on which the new literary language had to rely, and the very possibility of such reliance is thus quite

2. The Conflict Between Linguistic Theory and Actual Practice

doubtful. Uspenskii writes: "We have very little information about the foppish speech of the first half of the eighteenth century.., and so we have to limit ourselves to individual examples that illustrate Trediakovskii's connection with foppish speech" (loc. cit., 136). However, the examples are too few to make this case; there are only two. One is the use of the word *вкус* (taste) in the figurative sense, as a calque from the French *goût,* the other, the use of the plural *вы* as a polite form of address, about which Trediakovskii writes in his foreword to the translation of the Latin *Short and Powerful Speech* of 1744 : "In translating I changed… the serious Latin thou (ты) to our tender you (вы) of today, for general polite usage" (Pekarskii, IA, II, 104). Both of these innovations certainly appear as the result of the Europeanization of Russian society, and were therefore at first characteristic of the cultural elite. But it is doubtful, however, that the entire social elite, including "the court of Her Majesty" was involved with foppish behavior (cf. Kantemir's satirical observations about fops; and Kantemir certainly belonged to the elite).[16] It is even more dubious that foppish language was characterized not merely by individual borrowings and calques or direct use of foreign (French) expressions but by a well developed lexical and grammatical usage that could serve as a source of normalization on the order of the language of the court in France. Therefore, to orient the literary language on foppish speech, even if this existed in some sort of embryonic form, was not an option.

The idea of "purifying" the new literary language in connection with the linguistic and stylistic categories which Classicism promoted was just as unreal. A strict adherence to the theory would have left a new author without any linguistic material at all — in Russia the "pure" language would have turned out to be a language without words. Indeed given the absence of a neutral linguistic tradition any construction and any given word necessarily

---

[16] Both of these innovations should evidently be dated to an even earlier time than that which Uspenskii suggests. "Vkus" (taste) in the figurative sense appears at least as early as the translation of Molière's "Les précieuses ridicules" by Vymeni, Peter I's jester, in 1708 (compare Tikhonravov 1874, II, 266, 272; and Molière I, 274, 276). Of course, one may doubt that in this strange translation we find a direct reflection of actual spoken usage, although the common use of foreign languages in the Petrine period makes this semantic calque something to be expected (perhaps, through the German *Geschmack*). Using *вы* was also widespread in Peter's time, and many examples may be found in Peter's own letters and those of his contemporaries […] (PiB, II, 65, 126; Sumkina 1981, 40–51). […] In any case, there is no established connection between the plural you and foppish speech. No less indicative in this connection is that Trediakovskii defines the form as polite not only in 1744 but also much later (see Uspenskii's collection of examples, Uspenskii 1985, 135), when it is impossible to see a preference for foppish speech or orientation on spoken usage. This means that one cannot connect the use of the formal *вы* in Russia to the introduction of Vaugelas' ideas.

fell into one of the forbidden categories. If the author drew from the literary tradition, he would be using lexical and syntactic Slavonicisms, and thus be guilty of using learned and overblown expressions. If, on the other hand, he drew from spoken usage, he could be faulted for using low and vulgar language; insofar as in practice no tradition of cultured speech existed besides Church Slavonic, any non-literary elements might be said to belong to odious gutter usage. In Russia nothing resembling the polished spoken language distinguishing a person of "good society" from an artisan with no manners existed, as in the preceding period it was only the bookish tongue that possessed cultural value in Russia, while the non-bookish language lay outside of culture and enjoyed no social or cultural prestige (sf. Uspenskii 1987, 18). Neither could chancery (business) language serve as a source; as discussed earlier (§ I–1.4), in the period of the formation of the new literary language it was already a vanishing phenomenon, of no importance at all for the new linguistic consciousness; moreover, any reference to it could activate the criticism that this was "la langue de la chicane" (the language of pettifogging bureaucrats) that for Classicists was object of special disdain. True, there remained the possibility of supplementing the language with borrowings and neologisms, but this path was also closed, insofar as Classicist doctrine prohibited these categories as well.

Hence following European theories directly led to an impasse, and so there was only one way to resolve the situation, and that was to divorce theoretical declarations from linguistic practice. Classicist theory was only followed at symbolic moments; this was the case, in particular, with lexical and morphological Slavonicisms (see § II–1.3, § II–1.4). In practice, material derived from the traditional, Church Slavonic, linguistic legacy was preserved to a significant degree (predominantly in its hybrid form), through the intermediacy of the "simple" language of the Petrine epoch. The first codifiers of the new literary language took this path of separating practice from declarations. Their position was defined from the beginning by the given negative attitude toward the Church Slavonic language, and consequently to the Church Slavonic literary tradition. This, in particular, was Trediakovskii's position, and it is for this very reason that references to tradition are almost completely absent in his early works (at least when language is being discussed).[17] The single Russian author Trediakovskii

---

[17] In questions of versification Trediakovskii refers to the preceding tradition in several cases. Thus he rejects masculine rhymes, basing himself on the fact that "it is contrary to our ancient but very solid usage, like fire to water, or the truth to slander" (Trediakovskii 1735, 23; 1963, 382–3). Further, he derives the tonic principle "from the innermost qualities belonging to our verse," referring to "the poetry of our simple folk" (loc. cit, 24/283). On references to the Slavic Psalter as model for the odic tradition see below (§ II–2.2). Other references to

cites is Kantemir, with whom he was more or less in agreement, although Trediakovskii thought his works in major need of revision (1735, 86–7; 1963, 418–9). And so in theory Trediakovskii rejected the existing literary tradition and declared the language of the court to be the basic criterion of linguistic purity (and correspondingly he relegated Slavonicisms to the ranks of "impure" words). Linguistic practice, however, could not base itself on such fictitious sources, and it was therefore incumbent to find an acceptable European category in which to include those elements of the traditional bookish language which the new literature could not do without, but which were nevertheless admittedly in conflict with the purist ideal.

2.1 Poetic License and the Church Slavonic Literary and Linguistic Tradition

In this context Trediakovskii's views on poetic language and his view of the interrelationship between prose and poetry turned out to be crucial. The theoreticians of French Classicism had not held to one unified point of view on this question, and so their Russian followers were able to interpret things in a way which more or less corresponded to their own practice. At the same time, poetic texts were identified as models for correct linguistic usage, so that resolution of the question of what the poetic language should be had decisive importance for the entire process of normalizing the new literary language.

The basic view of French Classicism on this subject had come into being as a direct reaction against the views of the Pléiade poets, and, more broadly, against the entire theoretical heritage of the French Baroque. For Ronsard, Du Bellay, and Vauquelin, the poetic language differed from the prosaic primarily in its freedom and richness (see Brunot, II, 168–73; Brunot 1959, 228f); for this reason the main task in creating a poetic language was to "amplify the language," and moreover, any means were permissible for this enhancement — borrowings, archaisms, neologisms, etc. Mademoiselle de Gournay expressed this idea with great consistency and clarity when she wrote in defense against attacks by the Malherbistes that: I am so far from

---

the earlier literary tradition are exclusively negative (see, loc. cit., 2, 13, 68–9, 7; 3 verso, 375, 408, 410). It is curious to note that well the young Lomonosov rejects the preceding tradition even more consistently than Trediakovskii, in contrast to him, for example, arguing for allowing male rhymes and the absurdity of excluding them from poetry (Lomonosov, III, 8–9; VII^2, 15–16).

Chapter 2. The Start of Normalization of the New Literary Language

being reduced to retrenchments [throwing out "redundant" words] like the pretentious people at court that if there ran through the works of all our poets or through the streets of Paris three times more words, I would not repudiate a single one, excepting a half dozen which only the lowliest mob uses. Those other poets and fashionable scholars have strongly disagreed with me, [arguing] that they can provide me with a dozen words to say this or that [but] without the ones they pretend to despise so that I will be forced to eliminate them; [but] I want *fifteen* words and do not want to lose any of them. (Gournay 1626, 587) For the Baroque the language of prose was seen as an abbreviation of the language of verse and one in which it was impossible to allow similar freedom, that is, there were many more limitations imposed on prose than on the language of poetry.

Malherbe and his followers held directly opposing views (Brunot 1959, 227f). For them the greatness of the poetic language was not in its richness and freedom, but in its refinement. Accordingly it was the language of verse that turned out to be an abbreviation of the language of prose and demanded greater strictness and greater purity, so that many more limitations were imposed on it than on that of prose. This was the position that Vaugelas adopted and which became to a greater or lesser extent the norm for Classicism. Vaugelas wrote in part that

> Our French poetry derives one of its main charms from the fact that it always makes use of words used in prose... in contrast, the Greek and Italian languages have an infinity of terms particularly assigned to poetry, which seem wild, first of all to their own people, and as the whole world knows, uneducated Italians (les Italiens naturels) don't understand their poets unless they have studied them. (Vaugelas II: 411)

Bouhours expressed the same view (1671: 60–1). In this way the poetic language was held to even greater purist limitations than the language of prose; poetic language demanded naturalness and clarity, which were at the heart of the purist doctrine, and even more, an expressiveness and beauty which were not as crucial for prose.

This view was not, however, hard and fast dogma, and French Classicism's striving to broaden expressive means — "to find new expressions in verse," as Boileau wrote to Racine (III: 286) — often led not only to its disregard in practice but also to significant theoretical qualifications. Hence Chapelain had already expressed the opinion that Malherbe's verse was very beautiful rhymed prose (Chapelain I: 637; cf. Brunot 1959: 151, 585), and that epic (heroic) poetry demands far greater diversity than would usually be permitted, including in vocabulary. True, Chapelain was very careful in his pronouncements, and did not want to emphasize his disagreement with reigning purist practice. Thus in the preface to "La Pucelle" he writes that Virgil had taught him "that the character of narration, even in the epic, demands clarity above all; and that one should only strive to be beautiful by the choice of words that are pure, sonorous and energetic; by using grand and strong figures [of speech] without extravagance... I learned from him that stilted features (traits guindés), however spiritual they may be, are absolutely impermissible" (Chapelain 1656, l. C IV verso) At the same time he contrasts the genius of ancient poetry to the French genius: the genius of ancient poetry, including that of Virgil, is characterized by stylistic audacity, which is proper for the epic, and insufficient in French poetry. This suggested a moderate opposition to the rigorous purism of the Malherbistes. The same opposition is evident in his attitude toward Ronsard as one who carries on classical traditions, as opposed to poets who have success in women's boudoirs (Chapelain, I, 640; cf. Brey 1957, 18–9).[18]

In an analogous way, other authors of heroic poetry (mostly "moderns") also held poetic license to be a necessary feature of epic verse, which could not do without "uncommon" words ("certain bold terms, which serve to elevate [poetry] above the ordinary and which are painfully suffered by their [lady readers'] delicate ears, accustomed to the gentlest of terms that are most authorized by usage" [Desmarets 1657: l.e1–e1 verso]). Hence epic poetry turns out to be a special sphere of poetry juxtaposed to the everyday "prosaic nature" of Malherbean poetry.[19] This opposition is extended both to lexicon and syntax (Desmarets specially supports the necessity of inversions in epic verse — loc. cit, l. i4 — o1 verso), as well as to properly literary devices, e.g., the Classicist principle of naturalness is downgraded in all spheres of action. Desmarets speaks of this unambiguously: "I would wish that all poets who say that there should be no inversions in our language would create epic poems; we would see a poor and miserable *politesse*. The same goes for subject matter; the marvelous will be debased if it is not marked by the supernatural, because it is certain that it is necessary to pass beyond the bounds of nature, both in regard to things and in regard to words, if we want to produce works that will be more than ordinary" (loc. cit., l.o1).

Georges Scudery speaks of the same opposition to Malherebism in

---

[18] In the early eighteenth century Fénélon advocated a similar position on the language of poetry, also finding various merits in Ronsard and protesting against the impoverished language of purism [...]. (Fénélon, VII, 153).

[19] Desmarets lays out this position very clearly, directly contrasting it to that of strict purism. In his view, the way to the necessary excellence of epic poetry is precisely the creation of a special poetic language. [...] (Desmarets 1657, l.i2–i2 verso).

the foreword to his epic poems in which he insists on justifying those words "which will not perhaps be heard by the entire world" (Scudery 1654, 1. d4). Although the issue here was the use of special terms (see Scudery 1637, 1. A2–A2 verso; Scudery 1654, 1. d4–d4 verso), the principle remains the same—high style gives the right to deviate from common literary speech. Together with lexical departures in high style Scudery envisions the wide use of "rich rhetorical figures, that is to say, hyperbole, prosopopeia, metaphor, comparison, epithets, and all the others which poets and orators use" (Scudery 1654, 1. c3). Consequently, in Scudery as well anti-purist tendencies make up a complete system. One could cite many more similar examples (cf. Hatzfeld 1929 on Baroque poetics in the religious poetry of Classicism).

Thus for a series of French poets, primarily authors of heroic poems, the high style serves as a special sphere in which deviations from Classicist poetics and style is allowed, as if an island of legalized Baroque within Classicism. Understandably, Russian authors who wanted to bring Russian linguistic material into line with the demands of Classicist purism could not help but make use of this French precedent to justify and legalize their own "deviations" from European rules.

At the same time representatives of the "ancients" who condemned Chapelain for "big ugly words" (Boileau II: 339) and made fun of Christianized heroic poetry could reject the strict purism of Malherbe and Vaugelas, citing the example of classical poetry (i.e., Homer and Pindar; see Boileau's "Discourse on the Ode" and above § I–1.2). It is indicative that Rollin, so valued by Trediakovskii, wrote that "Poetry has a language that is unique to it and that is very different from that of prose. As poets in their works aim principally to please, to move us, to elevate the soul, to inspire great sentiments and to revive the passions, they are permitted to use expressions that are bolder, manners of speaking beyond that of common usage, more frequent repetitions, freer epithets, more ornate and extended descriptions" (Rollin, I, 127).

For their Russian pupils, conflicts among their French mentors allowed for the possibility of choice — in theory — between a strict or moderate purism, i.e., one which would allow some freedom of word choice in the poetic language. As we have shown, in Russian circumstances the demands of Classicist purism were impossible, so it is fully understandable that the possibility of including "impure" words in poetry which the French theoreticians allowed would be taken full advantage of by their Russian followers. The violation of purist principles was brought under the rubric of poetic license and hence at least partly legitimized by it.

In this context it was completely natural that in their poetic tracts

2. The Conflict Between Linguistic Theory and Actual Practice

both Trediakovskii and Kantemir allotted extensive sections to poetic license. Against the background of French Classicism's attitude toward poetic license, which was to limit it in every way possible, the connection between freely permitting liberties and the difficulties of instituting the new Russian literary language emerges quite dramatically (Gukovskaia 1957: 219). While chapters on poetic license were a natural part of Russian poetic manuals, in France the onset of the Classicist period had been marked by Pierre de Deimier's "L'Art poëtique" (1610), which dedicated two special chapters to the struggle against poetic license and alleged authorial privilege (see Brunot III: 16).

In fact, the category of poetic license did allow the literary language to retain that which according to strict purist norm would have had to be rejected. In Russian conditions this meant first of all "Slavonicisms," insofar as this genetic rubric was introduced into Russian linguistic and stylistic systems and they began to be perceived as spoiling the purity of the literary language. The petitions to Apollo which enumerated the poet's individual offenses, and for which the poet humbly begged pardon, were essentially lists of poetic liberties. Such lists reflected both the poet's linguistic consciousness (what he considered an offense and what he didn't) and his individual practice (which sins he committed and which he didn't).

Trediakovskii presents this sort of list in his *New and Brief Method* in the chapter entitled "Concerning Liberties Used in Composing Verse": "Verbs in the second person singular may end in *ши* instead of *шь*; and infinitives may end in *ти* instead of *ть*. For example: *пишеши* instead of *пишешь* and *писати* instead of *писать*. The pronouns *мя. тя* [may also be used] instead of *меня, тебя*; and the same for *ми, ти* instead of *мнѣ, тебѣ*; not infrequently *ти* is used instead of *твои*" (Trediakovskii 1735, 16; 1935, 377). Concerning the vocative case, Trediakovskii writes: "Many vocatives, which in our language resemble nominatives (except for these most blessed and lofty names: БОЖЕ, ГОСПОДИ, ИИСУСЕ, ХРІСТЕ, СЫНЕ, СЛОВЕ, that is, the incarnate WORD), may sometimes in verse end in the Slavonic manner. Hence instead of *Філотъ* one may put *Філоте*, as I did in one of my satires" (ibid, 18; 379).

Kantemir wrote his "Letter of Khariton Makentin" as a kind of revision of Trediakovskii's *New and Brief Method*, and in some cases he simply repeats, and in others contests and supplements it, reflecting the degree to which his literary practice and theoretical consciousness differed from Trediakovskii's. In the chapter "On License in Verse Measure" he writes: "Verbs in the second person singular may end in *ши* instead of *шь* and infinitives in *ти* instead of *ть*. for example *писати* instead of *писать*,

Chapter 2. The Start of Normalization of the New Literary Language

читати instead of *читать*" (Kantemir 1744, 23; II, 20). But that is as far as Kantemir's and Trediakovskii's recommendations coincide. Thus Kantemir asserts that "All of the word shortenings which the Slavonic language allows may, when required, be freely adopted in Russian verse, for example, it is fine to use *вѣкъ, человѣкъ, чистъ, сладкъ,* instead of *вѣковъ, человѣковъ, чистый, сладкій.* Much more rarely do I advise the use of *мя, тя, ми, ти* instead of *меня, тебя, мнѣ, тебѣ*" (ibid, 22; 18; the last sentence is clearly directed against Trediakovskii). Then under the special heading "Slavonic Endings in Adjectives are Permitted," which was cited above in § II–1.3, he writes: "With no less boldness one should use all Slavonic endings in adjectives rather than Russian ones; hence it is fine to use *сладкій* instead of *сладкой, изрядный* instead of *изрядной.*" On noun endings he states that: "Instead of instrumental in *ами* or *ою* it is fine to use the shortened forms in *ы, и* or *ой*; hence you may write *роги* instead of *рогами, совѣты* instead of *совѣтами, рукой* instead of *рукою*" (op. cit. 22; 18–9).

The differences in Trediakovskii and Kantemir's lists of poetic liberties demonstrate the lines along which linguistic consciousness developed during this initial formative period of the new type of literary language. What relationship do these lists actually have to the Church Slavonic literary heritage? It is apparent that they catalogue only that which on the one hand was felt as an "alien," "Slavonic" element, and on the other, that which the new literary language felt it had to legitimize. The lists do not include those elements that were felt as "Slavonic" and seen as unnecessary or inadmissible in the new language, that is, the markers of bookishness that had been banned from the "simple" language in the Petrine period. In this the general intention of the lists' authors was different from Adodurov's in his list of "Slavonicisms"; if it was important for Adodurov to signal the rejection of Church Slavonic, the task facing Kantemir and Trediakovskii was to legalize various traditional bookish elements, with the negative attitude toward "Slavonicisms" taken for granted.

The lists also do not include those elements which derive from the traditional bookish tradition but were not perceived as such and so didn't require justification. In the period in which linguistic consciousness was being transformed, the attribution of this or that element to a given category often changed, and it is these changes which reveal how and in what order individual markers entered linguistic consciousness and came to define new norms of literary usage. In this sense both the similarities and differences in Trediakovskii's and Kantemir's lists are significant.

In the linguistic consciousness of the period under discussion, the oppositions of *-ти/-ть* in the infinitive and *-ши/-шь* in the 2nd pers.

2. The Conflict Between Linguistic Theory and Actual Practice

present may be connected with the opposition between linguistic codes; corrections to manuscripts during the Petrine era testifies to this (§ I–1.3). True, this connection was not expressed in the fact that one of the variants was exclusively related to the traditional bookish tongue and the other to the non-bookish language, but rather in that for the bookish language *-ти* and *-ши* were the basic forms, and *-ть, -шь* supplemental ones, while for the "simple" language the correlation of variants was the reverse (Zhivov 2004). Hence the use of *-ти* and *-ши* in the new literary language required special explanation. Both Kantemir and Trediakovskii do this, with Trediakovskii reproducing Adodurov's solution (§ II–1.4), and Kantemir Trediakovskii's. Linguistic practice corresponding to the norms they advocated was generally accepted though the mid-1740's, and evidently derived from the tradition of syllabic poetry, in which infinitival rhymes were extremely common.

Trediakovskii used infinitives in *-ти* in *Voyage to the Island of Love* as poetic license. In the prose sections he only used infinitives in *-ть,* while in the poetry there were a significant number of *-ти* forms, together with those in *-ть,* for example, in the rhymes *творити — быти, смягчити — быти, небыти — забыти, здати — изъяти, любити — быти* (Trediakovskii 1730, 30, 356, 90, 105, 105). This was not only Trediakovskii's practice but the norm accepted by his circle of academic philologists as a whole.[20] Trediakovskii kept to this practice in his other poetic works of the 1730's, for example, in the "Ode on the Taking of the City of Gdansk" of 1734 and in his verses for the *New and Short Guide* of 1735. This was also Kantemir's practice. In his prose works of the 1720's, written mostly in hybrid Church Slavonic, Kantemir often uses infinitives in *-ти*; this form also appears often in his "Description of Paris" of 1726, written in Russian, where the *-ть* ending predominates (Kantemir, II, 360–2). Later Kantemir did not allow such variation. At the same time, in Kantemir's verse of all periods he used *-ти* for verbs with non-final stress, for example, in his First Satire: *провожати — коронати, терпѣти — имѣти, познати — называти, старѣти – имѣти* (Kantemir I, 17–9, 21); in the Sixth Satire: *продолжати — добѣжати, смерти — стрети* (ibid, 140, 142); in his translations of Horace: *подчиняти* (ibid, 394); and so on. The young Lomonosov also follows this practice in this period; one meets the *-ти* form in the "Ode on

---

[20] There is evidence of this, for example, in the *Notes to the Gazette (Primechaniia k vedomostiam)* prepared by academic translators. Thus in the first issue for 1734 while *-ть* is consistently in the prosaic text in the verses addressed to Anna Ioannovna, infinitive rhymes in *–ти* also occur […] (Primechaniia 1734, 4). Other occurrences of rhymes in *-ти* as poetic license also occur in other poems in this issue (a translation of epigrams by Villeroi, p. 74, and verses on fireworks, pp. 140–1).

the Taking of Khotin" (*покрыти — склонити*; Lomonsosov, I, 13); in the translated ode by Fénélon of 1738–9 (*начати — почерьпати, почивати — воздати*, ibid, 9, 11); and in the odes of 1741 (*начати — стояти, прельстити – всвеселити*; ibid, 28, 43). In this context it is understandable that Lomonosov does not object to this use of infinitives in Trediakovskii's *New and Short Guide*, while he does criticize other nonnormative verbal forms (cf. his ironic addition to the form вѣмъ — "вѣси, вѣсть"; Berkov 1936, 56). From the mid 1740's both Lomonosov and Trediakovskii cease using this poetic liberty.

An analogous pattern may be observed for the use of enclitic pronouns which in the previous period also served as markers of bookishness, that is, as an element related to the differentiation of linguistic codes (see Soluianova 1989). Trediakovskii recommends this liberty, which fully accords with his practice (he uses it often, as in the verses from the *New and Short Guide*). Kantemir frowns on its usage (perhaps, because of its connection with the old bookish tongue; see also Lomonosov's comments on the *New and Short Guide*, in which he underscores all of the enclitic pronouns; Berkov 1936, 56), and this is also consistent with his poetic practice, in which they occur far more rarely than in Trediakovskii (see the isolated cases in his "Speech to the Most Pious Sovereign Anna Ioannovna," his paraphrase of Psalm 36[21] and Anacreontic songs; Kantemir, I, 288, 305, 346, 349, 354, 355, etc.). In the Anacreontic songs the form occurs comparatively more often, which is evidently a function of their antique "classical" coloration. The use of specially bookish forms could model antiquity as a cultural paradigm (Church Slavonic elements serve here as correlative for ancient classical languages; see § III–2.1) or even model classical languages as such (with their structural peculiarities, for example, their developed verbal inflexion, vocative, enclitic pronouns, etc.). Attempts at such modeling, abhorrent for Classicist France, testify that in the 1740's Kantemir departed from purist doctrine (see below). These poetic liberties nevertheless remain a practice demanding special justification.

As far as the markers of infinitives and the 2nd pers. present form *(-ти, -ши)*, as well as enclitic pronouns, both Kantemir and Trediakovskii evidently concur. In terms of the genetic opposition between Russian and Church Slavonic that became so important these elements were defined as "Slavonic." The slight difference in formulations is due to their varying judgments on the permissibility of these "Slavonic" elements in the new literary language, judgments which to some extent correlate with each poet's particular linguistic practice.

---

[21] Psalm 37 in the Western Bible. (Translator's note)

2. The Conflict Between Linguistic Theory and Actual Practice

The general linguistic consciousness of the two poets is also manifested in the fact that they do *not* incorporate a series of genetic Slavonicisms into their lists of liberties. Here, for example, belong forms with *жд* in place of *dj or the gen. fem. sg. adjective endings *-ыя/-ия* which both authors use freely and without special explanation. In permitting Slavonicisms into the literary language that were in one way or another formally marked, Kantemir and Trediakovskii further opened the door for Slavonicisms of a properly lexical character, which do not rate mention in either of their lists of poetic liberties (although Kantemir could in principle also consider special cases, as in his note on the rhyme *простый — острый*: "I don't know if another such pair could be found" — 1744: 9; II, 6). One may suggest that tolerance for grammatical Slavonicisms eliminated the very problem of regulating the use of lexical Slavonicisms, at least in terms of the poetic language (see Vinokur 1959, 128).

Hence the task of "purifying" the literary language of lexical Slavonicisms proved to be more simulated than actual for the poetic language as the very notion of a special poetic language made it possible to bypass the thorniest problem of linguistic normalization — the problem of dividing up the language by genetic criteria and assigning stylistic value to each group — while still preserving apparent loyalty to purist theory (§ I–1.3). Although in the 1730's and early 1740's this method of evading difficulty is nowhere stated explicitly, it was clearly evident in poetic practice. Trediakovskii used lexical Slavonicisms without any limit in the poetry from *Voyage to the Island of Love*, in his ode "On the Taking of the City of Gdansk," and in the poems in the *New and Brief Method* (cf. Sorokin 1976, 49–50; Alekseev 1982, 89, 96). This liberty concerned not only non-pleophonic forms, but all pairs whose correlation did not involve morphological markers (*око — глаз, перст — палец, чело — лоб*, etc.).

Thus the opposition of lexical Russicisms and Slavonicisms is not notable in *Voyage to the Island of Love*, as they are not distinguished by formal characteristics. In any case, both are encountered in the verse as well as the prose, and oppositions like *око — глаз, чело — лоб*, and the like, are not included in consideration of genetic parameters and the imperative to get rid of any kind of "slavonicization." *Око, чело, перст,* etc. do not appear as poetic liberties but as a normal part of the vocabulary, with no regard for genetic derivation.[22]

---

[22] See, for example, *окомъ* (28), *очи* (29, 35*, 75, 120*) and *глаза* (31, 100, 120), *главы* (32*) (Тредиаковский 1730 — pages marked with an asterisk refer to poetry); cf. also: *перст указательнои* (29), *уста* (100), *чело* (75).

Analogous material is absent from the *New and Short Guide,* insofar as the prose and verse material are thematically juxtaposed. It is obvious however that in the poetry Slavonic vocabulary (Slavonic from the perspective of the later tradition) is used without restriction, and apparently even preferred to the Russian (for example, *око* and *очи* appear many times, while *глаз* and *глаза* are absent, and the same goes for pairs like *уста — губы*). It is possible that this is due to limits on "low" or "coarse" lexicon (given the blurry definition of what these categories meant). The following lines from Trediakovskii's second Elegy are indicative:

> Очи светлы у нея, цвета же небесна,
> Не было черты в лице, чтоб та не прелесна;
> Круглое чело, чтоб мог, в оное вселиться
> Разум данный с небеси, и распространиться.
> Алость на устах весьма мяхкость украшала,
> А перловы зубы в ней видеть не мешала;
> Чернотью ея власы соболю подобны,
> Паче шолку те рукам мяхкостью угодны.
> Всеб ея перстам иметь с златом адаманты,
> Груди всеб ея носить чистые брильянты.²³

(Trediakovskii 1735, 56/401–2)

(Her eyes are bright, of heavenly color [and] there is no feature of her face that is not charming. A round brow in which reason given from heaven can reside and proliferate. The vermilion of her lips adornsors them with softness and does not hinder the view of her pearly teeth. The blackness of her hair is like sable, softer than silk to the touch. All her fingers should have gold and precious stones, and pure diamonds highlight her breasts.)

The same freedom in using similar forms is also characteristic of Kantemir (for example, in the First Satire, *глаза* [Kantemir, I, 9, 15], *очи* [17], in the Second Satire *уста, устъ* [33, 42], *глаза, глазъ* [35, 42, 49], *очьми* [40]).

As shown (§ II–1.3), one result of the influence of purist theory on Russian linguistic thought was that a series of variants which were earlier felt as neutral now began to be connected with the opposition between Church Slavonic and Russian. The process of reinterpretation could proceed in different ways with different authors. However, this might not be directly reflected in linguistic practice, and the category of poetic language could facilitate this because having defined a given element as a Slavonicism, an

---

²³ The poem has a lot of marked "Slavonic" vocabulary, e.g., очи, чело, персты, злато. (Translator's note)

2. The Conflict Between Linguistic Theory and Actual Practice

author could at the very same time call it poetic license and continue to use it in his works without any qualms. One may regard the differences in Trediakovskii's and Kantemir's lists of poetic liberties as a reflection of this process of interpreting variants individually according to notions of genetic difference.

Their treatment of adjectival endings illustrates just such individual approaches. As shown (§ II–4), Kantemir was one of the first (after Paus) to consider nom. and acc. masc. sg. adjectival endings in *-ый/-ий* as a Slavonicism, permissible in poetry, while Trediakovskii does not mention adjectival endings as markers of the Church Slavonic — Russian opposition. An analysis of Trediakovskii's texts suggests that indeed he did not connect the alternation of the endings *-ой/-ый* with this. If in *Voyage to the Island of Love* we may note some preponderance of the ending *-ой/-ей* in prose and *-ый/-ий* in verse [examples omitted], in works of 1734–35 the ending *-ый/-ий* dominates in both prose and verse (due to the influence of the grammatical tradition), although Trediakovskii continues to use *-ой/-ей* in both as well. This demonstrates that connecting these alternations with the Church Slavonic — Russian opposition was one of Kantemir's linguistic innovations (as he apparently did not know of Paus' grammar), and was not a fact of the period's linguistic consciousness.

Kantemir and Trediakovskii also interpret short adjectives in their attributive function differently. Kantemir sees them as "abbreviated words which the Slavonic language legitimizes," i.e., Slavonicisms permissible in verse. In hybrid texts there was no regularity in the use of long and short adjectives forms in the attributive function (cf. Zhivov 1986b, 258), so that there seems no basis for considering the short forms as markers of bookish language (cf. however, evidence of a contrary character in Russian historical works of the late seventeenth — early eighteenth century — Solunianova 1989). The replacement of short forms by long ones in the attributive function which Sofronii Likhud implemented in editing the *General Geography* was apparently an attempt at normalization rather than removing marks of bookishness (cf. the replacement of long adjectives for short ones in the predicate function, Zhivov 1986b, 258). Be that as it may, this kind of forms, which were alien to oral speech, were not perceived as neutral and required special justification [...]. This could be reason to interpret them as Slavonicisms; apparently this was why Adodurov in his 1731 treatise indicates the "Slavonic" character of short adjectives (§ II–1.4). Trediakovskii objects to this interpretation, arguing that the given construction is not specially Slavonic. This is evident, in part, from the fact that he cites as allowable poetic license the combination *бѣлъ шатеръ* within a group of expressions which may be "used by our simple folk... in their special poetry" (Trediakovskii 1735, 18; 1963, 379). Trediakovskii thus indicates the possibility of the attributive use of short adjectives in Russian, which would naturally prevent its being considered a Slavonicism and ascribe it to the "natural" qualities of Russian. Here Trediakovskii uses the same strategy of legitimizing linguistic practices as in his treatises on tonic verse (see note 17 above).[24]

Kantemir and Trediakovskii also present different interpretations of the instr. pl. noun endings -*ами* /-*ы*. Kantemir, in considering the instr. pl. variants -*ами* /-*ы* and instr. sg. -*ою*/-*ой*, also allows for the short forms -*ы*/-*ой*. From this it seems doubtful that he considered the -*ы* ending specifically Church Slavonic; in any case he considered it non-normative but something to be preserved for poetic usage. Trediakovskii did not include it in his list of poetic liberties, presumably because he didn't think it worthy of preservation. These different interpretations correspond to the two authors' linguistic practices at the time they wrote their respective treatises.

In the early 1730's Trediakosvkii used the instr. pl. -*ы* ending as a poetic liberty. Thus in the prose part of *Voyage to the Island of Love* it never occurred, while in the poetry the endings -*ы* and -*ми* are fairly common. The proportion of older endings make up 67% of instr. pl. endings, that is, -*ы* and -*ми* occur (of course, not including a-declension nouns) twice as often as -*ами*; cf. such forms as *недруги* (Trediakosvkii, III, 658); *цвѣти* (662, 690); *глазы* (670). One must especially note neuter noun forms with -*ми* endings, which Adodurov condemned so strongly a year later (see

---

[24] As in the case of tonic versification and the advantages of trochaic, the reference to "the poetry of our simple folk" does not indicate the fundamental importance of folk art for Trediakovskii, nor (as Jakobson idly suggests) "his clear preference... for national, popular poetry" (Jakobson 1966, 619), but rather the notion of the natural qualities of language, which was significant for eighteenth-century philological thought, Russian as well as French and German. Generally speaking, asserting these qualities did not contradict the universalism of Classicist theory, but only demonstrated how universal principles were embodied in particular national traditions (hence there was no contradiction here with what W. Lehfeldt has called Trediakovskii's "supranational strivings" — Lehfeldt, 1992, 298). In precisely the same way, in speaking of Opitz' verse reform C. F. Hunold refers to "the specific traits of our language" (Eingenschaft unserer Sprache) (Hunold 1707, 50; cf. Klein 1995). To support his claim of "naturalness," Trediakovskii cited not Russian folklore but the poetry of Dubrovnik as a related Slavic tradition (cf. his reference to "the Dalmatian booklet," apparently one by Ivan Gundulić — Trediakovskii 1963, 442). By the force of this general conception, references to folklore could be used to justify poetic innovations. Lomonosov also took this position (cf. his discussion of the qualities of the Russian language in the "Letter on the Rules of Russian Versification"). It is interesting that he also interprets the attributive use of short adjectives in these terms; at least on the passage referring to folk usage from Trediakovskii that we have been analyzing he jotted noted an apparent example on the margin: *калена стрела* (Berkov 1936, 61).

2. The Conflict Between Linguistic Theory and Actual Practice

§ II–1.4), e.g., *плечьми* (666); *желаньми* (713); *вздыханьми* (713). In the mid-1730's Trediakovskii's practice changed. In the "Ode on the Taking of Gdansk" and the accompanying "Treatise on the Ode in General" of 1734 instr. pl. forms in *-ы* and *-ми* are completely absent, whether in poetry or not [...] and the same is true for the *New and Short Guide* of 1735. Thus the forms that in 1730 Trediakovskii found acceptable as poetic license lost that status. It seems natural to see this as part of the academic normalizing program (§ II–1.1).

Kantemir stood aside from this process. As an example of his prose of the 1730's one may look at his translation of Fontenelle's *Conversation on the Plurality of Worlds,* in which Kantemir practically never uses the old instr. pl. forms. Iu. S. Sorokin cites just one instance of such usage ("дорожки света...пересекаются меж собою безчисленными *образы,*" Sorokin 1982, 64–5). On this background, the use of instr. pl. forms in *-ы* and *-ми* in his verse of the same period appear undoubtedly as poetic license. These appear often (see Obnorskii 1913, 61–2), for example, *крайми* (Kantemir, I, 171), *латми* (I, 300), *басурманы* (I, 182), *греки* (I, 138), *латины* (I, 138), *персты* (I, 300), *писцы* (I, 70), *уставы* (I, 110), *холопы* (I, 139), etc. Thus Kantemir's poetic practice reproduces the same model used in Trediakovskii's early attempts at verse. Unlike Treiakovskii, however, Kantemir did not reject this practice in his subsequent writing, but on the contrary, declared it to be the norm.[25]

Trediakovskii considered the use of the vocative case as poetic license, while Kantemir did not mention it. This silence seems to clearly indicate that Kantemir did not consider the use of this form a poetic liberty. As a matter of fact, in his *New and Short Guide* (1735: 86–7; 1935: 418–19) Trediakovskii offered a corrected version of the start of Kantemir's first satire: "Ум толь слабый, плод трудов краткия науки!" in place of "Уме слабый, плод трудов не долгой науки!" Trediakovskii argued that this revision eliminated two poetic liberties from the line (the use of the vocative and the fem. gen. sg. form *недолгой*; Trediakovskii 1735, 86–7; 1963, 418–9). Kantemir for his part rejected this correction, and kept the vocative in the final edition of

---

[25] In the second half of the 1740's Trediakovskii again started to permit the use of the old instr. pl. forms as poetic liberty. Most indicative in this respect is his Psalter paraphrase (Trediakovskii 1989), where the old endings comprise 22% of the instr. pl. forms. This practice was further extended in his *Tilemakhida.* This change of linguistic practice was apparently connected to changes in his theoretical position, especially his view of the role of conversational Russian and of the nature of the Russian literary language, which began to equate with that of Church Slavonic (see § III–1.2 and § III–1.3), although the character of this connection is not obvious. What is clear, in any case, is that all of these changes in usage demonstrate the influence of theoretical positions on linguistic practice.

Chapter 2. The Start of Normalization of the New Literary Language

the satire (Kantemir I: 9, cf. p. 190 and I, 8, second pagination). Apparently he did not agree with Trediakovskii about what constituted poetic license and therefore was not about to eliminate them. As far as the vocative case, this is confirmed in his frequent use of them in his translation of Horace's "Epistles" ("Pis'ma") done in 1742 (here we have: Меценате, знамените Лоллїе, Юлїе, Флоре, Нумице, Атриде, музо, etc. — Kantemir 1744, 1, 22, 32, 37, 45, 57, 63, 69; I, 390, 407, 415, 426, 435, 440). We may conclude that while Trediakovskii considered vocatives Slavonicisms, Kantemir, despite the established grammatical tradition (see § II–1.4), did not see them as exclusively belonging to the old bookish language and beyond the norms of the literary language of the new type (cf. the enduring use of vocatives in Prokopovich's sermons, Kutina 1981, 31–32).

Possibly, Kantemir thought that eliminating the vocative would unacceptably impoverish the language, especially felt when one had to convey the richness of classical poetry. As we have seen, this was one reason that led him to permit the wide use of enclitic pronouns, and the same factor might also have been at play with the vocative.[26] In his translations of classical poetry, Kantemir in many ways anticipated the perception of Russian as a language that inherited the richness and complexity of classical tongues (§ III–2.1). Kantemir translated Horace's epistles in unrhymed verse, explaining that he did this "in order to remain closer to the original, from which the need to rhyme would cause me to greatly diverge" (Kantemir I, 385). The possibility of doing this was assured by Russians' possession of a special poetic language (that likened Russian to classical tongues), and its realization was to lead the way toward the entire literary language's perfection on its path toward richness and refinement. Kantemir wrote: "In many places I preferred to translate Horace word for word, even though I felt myself that for this it was necessary to use new words, images and phrases, and therefore not be completely comprehensible to readers who are not knowledgeable in Latin. I excuse this conduct because I undertook this translation not only for those who do not know Latin and who will be satisfied by reading Horace's epistles in Russian, but also for those who study Latin and want to

---

[26] Apparently, the classical context as a factor influencing the use of special linguistic forms, creating a model of "ancient" usage, had begun to be felt already in the seventeenth century. Analyzing the second editing of the translation of B. Varenius' *General Geography*, G. Hüttl-Folter noted that in the rare cases when the form of the aorist was preserved, it could be connected to the theme of classical antiquity (Hüttl-Folter 1987, 59–60). An analogous use of aorist forms may be seen in the seventeenth-century Russian translation of Pomponius Mela's *Geography* (GIM, Chud. 347; see Zhivov 1988, 59). In the Russian literary language of the new type such use of the simple aorist could not occur. Thematic motivation, however, could still play a significant role, conditioning the use of non-normative elements.

2. The Conflict Between Linguistic Theory and Actual Practice

completely understand the original. And still another benefit will come of this if in consequence these new words and phrases will enter common use and thereby enrich our language, a goal that shouldn't be forgotten in translating books" (ibid, 386). In the 1730's Trediakovskii did not share this view of the poetic language, and did not therefore strive to inculcate "ancient" qualities into it, and he saw the use of the vocative as simply a poetic liberty.

Among Trediakovskii's linguistic innovations not mentioned by Kantemir is the opposition of pleophonic and non-pleophonic forms, or, more accurately, the assertion that the poetic language was capable of freely transforming pleophonic and phonetically similar forms into non-pleophonic ones. As stated above (§ II–1.3), Trediakovskii treats as poetic liberties a series of elements that could be seen as examples of non-pleophonic lexicon. This gives him the possibility of using such lexicon freely. Kantemir also widely used this kind of vocabulary (together with the pleophonic), but apparently he did not consider that this required special justification (see if only in the First Satire [I, 10–19]: *предъ* (ter), *нравъ*, *премѣну*, *злата* (bis), *глава*, *чрез*, *чрезчуръ*, *златые*).

It is noteworthy that Trediakovskii, while allowing the given liberty, makes the special condition "that the word [to be] made use of as a poetic liberty... be somewhat in use" (Trediakovskii 1735, 20; 1963, 380). It would seem that Trediakovskii is appealing to usage that is in accord with Classicist linguistic theory. Obviously, however, in spoken speech *брегу* and *стрегу* (instead of *берегу* and *стерегу*), cited by Trediakovskii, were just as absent as *острожно* (instead of *осторожно*), which he rejects as inadmissible. In distinguishing between these forms Trediakovskii apparently had in mind that *брегу* and *стрегу* may occur in Church Slavonic, while *острожно* may not (the corresponding idea was expressed by the word *опаснѣ*). It follows that "somewhat in use" (neskol'ko i upotrebitel'noe) refers not to the spoken language but to the literary tradition, references to which Trediakovskii camouflages under the accepted category of "usage."

At the same time, in Russian conditions defining poetic license was not merely a purely academic endeavor but a commentary on and justification of one's own practice. Poetic works of the 1730's were composed as the first, standard-setting examples of Europeanized Russian poetry, and therefore arguments about their meeting linguistic norms took on special importance. It is indicative that among those allowable "non-pleophonic" forms which were "somewhat in use," together with *брегу* and *стрегу* Trediakovskii cites *брежно*. As has just been suggested, in defending the use of *брегу* and *стрегу*, Trediakovskii clearly had the Slavonic literary tradition in mind. *Брежно*, however, is declared permissible not because this form is not

Chapter 2. The Start of Normalization of the New Literary Language

artificial, but because Trediakovskii himself used this unauthentic word — absent in Church Slavonic texts[27] — in his "Ode in Praise of the Flower of Rose " (1735, 60; 1963, 403):

> Тернием кругом оградила брежно,
> Не касалось бы к нежной что не нежно.
>
> (Trediakovskii 1735, 60; 1962, 403)

(Carefully guarded all around by thorns, nothing indelicate would touch what was delicate.)

It is likewise characteristic that Kantemir, citing an example of a permissible instr. pl. in -ы/-и, gives the example *роги*, hardly the first word that would come to mind. An association with the opening lines of his "Petrida" probably came into play here:

> Я той, иже некогда забавными слоги,
> Не зол, устремлял свои с охотою роги...
>
> (Kantemir I, 297)

(I am the one who once, with amusing words,
Not spiteful, willingly directed my horns ...)

True, although *роги here* is not in the instr. pl. (but rather *слоги*, which rhymes with it), the connection with this concrete text seems fairly clear.

And so the theoretical notion of poetic license allowed for the creation of a special poetic language, which in Russian conditions turned out to be significantly closer to the traditional bookish language than a language without them would be. For Trediakovskii, this seems to have been the limit of the significance of the poetic language. In his linguistic views of the 1730's and early 1740's a special poetic language was conceptualized not as indicator of the specific linguistic situation, but as a separate (if extremely important) register, whose existence helped one get around the restrictive limits of Classicist purism. Kantemir went farther and connected the defense of poetic license to his general understanding of the linguistic situation. For him poetic liberties become not merely permissible deviations from a

---

[27] In late seventeenth century Church Slavonic texts one may meet осторожно and бережно, although in the *Slovar' XI–XVII vv.* the latter is not listed and the former is only attested in a non-bookish text (SRIa, I, 144; SRIa, XIII, 154). [...] Be that as it may, this type of example shows that the forms Trediakovskii proposed were completely artificial and not connected to orientation on the Church Slavonic tradition, which, on the contrary, assimilated their natural equivalents.

2. The Conflict Between Linguistic Theory and Actual Practice

linguistic norm but distinctive marks of a special poetic speech to which the impoverishing norms of prose language cannot and should not be applied.

In the "Letter of Khariton Makentin" Kantemir wrote:

> The French language... does not have a poetic idiom; it must use the same expressions in verse as in ordinary prose composition (v prostoslozhnom sochinenii)... Our language, on the contrary, may properly adopt unusual words from Slavonic in order to separate poetry from the ordinary language and thereby strengthen its verse... Italians, Spaniards, the English and perhaps even others with whose languages I am unfamiliar, who have means similar to ours, have been very successful in free verse. Why then do we not favor the judgment of so many peoples? (Kantemir 1744, 5–6; II, 2–3)

Kantemir thus declaratively rejects Classicist purism as it applies to poetic language, polemicizing with the French and preferring to follow the Italian linguistic and literary tradition (see Pumpianskii 1935, 83–100; Pumpianskii 1941a, 186–7; see also Grasshoff 1966, Baracchi 1990, 101f), which the French Classicists detested (Bouhours 1671, 50f). Moreover, his statements may have been immediately directed against Vaugelas' thesis cited earlier (Kantemir would most likely have been familiar with his "Remarks") that juxtaposed the French and Italian traditions, giving clear preference to the former.

However, the most immediate sources for this juxtaposition were evidently Voltaire's "Essay on Epic Poetry" (Voltaire, II, 353–80) and the negative response by the Italian poet and translator (and close acquaintance of Kantemir) Paolo Antonio Rolli, entitled "Critical Examination of M. Voltaire's Essay on Epic Poetry" (Rolli 1729; on his relations with Kantemir, see Grasshoff 1966, 119–21). In his essay, Voltaire had written that different languages have different natures, and that this is felt in the way that different national traditions develop the common classical heritage:

> You sense in the best modern writers the character of their countries through their imitations of the classics; their flowers and fruits germinate and are ripened by the same sun, but from the soil that nourishes them they receive their tastes, colors, and different forms. You recognize an Italian, a Frenchman, an Englishman, a Spaniard by his style as by his facial features, by his accent and manners. The sweetness and softness of the Italian language is insinuated into the genius of Italian authors. Verbal pomp, metaphors, a majestic style—these, it seems to me, generally speaking, characterize Spanish writers. Power, energy, daring are particular qualities of English; they love allegories and comparisons above all. The French possess clarity, exactness, elegance; they take few risks; they do not have the power of the English, which seems to them something gigantic and monstrous, nor the Italian sweetness, which to them seems to degenerate into a feminine softness. (Voltaire, II, 355)

Voltaire further analyzes Tasso's *Jerusalem Liberated* and while acknowledging it as a masterpiece nevertheless makes a series of comments on its weaknesses, having in mind primarily its deviations from what is natural, among other things, in language (ibid, 370). This is the conceptual framework which Kantemir develops. He also speaks of four languages, French, English, Italian, and Spanish, but gives preference not to French like Voltaire, but to Italian, Spanish and English, and he rejects that "dryness" (sécheresse) of French, of which Voltaire speaks (ibid, 379) as a model for Russian. We may suggest that Kantemir at least in part took the side of Rolli, who denied the simplistic correlation of the genius of the language and the character of literature, and in particular, who refused to accept that Italian was especially soft or effeminate. In any case, a special poetic language seemed to Rolli as something obvious, and he speaks positively of Trissino,[28] which naturally signified a decisive rejection of the assertion that the poetic and spoken languages had to be in agreement. Rolli could have had an influence on Kantemir in this area as well.

Apart from the Italians, Kantemir might also have followed the lead of Feofan Prokopovich, who had a significant influence on the formation of his literary views in the late 1720's – early 30's (§ I–2.2). In his view on the poetic language, Feofan developed the pre-Classicist tradition that held that, at least as far as lexicon, poetry was necessarily opposed to prose and did not employ commonly used vocabulary.[29] In principle, one could connect this line of development (Prokopovich – Kantemir) with the broader influence of Russian school poetics and rhetoric on the theoretical views of the creators of the new Russian language and literature; the fact that they repudiated the school tradition did not exclude such influence (cf. Zhivov 1988c). In This connection it is interesting to note the young Lomonosov's negative attitude to the French tradition. In the "Letter on the Rules of Russian Versification" of 1739 he wrote: "The French, who want to act naturally in everything, almost always bring about the opposite despite their intention; as far as us, and [poetic] feet, they cannot serve as an example; because, trusting to their fantasy, and not the rules, they paste words together in their verse so haphazardly that you can't call it either prose or poetry... I cannot rejoice enough that our Russian language in its boldness and heroic

---

[28] Gian Giorgio Trissino (1478–1550), Italian poet and dramatist, best known for his tragedy "Sofonisba" (published 1524) in blank verse, that attempted to be faithful to classical rules. (Translator's note)

[29] See the passage in Prokopovich's *Rhetoric* (Lachmann 1982, 35), based on a treatise by Nicholas Caussinus. […]

sound does not yield to Greek, Latin, or German, but, like them, can in itself have both its own and natural versification" (Lomonosov, III, 5–5; VII², 13). Thus, if Trediakovskii followed the reigning French tradition, Kantemir and Lomonosov sought models outside of France (at least, for particular aspects of their conceptions), and this also helped them seek solutions to the difficult problems of creating a "European" language and literature for Russia.

Defining a special poetic language had special importance for lexicon. As we have seen, Classicist purism posed the task of classifying vocabulary by genetic parameters, thus establishing the special category of lexical Slavonicisms in the new Russian literary language, and it posed the practically impossible task of ridding the language of them (§ II–1.3). The notion of a poetic language made it possible to bypass this challenge in practice and to leave the limits of the given lexical class unspecified.

The conception of the poetic language described here directly influenced attitudes toward the literary tradition and spoken usage. If, as has been noted, theory gave primacy to the spoken usage of the court and of "elegant company" at the same time as the importance of the literary (Church Slavonic) tradition was downplayed, in practice the unlimited acceptance of Slavonicisms in the poetic language made orientation on usage a speculative fiction and simultaneously sanctioned the tie with the preceding tradition. Literary theory imperturbably proclaimed European dogmas, and this facade served to reconcile enthusiastic supporters of European innovation with the literary and linguistic continuities imposed by the literary process itself.

2.2 The Language of the Ode and Church Slavonic Panegyric Poetry

The attitude of the new generation of Russian poets (Kantemir and Trediakovskii, and later Lomonosov and Sumarokov) toward the preceding tradition of syllabic poetry was outspokenly negative. In France, Classicism strove to transform the already existing literary and linguistic tradition, to which it related critically, but did not deny. In one way or another, Classicist theories were oriented on the "vices" of previous literature, and its prescriptions were aimed at remedying them. But correcting defects is necessarily the continuation of a larger literary process, taking continuity for granted. In Europe the literary past existed in its full scope, and served as the material from which Boileau and Vaugelas worked out the new literature and the new literary language.

The situation was fundamentally different in Russia. Classicism was formed as part of the new culture that negated the old (cf. Lotman and Uspenskii 1977), and as far as it was concerned, the literary past was virtually nonexistent. The negation of the previous tradition could focus on various issues, and it was only in the 1750's that the clash between syllabic and syllabo-tonic versification systems became dominant. Thus at first Kantemir simply disparaged the syllabic *virshi* of Sil'vestr Medvedev and Fedor Polikarpov:

> Сенька и Федька когда песнь пели
> Пред тобою,
> Как немазаны двери скрипели
> Ветчиною.
>
> (Kantmir, I, 284)

(When Senka and Fedka sang their song before you [Feofan Prokopovich] it was like squeakling doors ungreased by fat.)

Later he criticized the misuse by "base versifiers" of "imperfect [that is, infinitive] rhymes in *-ami,* because they are very unpleasant to the ear" (Kantemir 1744, 9; II, 6). Trediakovskii allowed such rhymes, but in "our old" verse finds the lack of tonic feet intolerable because they "were more like prose, going along with a certain number [of syllables], rather than verse that sings." He also calls ten-syllable and twelve-syllable meters "the most abhorrent monster in verse" (Trediakovskii 1735, 69; 1963, 408, 410). On his part, Lomonosov condemned replacing trochees with pyrrichs, spondees and iambs and criticized obligatory feminine rhyme in the "Letter on the Rules of Russian Poetry" (1739). Rejecting Trediakovskii in these issues, Lomonosov referred to the previous literary tradition as the source of his errors. In one case, he writes: "This baseless usage which was imported into Moscow schools from Poland cannot supply any kind of law or rule for our versification." In another case, he noted that "As is apparent, this rule originated in Poland, from where it arrived in Moscow and was intentionally established there. This custom is just as baseless as imitating Polish rhymes..." (Lomonosov, III, 5, 9; VII^2, 12–13, 16).

Even though Russian authors borrowed the critical formulas of French Classicism, in Russian conditions, by force of their total denial of the past, the corresponding target of criticism – the previous literary and linguistic tradition –was absent. The energy of Russian writers was directed not at criticizing their predecessors but at creating a new literature (a new literary language and new literary genres). It is indicative that while Boileau in *L'art poétique* names dozens of earlier French writers (if only to criticize them), in the programmatic works of Russian Classicists (Trediakovskii's "Epistle of Russian Poetry to Apollo" and Sumarokov's epistle "On Poetry") Russian authors are hardly mentioned (Sumarokov, it is true, speaks of Prokopovich and Kantemir in the draft of his epistle, precisely because they may be seen as the direct predecessors of Russian Classicism). On the other hand they do mention a multitude of classical and Western European writers who serve to embody the literary past; the new Russian literature is perceived not as a continuation of older Russian literature but as a continuation of the European tradition (cf. Klein 1990, 267–9). It was precisely this continuation that was to be created. We are dealing here with the phenomenon that A. S. Lappo-Danilevskii called epigenesis (1990, 21), which he juxtaposed to processes of organic development.[30]

The first Russian Classicists considered themselves the creators of a new literature, and hotly debated which of them was the first to establish "correct" poetry (see: Trediakovskii 1963, 441–2; Lomonosov, IX^2, 631; Sumarokov, IX, 220; and also: Kunik 1865 XL and ff; Berkov 1936, 68f). Significant in these arguments was, of course, not only the priority of creating the new poetry, but also of condemning the old.[31] Be that as it may, however sharp the declared break from the past was, it could not be complete or consistent. Using elements of the previous literary and linguistic tradition was unavoidable. Cardinal issues here became the appropriate versification system, the problem of literary stylistics, and that of the literary language— and in these questions the European tradition could give little help. As Trediakovskii observed in 1750, criticizing Sumarokov, and to some extent spurning his own European ideals, "Racine teaches one only how to sigh over nothing; and Boileau-Despréaux to sting everyone, [including] one's betters; but neither of these can tutor us in our language" (Kunik 1865, 449).

---

[30] One may also see something analogous to this in the later literary tradition. Thus, in the Romantic period the problem of national spirit in literature was resolved by looking to the ancient folk past. Curiously, however, Zhukovskii sought the basis for this outside of Russia: while his translations of Romantic ballads were steeped in organic pre-history, this turned out to be English or German.

[31] An important point to be made here is that practically all later literary histories have taken this avowed break with the past on faith, and based their periodization and ideas about the literary process on it. For one example, this scheme is presented in the short survey of Russian literature M. N. Murav'ev prepared for Grand Princess Elizaveta Alekseevna in 1793; the start of "European" poetry in Russia is connected with Kantemir, while the previous literary tradition (with the exception of Prokopovich's sermons) is declared to be nonexistent, with Lomonosov and Sumarokov as continuers of Kantemir's project (GARF, f. 728, op. 1, no. 1366, l. 1–9). Essentially, this stereotype still remains in today's literary consciousness, in which "ancient Russian literature" includes everything created through the seventeenth century.

Traditions here were stronger than declared antipathies. This did not apply to all genres; the verse epistle, elegy, meditative sonnet and madrigal were all new genres introduced by Trediakovskii in the *New and Short Guide* (he could hardly have known of the syllabic verse epistles, so they needn't be considered here), so that any influence of the older tradition on them would have only been felt at second hand (cf. Klein and Zhivov 1987, 235–8).

One direct influence of the literary tradition was in the sphere of panegyric poetry. However new the genre of the ode or panegyric song may have been, it fulfilled the same functional role as salutatory *kanty* or syllabic panegyrics, composed by those now detested versifiers of the "Spasskii Bridge" who could claim a more than half century tradition going back to Simeon Polotskii and the New Jerusalem poets (see Panchenko 1973, 103f). Independent of the specifics of verse form, poetic panegyrics occupied a strictly defined role in the celebratory ritual of civic holidays, and the ode might force out *kanty* as part of the ceremonies of the imperial cult only by becoming their full functional equivalent, that is, by fulfilling the very same expectations of their most august listeners – in their phraseology, composition and style – as had been cultivated by a half century tradition of highly solemn triumphal ceremonials. As G. A. Gukovskii wrote:

> The sphere in which literature and thought applied their energy was first of all the palace, which played the role of political and cultural center... [It was both] temple of the monarchy and a theater in which magnificent spectacles were to be played out, whose basic idea was to demonstrate the might, greatness, and unearthly character of the earthly power... The solemn ode and panegyric speech ('slovo') were the most visible types of official literary creation; they existed not so much on paper as in the ceremonial of official festivities... Poetry, and belles lettres in general, did not exist all by itself at that time; it figured as one element of a larger synthetic action put together by painters, tailors, upholsterers, actors, courtiers, dance-master (tantsmeistr), master of ceremonies (tseremoniimeistr), master of fireworks, architect, academicians and poets — which as a whole came together to fashion an imperial court performance. (Gukovskii 1936, 13–14)

The newly-introduced German science of ceremonials only served to strengthen and codify traditions that had already been established in Russia, and in these ceremonies the Russian ode took an equivalent place to odes in German and to panegyric *virshi* before them (cf. Pumpianskii 1983, 19; see also Berkov 1936, 24 on the ceremonial presentation of odes).

The ode's place in the tradition of panegyric literature and its function as expression of praise in verse as part of a developed "civil cult" (§ I–1.1) conditioned its linguistic inheritance from syllabic panegyric poetry,

2. The Conflict Between Linguistic Theory and Actual Practice

as well as its parallels to ceremonial sermons, which fulfilled an analogous function in the sphere of "church ritual." The phraseology and stylistics of syllabic panegyrics derived on the one hand from the Baroque sermon (see Pozdneev 1961: 340f; Panchenko 1973: 233), and on the other, from the Slavonic Psalter (cf. Pozdneev, op. cit.). These connections were now transferred to odic poetry (see; Morozov 1880, 97, 269; Sobolevskii 1890, 1–6); Zhivov 1981, 65–70; Uspenskii and Zhivov 1983, 47–48; Rothe 1984, 95; Klein and Zhivov 1987, 276f; Sazonova 1987). Together with the literary heritage came the linguistic, and therefore Church Slavonic vocabulary and phraseology became an unavoidable component of odic discourse. Theoretical constructions could only legitimize these consequences of the literary process. As in the case of poetic license, it was necessary to find alternative ways to legitimize the repudiated literary tradition.

Naturally, these alternative routes were not so much a solution to the problem as a way to mitigate the contradiction between doctrine and literary practice. At every step these contradictions made themselves felt and spoiled the image of model European development. This helps explain the opposition between critical and practical positions in the literary process of this period; theoretical postulates were realized primarily by criticizing texts written by others, and did not extend to the writer's own literary production, that freely departed from the strict European (French) model. This led to a situation in which authors constantly accused each other of the very same faults. Deviations in favor of the old literary and linguistic tradition were never justified openly, but only indirectly and with awkward qualifications. Accordingly, in the course of criticism, when the demands of purist doctrine made themselves strongly felt, these accepted deviations looked like unforgiveable errors, testifying to the writer's lack of skill and taste. Critical stance and practice existed in isolation from one another, as critical pronouncements and literary sins depended not so much on the author as on the goals of the particular work in question.

Thus Sumarokov charged Trediakovskii with a partiality for tautologies, also a characteristic feature of Baroque poetics (see, for example, the parodic song "Oh pleasant pleasantness," apparently intended for Tresotinius in the comedy of the same name of 1750, in which Trediakovskii was mocked [Sumarokov 1957, 284, 559]. Sumarokov discusses this in his "Answer to Criticism":

> *An ode's disorder must be orderly* [a quotation from Trediakovskii's "Letter from a Friend to a Friend"—Kunik 1865, 473]. Orderly disorder is his favorite expression, like beautiful beauty, pleasant pleasantness, bitter bitterness, sweet sweetness; but Boileau does not say that an ode has to have orderly disorder:

Chapter 2. The Start of Normalization of the New Literary Language

> Son stile impétueux souvent marche en Hazard.
> Chez elle un beau desordre est un effet de l'art.
> (Its impetuous style often proceeds randomly.
> In it beautiful disorder is an effect of art.)
>
> (Sumarokov, X, 108)

It would seem as if the issue here has to do with Trediakovskii's special bias, and that he simply does not notice its incompatibility with Classicist teaching. But in the very same "Letter from a Friend to a Friend," that is, in the very same criticism Sumarokov was responding to, he was accused of the very same failing. Trediakovskii comments on one of Sumarokov's odes:

> "To the feet of a pedestal"—is that good? To be sure a pedestal does not have to do with arms. And although we do have in the Psalms *покланяйтеся подножие ногу его* [Psalm 110: 1 "I shall make your enemies a footstool for your feet"], this is a translation, and perhaps in Hebrew the word pedestal doesn't come from the word for feet, just as the Latin scabellum is not from feet. To bring the proud down to the pedestal of a monarch, even without adding feet, is a very glorious and heroic thing, and painful for the proud. (Kunik 1865, 454)

Sumarokov's phrase "низкий дол" (low vale) that he uses in his periphrastic ode of Psalm 143 arouses similar criticism:

> In the fourth verse of this stanza the author applies the adjective "low" to the noun "vale." But we know of no vale that's not low, unless the author has some kind of high one in mind. This is precisely what poets call a stop-gap [*затычка*, a calque of the French *cheville*, apparently used here for the first time — V. Z.], when something unnecessary is added to a verse to fit the meter. But the author should know that adjectives are used to clarify the nature of things, for praise or censure or some other similar kind of clarification; for to say "watery water" or "sunny sun" is to say nothing. Similarly no one would say "low vale." (Kunik 1865, 445)

As we may observe, in their criticism both Sumarokov and Trediakovskii criticize the use of tautological word combinations, while at the same time making use of them in their writing.

An analogous discrepancy between critical and literary practice may also be seen in the relations between Sumarokov and Lomonosov. Sumarokov attacks Lomonosov for using "senseless" metaphors and for combining "distant ideas" which contradict the norms of Classicist poetics, and this has led scholars to speak of the Baroque character of Lomonosov's odes (cf. Tschižhewskii 1960; Tschižhewskii 1970; Morozov 1965; Morozov 1974). This theoretical conflict was certainly connected with the issue of continuity with the Church Slavonic literary tradition which "was completely

2. The Conflict Between Linguistic Theory and Actual Practice

unthinkable without metaphorical expression" (Rothe 1984, 95). Starting with Gukovskii (Gukovskii 1927 and 1927a), this conflict has been seen as the actual reflection of basic differences in poetic practice (cf. Lachmann 1981), but this leads to the underestimation of the rationalist aspect of Lomonosov's odic style and of the Baroque elements in Sumarokov's own odic poetics. The problem here is the mistaken assumption that critical and literary practices corresponded. But in Sumarokov there is no such correspondence whatsoever. It is revealing that in his own solemn odes he repeatedly uses the very same expressions for which he mocks Lomonosov's. For example, compare the second Nonsense Ode:

> Эфес горит, Дамаск пылает,
> Тремя Цербер гортаньми лает,
> Средьземный возжигает понт.
>
> (Sumarokov, II, 207)

(Ephesus burns, Damascus blazes, Cerberus barks with three throats, the Mediterranean sea is kindled)

to the Ode on the First Day of the New Year 1763

> Цербер гортаньми всеми лает,
> Геена изо врат пылает.
> Раздвинул челюсти Плутон.
>
> (ibid, 52)

(Cerberus barks with all his throats, Gehenna blazes from its gates, Pluto drew open his jaws.)

One more example. In the first Nonsense Ode:

> Отверз уста правитель моря'
> Сто крат сильняе стала буря,
> И Океан вострепетал
>
> (ibid, 206)

(The ruler of the sea opened his lips, the storm became a hundred times stronger, and the ocean convulsed)

And the Ode on Name-day of 1762:

> Вещает Царь Небесных стран:
> Природа бурей возшумела,
> Потрясся вихрем окиян,
>
> (ibid, 47)

(The tsar of celestial realms prophesies: nature boomed with a storm, shaking the ocean with a whirlwind.)

195

Chapter 2. The Start of Normalization of the New Literary Language

Such examples could be multiplied (see more in Klein and Zhivov 1987, 244–5). In advancing a literary theory, however, it was not enough to merely abuse one's rivals. It was necessary to put forward positive principles that would at least partially legitimize the peculiarities of Russian literary practice, first of all the hidden continuity with the Church Slavonic literary tradition. This task prompted the search for those European theoretical propositions that would make such legitimization possible. This search led Russian authors — Trediakovskii in the first place, but also Kantemir — to the theoretical constructions of the "ancients," although in their Russian reception these significantly differed from the originals.

Trediakovskii's "Discourse on the Ode in General" is a clear example of such legitimization. As noted (§ II–1.1), Trediakovskii chose Boileau's ode on the taking of Namur as model for the first Russian ode; this was an emphatically experimental work which was meant to convey Pindar's peculiar style and poetics, which went counter to the basic tenets of French Classicism (on the contemporary negative reaction to this poem, see Janik 1968, 226; and also Achinger 1970, 28–9). In defending the literary legacy of the ancients Boileau wanted to demonstrate to the French reader the beauty of classical poetry, and thanks to this he ignored his own purist precepts. As Voltaire noted, "as soon as Despréaux tried to raise himself up in the ode, he was no longer Despréaux" (Voltaire, II, 37).

Among the arguments with which Boileau countered those of the "moderns" (especially Charles Perrault), Boileau noted in particular that by criticizing Pindar's style, Perrault was also condemning the similar style of the Psalter (Boileau, II, 202). It is precisely this poetics, common to both Pindar and the Psalter, that Boileau wanted to convey in his ode.[32]

---

[32] The same thinking may be seen in Boileau's "Critical Reflections on Longinus," in which he also polemicizes with Perrault [...] (Boileau, II, 407). Speaking here about a Homeric hyperbole of the goddess of discord whose head touches the heavens (Iliad, 5: 443), Boileau refers to similar tropes in the Psalter. Reference to the poetics of the Psalter simultaneously serves as justification of the daring of classical poetry and its reproduction in Classicist works. This poetics functions as a model of the sublime that is not subject to criticism. One can find this idea in other French authors, for example, in Jean-Baptiste Rousseau, who also refers to the Psalter in connection with Longinus' treatise on the sublime (Rousseau 1823, I, 1; see below).

Curiously, Homeric hyperbole, having received Boileau's sanction, became a regular feature of Russian odic poetry, for example, in Sumarokov's ode to Elizabeth on the Prussian war:

> Но ону [пучину] Атлас презирает,
> Ея ногами попирает,
> Главой касаясь небесам... (Sumarokov, II, 24)

(But Atlas disdains the abyss, he tramples it with his feet, his head touching the heavens...)
One may find similar images in Lomonosov (e.g., Lomonosov, I, 147; II, 120).

2. The Conflict Between Linguistic Theory and Actual Practice

Thus Boileau's ode may be seen in a very complex literary and historical setting which allowed for more than one interpretation. Appealing to Pindar, which was polemically directed against the "moderns," could also be aimed at appropriating the special prestige which the Pléiade had accorded him; Boileau presents as it were a "correct" French Pindar, as opposed to the "incorrect" Pindar of Ronsard. He asserts the appropriateness of Pindar's poetics by alluding to the Psalter, because even the "moderns" could not allow themselves to denigrate its poetry openly.

Trediakovskii, as opposed to Boileau, was writing a model ode rather than an experimental one, and his goal was to lay the groundwork for a Russian odic tradition. Therefore, in following Boileau's "Discourse on the Ode" in his own treatise, Trediakovskii completely ignored that work's polemical context (§ II–1.2). Because of this, Boileau's "daring" modifications become for Trediakovskii the genre's required features. One of these features is orientation on the stylistics of the Psalter. Having discussed "odes written in foreign languages" in his own "Discourse," Trediakovskii wanted to present a model ode written in Russian, and the Slavonic Psalter is cited in this capacity:

> A Russian connoisseur may take note of the loftiness of the words — of the kind that should be in odes — in the psalms of the holy psalmic poet, that is, the blessed prophet and King David; for the psalms are nothing other than Odes, although the psalms have not been translated into verse in Russian, as they have not been in other Christian tongues, even though they were all [originally] composed in Hebrew verse, according to the Hebrew poetic practice of their day.[33] He will see in them nobility of subject matter, richness of adornment, and magnificence of language; he will see an amazing ascent to the heights, flying high by means of style, of a kind met in Pindar and Horace, and which Mr. Boileau-Despréaux enjoins; he will see and admit that this is the divine tongue itself. (Trediakovskii 1734, l. 14 verso.)

In this way, while apparently developing Boileau's views, Trediakovskii at the very same time legitimizes the connection of the Russian ode with the Slavonic Psalter, and consequently, also implicitly with the tradition of Church Slavonic syllabic panegyrics.[34]

The practical results of this theoretical development are clearly seen in the following example. In the first lines of Trediakovskii's ode, which

---

[33] Trediakovskii is referring to the standard European Bible translations (e.g., the King James version, Luther's Bible) that were in prose, rather than to the literary tradition of verse paraphrases (e.g., Simeon Polotskii's *Psaltir'*, published in 1680).

[34] Trediakovskii's view of the supreme importance of the Psalter as poetic model could also have been supported by arguments from Rollin, whom he so greatly valued. See Achinger 1970, 28–9.

were meant as a translation of Boileau's opening lines, he wrote:

> Кое трезвое мне пианство
> Слово дает к славной причине?
> Чистое *Парнасса* убранство,
> Музы! не вас ли вижу ныне?

(Trediakovskii 1734, l.B verso)

(What sober intoxication does the word give me for this glorious purpose? Pure adornment of Parnassus, Muses! Is it you that I now see?)

Compare Boileau:

> Quelle docte et sainte ivresse
> Aujourd'hui me fait la loi!
> Chastes Nymphes du Permesse,
> N'ést-ce pas vous que je voi?

(Boileau, II, 205)

(What learned and sacred intoxication has become the law for me today! Chaste nymphs of Parnassus, Is it not you that I see?)

This juxtaposition reveals that Trediakovskii made use of "Pindaric daring" in introducing an oxymoron into his ode, absent in Boileau's text. Indeed oxymorons were one of the defining features of Baroque poetics and were decidedly alien to Classicism, in particular to Boileau's version of Classicism. It is understandable that this violation of the norms of Classicist usage would provoke criticism from adherents of purist doctrine. Sumarokov, addressing the theoretical rather than the practical issue, wrote in his "Answer to Criticism" that "his [Trediakovskii's] favorite expression is to combine a noun with a most inappropriate adjective, for example, *трезвое пианство* [*sober intoxication*], a phrase in which he tried to imitate [the line from] Boileau's Ode: 'Quelle docte et sainte yvresse.' But it is hardly similar" (X: 95). Significantly, when Trediakovskii republished the poem in 1752, he corrected the lines to read:

> Кое странное пианство
> К пению мой глас бодрит!

(Boileau 1752, II, 21)

(What strange intoxication makes bold my voice for song!)

Even more significantly, the phrase "sober intoxication" was itself taken from the vocabulary of religious, ascetic literature, in which it described a state of mystic ecstasy (cf. the Greek "μέθη νηφάλιος," Latin "sobria ebrietas"); it was applicable to poetic ecstasy as well. The expression

2. The Conflict Between Linguistic Theory and Actual Practice

"μέθη νηφάλιος" goes back to Philo of Alexandria who uses it to describe the rapturous condition of the soul, a mystical union with the divine. The underlying notion corresponds to Platonic ideas and may be seen in the context of the developing Greek cult of the soul ("Seelencult"; see Rohde 1894). In the first century, as a result of the Hellenistic rethinking of Platonic theories and their combination with the rhetorical tradition (the doctrine of pathos-ecstasy and of psychological principles), this idea led to the spread of ideas about poetic genius and poets' prophetic gifts (see Lewy 1929, 54–63; Flashar 1959, 287–307; cf. Coulter 1976), which left a trace, in particular, in Pseudo-Longinus.[35] This tradition apparently served as the background for Boileau's "sainte ivresse"; in his poem Boileau evoked the ancient coloration, making use of Pseudo-Longinus, whose ideas he so greatly valued. Western European mysticism, which promoted this tradition in various forms, could have served as a mediating link.

However, Trediakovskii's "sober intoxication" points not to the classical but to the patristic tradition. This expression was fairly common in both Greek and Latin patristics, and may be encountered in Origen, Eusebius, and Gregory of Nyssa (Lewy 1929, 119–64). In Greek patristics, it had a centuries' long history, appearing, for example, in Symeon the New Theologian (see Krivoshein 1962; Krivoshein 1980, 71–2) and could also make it into hymnography (Lewy 1929, 146). Echoes of this may also be found in Slavonic writing, for example, in the Service to Ss. Constantine and Cyril "Touching the chalice of wisdom with your lips, you were filled up with salvific intoxication" (Service menalogion [Mineia sluzhebnaia] of the early twelfth century, for the month of February — GIM, Sin. 164; Lavrov 1930, 108). In this tradition the expression could signify both the ascetic's ecstatic state as well as the state of believers in general, deified by communion with the divine. This is from where Trediakovskii takes the phrase, applying it to poetic inspiration and thereby (apparently, unconsciously) returning words that were familiar to him to their classical roots. And so in his programmatic poem, meant as a model for the Classicist ode, Trediakovskii employed a cliché from the religious literary tradition that contradicted the norms of Classicist stylistics (he probably took the phrase from the Latin; it is obvious, however, that for Trediakovskii, graduate of the Slavono-Greco-Latin

---

[35] The idea is reflected in rhetorical manuals in the doctrine of genius, inspiration, and "furor poeticus." Poetic inspiration could be described in these terms as sacred intoxication, Dionysian ecstasy, in which the hidden nature of things is revealed to the poet. Pseudo-Longinus' treatise "On the Sublime" may serve as a striking evidence of this development; it says, in part, that the poet "must be sober even in Bacchic frenzy" (XVI.4); M. Flashar demonstrates that these words show the direct influence of Philo's teaching (Flashar 1959, 308–322).

Academy, Latin, Greek and Slavonic patristics represented a single literary and linguistic tradition).

The given example is especially meaningful because Trediakovskii was not just casually deferring to customary usage but consciously introducing a phrase from religious literature as an example of a something permissible in high odic discourse. Indeed, like Boileau, in his "Discourse" Trediakovskii mounts a special defense of his poetic liberties. In this connection, Boileau speaks only about poetics, defending the possibility of the miraculous in the Pindaric ode.[36] Trediakovskii expands on this point: "My fifth stanza is no less bold, which presupposes that Her Imperial Highness is present at the siege and leads the troops, instead of leaving that honor to his excellency, Count von Minnich" (Trediakovskii 1734, l. 16 verso). I note in passing that asserting the permissibility of the miraculous does not prevent Trediakovskii from later insisting on Classicist naturalness and simplicity as requirements of odic language and depiction. This strict approach is realized, again, in his criticism, as when he attacks Sumarokov for excessive "poetic liberties" and says of one stanza of an ode of his: "it is all what the French call *phébus,* 'what we may describe as 'blowing overblown bubbles' or 'trying to grab clouds with the mouth'" (Kunik 1865, 466). Cf. also his statement that the odic disorder sanctioned by Boileau does not mean that odes should "take off in all directions like a crazed cat" (ibid, 473). Thus in regard to the "miraculous," that which is acceptable in one's own poetic practice appears to be an unforgiveable violation of the rules in someone else's verse — what, as we have suggested, was an expected result of the conflict between doctrine and practice.[37]

In distinction from Boileau, however, Trediakovskii particularly dwells on issues of language. He wrote:

> I have tried to pindarize in all aspects, that is, to imitate Pindar in everything, and so I called a sword angry, and intoxication sober, and used many other similar, very daring figures, using the most magnificent words that I could, following the example of the ancient dithyrambic poets. This is seen in the entire ode, and especially in the fourteenth stanza, in the figure that is called hyperbole, which, although it is extreme, and little similar to truth, is permitted

---

[36] Boileau writes: "I have thrown into it as many magnificent words as I could, and following the example of the ancient dithyrambic poets, I have used the boldest figures, to the point of making a white feather which the king commonly wears in his hat into a star" (Boileau, II, 203). Boileau thus speaks of poetics in terms of content, juxtaposing the Classicist categories of the "natural" and "miraculous" (see Brey 1957, 231–9).

[37] The exact same situation is repeated when Sumarokov, repudiating Trediakovskii's criticism of his lack of clarity and grandiloquence, makes the very same charges against Lomonsov's odes (cf. Gukovskii 1927).

2. The Conflict Between Linguistic Theory and Actual Practice

by the law of most audacious dithyrambism, if one may freely put it this way. (Trediakovskii 1734, l. 15—15 verso)

For Trediakovskii pindarizing thus turns into a theoretical maneuver which allows him to connect the ode with the Church Slavonic literary tradition without breaking with Classicist theory.[38]

And so the pressure of literary tradition caused Russian Classicists to diverge from the system of poetic and stylistic rules that they had assimilated from their French teachers. Justification for this was the doctrine of poetic ecstasy, *furor poeticus*, which allowed a poet to violate laws at will. In Russian conditions this right acquired much greater importance than for the French, and it was insisted upon with greater determination and consistency; and it was by no means limited to the framework of "beau desordre" which the true Classicist would only accept with careful moderation, following Boileau's instructions. Pindarizing spelled the complete destruction of the norms of Classicist poetics, legalizing the Baroque poetics of the Russian ode. Baroque poetics, and through this the connection to the previous literary tradition, became normative, and emerged as evidence of the poet's prophetic gift. By calling poetic ecstasy "sober intoxication," Trediakovskii attributed a providential significance to it. This ecstasy also ultimately defined the connection of odic poetry and Biblical prophecy, that "very language of God" in which the destruction of logical connectedness reveals the truth that lies beyond simple comprehension. In this case, however, the criteria for evaluating a poetic work transcends those rational principles put forward by Classicism, and entirely depends on the acceptance or rejection of the poet's prophetic gift. In obvious contradiction to Classicist aesthetics, the very same formal characteristics could apply to both genuine and counterfeit poetry.[39] Prophetic foresight of the true poet is contrasted to the blindness

---

[38] The verb "pindarisovat" corresponds to the French "pindariser." At first this verb meant "to write, imitating Pindar; to write in an exalted way, like Pindar." This was just how the verb was used in the sixteenth century. Thus Ronsard wrote (Odes, bk. II, 2) "Le premier de France J'ai pindarizé" (Ronsard, I, 433). But Ronsard did have predecessors; at the start of the sixteenth century Saint-Gellais declared "J'ay d'autres fois voulu pindariser." By the end of the seventeenth century, however, the verb had acquired a negative connotation — "to write pompously, with affectation" (DFA², II, 279; DFA³, II, 340). This was clearly connected to the reevaluation of the sixteenth-century literary heritage and of Baroque poetics that contradicted the Classicist idea of naturalness (cf. Trésor 1988, 389). It is all the more characteristic that Trediakovskii "pindarizes," ignoring contemporary French usage; employing a term of French Baroque poetics, he seems to be declaring that the ode is a genre which has the right to violate Classicist canons.

[39] French writers fully understood the dangerous nature of the idea of poetic ecstasy for the normative aesthetic of Classicism, as well as for its linguistic and stylistic aspect. Thus Bouhours, who without qualms assigns all merits to French poetry and language and all faults

Chapter 2. The Start of Normalization of the New Literary Language

of false ones, whose lack of logical connectedness leads to a "muddle," and for whom "intemperate enthusiasm" replaces "sober intoxication." This is exactly the scheme Trediakovskii applies to an ode by Sumarokov, indicating its logical disconnectedness: "Is this not, my Lord, that very same intemperate enthusiasm? Or rather, is it not that muddled muddle, in which round and square are mixed up? It must have been that our author snapped up too much of those Hippocrene waters when he composed this" (Kunik 1865, 463). "Intemperate enthusiasm" here appears as negative antipode to "sober intoxication," demonstrating that Russian authors fully understood the anomalous character of odic poetics and stylistics.

For all that, the given anomaly became the standard feature of high style, and this strange imperative cannot help but be connected to the necessary continuity between the new poetics and traditional literature, which imposed itself by virtue of the linguistic material itself. The mutual connection we have described between the doctrine of poetic ecstasy, Baroque poetics and stylistics, and literary-linguistic continuity was by no means simply Trediakovskii's individual contrivance, but the natural result of the literary process. Indeed, one may uncover the same connections in Lomonosov as well.

In his "Short Guide to Oratory" of 1748, Lomonsov wrote:

> Rapture (voskhishchenie) is when a writer imagines himself in [a state of] amazement, in a dream state, produced by something very great, unexpected or strange and supernatural. This figure [of speech] is almost always accompanied by imagination (vymysel [i.e., something made up]), and is common in poets, for example: In Ovid's *Metamorphosis,* bk. 15, Pythagoras says:
>
>> Устами движет Бог; я с ним начну вещать.
>> Я тайности свои и небеса отверзу,
>> Свидения ума священнаго открою.
>> Я дело стану петь несведомое прежним;
>> Ходить превыше звезд влечет меня охота,
>> И облаком нестись, презрев земную нискость.

(God moves [my] lips; I begin to prophesy with him. I will reveal my secrets and those of the heavens; I will disclose the visions of the holy mind. I will begin to sing what was not known before. I am drawn to wander high above the stars and be carried along likeas a cloud, disdaining the mean earth below.)

And Boileau-Despréaux, beginning his ode on the taking of Namur, says:

---

to Italian and Spanish, [...] warns that that poetic furor may produce absurd results (Bouhours 1671, 60–1).

2. The Conflict Between Linguistic Theory and Actual Practice

What learned and holy intoxication makes the law for me today? Pure muses of Permessus, do I not see you. Hurry your most wise visage to the ringing to which my lyre gives birth. Then come the following lines:

> Какая бодрая дремота
> Открыла мысли явный сон?
> Еще горит во мне охота
> Торжественный возвысить тон.
>
> (Lomonosov, III, 264–5; VII², 284–5)

(What bold drowsiness has revealed a waking dream to my mind? Desire still burns in me to elevate my triumphant tone.)

As one may observe, the above passage combines precisely those elements that we have described in Trediakovskii: an indication of the connection between poetic ecstasy and supernaturally revealed knowledge (which, moreover, Lomonosov refers to as dreaming, that is, a delusion, fearing to equate poets with genuine holy men); backing this up by reference to the classical (Pythagorean) tradition; mention of Boileau's Namur ode as model of a poet's ecstatic speech; and a legitimization of Baroque poetics and style (in particular, invention and hyperbole) as the necessary means for expressing poetic prophecy. In fact, as a Russian example Lomonosov cites his own "Ode on the Arrival of Elizabeth from Moscow to St. Petersburg" of 1742 (Lomonosov, I, 97) in the first stanza of which, reflecting the poet's ecstatic condition, there are two whole oxymorons, "bold drowsiness" and "waking dream." Both of these are used in the same sense as "sober intoxication" in Trediakovskii, as an indication of poetic ecstasy; and as in Trediakovskii they correspond to Boileau's "sainte ivresse" (although in Lomonosov's prose translation he manages without the oxymoron). The similarity even extends to the details. Indeed, Sumarokov subjects these oxymorons to mockery as well. In the first Nonsense Ode, parodying Lomonosov, he writes:

> Не сплю, но в бодрой я дремоте,
> И на яву зрю страшный сон. ..
>
> (Sumarokov, II, 206)

(I don't sleep, but in my bold drowsiness I, waking, see a horrible dream...)

Sumarokov's perspective on Lomonosov is critical, and as one would expect he denies the authenticity of his prophetic gift. As we have seen, such negation removes all justification for breaking the norms of Classicist poetics and style, turning "sober intoxication" into "intemperate enthusiasm." In his polemic with Lomonosov, Sumarokov precisely follows the model Trediakovskii presented when criticizing him himself, as "bold drowsiness" and "waking dream" are also declared attributes of poetic muddle. This motif appears in the fourth Nonsense Ode ("Difiramb Pegasu" [Dithyramb to Pegasus]):

> В безоблачной стране несуся,
> Напившись Ипокренских вод,
> И их напившися трясуся
> Производитель громких Од!
>
> ....
>
> Род смертных, Пиндара высока
> Стремится подражать мой дух,
> От запада и от востока
> Лечу на север и на юг...
>
> (Sumarokov, II, 209–10)[40]

(I am carried through the cloudless realm, having gotten drunk on Hippocrene's waters, and, having drunk my fill, I tremble, producer of loud odes!... My spirit, kin of mortals, strives to imitate high Pindar. From west and east I fly to North and South...)

Here too there is a metamorphosis of "holy ecstasy" into delirious frenzy (see also Sumarokov's fable "The Monkey Poet," Sumarokov, IX, 169–70). Of course, this does not prevent Sumarokov from referring to Pindar as model of inspired poetry in other cases, and in his own high style poetry (Sumarokov, II, 193–5).

However incompatible these traits of high style poetry might have been with critical principles, *furor poeticus* in its special Russian variant became a regular marker of the ode as a genre, and by force of extrapolation, a constituent element of high style in general. The linguistic expression of this generic marker was "pindarizing," a departure from the linguistic and stylistic norms of Classicist purism elevated to a system, whose generic model was the Psalter. It should be emphasized again that in Russian

---

[40] The same motif is developed in the fifth Nonsense Ode ("Difiramv" [Dithyramb]):

> Позволь великий Бахус, нынь
> Направити гремящу Лиру,
> И во священном мне восторге
> Тебе воспеть похвальну песнь!..
>
> ....
>
> Крепчайших вин горю в жару,
> Во изступлении пылаю:
> В лучах мой ум блистает солнца,
> Усугубляя силу их.
>
> (Sumarokov, II, 214)

(Please, great Bacchus, direct my thundering lyre today in my holy ecstasy to sing you a song of praise!... I burn in a fever of the strongest spirits, I blaze in a frenzy: my mind sparkles in the sun's rays, redoubling their strength.

2. The Conflict Between Linguistic Theory and Actual Practice

conditions this connection with the Psalter took on not only literary but also linguistic importance. True, in connecting the ode with the psalms, Russian authors could fall back on indisputable French precedents, which had a long tradition, and which gave the ode a special status in terms of the Classicist canon.[41] However in France the connection of the ode and the Psalter did not properly relate to questions of language, as the Psalter remained in Latin, and the ode in French; and French translations of the Bible did not have the important cultural status as did the Latin and Slavonic Bibles; cf. Brunot, V, 25–31). The connection related to general aspects of poetics (the character of metaphors, logical development, composition, etc.) and not to specific shared linguistic elements. In Russia, on the other hand, appeals to the Church Slavonic Psalter legitimized not only elements of biblical poetics but also grammatical and lexical elements of the old bookish tradition, those which according to the new genetic definition were labeled "Slavonicisms." This linguistic aspect had broad relevance, defining not only the young Trediakovskii's poetic liberties but the general character of the poetic language. The Church Slavonic literary tradition had primary importance in its formation, and this continuity did not depend on any one particular author's theoretical position.

The young Lomonosov's linguistic practice is very revealing in this regard. As noted earlier (§ II–1.4), in the 1730's his general linguistic orientation, like that of Trediakovskii and Adodurov, was on spoken usage, and, as a consequence, against Slavonicisms. Apparently, he held a more radical position than Trediakovskii at this time. In any case, in his marginal comments on Trediakovskii's *New and Short Guide* he singled out traditionally bookish elements (that is, elements that in the linguistic consciousness of the time were felt as specific markers of the bookish language) such as *ти, тя, мя, такожде, токмо, тако, бо,* and his annotations related equally to prose and verse. One may conclude, then, that he did not accept poetic license as a means of legitimizing Slavonicisms, as did Trediakovskii and Adodurov (§ II–2.1). At the same time he labeled a series of words and expressions as "inusitatum," which indicates that his criteria in defining linguistic material was oral practice (see Lomonosov, III, notes, 6–11; Berkov 1936, 56–7;

---

[41] I will cite only two additional examples of how the connection between odic and biblical poetics allowed the ode to preserve stylistic features that in essence contradicted the ideals of Classicism (cf. Viëtor 1923, 117–9, 139–40). Mlle. De Gournay, defending her older contemporaries of the late sixteenth-early seventeenth century from attacks of the Malherbistes, describes classical poetry as full of metaphors and cites the Bible as a model, leaving no room for doubt [...] (Gournay 1962, 66). Several decades later, we find similar declarations from such a convinced Classicist as Jean-Baptiste Rousseau [...] (Rousseau 1823, I, 2–3).

Uspenskii 1985, 88–9). These, presumably, represent Lomonsov's views in 1739, when he was writing the Khotin ode.

This ode, similar to Trediakovskii's "Ode on the Taking of Gdansk" of five years before, was created as a model of the first correct ode, that is, as more "correct" than Trediakovskii's. It is hence extremely significant that this ode manifests the very same debt to the Church Slavonic literary tradition that marks Trediakovskii's. The Slavonicisms here are routine, and one may point not only to non-pleophonic lexicon and other forms of that type (*брег, огнь, седмь*, etc.), which might not have been associated with the Church Slavonic tradition, but also infinitives in *-ти* (such as in the rhyme *покрыти — склонити* in the third stanza), which served as one of the indicators of the bookish language and which Adodurov and Trediakovskii had allowed in poetry as poetic license (§ II–2.1). No less significant was Lomonosov's use of biblical phraseology, like "Небесная отверзлась дверь" (cf. Psalm 78 [77 in the Slavonic bible], 23, 25: "и двери небесе отверзе"; Rev. 4: 1: "и се двери отверста на небеси"; Hymns (stikhiry) for Candlemas: "да отверзется дверь небесная днесь"; cf. Greshishcheva 1911, 116–7); "Россия, как прекрасный крин,/Цветет под Анниной державой" (cf. Isaiah 35:1: "Да возрадуется пустыня и процветет яко крин"; see Solosin 1913, 245–6; Cooper 1972, 74), etc.

We should keep in mind that Lomonosov's Khotin ode and the accompanying "Letter on the Rules of Russian Versification" were polemically directed against Trediakovskii's treatises and his ode on the taking of Gdansk; at some points Lomonosov rejects Trediakovskii, at others agrees with him (cf. Berkov 1936, 66–7). In this context Lomonosov's mention of Pindar in the Khotin ode ("But for your lips' eloquence, Pindar,/ Thebes would have blamed [you] more harshly" [Витийство, Пиндар, уст твоих/Тяжчаеб Фивы обвинили…"][42] — Lomonosov, I, 20; VIII², 29) unquestionably indicates the character of his poetics: in 1739 Lomonosov "pindarizes" just like Trediakovskii, and just like Trediakovskii the result is to legitimize the influence of the Church Slavonic literary tradition on high style genres.[43] The passage cited above from the *Rhetoric* of 1748 merely

---

[42] According to legend, Pindar's native Thebes was angry at his praise of its rival, Athens. (Translator's note)

[43] It is worth mentioning in this context that the "Letter on the Rules of Russian Versification" mentions Boileau's very same ode on the taking of Namur (Lomonosov, III, 5–6; VIII², 13). True, Lomonsov doesn't speak of its poetics, but the fact that its first stanza is written in tonic verse, which, in Lomonosov's opinion, people overlooked due to their perverted taste. However it is clear from this mention that Boileau's ode was considerably more popular among Russian writers than in France; this was of course not connected with its metrical characteristics but with its special poetics.

confirms this effort, which as we have seen, was present from the beginning in newly forming Russian literature.

As concerns the pindarizing of the Khotin ode, a reservation is in order. As is known, the ode was written in emulation of Günther's ode on peace with the Porte (the victory of Prince Eugene) in 1718 (see the comparison between them in Kirchner, 1961). It was this very ode that Gottsched cited as example of the German Pindaric ode (Gottsched 1751, 432; cf. Viëtor 1923, 87). In 1739, Lomonosov definitely knew of Gottsched's opinion (cf. Dan'ko 1940), and when he mentioned Pindar (who is not named in Günther's ode) he could have had the German tradition of odic poetry in mind rather than Trediakovskii (cf. Cooper 1972, 42). In the larger European context, however, both Boileau's Namur ode and Günther's ode on Prince Eugene's victory belong to one tendency. Both Trediakovskii and Lomonosov subscribed to this trend, and, of course, Lomonosov could not have been completely indifferent to Trediakovskii's precedent.

The properly linguistic aspects of this effort had been established even earlier. In accord with the Boileau — Günther tendency of linguistic practice Lomonosov had already given theoretical justification for using the previous bookish tradition in rhetorically significant genres in his *Rhetoric* of 1744. He wrote: "One should avoid old unused Slavonic phrases which people do not understand, but at the same time not abandon those whose meaning people do understand, even if they are not used in simple conversation" (§ 123 — Lomonosov, III, 68; VII^2, 70). True, in the given passage Lomonosov is not speaking of the ode, but about sermons, so one might think that this statement has nothing to do with the poetic language. But that is hardly justified. In fact, although Lomonosov specially indicates that "Rhetoric teaches how to compose prose compositions, while Poetry [teaches how] to create poems" (§ 4 — Lomonosov, III, 18; VII^2, 24), the poetic examples that he constantly offers in the *Rhetoric* of 1744 clearly demonstrate that he considers the stylistic principles applicable for high style poetic as well as prose speech; the language of poetry is clearly equated with the style in which "oratorical discourses" are to be written (§ 23, 11). Compare in the *Rhetoric:* "Style in spiritual oratory should be important, magnificent, forceful, and, in a word, appropriate in material, person, and place; for... concerning matter esteemed for its holiness it is not proper to speak with base and frivolous words" (§ 123; ibid 67; 69–70). Trediakovskii speaks in similar terms about the style of the ode (Trediakovskii 1734, l. 12 verso): in this genre "noble, important matter is always described... in the most poetical and very high language" that is contrasted to "frivolous and peasant" speech (§ 1–1.1). The stylistic parameters of odes and sermons turn out to be identical, which unquestionably parallels the connections between these genres in the larger literary process.

The problem under consideration may seem extremely narrow; instead of the general question of the character of the literary language we have focused on the issue of the language of poetry, and even that was further reduced to the question of high poetic genres, primarily the ode. But however narrow it may be, it was precisely this question which turned out to be the key for the entire plan to create a new literary language.

Certainly, subsequent literary development pushed panegyric genres to the periphery of the literary process, and the new perspective (that of the nineteenth century) conditioned the inability of readers (and scholars) to accept "the odic theme of the inseparability of poetry and the state" (Pumpianskii 1983a, 316), their rejection of the poetry of rank and pomp which had inspired all of European Classicism from Malherbe to Kheraskov. Classicism and enlightened absolutism derived from common ideas about rational order and progress which were to remake the world, freeing it from fear, superstition, and fratricidal conflict (cf. Lotman 1983; Zhivov 1989). The state became subject of poetic ecstasy and philosophical meditation precisely because it was seen as vehicle for establishing cosmic harmony on the earth. Therefore a monarch's victories, his well being, the concluding of alliances and peaceful agreements were not merely materials for depiction but themes for philosophical and artistic reflection. Progress of the state was perceived as the progress of reason and enlightenment, and not merely as the individual progress of a particular society, but as the universal development of a principle that comprised a collective value (on the genesis of these ideas, see Yates 1975; Yates 1977; Kossellek 1979; Zhivov 1989). Such was the literature of the age of Louis XIV in France, German literature of the first half of the eighteenth century — and Russian literature from Feofan Prokopovich up to Derzhavin. If was for this very reason that "state" poetry, all of those "Henriades" and "Petridas," so wearying for later readers, as well as all of those innumerable coronation and name-day odes as well as those commemorating the capture of the latest fortress, bore the weight of fundamental philosophical concerns and was considered the single worthy arena for the thinking poet, the pinnacle of creative endeavor.

It was natural then in these conditions that Russians' attention in the eighteenth century was fixed primarily on the ode as the basic genre of high poetry, and the norms of literary usage were worked out in debates over high style discourse, at the same time as the language of lower poetic genres and of prose (oratory aside) were to some extent excluded from consideration. In the linguistic consciousness of the last two thirds of the

2. The Conflict Between Linguistic Theory and Actual Practice

eighteenth century, the language of high style poetry emerged as the measure against which the diversity allowed in other types of literary speech would be gauged. Hence what was permitted in the poetic language had far greater practical significance, and defined if not the real characteristics of the entire literary language, then at least its potential possibilities. Because of this the connection of the ode with the Church Slavonic literary tradition had decisive importance for the literary language, and the ode's linguistic and stylistic parameters, extended to other high genres (such as the heroic poem and tragedy — see Gukovskii 1936, 220), became the defining characteristics of the literary norm. In practice the continuity of the ode with the Church Slavonic literary heritage led to the extensive endorsement of traditionally bookish elements — "Slavonicisms" — as norms of the literary language. Linguistic theory which had prescribed orientation on spoken usage turned out to be in plain contradiction with actual linguistic practice, and so, from the mid-1740's, literary thought began to search for a new theory which would be able to resolve the discrepancy.

Chapter 3

The Changed Conception of the Literary Language; The "Slavenorossiiskii Language" and the Synthesis of Cultural and Linguistic Traditions

1. The New Nature of the Russian Literary Language and the Emergence of Slavonicizing Purism

As we have shown, in the early period of the formation of the Russian literary language, theoretical views stood in radical contradiction to established practice. In theory reliance on spoken usage was proclaimed, and the attitude toward the previous literary and linguistic tradition was sharply negative. In practice, however, there was continuity with the earlier literary and linguistic tradition, while reliance on spoken usage could not be realized. In Russian conditions the conception of the literary language taken from the French thus acquired new contours. In particular, while French Classicism based itself on both spoken usage and literary tradition, its Russian followers rejected the latter point. This rejection was motivated by Petrine linguistic policy, which defined Church Slavonic as a clerical language, unsuitable for the new culture. The theoretical rejection of the Church Slavonic linguistic heritage was predicated on the antagonism between secular and religious culture which developed during the course of the Petrine reforms. This antagonism was the background for the reception of Classicist linguistic theories. The opposition of Russian and Church Slavonic was accepted as a given, and the terms in which it could be described were extracted from French theories. These terms derscribed language in terms of genetic character and as a result, the Russian — Church Slavonic opposition was equated with the opposition between French and Latin, which in turn led to associating Slavonicisms in Russian with Latinisms in French.

Such a scheme created a series of problems, and this made the situation unstable. In the first place, the very use of a fictitious theory turned out to be more of a hindrance to linguistic development than a stimulus. The attempts which we have analyzed to get around the dogmas of the given theory and to introduce issues raised by literary practice into the theoretical framework by reinterpreting its basic notions clearly demonstrated the discomfort Russian linguistic theorists felt with the dogmatically accepted principles. Hence while the notion of relying on spoken usage seemed to coincide very well with the rejection of Church Slavonic influence on the new literary language, the need to consistently separate Slavonicisms and Russicisms which the theory demanded turned out to be so complex that a decade of attempts at resolving the problem did not lead to satisfactory results.

In the second place, a contradiction arose between the desire to create a literary language on European principles and attempts to construct a civic, as opposed to an ecclesiastic, tongue. Indeed, no analogy for the coexistence of two such languages with similarly differentiated functions existed in Europe. From the European point of view, limiting a literary language to the secular sphere alone would have attested to its weakness, its insufficient "richness," which would preclude describing high and low subject matter with equal success. The guiding idea of the French linguistic reformers of the sixteenth century was that one could deal with any subject, including science or religion, just as well in French as in Latin. By the next century, after Bossuet and Descartes, the question had long been settled: a properly organized literary language should be able to meet the needs of an entire culture in all of its manifestations, that is, to be polyfunctional (cf. Brunot, II, 83f). In Germany, at least in Protestant Germany, after Luther's Bible translation in the sixteenth century and the spread of German to both church service and scholarship (see Grimm 1987), the issue of polyfunctionalism had also been resolved for all practical purposes.

Peter's language policy, for all of its orientation on Europe, led to something far from European in its results (see § 0–6). And in truth, a special civic language opposed to the language of the church was more of a metamorphosis of the older linguistic situation, a reorganization of registers, than an emulation of European models proffering the ideal of a universal national tongue. One needs to keep in mind the special nature of Russian cultural (religious) consciousness that differed from that of European educated elites and that created obstacles for the creating such a polyfunctional literary language. In Catholic Europe the church service (apart from the sermon) remained in Latin,[1] but this did not affect the issue of polyfunctionalism. For seventeenth-century European cultural consciousness (that of the cultural elite), the church service was a fossilized ritual form that had no direct connection to perfecting mankind, and thus stood on the cultural periphery. The decline of sacramental consciousness put the sermon forward as the main means of enlightenment and moral progress. Of course, national languages had been introduced in sermons long before the seventeenth century. But in the seventeenth century theological and historical-ecclesiastical treatises also began to be written in French. Therefore in seventeenth-century perception, despite the fact that Latin preserved its liturgical function, the national languages, and French in particular, emerged as fully empowered masters not only in the sphere of secular culture but also in religious matters (see Brunot, II, 14f, 83f; Caput, I, 293). In Russia, however, even among the educated elite that had experienced the strongest influence of Western ideas, the liturgy was never perceived as on the periphery of religious life. Therefore the preservation of Church Slavonic in the liturgy, even after Russian began to be used in sermons (see § III–3.1), was a much stronger factor in linguistic consciousness; in religious life, Church Slavonic continued to be the main language, and Russian only served side by side with it. Hence in eighteenth-century Russia the literary language's polyfunctionalism ran into special difficulties unknown in the West.

    Caught up in the struggle against Church Slavonic, the first codifiers of the literary language might have been able to ignore this contradiction at first, but as the functional diapason of the new language widened, and when people began to write not only scientific-technical manuals and books about "sweet love," but rhetorical panegyrics and philosophical treatises as well, the lack of correspondence between their initial conception and the European ideal became more and more evident. Moreover by the middle of the 1740's a new cultural and historical situation had come into being. Peter's policies had born fruit: a new society and a new culture had been created. Although this new culture's antagonism toward traditional culture did not fully disappear, it took on new forms. A generation grew up which had been born into the new culture; for the urban nobility the opposition between traditional and modern culture no longer meant an opposition between old habits and the

---

[1] In France in the second half of the seventeenth century the situation changed somewhat. The Jansenists translated the Missal and New Testament into French, and these were known widely, despite the opposition of the Jesuits (Brunot, V, 25–31). True, these translations were meant for individual reading, not for church services, but in terms of the period's cultural and historical development personal use was more important than the cult function.

fresh convictions of a newly introduced ideology but rather an opposition between its own elite culture and that of unenlightened society. In particular, by the mid-1740's a definite synthesis between reformed Orthodoxy and the cult of the emperor had come into being (§ III–3), so that the struggle against "clericalism" ceased to be a real issue. The same was true for the struggle against Church Slavonic literary culture.

The start of Elizabeth's reign marked the rise of the problem of new national self-consciousness, of national identity. The Europeanized elite was no longer satisfied with merely being part of Europe, but began to formulate the notion of a "Russian European," and to think of itself not as a European missionaries who had landed among some obscure aborigines, but as the best part of its own nation, with authority based on its own merits and worth. It is not accidental that by the middle of Elizabeth's reign there appeared satirical attacks on dandies (for example, Elagin's epistle to Sumarokov, or the first comedies of this "Russian Racine" — see Poety XVIII veka, II, 372–77) — that is, against that segment of the elite that did not bother to connect its "Europeanism" (whether genuine or not) with national traditions (again, no matter whether real or ersatz). In this way the new culture acquired its own tradition, albeit still a very recent one, and more often than not sanctified with the name of Peter the Great. The new literary language likewise to some extent lost its novelty, as texts written in it began to accumulate and the very idea of writing ceased to be an act of unprecedented daring. For all of the differences among these texts in terms of concrete linguistic forms, they were united by the common goal of expressing a normalized literary language which would answer the demands of Classicist purism. A tradition of teaching the new literary language was also established, and this provided a framework in which aspects of normalization could be given theoretical grounding.

The existence of these texts served to legitimize references to literary tradition in terms of Classicist purism, and this created the possibility of theoretical appeals to texts rather than only to spoken usage as the criterion for linguistic correctness. Together with this, the texts testified to the fact that Russian could indeed fulfill the function of a literary language, and with some improvement could do this no worse than Latin or any of the European tongues. Therefore the issue became not Russian's equal status vis à vis the traditional bookish language (Church Slavonic) but its equality to other European languages, i.e., its capacity to express the whole gamut of European ideas and phenomena. As A. A. Alekseev noted, "during the period of rapid blossoming of national self-consciousness it was no longer enough to say that 'we are a new people,' as it had been in the Petrine epoch, it was necessary to take one's place on a level with Europe" (Alekseev 1982, 126).

Most eloquent testimony of this new perception of the Russian language is the denunciation made by I. S. Gorlitskii, Academy translator and author of *A French and Russian Grammar* of 1730, against Johann-Daniel Schumacher (I.-D. Shumakher), who spent a short time in 1742 under arrest for embezzlement. Gorlitskii complained that in the foreword to a short description of the Academy of Sciences commentaries, published in 1728, Schumacher had insulted the Russian language and Russian translators (among them Gorlitskii), writing of the language's poor state (and consequently its incapacity to present scholarly material) and of the probable imperfection of its translations, so that "to the offense of Russians, not without insult, translators, fully grown men, are being subjected to his premeditated poison" (Pekarskii, IA, II, 90).[2] Gorlitskii's pathetic assertion of national self-worth was part of the anti-German movement that became fashionable in the first period after the coup that brought Elizabeth to the throne. This movement, however, appealed not to ancestral traditions but to the Europeanized culture of Russian Petersburg, to Russia's worth as a European civilization — part of that search for national identity mentioned above. Including language into this circle of issues shows that the Russian literary language of the new type was perceived as one of the European languages, not inferior to others in value and therefore capable of expressing any achievement of European thought. It was this perception that served as stimulus to the formation of a new system of linguistic ideas and to the transformation of linguistic practice.

---

[2] Indeed, S. Ignat'ev and Prince B. Iusupov, who were in charge of the investigation of Shumacher, questioned "who ordered the foreword of the 'Kommentaria' composed and who confirmed it" (Materialy AN, V, 544–5). The answer to this question has not survived and the given issue did not figure into Shumakher's interrogation, so it appears that the investigators were skeptical about Gorlitskii's hurt national feelings. Naturally, in the address to readers that preceded the "Short Descripton of the Commentaries" there was nothing insulting to the dignity of the translators or defaming the Russian language. However, insofar as this was the first work by Academy translators, the editor expressed certain misgivings about the quality of the translation. Addressing the "benevolent reader," he wrote: "Do not find fault with the translation, that it is unintelligible or not very beautiful. You should know that it is a very difficult thing to translate well, because one not only has to know both of the languages from and to which one is translating perfectly, but one has to have a clear understanding of the thing being translated. In this case we looked them over very carefully so that they would be both comprehensible and pleasant, and we acted with greet diligence and care, and each translator was given those treatises to translate which we knew that he understood better, and moreover, the translations themselves were read and witnessed in the presence of all of the translators. And if these dangers were not successfully overcome, the only refuge that remains is to beg you to be tolerant of our weakness *until the language itself will be improved and the translators better trained*" (Kratkoe opisanie 1728, foreword, l. 2–2 verso — my italics, V. Z.) It was the last italicized phrase that provoked Gorlitskii's protest.

1. The New Nature of the Russian Literary Language

1.1 The Polyfunctionism of the New Literary Language

One indication of the beginning of a new system of linguistic views was the appearance in Russia of the common European topos which ascribes various virtues to each of the modern literary languages and which usually concludes with a paean to the language in question that unites all of the aforementioned merits. If in his "Speech to the Russian Assembly" of 1735 Trediakovskii had spoken about the creation of European languages as a glorious example which Russia must now follow, in his "Speech on Oratory" (Slovo o vitiistve) of 1745 the accent changed. Now he spoke about the equality to Latin that French had achieved, and then asserted that "other, many other most civil and enlightened peoples, such as the most shrewd English, the most well-thinking Dutch, the most profound Spaniards, most sharp-witted Italians, the most eloquent Poles, the most thorough Swedes, the most serious Germans... [all] today imitate the example and glory of the French, and achieve what they desire with eminent success" (Trediakovskii 1745, 71–73).

This is the path that also awaits the Russian language, which "without any doubt... can confirm this itself, if it first will undertake and accomplish many translations from other languages, and in this way purify the vocabulary (posloviia) of its writings, and, at the same time, by coming up with names for many diverse things, receive a rich abundance of words" (ibid., 79). The "Speech on Oratory" was itself meant to be such a model work as far as its language, which would clearly demonstrate the Russian literary language's capability of expressing any idea, however complex. Trediakovskii presented the Russian text in parallel with a Latin version, and if the Latin was meant as an example of linguistic perfection and rhetorical refinement, the parallel Russian text was to demonstrate that Russian was capable of the same. Trediakovskii read the speech in connection with his appointment as professor of Latin and Russian eloquence at the Academy of Sciences (Pekarskii, IA, II, 106–11). The very creation of such a position (which was, by the way, the decision of the Senate rather than the Academy—cf. Trediakosvkii 1851) indicates that the Russian language had achieved a new status, analogous to that of other European tongues.

In his "Epistle on the Russian Language" of 1747 Sumarokov presented the same scheme of linguistic perfection:

> Возмем себе в пример словесных человеков:
> Такой нам надобен язык, как был у Греков,
> Какой у Римлян был, и следуя в том им,
> Как ныне говорит Италия и Рим,

Chapter 3. The Changed Conception of the Literary Language

> Каков в прошедший век прекрасен стал Французской,
> Иль на конец сказать, каков способен Русской.
> Довольно наш язык в себе имеет слов...
>
> (Sumarokov 1748, 3)

(Let us ourselves follow the example of literate peoples. We need the kind of language that the Greeks had, like that of the Romans, and following them, like that which Italy and Rome today speak, in the way French became beautiful in the last century, and finally, as Russian is capable [of becoming]. Our language has a sufficient [number of] words in it...)

In the 1750's Lomonosov developed the idea of Russian's equality with other European languages, or even its superiority over them. He asserted, after Trediakovskii, that

> Cicero's powerful eloquence, Virgil's magnificent solemnity, Ovid's pleasant rhetoric do not lose their value in Russian. The most subtle philosophical fancies and reasonings, multifarious natural qualities and changes... may have proper and vivid expression in Russian. And if there is something we cannot precisely depict, we should ascribe it not to our language but to our own lack of art. (Lomonosov, IV, 10; VII^2, 392)

Russian (rossiiskii iazyk) is in no way less worthy than any other European language, on the contrary, "in its breadth and abundance it is great in comparison with all those in Europe." Lomonosov further states that

> the [Holy] Roman Emperor Charles V used to say that one should speak with God in Spanish, with one's friends in French, German with one's enemies, and in Italian with women. But had he been adept in Russian, he would of course have added that one may speak that language with all of the above. For he would have found in it the magnificence of Spanish, the liveliness of French, the strength of German, the tenderness of Italian, and, more than that, the richness and expressive conciseness of Greek and Latin. (Lomonosov, IV, 9; VII^2, 391)

Lomonosov took this anecdote about Charles V from Peplier (Rak 1975, 219; cf. Keipert 1981, 34). It circulated widely in the context of discussions about the character of various languages, for example, in Bouhours (1671, 72), Bayle's dictionary (Lomonosov, IV, note, 45–6), etc. M. I. Sukhomlinov cites several more examples in which particular European languages are associated with various traits (op. cit., 46–8). Many more may be cited from French and German literature.[3] In the mid-eighteenth century

---

[3] E.g., the textbook Die neuste Manier französisch zu reden (A New Method to Speak French) (Hamburg, 1710), cited in Brunot, V, 358.

1. The New Nature of the Russian Literary Language

this topos was still fully topical, as evidenced by Voltaire's "Essay on Epic Poetry," cited above (§ II–2.2). Declaring that "every language has its own genius," and characterizing the genius of each modern European tongue, Voltaire further asserted that "it is certain that our language is stronger that Italian and sweeter than English" (Voltaire, II, 379).

If the best European language was French, in principle, Russian could be no less great. Even earlier Lomonosov had written in the foreword to his *Rhetoric* of 1748:

> The language with which the Russian state maintains power over a great part of the world has a natural abundance, beauty and strength that yield to no other European tongue. And so there is no doubt that the Russian word can be brought to such perfection as will cause amazement in other [peoples]. (Lomonosov, III, 82; VII^2, 92)

The main focus of amazement for Lomonsov as well as for Trediakovskii and Sumarokov was France. It was precisely the French, "having purified and beautified their language via the diligence of skilful writers," who have accomplished this so that "the use of [their] language has not only spread throughout Europe but also into distant parts of the world and among European peoples, not only of their own tribe, and serves generally for mutual communication" ("On the Current State of the Verbal Arts in Russia," Lomonosov, IV, 247; VII^2, 581–2; on the connection between language perfection and its geographical spread, see, for example, Bouhours 1671, 45–7).

Characteristically, the above-cited passage from Lomonosov's *Rhetoric* about the flourishing of the verbal arts in Russia (i.e., the perfecting of the language) is connected with polyfunctionalism:

> In today's age although there is not as much use of the ornamental word as there was among the ancient Greeks and Romans, especially in judicial matters, [it is still used] in putting forth God's word; in correcting human morals; in describing the glorious deeds of great heroes; and in many political situations — to what extent it is useful clearly reveals the state of those peoples among whom the verbal arts do flourish. (Lomonosov, III, 82; VII^2, 91–2)

Assuming all of these roles, the Russian language was to take its place in the chorus of European languages; it was as if the oft-repeated idea of European polyphony was now to complete its journey in Russia, having encountered a language which united the excellences of all others.[4]

---

[4] Lomonosov writes of Russia's superiority over other European languages in several other works as well ("Foreword on the Use of Church Books," "Philological Research and Evidence," Lomonosov, IV, 225–6, 229–31, 233; VII2, 587–8, 590–1, 762; see also below).

Such perfection, however, did not harmonize well with the idea of separating the civic and ecclesiastic languages. In fact, in speaking of the perfection of French, Trediakovskii remarks that the French

> have so... far developed... their native tongue [that they can use] it for writing everything sacred, everything civil, everything concerning the sciences, everything historical, everything oratorical, poetical, critical, in a word, everything not only useful and beautiful but also entertaining; that they have [not only] turned it into the most pleasant, sweet, polite, and most abundant of all European tongues, but also made it necessary reading for all courtiers, judges, ministers, envoys, commanders, soldiers, citizens, scholars, merchants, as well as artists. (Trediakovskii 1745, 70–71).

It is obvious from this that the perfection of a "European" literary language was necessarily tied to its polyfunctionalism; among other things it had to serve as a vehicle for religious writing with no less success than for secular literature.

This perspective demanded an end to the dualism of civic and ecclesiastic tongues that had been a basic part of the linguistic program of the 1730's. How could this be done? It would have been logical to translate the Bible and liturgy into the vulgar tongue, as the Germans or English had done. The connection of a language's perfection with the translation of sacred texts into it was a vital part of the era's linguistic consciousness. On the German precedent, precisely on linguistic development in its Protestant part, Lomonosov wrote that "as [soon as] the Germans had begun to read their holy books and hear the church service in their own language its richness multiplied and accomplished writers appeared" (IV, 226; VII^2, 588; cf. Keipert 1991; Picchio 1992, 144). Evidently, it was possible to follow the French precedent, when theological works, religious historical writings, and sermons were translated. But this path was dangerous and laborious, contradicting traditional values of Russian society and offering little chance of success. Another path, however, also presented itself, perhaps less logical but on the other hand more sure and simple. That path was to somehow combine Russian and Church Slavonic, the new and old written languages, to the extent that one could speak of this as one language. If a category could be found which would permit defining Russian and Church Slavonic as two variants of one language then the demand for polyfunctionalism would be satisfied of itself; the new literature in Russian would subsume "all civic writings" and the old Church Slavonic literature embrace "everything divine."

This solution had already been suggested in the "Speech on Oratory" in which Trediakovskii juxtaposed foreign languages to the "natural"

1. The New Nature of the Russian Literary Language

language. Use of the "native" or "natural" language, unlike foreign ones, is specifically distinguished by the sought-after polyfunctionalism; it is characterized, in Trediakovskii's words, by "most frequent usage, practically on the hour." He continued,

> For wherever anyone goes in a well-ordered city one may hear one's native language. If a great bell summons one to church, one may hear prayers flowing there as well as the word of God preached in the native tongue. If, on business or for curiosity, one goes down to the palace of the supreme autocrat, there everyone... speaks the native language and congratulates each other in it, expresses their good wishes, greets one another, and so on, conversing in the native tongue both sincerely or hypocritically, but it is this language one hears and wants to speak to others for one's own self-respect... Let one appear in the senate before the senators; in the senate too one will present one's case in the native tongue, and what they decide will be written in the same language. If one enters the courtroom before a Judge, one will likewise defend oneself, present evidence or be charged on account of it in one's native tongue. Do you wish to go out into the street? There too one can speak one's native language and understand... the conversations of others. Let one go see a comedy during a holiday; at the theater too they are putting on the show in the native tongue... What else? [If one wants to] reply to a soldier who makes greeting, [one will do it] in the native tongue; hire a worker — in the native tongue; say hello to one's friends — in the native tongue; scream at one's servant — in the native tongue; give one's children a lesson — in the native tongue; utter affectionate words to one's better half or speak to her in anger — in the native tongue. (1745, 57–59)

One might have thought that Trediakovskii was describing not the functioning of the "natural" tongue in Russia, but some ideal situation in which the native language fulfills all of the listed functions (cf. Uspenskii 1985, 122). This interpretation, however, poorly corresponds to the fact that this multiplicity of usage is attributed to Empress Elizabeth:

> Who does not know that our most wise empress speaks not only German, but also the French language? But Her Majesty, [for its] magnitude, superiority, and extent, does not desire any other language besides the one with which this, our most beautiful Pulcheria, prays to God most piously, defends the law most Christianly, expounds the faith most Orthodoxly, acknowledges the single holy, catholic, apostolic Church, proposes statues most intelligently, spreads the glory of the empire most laudably, grants promotions most deferentially, gives rewards for merit most generously, carries on conversations most graciously; and gives advice, forgiveness, praise most fairly. (Trediakovskii 1745, 73–5)

Thus all of the various functions of the "natural" language are contained in the speech activity of one concrete person that consciously chooses the

Russian language, which refutes the interpretation of this passage as an ideal picture.[5]

And so, according to Trediakovskii, the single "natural" tongue is to be used everywhere, in both secular and religious spheres; he does not specify which language he has in mind here, Russian or Church Slavonic, but it is evident that given such a perspective the very opposition between the two is somehow eliminated. Trediakovskii evidently recalled the treatment of the two languages that Paus had once proposed.[6] As we know, from the start Paus had been of the opinion that Russian and Church Slavonic formed a certain unity or synthesis, and he justified the necessity of studying both together by arguing that otherwise church books, works on "high and spiritual" topics, as well as scholarly and historical texts would be incomprehensible (BAN, Sobr. Inostrannnykh rukopisei, Q 192, l. 3)—that is, he argued that the civil language was insufficient in the functional aspect. (In the introductory remarks he had begun by listing the functions which the "rußische slavonische Sprache" fulfills in the Russian empire—its use in daily life, in offices, courts and church — op. cit., l. 5).

If we remember Trediakovskii's radical assertions in the foreword to *Voyage to the Island of Love*, Adodurov's remarks on Slavonicisms in his essay on grammar (§ II–1.1) or his negative view of Paus' ideas, the change in outlook on the relation between Russian and Church Slavonic seems almost unthinkable. From a broader perspective, however, the notion of a certain unity of Russian and Church Slavonic seems quite usual and traditional. The Petrine era was not long over, but for many previous centuries there had not been any fixed separation between the two languages, and in any case

---

[5] Trediakovskii's statement that it is the empress who sets the example to her subordinates of using the "natural" language in part recalls Bouhours, whose "Les Entretiens d'Ariste et d'Eugene (Conversations of Ariste and Eugene)," a work that may have been familiar to Trediakovskii, says of Louis XIV: "But you know very well that our grand monarch holds the first place among fortunate geniuses and that there is no one in the kingdom who knows French as he knows it" (Bouhours 1671, 168).

[6] Trediakovskii most likely knew Paus' grammar. In any case, Adodurov read it in 1729–30, when he reviewed it together with M. Shvanvits. Trediakovskii lived with Adodurov after his return from France and unquestionably discussed with him those linguistic issues that Paus' book dealt with directly. After Paus' death, the rough draft of the grammar turned up in the library of the Academy of Sciences, where it remains to this day. That means that it was accessible to Academy philologists, including Trediakovskii. There is no doubt that in this early period any description of the Russian language provoked the mostly lively interest in the small circle of academicians that was occupied with teaching Russian, working out typographical rules, translations, and other tasks involving the language. Paus' grammar was the most extensive work of this kind, and it's hardly likely that Trediakovskii would have ignored it, even though in the 1730's he would have been critical of it.

the label "Russian" could be freely applied to the bookish tongue, to the non-bookish written language, as well as to the conversational tongue (cf. Dell'Agata 1986, 186). One may suggest that the traditional perception now underwent a new transformation, now taking on life in this modified aspect.

In the "Speech on Oratory" Trediakovskii touches on this issue only in passing, without going into detail. The unity of Russian and Church Slavonic is not so much asserted as presumed. The question, however, was too important not to demand further explanation. It was still left to define the nature of this implied unity; moreover, the old categories of the pre-Petrine period were no longer appropriate, as both "Russian" and "Slavonic" were now seen as literary, i.e., bookish, languages, with written traditions; both were codified, and their differences, defined in genetic terms, were the subject of continuing discussion. The task was complex, and we should note from the start that Trediakovskii and Lomonosov were only able to manage it in part, and did not significantly improve on the interpretation that Paus had suggested. To combine contradiction and unity was possible only using complicated and artificial arguments. Nonetheless in their works of the late 1740's and 1750's they attempted to resolve the problem.

1.2. The Single Nature of Russian and Church Slavonic

In the article "On the Spelling of Adjectives" (first variant — 1746), written one year after the "Speech on Oratory," Trediakovskii already indicated the way of bringing Russian and Church Slavonic together that he would subsequently develop. He wrote here about "the similarity of Slavonic and our language for the most part, about which everyone well knows... [Slavonic] is our language's source and root, and differs from ours but little" (Lomonosov, IV, notes ,12–13; cf. Vomperskii 1968, 87).[7] In essence this same formula (with the characteristic addition "and exact likeness") is repeated in the version of 1755: Slavonic is here called the "church" language, "which is source, and father, and exact likeness of our Slavenorossiiskii, or civic, language, and does not differ from it by even a finger, so to speak" (Pekarskii 1865, 103).

---

[7] Cf. the Latin variant of this passage, where "lingua slavonica" is seen as a language "quod sit nostrae fons atque origo, id omnibus est notissimum, et a qua nostra vix latum digitum, ut ita dicam, recedat" (which is our source as well as origin, and therefore which hardly differs from ours by a finger's breadth, as is very well known) (Lomonosov, IV, notes ,12).

Chapter 3. The Changed Conception of the Literary Language

The notion of "roots" and of the "root" characteristics of a language was not Trediakovskii's invention. In both France and Germany of the seventeenth and early eighteenth centuries the question of a language's natural characteristics — the constant attributes which remain unchanged despite all the innovations of custom (usage) and which define the spirit of the language (the "génie de la langue") — was the subject of lively discussion. Considerations of the differing geniuses of various languages are so common in the French literature that it doesn't make sense to cite particular examples (cf. Kozlov 1988). In the most general sense, the genius of the language is understood as the aggregate of its specific features that define its differences from others and its self-identity in various historical stages (this issue comes up in particular when discussing the change in the genius of the language in the transition from Latin to French). This general understanding could be concretized both in discussions of some specific feature of a language (for example, its precision, austerity, or on the contrary, its splendor) and also in appellations to a structural principle. The first argument may be found, for example, in Lamy (1737, 97), who writes:

> To completely understand the usage of a language one must study its genius and take note of its idioms or manner of speaking that are unique to it. The genius of a language consists of certain qualities that those who speak it affect to give to their style. The genius of our language is clarity and naïveté. The French seek these qualities in [good] style, and are very different in this from Orientals, who only esteem mysterious expressions which give one much to think about.

The second argument may be seen, among others, in Rollin. Speaking of the defects of French language education in comparison with the Roman, he writes:

> We must take the same amount of care in order to perfect our use of the French language. There are few people who learn it by principles. One may think that usage alone is enough to make one adept. It is rare that one applies oneself to deepen the [language's] genius and to studying all of its nuances. People often ignore all but the most common rules, something that sometimes happens even in the writing of the more skilled. (Rollin, I, 3)

Grasping the genius of the language is connected here with the serious study of grammar; the genius of the language here appears as something analogous to generalized grammatical rules (this idea is developed in the passage cited in § III, note 22). These two views of genius of the language are not opposed, and in many instances it is hard to tell precisely which one the author has in mind.[8] In Germany this issue takes a somewhat different route.

---

[8] Thus Pierre-Daniel Huet criticized Perrault for reading Homer in Latin, challenging his judgement on the grounds that the Latin translation missed the genius of the language. He

1. The New Nature of the Russian Literary Language

Writers primarily focus on the question of "root words," on etymology and word formation, and on how the ancient basis of the language is preserved in word creation (J. G. Schottelius' works are particularly important in this area — Schottelius 1663; cf. Blume 1978, 43). This was the historical linguistic basis for Humboldt's later theory about the inner form of a word.[9]

Trediakovskii's position needs to be interpreted in the context of these ideas. By suggesting that Slavonic is the root of Russian and that Russian hardly deviates from it, Trediakovskii wanted to say that the root qualities of these languages are identical, and that despite some formal differences they are of one spirit or of one nature. This position is stated explicitly in the *Conversation About Orthography* of 1748. Trediakovskii here again discusses the question of plural adjective endings, in great detail. Trying to prove that the final vowel in masculine plural adjectives should be *u*, Trediakovskii cites "the unity of our language with Slavonic" as his primary argument (Trediakovskii 1748, 295 / III, 199). When a foreigner expresses doubts and says that "Slavonic is not only not the same as your language, but not even similar" (ibid, 297/ 201), a Russian (i.e., Trediakovskii) explains what he means by unity:

> That language cannot but be the same as another which has the same nature as it does in all its parts, because in these things unity in nature means that they have the very same substance, that is, they are one and the same among themselves. Therefore our Russian (rossiiskii) language has the same nature as Slavonic in all its parts, insofar as: they have the same nouns and verbs; the same other parts [of speech], declinable and non-declinable; the same declension of nouns and conjugation of verbs... together with the same prepositions, which require the same cases; the same conjunctions; the same coordination not only of parts of the sentence, but as regards all governing aspects; the same rules, and the same exceptions to them. In sum, the Russian (russkii) language has the same spirit and shares a single soul with Slavonic, so that our language may be called Slavenorossiiskii, that is, Russian by nation (rossiiskii po narodu) and Slavonic by nature (slavenskii po svoei prirode). (ibid, 298–99; 202–3)

---

explained: "If you read Latin thoughts in French expressions, you speak like a pedant; if you think in French but express yourself in Latin, you speak like a schholboy. Each language has its own particular charms, which it can neither borrow nor lend" (Hepp 1968, 551). Here the notion of genius clearly means a certain correlation between the language's structure and the structure of thought, which extends both to grammatical and stylistic features (cf. also Régnier-Demarais's discussion of the different geniuses of various languages — Régnier-Demarais 1700, 32–7).

[9] The issue of genius of the language was often raised in connection with the problem of borrowings and linguistic richness, as borrowings could come into conflict with a language's spirit (see Bouhours 1671, 81–6; Fénélon, VII, 127). Lomonosov's note "Characteristics of the Russian Language" in "On Translations" may reflect this question (VII², 767; see Keipert 1981, 43–4).

Chapter 3. The Changed Conception of the Literary Language

In this way "unity in nature" is equated with fundamental structural characteristics, and in light of this identity particular individual differences turn out to be insignificant:

> All of the dissimilarity one finds between our language and Slavonic concerns only the so-to-speak surface of the language and not its inner being, as it consists either in newly introduced words (like our *ежели* for the Slavonic *аще*) or in the simplest usage introduced by the people, for instance, *голова* instead of *глава*, *пить* instead of *пити*, *молоко* instead of *млеко*. But this sort of dissimilarity in no way prevents our language from being the very same as Slavonic, just as it would be wrong to say that Novgorodian isn't Russian because they use *лони* and *дежа* for our *давно* and *квашня*. This difference *would* prevent it if it [Slavonic] were like Latin for French, or for Italian or Spanish, because in the total nature of their composition these three languages broke off from Latin, although it is clearly seen that they derived from it... (ibid, 300; 203)

Trediakovskii also bases the idea of Church Slavonic and Russian's unity also on the fact that Russians do not need training to understand Church Slavonic: "Besides, everyone, even our uneducated people, understands the Slavonic language used in our church books, which would not be at all possible if the Slavonic language was not one and the same as ours" (Trediakovskii 1748, 299–300; III, 203). Insofar as the new conception of unity presumes the identity of grammatical structure, learning Church Slavonic proves to be unnecessary. In accord with European models, training is understood as the appropriate grammatical study of the language, but Trediakovskii, characteristically, focuses not on elements of this education that had appeared in Russia since the establishment of schools in the later seventeenth century but rather on the centuries'-old tradition of learning the bookish language via the memorization of texts; he does not look at this tradition in terms of education, but constructs his own new conception that takes into account the differences between Russia and the West.

This new perspective radically contradicts Trediakovskii's previous views. As we have seen, in 1737 he had written that a Russian (Rossianin) will no more understand "when they speak Slavonic" than will "an Italian … when they speak Latin" (§ II–1.1). This change of opinion had direct consequences for categorizing Slavonicisms. For French purism Latinisms appear as "learned words" insofar as Latin required special training. For the young Trediakovskii this argument also applied to Slavonicisms. But if it was not necessary to study Church Slavonic, then Slavonicisms were not connected with school and couldn't be defined as "learned."

Hence the differences between Church Slavonic and Russian could be reduced to a limited collection of grammatical and lexical features

1. The New Nature of the Russian Literary Language

outside of which the languages were seen as identical. Trediakovskii's set of differences is itself very telling (although it is not clear if he considered it comprehensive). It includes the system of past tenses, the absence in Russian of the dual, the infinitive marker (*-ти* or *-ть*), pleophonic and non-pleophonic forms, and various auxiliary words. On differences between declension and conjugation, he writes: "the same declension of nouns and conjugation of verbs, except that in ours [Russian] the past tense has different personal endings, for example, *мы были* instead of *быхом,* however, this doesn't prevent even one of our illiterates from understanding that *быхом* or *бысте* or *бѣша* means the same as *мы были, вы были, они были*. And one can't say that our conjugations are not the same as Slavonic because, unlike Slavonic, there is no dual in them, because even in Slavonic this is not natural, but [adopted] from Greek and devised by grammarians" (ibid, 299–300; III, 202). In this way the fundamental grammatical markers which distinguished Russian and Church Slavonic in the linguistic consciousness of the previous epoch are clearly specified, but declared to be relatively superficial, not preventing comprehension of Church Slavonic by a Russian speaker, and consequently not destroying the languages' linguistic accord.

The course of Trediakovskii's thinking strikingly recalls that of Paus (§ II–1.4). Paus also went from asserting the functional union of Russian and Slavonic (and the limitation of either language taken separately) to suggesting their essential unity. Trediakovskii's view fully agrees with what Paus wrote. Responding to the question whether Russian and Church Slavonic are the same or not, Paus asserts that they are the same, "if one judges according to: 1) their elements and letters; 2) their position and roots; 3) their nature and analogy; 4) most of their grammatical inflections (grammaticalischen accidentibus)" (BAN, Sobr. Inostrannykh rukopisei, Q 192, l. 5). What Trediakovskii writes could be seen as an explication of Paus' position. Like Paus, he speaks of the identity of elements (true, not so much the letters, that is, the sounds, but nouns, verbs, adverbs and conjunctions); of the unity of their nature, expressed "in all its parts," that corresponds to Paus' "grammatical inflections (accidence)"; and finally, of the unity of rules and exceptions, by which is understood the notion of analogy as used by grammarians of the seventeenth and eighteenth centuries. So the similarity of Trediakovskii and Paus' views is not limited to the overall assertion of the unity of Russian and Church Slavonic, but also covers the way this unity was understood. It is indicative that both philologists, in choosing a generally known illustration of this unity, select the relationship between dialects. Trediakovskii notes that differences in particular inflections does not prevent the languages' essential unity, as "it would be wrong to say that Novgorodian isn't Russian." Paus cites a similar analogy, although naturally he refers to German rather than Russian dialects. According to Paus, "one can find the same amount of difference between Lower Saxon and standard German or Saxon and Low German" (l. 5).

Both Paus and Trediakovskii, while asserting the unity of the two languages, also indicate their frequent differences. Here to a great extent Trediaovskii also repeats Paus, who asserts that the differences between them arise as a result of "heutige Veränderung" (newly introduced words), that is, due to numerous deviations from the ancient "root" unity that make their way "into many grammatical forms (accidence)." It is precisely past tense endings and the dual that are classified as this kind of form. It is worth mentioning that in the grammar's prefatory letter that discusses the status of Russian and Church Slavonic, Paus specially remarks on past tenses. He writes that without studying Slavonic one cannot determine the difference between the three preterits (l. 3), that is, he distinguishes simple preterits as one of the main differences between the languages. He also writes about this in his "Observations" of 1732, noting that it is sufficient to get rid of the differences in preterite and infinitive endings in order to reduce the differences between the languages almost to naught (Winter 1958, 759; cf. the quote in § II–2.4). Again, Paus and Trediakovskii's shared position is the unity of Russian and Church Slavonic in their basic nature, with divergence in particular "accidental" cases.

At the same time, the set of differences that Trediakovskii identifies is much shorter than the extensive list that Paus presents. Of course, this may be related to the type of work they were writing: Paus was composing a grammar, so that every paradigm he adduced presents the problem of accounting for variants, whether Russian or Church Slavonic; while Trediakovskii was making a general argument included in a treatise on orthography. But this doesn't seem the issue. Trediakovskii enters into the discussion of Russian — Slavonic unity on account of plural adjective endings; he wants to prove that in harmony with "nature" the nom. masc. pl. must end in -и, while to distinguish fem. and neut. adjectives one may use the letters -е for fem. and -я for neuter which is "not against the character and nature of the language" (Lomonsov, IV, notes, 23). Paus establishes alternative endings (in both nouns and verbs), assigning the variants to Russian or Church Slavonic; in particular, for nom. pl. adjectives he gives *добрые* for masc., *добрыя* for fem., and *добрая* for neut., indicating that in Russian the neuter often has *-ие* or *-ые* (BAN, Sobr. inostrannykh rukopisei, Q 192, l.60ob–61). Trediakovskii, on the other hand, is concerned with choosing a normative variant for the new literary language, so he establishes this variant, ignoring the juxtaposition of languages and appealing to their common nature and to reason (that is, to analogy), and in some cases even to "the prescriptions of ancient grammarians" (Lomonsov, IV, notes, 20). The variability which Paus tries to organize by defining variants in terms of grammar to Trediakovskii represents a challenge for normalization: from variants based on different principles he wants to choose the one that best corresponds to the "nature" of the Russian language as it accords with Slavonic.

Paus' purpose is predominantly descriptive, and Trediakovskii's — normative. Insofar as for Trediakovskii the "nature of the language" — its root characteristics, revealed in its history, beginning with the most ancient times — serves as the criterion of normative choice, one may say that he combines Paus' idea of the single nature of Russian and Church Slavonic with the appreciation of ancient Slavonic qualities as they were seen to be organically present in contemporary Russian. By virtue of this the Russian literary language acquired a historical tradition that could satisfy the demands of a growing national self-consciousness. For Trediakovskii the nature of the language thus represented a structural starting point or backbone which was not harmed by peasant or illiterate usage, on the one hand, and on the other, not distorted by external influences (as was the case with duals; see below). Such a view of the nature of the language naturally drove Trediakovskii to seek the pure form (of both Russian and Church Slavonic) in the ancient past. And indeed Trediakovskii speaks of "the original, earliest [stage] of our language" as the model, which should serve as the norm of good usage in the literary language (Trediakovskii 1748, 292–3 / III, 197; cf. § III–2.1). In this historical perspective Russian and Church Slavonic merge, and this leads to minimizing their differences. These for Trediakovskii consist of those features which had become associated in linguistic consciousness with the basic, specific markers of the bookish (Church Slavonic) language. Here too, by the way, a certain revision was taking place.

Simple preterits take the main place in this group, and this corresponds to their traditional, many centuries'-long role as fundamental markers of bookishness. Participles, no less significant for the pre-Petrine literary tradition, are not included. The reason for this, evidently, is that they were assimilated by the Russian literary language of the 1730's in which they played the role, in part, of equivalents to participles in Western European languages (cf. Isachenko 1974, 255). The situation is different with the dual form. It did not juxtapose Russian and Church Slavonic insofar as it was "not natural" in Slavonic, i.e., not derived from ancient tradition. Indeed, Trediakovskii considers it a calque from Greek, artificially grafted onto Church Slavonic; in 1748 Trediakovskii juxtaposes ancient Slavonic to Greek influences, which corresponded to his earlier negative attitude toward the "Hellenoslavonic" tendency in Russian letters at the time of his condemnation of "Slavonicizing pomposity" (slavenshchizna) (§ I–1.2).[10] Adodurov, who connected Greek and Church Slavonic by the presence of the dual form, and used it to mark the difference between Church Slavonic and Russian, may have also shared the notion of its foreign origin [...] (Adodurov 1731, 13).

It is understandable that the search for genetic markers that was being undertaken in the 1730's (§ II–1.3,§ II–1.4) also left its mark on Trediakovskii's group of oppositions. Indeed, Trediakovskii characterizes "the simplest speech, introduced by the folk" by its pleophonic forms (*голова* instead of *глава*, *молоко* instead of *млеко*), that is, he cites the opposition of pleophonic and non-pleophonic forms that had not served to differentiate the bookish and non-bookish tongues in the earlier period.

After the unsuccessful attempts to eliminate "everything Slavonic" from the Russian literary language of the new type and to contrast Russian and Church Slavonic on the pattern of French and Latin, toward the end of the 1740's linguistic thinking sought a more adequate model, no longer rejecting, but reinterpreting old notions about their differences. The shuffling of ideas and categories that had taken place in the 1730's had dealt with material that had been prepared by the linguistic consciousness of the preceding period; from the end of the 1740's a new reorganization took place, in many instances in the opposite direction, but here too the starting point was practically the very same initial material, as the older linguistic thinking remained in force. A radical break with the past turned out to be not only difficult to accomplish, but unnecessary, as well as contrary to the needs of national self-determination. Therefore the past again assumed if not the principle then still a most respected place in linguistic (and overall cultural) discourse. This made it possible, on the one hand, to give theoretical basis to the synthetic character that the normative grammar of the new literary language acquired (§ II–1.4), and on the other, to resolve the problem of polyfunctionalism.

The changed conception of the relationship between Church Slavonic and Russian was directly reflected in the make-up of the literary language; now it no longer *opposed* Church Slavonic but *included* it. The "Slavenorossiiskii" literary language emerged as the union of Russian

---

[10] The idea of the dual as a category that Church Slavonic adopted from Greek had been expressed by Polikarpov; see the marginal note in manuscript "Chin tekhnologii" of 1721 [...] (RGADA, f. 381, no. 11241, l.67 verso). The special marked character of the dual (as archaic and specifically bookish) which Polikarpov ascribes to Church Slavonic could have influenced Trediakovskii's view of its artificial derivation.

and Church Slavonic ("slavenskii"), which was to serve as its "shield and affirmation" (Trediakovskii III, 372; cf. Uspenskii 1985, 175–6). This union characterized both its grammatical structure and corpus of words. Trediakovskii's *Tilemakhida* may serve as example of an attempt to realize such a synthesis; here Church Slavonic and Russian forms in conjugations of non-thematic verbs coexist (Alekseev 1981, 77), as well as dative absolute and gerundial constructions, etc. In general, Trediakovskii subordinates linguistic practice to his revised theoretical conception. Thus he stops using infinitives in *–mu* as poetic license, apparently insofar as infinitives with unstressed *–mu* were considered, as for Paus, as a fundamental difference between Russian and Church Slavonic (most indicative of this is his verse transposition of the Psalter, composed mostly in the late 1740's-early 50's). At the same time he began to use instr. pl. ending in *–ы* for nouns of various declensions, since this, according to his new views, was legitimized by the fact that both Russian and Church Slavonic have "the same declensions" (§ II–2.2, note 25).

Lomonosov arrived at a similar notion of the literary language, although a bit later than Trediakovskii. Like Trediakovskii, Lomonosov came to view the grammatical structure of the literary language as a distinct synthesis of Church Slavonic and Russian grammar. Undoubtedly, this idea of their coming together was made in full consciousness, as Lomonosov was a meticulous grammarian. Indeed in his "Notes for a Proposal of An Ending for Plural Adjectives," Lomonosov, as noted (§ II–1.4), rejected Trediakovskii's argument that, given the Russian literary language's lack of one specific form, one should use the ending *-uu/-ыи* for nom.-acc. masc. pl., based on Church Slavonic. Lomonosov objected that "the Slavonic language differs from Great Russian nowhere so much as in word desinences. For example, Slavonic adjectives in the singular masculine nominative case end in ый or їй, [as in] богатый, старшїй, синїй, while in Great Russian they end in ой and ей, [as in] богатой, старшей, синей" (Lomonosov IV, 1; VII[2], 83). Lomonosov equates the differences of nom. pl. adjective endings to other morphological forms that contrast Russian and Church Slavonic (in particular, simple preterits and л-forms). He thus rejects the academic synthesizing tradition that was introducing many Church Slavonic grammatical elements into the new literary language that were not perceived as specifically bookish. Lomonosov made this point in 1746, and one may connect it to the linguistic innovations that were conditioned by the rethinking of variability in genetic terms (§ II–1.4).

It is all the more remarkable that in his *Russian Grammar* of 1755, which described the structure of the Russian literary language in accord with

Chapter 3. The Changed Conception of the Literary Language

his ideas of the 50's, these endings are presented as coexisting variants (§ 161–IV, 77; VII², 452); no limits are apparently imposed upon their usage, except for the special case of past passive participles, about which he writes: "it is better to end ones that come from Slavonic in ЫЙ rather than in ОЙ, and more proper to end Russian ones in ОЙ rather than ЫЙ" (sec. 446 — ibid, 186; 548). Here the use of variant forms is connected with their derivation. It is significant, however, that both Slavonic and Russian forms equally go to make up the literary language, and moreover in his own practice Lomonosov preferred the first type (see Martel 1933, 80). Thus in the 1750's Lomonosov accepted the previously rejected synthesizing academic grammatical tradition, and at the same time apparently also embraced the attribution of this synthesis to ancient Slavonic practices, the basis on which Trediakovskii had rethought this synthesis.

It remained basically unclear just how far this kind of synthesis could go. It was obvious that it was definitely limited on the Russian side; in Lomonosov's *Grammar* the majority of forms and constructions which could be seen as dialect or as particularly vulgar were absent. There were also limits as far as Slavonic. Hence if Russian and Slavonic forms of nom. sg. masc. adjectives could be seen as variants, a series of other morphological oppositions attested to in the "Notes" of 1746 are not considered interchangeable (i.e., "In Slavonic *сыновómъ, дѣлómъ, рýцѣ, мене, пихомъ, кланяхуся*; in Russian, *сыновьямъ, дѣламъ, рýки, меня, [мы] пили, [они] кланялись*" — IV, 1; VII², 83), and in the *Grammar* only the Russian forms were given. Although in his "Materials for the Grammar" Lomonosov expressed his intention "to write about the difference between Slavonic and Russian" and "about Slavonic and [its differences from] our language, about how and when it changed and what should be taken into the writ[ten language] from it" (VII², 631 and 606), the intention remained unrealized. Therefore the extent to which Church Slavonic grammatical elements were to be allowed into the literary language remained undefined. At the same time it is significant that in practice Lomonosov could make use of Church Slavonic elements which he had passed over in silence in his *Grammar*; which was the case in particular with truncated participles (see Zapol'skaia 1985, 44–45).

This vagueness might have been significant rather than merely accidental, since in conceptualizing the literary language as a combination of Church Slavonic and Russian no theoretical basis was found for excluding any given Church Slavonic form. One gets the impression that at first there was a definite consensus which excluded the most marked Slavonic forms from the literary language, first of all the aorist and imperfect, which are virtually absent in both Trediakovskii and Lomonosov. Apparently this was based on the synthetic grammatical tradition that had developed in the process of teaching Russian in the Academy of Sciences (§ II–1.4). However, a consensus of this type could not serve as a reliable guide, and there were definite disagreements between the two writers (for example, in the *Tilemakhida* Trediakovskii uses instr. pl. in -ы/-и [cf. Alekseev 1981: 77], while these forms are absent from Lomonosov's *Grammar*, and only isolated instances of them may be found in his other writings [see Martel 1933, 81]). The door to assimilating Church Slavonic forms was open, and later authors could usher in as many as they wanted, occasionally using even the aorist and imperfect as well as other strongly marked grammatical Slavonicisms.[11]

It is noteworthy that if using this kind of form had earlier automatically served to shift a text from non-bookish to bookish registers (§ 0–3), this mechanism now no longer functioned. Church Slavonic and Russian forms could now freely coexist in the literary language, and using Church Slavonic forms did not serve as marker of linguistic register but accorded to particular stylistic goals. Stylistic mechanisms displaced those of lexical register (§ 0–1). One of the fundamental consequences of this change was the shift in understanding of the border between Church Slavonic and Russian. The two languages were no longer juxtaposed, for example, as one with and without the aorist tense (as they had been in the late seventeenth and early eighteenth century), but as one language with the natural, constant and necessary use of the aorist as opposed to one in which its usage was occasional and functional, depending on stylistic aims. Hence Church Slavonic ("Slavenskii") could be exclusively identified with standard Church Slavonic while the hybrid version could turn out to be not so different on the outside from the new

---

[11] Instances of the occasional use of aorist, imperfect, participles in -ай/-яй, dative absolute, etc., may be commonly found in eighteenth-century Russian celebratory and spiritual odes in relatively high quantity. In some cases this may be explained by semantic reasons, as is the case of the aorist *бысть* in the incohative meaning. This meaning, historically associated with this form, leads Lomonosov to use it, for example, in works where the aorist does not usually occur, e.g., the Ode on Ascension Day, 1746: "Со властью рек: да будет свет / И бысть! О твари Обладатель!..." (Lomonosov, I, 123; VIII², 140; cf. Martel 1933, 75–6).
We find a response to these lines with the same aorist form in Vladykin (1774, l. 4; cf. Cooper 1972, 146), in his 1774 ode on peace with the Porte: "Бог рек: да будет тишина, / И бысть! О вышний Обладатель..." One may find an analogous example in M. Popov's translation of *Jerusalem Delivered*: "По сих словах Гавриил бысть невидим и вознесся паки на небеса" (Tass 1772, I, 44 — meaning "became invisible"). Usages like this fulfill specific stylistic functions, which is also true in the other texts of the new literary language in which simple preterits and other marked Church Slavonic forms occur. On the use of simple preterits in psalm paraphrases by Sumarokov and V. Maikov, see below. Participles in -ай/-яй are not unusual in V. Petrov (see Petrov, I, 46; II, 216, 224, 225). On Radishchev's language in this context see Alekseev 1977, 112.

"Slavenorossiiskii" language. It is indicative that Sumarokov in commenting on the language of Prokopovich's sermons, which were written in hybrid Church Slavonic (Sumarokov, VI, 280; Lomonosov, VII², 821; cf. Zhivov 1985a), notes the impurity of the language but does not refer to it as Church Slavonic (see § III-3.2). This change in linguistic consciousness led the way to viewing Church Slavonic as the language of the church service and religious books (models of the standard language), that is, as the cult language, similar to Latin.

1.3 The New Interpretation of Purist Categories

The new literary language, envisaged as a synthesis of Church Slavonic and Russian grammatical structures, looked forward even more to a synthesis of their lexical stock; as we have noted, the two languages did not lend themselves to consistent differentiation in this area. The new synthesis presumed that now both Russian and Church Slavonic words were to be considered "pure"; the purist position was not rejected, but changed focus. Trediakovskii now spoke openly about the "pure" Slavonic tongue (cf. Trediakovskii 1748, 309; III, 210; Pekarskii 1866, 108–9). Lomonosov, setting out to write about "the purity of Russian style," apparently intended to base his argument on both the purity "of Slavonic expressions" as well as of Russian ones (in his "Foreword on the Use of Church Books" he wrote that the purity of German was connected with translating the "holy books" into it, and it was understood that the same factors came into play in Russian, that is, the Church Slavonic component in the literary language was definitely seen as pure — Lomonosov, IV, 226; VII², 588).

In his epigram of 1753–55 "Не знаю кто певцов…" (I don't know who of the singers…) Trediakovskii clearly speaks of the purity of the Church Slavonic component in the Russian literary ("civic") language:

> Славенский наш язык есть правило неложно,
> Как книги нам писать и чище коль возможно.
> В Гражданском и доднесь, однак не в площадном,
> Славенском по всему составу в нас одном,
> Кто ближе подойдет к сему в словах избранных,
> Тот и любея всем писец есть, и не в странных.
> У немцев то не так ни у французов тожь,
> Им нравен тот язык кой с общим самым схожь.

1. The New Nature of the Russian Literary Language

> Но нашей чистоте вся мера есть славенский
> Не щегольков ниже и грубый деревенски.
>
> (Uspenskii 1984a, 103)

(Our Slavonic language is truly the standard how to write books in the purest possible manner. The civil tongue (but not the vulgar) to this day has the same content as Slavonic [and] the writer who emulates it better in using choice words (not foreign ones) is the favorite of all. It's not the same for the Germans or for the French either; they like language that is close to the most ordinary. But for us the whole measure of purity is Slavonic, neither the language of dandies nor the coarse village tongue.)

Lomonosov apparently came to the understanding of Church Slavonic's purity somewhat later than Trediakovskii, which suggests Trediakovskii's influence on him. In any case, in the late 1740's Lomonosov does not yet connect purity with the Church Slavonic linguistic legacy. Speaking in the *Rhetoric* about the purity of style, he says that this depends

> on a thorough knowledge of the language, on frequent reading of good books, and on discourse with people who speak purely. The first is aided by diligent study of the rules of grammar; the second by selecting sayings, phrases and proverbs from good books; and the third by striving to speak purely before people who know and observe beautiful speech. As far as reading, I advise you to be supported by church books (for the abundance of sayings, not for purity), from which I experience no small benefit. Everyone should consider this necessary, for if one wants to speak beautifully, one should first speak purely and have [at hand] an ample number of decorous and select phrases for expressing one's thoughts. (Lomonosov, III, 219–20; VII², 236–7)

Thus linguistic purity is here connected to the knowledge of grammar and the conversational speech of people who "speak purely" (a purist demand quite familiar in early eighteenth-century Europe — § III–2.3), while the Church Slavonic literary tradition is cited not for its purity but for its abundant lexicon. And this abundance seems to be taken as a secondary characteristic, whereas purity serves as the basis for correct writing. It follows that the vocabulary of church books is interpreted as something to ornament one's speech, that is, not a stylistically neutral element but an indicator of what is lofty (on these two views of Lomonosov, see § II–2.2).

In the wake of this new view of the Church Slavonic component as pure, the interpretation of Classicist purist categories that had been accepted in the 1730's was no longer appropriate. The rubrics remained the same, but the lexical material to which they corresponded required redistribution. Insofar as **Slavonicisms** were now declared to be "pure" lexicon, they could no longer be ranked as "learned words." This category was fully disbanded and no longer played any role in the new purism. And indeed it had no place, since both Trediakovskii and Lomonosov, in consonance with their new views, no longer looked upon linguistic expertise as pedantry but as the necessary precondition for mastering the skills of the literary language. Trediakovskii constantly cited the usage of scholars and those skilled in languages (1748, 307–25; III, 208–224, etc.), while Lomonosov extolled the knowledge of grammar, arguing that those without it were hampered in their use of the literary language (IV, 128; VII^2, 496). Lomonosov's isolated statements about the inappropriateness of Slavonicisms (IV, 228; VII^2, 589, VII^2, 581) by no means signified that they were to be excluded from the "pure" lexicon, but rather referred to the stylistic norms of their usage (§ III–2.2).

At first glance it might seem that Sumarokov had a different view of Slavonicisms. According to Boris Uspenskii, "In the 'Epistle on the Russian Language' Sumarokov orients the Russian literary language on conversational usage…, declaring himself against Slavonicisms… The linguistic program corresponds to the program once advocated by the young Trediakovskii, whose follower Sumarokov was, in essence" (Uspenskii 1984a, 92; cf. his differing opinion expressed later, Grinberg and Uspenskii 1992, 195). Indeed, lexical and grammatical elements of Church Slavonic in Sumarokov's comedies could define a pedant by means of his language, for example, the words of the pedant Ksaksoksimenius in the comedy "Tresotinius": "Подаждь ми перо, и абие положу знамение преславнаго моего имени, его же не всяк язык нарещи может" (Bestow on me a pen and I will immediately make a sign of my most illustrious name, which not every tongue can pronounce) (Sumarokov, V, 322; cf. § III–2.2). The Church Slavonic elements used here—the adverb абие, the construction with иже – belong, however, to those marked signifiers of bookishness which defined the bookish language in late seventeenth — early eighteenth century linguistic consciousness, and which both Trediakovskii and Lomonosov considered outside the bounds of the literary (Slavenorossiiskii) language. Sumarokov also refers to "the words иже, яже, and еже that are no longer used and that sound good in our church books, but would be awful not only in amorous but in heroic conversations" (Sumarokov, X, 98). This however represents more a polemical position than Sumarokov's attitude toward Slavonicisms or conversational usage. Disputing with Trediakovskii, Sumarokov wants to pigeonhole particularly learned words, and together with Latin expressions he cites "obsolete" Slavonic words that were not characteristic of Trediakovskii's usage but because of their obscurity symbolize the pedant's false erudition. At the same time, echoing the French, he makes reference to usage (as do Trediakovskii and Lomonosov). This creates the false impression that Sumarokov is against

1. The New Nature of the Russian Literary Language

Slavonicisms in general. A series of his statements (cf. § III–2.1) as well as his own linguistic practice belie this idea. His language combines Russian and Church Slavonic elements, while specific forms of conversational usage are legitimized not as normative but as allowable variants, used sporadically. These forms Sumarokov's critics labeled "base" and "of the simple folk" (cf. Klein and Zhivov 1987, 258f), which corresponded not so much to their real sociolinguistic character as to the critical rubrics of French purism.

Before the commencement of Sumarokov's clashes with Trediakovskii and Lomonosov (the "Epistle on the Russian Language" was the opening salvo against Trediakovskii — see Grinberg and Uspenskii, 1992, 139–42), his linguistic views had been developing in the same direction as those of his future antagonists. His criticism was motivated not by differences of opinion but by polemical needs, as Sumarokov assumed the pose of the single right-thinking European author struggling against crude home-grown fabrications. This pretension prompts him to criticize Trediakovskii, and later Lomonosov, from a "European" position, moreover in many cases the direct transfer of French purist opinions into the Russian context likens many of his pronouncements to those of the young Trediakovskii. Still, this similarity is of a superficial character; more important, in defending his independence from the scholarly authority of his rivals, in many ways Sumarokov was rejecting the rigid regulation (the system of prohibitions) that both Trediakovskii and Lomonosov were striving for, and he evidently saw this as pedantry which his antagonists were trying to substitute for necessary authorial aesthetic judgment (see below, § III–2.2). In any case, Sumarokov's linguistic program did not advocate any prohibition on Slavonicisms.

With the change of perspective on Slavonicisms the rubric of **archaisms** was also reinterpreted. Earlier the Church Slavonic literary tradition had been consciously ignored, so that the use or disuse of any given word in terms of that tradition had no relevance to the new literary language. Now, however, when Church Slavonic was introduced into the new language's diapason, the Church Slavonic tradition once again became important, and important theoretically, not only in practice. Hence Trediakovskii could speak of "customary Slavonic words which everyone knows" (Pekarskii 1866: 109), and Lomonosov of words "although generally used little, especially in conversation, yet comprehensible to all literate people" (IV, 227; VII^2, 588). It was understood that such "pure" Slavonic words were to be juxtaposed to "impure" Slavonic words that had fallen out of use, that is, archaisms. And indeed Lomonosov especially singles out "unused and quite decrepit" Slavonic words, like *обоваю, рясны, овогда, свѣнѣ* and similar ones" (IV, 227; VII^2, 588), and in the "Materials for a Russian Grammar" he mentions

Chapter 3. The Changed Conception of the Literary Language

"old Russian church words" (VII², 607). Trediakovskii evidently held similar views, and one may conclude that in criticizing Sumarokov for using the word *седалище* in "Khorev" in the meaning of "seat" he considered this, in reference to the Slavenorossiiskii literary language, to be archaic.

At the same time it is very indicative that Trediakovskii assigned Russicisms that were attested in written sources but absent in spoken usage to the category of archaisms. In the foreword to *Argenida* of 1751 Trediakovskii wrote: "And in truth the Novgorodian Marfa Posadnitsa of [former] primitive times will not read my translation. It was done for today's polite and flourishing (vytsvechenyi) [age] in which our language no longer has either ОЖЕ or АЧЕ or any of the other great number of archaisms, that is, [words] of great antiquity" (1751, I, lxi–lxii; cf. Lomonosov's "Philological Research," in which he writes "about reading ancient books and about phrases from Nestor, Novgorodian texts, and others, which are not found in dictionaries" — VII², 763). References to archaic East Slavic elements understandably had no relevance to contemporary literary practice, but they precisely fit the Classicist rubric of archaisms, and better corresponded to it than specifically bookish (not "ordinary") Church Slavonic words. Hence the attention of linguistic theory to this lexical group.

Understanding archaisms as elements of Church Slavonic that had gone out of literary usage was also characteristic of Sumarokov. Speaking about the sources of the "richness" (abundance) of the literary language in his "Epistle on the Russian Language" of 1748 he wrote:

> Имеем сверьх того духовных много книг:
> Кто винен в том, что ты псалтыри не постиг,
> И, бегучи по ней, как в быстром море судно,
> С конца в конец раз сто промчался безрассудно.
> Коль, АЩЕ, ТОЧИЮ обычай истребил;
> Кто нудит, чтоб ты их опять в язык вводил?
> А что из старины поныне неотменно,
> То может быть тобой повсюду положенно.
> Не мни, что наш язык не тот, что в книгах чтем,
> Которы мы с тобой, не Русскими зовем.
> Он тотже, а когда б он был иной, как мыслишь;
> Лишь только от того, что ты его не смыслишь;
> Так чтож осталось бы при Русском языке?
>
> (Sumarokov 1748, 7)

(Besides this we have many religious books. Who is at fault that you haven't mastered the Psalter, and running through it like a ship on the swift sea, have rushed senselessly from end to end a hundred times? If custom has eliminated АЩЕ, ТОЧИЮ, who forces you to bring them back into the language? But that which hasn't been abolished from the past you may use everywhere. Don't think that it's not our language that we read in books which you and I call "not Russian." It's the same; and if it were different, as you imagine because you don't understand it, what then would be left of the Russian language?)

These lines assert the unity of Church Slavonic and Russian, and in consequence, that words taken from church books may be freely used in the literary language; excluding such words would lead to the catastrophic impoverishment of the language ("What then would be left of the Russian language?"). One should only avoid those Church Slavonic words which "custom has eliminated," that is, words which have become archaic. By "custom" (or usage) Sumarokov clearly has in mind not conversational usage but usage within the literary tradition.[12]

Changes also took place in the interpretation of ***borrowings***. If formerly the rejection of the Church Slavonic linguistic ethos had led to the use of borrowed forms as a permissible "civic" equivalent for banished "church" words (which did not, of course, contradict a fundamentally purist approach in theoretical constructions), then now, after that ethos had been assimilated into the "civic" language, the struggle against borrowings became a real and realizable task. At the same time, this struggle became a natural component of the new linguistic program; in creating a literary language which was opposed to Church Slavonic, borrowings could have a definite role, but in creating a literary language that was to be equal in worth to those of Europe, its liberation from newly-borrowed foreign elements was directly connected with the claim to self-sufficiency. It is therefore understandable why in the foreword to the *Argenida* Trediakovskii cites the absence of borrowings as the special merit of his translation: "I used almost no foreign words in the translating this Author, however many may be in use among us today. On the contrary, I tried purposefully to translate using all possible equivalent Slavenorossiiskii expressions, except for mythological ones..." (1751, I, lx–lxi). In conformity with this aim, in his "Three Discourses" of 1758 Trediakovskii wrote that "our Slavenorossiiskii [language] also suffers today from the alien Western words it has adopted" (1773, 241; III: 511),

---

[12] If we interpret custom (обычай) differently, the reference to religious books as a special source would not make any sense; if one could take from church books only that which had been preserved in conversational usage, then this usage would be a self-sufficient source, not needing additions from church books — Considering Sumarokov's orientation on French theory, such additions, lacking in any real content, would seem especially strange.

Chapter 3. The Changed Conception of the Literary Language

and in his republished "Ode on the Taking of Gdansk" of 1752 he excluded borrowed lexicon (see Alekseev 1982, 96).

Lomonosov's views developed in the same direction. It is indicative that in the treatise "Foreword on the Use of Church Books" he directly connects assimilating the Church Slavonic heritage into the literary language with getting rid of recent European borrowings:

> ...by assiduous and careful use of the naturally related Slavonic language together with Russian, those wild and strange and stupid words which are entering our language from foreign ones may be staved off... Because of the neglect of reading church books, today such improprieties steal into our language imperceptibly and defile the proper beauty of our tongue, subject it to constant changes, and lead to its decline. All this may be cut short in the way I have indicated, and the Russian language will assert itself in full strength, beauty and richness, and not be subject to change and decline. (Lomonosov, IV, 230; VII², 591)

In another place he wrote that "we should not accept foreign [words] so as not to fall into barbarism like Latin" (IV, notes, 245; VII², 768); cf. in the "Materials" his note "about the misuse and introduction of foreign words" and his other protests against borrowings and calques from German, French and Polish (IV, 95 and 203; VII², 467, 562, 622).

Sumarokov also repeatedly returned to the theme of borrowings as words which harm the language's purity, for example in his articles "On Ridding Russian of Foreign Words" and "On Root Words in Russian" (IX, 244–47 and 249–56), and it is characteristic that in his "Epistle on the Russian Language" of 1748 the admonition against borrowings is connected with the "richness" of Russian: only the ignorant who are unable to make use of Russian's richness fall back on borrowings (this richness, as we have noted, stems precisely from Russian's union with Church Slavonic — cf. § III–2.1). Sumarokov wrote:

> Другой, не выучась так грамоте, как должно,
> Поруски, думает, всево сказать не можно,
> И, взяв пригоршни слов чужих, сплетает речь
> Языком собственным, достойну только сжечь.
> ....
> Перенимай у тех, хоть много их, хоть мало,
> Которых тщание искусству ревновало,
> И показало им, коль мысль сия дика,
> Что не имеем мы богатства языка.
>
> (Сумароков 1748, 4, 6)

(Another, who hasn't learned to write as one should, thinks that one can't say everything in Russian, and having taken a handful of foreign words, weaves a

1. The New Nature of the Russian Literary Language

language of his own, worthy only to be burned... Borrow from those, the many or the few, whose efforts strove with art and showed by this how outlandish the idea is that our language isn't rich.)

Cf. also the remark of the parodic Francophile Diulizh in Sumarokov's comedy "Chudovishchi" (Monsters): "...I wish I didn't know Russian. What a miserly language!" (Sumarokov, V, 258).

In this period reviling borrowings became a commonplace of Russian letters. One may see a similar evolution in the views of V. N. Tatishchev as that which we observe in Trediakovskii and Lomonosov. We should note that his linguistic thinking was significantly less precise that Trediakovskii, Adodurov or Lomonosov, so making sense of certain of his views (for example, about progress in language, or on the role of Church Slavonic and its relation to Russian) is very difficult. Even so, he had a negative attitude toward borrowing (as the reason for languages' corruption and decline) from the very beginning. In the 1730's his protest against them was nevertheless limited.[13] Tatishchev permitted borrowing terminology, and might even consider it the "enhancement" of the language (Tatishchev 1979, 98–9), but he considered it "unbeneficial" to borrow terms that could easily find Russian substitutes. Tatishchev's correspondence with P. Rychkov in 1750 evidences a harsher attitude toward terminological borrowings, which are now perceived as "vile"; one may assume that he thought it necessary on principle to replace them with Russian (Slavic) neologisms. The change in attitude is highlighted by the fact that Rychkov was pupil and follower of Tatishchev, although his discipleship had taken place during Tatishchev's Orenburg period (1737–9), that is, his linguistic habits had developed under the influence of Tatishchev's views of the late 1730's. In accord with these habits a decade later Rychkov wrote a work on Russian trade and manufacture. Tatishchev sent him his response to this work in February, 1750:

> Your composition on Russian trade and manufacture is worthy of praise, although in some places it is insufficient, and in others flawed, and so I have sent it to Moscow to have it copied and then added to. Among these [flaws] the first and main one is the intermixing of Latin and French words, which all scholars consider vile. (Pekarskii 1867, 19)[14]

---

[13] [...] See his "Conversation of Two Friends About the Use of Science and Schools" (Tatishchev 1979, 56, 91, 97) and his letter to Trediakovskii of Feb. 18, 1736 (Obnorskii and Barkhudarov, II, 2, 88–91).

[14] Rychkov's answering letter from Orenburg of May 5, 1750, displays the spread of the new purist ideas: "That I sometimes include foreign words in my letters and compositions occurs because of nothing else but my insufficient knowledge of our own terms appropriate for such matters... I never used these foreign words without extreme need, and henceforth will try to

Evidently Kantemir's attitude toward borrowings changed in the last period of his writing. I have already cited his "Foreword to the Translation of Justinian's History" in which he claims the absence of foreign borrowings to be the translation's principle merit (§ II–1.2). No less indicative is the elimination of borrowings from the last version of the satires (cf. the examples in Veselitskii 1974, 40).

The conception of the category of vulgar and base words underwent an even more radical metamorphosis. Protests against "folk" (that is, peasant) usage might have been made even earlier, but then they were purely theoretical and had no influence on linguistic practice whatsoever (§ II–1.2). Now, given the changed situation in which the newly acquired stock of Slavonicisms offered the new literary language an inexhaustible supply of vocabulary that was obviously not low, any word perceived for whatever reason as a Russicism could be assigned the status of a vulgarism. Given the absence of a normalized conversational language, there could be no definite dividing line between "permissible" (pure) and "impermissible" (impure) Russicisms; the resolution of the question depended on individual taste, predilections, and the polemical or non-polemical context, and allowed for an unlimited variety of possible variations.

Lomonosov's view of this issue seems moderate. In his Grammar he codifies such forms as глядь, бряк, and хвать, noting at the same time that they represent "the special quality of the simple Russian language" (IV, 175; VII^2, 539). In the "Foreword on the Use of Church Books" he excludes from the literary language "detested words which are not proper to use in any style, except perhaps in low comedies" (ibid, 227; 589). Lomonosov does not clarify how one might distinguish these words, so we cannot have a concrete notion of his attitude toward vulgarisms. We have far more material on which to judge Trediakovskii's opinion on this question, but it is not unambiguous. In linguistic practice he commonly uses many properly Russian elements (see Alekseev 1981, 80–8), although in his theoretical and polemical writings he may sharply curtail their use. In the "Conversation About Orthography" Trediakovskii often juxtaposes correct usage to that which is "base and peasant," "pancakemonger's usage (блинниково употребление)," "usage which has been corrupted by simpletons," etc. (1748, 307, 312, 314, 315, 325; see also below). At the same time he speaks of pleophonic forms and

---

keep ours better in mind and if possible never use theirs again" (Pekarskii 1867, 24; incidentally, such expressions in this letter as "присланных ко мне ремарков," "метод вообще апробуется," etc., indicate that Rychkov was unable to rid himself of this bad habit).

1. The New Nature of the Russian Literary Language

infinitives in *-ть* as "used in the simplest speech, introduced by the folk" (ibid, 300). In his criticism of Sumarokov Trediakovskii is even more radical in juxtaposing Russicisms to Slavonicisms and assigning them "to street usage." Here he describes as "base usage" or as "street" or "low" liberties forms of the type *подобьем, молнья, Божьему, понятье, беумье*, instead of *подобием, молния, Божиему, понятие, безумие*, the endings *-ой/-ей* as opposed to *-ыя/-ия* in gen. sg. fem. adjectives and possessive pronouns, "*опять* instead of *паки*, *этот* for *сей*, *эта* for *сия*, *это* for *сие*," etc. (Kunik 1865, 450, 456, 469, 476, 477, 479).

In essence the juxtaposition of "pure" and "low" ("base") for Trediakovskii turns out to be a simple renaming of the former opposition between Slavonic and Russian, at least in the polemical context. It is characteristic that the old task of classifying linguistic variants continues in a new framework, with the only difference that those markers which had earlier differentiated languages now differentiated good and base usage. In his article "On Plural Adjective Endings" (1755 version), Trediakovskii wrote: "All of these adjectives of ours in the singular, masculine, nominative case, have an (й) [ending], which is called short, and before this short (й) there is always either (и) or (ы), and it is never otherwise in the pure language... Some people not only speak in the simple way, but also in writing use the letter (о) before the short (й) instead of (и) or (ы)... and this mistaken written usage strangely confuses the masculine singular nominative with the feminine dative singular" (Pekarskii 1866, 104). This is referred to in the epigram "I don't know who of the singers… (Ne znaiu kto pevtsov…)" as well (Uspenskii 1984a, 103).

New oppositions are now drawn into the division between "pure" and "base," for example, the opposition between prefixes *роз-/раз-*, which had not been connected to the juxtaposition of languages before (§ II–1). Hence we read in Trediakovskii's "Three Discourses" that "in our entire language there is no prefix РОС or РОЗ... there is only a similar one, but that is not РОС, but РАС and РАЗ... True, the rabble and the most base say *розбить* instead of *разбить, розвесть* instead of *развесть*... and so on; but such wordsmiths are always ridiculed by respected people who know the importance of language." (Trediakovskii 1773,195; III,474). This opposition is now extended into properly lexical word pairs, as in the epigram "I don't know who of the singers…":

        Не голос чтется там, но сладостнейши глас,
        Читают око все, хоть говорят все ж глаз

Не лоб там но чело, не щоки но ланиты,
Не губы и не рот, уста там багряниты.

(Uspenskii 1984a, 103)[15]

It is obvious that in these conditions Classicist purism's struggle against vulgarisms could be realized by rejecting spoken forms in favor of bookish ones (which of course could never have been foreseen by Western — or at least French — purist doctrine).[16]

As a result of this development the correlation of Russicisms and Slavonicisms which made up the correlative pairs changed. If earlier the Russicism had been considered the basic form, and the Slavonicism subject to certain restrictions, it was now the reverse. In particular, if formerly the use of Slavonicisms had been considered poetic license, now the corresponding Russicisms could be assigned that role. Hence Trediakovskii could refer to "several folk and poetic liberties, such as these: *иль* instead of *или*, *спать* instead of *спати*" (Pekarskii 1866, 106). Similarly, in the "Letter From a Friend to a Friend," he could condemn Sumarokov for writing *молнья* instead of *молния*, *к престолу Божьему* instead of *к престолу Божиему*, and call such usage "base liberty" and "the greatest [kind of]... street license" (Kunik 1865, 469).

The positions of Sumarokov and Lomonosov were somewhat less radical, but on the whole reveal the same interpretation of the category. Like Lomonosov, Sumarokov does not consider every Russicism that had a Slavonic correlative to be automatically vulgar. The pairs offer a stylistic contrast and create the possibility of choice that a skilful writer could take advantage of. For high genres the basic member of the pair was the Slavonicism, and their Russian correlative could be characterized as a poetic

---

[15] An untranslatable play on Russian — Slavonic word doublets (*голос/глас, око/глаз[а], лоб/чело*, etc.). (Translator's note)

[16] We should keep in mind that late seventeenth century French purism could understand "lowness" (basesse) in two senses, as vulgarity and as impropriety; for the latter, see for example Charpentier, who wrote that "dirty remarks, outrageous speech, baseness — are not to be tolerated. And if one wants to express some tender passion, it must not be by using those ugly expressions which Catullus and Martial so often used" (Brunot, IV, 281). This fear of impropriety passed into the so-called "war of syllables," in which the use of certain words and even syllables that could have improper meaning was forbidden — for example, the use of the verb "inculquer" (instill) because it includes the syllable "cul" (backside) (ibid, 279–97). This phenomenon had its echo in Trediakovskii, cf. his "Letter from a Friend to a Friend": "In choosing these words he [Sumarokov] does not realize which go badly in a serious composition, so that they signify something vile when used or combined, like writing *блудя* [possibly: fornicating] instead of *заблуждая* [going astray], or using *какоеб* instead of *какое*, while the *б* or *бы* could be connected to another part of the word" (Kunik 1865, 476) (NB. "еб" has an obscene meaning in Russian — translator's note.)

liberty that could be justified by special considerations (cf. Sumarokov, X, 97).[17]

As concerns *dialecticisms*, given the lack of a normalized conversational usage and the literary language's orientation on the literary tradition rather than on such usage, dialecticisms did not require special attention; orientation on the literary tradition tended toward a more inclusive attitude toward vulgarisms, and dialectical lexicon merged into the mass of rejected "vulgar speech."[18] The frequent references during the period to the special beauty and correctness of Muscovite speech (for example: Lomonosov II, 132; VIII², 542; IV, 52–3; VII², 430; Trediakovskii 1748, 305; III, 207; Sumarokov, X, 42; Rzhevskii 1763, etc.; cf. Bobrik 1993, 37–9) were a natural reflection of the purist thesis about the superiority of the dialect of the capital. This was also evident in Sumarokov's attacks on Lomonosov's provincial speech habits: "Pythagoras doesn't know the Muscovite dialect because he was born in a village in a district where not only the peasants but the nobility speak very badly" — Sumarokov, IX, 279; cf. also X, 16 and 26, etc.). However, in distinction to the French, who emphasized dialectical aspects of lexicon and grammar, the issue here exclusively concerned pronunciation, so that for the formation of a "pure" Russian literary language the question of the superiority of Muscovite speech had only peripheral importance.

Similarly, the category of *bureaucratic words* (prikaznye slova) was not clearly delineated at first, and like dialecticisms, also tended to be grouped with the mass of "low" vocabulary. Characteristically, in his "Epistle on the Russian Language" of 1748 Sumarokov did not ascribe special bureaucratic

---

[17] With such an approach "low" forms may to some degree acquire sociolinguistic significance (cf. Uspenskii 1984a, 97–8). This is the sense in which Sumarokov's objection to Lomonosov's phrase "Нептун чудился" (Neptune was amazed) should be read: "*Чудился* is a word most base, as base as *дивовался*" (Sumarokov, X, 84); the fact that Sumarokov is in fact wrong is not significant here (see Klein and Zhivov 1987, 267–8). It is indicative that at the same time as Sumarokov accepts the category of vulgarisms, he practically pays no attention to them, as sociolinguistic differentiation is simply given lip service in accord with the French model.

[18] It may be that Trediakovskii considered the word *накры* that he encountered in Sumarokov as an inappropriate dialecticism: "Moreover, what he means by *накры*, I don't know; and neither do many others whom I asked about its meaning; from the context one may guess that he means a tambourine (бубны), but that's not how it's said in Russian, although maybe in Chuhkon" (Kunik 1865, 481–2) [NB. "Chukhon" is a pejorative term for the Finno-Ugric language spoken by native peoples living near St. Petersburg — translator's note.] *Накра* is an old borrowing from the Turkish languages (Fasmer, III, 40) and may be met in Church Slavonic as well as Russian texts (Sreznevskii, II, col. 293–4). Trediakovskii, however, is emphasizing its unfamiliarity, and in mentioning the Chukhon language, may be connecting this to limitations on regional usage. But this is a special case; as a rule, in their polemical attacks, Trediakovskii, Lomonosov and Sumarokov all confine themselves to criticizing "base" usage without specifying the nature of the baseness.

jargon to petty officials (pod'iachie); his attacks on such language, clearly modelled on the struggle of French purists against "la langue du palais," began somewhat later, and it was these attacks themselves that established the rubric of "bureaucratic words" in Russian linguistic consciousness. Rather, he charged them with a general predilection for "incorrect" language, for the archaic, vulgar, and markedly bookish. He wrote sarcastically:

> Лиш только ты склады немного поучи,
> Изволь писать Бову́, Петра́ златы́ ключи.
> Подьячий говорит: писание тут нежно,
> Ты будеш человек, учися лиш прилежно.

(Sumarokov 1748, 6)

(If you just learn a bit by rote [i.e., elementary literacy], go write a "Bova," "Peter of the Gold Key" [pulp fiction]. The clerk says: the writing is so tender. You will be a human being [if you] just study well.)

One may observe a similar approach in Trediakovskii. Hence when he described a character personifying the ideal correct language in his *Conversation About Orthography*, he noted that "he is almost always at his job, at court and with courtiers; and when he has the time, he spends as much of it as he can at home, sitting with his books. Moreover, except for church, he has never once been in any public place, not in the street, the markets, offices, shops, or any places like them" (1748, 314; III, 213). "Offices" (prikazy) are among the list of places where one can be infected by "base" usage; bureaucratic language and bureaucratic words are not distinguished as a separate category, but are seen as just as incorrect as the language of "country muzhiks," "bootmakers" and "coachmen." Nevertheless, in one place in the *Conversation* the foreigner says, "It seems to me, ladies and gentlemen, that you have cleaned up (ochistili) my first article," and there is a footnote explaining that "This kind of expression (izobrazhenie) is used by clerks" (Trediakovskii 1748, 182; III, 119). Here a bureaucratic phrase serves as a special marker of "impure" usage and models the incorrect speech of a foreigner.[19] There is only infrequent mention of bureaucratic language in Lomonosov. In his "Materials for the Grammar," there is a note "On

---

[19] Cf. the following dialogue at the end of the book between the foreigner and the Russian: "*For.* Have mercy, sirs! What have you done! Is it right to print all of what I say? I've committed so many offenses against your language it's impossible to do worse! They'll mock me into dust... *Rus.*: ... you are needlessly frightened of mockery. Everyone will make allowance for you as a foreigner, knowing that it is impossible for you not to make mistakes, as you are not a native speaker" (Trediakovskii 1748, 434; III, 298–9).

1. The New Nature of the Russian Literary Language

Bureaucratic Style" (Lomonosov, VII², 606), but it remains unclear exactly which elements he connects to this style. All of the above suggests that the occasional assertion in the secondary literature that this or that author — Kantemir, Trediakovskii, Lomonosov — gradually freed his language from bureaucratic usage (e.g., Vinogradov 1938, 138–9, Alekseev 1982, 124, etc.) are anachronistic, and are not well grounded in the actual linguistic consciousness of the corresponding period (cf. § I–1.4).

One should keep in mind that in the eighteenth century the bureaucratic language did continue to exist as a special linguistic tradition, parallel to that of the literary language, but without any influence on it (§ I–1.4). This tradition was gradually dying out, but in the middle of the century was still preserved in the cultural memory of the linguistic community. It is paradoxical, however, that the majority of attacks on "bureaucratic" words and expressions that one meets in the writings of Russian Classicists are directed not at real elements of the administrative language but at elements which were only fictitiously assigned to it (cf. Levin 1964, 85–6). The many attacks on the conjunction *понеже*, for example, are well known as this word appears as the symbol of bureaucratic jargon in writings on language. Sumarokov writes about how petty officials behave arrogantly toward him (IV, 315), and mocking them, writes, "Яко бы больше нужды не имелось,/ В сильном понеже сочинить екстракт" (As though there were no greater need / To compose an extract [in thisthe style full of] *понеже*'s) (VIII, 323). Other attacks on this word exist as well (see Martel 1933, 67; Levin 1964, 85–9). Yet the word was not specifically bureaucratic either in the seventeenth century (§ I–1.4, note 16), nor did it become so in the eighteenth (see Levin 1964, 86). Likhud in his editing of the *General Geography* sometimes used it to replace the more bookish conjunction *ибо* (Zhivov 1986b, 253). The conjunction *понеже*, then, was completely neutral, and defining it as bureaucratic was totally artificial. That it was so was underscored by the fact that the opponents of *понеже* rejected it in a fully conscious way, at a certain definite moment, whereas before that they had used it more or less freely. After the 1750's Lomonosov no longer used the word (see Lomonosov VII², 892–3), and Sumarokov stopped using it at the same time (cf. the use of *понеже* in a letter of 1748 and its absence in subsequent ones — PRP 1980, 69f). One may observe an analogous process later in Karamzin as well (he uses the word in the 1780's but doesn't in the 90's — Levin 1964, 236).

This indicates that the reasons for rejecting *понеже* were not due to any real aspects of its linguistic use but because it was artificially equated with French "juridical" conjunctions which were the special targets of French purists (conjunctions like "ains," "jaçoit que," "ores que," "à raison de quoy" — Gournay 1962, 118; Vaugelas 1647, l. o2, 568; Brunot, III, 22–26 and IV, 388–97). Since the French had juridical conjunctions, the Russians had to have them too. Moreover, any conjunction which was more or less characteristic of the bookish language could have fulfilled this function as negative model. Just as the assimilation of French theory had stimulated considering linguistic variations in terms of a Church Slavonic — Russian opposition in the 1730's (§ II–1.4), so in the second half of the century assimilating these theories led to reconceptualizing them in terms of other oppositions, including "pure" versus "bureaucratic."

As a result of this artificial approach, a large number of Slavonicisms were interpreted as bureaucratic language even though they had nothing to do with it. Thus in Novikov's satirical journal *Truten' (The Drone)* a female fashion-plate writes that "From wimin's style you've made it a clerk's, edifying [us] for no reason: *обаче, иначе, дондеже, паче*" (Berkov 1951, 233–4); common Slavonicisms are thus declared to be bureaucratic. Even more typical, in Fonvizin's "Brigadier" the speech of the Councilor, ostensibly satirizing the linguistic habits of the courtroom, is actually simply parodic Slavonicizing. Insofar as the Slavenorossiiskii literary language could absorb lexical Slavonicisms without any limit, "unnecessary" Slavonicisms were placed into other rubrics. The bureaucratic language was forgotten in the second half of the eighteenth century (§ I–1.4) and its image underwent a metamorphosis; if in the seventeenth century it had been juxtaposed to Church Slavonic as Russian, in the second half of the eighteenth century it assumed the role of Slavonicized rather than "pure" Russian.

The attitude toward the category of ***neologisms*** was determined by three factors: the need to expand available vocabulary to describe new ideas and realia; the purist rejection of borrowings, which made neologisms especially important to satisfy this need; and, finally, disapproval of neologisms assimilated from the French. These contradictory factors led to a situation in which neologisms were largely permitted, especially in scholarly writing which required new terminology. Cf. Lomonosov's foreword to his translation of *Wolff's Experimental Physics* of 1748: "to name several Physical instruments, actions and natural substances, I was forced to seek [new] words which may seem somewhat strange at first, but I hope that with time and use they will become more familiar" (VI, 304; I^2, 425; on the problems of creating language of science see: Kutina 1964; Kutina 1966; Veselitskii 1972). French prohibitions were no less operative than the needs of linguistic practice, and perhaps also the example of German language building. As G. Blume writes concerning seventeenth-century German, "these experiments with new words (frequent for translation) are generally

1. The New Nature of the Russian Literary Language

typical for linguistic-historical epochs in which a language is used in forms of communication that have been uncommon for it up to that point (e.g., in new forms of literary communication). This was still the case in seventennth-century Germany, while at the same time in France a stage of [linguistic] consolidation had taken the place of experiment" (Blume 1978, 44). In this regard eighteenth-century Russia was unquestionably closer to Germany than France.

In theoretical declarations, however, neologisms were almost never mentioned; to sanction them would have contradicted purist theory, to limit them — to contradict literary practice. It is possible that the summons to read church books was particularly connected to the problem of neologisms (cf. Keipert 1981, 40). In them one could find ready words which could be used to name new phenomena (and the consequent semantic neologisms which arose were apparently acceptable to the purism of the time). It is understandable how in a polemical context the problem of neologisms could come to the fore. Hence in his condemnation of Sumarokov Trediakovskii charged that: "our author introduces words into his works that are not used, like *в последок* instead of *напоследок*, *не времянно* instead of *не навремя*, *мгновенно* instead of *во мгновении*, *отколе* in "Gamlet" (Hamlet) instead of *откуду*, *надвела* instead of *навела* in "Khorev," *бремянило* instead of *отягощало*, *сугублю* instead of *усугубляю*..." (Kunik 1865, 477). Trediakovskii, it appears, criticizes these innovations insofar as they do not rectify the lack of words but replace words that already exist.

This attitude toward neologisms, later fully developed by the Russian Academy, corresponded to the compromise position that had been worked out by French purism in the late seventeenth and early eighteenth century as a result of the intersection of Vaugelas' ideas and Cartesianism, which could not deny reason the right to effect linguistic innovations. As Lamy wrote in his *Rhetoric*, "When custom does not supply the appropriate terms to express what we want to say, we are entitled to recall those which usage has rejected unnecessarily... provided however that the new word is dressed according to fashion, and that it will not seem foreign, that is to say, that it has a sound which is not entirely different from the words we use; if one is taking it from Latin, for example, one may adapt it by analogy..." (Lamy 1737, 90–1; cf. a similar approach in Trediakovskii's revered Fénélon, VII, 124–27). In Russian conditions, the resurrection of words which had been "wrongfully rejected by usage" (which Lamy wrote about) led back to church books as source for the literary language. This is exactly the course Trediakovskii chose in creating philosophical terminology for his "Speech on Wisdom, Prudence and Virtue" of 1752. Defending his innovations, he wrote to the

Academy chancellery on Dec. 11, 1752, that "these terms are confirmed in all of our church books, from which I took them" (Pekarskii, IA, II, 167).

Neologisms turn out to be permissible insofar as their form is traditional and the changed meaning is not taken into account (see Uspenskii 1985, 183). One may see this approach to neologisms in Trediakosvkii's note to the word *ифика* in the foreword to Rollin's *Roman History*: "*Ифика*. This word, according to simple grammatical sense, in our language is *нравственница*, or rather, so that the ear won't be irritated with its novelty, *нравоучительница*" (RI, XII, 1). Remarkably, the neologism *нравственница* is rejected as unacceptable while the neologism *нравоучительница*, also absent in Church Slavonic, is permissible. It is apparently permissible because of its similarity to the word *нравоучитель* (a word that does not seem to be met in Church Slavonic texts but which is listed in Polikarpov's *Lexicon* — 1704, l. 201, 2nd pag.). It follows that the neologism's admissibility is not determined even by the existence of a formally identical word in the church books by its relation to word-forming models. This recalls the requirement of having a familiar resonance which both Lamy and Rollin cite; cf. also Gottsched's discrimination between two types of neologisms: "either completely new syllables and sounds which you don't otherwise hear in our language or a new grouping of old syllables and words which have never before been combined in this way" (Gottsched 1751, 235); neologisms of the latter type were to some extent permissible.

2. Rationalist Purism and the Richness of the Slavenorossiiskii Language

The metamorphosis of the purist conception that had taken place led to a situation in which the new literary language was able to derive sustenance from both Russian and Church Slavonic sources. The previous understanding of purism had limited an author's choice of vocabulary, at least in theory. Thanks to this one single change in the linguistic equation, the new conception generated an exceptional abundance of words, especially when contrasted with the former lexical poverty. As early as 1733 academic translators had written in "A Prediction" printed in the *Notes to the Gazette* (*Primechanii k vedomostiam*) of January 1 that "To this day we... have tried very hard to bring out into the light various necessary matters using a clear and easy presentation, materials which for the most part have been greatly obscured by special clever words. This was also no easy task, since the German language, in which we write, as well as the Russian, into which we convert our thoughts, still isn't sufficiently capable of depicting all ideas" (Berkov 1952, 72). Not twenty years would pass before an abundance of words—an embarrassment of riches — would be ascribed to the new literary language as its predominant characteristic (see Alekseev 1982, 118f). The main reason for this change was the acceptance of Church Slavonic's lexical stock, part of a new complex of ideas which turned Slavonicizing purism into an analogue for prevailing European linguistic theories.

2.1 The Richness and "Antiquity" of Russian

In his "Foreword on the Use of Church Books" Lomonosov wrote that "from church books we have acquired the richness with which to forcefully depict important and lofty ideas" (IV, 229; VII^2, 590). Thanks to this richness "we have proper and expressive means... for [expressing] very diverse natural qualities and distinctions" (ibid, 10; 392). Apparently thinking along the same lines, Trediakovskii wrote of Sumarokov that because he did not know church books he lacked "an abundance of select words" ("l'abondance des mots choisis," Kunik 1865: 496). At one stroke, legitimizing the Church Slavonic lexical heritage made the Russian literary language abundant, and gave it a special place among the literary languages of Classicism.

In fact, in European Classicist linguistic consciousness the ancient tongues (Latin and Greek) were fundamentally different from modern ones. Chapelain wrote:

> ...I do not believe that our modern languages are as capable of strong figures of speech, either in meaning or elocution, as those which reigned so happily among the ancients (les Anciennes). That apparently happened thanks to the fact that Greece and Italy had more time to cultivate their language from the moment when they began to enjoy studying the disciplines, which we did not have to perfect our own [language] since the moment we thought to embellish it. Or [perhaps] this was because of the genius of ancient times, which acquired its daring not only without pain, but even with pleasure, favoring the bountiful audacity of orators and poets who were admired for taking risks. Instead, our own genius rejects with disgust the smallest bold figure in stylistic matters of style and vocabulary, anything that deviates even slightly from the way of speaking current among those who are called "gentlemen" (honnêtes gens). (Chapelain 1656, l. dI — dI verso).

Thus the ancient languages were seen as free and bold in their use of words, whereas the modern ones were fettered by their connection to the linguistic practices of aristocratic society. Chapelain, however, fails to explain how the boldness of the ancient tongues is compatible with their purity. He clearly avoids two assertions that were unacceptable for Classicism, first, that the striving after purity leads to a language's impoverishment (about which Mlle. de Gournay speaks, and which Chapelain specifically tries to ignore), and second, that the ancient languages were not pure (an assertion which contradicted the Classicist emphasis on imitation and would lead to too sharp a break with the classics).

We should keep in mind that the literary and linguistic program of Classicism was in principle hardly based on tradition; the postulates of naturalness, propriety, verisimilitude, and correspondence to modern taste by no means led to cultivating continuity with the past. The classical cultural heritage, however, held a special place. In the framework of the contrast between the Classical Age and the barbarian Middle Ages that formed in sixteenth and seventeenth-century cultural consciousness, the values of Greece and Rome were endowed with all positive values, while the Middle Ages were declared a time in which good taste was corrupted. It was precisely at this time that the Middle Ages took shape in cultural consciousness as a special historical epoch (cf. Edelman 1946; Neddermeyer 1988), and the theoreticians of Classicism assigned the most heterogeneous characteristics to it, united mostly by their lack of correspondence to good taste. Rejecting the Middle Ages inferred a focus on antiquity. In this way the interest in the classics was not an organic part of the Classicist program but a consequence of the collateral battle that was being waged with previous cultural epochs. For Chapelain therefore antiquity held undisputable authority, and he had only to indicate the divergences between the genius of classical languages and that of French. However, the more consistent theoreticians of Classicism — the "moderns" — went farther and could train the whole arsenal of Classicist rigorism against the classics.[20] Be that as it may, a basic dissimilarity between ancients and moderns was asserted with classical tongues defined as naturally abundant in words and rhetorical figures and modern ones characterized by

---

[20] A substantial place in this critique was given to a deprecating analysis of Homer's language, and to a lesser extent that of other classical authors. Criticism of this type may be found in Pierrot (cf. Pierrot 1964, 312) and Fontenelle [...] (Fontenelle, II, 362; cf. Hepp 1968). This attitude toward antiquity was not universal in Classicism, and played almost no role in forming its linguistic doctrine, although one might suggest that Vaugelas' principles to some extent helped prepare the ground for "the moderns."

2. Rationalist Purism and the Richness of the Slavenorossiiskii Language

moderation and precision.²¹

This contrast between the richness of classical languages and the limited nature of modern ones (first of all French in its Classicist guise) was common among French theoreticians and constantly cropped up in their writings. There occur rather detailed explanations about what the richness of the ancient languages consists of and how modern ones differ. Rollin, for instance, writing about the education of children, wrote that "If they had some inkling (teinture) of the Greek and Latin languages, that would be the time to make them realize for their own good the genius and character of the French language by reading its [leading] writers and forcing them to compare them with the former [i.e, the classics]. It [French] is lacking in many benefits and advantages which are their principle beauty" (Rollin, I, 6–7). Rollin then lists the ways in which the ancient languages are superior: in the abundance of words and phrases (especially in Greek); in creating compound words; in the potential to create words by means of prefixes; in their free word order; in the variety of noun and verb inflections; in the existence of three rather than two genders; in the existence of comparatives and superlatives; and in the use of diminutives. Devoid of all this, French still has the advantages of clarity and comprehensibility which compensate for its poverty — the capability "to be such an enemy of all inelegance, and to bring such clarity to the spirit that one cannot fail to heed it when it is handled by a skillful hand" (ibid). In this way a system of oppositions was established that distinguished modern from ancient languages.²²

Evidently, Rollin's views ultimately derived from the traditions of Port-Royal and its understanding of the juxtaposition of "classical" and "vulgar" tongues. Thus, for example, in the Port-Royal *Grammar* it says of relative adjectives that "when one adds to the words that signify substances the connotation or mixed signification of the thing to which the substances relate one turns them into adjectives , e.g., *homme, humain, genre humain, vertu humain*, etc. The Greeks and Latins have an infinity of such words: *ferreus, aureus, bovines, vitulinus*, etc. But Hebrew, French and other vulgar languages have fewer; French uses a "de": *d'or, de fer, de boeuf,*

---

²¹ The juxtaposition of the richness of "ancient" languages to the poverty and purity of "new" ones was superimposed onto the earlier contrast between Greek and Latin: Latin was homogeneous and pure, while Greek was heterogeneous (in its dialects) and diverged from the ideal of purity. This latter contrast may be seen in the writing of the Humanists (for example, Lorenzo Valla — Bragina 1958, 122–3), although it was (mostly) no longer characteristic of seventeenth-century France; Greek and Latin were united in being contrasted to "new" languages.

²² See Rollin's list of the advantages of ancient languages [...] (Rollin, I, 6–7).

etc." (Arnault and Lancelot, 1803, 274–5). A similar remark is made about vocatives: "In our language, and in the other vulgar tongues, this case is expressed in common nouns which have an article in the nominative by the suppression of this article" (ibid, 286–7). These observations may be seen as asserting the greater lexical and grammatical richness of classical languages in comparison to vulgar tongues.[23]

This opposition was undoubtedly familiar to Russians in one form or another. Trediakovskii's broad familiarity with French literature allows us to presume that the discursive opposition between "ancients" and "moderns" was one of the elementary frameworks within which he and his contemporaries debated history and language. Trediakovskii knew the works of Rollin intimately, referring to him as "great" (Trediakovskii, RI, I, p. ДІ; cf. Trediakosvkii, DI, I, Preduved., l. 1 verso); of special importance was the "Treatise on Studies" (Traité des etudes) [...] that L. V. Pumpianskii (1941b, 251) suggested "had a great influence on Trediakovskii, and as a matter of fact, molded his literary views" (cf. Serman 1962, 211–3; Achinger 1970, 18f; Kibal'nik 1981). One may even assert that the mature Trediakovskii related ancient to Classicist literature through the prism of Rollin's synthesizing approach. His views on the relation between classical and modern literary languages might also naturally have come from Rollin.

The sources of Lomonosov's views are harder to clarify. Lomonosov knew a series of French writers (for example, Pomey), and we know that he made a conspectus of Boileau's translation of Pseudo-Longinus during his years of study abroad (Lomonosov, VII², 791); this presupposes knowledge of the prefatory "Reflections on Longinus" in which the comparative value of French and the classical languages is discussed. Here it is noted that French is very fastidious in word choice and therefore, "although it may be rich in beautiful terms for certain subjects, there are many for which it is very poor" (Boileau, II, 442). Formative for Lomonosov were also Gottsched's major works, which could have served in this case as an intermediary for the ideas of

---

[23] One may find a curious reflection of these ideas in Evgenii Bolkhovitinov, who wrote: "Concerning the abundance of the Greek language one may judge by the example that from one single verb [from the following list], φερω, ιστημι, τιθημι, and εχω, one could compile an entire dictionary full of words. In Greek the adjective "proud" may be expressed forty times using words that have the same meaning... As far as expressiveness, Greek participles and adjectives, which sometimes can express an action, likeness, and quality together, show this best. Most often one can see examples of this in Pindar, but no fewer in church hymns, especially Irmosy [heirmoi] and Oktoikh [Octoechos]" (Evgenii Bolkhovitinov 1800, 100. Characteristic here is the combination of Pindar and liturgical literature as a single source for Russian literature's high style (§ II–2.2).

2. Rationalist Purism and the Richness of the Slavenorossiiskii Language

Rollin and Lamy. Lomonosov also knew the Port-Royal *Grammar*.[24]

Within the binary framework of ancient and modern languages, Church Slavonic obviously belonged to the ancients; it had the same abundance of words as Greek and Latin, the same characteristics of word structure and formation, the same system of endings. According to the French theorists, Latin's richness developed thanks to the influence of Greek (Rollin, I, 42–3; cf. Trediakovskii 1745, 79); Church Slavonic's richness came from the same source. It is with this idea that Lomonosov began his "Foreword on the Use of Church Books":

> In ancient times, when the Slavonic people did not know how to depict its thoughts in writing, thoughts which were then very limited due to ignorance about many things and actions that were known [only] to educated peoples, its language was also not abundant in many phrases and expressions of the intellect, of the kind we read today. This richness was acquired first and foremost together with the Greek Christian law, when church books were translated into Slavonic for glorifying God. The outstanding beauty, abundance, importance and power of the Hellenic word is very highly esteemed; lovers of the verbal arts amply attest to this... One who has penetrated into church books in the Slavonic tongue can see clearly from the translation of the Old and New Testament, patristic homilies, from the spiritual songs by Damascene [John of Damascus] and other creators of canons how much of Greek abundance we see in Slavonic... (Lomonosov, IV, 226; VII^{2,} 587)

Hence Greek turns out to be the primary source of richness for all cultured languages (cf. Lomonosov's reference to "lovers of the verbal arts," that is, the European estimation of Greek's importance) with Latin and Church Slavonic its lawful inheritors.

Having become Church Slavonic's rightful heir, the new literary language also inherited its richness, and that which Church Slavonic received from Greek was now passed on to Russian. Having described the beauty and strength of Greek as imparted to Church Slavonic, Lomonosov continues: "and from here we increase the sufficiency of the Russian word, which is great in its own plenitude and able to absorb the beauties of Greek by means of Slavonic" (Lomonosov, IV, 226; VII^2, 587). Insofar as the Russian literary language was seen as of one nature with Church Slavonic (§ III–1.2), it was also party to the genius of ancient languages, and first of all, to their lexical abundance. "As far as the abundance of the Russian language,"

---

[24] There exist Lomonosov's notes on Gottsched with mentions of Rollin and Lamy (Lomonosov, III, notes, 34); on the direct dependence of his *Rhetoric* on Gottsched's *Complete Rheroric (Ausfürliche Redekunst)* see Grasshoff 1961; on the influence of Cartisean linguistic ideas on Lomonosov, see Signorini 1988, 523; Signorini 1991, 157–8.

writes N. Popovskii in 1755 (1755, 173), "in this the Romans have nothing to brag about in comparison. There is no thought that cannot be expressed in Russian."

Trediakovskii followed this same train of thought. Like Lomonosov, he now placed the Russian literary language (Slavenorossiiskii) on a level with the classical languages and also juxtaposed it to French (as a new and hence impoverished language). In the foreword to *Tilemakhida* he describes Slavenorossiiskii: "Nature gave it all the abundance and sweetness of the Hellenic tongue, and all the importance and gravity of Latin. Why should we voluntarily subject ourselves to French poverty and narrowness when we have the myriad richness and breadth of Slavenorossiiskii"? (Trediakovskii 1766, I, I; II, xii). In another place he asserts that Russian can "not only lushly pour forth like French, but also march splendidly like Latin and even strive passionately like Greek" (Trediakovskii, RI, XII, xxi).

Repeating in his "Three Discourses" the common European account about how the classical languages had fallen into decay as a result of the barbarian invasions which had changed their basic nature, producing French, Spanish, modern Greek, etc., in the process, Trediakovskii equated Slavenorossiiskii with the classical languages before their fall:

> Scarcely had the Northern peoples entered Italy did the Latin language begin to suffer. The Franks who conquered the Gauls immediately corrupted their Roman tongue, probably used since Roman times, and produced French... [A]pproximately the same thing happened in Constantinople with Greek on account of the Turks, and similarly our Slavenorossiiskii suffers today from accepting foreign Western words, which comes exclusively from our very close association with Western peoples. However, our language cannot suffer irremediable harm: literary Slavonic will maintain it, preserve it, and save it from injury, unwaveringly and for all time. (1773, 241; III, 511)

Trediakovskii believes that the "classic" Slavenorossiiskii language is being subjected to a similar assault of foreign words (apparently, French and German) as Latin and Greek had once been, but that it will be preserved unharmed by Church Slavonic, the source of Slavenorossiiskii's "classical" quality. Here Slavenorossiiskii's membership in the "ancient" languages and its fundamental difference from the "moderns" is declared unequivocally.[25]

---

[25] The argument about the ancient classical languages being destroyed by the barbarians cited in reference to the corruption of Russian also appears in Sumarokov, apparently not taken from Trediakovskii but simply a European commonplace. Noting the disappearance of one element of Russian's historical richness, the simple preterits, Sumarokov writes that "we are daily being deprived of the remaining beauties of our tongue, and with time we will lose them all. The Helene and Roman were deprived of their languages by barbarians, but we are being stripped of our beautiful language by ourselves" (Sumarokov, X, 23).

2. Rationalist Purism and the Richness of the Slavenorossiiskii Language

The new notion of the Russian literary language as "ancient" was also reflected in Trediakovskii's opinion about Greek's significance for Russian and for the poetics of Russian literature. If formerly Trediakovskii had completely dismissed such influence (§ I–1.2), and could state that Slavonic was "as far away" from Greek "as Chinese" (Trediakovskii 1737, 16n), now Greek and classical poetics turned out to be worthy models for emulation. His new conception of the literary language led Trediakovskii to Grecophilism (for a detailed discussion of this, see Uspenskii 1985, 169–70). This was reflected in many of his pronouncements.

Hence Trediakovskii again changed his views on orthography. If in 1748 he mocked Polikarpov's insistence that one write *Φ* and *θ* in Greek names in accord with their spelling in Greek (§ 2–1.2), in 1755 he introduced a distinction between *u* and *i* in the very same Greek names, referring to the practice accepted at the Academy typography of using *Φ* and *θ* (the same as in Polikarpov). The spelling of borrowings from Greek and Latin (the ones in Greek corresponding to *ι*) using *ï* rather than *u* had entered orthographic practice of the Moscow Typography in Polikarpov's day.[26] This was characteristic practice for bookmen of Grecophile orientation (see the discussion of Likhud's correction of the *General Geography*, § I–1.3). The Academy typography changed this norm so that in all cases *u* was used. In these conditions Trediakovskii's return to the old practice cannot help but be seen as a conscious decision. At first the importance of Greek as source of linguistic norms for literary Russian was completely rejected, and then asserted with no less insistence. In 1755 Trediakovskii wrote: "Those who defend this innovative usage of the Academy typography [argue] that it is easier and more convenient to write like that, because not all writers know how to spell some particular foreign word, and where to use the letter (i). All right, such clever simplicity in reference to (и) and (i) is praiseworthy. But why then isn't this most marvelous simplicity observed in the Academy typography when it concerns (Φ) and (θ) in foreign words?" (Pekarskii 1865, 113). It is remarkable that Trediakovskii refers to this rule as "established by very longstanding usage" (ibid, 112), that is, he refers approvingly to the very same orthographic practice of the Grecophiles that he had sharply denounced ten years before.

Trediakovskii also refers to the precedent of the "ancients" when he justifies the use of "single strokes" (edinitnye palochki), that is, dashes.

---

[26] See for example the corrections to the type-set copy of *Tsarstvo mira* (Kingdom of the World) (Moscow 1702): *славянолатинских* > *славянолатїнских*, *скїпетра* > *скипетра* (Gr. σκῆπτρον), *θїмїан* > *θимїан* (Gr. Θυμίαμα) (RGADA, f. 381, no.1032, l/ 1, 1 verso).

Chapter 3. The Changed Conception of the Literary Language

The introduction of dashes as "the antidote and scourge of homonymy (ravnoglasie) or ambiguous expressions" was meant to enrich the expressive means of the literary language, to increase its "ancient" richness and thereby bring it that much closer to the classical ones. Trediakovskii writes: "It is known from history that the ancient Greeks and Romans in theatrical and public (kantsel'nykh) declamations used different intonations, with some kind of notes, like musicians [use for] their choruses or dance-masters for their steps... I think that with great probability their notes served exactly the same purpose as my single strokes between words, above them [indicating] words' triple prosody, and below them the poets' usual marks indicating long or short syllables; they were basically similar to my method" (Pekarskii 1865, 115).

No less indicative was Trediakovskii's wide use of compound words in *Tilemakhida* and in many late works, and especially his use of compound adjectives. In *Tilemakhida* compound adjectives often correspond to simple French ones in the original (see Orlov 1935, 41–2; Petrova 1966). As A. A. Alekseev notes, "the single exemplar here was the Greek language of the *Iliad* and the *Odyssey*, while the chosen models for word formation came from Church Slavonic" (Alekseev 1981, 87). As D. Tschižhewskii demonstrated, the majority of complex words that Trediakovskii used had direct correlatives in Church Slavonic texts, and their stylistic functions may be seen as a transformation of the tradition established by Church Slavonic literature (Tschižhewskii 1940, 114–20). By using compound adjectives, Trediakovskii consciously tried to give the *Tilemakhida* an epic, Homeric coloration; at the same time he wanted to demonstrate that the new literary language was fully capable of absorbing the lexical abundance which came from Greek and Church Slavonic. Trediakovskii pursued the same goal when he used compound words (in many cases neologisms) in other works, for example, in his foreword to Rollin's *Roman History* the phrases нектароливная Сочность, Сп̃ренолестныхъ затѣей, вострубила доброязычно (see Trediakovskii, RI, I, p. E, AI), and in the foreword to *Tilemakhida* and elsewhere. As we have already noted, in European linguistic thought compound words were a marker of "ancient" languages, so that by introducing them into the Russian literary tongue Trediakovskii was trying to demonstrate its "ancient" character as well.[27]

---

[27] On compound words in connection to the problem of enriching the language, see: Fénélon, VII, 125 [...] ; Gottsched (who remarks on the similarity of Greek and German in this area) (Gottsched 1751, 235–6); and Rolli (on Greek and Italian, in connection with the Italian humanist and man of letters Gian Giorgio Trissino) (Rolli, 1729). In all these cases, complex words are seen as a characteristic feature of ancient languages, and juxtaposing them to modern ones defines one aspect of their richness. See also Bouhours' attack on complex words as elements which harm linguistic clarity (Bouhours, 1671, 63–4); in this

2. Rationalist Purism and the Richness of the Slavenorossiiskii Language

The changed conception of the literary language and the new attitude toward Greek that it produced also led to a reevaluation of unrhymed verse. In literary thought of the end of the seventeenth and eighteenth centuries, the possibility of using unrhymed verse was tied to a language's richness, and with the existence of a special poetic language which could be differentiated from prose by itself, without the aid of rhyme (cf. Kantemir II, 2–3). Pointing to the differences between Russian and French poetry and at the possibility of unrhymed Russian verse, Kantemir cites two issues: the existence of a special poetic language (discussed above, § II–2.2) and word order. French "must... without fail place pronouns before nouns, nouns before words [i.e., verbs, *verbum* — VZ], verbs before adjectives, and finally, [to put] a phrase governed by another word in its appropriate case, that is, it is not permitted in French to change word order, so that without these helping devices, it is necessary to decorate a line with rhyme; for without it the language would seem overly bare (prostoslozhnaia)" (Kantemir, II, 2–3).

As mentioned, Rollin wrote about free word order as a feature testifying to a language's richness.[28] Trediakovskii didn't directly treat this question, although the frequent use of inversions in *Tilemakhida* shows that he was sympathetic to this position. Other late eighteenth-century writers who directly or indirectly assimilated Trediakovskii's view of the "ancient quality" of Slavenorossiiskii developed the idea of the connection between this and free word order quite explicitly. Thus Moisei Gumilevskii wrote that "In translating into Russian one should not be hampered by the example of the Germans or French and make each period follow a single set [or monotonous] order. Having freed our language from this constraint, we can give it free movement, on the example of Greek or Latin. For among its many qualities it can be rich and superior to others and has the ability of coming closer to the language being translated without losing its own nature at the same time" (Moisei Gumilevskii 1786, 25–6). Evgenii Bolkhovitinov also writes of "the freedom of placement and order of words," that makes Russian similar to Greek (1800, 14).

Bouhours demonstrates the superiority of French over the ancients. Attention to complex words as a stylistic marker (in poetry or high style) has a long tradition (Aristotle, Demetrius Phalereus). Later commentators who see them as a marker of Slavenosrossiiskii's richness that makes Russian equal to the classical languages include Moisei Gumilevskii and Evgenii Bolkhovitinov (see below).

[28] For French theoreticians, the free word order of the "ancients" could be seen as "unnatural" and irrational, contradicting the aesthetic principles of Classicism [...] (see, for example, Bouhours, 1671, 65). The richness of ancient languages could thus be seen as false, and the "restrictedness" of French as the natural order of things; be that as it may, the basic opposition remained in force. Bouhours' attacks on the ancient languages clearly prefigured the arguments of the "moderns" in the "quarrel between the ancients and moderns."

Trediakovskii directly followed Kantemir's lead in the question of rhyme. By general consensus, in the seventeenth and eighteenth centuries the appearance of rhyme in European poetry was related to the age of barbarism, and the very need for rhyme was seen as a consequence of the change in the spirit of the ancient tongues caused by barbarian (Germanic) influence, which had given rise to the impoverishment of their phonetic structure and the replacement of lexical stock. Unrhymed verse was associated with the genius of ancient languages, rhymed with the genius of the new ones (see Lamy 1737, 173–4; New Latin Method 1696, 641; Fenelon, VII, 149–51; Rollin, I, 119f; Gottsched 1751, 77–9; etc.). Trediakovskii repeats this scheme. In his treatise "On Ancient, Middle and New Russian Verse" of 1755 he wrote that "Since Gothic times, I don't know how, such a strong spirit of attraction and inclination for rhyme was spread so universally, in the West and in the East, that not only the so-called living languages considered rhyme in verse as tender and sweet and as magnificent adornment but also the refined (stepennye) languages, Greek primarily and Latin, as I have said, now did not want to be without it" (1935, 424). Significantly, unrhymed verse in the ancient languages was considered noble, whereas rhymed was considered popular, that is, the juxtaposition of rhymed and unrhymed was connected with the opposition between noble and lower-class usage. Hence Trediakovskii wrote that the Greeks called rhymed verse "political, that is, of the common people," whereas unrhymed Greek and Roman hexameter verse, "consisting of itself alone, did not unify lines by rhyme; this noise (shumikha) at the end of the line would have been offensive to the ancient, noble, precious, unrhymed [poetic] gold of these peoples" (ibid, 424 and 439). By using unrhymed verse (primarily the unrhymed hexameter of the *Tilemakhida*), Trediakovskii emphasized that the Russian literary language in its "noble" and "rational" usage was similar in quality to classical ones.

Tilemakhida's hexameters thus had fundamental significance for Trediakovskii. According to French notions, rhymed Alexandrine verse was suited for epic poetry in the modern language, and fulfilled the requirements of purist doctrine, while unrhymed hexameter was characteristic of epic verse in "ancient" languages, to some extent free from purist strictures.[29] The main example of the latter was Homer. In the context of the quarrel between ancients and moderns, Trediakovskii's evaluation of Homer's language was undeniably noteworthy, and directly contradicted what Fontenelle had

---

[29] To what extent Trediakovskii relied on the German model in using hexameter is a separate question. In Germany too, following the classical example, and in particular using unrhymed hexameter, was conditioned to a great extent by opposition to the hegemony of the French literary tradition and assertion of the national distinctiveness of German poetry (see Klein 1995; Freydank 1985, 40f).

written (see note 20 above), despite the fact that he was clearly a figure of authority for Trediakovskii, at one time a model for emulation (see Uspenskii 1985, 148–9; in 1744 Trediakovskii had translated Fontenelle's "Speech on Patience [Discours sur la Patience]"). That which the "moderns" considered the weaknesses of Homer's language, his lack of good taste and linguistic purity, Trediakovskii took to be positive qualities, manifesting special richness: "Homer often goes from a loud voice to a soft one, from lofty to tender, from sentimental to heroic, pleasant to harsh and somewhat violent. There is a veritable untold richness of comparisons and metaphors, and, however diverse, always proper and appropriate" (Trediakovskii 1766, I, ix / II, xiii). This reevaluation of Homer's language signaled the general reassessment of the "richness" of classical languages which was now clearly seen as a positive feature that was desirable for the new Russian literary language.

Richness of language was also associated with the richness of poetry. Speaking of the "restrictiveness" of the French language, Trediakovskii suggested the metrical poverty of French verse that only had one hexameter form. Here French poetry was juxtaposed with Greek and Latin and their metrical wealth, a wealth that was also available to Russian poetry, which he asserted by creating a variety of Russian forms of the hexameter (Trediakovskii, I, 129, 139).[30] We also find a positive view of the Greek legacy in Sumarokov, who wrote that "Greek words were introduced into our language by necessity, and are an adornment to it" (Sumarokov, IX, 246). The idea of enriching languages as the result of translating Greek into Latin and then into other European languages had already been suggested by Kantemir in the "Foreword to the Translation of Justinian's History" (1738–44) (see Druzhinin 1887, 197), anticipating his younger contemporaries. By the last third of the eighteenth century this scheme had become a staple of Russian literary thought, a commonplace in discussions of the language and its characteristics.

The constant repetition of this scheme shows how directly it was connected to the conceptualization of Slavenorossiiskii and to the formation of Slavonicizing purism that was examined above (§ III–1.3; cf. Picchio 1992). I will cite a few examples. A. A. Barsov wrote that "we Russians have… a special, limitless fount of abundance… in our Slavonic church

---

[30] Trediakovskii's radical turnaround in his view of Greek's influence on Church Slavonic (and hence on the Russian literary language) may also be seen in his positive evaluation of Polikarpov in the 1755 treatise "On Ancient, Intermediate and New Russian Poetry." Polikarpov is referred to here as "a most skilled man in the Greek, Latin and Slavonic languages" (Trediakovskii 1935, 432) — which directly contradicts Trediakovskii's earlier opinion (§ I–2.2).

books which came directly from the Greek source" (Barsov 1775, 266). This idea was also repeated in the Russian Academy several times, echoing Lomonosov almost word for word: "The Greeks who brought the Christian law to the Slavonic tribes strove to spread it by transposing holy church books into the Slavonic tongue... From their transposition into the Slavonic language it acquired abundance, importance, power, concision in conveying thoughts, convenience in constructing words, and other beauties of Greek... The Russian language, having as its immutable basis the Slavonic tongue, has preserved these advantages deriving from holy church books" (SAR, I, vii–viii).

Moisei Gumilevskii shares the same opinion. He points to the Greek language as "the abundant source for enriching the Russian word" (Moisei Gumilevskii 1768, 8) and says that "our Russian language would still have been cramped and inadequate as it was in the days of St. Prince Vladimir if various translations had not given it abundance, in particular, from the church books transposed from Greek into the Slavonic language. Who alone could have thought up the word and idea of *собезначальный, матеродевственный, златоустный, воскресение, Троица* (*together-having- no- beginning [concerning the son of God]; Mother-virginal; golden-tongued; resurrection; Trinity*), etc., if the translation had not been made from Greek church books"? (ibid, 22). Correspondingly, the Russian language holds a special place among European languages for "not only tolerating complex, separate, variable, and derivative words better than other languages, but also being especially adorned by these changes" (ibid, 23–4; on complex words see above). In equal measure, Slavenorossiiskii's syntax is organized on the ancient model and not that of modern languages enjoying free word order (see above).

Even more expressive is M. N. Murav'ev's discussion in the introduction to his course on the Russian language that he read to Grand Princess Ekaterina Alekseevna in 1793; the author clearly wanted to impress the future Empress that the language of her subjects enjoyed special advantages unknown to other European languages. He wrote:

> The Russian language is a Slavonic idiom and enjoys an incontestable superiority among languages derived from a common source. Known later but perhaps no less ancient than Greek and Latin, the Slavonic tongue was carried from the east toward the north and expanded into an immense space which the languages of the Scandinavians and Germans and those of the Romans and Greeks all abandoned. It was especially the last that influenced its formal development. The great Vladimir, apostle and champion of Russia, having so to speak won over the religion of the Greeks, found himself obliged to cultivate the language in order to inculcate into belligerent peoples more abstract ideas

2. Rationalist Purism and the Richness of the Slavenorossiiskii Language

and that beneficial charity that is the spirit of the Gospel. The Holy Scriptures translated literally from the Greek text are blessed in the Slavonic with turns [of phrase] and expressions that preserve the genius of the original language. Slavonic, admitted in its turn to the ranks of ancient and classical languages, is at base just as precious as it is inexhaustible, and supplies the writer of genius with expressions both noble and sonorous. (GARF, f. 728, op. 1, no. 1366, l. 2–3; written on the notebook in Ekaterina Alekseevna's hand: "Exercises in the Russian Language which Mr. Moravieff composed for me in 1793").

We also find an eloquent defense of Russian's abundance deriving from Church Slavonic and of Church Slavonic's coming from Greek in Evgenii Bolkhovitinov. He sees the richness of language as the result of enlightenment. The Greeks, in his opinion, "gathered the knowledge of the whole world into their borders, and introduced the abundance, expressiveness and beauty of all languages into their own; in this way one language became the source of enrichment and perfection of others... indeed, from the time of the enlightenment of the Greeks all eminent nations have acquired enlightenment and the perfection of their languages from Greek" (Evgenii Bolkhovitinov 1800, 9–10). He further speaks of the Romans who purified and enriched their language by "translating Greek books into it" (ibid, 10–11), and of the Middle Ages, when "barbarism took the place of taste, and coarse language the place of eloquence" (ibid, 12). The subsequent development gradually perfected the modern literary languages, described here according to the familiar universal scheme (§ II–1,1), beginning with France ("France managed to translate all of the Greek authors and Fathers of the Church into its language before others, and therefore was able to purify, spread and perfect its language before them all" — ibid, 12), and continuing with Germany and England, their success all connected to their having turned to the same Greek source.

The path of Russian, however, was different from the European:

> But all of these examples are irrelevant for us. What could our Slavonic tongue have been in ancient times? If we could have known its condition before the time when Greek books were translated into it in Moravia; if we could compare the language of our ancestors that was used before their union with the Russes with what remains in church books, what difference would we find? Who could conceive that the language of a half-savage and nomadic people could have such a multitude of words, such flexibility and ease of expression, such an abundance of adjectives and so great a number of word variations as can be observed in no other language? To what is it due, if not to the Greek language, the means by which the Slavs received both the Christian faith and the richness of the word? But this is not the whole story. All languages derived from Greek a great part of their abundance and beauty; but not one drew from it with such expressiveness and precise faithfulness to the original as Slavonic. In what

other language could one translate with such expressiveness and precision the words *соприсносущный, собезначальный, матеродевственный, неискусобрачный, человекообразный, равносущный,* and the like? For this reason, all languages that wanted to borrow expressive words from Greek had to borrow the Greek words themselves. Slavonic alone found and finds in itself the power to imitate Greek perfectly, and to imitate not only words and expressions but also the freedom of placement and order of words, which, it seems, is impossible for other languages. And everything that Slavonic acquired was able to be enjoyed (and is enjoyed) by Russian. For beside the newly introduced words and expressions in place of the Slavonic, all other qualities of the Slavonic language are congenial and essential to this language [i.e., Russian]. For this very reason our language not only does not yield place to any of the European ones, but rather excels them in expressiveness". (ibid, 14–5; Bolkhovitinov oriented himself on Lomonosov's ideas, and judging by the examples of compound words, he knew Moisei Gumilevskii's treatise as well)

We should again note that given eighteenth-century universalist and normative thinking, any deviation from the strict demands of French purism required some kind of justification. The example of Greek and Greek literature could serve just such a role. This model could sanction linguistic experiments in individual works (see § II–2.2 on Boileau's Namur ode) and could also justify languages as a whole; the existence of Greek "beauties" could make up for the absence of French "purity." The classical ideal played the role of a screen that could cover up the awkward maneuvers of a provincial who was not able to keep up with the rigors of French manners; and Greek played the role of such a screen for more languages than just Russian.

The "ancient" character which the Russian literary language had now attained placed it in a special position among the literary languages of Europe. Those were limited in their means of expression, while Russian was free, not forced to make do with an impoverished vocabulary because it was overflowing with linguistic riches. Describing the "benefits which many languages lack," Lomonosov gives first place to "the advantage of rich means for powerfully depicting serious and lofty ideas which we have gained from church books"; it is precisely in the means for expressing such ideas (i.e., the high style) that "the Russian language is superior to many modern [i.e., not ancient] ones, by making use of the Slavonic language from church books" (Lomonosov IV, 227 and 229 / VII^2, 589–90). This is probably what Lomonosov had in mind by the notation in his "Philological Research and Evidence": "5. On the advantages of the Russian language" (ibid, 233/ 762). This context also clarifies what Lomonosov wrote in the summary "On translations": "From Latin to Russian rather than from French... Better to translate from autographs [i.e., from originals and not from translations]" (Lomonosov, VII^2, 767; cf. Keipert 1981); it is understood that Russian is closer to Latin than French, and their similarity, one may presume, is conditioned by their common status as "ancient."[31]

According to the contemporary view, the superiority of "ancient" languages over "modern" ones arose as a result of the stability of the literary tradition, which allowed it to diversify and develop without losing its abundance. Hence abundance was definitely related to the special tradition of the written language. In the perception of seventeenth-century French writers, conversational usage could appear in the guise of a monster that devours words and expressions; the expressions that had seemed good and refined yesterday on the very next day could become the object of scorn and mockery (cf. complaints about "bizarre usage" in the foreword to the French Academy Dictionary of 1718 — SFA, I^2, l. e3). Such a situation could hardly appeal to authors hoping for immortality. The dream arises of stable usage that would be affirmed in the best works and serve as unchanging model of conversational speech of select society. If literature was to be subordinate to the norms of conversational usage, then from the point of view of writers it was desirable that conversational usage first be subordinated to classical literary models. In this approach, the poverty of French was connected to its absence of classical works (in terms of language), and the richness of the ancients, on the contrary, was tied to the fact that it did have such models that had fixed the best conversational usage and given it consistency. Speaking of authors who are no longer read, Boileau wrote:

> And it must not be imagined at all that the fall of these authors, French as well as Latin, occurred because the language of their countries changed. It only happened because they in their languages never reached [qu'ils n'avoient point attrapé] *the point of solidity and perfection* which is necessary for longevity and for a work to achieve immortality. Indeed the Latin language, for example, in

---

[31] This understanding is also reflected in Lomonosov's notes, dated to the early 1750's, on Ivan Shishkin's translation of *Thoughts by Cicero, Translated for the Use of Educating Youth by Mr. Abbot d'Olivet*, which was based on a French compilation. According to the proofreader, "Mr. Councilor Lomonosov announced to me that we should wait on the typesetting of the book *Cicero's Opinions*, because he said that it was translated from the French in the way that the French usually translate Latin, i.e., taking only the idea of the original and adding some words from themselves and arbitrarily taking and eliminating others, and therefore [the book] is not similar to the Latin original, so that it is worth asking if we should really publish it this way or translate it over" (Pekarskii, IA, II, 486–7). Furthermore, according to Lomonosov the French do not and cannot reproduce the beauty of the Latin original due to the "modern" quality of their language. So in translating from French this beauty cannot be passed on to Russian while, thanks to Russian's richness, it may be achieved if the translation is made from the Latin original and strives to capture the literal meaning.

which Cicero and Virgil wrote, was already very changed [for the worse] by the time of Quintilian and even more by the time of Aulu-Gelle. However, Cicero and Virgil were even more esteemed later than in their own day because they had *established the language by their writings,* having attained the point of perfection of which I spoke. (Boileau, II, 428; my italics — V.Z.)

Boileau does not explain how, given the changeability of language, this moment of stability and perfection may be reached. He tries to reconcile two simultaneous goals—an orientation on literary models and on conversational usage, and this leads him to a contradiction that he cannot, and does not want to resolve.

However, a way out of the impasse is found. It consists in the fact that the Greeks and Romans took special care of their spoken language, not allowing it to deviate from the purity that had been achieved and fixed by their literary works. Thus Rollin wrote of the Romans: "Among them children were educated in the purity of their language from the cradle. This was regarded as the first and most essential concern before all other habits. It was especially urged on mothers, wet nurses, and servants. They were cautioned as far as possible never to let slip a vicious word or expression in the presence of children" (Rollin, I, 2). Lamy put it in even more radical terms: "The Greek language is elegant and... indisputably became the most beautiful and perfect of all languages. It is known that the Greeks dedicated themselves [s'adonnerent] entirely to the science of words; their philosophers blended grammar with philosophy... This language which they created in their studies and in their schools was soon heard spoken in a beautiful refined manner, spoken only in a polished way" (Lamy 1737, 95). Fénélon makes similar arguments in his letter to the Academy (Fénélon, VII, 124; cf. Caput, II, 21).[32]

In Russian conditions this scheme took on special content: the bookish tradition was identified with the Church Slavonic literary heritage, and lexical abundance turned out to be an abundance of the language of "church books," that is, the written language as opposed to the conversational. As Lomonosov noted, the "Slavonic people" did not have an abundant language when it still "did not know how to depict its thoughts in writing" (ibid, 225

---

[32] Nicole resolves the issue somewhat differently. He asserts that those who write for immortality cannot be sure that their usage will be followed, since the beauty they achieve "may only last as long as this usage"; they therefore "must find a more durable means to please, and make every effort that their works contain beauties that do not depend on opinion and whim." This means finding harmony between words and things, that is, following that rational order which dwells in the nature of things and is opposed to usage as the permanent is to the fast-changing (Nicole 1720, 184–5).

2. Rationalist Purism and the Richness of the Slavenorossiiskii Language

/ 587). Richness is explicitly connected here with a written principle, based on books. According to this line of reasoning, Russian's superiority before all other European languages consisted in the existence of a special written language with an ancient tradition, as opposed to the conversational language, one which had yet to achieve the "point of solidity and perfection" about which Boileau spoke. The Classicist premise concerning the unity of literary and conversational tongues as a condition for linguistic purity was silently ignored, and the bookish tradition declared to be the source of purity and of richness, and the pledge of the Russian language's greatness and beauty. "It is well known that in the French language," wrote Trediakovskii,

> friendly conversation is the model for beautiful composition (de la conversation à la tribune), because they have no other. But for us friendly conversation is popular usage, and most beautiful writing is another, most excellent kind of usage, different from simple conversation and more like bookish Slavonic... No one writes letters about household affairs without trying to make his writing different from simple conversation, and it could be called a general rule among us that he who comes closest to the Slavonic language in civil writing, or someone who uses more common Slavonic words which everyone knows does not write basely, and that is better. Our model for writing is not friendly conversation (la conversation), but the bookish church language (la tribune), which is alive within the religious community, just as the conversational language is alive among the citizens. This is our great advantage (shchastie) over many European peoples! (Pekarskii 1866: 109)

Trediakovskii presents the very same ideas in almost the same formulation in the epigram "Ne znaiu kto pevtsov…" (I don't know who of the singers…), where, speaking of Sumarokov, he writes:

> За образец ему в писме пирожной ряд,
> На площади берет прегнусной свой наряд
> Не зная что у нас писать в свет есть иное
> А просто говорить подружески другое.
> Славенский наш язык есть правило неложно,
> Как книги нам писать, и чище коль возможно.
> В Гражданском и доднесь однак не в площадном,
> Славенском по всему составу в нас одном.
> Кто ближе подойдет к сему в словах избранных,
> Тот и любея всем писец есть, и не в странных.
> У немцев то не так ни у французов тожь,
> Им нравен тот язык, кой с общим самым схожь
> Но нашей чистоте вся мера есть славенский,
> Не щегольков ниже и грубый деревенский.
>
> (Uspenskii 1984, 103)

(Street vendors are his model for writing, he takes his vile garb from the gutter, not knowing that for us writing for society is different, not the same as friendly conversation. Our Slavonic language is a truly the standart how to write books in the purest possible manner. The civil tongue (but not the vulgar) to this day has the same content at Slavonic [and] the writer who emulates it better in using choice words (not foreign ones) is the favorite of all. It's not the same for the Germans or for the French either; they like language that is close to the most ordinary. But for us the whole measure of purity is Slavonic, neither the language of dandies nor that of the coarse village tongue.)

Such an approach not only legitimized the Church Slavonic tradition as source for the Russian literary language, but made reference to it necessary in order to assert its richness and purity. Church Slavonic thus became the measure of the new literary language's purity and correctness (§ III–2.3), which anticipated a basic change in perception of the literary language as a phenomenon of culture.

2.2 The New Stylistic Normalization

Assimilating Church Slavonic's heritage into the new literary language created specific problems which had not arisen before. If earlier the literary text had been defined as Russian (in which Slavonicisms remained unrecognized, or were treated as poetic liberties), now, when Russian and Church Slavonic elements both had an equal right to enter the literary text, the problem ensued of the text's linguistic heterogeneity. In principle, the demand for linguistic and stylistic homogeneity was an integral part of the Classicist program which was consciously opposed to Baroque mixing of languages. Such macaronic combinations were also, understandably, condemned by Russian theoreticians, and used only when it was unavoidable. Hence, for example, Kantemir noted: "if there occur two adjectives, or an adjective and noun, then both should necessarily end with the same ending. For example, instead of *чистою рукою* one may write *чистой рукой* but *чистою рукой* sounds very bad to the ear" (1744, 22; II, 19).

Trediakovskii makes analogous statements. In the "Letter from a Friend to a Friend" of 1750 he criticizes Sumarokov several times for using heterogeneous (macaronic) combinations. Thus he writes: "In the first verse he has put *слабыя сей* instead of *слабыя сея*; for it irritates the ear very much when words are coupled, or both refer to one thing, and one is given in full and the other shortened. It is always better, but especially in verse, to give

2. Rationalist Purism and the Richness of the Slavenorossiiskii Language

the long form of both such words; but it is more bearable, when the meter demands it, if both are short [rather than mixing forms], as in the second line, *невидимой своей*" (Kunik 1865, 444). The combination "*любезной дщери*" (gen. sg.) provokes analogous criticism: "*любезной дщери* instead of *любезныя дщери* is incorrect, and sounds bad, because the noun *дщери* is the full genitive case, but the adjective *любезной* is shortened, or rather, corrupted due to popular ignorance, whereas in actual fact it is dative" (ibid, 462). This criticism is repeated a third time: "In the sixteenth stanza the fifth line has *красы безвѣстной* instead of *красы безвѣстныя*, a slipshod combination. Full and shortened forms do not go together well and irritate the ear, as I have already reported to you, my lord" (ibid, 469).[33] Here again the mixture of disparate forms in the same grammatical case provokes criticism. The same caveat, already clearly echoing Lomonosov, is made by I. Rizhskii, who writes: "A Russian who knows his language adequately, when using a pure Slavonic or Slavenorossiiskii word with a Slavonic ending will never follow it with a pure Russian [ending], but always Slavenorossiiskii, which in this case to some degree serves as a transition from one language to another" (Rizhskii 1796, 10–11).

However in all these cases the issue concerns the heterogeneity of grammatical markers; on the lexical level, Russian and Church Slavonic are hardly ever juxtaposed (see § II–1.3), and the question of macaronism is not posed. Legalizing Church Slavonic lexicon—any word taken from "church books" — as an element of the Russian literary language led to a situation in which both "pure" Russian and "pure" Slavonic words could be used in a text, and because of this, lexical macaronism became one of the basic problems of literary stylistics. The threat of macaronism resulted from that very embarrassment of riches of which we spoke earlier.

Russian theoreticians thought in the basic linguistic categories of European Classicism. It was natural then, that in order to deal with macaronism they would try and conceptualize the problem in terms of the categories supplied by western linguistic legislators. In the West, the problem of lexical selectivity — selecting "pure" words for a given text and genre- was resolved by classifying words into stylistic registers and correlating those registers with the hierarchy of genres of Classicist poetics. Words

---

[33] We may already observe the call for homogeneity, it seems, in Trediakovskii's *New and Short Method* of 1735, when he rewrote Kantemir's line "Уме слабый, плод трудов..." into "Ум толь слабый, плод трудов..." Trediakovskii notes that according to his rules the forms ум and плод should have been used, as opposed to "the old way of writing," the forms уме and плоде (Trediakovskii 1735, 86–7; 1963, 418–9).

were classified as high, middle and low (*sublime, médiocre*, and *bas* — cf. § II–1.2); genres were also divided into three groups, and high words were correspondingly mostly used in high genres, middle words in middle ones, and low words in the low. The basic principle of classification was thematic; to the high register belonged words signifying lofty subject matter, to the low — low matter, etc. Correlating these classifications with genres seemed self-evident, insofar as high genres mostly concerned lofty matters, low genres, low matters, and middle ones, those in between. This classification was not clear cut or exhaustive and was based on stylistic nuances not easily amenable to theoretical generalization.

The doctrine of three styles as it was understood by French thinkers of the late sixteenth-early eighteenth century may be illustrated by Lamy's description. He writes:

> It is the subject matter that must determine the choice of style. Those noble expressions that render a style magnificent, those grand words that fill one's mouth, give things an air of grandeur... When things are grand... the style that describes them must necessarily be animated, full of movement, enriched with all sorts of figures and metaphors. If the subject does not treat of anything extraordinary and may be considered without being touched by passion, the style then should be simple... There is an infinity of different styles, as are the kinds of things one can write about. Nevertheless the great artists have reduced all of the particular manners of writing to three types. The material of all discourse is either extremely noble or extremely base or somewhere in between these two extremes, that is, nobility and baseness. There are three types of style that correspond to these three types of material, that is, the sublime, the simple, and the middling (médiocre). (Lamy 1737, 317–8)

Lamy further examines what means are characteristic of high and low styles, and as in other similar treatises deals with rhetorical rather than linguistic means (types of rhetorical figure, permissible metaphors, etc.). Properly linguistic aspects are only occasionally mentioned and do not suggest any clear classification of the linguistic material. For example, "It is necessary that the word suits the thing: that which is grand demands words that convey great ideas... There are terms and expressions that one only uses on grand occasions" (ibid, 327). This kind of instruction presumes at the very most the stylistic value of certain individual words, but by no means the division of the vocabulary as a whole into three parts.

French lexicographers like Chapelain do not essentially go any farther than this, for example, when he suggests that the Academy dictionary supply words with notes "so that people will know which are of the sublime, medium, and lowest type" (Livet, I, 103). Nor does Faret, who writes that "it

2. Rationalist Purism and the Richness of the Slavenorossiiskii Language

would be good to establish definite word usage... one will find few of the ones which we use today to eliminate, provided that they are ascribed to one of the three types of writing for which they may be appropriate; those which, for example, are worthless for the sublime style may be tolerated in the middle and sanctioned for the lowest and comic style" (ibid, 23; cf. Brunot, III, 34). These general ideas would also be repeated in the eighteenth century, although then they tried to establish an inventory of vocabulary categorized by the three styles. But even these inventories contained only selective examples and by no means intended to present a complete lexical classification.[34] Nevertheless all of these discussions include the idea of linking lexical material to the three styles of traditional rhetoric. In the framework of Classicism's theory of genres this linkage was extended to genres.

This area of French stylistics did not concern itself with the problem of mixed styles, because macaronism had long been mercilessly condemned as the practice of stupid pedants who scattered little Latin words throughout their speech. This mixing was unthinkable in an artistic text. Anti-macaronism was a common cultural position for all of the Russian literary men of the period under discussion. More often than not, though, this remained something not remarked upon, something self-evident to everyone. A series of Sumarokov's statements represent a response to the anti-macaronic premise of French Classicism. Typically, he ascribes to Russian pedants a passion for Latin words as well as for marked Slavonicisms; Latinisms and Slavonicisms serve as two equivalent features of macaronic speech. Thus in the song "Часто по школам мелют только ветер" (which we may loosely translate as "Making Wind in School") pedants are mocked in the following couplet (Sumarokov, VIII, 323):

> Точию ergo ныне рцы в беседе,
> Будеш ты абие смешон еси.

([Something like:] If you merely quoth ergo in conversation today you will be taken for a fool forthwith)

The speech of pedants in "Tresotinius" demonstrates analogous characteristics. "Бобембиус: Мое твердо о трех ногах и для того стоит твердо, ergo оно твердо; а твое твердо не твердое; ergo оно не твердо (Bobembius: My 'tverdo' [the letter 't'] on three legs stands firm (tverdo) for

---

[34] One may find another illustration of this general thesis in Mme. Necker (Brunot, VI, 1017). For an example of an inventory see E. Mauvillon's treatise of 1751; (cf. Brunot, VI, 1018f). We may note that Lomonosov might have known this treatise, as Mauvillon was the author of a history of Peter I.

that reason,[35] *ergo* it is firm (tverdo), but your tverdo is not firm; *ergo* it is not firm" (Sumarokov, V, 306). "Ксаксоксимениус: Подаждь ми перо, и абие положу знамение преславнаго моего имени, его же не всяк язык нарещи может" (Ksaksoksimenius: Bestow on me a pen and I will immediately make a sign of my most illustrious name, which not every tongue can pronounce)" (ibid, 322; cf. § III–1.3). We see here that Latinisms are included in pedants' speech together with conspicuous Slavonicisms (the auxiliary verb *еси* used for no grammatical reason, constructions with *иже/егоже*, the adverb *абие*, etc.). — that is, elements that had long been eliminated from the new literary language (cf. § I–1.3). Clearly, the use of these marked elements had the same relationship to the problem of the new literary language's normalization (to the problem of admissible combination of elements that the language had assimilated) as the use of Latin expressions. As with the French, in the given case the problem here was not about stylistic normalization.

The complex of ideas connected to stylistic normalization that was framed by the so-called theory of three styles, going back to the classical rhetorical tradition, was well known to Russian theoreticians (cf. Vinogradov 1938, 92; Vomperskii 1970; Tschižhevskii 1970a; Isachenko 1976, 392–93). It was from here that the notion of the firm connection between lexical selectivity and genre derived. One may find general statements about this connection in Trediakovskii's "Discourse on the Ode in General" (§ II–1.2) and Sumarokov's "Epistle on Versification" of 1748 ("Znai v stikhotvorstve razlichie rodov, / I chto nachnesh, ishchi k tomu prilichnykh slov..." [Know the differences of genres in poetry, and find the appropriate words for what you undertake] — Sumarokov 1748,10; thereupon follow general recommendations by genre). However the general stylistic and semantic principles for "finding the proper words" did not correlate at all to the opposition between Russian and Church Slavonic—introducing genetic parameters into linguistic theory (§ II–1.3) did not touch on issues of style. Determining this relation now became a pressing problem for Russian stylistics: semantic and stylistic criteria for selecting vocabulary had to be combined with genetic ones. The way in which this issue was resolved was in large part predetermined by the way Slavonicisms had been interpreted earlier (§ II–2.1): permitting marked Slavonicisms as a matter of poetic license had opened the door to connecting the new literature with the Church Slavonic panegyric tradition, elements of which could easily be reconceptualized as belonging to a "high" lexical register. The next step

---

[35] A pun on the name of the Slavonic name of the letter "tverdo," that also means "firm"; there was a disagreement whether it was better to write it with one leg (Т) or with three (like an upside-down Ш). (Translator's note)

2. Rationalist Purism and the Richness of the Slavenorossiiskii Language

was to correlate Church Slavonic vocabulary (as far as it was understood as such) with high genres.

This correlation was distinctly manifested in Trediakovskii's "Letter From a Friend to a Friend" of 1750. Here Trediakovskii repeated French Classicist postulates about the poetics of genre, e.g., "the ode, like the tragedy, cannot tolerate street usage" (Kunik 1865, 482). He also wrote about the demand for a literary text's stylistic homogeneity: "Let us now examine [Sumarokov's] tragic and epistolary speech. But what unevenness do I see here? I see high and low together, brightness and darkness, arrogance and pusillanimity, little that is proper and much that is indecent; in a word, I see chaos itself. Everything is based not on Grammar nor on our correct books but on street usage. In the first place, he is not able to choose words well: hence in his tragedies he writes *опять* instead of *паки*, *этот* instead of *сей*, *эта* instead of *сия*, *это* instead of *сие*" (ibid, 476). Here the choice of words for tragedy is already related to the opposition of Russian and Church Slavonic, and in the correlative pairs the words to be chosen for tragedy are Church Slavonic rather than Russian; it follows that Church Slavonic is defined as high style. In another place Trediakovskii writes about this even more clearly: "Did our respected author recall that he was composing an ode, that is, the highest genre of poetry?... Why then did he not make an effort to choose [appropriate] words? The ode does not tolerate common popular speech; it completely distances itself from it, and accepts only what is lofty and magnificent. Because of this, why did he not use *воззри* instead of *взгляни*?" (ibid, 456). And elsewhere: "In the seventh verse the word *миг* is base, and consequently not odic. Instead of this one should say *мгновение ока* in high style." (459). Even earlier, in his report on Sumarokov's "Hamlet" of 1748, Trediakovskii had written: "Everywhere is strewn an uneven style, that is, in places it is in Slavonic and above the theater, and in others very much according to street usage and below that of tragedy" (Pekarskii IA, II: 130). Hence for Trediakovskii stylistic homogeneity and related lexical selectivity were a necessary condition for correct composition. At the same time, a word's stylistic characteristics were clearly correlated with its genetic profile, and Church Slavonic was construed as high style and associated with high genres.

It seems that for Trediakovskii it was precisely the high genres that were subject to normalization and it was not necessary to observe such strict linguistic regularity in other genres. In any case, such a position probably underlies the following criticism, also addressed at Sumarokov: "you see, my dear sir, that this stanza is full of the adverbs *противу* and *против* as well as the verbs *воружись* and *воружи*. And since there is no discrimination between words in it, it cannot be called an odic stanza" (Kunik 1865, 458). Thus for the language of the ode morphological normalization was essential, and this normalizing demand was visibly extrapolated onto all genres of high style. Trediakovskii's own practice in high poetic genres (for example, *Tilemakhida*) did not meet these harsh demands (see Alekseev 1981), as one sees here variability and Russian forms even when they had "high" Church Slavonic correlatives. Such divergence between polemical stance and linguistic practice, as we have seen, was by no means unusual for this period (§ II–1.2).

Indeed Trediakovskii's stylistic prescriptions were in many ways subordinate to polemical considerations. They were not systematic and left many questions unresolved. It was only clear that, given a choice, one should select Slavonic elements for high genres rather than their Russian equivalents. Nothing was said about how or in what cases Russian words could be used in high genres, or about what principles of lexical choice should apply in genres that were not high. Lomonosov approached these questions systematically, although for this very reason in isolation from literary practice. He based his solution on a refusal to separate all vocabulary into high, middle, and low, although the idea of connecting lexical selection and generic hierarchy remained in full force. For thematic classification of words into high, middle, and low (something that would have been rather hard to define in reference to concrete material and relevant for only isolated stylistic nuances, rather than for separating the entire vocabulary by registers) Lomonosov substituted classification according to genetic markers, which by definition could give an unambiguous description for any word. This classification represents the final application of genetic parameters to vocabulary, something that had become such a pressing need since the start of the normalization process (§ II–1.3). Lomonosov's genetic classification is correlated to genres, a theoretical *tour de force* that was the basis for his celebrated theory of three styles. As a result of this correlation genetically heterogeneous words could appear in a single text (genre), although macaronic word combinations were to be limited. Obviously, the theory of three styles resolved (at least in theory) quite different problems from those which Classicist stylistic doctrines were concerned with.

How was this limitation of marcaronism to be achieved? Three levels are defined within the bounds of "pure" vocabulary:

> 1) "Slavonic" words absent in Russian, "which although little used generally, and especially not in conversation, are understandable to all literate people, for example, *отверзаю, Господень, насажденный, взываю;*"

2. Rationalist Purism and the Richness of the Slavenorossiiskii Language

2) "Slavenorossiiskie" words i.e., words common to both Russian and Church Slavonic, "which were used both by ancient Slavs and today by Russians, for example, Богъ, слава, рука, нынѣ, почитаю;"

3) "Russian popular (prostonarodnye) words," i.e., Russian words "which are absent in what remains of the Slavonic language, that is, in church books, for example, говорю, ручей, которой, пока, лишь." (Lomonosov, IV, 227; VII², 588)

Two additional categories are not included in this classification, but are specially mentioned as impermissible in the literary language. From "Slavonic" words are "excluded" words that are "unused and very obsolete" like обаваю, рясны, овогда, свѣнѣ; from "Russian popular" words are "excluded... words that are despised, which it is improper to use in any style, except perhaps vulgar comedies"; for this last category Lomonosov does not supply examples, presumably out of concern for propriety (ibid; cf § III–1.3). If we do not count the introductory sections of J. W. Paus' *Slavono-Russian Grammar* that asserted the unity of Russian and Slavonic "as far as their material and basic vocabulary" (§ III–1.2), Lomonosov's classification explicitly asserts the common lexical fund of Russian and Church Slavonic for the first time. This allows Lomonosov to disregard the problem of making a complete juxtaposition of Russian and Church Slavonic vocabulary that had brought earlier attempts at lexical normalization to a dead end (§ II–1.3).

Lomonosov further relates this classification to the hierarchy of genres. High genres ("high style") required words from Slavonic and Slavenorossiiskii, low ones ("low style") — words from Slavenorossiiskii and Russian, while middle genres ("middle style") could use words from all three (Lomonosov IV, 227–8; VII², 588–90). In this way the problem of macaronism was resolved for the high and low styles. The middle style, which permitted both "Slavonic" and "Russian" words, needed special qualifications. And indeed Lomonosov wrote that "In this style one should observe all possible evenness, which may in particular be lost if a Slavonic word be put next to a popular Russian one" (ibid, 228; 589). The scheme which Lomonosov proposed resolved the problem of what to do with the abundance of words created when uniting Church Slavonic and Russian vocabulary by regularizing that abundance according to Classicist stylistic notions. Here too European categories acquired new meanings, and could even lose their original strictly stylistic intent (cf. Martel 1933, 56), but they offered a way to describe the specific relations of Russian and Church Slavonic elements within the new literary language.

At the same time, Lomonosov's structure contained a certain duality in its understanding of Slavonicisms. On the one hand, they were given the status of pure vocabulary, an organic part of the new literary language, and in that capacity were not subject to limitations as far as their linguistic "purity." On the other hand, for Lomonosov Slavonicisms possessed a definite stylistic quality and were therefore subject to stylistic limitations. In the scheme outlined above, however, such limitations also applied to Russicisms; Slavonicisms and Russicisms were arranged in a perfectly symmetrical pattern, and in the demand not to use them side by side no special "loftiness" was ascribed to Slavonicisms. At the same time, Lomonosov also made statements specifically about the stylistic normalization of Slavonicisms. Describing the lexical make-up of the middle style, for example, Lomonosov wrote that "one may accept some Slavonic words used in the high style [into the middle style], however only with great care, so that the style will not seem overblown (nadutyi)" (Lomonosov, IV, 228; VII^2, 589). Similarly, in his notes "On the Current State of the Literary Arts in Russia" he remarked in one point of his plan, "Slavonicizing (slavenchizna) out of place. Дщерь» (Lomonosov, VII^2, 581). He apparently had in mind the stylistically unjustified use of Slavonicisms. Here Slavonicisms were equated to the high words of European stylistic theories, whose similar stylistic restrictions were well known in Russia. The very term "nadutyi" used to describe "high" words not corresponding to lofty material was a calque from the French "enflé," "gonflé," from the Latin "ampullatus" (see Uspenskii 1985, 92–6).

     This kind of discussion may be found in almost all rhetorical (stylistic) manuals, for example, in Lamy (1737, 323).[36] As with their other descriptions of style, they are concerned with rhetorical rather than properly linguistic issues. One may find similar general prescriptions without any reference to concrete linguistic issues in M. N. Murav'ev's "Treatise on Various Styles," composed in the spirit of comparable Western works (Murav'ev 1783, 23–4). As far as vocabulary, stylistic limitations only apply to a small number of synonyms that contain specifically "high" lexicon. It was precisely because of such things that Lomonosov had to radically reinterpret such schemes. Putting Slavonicisms in place of the high words of this scheme would have always marked them out in relation to Russicisms, and Lomonosov was clearly not inclined to such an interpretation. Therefore the stylistic category of "overblown," of unjustified loftiness, is of lesser importance to him, a

---

[36] Scudery gives a very clear formulation of this idea: "every virtue has some vice that is very close to it, and which resembles it, as for example, liberality and prodigality, bravery and rashness. In the same way every kind of perfect style has as its cousin a defective one, and it is very easy to pass from one to the other. The magnificent easily degenerates into the overblown and swollen; the mediocre — into the feeble and sterile; and the low — into the gross and overly popular" 1654, l. c2 verso).

2. Rationalist Purism and the Richness of the Slavenorossiiskii Language

secondary issue in relation to the classification of vocabulary into three genetic groups.

And so we may note two ways in which Lomonosov understood Slavonicisms: as stylistically neutral elements (in high and middle genres), and as specially "high" elements whose use required special justification. This duality ultimately stems from the fact that genetic parameters are artificially connected to stylistic ones; "Slavonicism" as a stylistic category is simultaneously an extension of "high Slavonic words," that is, marked bookish elements (see § II–1.3), and also a result of the new understanding of "Slavonic," into which category fall stylistically neutral elements to which the new theory ascribed "Slavonic" origins. In subsequent linguistic and stylistic theories, both of these understandings of Slavonicisms that appear in Lononosov were further developed.

Be that as it may, Lomonosov outlined a plan for a new literary language which combined national literary and linguistic traditions with Classicist conceptions of linguistic correctness and purity. The borrowed rubrics not only provided a way of describing the Russian literary language's stylistic and linguistic characteristics but also, because they were informed with different content, prompted the formation of new stylistic categories that little accorded with their original designation. Applying European models to Russian material thus entailed radically rethinking them.

The system of stylistic evaluation based on genetic criteria which Lomonosov worked out in his "Foreword on the Use of Church Books" for vocabulary may also be observed in his works on grammar. Here, however, it took on significantly different forms, insofar as the situation in which lexicon and grammar found themselves posed different challenges to normalization. As already mentioned (§ II–1), the normalization of grammar presumed stylistic differentiation as one possible way of dealing with variability and deciding between variants. We find attempts at such normalization in Lomonosov's *Russian Grammar,* although the system of evaluation lacks the kind of precision and logical connection that we see in "Foreword on the Use of Church Books." The issue here, clearly, does not have to do with the specifics of grammar but with the fact that the classification of vocabulary resolved an artificial theoretical problem—to combine the rhetorical theory of three styles with classifying lexicon genetically, and to create an analogue for the Classicist stylistic conception—while in grammar no such artificial problem arose. For this reason stylistic criteria applied on the grammatical level were inconsistent, selective, and to some extent fortuitous. Nevertheless, they are of significant importance for understanding Lomonosov's linguistic and stylistic ideas.

As discussed above (§ II–1.4), in his work on grammar, Lomonosov operated within the academic grammatical tradition that took a synthesizing approach, combining Russian and Church Slavonic elements. If in the 1730's this synthesis ran somewhat counter to the general linguistic trend that demanded the segregation of the two languages, now this was no longer an issue. It is indicative, as we have seen already (§ III–1.2), that in his grammar Lomonosov gives as coexisting variants the nom.-acc. masc. sg. adjective endings *-ый, -ой,* and *-ей* (§ 161 — Lomonosov, IV, 77; VII^2, 452), while for the previous decade he had considered these very same endings as belonging to different languages. As a result of grouping together this kind of elements the same problem arises in grammar as it had in vocabulary — how to deal with the newly acquired abundance that threatened macaronism. However, in grammar this problem was quite limited, insofar as the abundance itself was restricted. Thus, for example, following the academic normalization of infinitive forms, in his grammar Lomonosov gives only the unstressed variants *-ть* and *-чь* (Lomonosov, IV, 132, 135, 141, 153, 160; VII^2, 500, 503, 508, 510, 525), while endings in *-ти* and *-чи* are eliminated and pose no problem.

The problem of abundance only arose when the academic grammatical tradition had not worked out a uniform solution and permitted unmotivated variability. It was precisely for these few cases that Lomonsov tried to establish a stylistic differentiation between variants. Here he proceeded in the same way as in his anti-macaronic recommendations concerning the middle style. He did not exclude either of the variants, but strove for "all possible evenness," prescribing caution that elements of different stylistic coloration not be combined. For such prescriptions he did not need a three-part grouping of the kind he used for vocabulary, but only a binary opposition of "high" and "low" elements, or in genetic terms, "Slavonic" and "Russian." The category of "Slavenorossiiskii" that was such an innovation in classifying vocabulary corresponded to the longstanding grammatical tradition in grammar, to that synthetic approach to Russian grammar for which the juxtaposition of Russian and Church Slavonic was not important, but considered the basic elements of the two languages to be the same. Therefore the question of heterogeneity only came up relative to those grammatical elements for which, at least in Lomonosov's opinion, genetic characteristics continued to be in force.

The number of such elements was small, not only relative to Paus' extensive list but also to Adodurov's more modest inventory (cf. § II–1.4). Furthermore, in many cases it was innovative, that is, it put into play things which had not formerly been connected to the opposition between languages, while many elements that had earlier been defined by genetic characteristics

2. Rationalist Purism and the Richness of the Slavenorossiiskii Language

were no longer treated that way, and, moreover, the choice of variant followed the academic grammatical tradition. Thus, for example, if Adodurov contrasted Slavonic forms of the comparative degree with the suffix *-ш-* (*честный — честнший*) to the Russian forms like *умнѣе, богатѣе, дороже* (Adodurov 1731, 11–12), Lomonosov describes only forms of the type *смирнѣе, веселѣе* (§ 212 — Lomonosov, IV, 94; VII², 466), ignoring forms of the type *честнший* and *свѣтлѣйший*.[37] Lomonosov categorizes passive participles in *-мый*, gerunds in *-я* (juxtaposed to "Russian" gerunds in *-ючи*), the secondary gentitive and secondary prepositional cases of masc. nouns[38] and ordinal numerals the type *вторыйнадесять* as innovations of stylistic significance, that consequently implicitly possess the relevant genetic characteristic, i.e., are Slavonicisms. These innovations were virtually separate from linguistic practice. Participles and gerunds were so firmly entrenched in the literary language that their stylistic or genetic distinctiveness was on the whole not felt, the second gentitive and second prepositional cases were used just as they had been before the *Russian Grammar,* despite the rules Lomonsov had proposed, and ordinal numerals of the type *вторыйнадесять* were not at all assimilated by the literary language. Of the known oppositions from the previous grammatical tradition Lomonosov's recall the endings of the nom.-acc. masc. *-ый/-ой*, gen. sg. masc. and neut. *-аго/-ого*, and gen. sg. fem. *-ыя/-ой* (cf. these oppositions in Paus' grammar — § II–1.4).

This exhausts the stylistically marked elements in Lomonosov's grammar that for that reason required special regulation. Their small number indicates that Lomonosov was continuing the synthetic tradition of the Academy's philologists, and by no means proceeding from a notion of Slavonic — Russian bilingualism. Therefore, it is unjustified to claim, as does

---

[37] It seems that B. A. Uspenskii is not entirely correct in considering comparative forms in Lomonosov's grammar of the type *свѣтлѣйший, свѣтлѣе* as marking an opposition between "high" and "simple style" (Uspenskii 1994, 202). Like the form *свѣтлѣе* that does not occur in Lomonosov, this opposition has been created by the researcher himself. Lomonosov cites *свѣтлѣйший* primarily as a form of the superlative degree, noting that "At the same time one should know that [forms] ending in ШІЙ and without the prefix ПРЕ [that is, forms like *свѣтлѣйший*] are used more for the superlative than comparative degree" (§ 215 — Lomonosov, IV, 94; VII², 467). One may conclude from this that Lomonosov is implicitly ascribing the form *свѣтлѣйший* to the comparative degree in Church Slavonic, whereas the comparative degree of this type might not belong to the synthetic "Slavenorossiiskii principle" that he describes, and so is not used in Russian, either in the "high" or the "simple style."

[38] In the *Tekhnologiia* Polikarpov mentions the second genitive as a special feature of Russian that contrasts it to Church Slavonic. In Russian, he writes, "the genitive singular of inanimate nouns ending in Ъ is usually У and not А, as in *указъ, указу*" (Uspenskii 1994, 110). It is unlikely that Lomonosov knew Polikarpov's work. Significantly, the academic tradition before Lomonsov ignored this feature.

Uspenskii in his analysis of Lomonosov's grammar, that in his conception "the Russian literary language contains within itself the projection of Church Slavonic — Russian bilingualism; the relationship between languages (within the framework of the linguistic situation) is transferred onto the relation between styles (in the framework of the literary language)" (Uspenskii 1994, 145). As stated above, in his creation of grammatical rules, Lomonosov strove to establish that same "evenness" as in texts of the "middle style," that is, to eliminate possible macaronism. The problem of macaronism was posed on two levels, the creation of forms (the micro level) and of word combinations (the macro level). In the first case creating "impure" (macaronic) words was forbidden, and in the second, the "impure" (macaronic) combination of elements.

To the micro level belong Lononosov's remarks about participles, gerunds, and forms of the comparative and superlative degree. Thus, apropos of present participles he writes:

> It should be noted that these participles can only be formed from those Russian verbs which are in no way different, either in pronunciation or meaning, from the Slavonic... It is quite unacceptable to create participles from verbs which mean something base, and are only used in simple conversation, because participles have a certain loftiness, which is the reason it is fitting to use them in high genres of poetry. (§ 343 — Lomonosov, IV, 127–8; VII², 496)

This is especially emphasized for present passive participles:

> Present passive partiociples ending in МЫЙ also come from Russian verbs which were used by the Slavs, for example, *вѣнчаемый, пишемый, питаемый, подаемый, видимый, носимый*. But for the most part they are more properly used in rhetorical or poetic works than in simple style or in popular speech. Participles from Russian verbs not used by Slavs, for example, *трогаемый, качаемый, мараемый*, are very brutish and intolerable to the ear. (§ 444 — Lomonosov, IV, 185; VII², 547–8)

At the same time, variant suffixes and endings are given for passive participles that depend on the genetic basis of their roots:

> Past imperfect passive participles made from both new Russian and Slavonic verbs are very commonly used; *питанный, вѣнчанный, писанный, видѣнный, качаной, мараной*. The difference between them is that the ones from Slavonic are better ending with ЫЙ rather than ОЙ, and those from simple Russian better end in ОЙ than ЫЙ. The first ones decline like true [adjectives], for the second the ending ОГО is more fitting in the masc. and neut. gen. sg. than АГО. They also have one "н" at the end. (§ 446 — Lomonosov, IV, 186; VII², 548)

2. Rationalist Purism and the Richness of the Slavenorossiiskii Language

Similar restrictions are put on creating gerunds, only the issue has to do not with "Slavonic" but with "Russian" roots, insofar as these forms themselves are seen as not Slavonic. "And besides, it should be noted that gerunds in ЮЧИ are more suitable [formed] from properly Russian verbs than those derived from Slavonic; and, on the contrary, gerunds in Я are better formed from Slavonic rather than Russian [verbs]. For example, it is better to say *толкаючи* than *толкая,* but on the other hand, it is better to use *дерзая* than *дерзаючи*" (§ 356 — Lomonosov, IV, 131; VII^2, 499).

Similar prescriptions are laid down for the comparative and superlative degree: "Slavonic comparative and superlative degree in ШІЙ are little used except in serious and lofty style, especially in verse: *далечайшій, свѣтлѣйшій, пресвѣтлѣйшій, высочайшій, превысочайшій, обильнѣйшій, преобильнѣйшій*. But here one must be careful not to use this in adjectives of low meaning or in those not used in Slavonic: *блеклѣйшій, преблеклѣйшій, прытчайшій, препрытчайшій* and the like (§ 215 — Lomonosov, IV, 94; VII^2, 467).

Insofar as the formation of the given elements is connected to their genetic character, they acquire special stylistic weight and their use is therefore limited to texts in either low or high style. Hence Lomonosov says that active participles "are used only in writing, and in simple conversation should be replaced by the relative pronouns: *который, которая, которое*" (IV, 127). Similar comments are made about the other elements that are characterized genetically. Here, as with vocabulary, combining hereogeneous elements is limited by these criteria to middle style texts.

At the same time, the combining of genetically opposed variants is also limited on the macro level. Precisely this kind of limit is put on variants of the gen. sg. ending *-а/-у* and the prep. sg. *-ѣ/-у*. Cf. on the gen. sg. in the materials for the *Grammar*: "Here it should be noted that nouns which on the strength of the above described rules end in *у* rather than *а* in the genitive... should usually take *а* if they are closer to the Slavonic dialect but not so often in... the common Russian language as in written and high style: *...залогъ, га; восходъ, да.* [This is so] especially when important adjectives are combined with them: *божественнаго залога, солнечнаго возхода*" (Lomonosov, VII^2, 647–8; cf. in the grammar § 72, IV, 83; VII^2, 457). On the prep. sg. it says: "As in many other cases, one must also observe here that in the high style where the Russian language becomes closer to the Slavonic, the ending in ѣ predominates:*очищенное въ горнѣ злато; жить въ домѣ Бога вышняго; въ потѣ лица трудъ совершать; скрыть въ ровѣ зависти; ходить въ свѣтѣ лица Господня*, but the same words in simple style or everyday conversation prefer *у* in the prepositional: *медъ*

Chapter 3. The Changed Conception of the Literary Language

въ горну плавить; въ поту домой прибѣжалъ; на рву жить; въ свѣту стоять" (§ 190–IV, 87–8; VII², 461). Lomonosov makes similar comments on ordinals: "From eleven to nineteen derivatives are created by adding 'надесять': *первойнадесятъ, второйнадесять* and so on; they are used only in important materials and in dates: *Карлъ вторыйнадесять* rather than *двенадцатой*, *Лудвигъ пятыйнадесять* rather than *пятнадцатой*; *сентября пятоенадесять число* rather than *пятнадцатое число*" (§ 259 — IV, 105; VII², 476).

Thus in grammatical descriptions three classes of material are not distinguished, as in lexicon, but only two, Russian and Slavonic, or low and high. This dual division is quite sufficient to expose heterogeneous combinations and to formulate recommendations how to avoid them. Hence the given scheme shows clearly that the three-part divison of lexicon is completely artificial and does not so much resolve the problem of getting rid of macaronism as it serves to formulate the problem of macaronism in categories that are traditional for Classicist stylistics, and at the same time eliminating this problem from discussions of the corpus of "pure" lexicon. The three lexical classes correspond to the classical scheme that describes the corpus of "pure" vocabulary so that the presence of genetically heterogeneous elements ceases to contradict purist theory.[39] In lexicon it was not so much real problems of stylistic normalization that were being resolved as the issue of linguistic heterogeneity that arose due to the necessity of normalizing the lexical abundance that was revealed in the literary language as the result of assimilating the Church Slavonic component. As has been noted in the scholarly literature concerning linguistic practice, including that of Lomonosov (Martel 1933, 56), this laying out of rules did not have a noticeable effect. Reglamentation was not immediately needed for practice but mainly for conceptualizing the new type of literary language as it related to European standards.

It was precisely on this last point that Sumarokov's position opposed those of Lomonosov and Trediakovskii. Although Sumarokov was significantly less interested in theory than they were and did not write extensive linguistic

---

[39] In this regard it is very significant that I. Rizhskii, who follows Lomonosov's basic system and poses the problem of macaronism in his terms, employing the same dualistic opposition of high and low style (specifically in the discussion of lexicon). He writes: "A writer… should… take care that every word he uses, every phrase, not be higher or lower than the idea he is expressing, and that they perfectly correspond to the genre and content of the work. For almost every type of composition has, so to speak, its own language. For this reason pure words of Slavonic and Slavenorossiiskii only belong in high style genres; and in contrast pure Russian [words] are characteristic of those compositions whose content is close to that of everyday social conversations" (Rizhskii 1796, 11–2).

2. Rationalist Purism and the Richness of the Slavenorossiiskii Language

treatises, his polemical writings and the linguistic comments scattered among his various works manifest a considerable similarity between his views and those of his literary rivals. As we have shown, Sumarokov shared the common opinion of early Russian poets concerning the richness of Russian, about the connection of this richness with Church Slavonic and church books, about the positive role of Greek in creating this richness, and so on. His objections to Trediakovskii and Lomonosov were on another level. Sumarokov held that his learned colleagues were advocating too strict a normalization that did not allow sufficient room for a writer's individual aesthetic judgment. In his opinion, stylistic choice should be determined not by formal parameters (for example, Russian or Church Slavonic provenance), but by authorial taste that could evaluate the appropriateness of a given element in the particular context.

Thus, for example, responding to Trediakovskii's criticism that he "was poorly able to select words, for in his tragedies he writes *опять* instead of *паки, этот* instead of *сей, эта* instead of *сия, это* instead of *сие*" (Kunik 1856, 476), Sumarokov does not challenge Trediakovskii's standards for stylistic evaluation but his pretensions to objectivity and his academic encroachment on the freedom of authorial creratvity. In his "Answer to Criticism" Sumarokov writes, "*Этот, эта, это* instead of *сей, сия, сие* I consider poetic license that one may not use in odes but that one may use in tragedies in some cases, because they are neither foreign words nor popular ones; and indeed I employ them very rarely" (Sumarokov, X, 97). Sumarokov thus accepts both the correlation of stylistic and genetic characteristics as well as the general evaluation of individual stylistic elements. Like Trediakovskii, he considers *сей, сия, сие* as high style words which should exclusively be used in odes, and *этот, эта, это* as low ones that have no place in them. In his opinion, however, the genre of tragedy is different from the ode insofar as it presents the speech of various characters that may not always manifest a single style (one may find this argument in French literary criticsm as well, for example: Scudery 1654, l. S3). The author of tragedy should thus be free in making linguistic choices and scholarly rules of normalization should not be imposed on an author's sense of what is proper or improper in a particular instance. Sumarokov argues that he uses elements that Trediakovskii sees as questionable "very rarely," but that his ability to make use of them is important. This position is stated even more specifically in his response to Trediakovskii concerning the use of *опять* instead of *паки*: "He considers it a fault that I write *опять* instead of *паки*, but is it appropriate to put *паки* into the mouth of a seventeen year old maiden when she is in the throes of amorous passion when *опять* is perfectly common"? (Sumarokov, X, 98).

Chapter 3. The Changed Conception of the Literary Language

According to Sumarokov, language achieves value not as a result of scholarly regulation (normalization) but through the taste and talent of authors "whose labors have ardently sustained art" ("Epistle on Poetry," Sumarokov 1748, 4, 6). He therefore demonstratively contrasts his artistry to the pedantic presumptions of his rivals. His use of infinitive forms is a good example. As stated earlier (§ II–2.1), from the mid 1740's both Trediakovskii and Lomonosov had stopped using infinitives in -*ти* as poetic license, and this form had ceased appearing in common (prosaic) use even before, in the early 1730's (§ II–1.4); in both of these cases the change accorded with academic norms. Sumarokov clearly does not want to be restricted and in his linguistic usage demonstratively rejects attempts to limit his freedom.

Sumarokov's early poetic works use both infinitive forms. For example, in the "Epistle on Poetry" of 1748 we find together with frequent infinitives in -*ть* the forms *владѣти, чувствовати, погубити — изтребити, терзати* (Sumarokov 1748, 4, 10, 14, 18). One might presume that he is using this form as poetic license, yet he continues to use it even later, and many examples may be found for instance in his eclogues: *имѣти* (in "Kalista" — Sumarokov 1769, 251; 1774, 30), *убрати* ("Sil'viia" — 1769, 271; 1774, 50), *имѣти, быти, молвити, искати* ("Beliza" — 1774, 32–3), etc. Sumarokov values the variablity of the infinitive and does not want to renounce it, as it expands the flexibility of the poetic language. In particular, his corrections to the eclogue "Del'fira" suggests this: compare "И можно бъ было вдругъ ихъ все *окинуть* глазомъ'" (1769, 261) changed to "И можно бъ было вдругъ *окинути* ихъ глазомъ" (1774, 39) and "Что было *отвѣчать!*" (1774, 40) changed to "*Отвѣтствовати* что" (1774, list of corrections).

Variability of the infinitive form is also a feature of Sumarokov's prose, and this is clearly not a question of license but rather a purposeful striving for diversity rather than restricting the linguistic material that the Russian literary language acquired as a result of its "unity" with Church Slavonic. Thus in his "Several Articles on Virtue" infinitive forms in -*ти* and -*ть* occur in approximately equal measure (with a slight preponderance of the former). The following passage well illustrates the nature of this variability:

> Не *дѣлати* зла, хорошо; но сие благо еще похвалы не заслуживаетъ: столбъ худа не дѣлаетъ; но столбъ за то еще почтенія не удостоевается. Не *дѣлать* худа, неесть добродетель: добродетель есть *дѣлати* людямъ добро, коли можно: похвально и то, что я могу и не *дѣлать* людямъ худа; но то еще не добродетель. Но можетъ ли еще ето *быти,* что бы кто не смогъ людямъ *дѣлати* добра? (Sumarokov, VI, 239)

2. Rationalist Purism and the Richness of the Slavenorossiiskii Language

Sumarokov's comedies, in which both infinitive forms occur in the language of all of the players, whatever their character and speech type, may serve as no less eloquent an example.

Another aspect of Sumarokov's linguistic practice is particularly telling. Although declaring Russian and Church Slavonic to be of one nature made the occasional use of simple preterits potentially possible in literary texts of the new type (§III–1.2), neither Trediakovskii nor Lomonosov took advantage of this. In contrast, Sumarokov did not wish to relinquish this means of expression, as he was concerned not so much with normalization as with the diversity of stylistic expression.

This was the reason for the individual instances of simple preterits and perfectives with auxiliaries that occur in his psalm paraphrases and other biblical texts that went into the three volumes of Sumarokov's *Spiritual Verse*. Thus in the paraphrase of Psalm 29 we find: "Отвратил лице свое и *ужасохся*"; "К тебе Господи *воззвах* и *помолихся*" (Сумароков, 1773–1774, III, 17); in the paraphrase of Psalm 42: "*Прильпе* душа моя к тебе" (27); in the paraphrase of Psalm 77: "И *взыде* гнев на Израиля" (31). Alongside simple preterits appear forms of the perfective with auxiliary verb in the 2nd pers. sg.; cf.: *сѣлъ еси* (Psalm 9, 12), *извлекъ мя еси, исцѣлилъ еси, превратилѣ еси* (Psalm 29, 17–18), *далъ еси, избралъ еси, усыновилъ еси, смѣшалъ еси* (Psalm 79, 35–6). Significantly, all of these forms (simple preterits and perfectives with auxiliary verb) are only found in his psalm paraphrases done in free verse (Pletneva 1987). As M. L. Gasparov notes, free verse "in connection with a high linguistic register [was considered] a mark of inspiration, when the author himself lost control of the stream of divine speech pouring from his lips" (Gasparov 1984, 60). Curiously, in these psalm paraphrases written in free verse we only encounter infinitives in *-ти,* apparently corresponding to inspired, prophetic speech (in those not written in free verse the two infinitive forms freely vary — see Pletneva 1987). In this manner, Sumarokov displays his poetic freedom, using forms that according to the normalizing approach were considered a completely impermissible anomaly.

From this perspective, the normalizing activity of the academic philologists looked like senseless pedantry, as opposed to the activity of a genuine poet. At first Sumarokov charged Trediakovskii with this kind of pedanticism. Depicting him in the pedants Tresotinius and Ksaksoimenius in the comedies "Tresotinius" and "Chudovishchi" (Monsters), Sumarokov not only mocked his literary opponent (see Grinberg and Uspenskii 1992), but also defined his own anti-normalizing literary and linguistic position. Furthermore, Sumarokov's theoretical statements accord with his comedies' usage. In his later article "On Spelling," Sumarokov criticized the practice of writing *i* instead of *и* in words borrowed from Greek and Latin that had been endorsed by Trediakovskii in his treatise of 1755 (see above § III–1.1). He wrote: "Ancient and modern pedantry writes the following words, for example, using the letter 'I' — *Императоръ, Ираклiй* and the like; because, they say, that's how they were written in Latin and Greek; but Romans did not even have an И, so did they have any choice? And must Russians be forced to study Greek or Latin for the sake of Russian spelling? According to this pedantic rule, one would have to use 'I' everywhere in words from Greek and Latin, and not only at the start of a word. What could be more absurd!" (Sumarokov, X, 27).

The charge of pedantry was directed not only at Trediakovskii but at the entire academic tradition, including Lomonosov. Challenging the authority of Lomonsov's grammar and arguing that "it has not been established by any learned assembly" (Sumarokov, X, 38), at the same time Sumarokov noted that its authority was based "on the principle that Mr. Lomonsov was an academician; they thus place faith in the Academy, although he [alone] did not constitute the Academy, but was only a member; and neither the Academy nor Russia sanctioned it; and indeed the Academy could not do so, because its concern is with the sciences and not the language arts" (ibid, 6–7). Thus the regulation of language and literature undertaken by the Academy of Sciences is declared worthless, and to have no connection to that carried out by the French Academy (which was dedicated not to the sciences, but to the verbal arts). Scholars working at the Academy were incapable of perfecting language and literature, and the entire academic tradition merely consists of creating senseless rules, "an unnecessary waste of time" (bezdelki) that only give the appearance of wisdom, but in actuality only hinder an author's "imagination and thought."

This is precisely Sumarokov's opinion of the rule introduced by Academy philologians to use strees marks to differentiate homonymns. The practice may be illustrated with examples from Lomonosov's *Short Manual of Oratory* of 1748: *рѣки́* (gen. sg., to differentiate it from the nom. pl. *рѣ́ки*), *берега́* (nom. pl., to differentiate it from the gen sg. *бе́рега*), *правила́* ("instructions, prescriptions" — to distinguish it from *пра́вила*, "helms, rudders"), *вѣку́* (prep. sg. — to differentiate it from the dat. sg., *вѣ́ку*), *слова́* (acc. pl. — to differentiate it from gen sg. *сло́ва*), *своюˊ* (acc. sg. fem. of the pronominal *свой*) to differentiate it from *сво́ю* (1ˢᵗ pers. sg. of the verb *своить*), etc. (Lomonosov, III, 100–4). Accent marks are used to differentiate both lexical and grammatical homonymns, and the very identification of possible homonyms often required a certain amount of ingenuity.

2. Rationalist Purism and the Richness of the Slavenorossiiskii Language

This practice provoked an angry philippic on Sumarokov's part that was clearly fueled by his resentment over the pretensions of non-noble academicians to dictate rules to upper-class literature:

> The ancients placed accents on syllables, but they did this for the simple folk, to teach them how to pronounce Slavonic expressions and to get them used to correct pronunciation, something we don't need anymore. And when stress marks were left in, practically by order of Peter our first emperor, the theoreticians, not knowing why the stresses were used, asked for approval to put them on expressions that were written in the same way. What's the need of this? The context clearly indicates what the meaning is. *Потóмъ* and *пóтомъ* may be told apart without accents... *Я въ Парижѣ былъ, а потом поѣхалъ я въ Лондонъ*; isn't it clear that this means *потóмъ* and not *пóтомъ*? *Я потомъ моимъ сие приобрѣлъ*: isn't it clear that this means *пóтомъ* and not *потóмъ*? [...] Instead of trying to come up with good expressions and using them, employing rhetorical and poetic beauties, the intelligent writer has to burden his mind with this, and interrupt his thougthts and imagination. But an intelligent writer will not pay attention to this kind of unnecessary waste of time. It is only a pity for students, although not for their teachers, because teachers do this on account of outrageous pedantry, while students are tortured unjustly, due to their youthful ignorance. Immature students are thus tortured by bondage to their instructors, while their teachers sweat their brains out for appearance sake, or rather, have lost their brains. (Sumarokov, X, 33–4)

Sumarokov had already written about this in his earlier article "To Typographical Typesetters," insisting that "every Russian will understand when one should say *сéрдца* and where *сердцà* without the typographer's help" (Sumarokov, VI, 307; see also VI, 311).

Naturally, this argument is not only about spelling but also expresses Sumarokov's attitude toward scholarly normalization of the language as a whole. It extends too, in particular, to Lomonosov's attempts at normalization in vocabulary and grammar. Sumarokov clearly accepts the general concept of the relation between stylistic and genetic parameters, and when Trediakovskii criticizes him for incorrect or "base" usage, Sumarokov does not so much insist on his correctness as speak of the admissibility of this or that "little liberty" (Sumarokov, X, 97–100). Sumarokov is just as much a purist as his rivals, and his view of Classicist purism is on the whole connected to the very same rethinking of Western stylistic categories that we have seen in Trediakovskii and Lomonosov from the end of the 1740's. The differences are in the emphases, and here the most important thing about Sumarokov is his skeptical attitude toward rules. For Sumarokov, rules (or at least "unnecessary" rules) are the gratuitous nitpicking of pedants, while for Trediakovskii and Lomonosov they are of principle importance and represent one of the key aspects of the version of purism they were developing.

2.3 Rationalist Purism and Its Russian Metamorphosis

Certainly not all of the European theoretical concepts assimilated during the process of normalizing the Russian literary language could be adapted to fit the Russian linguistic situation with equal success. Special difficulties arose concerning the notion of usage. As has been noted, it was this idea that lay at the heart of Classicist purism. Vaugelas and Buffier, to whom Trediakovskii made reference (e.g., 1748, 316; III, 215), used the term to mean the practices of conversational speech, which according to their view defined the norm for the living tongue, independent of rules, reason, or literary tradition. Vaugelas described usage as a tyrant that reigns over language ("this usage…which the whole world calls king, or tyrant, the arbiter, or master of languages" — 1674: l.aI verso). This tyrannical usage has clearly expressed sociolinguistic characteristics as Vaugelas defines it as "the way of speaking of the sanest part of the Court" (la façon de parler de la plus saine partie de la Cour) (ibid). Purity and perfection of the literary language consist in excluding everything that does not correspond to usage at court. Understandably, a literary language oriented on the Church Slavonic literary and linguistic tradition had almost nothing to do with purist ideals of this type. It is therefore obvious that the notion of usage had to undergo a most radical kind of reinterpretation in the linguistic models which Trediakovskii and Lomonosov were creating in the late 1740's and 50's.

Although Trediakovskii refers to Vaugelas in his interpretation of "usage" he apparently follows French authors of the late seventeenth and early eighteenth century who distinctly modified Vaugelas' postulates. This modification proceeded in two directions. In the first place, the interrelation between usage and the literary tradition was reexamined. Vaugelas himself had referred quite often to the language of "the best writers" (cf. Gukovskaia 1957, 221f, 234–35), although such references may not have had independent significance, because Malherbe and Coeffeteau may have been important for him only insofar as they had established the best conversational usage in writing. Thereafter, however, writers' authority played an ever greater role; both in Bouhours and in the works of the Académie Française the literary tradition became an independent source for the linguistic norm, at the same time as the canon of model authors was significantly expanding; together with Malherbe and those who based themselves on court usage there appeared writers with different linguistic orientations. In certain situations the literary tradition became the basic norm, with declarations about conversational usage taking on the symbolic function of demonstrating loyalty to Classicist principles. This kind of metamorphosis is observed, for example, in Gottsched. While he speaks of the necessity of following conversational usage, in German conditions this ran into the language's diversity of dialects and absence of a single conversational norm. After Vaugelas, Gottsched distinguished between the speech of the mob and that of the court, but was unable to choose which usage should be followed from among the many German courts (Gottsched 1757, 3). In this situation the role of the literary tradition unavoidably becomes more important. Conversational usage alone only creates the primary material, while talented writers enrich and regularize it, so it is precisely they who should be followed in sustaining the language's purity. [...] Gottsched's works were known to Lomonosov, and possibly also to Trediakovskii, and so this modification of ideas about usage might, in principle, have had direct influence on the Russian authors.

In the second place, Vaugelas' theories were modified as a result of their contamination by Cartesian ideas. In essence Vaugelas, on the one hand, and the Cartesians Arnauld and Lancelot, on the other, were occupied with different aspects of language: Vaugelas' attention was focused on the normalization of the literary language, while the grammarians of Port-Royal were concerned with the universal rules of human reason as they were revealed in various linguistic systems. When directly juxtaposed, however, the understanding of language in the two groups was different and in obvious conflict: whereas the Cartesians held reason to be the basic principle of a language's construction, the followers of Vaugelas maintgained that it was usage, conceptualized as an irrational principle.

Since the end of the seventeenth century attempts had begun to reconcile usage and reason (cf. Caput, I, 245). These attempts were most clearly reflected in Lamy's *Rhetoric* and had undoubted influence on both Rollin and Gottsched and on a series of other writers (for example, Thomas and Grimarest) with whom the Russians were familiar in one way or another. The basis of this developing rationalist purism was the notion of "intelligent usage." On the one hand, language is conceived of as a system of conventional signs formed by usage (custom); reason, trying to communicate thought, necessarily subordinates itself to this conventional system; consequently usage is also a rational act. Lamy writes:

> Reason and necessity force us to follow usage, because it is the nature of the sign to be known among those it serves. Indeed, words have been figures of our ideas only because they have been made to refer to certain things by usage; they should only be used to signify those things that they conventionally mean as signs. One may call the animal we call a horse a dog, and a dog a horse, but the idea of the first is attached to the word horse, and the second to the word

dog, and one can't confuse them and take one for the other without causing great confusion among people, like that which came to pass when they wanted to build the Tower of Babel. The bizarre practices of those who do not wish to follow longstanding custom are to be despised; it's even more bizarre to undertake the folly of trying to reject the ordinary manner of speaking. To adopt unknown terms is to wrap in obscurity that which we would explain. (Lamy 1737, 89–90)[40]

It is obvious from this that not only that which is subordinate to general usage but even the concrete rubrics of Classicist purism are seen as based on reason.

On the other hand, if for Vaugelas usage was to a large degree juxtaposed to rules (as to the rational principle in language) and could give rise to an unlimited number of unexplainable exceptions, for rationalist purism it was not the zone of exceptions that was significant but the zone in which usage and rules coincided. Linguistic activity is regulated by analogy, which usage follows, deviating from it only in a limited number of cases. A zone of unexplainable exceptions exists (on this basic point rationalist purism still repeated Vaugelas), but purifying the language consists precisely in reducing it as much as possible. Consequently the idea of two types of usage, good and bad, was also revised: if for Vaugelas good usage was that of the court and bad that of the mob (i.e., socio-linguistic criteria), for rationalist purism good usage was the usage of the "rational," of the learned, those who knew grammar (as a bow to tradition, courtiers could be included here as well), while bad usage was that of the ignorant (the same mob, but in a different sense). Therefore purifying the language became linked with rules, grammatical tradition, and the rational principle in language. Vaugelas' irrationalism could come under attack, and enlightenment be connected with grammatical normalization and establishing rules (cf. Caput, II, 20).

Lamy, like Vaugelas and many of his followers, distinguishes good and bad usage:

> When we elevate usage to the throne and make it arbitrary sovereign of languages, we do not pretend that we are putting the scepter in the hands of the populace. There is a good and a bad usage, and just as good people serve as example to those who want to live well, so too the habits (coûtume) of those who speak well is the rule for those who would like to speak well. *Usum qui*

---

[40] Here Lamy develops the ideas of Pierre Nicole, who in part wrote: "All that does not conform to reason wounds us, and nothing is more contrary to reason than to reject the words we use and replace them with strange and extraordinary ones." At the same time, "good usage" is contrasted to "these new fashions of speaking which we see born every day at court and in the salons (ruelles) " (Nicole 1720, 183–4).

2. Rationalist Purism and the Richness of the Slavenorossiiskii Language

sit arbiter dicendi, vocamus consensus eruditorum, sicut vivendi, consensus bonorum.[41] (Lamy 1737, 93)

Although as in Vaugelas socio-lingusitic criteria are used in defining good usage, the replacement of court society by scholars shows that for Lamy what is important is not the refinement of court speech but the power of reason and the knowledge of the erudite. This break with Vaugelas becomes obvious when Lamy speaks of the ways to tell good from bad usage. The first means is experience, which does not contradict Vaugelas. However, the two next criteria, reason and analogy (i.e., grammatical rules) directly link good use with the rational principle. Use by itself does not guarantee linguistic purity; only reason that comprehends the fundamentals of language and establishes rules is capable of distinguishing good from bad usage (cf. Lamy 1737, 94–5).[42]

Thus the choice between two competing expressions is made not by court fashion but by scholarly reasoning, by weeding out that which does not correspond to the universal rational basis of the language. Naturally, in such an approach to good usage "rational" rules of grammar play the most important part:

> This manner of understanding usage, by comparing many expressions and by [determining] their interrelations, is called analogy, and is the means by which languages have become fixed. It is by this means that grammarians come to know the rules and good linguistic usage, and have composed grammars that are very useful, if they are done well, because in them one can find the rules which otherwise one would be obliged to search for by the tedious work of analogy. (ibid, 96)

Thus although the dominance of usage over language was not challenged, the bounds of its power were significantly reduced. The lack

---

[41] "We will define usage as the practice agreed upon by the educated, just as when our way of life is concerned we define it as the agreed-upon practice of good people." Adapted from Quintilian, *Institutio oratorio*, I, vi, 45. (Translator's note)

[42] Lamy writes: "The second way we have to understand good usage is reason, as I will show. All languages have the same fundamentals, which men would realize if by some chance (like that which we have pretended) they were obliged to invent a new language. With the understanding that we have given of these fundamentals it is easy to become the master and judge of a language and to condemn the laws of usage which are opposed to those of nature and reason. If we do not have the right to establish new laws, we do have liberty not to follow those which are bad. Languages only become refined when men begin to reason, when expressions that corrupt usage has introduced are banished. But these can only be perceived by educated eyes and by an exact knowledge of the art which we are examining. Reasonable usage is established by the choice of appropriate expressions that renew language, and by non-usage (if one may be permitted to express it this way) of corrupt ways of speaking" (Lamy 1737, 94–5).

Chapter 3. The Changed Conception of the Literary Language

of clear borders between reason and usage led to a situation in which the immediate orientation on conversational speech could become purely declaractive, and play virtually no role in a writer's linguistic practice.

These two modifications of Classicist purism were not opposed to one another and could therefore combine in various ways. The source of language's purity could thus be defined as the literary tradition, as reason (rules and grammar), and also as the conversational speech of the social elite. Moreover, the various combinations of these factors were precisely what produced the variety of European Classicist conceptions of purism of the late seventeenth and first half of the eighteenth century. It is probably not worth trying to reduce all of the influences of French purist theory on Russian thinking about language into one single approach connecting Trediakovskii and Vaugelas. Russian theoreticians who declared the Russian literary language to be of one nature with Church Slavonic were undoubtledly familiar with a broad range of purist doctrines, and all they had to do was to select from among this diversity that set of formulae which could most easily be adapted to the Russian situation and to the notion of Slavonicizing purism, which from the late 1740's became the dominant conception of the new literary language.

Obviously, from the three sources of linguistic purity—conversational usage, literary tradition, and grammatical rules — only the latter two were relevant for Slavonicizing purism, whereas conversational usage was merely a fictive rubric. These were the very sources of which Lomonosov spoke in sections 164 and 165 of his *Rhetoric* of 1748 which were cited above (Lomonosov, III, 219–20; VII^2, 236–7). Stylistic purity here depends "upon a well-grounded knowledge of the language, upon frequent reading of books, and upon converse with people who speak purely. Diligent study of grammatical rules will aid in the first, in the second, selecting phrases, proverbs, and sayings from good books, and in the third, trying to speak purely in the presence of people who know and who observe the language's beauty. As far as it pertains to reading books, above all I recommend keeping to church ones..." It is noteworthy that while the first two pieces of advice are quite concrete (church books represent literary tradition, and Lomonosov's own planned *Russian Grammar* is alluded to as the basis for studying the subject), the final piece of advice ("people who know and who observe the language's beauty") is merely a bow to prevailing theory; the phrase suggests more than anything else orators and grammarians, and reference to their authority is but another way of appealing to the authority of grammar and rhetorical rules. Within this framework, the relationship of usage to grammar is precisely reflected in the foreword to the *Russian Grammar*:

"And although it [grammar] derived from general linguistic usage, it is the rules that show the way to actual use" (Lomonosov, IV, 11; VII², 392). Understandably, grammar's dependence on usage is somewhat undefined, while usage's subordination to grammar is fully concrete; grammar is compiled and functions as something normative, i.e., prescribing "rational" order to usage (cf. Signorini 1988, 528–9).

One may find multiple definitions of the sources of linguistic purity in Sumarokov, which indicates that he was party to the same change in linguistic worldview that Trediakovskii and Lomonosov had undergone. Criticizing the nom.-acc. sg. masc. form *бывшей* which he encountered in Lomonosov (and to which he preferred *бывший*), Sumarokov wrote in the article "To Senseless Rhymsters": "And what is even more strange is that many follow this rule, founded neither on the nature of the language, nor on ancinet books, nor on usage" (Sumarokov, IX, 279). This is repeated in the later article "On Spelling": "This newly introduced rule has no basis either in the character of the language, nor in ancient books, nor in usage, but only in Mr. Lomonosov's arbitrary opinion" (Sumarokov, X, 6). Thus together with usage, "the nature of the language" (which in practical terms means grammar) and "ancient books" (i.e., church books, of course, that substitute for literary tradition) represent the sources for linguistic correctness and purity. Essentially, the difference from Lomonosov is merely one of formulation.

True, in some specific cases Sumarokov may oppose usage and rules, but this is exclusively for polemical purposes. When Trediakovskii accuses him of breaking the rules, Sumarokov defends himself by arguing usage. Thus for example in regard to writing neuter nouns in *-ие* with *-ье* Sumarokov notes: "He calls the liberty of [writing] *паденье, желанье* instead of *падение, желание* base usage. But everyone uses this form, and it would be better if he said that this was incorrect rather than base usage" (Sumarokov, X, 99). Although Sumarokov by no means asserts that one should follow usage and disregard the rules, he considers little violations of the rules to be acceptable poetic license, at times producing special poetic charm. Responding to another of Trediakovskii's objections, Sumarokov states, "I follow usage with the very same keenness (rachenie) as I do the rules; correct words make for purity and eliminate coarseness from one's style. For example, *Я люблю сего, а ты любишь другаго* is correct, but coarse; *Я люблю етова, а ты другова* — from usage and from the elimination of three syllables in *го* and *аго* the sound is more pleasant" (ibid, 97–8).

In any case, usage does not become the main, not to say single, source of linguistic purity and refinement, the more so since Sumarokov as well as Trediakovskii (as well as Western authorities) recognize the danger of "bad and popular (prostonarodnoe) usage" (ibid, 22). Grinberg and Uspenskii are hardly correct in suggesting that for Sumarokov "poor" or "base" usage is evaluated "strictly in its socio-linguistic aspect" (Grinberg and Uspenskii 1992, 209). In any case in his late article "On Spelling" (1768–70) Sumarokov writes about how illiterate authors (those who have not studied grammar) who sow bad usage have popular success with "the most noble of readers," i.e, the social elite, "and others write and versify without having studied anything anywhere, and not only experiment in composition but compose in the loftiest genres of verse. And that their compositions are vile neither they nor the greater part of their readers will believe; they are praised for their prattle. Oh, ignorance, what is more respected, beneficial, and easier on earth!" (Sumarokov, X, 38). It is clear that, as for Lomonosov and Trediakovskii, good usage is connected not with social class but with education.

Hence for Sumarokov and his contemporaries usage turns out to be mostly a fictitious criterion. Sumarokov refers to it inconsistently and unsystematically, in general only to justify the imperfections of his language (which he acknowledges as such), and it remains unclear what he meant by usage, whether this refers to oral usage (the basis for Vaugelas' purism) or written usage (to which Vaugelas did not appeal) (cf. Grinberg and Uspenskii 1992, 209). For this reason the other two sources of linguistic purity — grammatical rules and the literary tradition — turn out to be far more important for Sumarokov (this in full agreement with his literary rivals). Sumarokov repeatedly writes about the importantce of studying grammar and grammatical rules, especially in his later years when Lomonosov had died and Trediakovskii, who had criticized his insufficient erudition, had left the scene, and he began to feel and present himself as the single practicing maître. It is not accidental that he republished his two epistles of 1748 with the new title "Instructions for Those Wanting to Be Writers" (Sumarokov 1774a, cf. Klein 1993, 56–7). He writes that "ignoramuses and illiterate people" are spoiling the language (Sumarokov, X, 46) and that "it will become even more corrupt until they cease regarding spelling and grammar as unnecessary things" (ibid, 20). He complains that "many of our writers almost always make mistakes because they don't know grammar" and that "they don't teach Russian grammar in schools" (ibid, 22 and 37).

Even in his earlier years Sumarokov had protested not against rules themselves but against excessive regulation. The absence of rules, he felt, diminished the expressive possibilities of the language. Thus in the article "To Typographical Typesetters" he writes: "The fewer rules, the easier to learn a language, and some think that this easiness is no little part of a

2. Rationalist Purism and the Richness of the Slavenorossiiskii Language

language's value; but a diamond that is lighter is not cheaper. It seems to me that one may find more value in moderate difficulty in a language because this creates more variety, and where there's more variety, there is more loveliness and beauty if variety does not undermine harmony. A language's difficulty demands more time spent on study, but also produces more satisfaction" (Sumarokov, VI, 310–11). Characteristically, Sumarokov relates rules to that which he values above all else — diversity. It is evident that in his opinion the lack of rules necessarily leads to "disconnected usage" that damages the very means of linguistic expression.

No less important for him was literary tradition. His references to the ancient books have already been cited. Together with this he also speaks of model authors. In general, grammar and the literary tradition serve as equally important factors for correcting the language. He can write that "our wonderful language" is threatened with "complete... destruction if contrary to desire conceited ignorance will continue for many years, and if it is not eradicated by our great writers and skilled grammaticians" (ibid, 59); both authors and grammaticians are declared to be equally necessary creators of the language. Moreover, Sumarokov may declare with some irritation that "we do not have either grammaticians or a knowledge of grammar shown to be based on nature and usage, nor [do we have] correct authors, while we do have an excess of writers, not to mention poets" (ibid, 37). From this, however, only follows Sumarokov's own self-assertion as the authoritative, single correct author on whom the developing norm should rely. In this connection Sumarokov may speak about the leading role of model authors in comparison to the role of normative grammar. He makes this point while bringing the authority of Lomonosov's grammar into question: "So why should one follow Lomonosov's Grammar? The grammar of all peoples is found in nature; and very good writers always preceded grammar; because people speak and write not following grammar but according to reason, founded on the nature of things, while grammar is based on [what] people [speak] and the more so on [particular] authors. When Homer wrote the Greeks did not have a written grammar, but this great poet and father of poets knew grammar" (ibid, 37). Sumarokov hoped to claim for himself this position of model author whose texts created the basis for a normative grammar, thus denying Lomonosov the main role in establishing rules for the Russian literary language. These, however, were only the details of literary conflict, while the recognition of grammar, model authors, and vaguely defined usage were agreed-upon sources of linguistic purity for both Lomonosov and Sumarokov, and as we will see below, for Trediakovskii as well.

Chapter 3. The Changed Conception of the Literary Language

By the second half of the eighteenth century Classicist purism and these three sources of linguistic purity had become universally accepted. One may find its traces, for example, in A. Rzhevskii's article "On the Moscow Dialect." This dialect is examined here as a creation of the "beautiful sex" (cf. on French linguistic theory's orientation on women's speech and the Russian response — Uspenskii 1985, 57–60, 63, 154–5), but this conversational usage in pure form does not satisfy Rzhevskii. He writes, "Won't our beautiful inventors of the new dialect do us this indulgence and in their writings use the language which is used by those who know Russian"? (Rzhevskii 1763, 74–5); here the usage of "those who know Russian" (that is, who are familiar with the grammatical tradition) is added on to simply conversational usage. A bit further the literary tradition also appears:

> I can guess beforehand that many will say, why not write just like we speak? This liberty would be overly excessive, so that at last not a trace would remain of our ancient tongue. We rejected the old dialect in conversation, now we will reject it in our writing; we will then import foreign words into our language [so that] in the end we can forget about Russian altogether, and that would be a great pity. Not one other people has committed such a murder of their native language, but as it is our language is already threatenend with final extinction. (ibid, 75)[43]

One can also cite A. Barsov's "Answer to the Letter of an Anglomane" where a general recommendation on how to achieve good taste in language is given as: "methodical and fundamental study, intelligent reading of the leading works of each type, ... non-servile imitation of select examples from these, [and] taking note of the pleasant usage of rational, distinguished, and well-educated people." In addition to this, it is noted that Russians have church books that affirm their language's richness (Barsov 1775, 265–66). We find an analogous discussion in I. Rizhskii's *Rhetoric*:

> Every writer must have a fundamental knowledge of his native language. The knowledge of grammar, reading of the best Slavonic and Russian books, especially those published in the most recent times, and intercourse with people educated in letters serve as the sole means to this... Finally, in case of doubt as to the purity of some word or expression, the Imperial Russian Academy's Dictionary of the Russian Language can serve as the most reliable guide. (Rizhskii 1796, 9–10)

---

[43] This argument recalls that of such an enemy of strict purism as Fénélon, who had written that "Grammar cannot fix a living language in place, but it can perhaps diminish the capricious little changes through which fashion reigns over words just as it does over customs. These changes based on pure fantasy may confuse and alter a language instead of improving it" (Fénélon, VII, 124).

2. Rationalist Purism and the Richness of the Slavenorossiiskii Language

The most consistent and theoretically well considered reinterpretation of the notion of usage is given by Trediakovskii. In the first version of his article "On the Plural Ending of Long-form Adjectives" (1746), usage and reason are presented as mutually interactive principles. Trediakovskii still repeats Vaugelas' conception of the relation between usage and rules; he writes that "Usage must be recognized as the most authoritative force in a language, because it alone possesses, in Horace's words, the power, and the right, and the rule over speech. For this reason it is stronger than all precedent grammatical rules prescribed against the living language, because usage does not procede according to rules, but rules are defined by consideration of usage. Otherwise all rules would be in vain, because they would apply to what did not exist in the language" (Vomperskii 1969, 88; Lomonosov, IV, notes, 16–7). Nonetheless, just like Lamy he gives reason power to choose in case of ambiguous usage: "When many usages contradict one another, nothing better than proper reason (pravyi razum) can judge between them, to decide which of them one should follow" (Vomperskii 1968, 98; Lomonosov, IV, notes, 17). At the same time changing usage never deviates from a language's nature, that is, for all of the changes, the basic features of the language's structure are preserved: "However changeable usage may be in and of itself over the course of several years, changes introduced by usage never occur which are completely at odds with the nature of the language. Otherwise this would not be the language's changing usage but its compete annihilation" (ibid). In case of uncertainty, usage should be harmonized with the rules which describe the grammatical structure of the language, and if no such rules may be found, then with the opinion of educated people who are best able to understand the language's nature. "If there are two or more usages, of which none may be defended by proper reason, then one should give preference to that which the greater number of the best and most learned people prefer" (ibid).

In later variants of this article, the statement concerning the priority of usage over rules is no longer repeated, which is the more remarkable in that such formulations are standard in Western manuals of the rationalist tendency.[44] Juxtaposing Trediakovskii's article with these manuals suggests that Trediakovskii's basic rejection of conversational usage goes farther and takes more conscious forms than in standard rationalist purism. This may

---

[44] Cf. in Lamy (1737, 97): "Analogy is not the mistress of language. She does not descend from the heavens to establish her laws. She only exhibits those of usage. *Non est lex loquendi, sed observatio* [There is no law how to speak except for observation], as Quintilian says." Similar statements may be found in Gottsched [...] (e.g., Gottsched 1757, 7).

Chapter 3. The Changed Conception of the Literary Language

already be seen in the *Conversation About Orthography*. Here although Trediakovskii states that the rules should be made to agree with usage, and not the other way around, he introduces the new idea of two usages, one the "rational" or "sensible" usage and the other that of the "senseless mob":

> And could it occur that there would *not* be two [types of usage]? Is it reasonable to call the usage of village peasants common usage? .... Or would it be fitting to appropriate the speech of a bootmaker or coachman? However, these people speak the same language as those who know (that is, those who either have a good education, or who have dealings with the court, or are of noble birth, or who have excelled in the sciences, or in the reading of books), but not as correctly, according to the nature of the language, or as skillfully. The first speak as they are able, according to their needs; the second, as one should speak, with discrimination. And since a language's usage is not something blind but sensible (blagorazumnoe), established by sensible people and accepted from those who are skilled, it has great power over the language. It is also rational (blagorassudnoe), so that if something in the language happens to change or if something new is introduced, it won't be changed or introduced haphazardly or with haste, but first considered against the language's rules which were purposefully made by the language in order to determine whether changes or innovations are contrary to its nature... (Trediakovskii 1748, 315–6; III, 214; cf. also 320–6; 217–21).[45]

Trediakovskii also repeatedly emphasizes the role of reason in determining "sensible" usage in his frequent assertions that the language should be oriented on "what either the larger or most enlightened part of the population uses. By 'the larger part' are meant not peasants but respected citizens, and by 'most enlightened' not simpletons but learned people, and these two groups are not different but one and the same insofar as their importance, because it is more fitting to trust the purity of the language of honest and enlightened people rather than that of the senseless mob" (Pekarskii 1865, 107; cf. Trediakovskii 1748, 324–5; III, 220–1). All these statements take the language of learned and rational people (i.e., those who know grammar) as their basis on principle, while references to the social elite merely testify to Trediakovskii's reticence to openly break with his European models. Trediakovskii's change in view is fully evident in the corrections he made to in his "Speech to the Members of the Russian Assembly" when he republished it in 1752. To his former arguments about usage, he added:

---

[45] Trediakovskii presents the situation of two usages as something universal rather than specifically connected to the Russian situation—the fact that in Russia good (reasonable) usage is equated with the special bookish language. In discussing usage, Trediakovskii assiduously downplays this issue. See the *Conversation About Orthography* [...] (Trediakovskii 1748, 307–8; III, 208–9).

"generally accepted beautiful written usage (pishemoe obyknovenie) cannot but be based on reason, however much usage not based on precise understanding of usage may be asserted" (1752, II, 16; cf. Uspenskii 1985, 183).

Trediakovskii's reasoning in and of itself does not greatly differ from that of ordinary rationalist purists, for example, Lamy in his *Rhetoric*. In Russian conditions, however, European concepts take on their own special content. Trediakovskii asserts that the changes usage introduces must harmonize with the language's nature, and that only those who understand that nature may determine correct usage. But the nature of the Russian literary language had been declared to be one with that of Church Slavonic (§ III–1.2). Therefore, correct usage in Russian always had to be harmonized with Church Slavonic, and in order to determine if that were the case knowledge of Church Slavonic was obviously necessary. All references to the usage of "respected citizens" who are of "exceptional deportment" (obkhoditel'stvom vytsvechennykh) were in this case the purest of fictions, and all seeming socio-linguistic indicators denoted phenomena of another order; what took on real significance was the opposition between the bookish language, based on Church Slavonic, which defined proper usage, and the conversational tongue, which, insofar as it was juxtaposed to the bookish language, was declared to be "not usage but delusion, whose real father is ignorance" (Trediakovskii 1748, 325; III, 221).

The decisive rejection of conversational usage as source of the linguistic norm signified a radical break with Vaugleas' tradition, no matter what compromise formulations may have tried to disguise it. It is clear that Trediakovskii well understood how his ideas looked from the standpoint of orthodox Classicism — he was liable to charges of linguistic pomposity, the loss of simplicity and naturalness. Indeed French Classicism constantly emphasized the need for simplicity in a well-developed language, and simplicity was juxtaposed not to the lofty but to the pompous.[46] Trying to rebuff accusations in advance, Trediakovskii tries to discredit those for

---

[46] Thus comparing two translations of Ariosto's "Joconde" by Bouillon and La Fontaine Boileau wrote that "A well educated man, as I see him, and in the opinion of Terence and Virgil, won't let himself be carried away by Italian extravagances or reject the path of good sense. Everything he says is simple and natural; and what I value in him above all is a certain naiveté of language that few people have a good idea of, although it constitutes the whole charm of his speech. This is that inimitable naiveté which was so highly valued in the writings of Horace and Terence..." (Boileau, II, 293). Boileau also cites the ideal religious example of simplicity in language, according this style a kind of religious sanction. He contrasts the naturalness of the language of the Bible to the overblown quality and excess ornament of empty rhetoric [...] (Boileau, III, 22). Lamy also writes that the genius of French consists in its precision and simplicity (naiveté) (Lamy 1737, 97; cf. Bouhours 1671, 55f).

whom conversational usage remains the ideal. He writes that "at court some do not accept [the idea of] two usages in language, and refer mostly to the incorrect type (nepriamoe) [of usage], spoiled by simpletons" (Trediakovskii 1748, 314; III, 213). After almost twenty years he repeats the same attacks: "When some of our people accustomed to French and German, not knowing anything but the civic language, espy in civic writing two or three Slavonic or Slavenosossiisski phrases, they exclaim in seeming indignation, *that's not in Russian!*, their complaint is not that these phrases are contrary to the character of the Russian language, but that they are not of the gutter, not of the marketplace, in a word, not vulgar, and also that they are known to the educated" (Trediakovskii 1766, I, lx, note; II, lxxiv). The simplicity of authors who orient themselves on conversational speech is declared to be a false simplicity, and a different equivalent is found for simplicity as a positive trait of a well-developed language (the simplicity of French purist writings): "I know your false opinion of simplicity, that is, the desire to speak and write commensurate with linguistic purity, as if this noble and praiseworthy simplicity (consisting of only natural and not embarrassing and ornate descriptions) did not do clear harm to the language; [but] one may write simply and without flourishes and still maintain purity and correctness of speech" (Pekarskii 1865, 108–9). Thus "simplicity" is not juxtaposed here to the use of specifically bookish forms, but emerges as a feature that also belongs to the special bookish language; simplicity comes not from an orientation on colloquial usage but from the absence of unnecessary (Baroque) rhetorical ornamentation. In this way the extremely important Classicist notions of simplicity and clarity that also in part define its linguistic and stylistic theories are carried over from the sphere of language to that of rhetoric and poetics. As a result, Church Slavonic grammatical learning ceases to be opposed to simplicity.

Trediakovskii attributes universality and stability to correct usage: "correct (priamoe) usage is universal and stable, because if it were not, this would already not be usage, but some sort of absurd hodgepodge of language, to its impairment" (Pekarskii 1865, 107; cf. Vomperskii 1968, 98; Lomonosov, IV, notes, 17). These attributes by themselves do not contradict European theories, in which universality signifies the supra-dialectical charccter of the literary norm, and stability the relative strength of this norm in the literary tradition. In the context of Slavonicizing purism they take on a different meaning, and serve to contrast the bookish and conversational languages. Church Slavonic and Russian, sharing a single nature, emerge as universal, insofar as (in opposition to conversational speech) they can never be based on dialect, and given the absence of a normalized colloquial

2. Rationalist Purism and the Richness of the Slavenorossiiskii Language

language, any conversational speech may be seen as dialect, as needed. It is also understandable how Church Slavonic and the literary language based on it may be characterized by stability; in a specifically written language only those changes are recognized that represent a conscious substitution of one (stable) norm for another (just as stable) one. And each time this norm is engrained in the literary tradition, for the simple reason that it does not exist outside of the literary tradition. In these conditions colloquial speech since it is not normalized is characterized by changeability, and hence the lack of stability. This is precisely Trediakovskii's argument as he proves "that (и) is the natural ending of our masc. pl. nouns" (Pekarskii 1865, 106). It is natural first of all because it belongs to Church Slavonic and is attested in church books. Colloquial usage cannot serve as a guide insofar as "among the people these endings are for the very greater part haphazard (bezrazbornyi)," and "consequently... this usage is neither universal nor everywhere constant" (ibid, 108).

Insofar as correct usage is based on Church Slavonic, its source is not living speech (whether of the social elite, the court, learned people or any other group) but writing. This again corresponded to European theories that gave priority to model authors over conversational usage of whatever kind. However, in place of the model authors that Russian literature had yet to produce church books were substituted, and it was from them according to Trediakovskii that one should learn correct usage. This is just how he argues concerning masc. plurals in -u: "the ending in (и) is of all others the most generally used (obshchestvenneishee), and... in masculine plural adjectives it is precisely natural, as pure Slavonic. Consequently, one should prefer this ending in the pure language, the more so since it is used in the main and most enlightened sources, that is, in all church books, which never vary in this and are hence classical" (ibid). This statement shows in all clarity how the Church Slavonic literary tradition took the place of both usage by enlightened citizens and the works of model writers as the standard of the linguistic norm; church books were declared to be "classic," i.e., they were to serve as the guide in learning the language (cf. Uspenskii 1984a, 117).

On account of this church books became the norm for the Russian literary language, and deviations from this norm began to be seen as a result of ignorance of church books. This is precisely what Trediakovskii reproaches Sumarokov for. "The author used the verb *спасаю* with the genitive case without the preposition *от*. We would have written it this way: *Ты от грознаго меча спасаешь*, and not *Ты грознаго меча спасаешь*. But the author was pleased to write a new way, and he clearly revealed himself as one who has never read the canon of prayers called the 'Paraklis,' for there it precisely and rightly says, *от тяшких и лютых мя спаси.* Would it not be better for our author to take up our [church] books to learn correct composition?" Trediakovskii juxtaposes the orientation on church books to an orientation on European models: "Racine only teaches one to sigh about nothings, and Boileau-Despréaux to sting everyone, including one's betters; but neither of them can instruct us about our language" (Kunik 1865, 449). In another place Trediakovskii writes: "The author rarely goes to great vespers and all-night vigils, or at least not in the time when the first voice is sung, for otherwise he would have known that in the 'Universal glory' that begins the 'Bogorodichny' [hymns in honor of the Mother of God] the word *поборник* does not mean *enemy* but *defender* and *helper* " (ibid, 480). And finally, summarizing Sumarokov's linguistic errors, Trediakovskii returns to his ignorance of church books as their main cause: "Such deficiencies, and so many of them, both taken separately and in his writing as a whole, stem from this first and most important source, [and that is] precisely that in his young years the author did not read enough of our church books, and therefore he lacks both an abundance of choice words and the skill to put words together correctly" (ibid, 495–6).

If Sumarokov is unable to harmonize his language with that of church books, Trediakovskii himself, to the contrary, is up to the task. When in 1752 the Academy (Miller [Müller] and Taubert) reviewed his "Speech on Wisdom, Prudence and Virtue," Taubert called for an additional review, in part due to "the author's use of many philosophical terms whose validity neither he nor Professor Müller were capable of judging." To this Trediakovskii answered that "these terms are supported by all of our church books, from which I took them" (Pekarskii, IA, II, 167). In Trediakovskii's opinion, it was obvious that using church books completely legitimized the linguistic innovations that he was introducing into new literary usage; insofar as he considered church books as "classics," any elements taken from them could not be seen as innovation.

As a result of this new adaptation of European theories to Russian linguistic reality the perception of Church Slavonic and the Church Slavonic literary tradition radically changed. Trediakovskii frankly declared: "For us friendly conversation... is not the rule for writing, but the bookish church language,... which is just as alive in Russian religious society as the conversational tongue is the civic" (Pekarskii 1866, 109). If Church Slavonic was formerly conceived of as a special ecclesiastical tongue with no direct relation to the new literary language which was to serve the new secular culture, now the closest mutual connection between it and the Russian literary language was asserted. Church Slavonic now emerged as source for the

2. Rationalist Purism and the Richness of the Slavenorossiiskii Language

Russian literary norm, and even while remaining in principle an ecclesiastic tongue, at the same time it turned out to be a necessary component of the new Russian culture. Without reference to the church tongue it was impossible to achieve correctness, purity, and abundance — those qualities which were to give Russian parity with European languages. It turned out that European beauties blossomed not on distant shores but right here at home, within the churchyard of the Greek Orthodox Slavonic church, any association with which had earlier been forbidden.

As a consequence of this new perception, the church tradition was now considered the preserve not only of pure faith but of pure language. An author unsure of the correctness of his writing or experiencing difficulty in selecting words was supposed to look directly to church books. Insofar as Russian and Church Slavonic were declared to have the same nature, Russian's nature was held to be imprinted in church books; here it was expressed in pure and unchanging form. Hence church books were transformed into a constant standard with which to measure the literary language and which shielded it from the danger of betraying its nature and becoming impure. Lomonosov wrote that "the Russian language will remain in full strength, beauty and richness, firm and inaccessible to change and decline as long as the Russian church will be adorned by singing the glory of God in the Slavonic tongue" (Lomonosov, IV, 230; VII^2, 591). Trediakovskii expressed precisely the same idea: "our Slavenorossiiskii language... can never be irremediably harmed: literary Slavonic will maintain it, preserve it, and save it from injury unwaveringly and for all time." And in another place he wrote that "the Russian language is one of the Slavonic languages, and indeed the most integral (tseleishii) of them, if it hasn't been spoiled; however, nothing will harm it forever: its shield and buttress is our immortal church tongue" (1773, 241 and 372). And so the Church Slavonic literary and linguistic tradition was fully reinstated, and this could not help but have important culturological consequences.

3. The Synthesis of Cultural and Linguistic Traditions: The Slavenorossiiskii Language and Its Functioning

The Petrine linguistic reform and the entire early period of the Russian literary language's formation had rejected Church Slavonic and been based on an anticlerical, exclusively secular notion of the new culture.

Church Slavonic was perceived as a narrowly church language, and the new literary language was to be the vehicle of specifically worldly, secular culture (see § I–2.1). At the end of the 1740's this conception changed, and the civic language was declared to be based on the ecclesiastic tongue. Of course this change did not mean that the reigning anticlerical cultural conception was suddenly transformed into a clerical one, but nevertheless the change was clearly symptomatic, for had the anticlerical bias remained in force, such a development would have been unthinkable.

The new conception of the literary language put it outside the opposition between clerical and anticlerical tendencies. This was a natural consequence of the fact that the struggle between these two political factions had come to an end. Indeed the cultural synthesis of absolutism presupposed a unified state culture in which both secular and spiritual interests would be subordinated to the all-encompassing and undivided power of an enlightened monarch. Culture became a state monopoly that necessitated its unification into one well-functioning state mechanism, moved by a single aspiration for historical progress and the triumph of reason. The theme of the state, its progress, prosperity, and power, became the main subject of philosophical reflection and it was this that served to inspire both civic leaders as well as poets and preachers. The unity of state-inspired ecstacy was to define cultural unity.

European theories about the enlightened state were founded on a specific cultural mythology whose roots derived from Renaissance attempts to find principles which could organize humanity in a harmony reflecting that of the cosmos. To a significant extent the ideology of enlightened absolutism was a reaction against the failure of the idea of social accord and the harmonious transfiguration of the world that European culture had experienced during the course of the Thirty Years War; the fruits that had been expected of the magic of science and universal love were now, from the mid-seventeenth century, expected to come from the monarch, who was putting an end to religious strife by force and through his unlimited will implanting harmonious concord. The mythological thinking of the Renaissance had undergone a profound transformation, but had not lost its mythological quality.

In the eighteenth century this mythology extended its influence to Russian soil. The realities of communal life, individual spiritual needs, as well as contradictory social and group interests were all relegated to the background in this mythology, and merged into the same class of phenomena as superstition and ignorance and all those things which prevented achieving the ideal. Naturally, historical facts never corresponded to this ideal picture in any way. In particular, the reconciliation of church and state in Russia was just as much a fiction as the enlightened monarch. Various priests evaded performance of celebratory services on important holidays (cf. Zol'nikova 1981, 152f), mass defections into the schism continued, and in the upper echelons of the church hierarchy much dissatisfaction continued to fester, rising to the surface in the case of Arsenii Matseevich, one of the few Russian clergymen to publicly oppose Catherine's confiscation of church property (see Popov 1912). The formation of the new cultural consciousness took place in spite of these historical processes, and was itself a historical process of primary significance. A new world view was developing and some reason was easily found to exclude everything that did not fit into it, if only on the grounds that the inappropriate phenomena had to do with people and social groups with which the new culture's enlightened brilliance should not concern itself; and if some unsuitable event did occur, and involve an inappropriate person, he could immediately be consigned to the category of "other," as happened to Arsenii Matseevich, who was transformed from the Metropolitan of Rostov into "Andrei the Liar," and the harmonious picture quickly restored.

The carrier of this new perception was that same "already new people" (Kantemir I, 46) to which the Petrine reforms gave birth and which had assimilated those reforms as its rightful heritage. It was this people which had created the Europeanized culture of imperial Petersburg, and it was in the context of this culture that the conflict between church and state had played itself out. The struggle for church independence ceased to be a cultural phenomenon, as it had been in the time of Stefan Iavorskii and Feofan Prokopovich's clashes, and it was relegated to the status of "unenlightened" protest, the ignoring of which was a most essential part of eighteenth-century enlightenment culture. The changing conceptualization of the literary language described above that demanded a radical reevaluation of the relationship of secular and religious culture permits us to date the formation of this new ideal picture of state harmony to the second half of the 1740's.

The center of imperial Petersburg was the court. It was not only the focus of the new culture's existence in its concrete manifestations, but also the realization of that cultural absolute which was thought of as the motive force behind all cultural development. In the ceremonial life of the court, the religious hierarchy occupied just as central a place as the secular. The culture of European absolutism which the court implanted itself contained a religious as well as secular component. The Empresses' confessor, the heir to the throne's tutor in theology, the court preacher were just as much literary agents of the court as those who composed celebratory odes or academic greetings. High offices were filled by those who sought to distinguish themselves in the new field of religious — state oratory. In the 1740's the passion for polemics quitted religious literature, and the age of Feofan's controversial works, the *Rock of Faith*, the *Hammer on the Rock of Faith*, and the pamphlet that answered it, Feofan's *Insupportable Yoke* and Feofilakt Lopatinskii's *Supportable Yoke*, Markell Rodyshevskii's notebooks, etc.— came to an end. The clash of convictions was over, and religious literature became a necessary, even compulsory, component of state enlightenment and the propaganda of absolute monarchy.

In 1767 Catherine the Great and her retinue made a journey down the Volga. During the trip the assembled company took up an unusual occupation for courtiers: they translated Marmontel's *Belisarius* (1766). The book was well known in Europe. It was simultaneously an admonition to enlightened monarchs, denouncing despotism and exalting a rational concern for one's subjects, and a manifesto of enlightened deism, juxtaposing rational religion to clerical obscurantism. In France the Sorbonne had condemned the book for freethinking, but in Russia it enjoyed another fate. Declaring for all to hear that she was no despot or tyrant, Catherine herself translated the chapter condemning autocratic rule, published the book and had it dedicated to Archbishop Gavriil (Petrov). The dedication was written by Count Andrei Shuvalov, devotee and friend of Voltaire. It said in part:

> The ancients preserved the practice of dedicating their works to people whom they sincerely respected. We follow their example, presenting our translation to Your Right Reverence. Your virtues are well known to us, especially the gentleness, humility, moderation, and enlightened piety which abide in you, and which should adorn the soul of every Christian, the more so in a pastor of your rank. All peoples and people of all stations in life need moral admonition. Social happiness depends on the good behavior of its members, and so it is useful to remind them often of the duty of man and citizen, and... to enflame their hearts with the zeal to imitate worthy people who lived before them. *Belisarius* is such a work... We sincerely admit that *Belisarius* has captured our hearts, and we are assured that this work will be pleasing to Your Right Reverence, because your thoughts, as well as virtue, are similar to those of Belisarius. (Marmontel' 1768: 1.3–4 verso)

This flattering dedication reads like an imperial edict which expresses the royal conviction that Gavriil's views are similar to Marmontel's. In this way the obligation to profess the worldview which so attracted the Empress was laid upon Gavriil, and together with this, the expectation that he would dress it up in words familiar to the Orthodox ear. He had to assimilate deistic religious toleration (as we have noted, in the context of eighteenth century

3. The Synthesis of Cultural and Linguistic Traditions

Russian autocracy, religious toleration was not an ideal of religious belief but a practical means of combating church independence). He was to preach civic duty and humbly concern himself with his flock's morality (for more detail see Sukhomlinov, I, 117–25). He was to present a version of Orthodoxy that could be integrated into Enlightenment discourse.

The question of how Gavriil carried out the empress' will and how this conformed to his devotion to Orthodox principles makes him one of the most paradoxical and at the same time deeply symbolic figures of the second half of the eighteenth century. No other eighteenth-century religious writer so consistently carried out a rapprochement between Christian teaching and Enlightenment ideology, asserting the unity of faith and reason, of divine providence and natural right. At the same time, while serving as one of the relgious grandees of Catherine's court, Gavriil remained an ascetic in his private life, and an advocate of monastic endeavor. His brilliant career proceded as if against his will, while his true spiritual desires were fully reflected in his support for monastic revival and a return to the patristic ascetic tradition. His literary works represent only his enlightenment aspect. His sermons and exegetical compositions are marked by rationalism and an emphatic absence of rhetorical embellishments, rare for the day. Gavriil's activity as member of the Commission to Compose a New Law Code and of the Russian Academy speak to his scholarly diligence and keep the mystical, monastic side of his life completely hidden.

Gavriil graduated the Moscow Slavono-Greco-Latin Academy in 1753 at the top of his class, but not desiring to take monastic vows, did not remain there, but requested the job of prosfornik (the one who prepares bread — *prosfira* or *prosfora* — for communion), so that he "would have a small bit of bread and always be near a church" (Titlinov 1916, 12–3). The church authorities, however, valued the existence of educated people too highly to allow them individual spiritual exploration. In 1758 Gavriil became a teacher in the Trinity Lavra Seminary and was almost forcibly brought to take monastic vows by the Lavra's Archimandrite Gedeon Krinovskii (for more on whom see below). Gedeon's protection guaranteed Gavriil's swift early rise. Right after his vows he became an hieromonk (ieromonkh) and rector of the seminary, and soon after that deputy (namestnik) of the Trinity Lavra. On August 8, 1761, he was appointed rector of the Slavono-Greco-Latin Academy and Archimandrite of the Zaikonospasskii Monastery. In this capacity he became known to Catherine, who evidently valued his erudtion and his knowledge of European languages (French and German), not all that common among the clergy, as well as his unusual breadth of views. The empress saw in him, in her words, a man who was "sharp and reasonable (rezonabel'nyi) and not an enemy of philosophy" (Znamenskii 1875, no. 4, 109). The young archimandrite seemed to Catherine to be a fitting candidate for the role of enlightenened hierarch, whose erudition and toleration would adorn the most liberal court in Europe, and whose strict piety would satisfy the expectations of the Orthodox population.

From then on Catherine herself took a hand in Gavriil's elevation. In 1763 he was named Bishop of Tver, in 1768 member of the Commission to Compose a New Law Code, in 1769 member of the Synod, and in 1770 he was named Archbishop of St. Petersburg and Revel (and simultaneously abbot of the Alexander Nevskii Monastery). Thus before the age of forty Gavriil occupied the most important archbishop's pulpit in Catherinean Russia. On January 1, 1775, he also took over administration of the Novgorod diocese (that was often combined with Petersburg's), and in 1783 was elevated to the rank of Metropolitan. He enjoyed the empresses' good graces all the way until her death, and for all that time was essentially the head of the Russian Church. As P. V. Znamenskii writes, "without upsetting anyone with unnecessary complaints and grumbling over the anticlerical spirit of the age and the violation of church rights, he put all of his energy into strengthening the inner power and means of the church... He strove to raise the moral character and education of the clergy under his care, and organized a Nevskii Seminary... The special object of his attention as archbishop were the monks, in whom he saw the mightiest power of the church" (Znamenskii 1875, no.8, 343).

Whatever Metroplitan Gavriil's private views, in his activity as a publicist he followed the directives of secular power, only modifying them slightly with his own views and tastes. In particular, if we turn to his sermons, we find in them rational moderation, summonses to fulfill one's civic duty, and very little of traditional Orthodox piety. It is indicative that in the foreword to the *Collection of Sermons for All Sundays and Holidays*, which he published together with Platon (Levshin) on Catherine's orders, it was asserted that "the service of God does not consist only in giving thanks and prayer, and in accomplishing the sacraments... but much more in teaching God's law..." (Gavriil and Platon I: l. 1). The priority accorded preaching that was declared here (as "moral admonition" needed by "all peoples and people of all walks of life") fully conformed to the rationalist religiosity of the Age of Enlightenment, and is quite far from Orthodox tradition (see § III–1).

The main thing that Gavriil tried to avoid was panegyrical brilliance, and this distinguishes his sermons from the usual homiletic production of the period. A significant portion of his sermons is limited to ethical issues, and sooner resemble moralistic tracts than examples of oratorical prose. This is true even of his panegyrical speeches in which generic requirements

3. The Synthesis of Cultural and Linguistic Traditions

were less strict, although rhetorical embellishment was one of their generic markers. Thus, for example, Gavriil dedicated the "Speech on Catherine's Name-Day" in 1777 to the theme of hamonizing man's will with God's. He says in it that striving for the common good and for harmony "directly relates to man's perfection... because here both feelings accord with reason and benefit with the benefit of others and intent with God's intent." In resolving the problem of theodicy he argues that "God would not be good if he did not connect bad consequences with bad acts," but he further discusses the impossibility for man to know genuine righteousness given the general imperfection of social life, in which the life of a righteous man "enters into the current of evilly intentioned people." This moralistic sentiment exhausts the speech's theological content. The most important thing for harmonizing man's will and God's is education, which allows people to absorb "the two shortest commandments: love God and your neighbor." Violating the divine order leads to the partial forgetting of these commandments, which "eternity" prescribes. Gavrill further includes a prayer, in which he asks "that we begin this [eternity] here, that the knowledge of this state [divine order] be practical." To this discussion Gavriil adds a few concluding phrases dedicated to the empress. He says that God "entrusted the preservation of his law, and by this our happiness, to our Most Pious Monarch" and that "Her cares, desires and labors" are directed toward the fulfillment of this task (Gavriil 1777, 2f). A panegyric is thus transformed into a moralistic exhortation.[47]

This lowering of style was clearly a conscious choice on Gavriil's part, and suggested a contrast for him between rhetorics and truth. A note was preserved among his papers that probably refers to his work as official preacher and panegyrist: "Forgive me, Most High One, if according to human custom I experienced desires in which my heart took not the smallest part" (RNB, Sobr. Peterb. Dukh. Akademii, no. 422, l. 1). The mantle of philosopher-hierarch and chcourtier-hierarch appear as a kind of decoration in the grandiose theater of Catherine's empire, summoned to hide and not

---

[47] In this context, Sumarokov's evaluation of Gavriil's art of preaching is understandable: "Gavriil, Archbishop of Petersburg, is more a composer of most intelligent philosophical dissertations than of public speeches; because he strives more for dissertation than for rhetorical figures it is impossible to compare him with other preachers. I will only say of him that the beauty of his smooth and imposing style earns fitting praise for his worthy name from the entire enlightened world, and that in posterity he will always be the honor of our age. Gavrill is like a river that fills its banks without noise and by orderly flow, never exceeding its borders" (Sumarokov, VI, 282–3). M. I. Sukhomlinov's judgement that "in his panegyrics Gavriil did not fully evade the rhetorical rut of that time" (Sukhomlinov, I, 103) is only true of a few of his panegyrical speeches which occupy a marginal place in his literary legacy.

reveal the true nature of the actor; this theater pretends to offer a complete picture of reality, and tries to subsume the real life that is taking place beyond its theatrical decorations. For as G. Florovskii writes, "for himself this magnificent and important Catherinean church leader... was a strict man of fasting, prayer, and an ascetic, and not only by intention, but in life" (Florovskii 1937, 123).

In this respect the best description of Gavriil comes from the notes of his cell-mate Feofan, later Archimandrite of the Kirillov-Novoezerskii Monastery (Feofan 1862). Through Feofan Gavrill was connected to the institution of *starchestvo* and in general to the entire developing movement of monastic renaissance, which he zealously supported. In his wide eparchy he rebuilt monasteries and chose abbots for them from among experienced aescetic monks. He held out for this against the Synod, which opposed his desire to fill these positions with unschooled monks (that is, those who had not had official academic training). In particular, he revived the well-known Valaam Monastery and saved the Moscow Simonov Monastery from closing. He affirmed communal living in monasteries and in 1796 compiled rules for such living, which he distributed thoughout the eparchy. At the same time he sent monasteries the books of Ioann Lestvichnik and Isaac the Syrian, fundamental works of Orthodox asceticism (Pokrovskii 1901, 503–8). With his direct support the *Dobrotoliubie* (Gr. *Philocalia*), translated by the elder Paisii Velichkovskii and overseen by Gavriil's order in the Alexander Nevskii and Trinity Lavras, was published in Moscow in 1793. This book more than any other determined the shape of Russian Orthodox spirituality for all succeeding decades. It is this ascetic image of Gavriil that casts a shadow of simulation or ambiguity on his image as an authoritative figure of the Catherinenan enlightenment, as well as on the entire official church culture of Catherine's reign.

This disconnect, this lack of any organic connection between the public and private spheres, not only makes Gavriil's image as sketched out from official sources deceptive, but also applies to Russian enlightenment culture as a whole as created and controlled by Catherine. It appears as a kind of mirage, but an imposed one, demanding the cooperation of everyone who came into contact with it. The church was just as drawn into this as was secular society, forced to find itself a place within the framework of the very same enlightenment mirage. As a result the religious hierarchy battled no longer for the church's independence, as in the Petrine period, but for its position *within* the state system, while keeping apart, as Gavriil put it, from "useless kicking against the pricks" (Sheremetevskii 1914a, 46). The very same Gavriil, serving on the Commission to Compose a New Law Code, achieved his main goal of acquiring special status for the clergy, separate from that of the "middle class" in which craftsmen and merchants were included, and immune to corporal punishment (actually, he only brought this to full completion under Paul). Striving to secure a place in the imperial order and, as possible, to compete with the nobility, the clergy had to assimilate at least the external signs of the reigning noble culture. These signs included, in particular, the new literary language, which had been worked out by the elite educational culture of the nobility. The court preacher had to speak the language, if not of secular society, than at least one that was pleasing and comprehensible to it. The unity of the literary language, having become an attribute of imperial standardization, also became an object of personal concern. In this way took shape the prerequisites for changing the language of religious literature, the merging of a special linguistic register of the literary tradition with the new type of literary language with its aspiration of universality.

3.1 The Evolution of the Language of Religious Literature

As we have seen (§ III–1.2), the changed conception of the literary language did not eliminate its opposition to Church Slavonic, but only modified the character of the opposition. Church Slavonic functioned primarily as the language of church books (Holy Writ and liturgy), in which markers of Church Slavonic were obligatory, whereas in the new literary language (Slavenorossiiskii), also based on church books, markers of Church Slavonic had a definitely optional character and might only appear for special stylistic ends. Thus in theory the language of secular culture was as close as possible to Church Slavonic but did not coincide with it (we are not speaking now of those aspects of the new literary language's normalization in which it was opposed to Church Slavonic, as these did not attract attention in discussions of secular versus religious languages). Having produced a new conception of the literary language, secular culture cleared the way for a cultural and linguistic synthesis of secular and religious traditions, for creating a new literary language as something universal. The language of the reigning culture was no longer that of the *Voyage to the Island of Love,* but an original synthesis which combined the linguistic heritage of Trediakovskii's novel with that of church books. It was this which aspired to the role of universal literary language for an enlightened Russian monarchy.

Chapter 3. The Changed Conception of the Literary Language

This situation posed a dilemma for religious literature. If Church Slavonic (as it was newly understood) was chosen as its vehicle, the borders between it and the new literary language would coincide with the separation between religious and secular literature. However, if religious literature chose a language which differed from that of church books, the borders between Church Slavonic (again, in the new understanding) and "Slavenorossiiskii" would be based on the opposition between the language of cult and that of culture (the latter combining religious and secular functions). The first solution was associated with clericalism, while the second had ample European precedent — this was the situation in France, and Germany was also moving in this direction in the eighteenth century, even in Catholic areas. Using Church Slavonic in the liturgy and Slavenorossiiskii in sermons and theological writings was analogous to the French having their liturgy in Latin and religious literature in French. Hence it was natural that Russia take the second route.

Most indicative of this development is the history of the language of homilies. Before the seventeenth century the sermon had been practically absent in Muscovite Russia; its place was taken by readings from the church fathers. In the seventeenth century, the Bogoliubtsy (Zealots of Piety) developed the sermon as an important weapon for propagandizing their ideas (cf. Zen'kovskii 1970, 133f), but this Great Russian trend was soon overtaken by sermons of the Ukrainian type. Without a long tradition, the sermon did not become an everyday activity of every priest, as it was, for example, in France and Poland, but a special activity by the learned clergy. In contrast to Vilnius, L'vov and Kiev, where sermons in a language accessible to the local population had prime importance in the battle between the Orthodox and Uniate churches, in Great Russia the sermon might not so much serve the religious enlightenment of the audience as demonstrate the pastor's own sophistication. In any case the sermon was part of educated culture, and for a long time preserved an association with recently introduced scholarly religious pursuits that contrasted with traditional piety.

In these circumstances, it was natural that the language for sermons in Russia be Church Slavonic, and moreover its standard variety, that as a rule revealed the grammatical art of the orator. This was one of the significant factors that preserved the situation in which Church Slavonic served as the single language of culture. In particular, it is indicative that in Moscow Ioannikii Galiatovskii's sermons, written in the Ukrainian "simple tongue," were translated into Church Slavonic (Kharlampovich 1914, 435; Uspenskii 1983, 91). Also written in standard Church Slavonic were Simeon Polotskii's

3. The Synthesis of Cultural and Linguistic Traditions

sermons that to a significant degree clearly shaped the later Russian tradition of homiletics.[48]

The book of sermons called *Statir*, written by an unknown clergyman from Perm in 1683–84, eloquently testifies to how this tradition was formed (RGB, Rumiants. 411; about this text, see: Vostokov 1842, 629–33; Sukhominov 1908, 434–8; Alekseev 1965; Uspenskii 1983, 116–8). In the foreword to the book, the author writes that the educational works available at this time were too complex for his provincial audience. This refers both to traditional translated works (for example, the sermons of St. Ioann Zlatoust [John Chrysostom]) as well as to new and original ones (for example, those of the highly esteemed Simeon Polotskii). Zlatoust's writing was "very incomprehensible, not only for the audience but also for those [priests] who read him, because the people who live in this area [are] very simple; not only laymen, but also clergymen, regarded Zlatoust's writing as if it were composed in a foreign language" (l. 5 verso) Similarly, "the language of the *Obed* and *Vercheria* [books of sermons] by the industrious and most wise Father Simeon Polotskii sounds like the height of erudition to the least educated people and is not understood by those rude in reason" (l. 5–5 verso). At the same time, linguistic analysis of the author's own language shows that he makes no conscious deviations from traditional Church Slavonic usage (Zhivov 1991). He consistently uses simple preterits, in proportions typical for traditional as opposed to hybrid usage, and tries to avoid the variativity characteristic of the hybrid language, although he is unable to normalize his language in accord with the standard grammatical approach. At the same time, there are no grounds for connecting his declarations about "simplicity" with the elementary nature of the author's sermons, either in terms of their rhetoric or content, as do Sukhomlinov and Uspenskii (Sukhomlinov 1908, 437; Uspenskii 1983, 117). The author's desire for simplicity and accessibility remains declarative, motivated by the fact that he does not feel himself capable of fully reproducing the learned, bookish language in which books are published in the capital. "Simplicity" here serves as just another way of describing the author's relative lack of education. [...] It is all the more indicative that he considers it necessary to write in the

---

[48] This is suggested in particular by the specific statistical distribution of new and old endings of *o*-declension nouns in plural oblique cases (the greatest number of new inflextions in the instr. pl., the least in the dat. pl., with the loc. pl. occupying an intermediate position) that are found in Simeon's sermons and then repeated in homiletic literature for more than half a century. The adoption of such practices may only be explained in terms of specific written routines tied to a particular genre, when one cohort of preachers reads and assimilates the linguistic properties of texts created by the previous generation (see Zhivov 1993, 95, 103; Zhivov 1995, 74–7).

standard bookish language, and sees his own work as an innovation oriented on educated models. Indeed the very idea of preaching rather than reading from the Prologue[49] was perceived as a novelty that came into conflict with traditional piety. The author tells how he got the idea of compiling a book of sermons: "I heard how in Russia in many cities very wise clergymen recite sermons (poucheniia) that they improvise on their own (ot ust) and do not read from books, and people very happily listen with great amazement. For Kiril Stavromeniiskii[50] in his book praises oral teaching very much, although because there are so few wise teachers in the church people are forced to read aloud from books. Thus I took him as a model, wanting to attract listeners…" (l. 5). The author was clearly attracted by the new phenomenon in Russian religious life, ready to follow the example of the Ukrainian author and to see himself as an innovator. This innovation led to clashes with his congregation and with other clergymen, in part recalling the persecutions to which Ivan Neronov and Archpriest Avvakum had been subjected in their day. To describe this conflict a different imaginative framework was selected — the opposition of knowledge and ignorance, enlightenment and error. […] Thus at the end of the seventeenth century a preacher could only act as a reformer, entering into confrontation with the ignorant mob.

Insofar as homiletics was an educated innovation, the language of sermons necessarily had to be Church Slavonic. The voices that called for the comprehensibility and accessibility of religious pedagogical texts in the second half of the seventeenth century had in mind not an opposition between Church Slavonic and Russian, but between rhetorically adorned language (in sermons made complex by Baroque "concetti") and language without such adornment (§ 0–5). Several times St. Dimitrii Rostovskii finished his sermons with an apostrophe to his unlettered listeners, offering them a special additional statement which presents a summary of the moral of the sermon. In one of them he says: "I think that not everyone will be able to keep what I have said in their memory (pamiatstvovati) except for the learned (kniznyi); the simple and unlearned will go away without benefit. So I will say something for them worth keeping in memory in a way they will understand (pamiati dostoino)" (Dimitrii Rostovskii, I, l.51 verso). Analogously, in a sermon on August 19, 1701: "It is already… time to end with an 'Amen'… but… I think… that everything I, a sinner, have said was not intelligible to the unschooled, and I fear they will go away without profit, and I do not want to

---

[49] A collection of saints' lives and edificatory stories geared to the church calendar. (Translator's note)

[50] The author of the Statir evidently had in mind Kirill Trankvillion-Stavrovetskii and his *Uchitel'noe evangelie*.

3. The Synthesis of Cultural and Linguistic Traditions

appear as a bombastic orator but as a useful teacher, so I will say something short for the profit of the simplest people" (ibid, V, 1.56 verso). After these statements follow texts in correct Church Slavonic, stripped, however, of Baroque rhetorical devices. Thus standard Church Slavonic remained the basis for homiletic practice.

The situation changed during the Petrine period, and is connected first of all with the activity of Feofan Prokopovich. After Feofan's move from Kiev to Great Russia the language of his sermons gradually changed from standard Church Slavonic to hybrid (for more detail, see Kutina 1981 and 1982; Zhivov 1985a; cf. § I–2.2). In his language appear variations in the inflection of nouns and adjectives, as well as variations in lexical and morphonological correlatives; dual forms disappear (except for lexicalized ones); the use of aorist and imperfective is lessened; participles lacking in agreement (gerunds) appear; syntax is simplified, etc. — all of which are characteristics of hybrid Church Slavonic. But however powerful the process of simplification may have been, the language remained Church Slavonic, which is unquestionably attested by the same simple past tense forms, by the use of active participles of the type *видяй, изволивый*, by the use of dative absolute, and so on. Having assimilated hybrod Church Slavonic as the main language for his sermons, Feofan subsequently moved to a less refined variety of that language, away from one in which, in particular, simple preterits were used relatively often and remained the principle means of expressing the past tense, to a language in which these forms only occurred occasionally, and only when motivated by theme or composition.

The movement toward comprehensibility and simplicity which Feofan clearly instigated did not, however, take the sermon beyond the realm of Church Slavonic, and the fact that it was used consistently in sermons was fully conscious. Feofan actually could have written in the "simple" (i.e., not Church Slavonic) language; for him the "simple" language was connected with the absence of those very marks of bookishness he preserved in the sermons (see the discussion of his editing of the *History of Peter the Great*, § I–1.3). For Feofan standard Church Slavonic, hybrid Church Slavonic, and the "simple" tongue were functionally distributed — standard as the language of cult and scholarly theological tracts, hybrid for sermons and religious literature aimed at a wide audience, and the "simple" as the language of secular literature (see Zhivov 1985a, 78–81). One cannot help but see in this division a realization of the opposition of civic and secular that was a basic element of Petrine cultural policy (§ I–1.2).

This functional distribution of languages that was certainly quite purposeful clearly demonstrates that the Slavonic grammatical elements in Feofan's sermons were not the accidental vestiges of the former tradition but, on the contrary, quite intentional, placed in the text to define its linguistic register. It is therefore methodologically incorrect to consider these determining markers of bookishness on the same level as variations that are irrelevant for defining the language such as mixed endings in noun declensions or pleophonic and non-pleophonic forms. Each sermon must be analyzed as a whole (excluding quotations), and not as fragments, and in this whole the first task is to identify the markers of the linguistic register. Otherwise even the most detailed linguistic analysis may lead to mistaken results.[51] Thus L. Kjellberg, analyzing a fragment of Prokopovich's sermon of March 1, 1725, writes: "In this specimen of pompous rhetoric the language is not yet free... of the heavy dross of Slavonic. Aorists and imperfects have disappeared in favor of preterits in -л-, but auxiliary Slavonic words like *аки* and *паче* are kept as well as participles of the type *раждшiй* and *сый* with which the language is riddled. It is true that one finds a Russian ending in the dative pl., in *по лѣтам,* but the regular Slavonic inflection in *добрiи Россiйстiи сынове*" (Kjellberg 1957, 14). Yet simple preterits are encountered in the sermons as a whole. A piecemeal examination and lack of discrimination between relevant and irellevent markers for distinguishing linguistic registers leads Kjellberg to characterize Prokopovich's language as "Russian with distinct Slavonic contributions" (ibid, 18). A differential analysis supports L. L. Kutina's conclusion that the language of his sermons is "simple Slavonic" (see Kutina 1981, 44; Kutina 1982, 8).

It is possible that it was directly due to Feofan's practice that the language of Russian sermons after the 1730's (or even somewhat earlier) became hybrid Church Slavonic. Although the concrete material remains almost completely unexamined from a linguistic perspective, selective analysis indicates that in all sermons of the period there is a definite merging of genetically Russian and genetically Church Slavonic elements in areas which are neutral insofar as the juxtaposition between the bookish and non-bookish markers is concerned, and at the same time, a series of marked Church Slavonic elements used to demonstrate bookishness place the text within the bounds of Church Slavonic (see § 0–2). The mechanism used to create texts in hybrid Church Slavonic allows for a high degree of variability, both on the level of the concrete correlation between marks of bookishness and the neutral background, and, within the framework of this neutral background,

---

[51] Such an approach, which in addition substitutes general impressions for concrete analysis, results in the kind of crude and improbable description that we find, for example, in E. Budde, who writes that "Feofan Prokopovich ... despite his religious rank, wrote and gave sermons in an almost conversational Russian" (Budde 1908, 50).

3. The Synthesis of Cultural and Linguistic Traditions

also on the level of the relation between grammatically normative and non-normative, old and new forms. This is also evident in the sermons of this period. Indeed, among them one encounters those in which marked Church Slavonic elements (markers of bookishness) occur in almost eveny sentence, as well as those in which such elements only occur occasionally, in a few cases, functioning not as a regular grammatical feature but as the semiotic marker of register.

I will cite several examples. I will begin with Dimitrii Sechenov's sermon on Annunciation, 1742. The use of the aorist and imperfect in this semon is constant and not connected with any definite thematic, compositional or stylistic purpose, cf. *ожидаху, желаху* (Dimitrii Sechenov 1743, 4); aorists *откыся, познася* (3); *видѣ слыша, видѣша, пріиде, бысть, явися, избра, дарова, созда* (4); *видѣ* (5); *содѣла* (7); *избавлени быхомъ* (12); etc, The 2nd pers. sg. л-forms are used with copula, i.e, are regular perfective forms: *сподобилася еси* (8), *даровала еси, наслѣдовала еси* (11). Notably, л-forms make up only somewhat more than 50% of all past tense forms, that is, significantly less than in Feofan's later sermons. Present participles of the type *изволяй* (6) and *творяй* (7) are encountered. Specific features of bookish language appear such as relative clauses with *иже*: *ихже око не видѣ* (5) *иже созда* (8). Exclamations are used as a constant rhetorical device, and the exclamatory genitive regularly occurs, e.g., *О несказанныя Божія къ человѣку любви!* (4), *О чудесе новаго...* (9). The dative absolute is also met: *церьковъ Россійская... прославлялася, братіи нашей православнымъ хрїстїаномъ подъ рукою агарянскою и еретическою сущимъ...* (12) For the functioning of the aorist as a mark of bookishness (lacking in properly grammatical significance), its use in a series of coordinated verbal forms together with л-forms is indicative, cf. the sequence of coordinated verbs like *погубилъ, отдася, подпаде, огорчилъ, прогнѣвалъ, попралъ, попралъ, презрѣлъ, вмѣнилъ* (5) or *собралъ, вручи* (12), etc. There also occur variations according to non-relevant markers. Instr. pl.: *усты* (4, 10), *съ скоты, звѣрьми, и гады* (5), *дѣлы* (12), *надъ враги* (12), *дарами* (10), *трудами* (16). Prep. pl.: *печалѣхъ* (10), *ушесѣхъ* (13), *по мракахъ* (4), *ущербахъ* (11). I will also mention a pleophonic form: *головы поотрубали* (16), although non-pleophonic forms are the norm. To varying non-relevant indicators belong infinitival markers: *сказать* (3), *видѣти, пожити, изчислити, измѣрити* (4), *быть, описати* (5), *знать* (9), *истребить, испразднить, отгнать* (13), etc. These variations clearly are not accidental mistakes, but indicate the hybrid language of the sermons.[52] The same variability of the hybrid language may be seen in Kirill Florinskii's speech on Empress Elizabeth's birthday, December 18, 1742 (Kirill Florinskii 1741; cf. Kjellberg 1957: 15–16).

Amvrosii Iushkevich's sermons are of another kind. Marked Church Slavonic elements are limited to a very small number and play a purely symbolic role. As an example, I will analyze his sermon on the interment of Anna Ioannovna of December 23, 1740. Of the relevant markers, imperfects are completely absent. Aorist forms are only used in four cases and are motivated by standard contexts for internment speeches: *[Импратрица] отыде въ горнюю къ Отцу Небесному обитель* (Vnutrennii byt, I, 479), *благоутробія мати ваша скончася, тріумфальныхъ побѣдъ вашихъ лаври и торжествъ россійскихъ вѣнцы мразомъ смерти увядоша* (480), *столпъ крѣпости отъ лица вражія разрушися* (480). Forms of the 2nd pers. sg. perfect with copula occur several times: *погружалъ еси (двоеглавый орле)* (480), *превозносилася еси* (481), *наказалъ еси* (482), *утѣшилъ еси* (483), *опечалилъ еси* (483), *опредѣлилъ еси* (483).[53] Together with relative clauses with *который*, clauses with *иже* are also used: *всепресвѣтлѣйшее солнце твое, въ немъ же зѣницы твоя погружалъ еси* (480), *императора Іоанна, его же въ вѣчномъ совѣтѣ опредѣлилъ еси царствовать надъ нами* (483). In one place a striking syntactical Grecianism is used, a construction *яко* + infinitive in the function of a consecutive subordinate clause: *...и толико побѣдами благополучными, прославилась, яко исполнится на ней словесам Духа Святого* (481; cf. Issatchenko 1980, 87). A genitive of exclamation occurs several times: *О вѣсти печалнѣйшія!* (479), *О прежесточайшія и неуврачуемыя язвы сердецъ нашихъ!* (480). In the sphere of markers not relevant for juxtaposing languages there is significant variability: dat. pl.: *монастырямъ* (479), *словесамъ* (481), *врагомъ* (480,

---

[52] Only unfamiliarity with the language of homiletic literature and lack of linguistic background may explain G. P. Blok's assertion in the commentary to Lomonosov's "Gimn borode" [Hymn to the Beard] that "Dimitrii's style of oratory, close to conversational language, often fell into the most vulgar popular speech" (Lomonosov, VIII[2], 1076). The example of "vulgar popular speech" cited from Sechenov's sermon — "слово отрыгнем Царице Матери" (Lomonosov, ibid; Dimitrii Sechenov 1743, 12) — strikingly illustrates the arbitrary nature of attempts to characterize linguistic elements based on modern notions of vulgarity. This phrase is a quotation from the first line of the first song of the canon for Annunciation, and *отрыгнем* is a normal Church Slavonic verb that has no popular connotations whatsoever (see Sreznevskii, II, col. 767; SRIa, XIV, 24–5). In the last analysis, Blok's statement was shaped by the grouping together of "indecent" and "popular" which derives from French purism of the mid-eighteenth century and has no connection at all to Sechenov's language (cf. § III–1.3). [...]

[53] The last four examples are not very significant insofar as they are used in address to God and may thus be seen as a marker of prayer within the sermon, that is, they function as a kind of specially marked "alien speech" that deviates from the usual texture of the sermon.

3. The Synthesis of Cultural and Linguistic Traditions

483). Instr. pl.: *громами* (480), *падежами* (480), *съ... грады* (480), *дѣлы* (481). Adjectival endings, normative for Church Slavonic, are relatively stable, although despite the dominating gen. sg. fem. ending *-ыя/-ия* we find *отъ которой* (482). In general, infinitives in *-тъ* are used (*печалиться* [479], *плакать* [480], *прославлять* [481], etc.), although there are also infinitives in *-ти* (*свидѣтельствовати* [481], *исполнитися* [481]). Short active participles are used without agreement (as gerunds), moreover together with the neutral affixes *-а/-я* and *-вши* are met the specifically bookish *-вше*; thus with a sg. masc. subject *потерпѣвше* (479), sg. fem. *оставя* (479), *бывше* (482), *пріобретше* (482), *вѣдая* (482); pl. *видя* (483). Forms of the vocative are used rather consistently (*орле* [480], *граде* [480], *невѣсто* [480]), although the nominative may also occur in address (*церковь* [480]).

The same linguistic features appear in Amvrosii's sermon on Empress Elizabeth's birthday, December 18, 1741, although the proportion of marked Church Slavonic elements is smaller and the proportion of genetic Slavonicisms among non-relevant markers is noticeably larger. In this rather lengthy text forms of the aorist are encountered only three times, at the start and ending of the sermon: *тогда пріиде Давідъ* (Amvrosii Iushkevich 1741, 4), *но не восхотѣхъ ему ни единаго зла сотворити* (5), *яко рука Господня укрѣпи мя* (16). Forms of the 2nd pers. sg. perfect with copula appear only in the prayer concluding the sermon: *даровалъ еси, обрадовалъ еси* (16). Genitive of exclamation occurs several times: *О нашего неблагополуія!* (5), *О радости! О торжества несказаннаго!* (12). *Иже* — constructions are not encountered, and an active participle occurs one time (*владѣй* [6]). One might possibly consider the pronouns *мя* (3), *тебе* (acc., 4), *ю* (16), etc., as marked Church Slavonic elements (although the first person personal sg. pronoun is only *я*), and one could also include here functional words of the type *аще, ово... ово*, etc. Indicators of the Church Slavonic register proper are limited to these. In the sphere of non-relevant markers we find broad variablilty and it involves all noun inflections. Thus, for example, instr. pl. *грѣхами* (3), *образы* (4), *врагами* (5), *дѣлами* (7), *потомками* (7), *дарами* (7), *трудами* (7, 12). *словами* (7), *солдатами* (12), *потомками* (13), *претекстами* (14), *печальми* (4), *учительми* (9), *родительми* (9), etc. In adjectival endings in the presence of the stable *-аго/-яго* in gen.-acc. sg. masc. and neut., in the nom.-acc. sg. masc. occur the variation: *который* (3, 11), *истинный* (3), *дикой и незнаемой* (7), *Россійскій* (7), *Россійской* (8), *морскій* (7), *неславный* (9), *темный* (9), *иностранной* (13), *незнаемой* (13), etc. The same with gen,. sg. fem.: *живыя* (4), *всякія* (4), *своея* (7), *послѣднѣй* (7), *всякой* (9), *самыя блаженныя* (9), etc. Infinitival forms are just as variable: *толковать* (3), *запамятовать* (3), *сыскаться* (3), *сказать*

(3), *взяти* (4), *воспитати* (4), *научити* (4), *мстити* (5), *удивлятися* (5), *владѣть* (6), *забывать* (7), *промышлять* (8), etc. Lexical morphological markers also vary, for example, pleophonic and non-pleophonic forms: *здравїе* (4), *главы* (4), *гласы* (6), *головами* (10), *голову* (13), *глада* (13), *гладомъ* (13,15), *кратко* (13), *головы* (15), etc.[54]

These more or less contrasting examples may serve to demonstrate the linguistic heterogeneity which hybrid Church Slavonic demonstrated in the homiletic literature of the 1730's and 40's. As far as I can judge from the material with which I am familiar, marked Church Slavonic elements which indicate the linguistic register of the sermons are universally attested, as are variations in the sphere of non-relevant indicators. The proportions, however, fluctuate, and these fluctuations describe a weakly differentiated continuum whose diapason was suggested by the examples we analyzed. It is possible that certain lines of continuity will be able to be isolated, and that the choice of this or that type of hybrid Church Slavonic will be shown to be more than simply fortuitous. This, however, requires special research. Together with the extreme cases, one may also cite many examples of an intermediate character.

To such intermediate texts belong, for example, the sermons of Grand Prince Peter Fedorovich's tutor in Divine law, Simon Todorskii. In his sermon on the occasion of the Grand Prince's birthday on February 10, 1743, we may observe a relatively high proportion of marked Church

---

[54] In principle, the concentration of the basic markers of bookishness at the start and end of a work and their almost complete absence in the middle allow us to see it as bilingual. In this case one may consider what is happening in Amvrosii's sermon as switching linguistic codes, hybrid Church Slavonic alternating with Russian (which is significantly Slavonicized in the sphere of non-relevant markers). Church Slavonic is used at the beginning and end of the sermon, where the Biblical story of David and Saul is presented, and which includes a general moral teaching and a prayer addressed to God. Russian is used in the middle, where the history of the recent palace coup that brought Elizabeth to the throne (on November 25, 1741) is told, and from the perspective of an eyewitness. The change in the narrator's position may be seen to motivate the change in linguistic code, a mechanism that is known in literary monuments of the sixteenth and seventeenth centuries (see Uspenskii 1983, 46–9; Zhivov and Uspenskii 1983, 162–4). The complex character of this text led L. Kjellberg into error (1957, 18). He characterizes Amvrosii's language as "Russian with weak Slavonic contribution" and asserts (as the material above indicates, without sufficient basis) that "Amvrosii speaks the normal Russian literary language of his time; it hardly includes more Slavonicisms than that of secular writers of the same epoch" (16). As we have shown, in the given era neither Lomonosov nor Trediakovskii used Church Slavonic elements as markers of linguistic register, while in the sphere of non-relevant markers there was significantly more normalization by the late 1730's than we see in Amvrosii. Amvroisii's later sermon on Elizabeth's coronation of 1743 (Amvrosii Iushkevich 1744) testifies to his lack of interest in reformed ideas on language. While the dominant form of expressing the past tense here is the *л*-form (more than 80%), fairly common simple preterits unambiguously indicate hybrid Church Slavonic.

3. The Synthesis of Cultural and Linguistic Traditions

Slavonic elements on the background of rather broad variations in the sphere of non-relevant markers. In a series of cases we meet imperfectives: *смиряху* (Simon Todorskii 1743, 6), *озлобляху* (6), *бываху* (6), *насильствоваху* (6), *укрѣпляхуся* (6), *освѣтише* (11), *предлагахъ Его Высочеству* (14). Aorists are also used: *пристави* (6), *рече* (7), *бысть* (17), *якоже вкрацѣ показася* (17). I also note the pronoun *яже* (9), the participle *сый* (12), and the athematic declension *имамы рещи* (6, 10). The variativity of the neutral background material is clearly reflected in noun declensions: dat. pl.: *неправедникамъ* (3), *кедрамъ* (4), *дѣламъ* (6), *праведникамъ* (6), *сыномъ* (6), *княземъ* (8, 9), *лицамъ* (8), *бѣсомъ* (11); cf. also in the coordinated constructions *неправедникамъ, ябедникамъ, донощикамъ и безсовѣстнымъ представителемъ* (7), *дѣтемъ и наслѣдникамъ* (8). Instr. pl.: *зубы* (4), *обрядами* (5), *регламентами* (7), *указами* (7), *титлами* (11), *съ Кабинетъ-министрами и Генералами Фельдмаршалами* (12), *неудобствами* (13), *резонами* (14), *сѵмволами* (15) (the ending *-ами* is close to the normative). Prep. pl.: *туманахъ* (3), *дворѣхъ* (4), *дѣлѣхъ* (6), *глазахъ* (7), *наслѣдникахъ* (8, 13), *праведникахъ* (8), *дѣлахъ* (9, 10), *лѣтахъ* (11), *судѣхъ* (11), *репортахъ* (14), *государствахъ* (14). There is a similarly strong variability in infinitival markers: *уязвити* (3), *потрафить* (3), *заклати* (4), *повредиться* (4), *множитися* (4, bis), *искоренити* (4), *признать* (4), *умножати* (4), *сохраняти* (4), *изъимати* (4), etc. Cf. also in parallel constructions: *уничтожать и искореняти* (8), *наставити и обучить* (8). Short participles are used without subject agreement, cf. with sg. masc. *привыкнувши* (8), *возлюбивши* (9), with pl. *устрашаяся* (7), *шествуя* (9), etc.[55]

This sort of data allows us to assert that the introduction of hybrid Church Slavonic into homiletic literature by Feofan Prokopovich (together, evidently, with Gavriil Buzhinskii) created a tradition that was followed by later religious orators. This new tradition clearly had both cultural-linguistic as well as literary motives. Among the first include the status of the hybrid language itself. On the one hand this was a special ecclesiastic language which

---

[55] The proportion of marked Church Slavonic elements is even higher in another of his sermons, on the marriage of Petr Fedorovich and Catherine, presented on August 25, 1745 (Simon Todorskii 1745). Here is some data on the markers of bookishness (in the sphere of non-relevant markers the picture is more or less analogous to that of the sermon of 1743). Here we find aorists: избра (5), бысть (5, 10), благослови (5), рече (7), возвысися (5), умножишася (5), возревноваша (5), прїидоша (6), рѣша (6), спаде (7), возлюбленъ бѣ (8), выну бѣ сходящее (8), остави (13); and a perfect with auxiliary verb: подвигнулся еси (7). On the whole, forms of the imperfect, aorist and perfect with auxiliary make up more than 26% of all past tenses. I also note the forms: азъ Россїянинъ сый (9), имамы рещи (8), еже речено бысть (10), егда (4, 9), аще (3, 10), абїе (11).

was juxtaposed to the language of worldly literature which was perceived at the time as specifically secular. On the other hand, the hybrid language, as already noted (§ 0–5), was the closest thing to a candidate for a popular, accessible language that still maintained its connection with the religious literary tradition. We should recall that during this period the sermon still belonged primarily to cathedrals and churches of the capitol cities, and that their audience mostly consisted of representatives of the new secularized culture, that Europeanized nobility which, according to Sumarokov's testimony, called church books "not Russian" (1748, 7). Therefore the choice of the hybrid language might have been conditioned by the desire to at least partially cater to the linguistic tastes of the audience.

The literary tradition that arose in this context was directly modeled on Prokopovich's sermons. One may find direct echoes of his images, rhetorical structures and themes in the most diverse preachers of the epoch, for example, in Amvrosii Iushkevich when he enumerates Peter the Great's achievements (Amvrosii Iushkevich 1741, 7–9; cf. Feofan Prokopovich I, 111f; II, 147f.), or in Simon Todorskii, when he alludes to Prokopovich when he says that the ancient pagans would have considered Catherine a goddess (Simon Todorskii 1745, 10; cf. Feofan Prokopovich, II, 140) or writes that Elizabeth "was as close to death as the cannonball which fell at her feet" (Simon Todorskii 1745, II — an allusion to the well-known image of Peter's hat with the bullet hole in Prokopovich's "Sermon on the Battle of Poltava" of 1717 — Feofan Prokopovich I, 158; see the quote in § I–2.2). New linguistic or historical and cultural stimuli were needed to shake the authority of a tradition which had become so well established.

Such stimuli appeared in the 1750's, when the struggle against clericalism was no longer relevant, when the reigning Europeanized culture had asserted a monopoly over enlightenment and the Russian literary language was reconceptualized as "Slavenorossiiskii," standing in the closest possible proximity to "the church language." The possibilities for homiletic literature which this new situation opened up were first grasped by the young monk (ierodiakon) and student of theology at the Moscow academy Gedeon Krinovskii. Thanks to his eloquence he was appointed court preacher on January 8, 1753, when he was not yet 30.

Gedeon's brilliant career was rather unusual but very indicative of an era when the ability to grasp the latest cultural fashions and put them into action could open up the way to the highest positions in capital society, a society as yet without fixed traditions and eager to accept and follow those adept in expressing new ideals and cultural prescriptions. After he graduated from the seminary in Kazan, Gedeon took monastic vows and remained there

3. The Synthesis of Cultural and Linguistic Traditions

as a teacher. In 1751 he left Kazan for Moscow, where he was able to enter the Moscow Academy. As a student there he attracted attention as a preacher. He was appreciated by I. I. Shuvalov, who recommended him to the Empress. His appointment as court preacher was the first step in his quick ascent. In 1758 be became member of the Synod and almost immediately thereafter archimandrite of Russia's leading monastery, the Trinity-Sergius Lavra. In 1761 he was ordained Bishop of Pskov and gave up his post as court preacher. In 1763 he took sick while on the road to Pskov and died on June 22 (see: Titov 1907; Seremetevskii 1914). P. V. Znamenskii describes Gedeon as "a lively and emancipated monk, and a court one as well, obliged for everything to the secular power which had so elevated him above his brethren.. And he lived like a grandee" (Znamenskii 1875, no. 2, 106). Toward the end of his life, Gedeon, despite his youth, was probably the single most influential church hierarch. The two most important church figures of Catherine's reign, Petersburg Metropolitan Gavriil Petrov and Moscow Metropolitan Platon Levshin, both owed their early advancement to his patronage.

Gedeon's first brilliant steps were tied to his sermons. How did he transform the sermon to ensure himself such success? Today's reader will not be struck by his sermons' absorbing presentation, depth of thought, or heightened spirituality. But for his contemporaries Gedeon's style was distinctly different from the rhetorical embellishments of previous religious orators. Platon Levshin wrote that it was as if his listeners "were beside themselves and were afraid that he would stop speaking" (Seremetevskii 1914, 325). Sumarokov also considered Gedeon deserving of praise (VI, 281).[56] P. V. Znamenskii writes: "Society was pleasantly struck by his new ways, which were so completely alien to the methods of the old, Kievan school, and all those rhetorical ornaments and conceits of argumentation, comparisons and tropes... which strike one so unpleasantly in the speech of previous preachers, not excluding... Feofan Prokopovich. His clarity and simplicity of thought, lively fantasy, precise and simple style which were accessible and comprehensible to the least educated listener... captivated his entire audience" (1875, no. 2, 105).

---

[56] Sumarokov wrote that "Gedeon is the Russian Fléchier; he is even more colorful than Feofan; it is unfortunate that there was little strength and fire in him, and that for lack of fervor he often filled his sermons with anecdotes and fables, the poor stock of true eloquence. Agreeability, gentleness, subtlety were his traits, and after Feofan, the devastated Russian Parnassus or church, deprived of rhetorical sweetness due to the death of the great archbishop, delighted Russia with this Gedeon, a man of great merit in oratory" (Sumarokov, VI, 281). Sumarokov thus skips over the entire period from Feofan to Gedeon as unproductive, with Gedeon serving as the continuer of the tradition Feofan founded.

These descriptions correspond in large measure to what Gedeon said of himself (and it is possible that they were formulated under the influence of Gedeon's own declarations). In the foreword "To the Reader" he wrote:

> The author agrees with the opinion stated in one of Seneca's works that both the one who speaks and the one who listens must have a single intent; that is, one should act and the other be acted upon; one should not try to do anything besides presenting people what one has in mind to say in as intelligible a way as possible. And since among the people there are always some who are simple and unlearned, for whom sermons in high style are difficult or impossible to understand, in order to put one's intentions into action one must necessarily take steps to make one's words easily comprehensible to even the most unlettered of the simple folk (Gedeon Krinovskii, I, foreword, 1.5 verso)

Similar reasoning may be found in Gedeon's admonitions to young priests that he included in the last volume of his sermons. Although there he is concerned with rhetorical structure, he likely also had in mind his own linguistic practice when he wrote:

> ...Everyone knows how very few Russian authors there are in print in our fatherland that could serve as an example for you, without mentioning that some of those should not only not be imitated by you, the young, but are also hard to understand for mature minds; but here you will find a style without added profundities and frills with which you can bring benefit to the people to whom you have dedicated yourself. I never tried to tether myself overmuch to rhetoric, but where she herself wanted to serve the word of God, I used her... I only regret that so many people keep silent because they are unable to speak eloquently, and so the benefit which the people could get is lost from sermons even though not written in oratorical manner. Others demand several months to prepare for one sermon... Moreover I am not saying that you should not zealously apply yourself to rhetoric... But I do not condone constrained rhetoric, that which in Latin is called *affectata*; for the moment I can show you the easiest image, until little by little you can ascend higher and to perfection itself. And I further admonish you, that you prefer benefit to the church above that which might come from eloquence. (Gedeon Krinovskii, IV, foreword, 1. 4–4 verso)[57]

Here Gedeon gives a characteristic appraisal of the earlier (Church Slavonic) literary tradition as "hard to understand," which is directly analogous to Feofan Prokopovich's opinion (§ I–2.1); at the same time, as with Feofan, criticism of the past serves as a natural counterpart to his own innovation.

As is well known, such declarations as Gedeon's were not something new in the history of Russian homiletics (see § 0–5). Simeon Polotskii had

---

[57] See also Gedeon's attack on proponents of rhetoric in relgious oratory in his sermon on the twenty-first week after the Descent of the Holy Spirit (Gedeon Krinovskii, IV, 81).

3. The Synthesis of Cultural and Linguistic Traditions

called for simplicity (1681, l. 7 verso), and so had Prokopovich (in his *Rhetoric, Spiritual Regulation*, and other works; cf. Kochetkova 1974). Summonses such as these, for all their lack of concreteness and indistinct formulation, were in each instance not only connected to a reevaluation of the previous tradition but a reevaluation of the character of its language as well. Indeed in both cases cited above summonses to simplicity contained the rudiments of particular linguistic programs: for Simeon Polotskii this was a rejection of rhetorically embellished and grammatically refined language in favor of unadorned language (a choice between adorned and unadorned within the framework of standard Church Slavonic), while for Prokopovich it was a rejection of standard Church Slavonic in favor of the hybrid variety. Gedeon's declarations also advocated a certain linguistic agenda that indicated a break with previous tradition.

The innovative linguistic character of Gedeon's sermons was first noted by Filaret Gumilevskii, who wrote that "In reference to his language he no longer follows the example of previous preachers but uses the popular tongue, augmenting it with the liturgical; his word endings, inflection, and syntax are all Russian" (1884, 332). This switch from hybrid Church Slavonic to Russian was achieved, as in the history of the language of secular writing (§ I–1.1), by excluding from texts those very markers of bookishness which had earlier been introduced to indicate its Church Slavonic character. In the context of rejecting rhetorical complexity, excluding marked Church Slavonic elements may be understood in principle as testimony to their new conceptualization, not as indicators of linguistic register but as elements of an elevated (affected) style. If we accept this point of view, it turns out that Gedeon's linguistic position precisely accords with those of the secular authors of his time (§ III–1.2), and it is possible that he acted under the influence of their ideas.[58]

---

[58] L. Kjellberg disputes Filaret's opinion, suggesting that Gedeon was not an innovator, but simply developed the trend that Feofan had begun, the gradual replacement of Church Slavonic with Russian; in Kjellberg's opinion, this replacement was motivated by the rejection of Baroque and the corresponding stylistic simplification (see Kjellberg 1957, 43). [...] As discussed earlier, in my opinion Kjellberg does not distinguish markers relevant for the opposition between Russian and Church Slavonic from those that allow free variation in both Russian and Church Slavonic texts. Filaret Gumilevskii is more sensitive to changes in language, evidently because to some extent he still shared the old linguistic consciousness. The mistaken definition of the type of language in my opinion leads Kjellberg to an incorrect description of the development of the Russian sermon (see his scheme: Kjellberg 1957, 18). The idea that rejecting the Baroque would automatically lead to a gradual replacement of Church Slavonic by Russian also seems incorrect. On the one hand, elements of Baroque style were firmly embedded in Russian religious literature, no matter what the language, and on the other, in Russian linguistic consciousness the switch from Church Slavonic to Russian

Getting rid of specifically Church Slavonic elements presented special difficulties for religious literature which secular writing did not encounter. In sermons, quotations from Holy Writ cited in the canonic Church Slavonic version were constantly encountered; in sermons in Russian this created a situation of bilingualism, analogous to French sermons which cited the Bible in Latin. Quotations are elements of alien text and do not define the linguistic character of the author's text (hence they were not taken into account in the descriptions of homiletic language analyzed above). However, quotations in Church Slavonic could induce the use of marked Church Slavonic elements in the immediately accompanying text, which could act as a kind of transitional link between authorial and alien speech.[59] This kind of secondary mechanism needs to be taken into account in describing the language of homiletic literature.

Kjellberg (1957) analyzed the language of Gedeon's sermons in detail and in the analysis below I will rely on his data. The most precise linguistic indicator is the use of the past tense, and here the following picture is observed in Gedeon's writing. In Gedeon's own texts imperfect forms are not used even once.[60] Instances of the aorist induced by biblical citations are quite common. To them belong first of all the aorist *рече* used to introduce quoted material (although the form *говорилъ* or *сказалъ* may also perform this function — Kjellberg 1957, 182). There are many other similar cases of induction. Apart from them there are only isolated instances of the aorist; the form *бысть* occurs several times, and in one sermon the forms *согрѣшихъ, согрѣшихомъ* often recur ("Согрѣшихъ, прости Господи!," "Согрѣшихъ, прости помилуй мя падшаго," etc., ibid, 183). The latter examples are a formulaic response to confession, and the aorist *бысть* has special qualities that ensured its preservation in secular literature (§ III–1.3). Hence we may consider that as grammatical forms the aorist and imperfect are absent in Gedeon's own text. In essence the forms of the past tense with copula are also missing, apart from the separate 2nd. pers. sg. form used to address

---

could not be gradual, but presumed a sharp break in linguistic and cultural positions that was revolutionary in character.

[59] A prime example of this may be seen in Amvrosii Iushkevich's sermon analyzed above. Here the quoted text induces the use of the 1st pers. sg. pronoun *аз:* "Сам Бог к Давиду глаголет: аз помазах тя на царство во Израили. Рассудите сия словеса божия, говорит Бог явственно: Аз, не фортуна, не случай, не народ Израильский; но Я, который небом и землею владею..." (Amvrosii Iushkevich 1741, 10).

[60] As the single example of imperfect in Gedeon Kjellberg cites the phrase: "Хрїсту нашему тако подобаше пострадати" (Gedeon Krinovskii, I, 261). However, this is an almost direct quotation from the Gospel: "И тако подобаше пострадати Христу" (Luke 24: 46, cf. Luke 24: 26), so in this case we are not dealing with Gedeon's own text.

3. The Synthesis of Cultural and Linguistic Traditions

God, where it has the special function of signaling prayer (ibid, 184). Active participles of the type *грядый, распныйся* are used rarely, as a rule only in paraphrases of Biblical expressions (ibid, 192–3). Hence the entire system of marked Church Slavonic elements is absent, which allows us to regard the language of Gedeon's sermons as Russian.

It is hard to say to what extent Gedeon conceived of all the linguistic factors that were involved in the switch from Church Slavonic to Russian. For linguistic consciousness of the middle-eighteenth century the opposition between the two languages probably looked less clear and precise than it had at the start of the century; one possible factor was the affirmation of the "Slavenosossiiskii" language of secular culture, and the assertion that it shared a single nature with Church Slavonic (§ III–1.2). Significantly, in the first edition of his sermons Gedeon could use constructions with single negation that functioned as markers of the bookish language at the start of the century (see Zhivov 1986b, 252). These constructions were eliminated in the second edition (Kjellberg 1957, 76), i.e., the negative particle was added before the verb, which very much recalls Sofrinii Likhud's corrections to the *General Geography* (§ I–1.3). Kjellberg cites such examples as "что ни самъ Сатана дѣлаетъ I 95 /*не дѣлаетъ* 107v," "ничто больше слѣдуетъ II 162 / *не слѣдуетъ*" (Kjellberg cites the changes to the second edition in italics after the back slash). This suggests that Gedeon only gradually became aware of the significance of single negation that led to their removal from the second edition.

Having gotten rid of marked Church Slavonic elements, Gedeon at first apparently thought that he had accomplished his task, and that he had created sermons in Russian. In the first edition of his sermons, the same kind of variability of non-relevant markers as had distinguished the first texts in "simple" Russian (§ II–1) may be observed. Gedeon's language would seem to have needed to undergo the same whole process of normalization as had the secular literary language from the 1730's through the mid-1750's. Thus in noun declensions the gen. and loc. sg. in *-у/-ю* is used unsystematically (Kjellberg 1957, 119); in the nom. — acc. neut. pl. the endings *-а/-я* and *-ы/-и* (*права — правы*) alternate (ibid, 122–3); and in the dat., instr., and loc. pl. a confused mixture of endings in *-ом/-ем, -ы/-и/-ыми, -ѣхъ/-ехъ,* and *-амъ/-ямъ, -ами/-ями, -ахъ/-яхъ* may be observed (ibid, 126–31). In adjectival declensions, nom. and acc. masc. sg. endings vary as *-ой* and *-ый* (ibid, 136–37); in masc. and neut. gen sg. the ending *-ова* is occasionally encountered (with *-аго/-яго* dominating; ibid, 138–9); in gen. sg. fem. the endings *-ой/-ей* and *-ыя/-ия* alternate (with the former predominating; ibid, 140); and there is a complete jumble of nom.-acc. pl. endings (ibid, 145–50).

Chapter 3. The Changed Conception of the Literary Language

There are also variations in: the pronouns *мене, тебе, себе/меня, тебя себя* (ibid, 171), present tense 2nd per. sg. endings (*-шь/-ши*; ibid, 180); and in part of infinitive endings (a rare *-ти* with most in *-ть*; ibid 188).

The first edition of Gedeon's sermons was published by the Academy typography (in the civic script) in 1755–59, and the second by the Moscow Synodal typography in 1760. For the republication the texts were revised in a particular way, and we may assume that this was done consciously either by Gedeon himself or on his direct instructions (see Kjellberg 1957, 80–1).[61] This revision included the following changes. In nom. pl. of the o- declension the ending *-и*, which appears in rare cases, is replaced by *-ы*; in the nom. -acc. neut. pl. the ending *-ы*, which sometimes appeared in the first edition, was in many cases replaced by *-а*, and in the dat. and loc. pl. the endings *-омъ/-емъ* and *-ѣхъ/-ехъ* were mostly replaced by *-амъ/-ямъ, -ахъ/-яхъ* (ibid, 74). In gen. sg. fem. adjectives, *-ой* was largely replaced by *-ыя*, and nom.-acc. pl. endings have been normalized with the ending *-ыи* virtually eliminated (ibid, 74, 151). The pronouns *мене, тебе, себе* have as a rule been replaced by the forms *меня, тебя, себя*; and in many cases infinitives in *-ти* have been replaced by those in *-ть* (ibid, 74–5). The intent of these changes is unquestionable: the variable forms were being regularized, and moreover according to the norms of the secular literary language (cf. Koporskii 1960, 126). In this way the language of sermons was to a significant extent merging with that of secular literature, and leading to the formation of a single literary language for both religious and secular writing.

In subsequent years the process continued to develop further. Two eminent church figures of Catherine's epoch, Gavriil Petrov and Platon Levshin, who had advanced thanks to Gedeon's support, carried on his work. Their sermons, written in Russian, set the tone for all homiletic literature. They served as the model which was sanctioned as virtually compulsory with the publication of the *Collection of Various Sermons for All Sundays and Holidays* in 1775. These sermons had to be read in every church except if the pastor was giving a sermon himself. It is obvious, however, that even if a clergyman decided to juxtapose his own creation to those approved by the Synod he would still be following the norm they had set. This norm related to language as well as subject matter.

---

[61] The hypothesis that Gedeon himself did the editing (see Kjellberg 1957, 80-1) has some support in the errata lists that accompany the third and fourth volumes of the first edition. Here we find in particular the correction of о талантѣхъ to о талантахъ, утѣшени to утѣшены, and мали and зли to малы and злы, which correspond to the changes incorporated into the second edition.

3. The Synthesis of Cultural and Linguistic Traditions

In fact the *Collection of Various Sermons* had been created to make moral admonitions efficacious, clear and comprehensible, and its appearance meant that the old religious didactic literature was now being declared ineffective and obscure (the very same idea which Feofan Prokopovich had propounded in the *Spiritual Regulation* when he had declared the Slavonic translations of Chrysostom and Feofilakt Bolgarskii to be incomprehensible — see § I–2.1). From the point of view of the compilers of the collection, this incomprehensibly stemmed in particular from the Church Slavonic language. It followed from this that if one wanted to speak and be understood, one had to speak Russian. In the foreword to the collection, written in the name of the Synod, the authors rejected the practice that "admonitions (poucheniia) from the Holy Fathers and lives of the saints from prologues, menologions for reading, and [selections] from other books of exhortations are read in church, which they say are sufficient for instructing any person" (Gavriil and Platon, I, l.3). Echoing Feofan, the compilers counter that "the exhortations of the Holy Fathers and those contained in the books cited, although they do contain moral admonitions, are limited, and not fully complete... besides that they are unclear (temny) in some places, made worse by not very good translation, and their obscurity is also increased by the Slavonic style, and therefore unintelligible not only to simple folk but sometimes also to the educated, or, if they are somewhat comprehensible, then because of their ancient style and lack of clarity, as well as sometimes their length, not very pleasurable or persuasive" (ibid, l. 3 verso; the last two epithets were standard requirements of oratory as defined by rhetorical manuals: "delectare et persuadere"). Having justified the rejection of traditional religious literature, the compilers continue: "Hence it was decided as useful and necessary to supply God's church with new sermons which would contain teachings concerning all the responsibilities of a true Christian and good citizen, and that this teaching be presented in a clear style, and hence intelligible to all, clearly organized, and so able to be long preserved in memory, and at the same time pleasant and full of sweet speech (sladkorechie) as befits the holiness of church, and for these reasons not boring but pleasurable and persuasive" (ibid, l. 3 verso).

In the majority of sermons included in the collection, this program is expressed by the rejection of marked Church Slavonic elements, at the same time as there is a definite normalization of those markers not relevant for the juxtaposition of Russian and Church Slavonic, the principles of which were similar to those on which the normalization of the secular literary language was based. However the language of the collection is not fully homogeneous, which clearly reflects the variety of sources which the compilers used. The collection contains works by Gavriil, Platon, and Gedeon Krinovskii, i.e., authors who had replaced Church Slavonic with Russian in their sermons. No other Russian authors are included. A series of sermons are translations and reworkings of Western preachers — Saurin, Bourdaloue, Mosheim and Gesner. From patristic literature only the sermons of John Chrysostom were selected. Still another source was *The Stumbling Block* by Il'ia Miniat (Elias Miniates), a Greek religious writer of the late seventeenth-early eighteenth century. "By number of works included the first place among all authors belongs to Platon. The selection, changes, reworking, and editing belong to Gavriil" (Sukhomlinov, I, 112). Indeed, all of the sermons were subject to shortening and revision, so that in a literary sense they have a certain unity. For example, in revising Gedeon Krinovskii's sermons, Gavriil typically removes his frequent amusing *exempla,* leaving mostly fragments containing moral exhortations. The prominence of supra-confessional moralizing is underscored by the inclusion in the *Collection* of non-Slavic (primarily Protestant) authors, and to a great extent Mosheim's *Sermons (Heilige Reden*) of 1765 served as the rhetorical model. All of this indicates that the repudiation of the Church Slavonic linguistic tradition was directly linked to the rejection of traditional models of Orthodox homiletics (for example, the works of Efrem the Syrian, Gregory the Theologian, and John of Damscus).[62]

In the absolute majority of texts the language leaves no doubt that this is the Russian literary language of the mid-eighteenth century, into which are interspersed citations from Holy Writ in Church Slavonic. Isolated texts, however, constitute exceptions. Such are the two sermons for Easter (Gavriil and Platon, I, l. 98–101 verso). In these works, especially the first, marked Church Slavonic elements are quite numerous. On the one hand, their use is based upon the listeners' close familiarity with the Easter service, and on the other emphasizes the special festive nature of the holiday, its exceptionality. Aorists and imperfectives are offered to listeners as magnificent and unusual embellishments, and one may see in this a special kind of transformation of the notion of marked Church Slavonic elements indicating an especially elevated style which was formulated during the creation of the "slavenorossiiskii" literary language (see § III–1.2).[63] Significantly, in all

---

[62] Indeed the basic goal of the collection was not introducing people to the holy life of the church but to provide rational enlightenment and instruction. It was asserted that "the ignorance of God's law is the reason for all of the improprieties and abuses in any office," together with the "superstitions" that "shame our faith." It is specifically ignorance and not primal sin or human attraction to evil that destroys the divine order and results in "undermining the general good," "destroying social tranquility and well-being" (Gavriil and Platon, I, l.2). Clearly, Enlightenment ideals of social harmonly are apparent under the outward form of Christian phraseology and "God's law" serves as equivalent to the prescriptions of reason.

[63] The use of simple preterits in the Easter sermons (especially the first one, in which there are a great number, so that they can't be seen as a chance deviation from the norm) is connected

3. The Synthesis of Cultural and Linguistic Traditions

other sermons, including those for Christmas, simple preterits are absent. For determining the status of marked Church Slavonic elements in the *Collection* as a whole, it is indicative that in preparing it for publication Gavriil would have eliminated simple preterits from the texts he was editing. Thus, revising John Chrysostom's sermon for the last Sunday before the Great Fast (Syropustnaia nedelia), among other changes the following were included: "…иже между древними проки столпы <быша> *были*, они хотя и по иннымъ добродѣтелемъ славны и знамениты <быша> *были*" (RNB, Sobr. Peterburgskoi dukhovnoi akademii, no. 99, l.55 verso). Thus a text without simple preterits is normal. In this way marked Church Slavonic elements go from serving as an indicator of linguistic register to become markers of style.

The shift from Church Slavonic to Russian was not only limited to sermons, but gradually spread to other genres of religious literature. In 1765 Platon Levshin's *Orthodox Doctrine* was published (at that time he was still a hieromonk and tutor of religion to Grand Prince Pavel Petrovich) (Platon Levshin 1765). Its short presentation of Orthodoxy's dogmatic theology was written in the Russian language, quite close in its features to the language of Gedeon Krinovskii's sermons. In 1766 Platon's translation of John Chrysostom's sermons (besedy) about the Book of Genesis was published. In the foreword to this edition it says that "In this translation we did not use Slavonic language at all so that our translation would not be obscure and incomprehensible to many people; we judged it better to retreat a little from the venerable Slavonic tongue of ancient times so as to create the least possible obstacle for readers to receive the desired benefit. But neither is there in this translation vulgar speech (vygovor prostonarodnyi), which would have been an unnecessary deviation from the respectful antiquity of Slavonic and a degrading to this holy book's contents" (Ioann Zlatoust I: foreword, l. 4). Analysis of the foreword itself reveals the wide use of lexical Slavonicisms combined with an absence of marked Church Slavonic grammatical elements. This compromise is what Platon had in mind when he spoke of rejecting "vulgar speech" — apparently, that the language of the translation will emulate the model established in secular literature by Lomonosov and Trediakovskii. This translation not only consolidated the Russian language's hold on sermons by sanctioning it for reading (rather

---

with their special rhetorical structure that is based on the structure of the Easter canon. […] The antonymic structure of the canon is repeated in the section of the sermon that contains the main group of aorists (Gavrill and Platon, I, 98 verso –99). It is this specific rhetorical structure that permits us to speak of the special stylistic use of simple preterits within the framework of the new type of literary language that the collection as a whole represents.

than declamation — the foreword suggests that the sermons be read in church during the Great Fast — ibid), but established it as the language for translations of patristic literature.

It is interesting to note that in this case the rejection of Church Slavonic is not only justified by reference to its "obscurity" but also to the "false rhetoric" of vainglorious preachers. Thus the entire complex of ideas that had taken shape during Feofan Prokopovich's battle with his enemies (§ I–1.2) and then reflected in Gedeon Krinovskii (see above) was recycled for another epoch. Indeed, Platon writes in the foreword about preachers who seek

> to give the audience an inflated opinion of themselves with their oratory. Those preachers do themselves dishonor who even in the holiest place do not abandon this passion, but pile word upon word, adorning their speech with various little flourishes, ignoring the importance and solidity of the truth, not speaking out of the emotion which divine zeal inspires in a Christian teacher but flattering themselves with the idea of being accorded the title of sweet-tongued from some listeners. However, such words grow cold on the lips of this sort of preacher, who themselves, not possessing the inner holy fire, are unable to inflame the listener. (Ioann Zlatoust, I, foreword, l.1 verso –2)

This empty use of rhetoric is contrasted to the language of Chrysostom himself:

> ...the style of his speech was smooth, clear, humble, penetrating, pleasant, the most natural, with nothing forced, no empty inflated words, no overly clever oratory, only the power of things themselves, producing the ordered connection of truth... He was very fortunate in coming up with an assortment of comparisons which brought vitality, appeal and concreteness to his speech, and truly there was in him that which is considered characteristic of a great orator, that is, he appealed to both the educated and the simple, was understood by both, and praised by both. (Ibid, l.2 verso)

The given publication could have served as a model of this style. Thus "in 1770 the Holy Synod instructed the rector Ilarion and prefect Il'inskii to review and revise the translation of Basil the Great's sermons, made in Moscow by the hieromonk Sofronii Mladenovich. They were directed to make the revision 'as clear and precise as possible, i.e., not in lofty Slavonic but in the purest Russian style, and as far as possible to make it similar to the translation of the published conversations of John Chrysostom on the Book of Genesis,' that is, Platon's translation was presented to the editors as a model" (Smirnov 1867, 358). In 1792 selected sermons of Chrysostom came out in Russian translation by the priest Ivan Ivanov (Ioann Zlatoust 1792), also following the model laid down by Platon. The translation was

3. The Synthesis of Cultural and Linguistic Traditions

evidently also ascribed to the priest Ioann Sidorovskii, member of the Russian Academy, whose translations were sometimes confused with those by Ivanov (Sukhomlinov, I, 271), although it is indeed possible that he took some part in it. The following epitaph was carved on Sidorovskii's gravestone (Sukhomlinov, I, 273):

> Течение Иоанн окончил Сидоровский
> Кой в церкви расплодил язык славеноросский;
> Чем древле Златоуст во Греции гремел,
> Он сделал чтобы росс легко то разумел…

(The course of Ioann Sidorovskii's [life] has come to an end; he made the Slavenosossiiskii language fruitful in the church; that which Chrysostom thundered in Greece of old he made clearly understood to Russians…)

This gravestone inscription ascribes the Chrysostom translation to Sidorovskii and connects the growing use of Slavenorossiiskii in church literature to this work. Whether justified or not, it is notable that Church Slavonic (the language from which Chrysostom was translated) is understood to be inaccessible and that the Slavenorossiiskii language is for that reason welcomed for religious writing. Thus the same scheme as laid out as official Synod policy in the foreword to the *Collection of Various Sermons* of 1775 is here presented in abbreviated form.

The reform of religious language also extended to hagiography. In 1782 Platon published the "Life of St. Sergius of Radonezh" which he had compiled; although marked Church Slavonic elements were not all excluded from this work (cf., for example, the occasional use of the aorist: *Сергїй родися, сотвори прилѣжную молитву, даде ему часть просфоры* — Platon Levshin 1782, 3 and 6 verso), their use was motivated by stylistic needs and they were perceived as isolated elevated elements which had happened into a text written in the usual literary language; only symbolic traces were left of the traditional hagiographical language.

One could multiply such examples. The "Slavenorossiiskii" literary language gradually forced Church Slavonic out of all branches of religious literature, so that the use of Church Slavonic was reduced to the liturgy alone. This made the question of translating Holy Writ into Russian (for reading rather than for church service books) an actual one. In 1794 a Russian translation of Paul's Epistle to the Romans was published, the work of Mefodii Smirnov (see Uspenskii 1983, 100), and with the founding of the Russian Bible Society in 1812 work on a systematic translation of the Bible began. The Western model of a single polyfunctional literary language triumphed over the bilingualism of civic and church idioms which had arisen as a result of Petrine cultural and linguistic policy.

3.2 The Unified Language of a Unified Culture

The synthesis of Russian and Church Slavonic in "Slavenorossiiskii" and the spread of this one language into all branches of writing reflected a new view of literature. The opposition between religious and secular here, as in the language, lost its relevance. In Catherine's reign literary activity acquired the status of something of state importance in which the empress herself took part. Having acquired this status, literature as well as language began to embody the hegemonic character of the regnant culture, not only in intent but in actual functioning, dominating over all spheres of social life. In consequence, literature was also perceived as a unified whole, generating a system of genres in which sermons and theological tracts occupied their own place along with odes, elegies, and comic operas. Describing the styles (shtili) which may be distinguished "in deciding the places for which words are proposed," Amvrosii Serebrennikov in his *Russian Oratory* lists the styles of: "the church, or didactic [style], [and those of] the court, the courts, school, theater" (Amvrosii Serebrennikov 1778, 158). The principles of constructing speech and models for imitation vary according to venue, but these differences do not prevent the unity of "Russian oratory."

This new unity of literature was manifested in many ways. In 1743, Trediakovskii, trying to receive the place of professor of eloquence in the Academy of Sciences but despairing of getting it from the Academy's conference, asked that the members of the Synod attest to his "abilities in eloquence, in Latin as well as Russian," and was given a statement that "his works are clearly produced according to the precise rules of eloquence, adorned with pure, select words, so that from all this it is clear that he has advanced in eloquence, that is, in Russian and Latin oratory, not just a little but to such an extent that genuine mastery should be credited to him" (Pekarskii, IA, II, 100). Trediakovskii received the position, but not by appointment through the Academy but by the Senate (ibid, 107); the Synod's recommendation was perceived as external interference, and Trediakovskii remained an outsider. Trediakovskii's attempt to publish his *Feoptiia* and verse paraphrase of the Psalter in the Synodal typography and with the Synod's approval encountered even more resistance; evidently M. Kheraskov, not wanting to acknowledge the religious authority's power over literature, played some part in this

3. The Synthesis of Cultural and Linguistic Traditions

(Shishkin 1989). Religious literature was perceived as a special sphere that did not have a direct relationship to secular literature, and religious writers as a separate fraternity living its own life and not capable of making judgments about the new literature.

During Catherine's reign the situation fundamentally changed. In 1783 the Russian Academy was founded, and its members included church figures as well as secular ones, and were gathered together as representatives of a single literature, moved by a common desire to perfect the verbal arts. They were occupied by one labor which was for the good of all literature, no matter whether secular or religious. The Academy's first task was the *Dictionary*, and in line with the established view on literature and the literary language Holy Writ and the liturgy as well as other works by religious and secular authors served as sources for it (see Sukhomlinov, VIII, 19–44). Hence the religious literary tradition became a model together with the secular. After asserting in the foreword that "the Slavenorossiiskii language mostly consists of Slavonic, or to put it more clearly, has its basis in it," the compilers note that to distinguish styles (slogi) the dictionary cites examples from "Slavenorossiiskii, that is, from religious books and from those of the best secular writers, according to which their usage in lofty and beautiful style is defined" (SAR, I, vi, xiv). This combining of church and secular sources influenced not only lexographical work but the literary process itself.

Given the importance of imitation as a category of Renaissance and post-Renaissance poetics, the choice of models came in large measure to define the character of literary creation. Therefore lists of model authors and works emerged as important indicators both of a literature's direction and that of its literary language. The list contained in V. S. Podshivalov's *Abbreviated Course of Russian Style*, for example, is remarkable:

> As regards the reading of good books which may aid in gaining a fundamental knowledge of the Russian language, among these are considered the works of Lomonosov, Feofan, Gedeon, Platon, and St. Dimitrii, and especially his *Menalogion for Reading*, or his *Lives of the Holy Fathers*, for prose; and for poetry also those of Lomonosov, Kheraskov, Maikov, Sumarokov, and other most recent ones like Derzhavin, Kniazhnin, Dmitriev, Bogdanovich, etc. After these works follow good translations, as are considered Bielfeld's political admonitions, Cyrus' travels, the *Destruction of the Peruvian Empire*, the *Life of Egypitan Tsar Sif* (sethos), the first volumes of Cleveland, passionate *Roland*, the *Life of Marquis G**... and many others, among which the main place is taken by translations from Greek of the whole circle of church [books], that is, the Bible or Holy Writ, ... Chrysostom's sermons, the *Margarit, Irmologion*, etc. (Podshivalov 1796: 32–33).

However Podshivalov's personal tastes influenced this list, the very combination of Gedeon and Lomonosov, the Bible and the first volumes of Cleveland (Abbé Prévost), is sufficiently eloquent testimony to the conception of a unified literature. One may find similar lists in Amvrosii Serebrennikov's *Russian Oratory* and a whole series of other works. Serebrennikov, it is true, gives his list of recommended literature according to "styles" (types of literature), and for this reason does not offer that sort of motley flood of names and titles as we find in Podshivalov. However, here too we do find a similar simultaneous orientation on secular and religious texts. For example, speaking of models of "the philosophical style," he writes: "In this type of writing especially worthy of emulation are the Right Rev. Gavriil, Archbishop of Novgorod and St. Petersburg and the Right Rev. Platon, Archb. of Moscow for sermons, Mr. Lomonosov for public speeches" (Amvrosii Serebrennikov 1778, 157–8).

No less remarkable a discussion may be found in Damaskin Semenov-Rudnev in the foreword to the edition of Lomonosov that he edited. He repeats the scheme explaining the formation of Slavenorossiiskii's abundance that derives from Lomonosov and Trediakovskii (§ III–2.1), but supplements it with thoughts about the relationship between secular and religious writing:

> Our Slavenorossiiskii language also had the fortune to acquire its well-being, abundance and solemnity first from Greek, and then from Greek and Latin. Until today's eighteenth century only Greek books that were needed for the church service were translated and printed, as well as the Bible, saints lives, and the famous works of the teachers of the eastern church. Later also appeared some translations of some Latin writers. By the medium of these translations almost all of the splendor, magnificence, abundance and solemnity of the Greek church language transferred into our language. But the most ancient authors who wrote with splendid taste, that is, Homer, Pindar, Isocrates, Demosthenes, of the Greeks, and Cicero, Livy, Virgil, Ovid of the Latins, — their beauty and tenderness were not yet communicated to it. Then our most wise monarch Great Catherine the Second... noticing [this], was pleased to allot a rather large sum of money as a reward for translations... Since that time have appeared and are today appearing very many excellent books, translated from contemporary European languages as well as from Greek and Latin. But it is unfortunate that many of those who have translated these books have read few or no church books, which is evident from their strange spelling and the composition of their words; and they especially did not take into consideration those writers who out of all of our enlightened society are considered the most skillful stylists. Among these writers the late Mikhail Vasil'evich Lomonosov rightfully occupies the first place. He was quite adept at Greek and Latin as well as several modern languages, and moreover read the church books that had been translated from Greek diligently, and so improved and enriched his speech so that one cannot help but consider him an exemplary author. (Lomonosov 1778, I, l. 4–5)

3. The Synthesis of Cultural and Linguistic Traditions

Damaskin Semenov-Rudnev thus not only simultaneously declares the Bible and Lomonosov's works to be normative, but this synthesis of the religious and secular also extends to Greek and Latin literature, in which, in his opinion, patristic works should be supplemented with Homer, Pindar, Virgil and Ovid.[64]

The conception of a unified literature was based on the Western model and conferred upon the new literary language that universality which it lacked as a consequence of the specific nature of Petrine cultural politics which had segregated civil and religious speech (§ III–1.1). At the French academy learned abbots attended meetings together with secular men of letters, and their works merged into one literary process; the sermons of Bossuet and Bourdaloue were considered equally good models of French as Jean-Baptiste Rousseau's odes or Racine's plays. The switch to writing sermons in Russian brought Russia closer to this ideal, as was indeed thought by contemporaries. Sumarokov wrote a special article "On Russian Religious Oratory," and the very fact that he did so is extremely significant, because it marked the unconditional inclusion of religious oratory into the diapason of Russian letters. When giving his short characteristics of individual Russian preachers (whose ranks are completely predictable: Feofan Prokopovich, Gedeon Krinovskii, Gavriil Petrov, and Platon Levshin), Sumarokov directly relates them to Western authors. He writes of Feofan, "This great rhetorician is the Russian Cicero" (Sumarokov, VI, 280); the reference to a Latin author evidently means that Feofan is situated as it were on the border between old and new literature. Further, Gedeon "is the Russian Fléchier" and Platon "the Russian Bourdaloue" (ibid, 281 and 283).

In and of itself the transfer of French concepts and titles is a regular feature of eighteenth-century Russian literary thinking; hence Lomonosov was considered in his time "the Russian Malherbe" and Sumarokov "the Russian Racine." Including famous church orators in this pattern indicated that Russian letters had achieved the same fullness as French. Significantly, this achievement was in one way or another connected with writing sermons in Russian: "Slavenorossiiskii" thus achieved the polyfunctionalism characteristic of the French literary language (§ III–1.1). Sumarokov's disciple F. G. Karin wrote directly about this:

---

[64] It is precisely this synthetic approach, and by to means some sort of undivided cultural consciousness, smoothly moving "from ascetic sto sinful passions" and "from Christian miracle to miraculous adventures" (as Hans Rothe suggests — Rothe 1984, 94) that explains the desire to unite disparate spheres in search of the sources for the new culture, as well as sources of purity for the new literary language.

> Feofan was the first who departed from the Slavonic linguistic prototype (pervoobraznost'); to do this he introduced everyday usage, so that given the harmony of his expressions, which reflect everything touching his thoughts or the content of his sermon as if in a mirror, he would be understood by everyone... We are indebted to him for the fruitful issue that we have produced, our own Bossuets, Fléchiers, and Massillons. Today our church pulpit does not yield place to any one of the holy pulpits in Europe, and has risen to such a degree of perfection as could only be desired. (Karin 1778, 6)

The unity of letters presupposed a unity of stylistic criteria. In the second half of the eighteenth century, secular writers could judge the stylistics of religious literature, applying the same precepts as in secular literature; religious writers could equally draw up their own prescriptions for all of Russian literature, relying on the theories worked out in the mid-century polemics over language. Hence Sumarokov in the article cited above wrote that "I see in Church Orators my brethren in rhetoric alone, and not in holiness; and so I have a right to speak about them, just as much as they have a right to speak about me, insofar as such mutual judgments belong to those who admire literature" (Sumarokov, VI, 277). At the same time Sumarokov criticizes Baroque sermons, approaching them with the Classicist demands for naturalness and comprehensibility, and addressing the same complaints about them as those he had made, for example, about Lomonosov's odes:

> Many religious orators who have no taste do not allow either their heart or their natural understanding into their works, but, intellectualizing without basis, imagining indistinctly, and hoping for the usual praise of the mob (which goes into raptures over everything it doesn't understand), dare to make their way to Parnassus up crooked paths, and instead of Pegasus bridle a wild stallion, or sometimes an ass, and are pulled up a crooked road onto some sort of hillock where not only the Muses but their names have never been heard of, and instead of fragrant narcissus they gather dandelions. (ibid, 279)

In relation to religious oratory Sumarokov expresses his habitual complaint — natural in the context of his Classicism — against "inflated sentences ornate beyond measure, neither in agreement with mind nor heart" (ibid, 280). Characterizing Gedeon's sermons, Sumarokov points to their "pleasantness, tenderness, subtlety" (ibid, 281), and here he obviously has in mind linguistic considerations analogous to those he defines for secular authors using the same terms.

To understand this process the attitude toward Prokopovich which came into being during this period is instructive. As we have seen from the material cited above, Prokopovich was put forward as one of the new model authors, and was often named along with Kantemir and Lomonosov as father of the new Russian literature. Both the association between Prokopovich's sermons and the Petrine cultural policy which had brought about the new literature as well as the conception of a unified literature, in which his sermons took equal place alongside Lomonosov's odes, evidently influenced this view. At the same time the hybrid Church Slavonic in which Feofan wrote was reconceptualized, and could now be perceived as "Slavenorossiiskii," which could include a large quantity of marked Church Slavonic elements. However it was quite impossible to reclaim this language under the criteria of Classicist purity, and for this reason tributes to Feofan are almost always accompanied by complaints about his impure language. This ambiguity may be traced as far back as Lomonosov, who removed words of praise for Feofan as an orator from his *Rhetoric* (see Lomonosov, VII², 174); it is assumed that he did this because he did not want "to make an example of an author who did not observe 'purity of style'" (Kochetkova 1974, 65; cf. Lomonosov, VII², 821). On Lomonosov's advice Sumarokov also excluded a positive reference to Feofan from his "Epistle on the Russian Language" of 1748, apparently for the same reasons.[65] The excised section contained both a comparison of Feofan to Cicero and a remark about the impurity of his language

> Последователь сей пресладка Цицерона
> И красноречия Российскаго корона.
> Хоть в чистом слоге он и часто погрешал;
> Но красноречия премного показал.
> Он Ритор из числа во всей Европе главных,
> Как Мосгейм, Бурдалу, между мужей преславных.

(Grinberg and Uspenskii 1992, 223, Lomonosov VII²: 821)

(This [was] a follower of sweet-tongued Cicero and crown of Russian oratory. Although he often sinned with impure style, he demonstrated great eloquence. [He was] among the best rhetoricians in all of Europe, along with the most famous men like Mosheim and Bourdaloue.)

What these defects were Sumarokov explained later: "Ukrainian turns of speech and foreign words which were required for some unknown reason

---

[65] This is suggested by the commentators to the second academic edition of Lomonosov (Lomonosov, VII², 813, 821). M. S. Grinberg and B. A. Uspenskii note that there is no documentary evidence of this interference and hypothesize that it was sooner the result of "a tactical ruse" by Sumarokov, who succeeded in having the epistles published by the Academy of Sciences (Grinberg and Uspenskii 1992, 224). In any case, Lomonosov and Sumarokov held the same opinion of Feofan's style that fit their overall theoretical position.

Chapter 3. The Changed Conception of the Literary Language

somewhat disfigured his works; but they were quite made up for by another sort of purity" (Sumarokov, VI, 280).

We may also cite S. F. Nakoval'nin's assessment in the foreword to Feofan's *Sermons and Speeches*:

> If someone would want to diminish his honor, [saying] that he employed an uneven style in his sermons, mixing in Slavonic, which was the basis of his writings, and sometimes popular expressions and sometimes language not used in Great Russia; then first of all one may easily answer along with Cicero and Horace that use by intelligent men does honor even to vulgar speech, and secondly, that he may be excused because he was occupied by many most important affairs and did not have the time to delve into all of the subtleties and beauty of language. (Feofan Prokopovich, I, foreword, 1. 2–3)

A. S. Shishkov later gave Feofan a similar evaluation: "His Slavonic style, sometimes mixed with popular turns of phrase, could in some places have been more even and pure, but these are trifles not noticed in great creations... They do not interfere with our appreciating his great merits, which consist in the order and depth of his thought, in the fecundity of his imagination, the appropriateness of his embellishments and power of his language" (Shishkov 1813, 9–10). Karamzin has a similar remark about Feofan. He calls him a "natural born orator" but nonetheless asserts that "in his speeches, both secular and religious, are strewn a multitude of the flowers of eloquence, although their style is impure, and one may say, unpleasant" (Karamzin, I, 574). The similarity of Karamzin's and Shishkov's views is very striking (§ IV–1), and demonstrates that for purism of any type the very idea of hybrid language is unacceptable. At the same time, we see here a convergence of purist conceptions which derive from Classicist linguistic doctrine which did not lose its force even though these conceptions were diametrically opposed to one another.

The unanimity of stylistic criteria as applied to both secular and religious wrtings guaranteed the interaction of linguistic practices in these two branches of literary activity. As discussed above (§ III–3.1), in preparing a second edition of his sermons Gedeon Krinovskii carried out a definite normalization of the language (noun and adjective endings, forms of the infinitive), and the principles of this normalization coincided with those that had already been implemented in secular literature. This means that in his linguistic practice he accepted those notions of what was or wasn't normative, pure or impure, that had been worked out by secular philologists who were trying to normalize the "civic tongue." The interaction of stylistic notions may also be seen in the way religious and secular writing made use of simple preterits. As we have seen in the analysis of the sermons for

3. The Synthesis of Cultural and Linguistic Traditions

Easter included in Gavrill Petrov and Platon Levshin's *Collection of Various Sermons for All Sundays and Holidays,* simple preterits were a violation of the norm that functioned as a sign of special divine ecstasy. The same thing may be seen in Sumarokov's psalm paraphrases (§ III–2.2) and in those of several of his followers. It is natural to conclude that this resulted from the mutual influence of secular and religious writing.

Similar lines of development emerge upon analyzing infinitive forms. Although Lomonosov and Trediakovskii rejected the *-mu* form as non-normative, other authors continued to use it. This is the case, for example, in Fonvizin's translation of Bitaubé's "Joseph," in which in the translator's opinion "it was necessary to maintain the solemnity of the Slavonic language" (Fonvizin 1769, foreword, l. 1 verso; typically, in the foreword Fonvizin uses infinitives in *-mь*). It is also true in M. Popov's translation of Tasso's *Jerusalem Liberated* (Tasso 1772). Sumarokov also continued to use the *-mu* form, from somewhat different motives (see § III–2.2); in his psalm paraphrases, written in free verse, there only occur infinitives in *-mu,* evidently indicating a form absent in conversational usage that therefore denoted inspired prophetic speech. This use of *-mu* for stylistic purposes is described in A. A. Barsov's *Russian Grammar*: Barsov writes of the infinitive form: "Its direct and full ending similar to the Slavonic is in *mu,* which now may be used only in verse or in high or church style, but otherwise it is abbreviated as *mь*" (Barsov 1981, 592). Barsov's mention of "church style" is not accidental; in the religious tradition variation of infitive forms had not been eliminated, which could lead to conceptualizing the *-mu* form as one of its specific features, and hence as a stylistic element appropriate to high spiritual thematics.[66] It is natural to conclude that the stylistic weight of *-mu* forms in secular literature derives from this practice of religious literature, and in turn that religious writers might have assimilated the view of this form as a stylistuically charged non-normative element; hence this form could appear as we have seen in Gavrill Petrov's Easter sermon, differentiating it from all of the other texts in the *Collection of Various Sermons.* Thus here too the interaction of the two literary traditions is apparent.

Together with this sort of stylistic equivalence another kind of interaction may be seen, when it is as if the specific linguistic peculiarities

---

[66] The changes that S. Nakoval'nin made to Feofan Prokopovich's texts when they were republished in the 1760's are indicative of this perspective. Nakoval'nin himself, judging by the forword to Prokopovich's *Sermons and Speeches*, did not himself use the -ти form. In Feofan's sermons, however, in many cases he replaced -ть with -ти forms (e.g., in the sermon on Peter I's burial; compare Feofan Prokopovich 1725 and Feofan Prokopovich, II, 128–32). Nakoval'nin clearly sees the -ти form as characteristic of religious writing, and edits Prokopovich accordinngly.

of the secular and religious literary traditions cancel each other out. Thus in religious literature the old inflections in oblique pl. cases are most rarely met in instr. pl. This tendency is encountered in all homiletic literature from Simeon Polotskii to Gedeon Krinovskii (see note 48 above). This does not involve the changeover from hybrid Church Slavonic to Russian, which emphasizes the fact that the variability of the given endings does not correspond to the opposition between languages but reflects the uncontrollable continuity of linguistic habits. The evolution of the secular language leads to a completely opposite result. Of all the old inflections only the instr. pl. in -ы remained in use; the expressive distinction between the old and new endings in the instr. pl. rendered it significant, a stylistic means which Tatishchev, Trediakovskii and Lomonosov all made use of (cf. Martel 1933, 81; Makeeva 1961, 104). With the merging of religious and secular literature and the creation of a single literary language these opposing peculiarities neutralize each other. In secular literature, starting with Sumarokov and his followers, the instr. pl. in -ы ceases to be used for stylistic reasons, and this leads to the uniform usage of the new endings. The same practice is established in religious literature after Gedeon Krinovskii, as can be seen, for example, in the *Collection of Various Sermons*. In this way, in cases where there are corresponding yet distinctive traits the interaction between the two traditions leads to the broadening of the stylistic repertoire of the literary language, while in cases where there are opposing features this leads to the smoothing away of differences. It was precisely the result of this kind of process that established a single universal norm for the new literary language in service of one united literature.

The "duality in unity" (dvuedinstvo) of Russian literature which came into being in this way emphasizes the duality in unity of the literary language. The thesis about its combination of Church Slavonic and Russian became a commonplace and was proclaimed as a starting point which needed no special proofs. In the Russian Academy's statutes it is presented almost in passing, as an explanation of the Russian language's special richness: "A language's richness follows plainly from the abundance of words and locutions (phrases), when each thing, each idea or action may be depicted in its own words or locutions. The Russian language may chiefly pride itself on such abundance, being made up of so-to-speak two languages, i.e., the ancient, or Slavonic, and the one derived from it, which is used today" (Sukhomlinov, VIII, 425).

We find analogous reasoning in V. Svetov's article "Several General Notes on the Russian Language": "Starting from the unification of the Slavonic and Russian dialects if we add the words used by Russians during the middle ages that are preserved in ancient chronicles and deeds,

3. The Synthesis of Cultural and Linguistic Traditions

and if we also demand explanations, what a huge dictionary will some day be compiled!" (Svetov 1779, 82). The issue here, of course, is not merely about compiling a big dictionary, but about the lexical reserves of the literary language which combined both Russian and Slavonic sources. The possibility of this combination and its stylistic parameters are specially defined. The author differentiates between the "Slavonic," "Slavenorossiiskii," and "New Russian" (Novorossiisikoi) languages: "The ancient Slavonic language, that I call dead, was used only in conversation before the invention of writing. After the acquisition of letters the Bible was written in Slavenorossiisikii, as well as chronicles and other handwritten documents; New Russian is justly considered that which educated Russians speak and write today, and had its origin in the time of the Renewer of the Russian Word [i.e., Peter I]" (ibid, 80–1). In making these definitions, the author notes that in the high style New Russian combines with Slavenorossiisikii, and as an example of this he gives "church sermons" as well as "other works" in verse and prose:

> However, observing the purity of the New Russian language in ornate works, they [writers] also with reason borrow equivalent phrases from books in Slavenorossiisikii, and thereby beautify their style to no small degree. We see this in the most recent church sermons and in other works written in verse and prose. For in high style works in verse and prose it is most appropriate to preserve ancient Slavenorossiisikii features in place of the new, for example: *восходящу солнцу на высоту небесную*, as opposed to (if in simple language), *когда солнце восходило* or *когда разсвѣтало*; also *гнѣвъ Божїй пролїется* instead of *Богъ прогнѣвается*; *вижу восходящую брани тучу*, instead of: *се война подымается,* and so forth. (ibid, 81)

It is very indicative that the Church Slavonic elements (or what the author considers them to be) are included in the high style while still "observing the purity of the New Russian language." In the framework of the new literary language they are thus defined as "pure" lexical elements par excellence.

In connection with the "dual unity" of the literary language the notion of linguistic purity is also bifurcated. An eloquent example of this may be found in Amvrosii Serebrennikov's *Oratory (Oratoriia)* (cf. Sukhomlinov, I, 189–98). Amvrosii's handbook may be seen as an eclectic attempt to synthesize various linguistic theories about style which had been developing in eighteenth-century Russia, and thus may serve as a record of the evolution that the linguistic and stylistic theories of French Classicism had undergone in being adapted to the Russian situation.

Oratory openly declares the fundamental principles of Classicist purism, and in Amvrosii's formulations can be heard an echo of Vaugelas, apparently through Trediakovskii's mediation (Sukhomlinov, I, 194). Here the necessity of "purity of style" is asserted and usage is indicated as the main criterion: "Purity of style requires pure expressions... Pure expressions," he explains, "are those which 1) are universally approved, 2) comprehensible, and 3) used in important works by our best writers" (Amvrosii Serebrennikov 1778, 98). In the definition of "universally approved" expressions we find Vaugelas' notion of usage before its characteristic Russian transformation (§ III–2.3): "Universally approved expressions are those which the best people of capital cities use in general conversation" (ibid, 99). This approach had no practical significance, however, and Amvrosii quickly combines usage with the literary tradition, which necessarily served as the real criterion. "But it is less dangerous and more convenient to learn this purity from important works by the best Russian writers. Such are all of Mr. Lomonosov's works, Mr. Sumarokov's and others" (ibid). References to "an educated ear" and "grammatical rules" supplement the assortment of reference points that Amvrosii substitutes for the criteria of usage (§ III–2.3).

Amvrosii's interpretation of linguistic "coarseness" is very indicative. After stating that "coarse expressions harm the purity of style," he goes on to define them, and here it becomes obvious that coarseness is by no means contrasted to refinement of speech or to language practices of the social elite (as it would be in a direct adaption of Vaugelas' doctrine) but grammatical correctness that demanded of a writer not habituation to good society but educational experience. "Coarse speech and expressions," Amvrosii writes, "are those which: 1) are strange to the educated ear, and used only by the simple folk; 2) whose writing is contrary to general speech or to the grammatical rules; and 3) which take pure expressions and create or end them in a new way, for ex., *швыряю*, that is, *бросаю*; *притча* instead of *случай*; *получить убыток*, *потерять человека* instead of *убить*; *презирать кем* instead of *кого*, *предвершение, раболепность*, and so on" (Amvrosii Serebrennikov 1778, 99–100).

Together with this Amvrosii recognizes the reality of Russian — Church Slavonic bilingualism. This recognition of the two languages as independent systems evidently does not seem to be something that he must camouflage by references to their continuity or shared nature. This acceptance of bilingualism may be connected to a new perception of Church Slavonic as the cult language, which in the form of quotes and paraphrases may be freely introduced into Russian texts; as we have seen, this practice had become quite standard for Amvrosii thanks to the newly formed tradition of Russian sermons (§ II–3.1). Hence Amvrosii may write: "We have two languages, Slavonic and Russian, and therefore there may be pure Slavonic turns of phrase unknown in Russian, and conversely Russian ones which sound

3. The Synthesis of Cultural and Linguistic Traditions

strange in Slavonic. However, since today no one in our country speaks pure Slavonic, which is contained only in Church books, and since Russian is not as abundant and lofty, here and in the following chapters we will have in mind a style combining Slavonic and Russian" (ibid, 98).[67] This unlimited assimilation of Slavonicisms into the literary language corresponds, as we have seen, to the unification of secular and religious traditions into one literature, and this is directly reflected in Amvrosii's list of models of high style. Here "one should study books by ancient and new writers, such as the holy Greek Fathers, and especially the creators of the canons, the panegyrists; and more than anything else the narratives, songs, psalms, prophecies and moral teachings of Holy Writ; of the Russian writers Mr. Lomon[osov] in odes, Mr. Sumarokov in odes and tragedies..." (ibid, 155).

And so the opposition between worldly and spiritual, secular and clerical, ceased to play any role either in choosing works to imitate or in selecting the very means of expression. In these conditions, Church Slavonic linguistic material is conceived of as neutral, and this was the dominant perception of the period, that is, Lomonosov's interpretation of Slavonicisms (§ III–2.2) was accepted; according to this view Slavonicisms were not specially connected to "elevated" or "rhetorically embellished" speech but functioned as a neutral means of expression which could be used in any genre except those in which they would conflict with specific Russicisms. It was precisely as a result of this reconceptualization that the so-called "Slavenorossiiskii" language developed, a language in which in V. D. Levin's words "the role, place, and function of archaic, 'Slavonic' lexicon... were very significant and were not limited to traditional high genres," or in other words, "high lexicon... was disassociated... from high style" (Levin 1964, 50 and 56; both

---

[67] Corresponding to this mixed character of "pure" vocabulary are the words that make up the rubrics of those which "damage purity." Here in the first place go "coarse expressions" and borrowings, while archaisms are practically absent. Archaisms are included in the more general category of "incomprehensible expressions": "Incomprehensible expressions may be either extremely ancient, newly invented, used in an incorrect (otmennom) meaning, or borrowed from foreign languages, for ex., Тиун, горволь, слана, самостоятельность, шамад, бреш" (Amvrosii Serebrennikov 1778, 100).
Following Lomonosov, Amvrosii normalizes the simultaneous use of Slavonicisms and Russicisms, although characteristically his prescriptions relate not only to the middle style, as in Lomonosov, but to the literary language as a whole (this reflects the interpretation of Slavonicisms as a neutral element — see § III–2.2): "Because our style consists of Slavonic and pure Russian expressions, and these languages are different from each other, one must be careful in choosing [words], so that one does not place a pure Slavonic expression next to a pure Russian one... Because there is nothing more offensive to the ear that this kind of absurd combination, which must be particularly avoided in verse" (ibid, 102; cf. the similar discussion in Rizhskii 1796, 11).

Chapter 3. The Changed Conception of the Literary Language

the epithets "high" and "archaic" are in this context anachronisms: they represent the scholar's value judgements which do not accord with those of the epoch in question).

It is indicative in this connection that Slavonic linguistic material was now seen as naturally corresponding to the "pure" vocabulary of Western European languages which were oriented upon spoken usage, and in this capacity was widely put to use in numerous translations of the period (see Lotman and Uspenskii 1975, 204–207 and 238–39). Moreover Slavonicisms turned out to be directly juxtaposed to borrowings, and were correlated with them as "pure" to "impure" elements, so that the struggle against borrowings and the introduction of Slavonicisms functioned as two sides of one process (in comparison, we may note that the struggle against borrowings in French never led to using archaic lexicon or Latinisms). Church books became not only the ideal measure of the correctness of the Russian literary language but also a practical source for replenishing vocabulary (Trediakovskii may serve as model of this practice, as he justified his neologisms by reference to church books; see § III–1.3). Hence in Amvrosii's handbook referring to church books is directly prescribed: "If something new has been invented, then it is permissible to think up new expressions [to describe it]; but one must be very careful of coming up with a new phrase for something that has long had its own name. Diligent reading of Slavonic church books will do much to avoid this" (Amvrosii Serebrennnikov 1778, 100–1).

This view directly corresponds to M. Popov's well-known remarks that precede his translation of Tasso's *Jerusalem Delivered*. Noting that he "tried to observe... such a style as was demanded by the weight and dignity of this poem, in which magnificence, love and tenderness reign everywhere" (Tasso 1772, p. S), Popov continues:

> In translating such an excellent and difficult work as is this type of poem, it was inevitable that many words were encountered which either we do not have in our language or which we still do not know about because we do not take pains to delve into the vast and rich Slavonic language, which is the source and beauty of Russian, and which over time of course will not yield in abundance to any other language in the world. I too could not avoid facing these difficulties, and could not free myself from them other than searching in religious books or in newly translated ones for words of the same meaning as those which I encountered in French; or I translated completely anew. For a poem will not tolerate foreign words unless unavoidably necessary; but they should not be tolerated anywhere. (Tass 1772, p. i)

Popov further presents an extensive list of his discoveries, in some cases supplying direct references to the Bible, for example: "Catapulte, f....

3. The Synthesis of Cultural and Linguistic Traditions

Стрелостоятельница, Macc[abees] B[ook] II, Chap. VI, l.20:51," "Espion, m. Соглядатай, Macc[abees] B[ook] II, Chap. V, l. 38, Созиратель, Chap. XII, l. 26," "Trophée, m. Всеоружие, Macc[abees] B[ook] II, Chap. XIII, l. 29" (ibid, p. AIf).

The same conception was also formulated by the translators of *Works of the Most Wise Plato,* I. Sidorovskii and M. Pakhomov:

> In presenting [this material] on the life, type of work and language of this philosopher, we consider it not inappropriate to briefly inform readers about this translation into Russian as well. To some it may appear that the style used in this translation is unsuitable for a style typical of everyday conversation... insofar as they will find a great multitude of expressions more characteristic of oratorical rather than conversational style. The reason for this is that Plato himself used a middle style between that of prose and poetry. Because of this it was necessary to observe a similar style in this translation and to approach somewhat the character of the Slavonic language. In some places we also depended on some expressions borrowed from ancient Slavonic, and some created anew, without however ignoring their own meaning; for in this case we also imitated a writer who similarly borrowed some [expressions] from the ancient Hellenic tongue, and some created anew... (Plato 1780, xii–xiii).

The authors here evidently relied on Trediakovskii's practice, although either directly or indirectly the source of their innovations as translators again turns out to be Holy Writ.

The cultural synthesis of the second half of the eighteenth century thus led to the emergence of a unified literature which embraced both secular and religious works, and also to the development of a single literary language which combined basic principles of Russian and Church Slavonic. Insofar as such a union was openly admitted, the old bookish tradition could freely influence the new writing, and this conditioned the priority of the "Slavonic" component over the "Rossiiskii" in the unified "Slavenorossiiskii" tongue. Corresponding to this development, the conception of the literary language also changed; the purist doctrine of French Classicism transformed into that Slavonicizing and rationalist purism whose theoretical basis had been established in Trediakovskii's and Lomonosov's works, and which thereupon became a commonplace of Russian linguistic thought. The cultural unity created in this way was illusory and fated to a brief existence; with its decline the epoch of "Slavenorossiiskii" was also to come to an end. The new developments produced by this decline will be examined in the following chapter.

Chapter 4

The New Cultural Differentiation; Linguistic Purity as an Ideological Category

1. The Emancipation of Culture and the Polemic Between Archaists and Innovators

The cultural synthesis of the second half of the eighteenth century was short-lived. Universal reconciliation of social interests and unceasing progress toward prosperity were the kind of fictions whose lack of verisimilitude became glaringly obvious after a certain point, even to those who had a basic stake in them. Unpleasant shocks followed one after another. The Pugachev rebellion, which paralyzed with fear not only distant provinces but the capital cities themselves demonstrated with all clarity the ephemeral nature of the alleged social contract which, according to those who had been brought up on Petrine cultural attitudes, the oppressed people had made with the enlightened monarch. "All of the common people were for Pugachev," wrote Pushkin in his "Notes on the Uprising" of 1834, which was meant to remind Nicholas I about the dark underside of monarchist ideas of social harmony. "The clergy [also] wished him well, not only the priests and monks, but the archimandrites and high clergy. The nobility alone openly took the side of the government" (Pushkin, IX, 375). By century's end the ideal of aristocratic culture, the "Europeanized culture of grandees" as G. A. Gukovskii called it (Gukovskii 1936, 32), that had claimed universal applicability no longer inspired that confidence.

The degree of disillusionment was determined by the extent of lost hopes. Analyzing the literature of the 1760's–80's, Gukovskii wrote that "Noble literature (and not only noble literature) of the eighteenth century was characterized by the notion that the rational word could perform miracles.

1. The Emancipation of Culture and the Polemic Between Archaists and Innovators

The woes of the world stem from misunderstanding, from the fact that people do not know the truth. Depraved people do not see that vice is absurd, and virtue necessary and beneficial. One should simply open the people's eyes, and everything will turn out fine, the wicked will quickly reform, and life will become beautiful. The results of this operation should be felt instantly. It was assumed that a few literary works would be enough to successfully cure the ills of society" (ibid, 36). By the 1780's more cautious appraisals sounded. On June 18, 1782, A. V. Khrapovitskii jotted down that "In sixty years schisms will disappear; as soon as popular schools are instituted and established ignorance will be destroyed of itself; then no coercion will be needed" (Khrapovitskii 1874, 2). Another ten years and practically nothing would remain of this Enlightenment confidence.

In 1781 Nikita Panin retired and Potemkin's party assumed full power, signifying the absolute nature of Catherine's rule and the triumph of the empress' pragmatic will over the rule of law, not only in practice (which had never been a question) but also as an idea. The Panin party lost influence not only because Catherine's politics changed (on this see Ransel 1975), but also because the discourse that Panin had promoted, and which had combined the ideas of monarchy, law, and universal prosperity, had become obsolete before everyone's eyes. This discourse may have remained, but only as the utopian description of an ideal order (Gleason 1981, 6–7) and not as a stimulus for social action. Fonvizin, who had gone into retirement after Panin, wrote that

> The sovereign who expects to base his absolute rule on the lack of state laws is not the most powerful. In thrall to one or several of his slaves, how can he be absolute?... Being like a transparent body through which all the inner motive springs are completely visible, he will write new laws in vain, declare the well being of his people, and glorify the wisdom of his reign; [but] the new laws will be nothing more than new rituals, making confusion of the old laws; the people will remain oppressed, the nobility humiliated, and despite his own aversion to tyranny, his rule will be tyrannical... Such a state of things cannot long endure... What then is the state? A colossus, held up by chains. The chains rip apart, the colossus falls and is destroyed by itself. (Fonvizin, II, 258)

One could acknowledge this state of affairs, and calling it "autocracy" instead of "despotism" seek justification for it (as Derzhavin did to a significant degree), but it was no longer possible to find poetic inspiration in it.

Insofar as the panegyric tradition of Classicism was based on the moral pathos of Enlightenment, centered on the court and the state, the change we have described served to dry up the very waters of inspiration. For true talent yesterday's ecstasy now sounded like insufferable deceit, the more so with each passing decade. Derzhavin, having been appointed state-secretary, fell silent, despite the fact that he had seemed to have promised to delight Catherine with ever new masterpieces on the order of "Felitsa." In his memoirs he recalls that "He could not enflame his spirit so as to preserve his former lofty ideal when he saw the human original up close, with its great weaknesses. As many times as he tried, sitting for a week locked up in his study, he was not capable of producing anything that would satisfy him; everything came out cold, strained and common, like the work of assembly-line poets, in whose works you hear only words, but no ideas or feelings" (Derzhavin, VI, 693–4; cf. 654). The odic tradition had exhausted itself. In 1784 Kniazhnin wrote:

> Я ведаю, что дерзки оды,
> Которы вышли уж из моды
> Весьма способны докучать.

(Sobesednik, XI, 5)

(I know that daring odes that have gone out of style may thoroughly annoy us.)

Actually, the end of the odic tradition might already have been signified by Derzhavin's "Felitsa." The "amusing style" and the portrait of the empress in human perspective testify to the inner rejection of that system in which the object of poetic ecstasy was the victorious empire itself, impersonal and supra-personal. As V. F. Khodasevich rightly notes, "Felitsa" was not the transfiguration of the ode but its destruction (Khodasevich 1975, 121). Of course, praise of the empress does not cease, but new themes appear. In Kniazhnin's epistle just cited he writes of the blossoming of Catherine's Russia:

> Что Россы в толь блаженной доле
> До ней и не бывали в век;
> Что здесь стесненный человек
> Досель, земли обремяненье
> На все имевший запрещенье,
> Днесь мыслить и щастливым быть,
> От ней имеет разрешенье.

(Sobesednik, XI, 4–5)

(That before her Russians never experienced such a blissful lot; that a person, before under restraint, a burden to the earth, forbidden to do anything, now has permission from her to think and to be happy.)

Private thought and individual well being here acquire the importance that state power and the wisdom of the laws used to enjoy (cf. Schenk 1972, 6;

1. The Emancipation of Culture and the Polemic Between Archaists and Innovators

Makogonenko 1987, 273–5),[1] and from this new perspective the triumphant theater of the court is exposed as a senseless sham.

This aspect of the literary process was one of the specific consequences of a profound change in worldview. The philosophical theme of the state was depleted, moved to a secondary position, and the liberated mental space became filled with new subjects. This development was common to all of Europe, and Russia took part in it as a participant in European culture. However, European culture itself acquired a special character in Russia, its features intensified and hypertrophic. Certainly, the ideology of Enlightened monarchy was universal, to a greater or lesser extent influencing state power and the reigning cultural factions. The monarch and the court were, understandably, its essential components, and if, say, Voltaire was not satisfied with them in their French variant he could seek them elsewhere, in Sans-Souci or Petersburg. The very freedom of choice, however, suggests the profound differences between the French Enlightenment and that in Russia.

For France, the epoch of Enlightenment may be said to have begun at that moment when the state lost its command over culture, which happened at the start of the eighteenth century. Of course, the state did not cease to be a cultural focus, and supplied themes for philosophy, literature and art; for this reason the search for an enlightened monarch was an organic part of the French cultural process. However, if earlier it was precisely the state that brought Enlightenment in its wake, it was now as if Enlightenment had overtaken the state and assumed the role of showing it the way. The task of observer and singer of the state's praises was replaced by that of the critic, planner and teacher. For Boileau the expression of state philosophy was the panegyric, for the Encylopedists — the critical essay. Answering the question "What is the Enlightenment?," Kant defines it as bidding farewell to mankind's immaturity, a parting in which the spheres of subordination and free speech are clearly demarcated (see Foucault 1984, 32–50). European enlightenment culture clearly belongs to the latter sphere, and one may describe this process as the emancipation of culture. Having overtaken the state, culture ceases to be controlled, and acquires autonomy and spontaneity.

---

[1] The period of Derzhavin's "amusing" odes ("Felitsa," "Blagodarnost' Felitse," "Videnie Murzy," "Izobrazhenie Felitsy") lasted less than a decade. In the 1790's Derzhavin returned to the high ode of the more traditional type (the odes "Na shvedskii mir," "Na vziatie Izmaila," etc.). Of course, the odes of this later period by no means lack experimental aspects; together with innovative stanza structure one may note a significant change in their system of imagery (for example, the introduction of Preromantic "Ossian" elements). However, it seems that Derzhavin's main poetic preoccupation was now primarily with other types of verse, with Anacreontics and with the Horatian tradition ("Lebed'," "Evgeniiu. Zhizn' zvanskaia," etc.).

Nothing comparable takes place in the early eighteenth-century Russia of Kantemir and Prokopovich.

In Russian Enlightenment the element of criticism is practically absent. It is replaced by a unique mythology of Enlightenment in which the enlightened monarch acts as creator-demiurge, founding a new Golden Age, and in which Enlightenment itself figures as one of the aspects of universal harmony produced by autocratic power.[2] This mythological background remains in full force at the beginning of Catherine's reign, and it is precisely this that the empress' reform projects take as their starting point, the basis on which Catherine assimilates French Enlightenment ideas. As the creator of a new world and messiah, the Russian monarch was committed to the most radical ideas of her age. The newer this new world was that was to arise on the Petersburg swamps so as to transform the universe, the more glorious the role of the Russian monarch who was revealed as the one who would bring about cosmic harmony, and the more this supported the myth of tsar-savior and demiurge.

This mechanism was true both for Peter the Great's radicalism and for Catherine's. In our opinion, it explains why the ideas of French Enlightenment became the semi-official ideology of Catherine's monarchy. If in Western Europe the Enlightenment represented the old age of absolutism, when it was offered a limiting contract with free reason (cf. Foucault 1984, 37), in Russia it was autocracy's childhood, in which the monarch, like a young god, appeared as the apotheosis of omnipotence. This mythological childhood, however, also had another aspect; as any official ideology, mythological or not, it could easily coexist with "despotism." The explanation for this evidently has to do with the fact that in eighteenth-century Russia there was no direct connection between state ideology and the actual mechanism of ruling the country.

One well-known example is enough to illustrate this state of affairs. In 1767 Catherine published her famous *Nakaz* (*Instruction*) which in large part reproduced the ideas of Montesquieu, Beccaria and the Encylopedists. In one of its articles it says that "In Russia the Senate is the repository of the laws" (IV, 26 — Catherine 1770, 16), and in another the Senate is accorded the right "to remonstrate (predstavliati) that a particular ukaz is contrary to

---

[2] The pastoral poetry of Russian Classicism is very indicative in this regard, as it is practically bereft of that critical potential inherent in its French models (the idyllic childhood of humanity as a device to expose its ugly old age). Russian pastoral verse testifies to a perception of history based on "a belief in a level of cultural progress never before reached" (Klein 1988, 57). As J. Klein shows, this change of cultural context is manifested even in Russian translations of French idylls (ibid, 45–56).

the Law Code, that it is harmful or obscure, that is must not be imposed" (III, 21 — ibid, 12). By "the Law Code" was understood the basic laws (a kind of constitution) and the right "to remonstrate" was immediately recognizable as the French parliament's "droit de remonstrance." It thus appears as if Russian autocracy is limiting itself by fundamental law in a most enlightened fashion (cf. Madariaga 1981, 151–5). But as is well known, there was nothing in reality that accorded to this appearance. There was no such Law Code in eighteenth-century Russia and at no time in Catherine's reign did they succeed in establishing fundamental law (on the failed attempts to create a law code, see Obozrenie 1833; Lappo-Danilevskii 1897). At the same time, moreover, the Senate in no way functioned as a representative body, or made any such remonstrances. This state of affairs is typical of many other articles of the *Nakaz*. It is fully obvious that the *Nakaz*, easily one of the most progressive juridical monuments of the eighteenth century, was at the same time a fiction that had no practical significance; this is a generally accepted fact and has often been analyzed by historians. What is of interest to us is that the *Nakaz*, like the entire state ideology, was a mythological act, and fulfilled a mythological function; it was the attribute of a monarch who establishes universal justice and creates world harmony.

It was just this way that Enlightenment culture arose in Russia, as first of all the mythological action of state power. Russian Enlightenment was a Petersburg mirage. Some Russian Enlightenment figures truly believed in its existence and others were its involuntary participants, but this does not alter it mythological essence. Above the Neva hung Semiramida's gardens, Minerva after a triumphant public prayer service inaugurated a temple to Enlightenment, Fonvizin denounced vice, and the people dwelled in bliss. This mirage was that same prototype of universal transfiguration in whose context the Russian monarch was magnified into a figure of cosmic consequence. And it was this same mirage that was reduced to nothing by the end of Catherine's reign. Insofar as Enlightenment culture in Russia (as opposed to France) was state culture, and directly embodied in Russian state mythology, the end of the epoch of Enlightenment assumed special importance. In Russia the Enlightenment firmly tied culture, secular as well as religious, to the state. This deep, fundamental connection was still fully active at the beginning of Catherine's reign, from the masquerade "Minerva Triumphant" organized by Sumarokov to the creation of the Russian Academy (which, of course, were modeled not on the activities of eighteenth-century French monarchs but those of Richelieu). Therefore the end of Enlightenment in Russia spelled the emancipation of culture, which was the direct opposite of what happened in France, where the emancipation of culture was marked precisely by the onset of Enlightenment.

The rift between state and culture had manifold consequences. It had a radical effect on all three components that made up the state cultural synthesis of Russian Enlightenment — religious culture, secular culture, and state cultural policies.

Insofar as by the end of the eighteenth century Enlightenment dogma had been compromised in the eyes of the government and ceased to serve as official ideology, church leaders were no longer obliged to harmonize their works with the spirit of Marmontel and Voltaire (§ III–3). Although administratively state control over the church only increased, Orthodoxy no longer needed such mimicry, and religious leaders no longer felt the need to present themselves as adherents of Western Enlightenment values that were not tainted by "ancient superstitions." In consequence, attempts were begun to make religious literature address the real needs of the population, without the need for philosophical subtleties or rhetorical beauties (§ IV–2). The challenge became to restore "the true face of Orthodoxy," however strange this face appeared in the imagination of particular contemporary churchmen. The process began of turning back to traditional wellsprings of Orthodox piety (translations of patristic literature, the development of ascetic theology, etc.) and attempting to connect this with eighteenth-century scholarly achievements (see Florovskii 1937, 110f; Nichols 1978).

At the same time the end of the era of state Enlightenment did not pass without effect on religious culture. Having tasted freedom from being yoked to a secular culture that was absolutely alien to it, religious culture was now not only emancipated from the secular, but consciously rejected it. The desire to isolate itself from those processes that secular culture was experiencing and to limit its circle of interests and concerns so that they did not intersect with problems of secular culture became a major feature of Orthodox religious culture right down through the 1860's. Owing to this Pushkin and Optina elder Moisei (as well as many others on both sides of the cultural divide) lived as if in mutually impenetrable worlds, knowing nothing of each other and having no need for each other.

State cultural policy also underwent radical change. Earlier the state acted as creator and master of culture, and it was for just this reason that Enlightenment could become official ideology. If for Louis XVI the Enlightenment as an independent intellectual movement was very threatening and full of bad augury, for Catherine it was a component of state mythology in which she herself was the central figure. Russia's cultural and historical development seemed controllable and fully encompassed by the Petersburg mirage; and there was nothing dangerous felt in this. In the 1750's, when

1. The Emancipation of Culture and the Polemic Between Archaists and Innovators

Catherine was reading the Encylopedists and preparing to reveal the new image of an Enlightened leader to Russia, the educated elite, which alone could serve as audience for her progressive declarations, was so few in number that it seemed possible not only to keep track of each person's ideas, but to direct them. In the 1760's, however, the social parameters of secular education significantly changed. As Gary Marker remarks, "the intellectual world of the1760s and 1770s looked very different from the world of 1740s... Ideas, politics, mentalities, and professional activity had not changed very much...There simply were many more laymen — both gentry and nongentry —coming out of secondary school and engaging in intellectual activity in the 1760s than there had ever been before" (Marker 1985, 70–1). Catherine did not give up quickly, and clearly did not abandon hope of bringing order to the after all not so greatly increased ranks of her enlightened subjects when she published *Odds and Ends* in 1769, but this undertaking turned out to be far more difficult to fulfill than conquering the Crimea. Society turned out to be insufficiently obedient and continually deviated onto unanticipated paths. Such is the emancipation of culture.

Cultural emancipation meant that culture developed beyond the bounds of mythology, took root in real life, and ceased to be controllable. In consequence, state cultural policy took on a defensive character. The end to free typographies, new censor restrictions, Fonvizin's disfavor and the arrests of Novikov and Radishchev were all signs of the new state of things. The change affected the clergy in a particularly peculiar way. If before this time the clergy had always been under suspicion for not sympathizing with state policies, now it was cast in the role of one of the main pillars of the system. Special attention was given to protecting "church books, or those relating to Holy Writ, faith, or to interpreting divine law and holiness" (PSZ, XXII, 875 — no. 16556, Feb. 27, 1787; cf. Khrapovitskii 1874, 42), censorial committees were created with the obligatory participation of a member of the clergy (PSZ, XXIII, 933 0 no. 17508, of Nov. 16, 1796), and in general the clergy unexpectedly became model and custodian of the new official worldview. The basis of "official Orthodoxy" which reached full flowering under Nicholas I was laid here; while this did not give the church freedom, now for the first time since Peter's era traditional spirituality ceased to be abhorred and could therefore develop in its own direction.

Secular culture also underwent profound changes. First of all, the religious life of secular culture changed significantly; it was now the clergy's responsibility, assigned to it by the state, to keep track of this. The disintegration of the state-oriented cultural synthesis meant that faith in progress and enlightenment by themselves ceased to satisfy the religious needs of society,

Chapter 4. The New Cultural Differentiation

and the result was new spiritual searching. For educated secular society this took place outside of the Orthodox tradition; Europeanized culture, having been freed, demanded Europeanized religion. As Georges Florovskii wrote, "these were people who had lost the eastern path and who had lost themselves on Western ones" (Florovskii 1937, 14). Spiritual searching was expressed in Freemasonry (in the forms it took in the 1780's), in Pietism, and in various mystical enthusiasms.

The attitude of the government and the church toward these pursuits was equivocal and often changed.[3] The persecution of Europeanized religious non-conformism was begun by Catherine, who felt threatened by the free moral development of society. At first church leaders who were accustomed to government-sanctioned free-thinking did not see any threat; Platon (Levshin) highly valued Novikov's Christian virtues and among his publications described as dangerous not the Masonic literature but "the vile and absurd fruits of the encylopedists" (Pypin 1916, 185). Emperor Alexander, on the contrary, attempted to impart an official character to Europeanized religiosity (a belated attempt to recreate, in a new guise, the lost synthesis of state and culture), but ran into opposition from the clergy that had acquired a certain independence of thought and the will to defend its own values.

The collapse of the state-cultural synthesis also affected the character of the literary process. The state theme was no longer central, and poetic inspiration sought new sources that belonged to the sphere of autonomous culture. This was felt in the development of small genres, first of all in love poetry. As Derzavin wrote in 1797:

> Так не надо звучных строев:
> Переладим струны вновь;
> Петь откажемся героев,
> А начнем мы петь любовь.
>
> (Derzhavin, II, 137)

(We do not need resounding displays. Let's retune our strings again; we will refuse to sing of heroes, and rather start to sing of love.)

This literary development determined the new tasks of poetics and style. The ode and the poetry of high genres in general ceased to serve as the

---

[3] It would be strange to explain the interest in Western mystical and pietistic movements merely by a lack of religious education, as does Hans Rothe [...] (Rothe 1984, 84–5). The issue was that the Russian educated class did not acknowledge the Orthodox tradition primarily because it was perceived as "non-European," that it did not give nourishment to the "European" soul and intellect. In was precisely the combination of the spiritual upset that resulted from the crisis of Enlightenment plus the lack of receptivity to national spirituality that led to supra-confessional religious pursuits, including the fascination with mystical literature.

1. The Emancipation of Culture and the Polemic Between Archaists and Innovators

sphere in which norms for the literary language were set (§ II–2.2). The high genres remained for the most part traditional both in poetics and language, and withdrew to the periphery of the literary process. If before elements of odic poetics had at times flickered in the elegy or heroid, now the interaction between genres worked in the reverse direction and panegyric verse now took on certain features of love poetry. If the poetic pathos preserved something of its force, it was no longer in the triumphant ode, but in verse dedicated to the theme of the poet himself and to poetry. This change in the focus of poetic ecstasy also indicates the end of the synthesis of state and culture and signals the emancipation of culture.

Indeed the religious and mythological potential that had earlier been linked to the state and monarch as architects of cosmic harmony was now transferred to culture itself, and the poet took on that demiurgical charismatic authority that had earlier devolved on the emperor. For this reason philosophical lyrics dedicated to the poet and to poetry (from Karamzin's "Poeziia" to Tiutchev's "Uraniia") took the place of the ode, and it was precisely this kind of verse that occupied the central place in high-style poetry. The poet emerges as the sacralized figure who mediates between the divine and the human (cf. Zhivov 1981, 70–6):

> Благоговей, земля! Склоните слух, народы!
> Певцы бессмертные вещают Бога вам.
>
> ("Uraniia")

(Be reverent, earth! Incline your ear, peoples! Immortal singers announce God to you.)

Thus the mythology of the state produced the mythology of the poet. Here in my opinion is one of the main sources of that special attitude toward poetry and literature that distinguishes modern Russia; the poet and writer rather than politician turn out to be the ones who maintain social harmony and regulate social good. Naturally, these ideas were not relevant for the entire society; one can see how the educated class provided itself with its own idols that were profoundly alien to those raised on traditional culture.

The emancipation of culture was thus a process that led to the further cultural differentiation of society and to the formation of opposing cultural traditions. Moreover this new differentiation was superimposed upon the old opposition between Europeanized culture, created as a result of the Petrine reforms, and traditional Russian culture that was to a significant extent preserved by the lower social classes and in one way or another remained significant for the educated class that was cut off from them. But even in the context of the former, the transparent wholeness of the dominant Enlightenment discourse was lost, and Russian Europeans ceased to understand one another, just as the unenlightened majority that had preserved the traditions of the fathers and grandfathers did not understand them. This cultural multilingualism conditioned a whole series of conflicts and controversies, leading to the constant semiotization and ideologization of linguistic and cultural behavior, and did not contribute at all to the establishment of a single, universal literary language. This contradictory situation served as the context for the further history of this language in the late eighteenth and early nineteenth century.

1.1 The Collapse of the Cultural-Linguistic Synthesis and the Karamzinian Program

The disintegration of the cultural and linguistic synthesis of the second half of the eighteenth century undermined the position of the "Slavenorossiiskii" literary language. The reaction against it was most clearly expressed in the linguistic program of Karamzin and his followers. This program has been the subject of numerous specialized studies (cf. Vinogradov 1935, 45f; Vinogradov 1938, 157–88; Kovalevskaia 1958; Levin 1964; Lotman and Uspenskii 1975; Uspenskii 1985), and so there is no need to recount it here. I will dwell only on those aspects of particular interest for our inquiry.

The most significant is the moment of rejection itself. Karamzin made his appearance as a linguistic reformer, making a break with the past, and the past with which he broke was precisely the Slavenorossiiskii linguistic synthesis of the preceding period. Karamzin's own periodization of the literary language may serve as evidence of this: "Dividing our language (slog) into epochs, the first should start with Kantemir, the second with Lomonosov, the third with the Slaveno-Russian translations of Mr. Elagin and his numerous imitators, and the fourth with our own time, in which a pleasant style (slog) is being developed" (Karamzin. I, 577). The preceding period, associated with the names of Elagin and Fonvizin, is seen by the Karamzinists as an epoch of the indiscriminate and unjustified influence of the church language which they held should have no association with the pleasant style. Commenting on the fact that in childhood Fonvizin read in church as a sexton, Viazemskii writes:

> "I do not agree with the author, who ascribes his knowledge of Russian to these pious exercises. We do not consider sextons and seminarists who clearly read more holy books than he did to be connoisseurs of the language and ideal

models. The influence of the Slavonic tongue, despite Fonvizin's opinion and that of many of our literary men, was not only not beneficial, but perhaps harmful to the author. He used it without thinking and was not able to cope with harmonizing the church language with the language of society..." (ibid, 18–9).

This harmonizing is declared to be impossible in principle and the benefit of church books nonexistent. The Slavenorossiiskii language turns out to be a fiction devised by writers unable to cope with the language in order to cover up their failings. Dashkov writes of "the imaginary Slavenorossiiskii language" (1811, 3; cf. Dashkov 1810, 258–9 and 264–5), and Viazemskii agrees that in language "there are no such two-headed creations as Siamese twins, and that is just as well, because such a language would be a monstrosity" (ibid, 36). Viazemskii is writing here about Fonvizin's translation of Bitaubé's "Joseph," which serves for him as a model of macaronic style that fundamentally sins against linguistic purity. His comments are not meant as a personal attack on Fonvizin but as a principled refutation of the ideas on which the "Slavenorossiiskii language" was based. In fact, Fonvizin's foreword had posed the problem of harmonizing Russian and Church Slavonic as the central one facing the literary language and he conceived of his translation as a model of their harmonization, conceptualized as a basic stylistic compromise.[4] It is just this compromise that Viazemskii cannot accept:

> According to some traditions, Fonvizin is considered the first writer in Russia after Lomonosov able to successfully combine the Slavonic and Russian languages. Novikov said of this translation that in it the translator preserved the seriousness of Slavonic and the purity of the Russian language [Viazemskii is citing his *Attempt at a Historical Dictionary of Russian Writers* — Novikov 1772, 231]. Everyone has repeated his words. [But] in the first place, it should have been indicated what kind of combination was being referred to, because it is impossible to simply claim that Russian lacks dignity or that Slavonic

---

[4] Fonvizin wrote: "All of our books are written either in Slavonic or in today's language. Perhaps I am mistaken, but it seems to me that in translations of such books as *Telemachus, Argenida, Joseph* and others of this type one must hold to the solemnity of the Slavonic language, but at the same time observe the clarity of ours. For although the Slavonic language is clear in itself, it is not so for those who do not use it. Consequently, the style must be such as we do not yet have. *Telemachus* is translated into Slavonic; and in *Argenida* I found many of our contemporary expressions, which it seems to me do not well accord with this book's seriousness. And so the greatest difficulty consisted in choosing a style. A multitude of Slavonic words and expressions came to mind, but I was forced to reject them as not having a precedent, for I feared to muddle the language's clarity or spoil its tender sound. Our modern words and expressions also came to mind, but I abandoned them [as well] as not having precedents, fearing that they were not commensurate with the solemnity of the author's idea" (Fonvizin 1769, foreword, l.1 verso — 2; Fonvizin, I, 433–4).

lacks a characteristic purity of its own (pertaining to its own usage). One can speak of the combination of individual words or on the other hand about the combination of forms, turns of phrase, or characteristics of two languages... The first combination is useful and even necessary... The second combination is unrealizable and undesirable; it cannot be natural, and consequently, it cannot be graceful... All of our writers have held and hold to the first combination, [but] the second I can find nowhere, neither in Lomonosov, nor in Kostrov, nor even in Petrov, who more openly than anyone else bound himself to the Slavonic yoke. I say nowhere, for I cannot consider something with no harmony as a combination... Lomonosov's prose language is a body enlivened now by the German and now by the Latin spirit, to which Slavonic words are added. Fonvizin's language, using the same additions, often loses its way due to Gallicisms. In neither this nor the other is there pure Russian or pure Slavonic, nor even pure Slaveno-Russian, if there can even be purity amid so much excess. (Viazemskii, V, 35–6)

Irremediable macaronism ("excess") is ascribed to Slavenorossiiskii, so that any way of detecting purity is called into question.

Continuing to apply categories taken from European linguistic and stylistic theories, the Karamzinists rejected the basic thesis of the common nature of Russian and Church Slavonic on which the entire edifice of the Slavenorossiiskii language had been constructed (§ III–1.2). The assertion of their common nature was now polemically reversed: parting company with the literary past, the Karamzinists now apply to the history of Russian the well-known scheme in which Latin's transformation into the Romance languages resulted from its contamination with barbarian dialects—that very scheme whose inapplicability to Russian Trediakovskii had tried to prove (§ III–2.1). Hence Dashkov could write that "while the basis for Russian is Slavonic," however "into the Russian dialect were incorporated numerous Tatar and other foreign words" and therefore "this dialect became completely separate from its roots due to the dissimilarity of many words and the difference in conjugations and even in the rules of syntax, and in this way became a separate language, just like other European ones" (Dashkov 1811, 32). Elsewhere he notes that "The language which we speak split off from Slavonic long ago because of the introduction of many Tartar words and expressions that were formerly completely unknown" (Dashkov 1810, 260). Viazemskii similarly writes of the impossibility of combining "forms, turns [of speech], and characteristics [i.e., the different natures] of the two languages, or even of one and the same language which has become different in its progressive stages of development" (Viazemskii, V, 35).

This was the reason why proving the South Slavic character of Church Slavonic was so important for the Karamzinists; if this were the case Church Slavonic would not represent the "roots" of Russian but was opposed to it by nature from the start. Hence Slavenorossiiskii mixed the natures of two different languages and was therefore fundamentally impure. Batiushkov wrote Gnedich on October 28–9, 1816: "Kachenovskii read a treatise on Slavic dialects... He asserts that the Bible was written in the Serbian dialect; I think that Karamzin says the same thing. And the Slavonic language has completely disappeared... No, I have never had such hatred for that mandarin, slavish, Tatar-Slavonic language as I do now! The more I delve into our language, the more I write and think, the more I become convinced that our language does not tolerate Slavonicisms, and that it takes the utmost mastery to purloin ancient words and give them a place in our language, whose grammar, syntax, in a word, everything, is contrary to the Serbian dialect" (Batiushkov, III, 409; for more detail, see Uspenskii 1985, 37–41).[5]

In denying Russian and Church Slavonic a common nature, the Karamzinists defined Church Slavonic (as well as Slavenorossiiskii) as a "special bookish language which one must learn like a foreign one" (Makarov, I, 2: 38–9). As a result Slavonicisms were seen as borrowings which had to be eliminated from the "pure" language. The Karamzinists' goal was precisely this, to show that Slavonicisms belong to the "impure" elements. One but not the only way to do this was to classify them under the rubric of borrowings. They could just as easily have categorized them as archaisms, which corresponded to the view of Church Slavonic as outdated and incomprehensible. Thus Makarov assigned "the development of a new language" to Lomonosov's era, and asserted that after that time Church Slavonic had become just as unintelligible as the language in France before Malherbe. Equating the Russian linguistic situation to the French, Makarov asked: "Can any Frenchman today really understand Montaigne or Rabelais?"(ibid, 20, 22). Insofar as literary texts before Lomonosov turn out to be incomprehensible and unrelated to modern usage, "more than two thirds of Russian vocabulary remained unused" (ibid), i.e., Slavonicisms are now treated as words that have gone out of use, or archaicisms. In demolishing the Slavenorossiiskii synthesis, the Karamzinists also repudiated the notion of Russian's (Slavenorossiiskii's) special richness; since Slavonicisms are

---

[5] That which was a revelation for Batiushkov was by no means so for Russian linguistic thought as a whole. One way or another, both Adodurov, and Trediakovskii, and Lomonosov, and, very explicitly, A. A. Barsov, had all spoken of the south Slavic basis of Church Slavonic (see Uspenskii 1985, 108–11). However, for them this fact was not evidence of the different nature of the two languages; one simply needed a broader approach to the notion of a language's nature, as common features were present to a greater or lesser extent in all Slavic languages.

Chapter 4. The New Cultural Differentiation

a borrowed element, the treasure-house of Slavnorossiiskii turns out to be bankrupt. Karamzin specifically addresses this issue in his note "On the Richness of Language" of 1795: "The true richness of a language consists not in the multiplicity of sounds, nor in the multiplicity of words, but in the number of thoughts which it can express. A rich language is one in which you can find words not only to describe your main ideas, but also to clarify the differences among them, their nuances, with greater or lesser emphasis, simplicity or complexity. Otherwise it is poor: poor despite all of its millions of words. Of what benefit is it that in Arabic certain physical objects, for example, swords and lions, have 500 names, when the language is unable to express any subtle moral ideas and feelings?" (Shevyrev 1854, no. 12, 184; see also Karamzin, III, 641).[6] Viazemskii writes exactly the same thing in the article "On the Misuse of Words" of 1827 (from which we quoted above) apropos the lack of a precise equivalent in Russian for the French verb "déguiser": "we still lack various words, despite all of the exclamations of our patriotic or (excuse me!) fatherlandophilic philologists and (once again!) wordophiles, who marvel at the richness of our language, a richness, we add in passing, of material, physical reserves, but we often remain in debt when we require words that are more subtle, abstract, or ethical" (Viazemskii, I, 270).

The entire edifice based on assigning the Russian literary language "ancient" status (§ III–2.1) falls apart, and the sources of its "ancient character" are mocked. In this context the change in attitude toward Greek influence on Church Slavonic is especially indicative. For the Karamzinists this influence does not impart any special qualities to Slavonic, but distorts its nature. Karamzin writes: "The authors and translators of our religious books completely modeled their language on Greek; they put *prepositions* everywhere, they drew everything out, they combined many words, and this *chemical operation* altered the initial purity of ancient Slavonic. The *Song of Igor's Campaign*, a precious remainder of it, shows that it was quite different from our church books" (Karamzin, III, 604). Makarov's statements are fully analogous: "Our ancestors succeeded in taking from the Greeks many terms and several metaphors; abandoning the ancient Slavonic dialect, they succeeded in forming their language according to the character of Greek. *Did it flourish* with *borrowed beauties* we cannot say with certainty; for that one

---

[6] The reference to Arabic clearly recalls French protests against the extravagance of eastern languages. Bouhours, for example, speaks about this with disdain, discussing richness in terms of the ability to express necessary ideas, and expressing skepticism toward lexical abundance per se. He wrote in particular that "Abundance is not always the mark of languages' perfection. They are enriched up to the point that they start to become corrupted if their richness consists exclusively in a multitude of words [alone]" (Bouhours, 1671, 85–6).

would have to see and *understand* the pure Slavonic language, which we no longer can today" (Makarov, I,2, 18–9; for more details see Uspenskii 1985, 22–3). It is obvious that we are dealing with the very same scheme that was constructed by Trediakovskii and Lomonosov, and that was so often repeated thereafter (§ III–2.1), which asserted that richness and beauty had passed from Greek to Church Slavonic and from Church Slavonic to the Russian literary language; in the Karamzinian version it is not richness and beauty that pass from Greek to Church Slavonic and Slavenorossiiskii but impurity and a profusion of useless words.

Protest against compound words (on their significance see § III–2.1) naturally also finds a place in this inverted scheme. Thus Dashkov, polemicizing with Shishkov, who had translated two articles by La Harpe and supplied them with his own commentary, writes:

> La Harpe speaks of complex Greek words like a person who is living in poverty and who is amazed by someone else's wealth. Mr. Translator applies La Harpe's words to our language. We can find no fewer multimomentous words in our language than in Greek... Of course, the compound adjectives *светоносный, лучезарный, искрометный* are very useful to our poets and orators. But Mr. Translator does not stop here, and continues: We say *древо благосеннолиственное*. Let them find me in French a word including three different ideas in it! Who says *древо благосеннолиственное*? Not only do we not, but in the entire Bible I don't think there's any such word. (Dashkov 1810, 297–8)

Further, Dashkov asks, "Must one seek huge and heavily sonorous words in tender compositions?" and cites some remarkable examples of this kind of creation: *длинногустозакоптелая борода, христогробопокланяемая страна*, etc. (ibid 299). Shishkov himself makes note of the Karamzinists' attitude toward compound words: "One of them.. does not wish to believe that *благодатный, неискусобрачный, тлетворный, злокозненный, багрянородный* are Russian words because they haven't read them either in Liza or Aniuta [i.e., sentimentalist texts]" (see Vinogradov 1935, 50).

Attitudes toward hexameter are also evidently related to this (on Trediakovskii in this connection, see § III–2.1). In general, disagreements about hexameter are not related to the debate between archaists and innovators (as it could be defended by both the Armazinian Uvarov and the archaist Vostokov — see Gasparov 1984, 125–6), however, hexameter's connection to Greek, and via this to Slavenorossiiskii evidently remained significant for the Karamzinists. Thus Viazemskii wrote in 1827: "If the best hexameters in the Russian language, that is, the hexameters by Zhukovskii and Gnedich, are called Russian verse only by abusing the term, what can we say about bad hexameters, about the abuse of an abuse?" (Viazemskii, I, 276). Denying hexameters membership in Russian poetry, Viazemskii seems to have considered this meter alien to its structure and ultimately to the nature of the language.

And so Slavenorosiiskii's exceptional richness turns out to be but a heap of words not fit for use in a pure language, similar to what French writers lacking in noble taste had left behind (e.g., Montaigne, whom Makarov cites, or Ronsard). This false richness requires someone to clean it up, a new Malherbe, and this is the role that Karamzin assumes. "Karamzin," writes N. I. Grech,

> by means of his lucid mind and tender feeling divined and used a true Russian combination of words, and — like Malherbe — figured out where each word should go... He saw and proved in practice that the Russian language, based on its own and not on ancient principles, was constructed like other modern languages, simple, direct, logical; that the expressiveness of its declensions and conjugations gives it the right to dispose of words according to the demands of meaning, and not according to Cicero's twisted locutions. Lomonosov created the language. To Karamzin we are indebted for Russian style. (Grech, I, 127).

Trying to assimilate features of ancient languages, in the first place free word order (on its interpretation as an element of linguistic richness, see § III–2.1), and the construction of rhetorical periods based on this are now seen as a mistake, similar to those committed by the poets of the Pléiade. In this light Lomonosov's linguistic instructions are also perceived as erroneous. Thus in the place of Malherbe-Lomonosov comes Malherbe-Karamzin.[7]

Indeed, for the Karamzinists the French model of literary and linguistic development acquired new significance. They again appealed to French purism while rejecting the interpretation which the Classicist doctrine had been given in Russia in the mid-eighteenth century; they tried to assimilate Vaugelas' linguistic theories in their original form, according to which usage

---

[7] Pushkin makes the comparison of the "Slaveno-Russian" trend with that of Pléiade (in connection with the question of linguistic richness and the influence of Greek): "Talented people, struck by the insignificance and (one must say) the ignobility of French poetry, took it into their minds that the povetry of the language was the reason and they began to try and remake it on the model of ancient Greek. A new school developed whose opinions, goal and efforts recall that of our own "Slaveno-Russians,"among whom there were also people of talent. But the labors of Ronsard, Jodelle and Du Bellay were in vane. The language refused to go in direction that was alien to it and instead took its own road again. Finally, Malherbe arrived, with such brilliant clarity, with such strict justice that he is considered a great critic" (from "On the Insignificance of Russian Literature,"1834 — Pushkin XI, 270. Following this passage comes the well-known quotation from Boileau).

1. The Emancipation of Culture and the Polemic Between Archaists and Innovators

and taste were put forward as the main criteria for the purity of language without reference to "reason" or rules of grammar, not to mention church books (see Tomashevskii 1959, 44–6; Uspenskii 1985, 61–5). The orientation on conversational usage naturally led the Karamzinists to juxtapose Russian and Church Slavonic. Insofar as this opposition was a given, it determined the interpretation of the purist rubrics — generally speaking, the very same as the first codifiers of Russian had followed (§ II–1.2). Linguistic thought, having completed a circle, now returned, as it were, to its initial starting point.

This was not a complete return, however, as the literary and linguistic situation in which the Karamzinists were operating was significantly different from that of the 1730's. Indeed, when Trediakovskii had imported French stylistic principles onto Russian soil he had come up against insuperable difficulties on account of Russia's total lack of its own modern literary tradition (§ II–1). The French program demanded the purification of the literary language, but in Russia, as opposed to France, there had been nothing yet to purify: a literary language distinct from Church Slavonic and depending on a secular linguistic tradition did not exist. By the end of the eighteenth century the situation was quite different, and a language reformer could already refer to a wide variety of properly literary texts that had come into being over a long span of development. A reformer could reject the stylistic or aesthic principles of these texts, but independent of his predilections they had established multiple precedents for the use of a whole series of words, expressions, and constructions which were no longer associated either with traditions of church literature or with common "vulgar" usage.

In the early period of codifying the literary language the question of what a Slavonicism was (as a thing to be rejected) had been quite tangible, but after a half century linguistic consciousness had undergone significant development, and the question could no longer be posed in the same way. Viazemskii, analyzing Fonvizin's language, wrote: "what do the so-called Slavonicisms consist of in Fonvizin's translation of *Joseph*? In the words *паче, паки* and the like, and in his preserving the letter *u* in the infinitives —that's all. These Slavonicisms recall the caricatures of French vaudeville, characters who try to pass themselves off as Italians by peppering their French with the words *perchgi, ogiè*, and so on" (Viazemskii, V, 38). The Karamzinists simply eliminated Slavonicisms of this sort—elements which were perceived as strictly bookish, as characteristic of high genres, and which could be easily replaced by corresponding Russian elements.

Elements of another sort which were also genetically Slavonic but which had become established in various literary genres were preserved as neutral and were not subjected to restrictions; it was no longer even necessary to question whether or not they were Slavonicisms. This was precisely the case with participles (see Lotman and Uspenskii 1975, 203–4). Podshivalov, who in many ways was close to Karamzin and the Karamzinists, had already written that it was not necessary "to avoid the use of participles that are more characteristic of the Russian language than the constant *который, который*" (Podshivalov 1796, 52–3); the genetic aspect of participles that was still important for Lomonosov (§ II–2.2) thus became irrelevant. Somewhat later and in harmony with the new linguistic ideas, Pushkin formulated this approach clearly and openly. He noted that "it is not the pronouns *сей* and *оный* alone, but participles in general and a multitude of necessary words are usually avoided in conversation. We don't say *карета, скачущая по мосту, слуга, метущий комнату* [*carriage, dashing across the bridge, servant, sweeping the room*], we say: *которая скачет, который метет* [*which is dashing, who is sweeping*] and so on, replacing the expressive brevity of the participle with a flaccid phrase. It does not yet follow from this that participles should be banned. The richer a language in expressions and turns of speech the better for a skilled writer. The written language is enlivened every minute with expressions born in conversation, but it should not deny that which it has acquired over the course of centuries" (Pushkin, XII, 96). "That which it acquired over the course of centuries" does not require genetic validation and is used by virtue of the tradition that had been created from the time of the early Trediakovskii up through the young Karamzin.

Finally, there were elements of a third type: Slavonicisms which were allowed for stylistic purposes or as poetic license. Although these were consciously recognized as Slavonicisms, it was still hard for the Karamzinists to ban them in the face of established literary tradition; stylistic differentiation substituted for banishment. Thus Dashkov wrote that "in our literature a lofty style cannot exist without the aid of Slavonic, but this necessity to use a dead language in order to support a living one... demands great prudence of us" (1810, 263). Viazemskii makes similar assertions: "Slavonic words are good when they are needed and necessary, when they make up for the lack of Russian ones. Then they are legitimate, and what cannot be cured must be endured. In the poetic language they are good as synonyms, as aids which poetic license permits and which at times serve the euphoniousness of the line, the rhyme, or the meter" (Viazemskii, V, 36). This position in essence corresponded to that version of Lomonosov's stylistic theory in which "Slavonic" elements appear as specifically lofty (§ III–2.2). In this instance the basic approach to Slavonicisms shares features with that of Podshivalov. Reviewing poetic liberties, he distinguishes "well known words which would not be accepted in standard prose" (Podshivalov 1798, 54), in this way himself creating a rubric to legalize Slavonicisms that have become engrained in the literary tradition.[8]

The special status of these Slavonicisms that were permitted in poetry and legitimized by tradition distinguishes them from those of the first type, i.e., marked Slavonicisms "for whose understanding one needs a new dictionary" (Podshivalov 1798, 57). Emphasizing the alien nature of these to the literary language, Podshivalov does not even include them in the category of archaism or borrowing but calls them neologisms, the kind that even poetic license totally rejects. He writes "about those who with surprising nonchalance grace our language with *неделимцы, пругло, самопруглости, ячность, янство, големый, неголемый* and so on," and he concludes that "this kind of unbridled license is in no way forgivable" (ibid, 57–8). In this way real Church Slavonic words that zealous proponents of the Slavenorossiiskii conception might in fact draw from church books like *пругло* and *големый*[9] were purposefully likened to the infelicitous invention of new words. Marked Slavonicisms were thus juxtaposed to those assimilated by the literary tradition. The latter lexical Slavonicisms were so well absorbed that the issue was not really about banning them from poetry, but about permitting the corresponding Russicisms into poetry. Viazemskii wrote: "One can't help regret that the peculiar kind of preference accorded Slavonic words over Russian ones has crowded many of them out of the poetic language, as if they were low. Now one cannot quite bring oneself to say *рот, лоб, губы* (mouth, forehead, lips) in verse, although in conversation, even the most correct, you wouldn't say about a familiar beauty: her *чело* and *уста* (brow and lips) are superior to others" (Viazemskii, V, 36).

The existence of a recognized literary tradition brought the Russian cultural and linguistic situation closer to European models, so that the linguistic positions of Karamzin and his followers were far less radical and utopian than those of the young Trediakovskii and the other philologists of

---

[8] Podshivalov also speaks here of syntactical inversions: "A poet is sometimes allowed to place words in an order different from that which the character of the language demands," although "the reader does not like [having to] overcome difficulties and will not forgive the poet this liberty very willingly; but this is only when rare beauty and enchanting pictures make him forget himself, and, so to speak, his strict scruples nod" (Podshivalov 1796, 55–6). In eighteenth-century linguistic consciousness inversion represented a syntactic Slavonicism (cf. Uspenskii 1985, 28–9; Zhivov 1986b) that was necessary in poetic speech.

[9] The word *големый* also serves as a sign of inappropriate Slavonicization in Karamzin and Dmitriev (see Uspenskii 1985, 32), just as it had half a century earlier in Prokopovich (§1–2.1).

the 1730's. Only one major parameter had not changed, and continued to differentiate the Russian literary situation from the French, and that was that normalized conversational speech that was to juxtapose the language of the court and good society to that of other social groups remained just as much an unfulfilled ideal in the early nineteenth century as it had been seventy years before. French reigned both at court and in "the best homes," and therefore conversational usage of the social elite remained just as fictional a criterion of linguistic purity as in Trediakovskii's day. However, unlike Trediakovskii, the Karamzinists did not try to hide this problem. They posed the challenge of perfecting conversational speech and as an instrument to achieve this pointed to belles-lettres. Karamzin wrote that "the French write as they speak, but Russians should speak about many subjects as a talented man will write" (Karamzin, III, 529). Makarov makes the same point (see Uspenskii 1985, 18). At the same time, the criterion of spoken usage is replaced by the criterion of taste (see Levin 1964, 122–6; Uspenskii 1985, 19–21). This was not foreign to Vaugelas' theory- otherwise, how to distinguish a model courtier from a grandee who did not belong "to the healthiest part of the court"? But if for Vaugelas taste was a subordinate, auxiliary criterion of conversational usage, for the Karamzinists it took central place.

In this new cultural and linguistic situation the approach to purifying the literary language of Slavonicisms was significantly different from that of the 1730's. The main difference was due to the literary tradition—the use of genetically Church Slavonic elements that had been sanctioned by writers from Lomonosov to Fonvizin and Derzhavin. This tradition helped determine linguistic consciousness and was common to both the archaists and innovators. While principles of usage and evaluation of various types of Slavonicisms differed, the types themselves were defined more or less identically and provoked almost no disagreement. The argument was over the permissibility or need for strictly bookish elements, specific to lofty genres, and over stylistic limitations on the use of corresponding Russianisms and Slavonicisms. Significantly, these debates ignored the large body of genetically Slavonic elements which were perceived as neutral, so that no one argued about them. Problems of linguistic norms gradually gave way to issues of literary style, that is, the debate concerned not the choice of which road to take but what mode of travel to use, and this prepared the ground for Pushkin's synthesis.

1.2 The Polemic over Language and Problems of Cultural Self-Consciousness

Karamzin's reform was a reaction against the literary and linguistic situation that had come to exist in the second half of the eighteenth century and which was defined by the conception of the "Slavenorossiiskii" literary language. The start of the reform relates to a time before the polemic between archaists and innovators, and therefore its basic substance must be understood not in reference to the dispute between these literary trends but in reference to the previous literary epoch. Furthermore, the later dispute introduced new issues into the Karamzinian position that cannot be reduced to a protest against the recent literary past; these issues were polemically connected to the further original elaboration of the "Slavenorossiiskii" conception in the period after the demise of the linguistic-cultural synthesis of the 1760's-80's, that is, to the new interpretation of this conception in the works of Shiskov and his allies.

We should keep in mind that the Karamzinist and Shishkovite positions, for all their antagonism, were modifications of one and the same basic doctrine of Classicist purism. Such ideas as purism, clarity, unnaturalness, and overblown style (nadutost') were common theoretical ideas, understood identically, but informed by different linguistic content. The main line dividing the opposing camps was, in essence, their attitude toward Church Slavonic: for the Karamzinists, this language differed in nature from Russian, and hence created impurity when combined with it; for Shishkov and his followers, Church Slavonic and Russian were of the same nature, and therefore their combination did not cause impurity. This basic point of conflict defined their entire further corresponding receptions of purist doctrine.

For the Karamzinists the open rejection of the Church Slavonic tradition did in fact facilitate the free assimilation of elements of the colloquial language into the literary tongue; for Shishkov, on the contrary, embracing Slavonicisms made them the predominant element in the literary language and thrust conversational forms aside into the rubric of popular speech (vulgarisms). Insofar as banning Slavonicisms was liable to cause a definite depletion of available word-stock, the Karamzinists foresaw the possibility of filling the gap by means of borrowed words; in any case, they preferred borrowings to seeking out obscure terms from church books. Of course, the Karamzinists also condemned the use of borrowings, but this violation of the French canon seemed more tolerable than the Slavenorossiiskii alternative.

Chapter 4. The New Cultural Differentiation

This dualism in relation to borrowings (recognizing them as impure but tolerating their use) is clearly seen in Viazemskii's statements defending borrowings due to the absence of necessary words: "One may say of our language that it is very rich and very poor. Many words necessary for depicting small shades of meaning and feeling are lacking... To take words from neighbors like foreign currency is not good, although we do use Dutch guldens, and no one disdains them. That's the whole point, that a skilful writer is permitted to put Dutch guldens into circulation when he has none of his own. That is what Karamzin did. The English also do this" (Viazemskii, VIII, 26; cf. Uspenskii 1985, 24).[10]

To the contrary, Shishkov and his supporters, counting on the resources Church Slavonic had to offer, decisively and uncompromisingly rejected borrowings. Accepting Slavonicisms into the literary language led the archaists to practically eliminate the rubrics of archaic and scholarly words, rubrics which for the Karamzinists were especially relevant insofar as they served as labels which discredited the Slavonicisms they would banish. As far as the other rubrics, the positions of Karamzin's and Shishkov's followers were essentially identical. Both for example rejected bureaucratic and dialectical vocabulary. Their position on neologisms was also similar: both saw them as a necessary exception to the purist program, one which was impossible to avoid in order to create Russian equivalents of borrowed words; they argued not about the fundamental permissibility of calques, but over individual cases which were not to the taste of one of the opposing camps. Karamzin supposed it necessary "to compose or think up new words, similar to the way the Germans composed and thought up new words when

---

[10] There are French precedents for references to the English language and its freedom from purist restrictions (see Brunot, VI, 2, 1002). They may also be encountered in eighteenth-century Russian writings on language, in particular, in connection with the same issue of borrowing. Thus in the notes to a translation of a work concerning the improvement of the English language published in *Opyt trudov Vol'nogo Rossiiskogo sobraniia*, M. I. Pleshcheev, writing under the pseudonym "Anglophile," wrote: "The spread of the to some extent established practice in our language, introduced some time ago, of throwing out all foreign words that are already in general use, and, I make bold to say, already naturalized, and to replace them with Russian words that no one understands, or at least do not have as clear a meaning as the former, is very odious. We see that there is no people whose arts and sciences prosper to any extent who would not borrow from other peoples... The English, although they have an abundant language, accept many technical terms that are used by other peoples without changing them" (Pleshcheev 1776, 35–6). In many other respects Anglophile's remarks also coincide with those of the Karamzinists, but what was the extravagant opinion of a lone voice in 1776 became the position of an influential literary movement in the early nineteenth century. Insofar as such views became institutionalized, they became less radical, and the use of borrowings changed from being a question of principle into an acceptable deviation from reigning purist doctrine.

they began to write in their own language" (Karamzin, II, 345). This kind of summons found an analogue in the proposal by the compilers of the Academy dictionary to "as far as possible avoid foreign words and try to replace them with those... newly composed according to the character of Slavenorossiiskii" (Sukhomlinov, VIII, 127–8). In his view of neologisms, Shishkov accepted the Russian Academy's authority.

Debates over calques that are especially notable in Shishkov's polemics with Karamzin himself, rather than with his followers (cf. Garde 1986, 281), were clearly shaped by their differing views of the nature of the Russian language. For Shishkov individual calques from French do harm to it, while for Karamzin Russian is close in nature to other modern European languages, so that calques from them cause no damage.

Externally, Shishkov's attitude toward Church Slavonic was no different from that of Trediakovskii or Lomonosov; like them, he maintained that "the strength and richness of the Russian language derive from Slavonic" (Sukhomlinov, VII, 192). However, this external similarity doesn't erase important differences. For Trediakovskii and Lomonosov acceptance of the Church Slavonic linguistic legacy was dictated by the desire to legitimize literary practice and to come to terms with the seemingly impossible task of removing Slavonic elements from the literary language (§ III–1); at the same time their approach was connected to the search for a normalizing principle to regularize the new literary language.

Shishkov faced no such problems. Church Slavonic material had become firmly established in literary practice, and those restrictions which the "new style" imposed by no means required their complete removal (§ IV–1.1). Slated for removal were only marked Slavonicisms and lexical details which had no defining significance for "Slavenorossiiskii" literary practice. For Shishkov, on the other hand, it was precisely lexicon and phraseology that were significant; he did not defend or use elements of the Slavonic grammatical system such as infinitives in *-mu* or single negation, and he had practically no interest in questions of grammatical regularization. However, marked lexical Slavonicisms were precious for Shishkov, precious not even so much for their usage, but simply to be preserved as part of the literary language as a connection to the Slavic past and a symbol of its fidelity to the national spirit.

From Shishkov's point of view Church Slavonic's importance was not that, having become normative, it would serve as gauge of the literary language's correctness (cf. § III–2.3), but rather that it was the language of the ancient Slavs. The problem of the Church Slavonic linguistic legacy was connected to the problem of nationality. The Karamzinist reform seemed to him a break with national origins, a step on the path leading to the ruin of Russian culture. The very notion of nationality as the basis of culture, of folk genius which is revealed in ancient civilization, as opposed to modern cosmopolitan civilization that strips away the unique features which make culture fertile, and the connection between language and national spirit were all ideas typical of the Preromantic period, and one cannot help noticing the influence of Herder on the writings of Shishkov and his adherents, whether direct or second hand (on the archaists' Romanticism see: Lotman 1971, 15–21; Lotman and Uspenskii 1975, 174f). In Russian conditions, the idea of nationality clearly belonged to the group of ideas that arose on the ruins of the Enlightenment mythological synthesis and which were aimed at defining a new basis for uniting society.

From Shishkov's perspective the Gallomania of the end of the eighteenth and start of the nineteenth century was a national catastrophe whose effects were more visible in language than in any other sphere. In high society, French was gradually squeezing out Russian; they read French and spoke in French. The educated gentry, which according to Shishkov should have been preserving and developing the national heritage, didn't read Russian and didn't even know how to read Church Slavonic. "Our ancient, deeply rooted, imposing, magnificent Slavonic tongue is despised," he wrote. "No one uses it, and even the clergy itself, dragged along by the strong arm of custom, is beginning to turn away from it" (Shishkov, XII, 249). The Karamzinists' attitude toward this problem was not uniform, and they too could raise objections to the widespread use of French.[11] However, for the archaists, the Karamzinists' general orientation on French culture, the young Karamzin's use of dandy jargon in his works (Uspenskii 1985, 25–30 and 46f), and Makarov's shocking statements (see Lotman and Uspenskii 1975, 185–192), among other things, all served to associate the proponents of the "new style" with Gallomania (see the caricature of the "Gallorus" in S. Bobrov's "An Incident in the Kingdom of Shadows" [Proisshestvie v tsarstve tenei]). The Karamzinists were ruining Russia with the help of the Gallomaniacs, and after the great fire of Moscow, Shishkov had them

---

[11] I. I. Dmitriev wrote (as late as 1835), "Stop the corruption of the national language if you do not wish to be reproached for an unintentional alliance with France. Do not be surprised! France destroyed our noble language in the domestic life of our upper class. From whom can our children learn it now? Learn it from seminarists, or in the lackeys' and maids' rooms? I really worry sometimes that the peasants will start to speak French, and we their language" (Dmitriev, II, 315). This sort of statement would have fully satisfied Shishkov. In the earlier period the Karamzinists did not condemn the misuse of French so harshly, but the critical attitude toward Russians' French-speaking, conditioned by concern for the development of the native tongue, was present even then (see Uspenskii 1985, 24–5; Garde 1986, 281).

in mind when he exclaimed, "Now I would like to shove their noses in the ashes and say to them loudly—'Is this really what you wanted?'" (Lotman and Uspenskii 1975, 192). For him Karamzin's linguistic innovations spelled the start of the road to disaster which had begun during the latter part of Catherine's reign.

Thus for Shishkov and his supporters Russia's black day coincided with the disintegration of the cultural and linguistic synthesis that undermined the unity of the integrated Slavenorossiiskii literary language (§ IV–1). From this perspective, linguistic and literary issues took priority over issues of culture and history. In fact, ideas about national self-consciousness and its connections with ancient folk culture had been alien to the enlightened absolutist notions of Catherine's reign. The past was then mostly associated with prejudice rather than any kind of positive values. True, national customs sanctified by time had not been swept aside under Catherine as they had been under Peter, and at times were even put on display in order to gain popular sympathy, but for the inner circle this was mostly a masquerade with no serious intellectual content. Catherine, sensitive to the change of cultural paradigms, published *Notes Regarding Russian History* in 1783–4 in *Sobesednik* that affirmed official patriotism with a nationalist tinge (cf. Kamenskii 1992, 389–90), but the issue here was more a legitimization of her own enlightened activity and the prerogatives of the reigning monarch than a search for national "roots." The ideology of enlightened absolutism was fundamentally universalist and was concerned with states, not nations.

Shishkov's Romantic ideas would have been out of place under Catherine, and were produced precisely at the time of the disintegration of the earlier official ideological system, when, having repudiated the notion of a universalist state, the search had begun for other, more organic bases for human society and other, deeper sources of human culture. Such searches were taking place all across Europe, and in this Shishkov was far from original— as he was not original in his utopian view of the past, which for him was more an ideal reconstruction than a realm for investigation. The actual past had no definitive significance for him, and for this reason the ages of Peter and of Catherine could be considered as constructive rather than destructive; the people's spirit was preserved in language, and therefore literary and linguistic considerations took priority over historical and cultural ones (Peter's attacks on Church Slavonic remained beyond Shishkov's concern). The Slavenorossiiskii language fully satisfied Shishkov, and because of this he saw Russia's age of well-being not as having ended with Peter (as it did for the later Slavophiles), but with the spread of the "new style."

From this perspective the contrast between the two sides' historical-linguistic and historical-literary views is striking. The archaists valued what was "ancient" (drevnost') and they included the eighteenth century in this category. In these terms, Lomonosov had not created a new literary language but had devised a way of preserving the old one, adapting it to new circumstances. P. A. Katenin wrote that

> ignorant people perpetually disfigured their speech by mixing in Tatar, Polish, and other words, while literate people continually cleansed and elevated it, holding fast to root words and Slavonic turns of phrase. Translations of holy books were always before their eyes, like a faithful guide, which if followed could not steer them wrong; and it is to this that we are obliged (even in recent times) for the resurrection of our language under Lomonosov, for without him it would not have become the pure, authentic language (I make bold to say, unique in all of Europe) that it is but would rather have become coarse, clumsy, and base, more motley than English or Polish. (Katenin 1822, 173).

To the Karamzinists, on the contrary, Lomonosov was seen primarily as reformer of the language, a forerunner of Karamzin who opened the way for him. This was precisely N. A. Polevoi's opinion:

> If we must compare Karamzin with anyone, we should compare him with Lomonosov: Karamzin began from the point at which Lomonosov stopped, and finished that which Lomonosov initiated. The achievement of each was equally great, important, colossal in relation to Russia. Lomonosov had found the elements of the Russian language in disarray, confused; there was no literature. Imbued with the study of Latin writers, he was able to discern the spirit of the language, bring it into order, formulate the initial Russian literature, he studied grammar, rhetoric, wrote poetry, and in his day was an orator, a prose writer and historian. After him and before Karamzin, over the course of 25 years, very little was done. Karamzin... brought up on the study of French writers and imbued with the best of European enlightenment, which was all definitely French, brought what he had acquired home to his native soil. (Polevoi, II, 607; for more detail see Vinogradov 1935, 28–38)

A more radical approach could go even further and reject Lomonosov, ascribing the start of Russian literature to Karamzin; in this view, Slavenorossiiskii is consigned to the dark ages, and the dawn of Russian letters portrayed as that precise moment which the archaists saw as its decline. Viazemskii, who was usually more moderate, once made this argument. In his "Information About the Life and Verse of Ivan Ivanovich Dmitriev" of 1823 he wrote:

> In 1791 Karamzin, who had returned to Russia, his mind enriched with observations and memories collected during his journey through the lands of classical European education, began to publish the *Moscow Journal,* from which time let it be said (not to antagonize adherents of the old law) begins

a new calendar for our language. In this publication, the cornerstone of our correct and radiant resurrected literature was laid on top of gloomy Gothic ruins. (Viazemskii, I, 122)

Reading these lines we should keep in mind that in European Classicist literary criticism the adjective "Gothic" was attributed to the language of the barbarian Middle Ages, when the concept of a correct language was lost and Quintilian's wise precepts were forgotten.

As we have noted, both the Sentimentalist Karamzin and the Romantic Shishkov accepted purist linguistic doctrine developed by French Classicism. For both sides Europe was the model (recall that Shishkov translated La Harpe and adored Bateaux). The question was not whether Russia should stand with Europe or alone but what it meant to stand with Europe. For the Karamzinists this meant assimilating European ideas and achievements, remaking oneself according to European standards. In the *Letters of a Russian Traveller* Karamzin wrote that

> To select the best in everything is the action of an enlightened mind, and Peter the Great wanted to enlighten our minds in all respects. The monarch declared war on our old ways first of all because they were coarse, unworthy of the age; and second of all because they prevented the introduction of other, most important and useful foreign innovations. It was necessary, so to speak, to screw the head off of deeply-rooted Russian stubbornness in order to make us flexible, ready to learn and accept... The Germans, French, English had outstripped Russians by at least six centuries; Peter set us going with his mighty hand, and in several years we almost caught up to them. All of those pitiful jeremiads about changing the national character and the loss of the Russian moral physiognomy are either nothing more than a joke or the result of the lack of solid thinking... We're not the same as our bearded ancestors—so much the better! External and internal crudeness, ignorance, idleness and boredom were their lot, even [those] of the highest status; for us all paths are open to refining our reason and to noble spiritual pleasures. Everything national (narodnoe) is nothing before what is human. The main thing is to be human beings, not Slavs. (Karamzin 1984, 253–4)

While Karamzin's views subsequently changed and he no longer equated nationality with crudity, and saw in Peter not just a creator but also a destroyer (see § I–1, note 1), for him the European path of development continued to be tied to a rejection of national antiquity. In a speech at the Academy delivered on Dec. 5, 1818, Karamizin said:

> Peter the Great, having transformed the fatherland with his powerful hand, made us like other Europeans. Complaints are useless. The connection between the minds of ancient and modern Russians has been severed forever. We do not want to imitate foreigners, but we write as they write, because we live as they

> live... The *special* beauty that comprises *folk* (narodnoi) literature yields to universal beauty; the first changes, the second is eternal. It is good to write for Russians, but even better to write for all people. (Karamzin, III, 648–9)

(We may note in passing the assumption of universal aesthetic values that is so characteristic of Classicist aesthetics.)

Several conclusions about language directly followed from these ideas. Makarov wrote that "We adopted from foreigners sciences, arts, customs, amusements, sociability; and we began to think like all other peoples (for the more peoples are enlightened, the more alike they are), and the language of Lomonosov became insufficient, just as Russians' enlightenment under Elizabeth became insufficient for Catherine's glorious age" (Makarov, I, 2, 21). Makarov asserts that "language always follows behind the sciences, the arts, behind enlightenment, behind mores, behind customs." Accordingly, the new literary language can have no relation to the ancient language and is fully justified in cutting itself off from Slavenorossiiskii of the previous period; "in regard to customs and ideas, we are not at all the same people as were our ancestors; consequently we want to compose phrases and produce words that correspond to our contemporary ideas, thinking like the French, like the Germans, and like all modern enlightened peoples" (ibid, 23 and 29).

For Shishkov, rejecting national antiquity meant excluding the nation from the family of enlightened peoples, because it is only savages that have no history and a past sanctified by tradition. The pantheon of European peoples was a pantheon of historical peoples. The archaists did not juxtapose nationality (narodnost') to what was human or enlightened because this was its necessary and most important component. Nationality was preserved in language, and ancient literature revealed its foundations with a fullness inaccessible to contemporary literature. From this perspective crudeness or a lack of clarity were not a significant deficiency in language, because the people's spirit was not a logical construction—it remained a mystery, and so a veil of obscurity was fitting (this was the general opinion of European Romanticism). Shishkov did not distinguish between ancient Russian and Church Slavonic, and considered the Slavonic translation of the Bible part of ancient literature. Indicating that it had been written "in the ancient Slavonic style, already not very clear for us," he noted that "here too, however, even through the murkiness and darkness inimitable beauties shine forth from it, and, in truth, the most powerful poetic expressions, few in words but profound in meaning" (Shishkov 1818, 72). For all their peculiarity, the writing of the archaists reflected more up to date European trends than those of their opponents.

1. The Emancipation of Culture and the Polemic Between Archaists and Innovators

The conflict between archaists and innovators played out within the framework of a debate over what was genuinely European. At first the Karamzinists' attitude toward Russian antiquity was completely negative, and interest in the ancient tongue was met with mockery. The Shishkovites were called "varangiorussians," which was meant to suggest that Shishkov and his cohort proclaimed barbarian darkness. Old Russia didn't exist for the Karamzinists; Zhukovskii satisfied the Romantic need for the past by delving into German and Scottish traditions. In the 1820s, however, these things changed, or rather, the change of cultural paradigm that had begun during the Napoleonic invasion crystallized. Nationality (narodnost') became a constant preoccupation of literary life, and it is hard not to give credit for this to Shishkov and his supporters. However skeptical and mocking the attitude of members of Arzamas to individual Shishkovites, their jokes retained some of the flavor of the previous century, while the archaists' ideas about nationality entered the circle of problems that defined the new era.

Viazemskii's arguments reflect the changes which the Karamzinists' cultural consciousness underwent in the 1820's and 30's, and may even be taken as a direct echo of Shishkov's ideas. Speaking of gentry education of the time, he writes:

> I regret that modern education... has not been able to better harmonize the necessary conditions of Russian origin with the independence of European cosmopolitanism. Karamzin, defending Peter the Great from accusations that he deprived us of a Russian moral physiognomy (in the physical sense as well, having shaved off our beards), says that "Everything national (narodnoe) is nothing before what is human. The main thing is to be human beings, not Slavs." This is a lofty truth and a wonderful principle of political wisdom, which may be supplemented and clarified by saying that one should first, or to a greater extent, be a citizen than a family man. But when applied to individual education, i.e., something personal rather than national, one should not lose sight of the fact that in order to be a European one must begin by being a Russian. Russia, like other states, participates in the common affairs of Europe, and hence must have her sons stand up for her as her fully empowered representatives. A Russian reborn as a Frenchman, a Frenchman as an Englishman, and so on, will always remain an orphan at home, and not be adopted by alien lands. (Viazemskii, V, 19–20)

One might presume that these sentiments develop those of Karamzin, formulated during the last period of his life while he was working on the *History of the Russian State,* and had distanced himself from the ideas associated with "Karamzinism." Indeed, in the foreword to the *History* we find significant reservations concerning pure "cosmopolitanism," recalling

Chapter 4. The New Cultural Differentiation

Viazemskii's later statements and very far from the radical declarations made in *Letters of a Russian Traveller*. Karamzin writes:

> The genuine cosmopolitan is a metaphysical being, and such a rare phenomenon that there is no need to speak of him, neither to praise or condemn him. We are all citizens, in Europe and in India, in Mexico and in Abyssinia; the personality of every person is connected to his land of birth; we love it because we love ourselves… The name Russian has a special magic for us; my heart beats more strongly for Pozharskii than for Themistocles or Scipio. (Karamzin, IGR, I, 14)

The recognition of native history as a necessary part of the nation's cultural consciousness seems to have influenced Karamzin's partial change of attitude toward Church Slavonic and Russian. He continued to view them as different, and as deriving from different sources. Speaking about the activities of SS. Cyril and Methodius, he writes that

> These two brothers and their helpers established the rules of the Slavonic bookish language based on Greek grammar and enriched it with new expressions and words taken from the dialect of their homeland, Thessalonika, that is, Ilyrian or Serbian, with which we today see the similarity to our Church Slavonic. However, all dialects at that time were less different among themselves, as they were far closer to their common source, so that our ancestors could assimilate the Moravian Bible for themselves all the more easily. Its style became the model for modern Christian books, and even Nestor imitated it. But the distinct Russian dialect was preserved in oral usage, and so from that time we had two languages, written and popular. This explains the difference of language between the Slavonic Bible and the *Russkaia Pravda* (issued soon after Vladimir), the Nestorian chronicles and the *Song of Igor's Campaign*. (Karamzin, IGR, I, 172–3)

Church Slavonic and Russian thus continued to be seen as separate languages, but their interaction was no longer seen only as the pathological combination of the incompatible. It is indicative that the influence of translations from Greek that generated the "richness" of Slavonic is no longer considered a senseless "chemical operation" (§ IV–1.1), but rather as something positive. Compare: "The Slavs, having accepted the Christian faith, adopted new ideas along with it, invented new words and expressions, and their language of the middle ages without doubt differed as much from the ancient as it does from ours today" (ibid, 89). Karamzin's attitude toward the richness of the Russian language evidently also changed; thus he wrote that "Victories, conquests and the greatness of the state, raising the spirits of the Russian people, had a beneficent influence on its language as well, which, under the pen of a clever writer with talent and taste could equal those

1. The Emancipation of Culture and the Polemic Between Archaists and Innovators

of the best languages of ancient and modern times in its power, beauty, and agreeability" (ibid).

This change of theoretical position also had an effect on Karamzin's linguistic practices, which in the later period allowed for a much broader use of "Slavonic" elements, both on the grammatical and lexical levels, than at the start of his literary career. This is obvious if one juxtaposes the language of the *History* to that of the *Letters of a Russian Traveler*. The differences, it is true, could be explained by the dissimilarity of genre, but an examination of linguistic features that clearly have no relation to the system of generic markers prompts us to take them as evidence of a change of his linguistic position. Thus, for example, in the *Letters of a Russian Traveler* there is a constant alternation of bookish forms of nom.-acc. sg. masc. adjectives with the endings *-ый/-ий* and *-ой*, and this variation allows Karamzin to construct "a real stylistic score (partitura)" (Lotman, Tolstoi, Uspenskii 1981, 319). The picture sharply changes in the *History*. Karamzin almost always uses the normative bookish *-ый/-ий* endings in unstressed position and *–ой* in the stressed. Thus he rejects the unrestricted use of forms that deviate from the bookish norm, and that which he earlier had used everywhere for stylistic contrast he now only falls back on in rare individual instances (see Afiani, Zhivov, Kozlov 1989, 405–6). It is also characteristic that in the *History* the prepositions *пред* and *чрез* are almost always used in the non-pleophonic form, whereas in *Letters of a Russian Traveler* they usually appear as the pleophonic *перед* and *через*. The *History* also expands the use of lexical Slavonicisms, which moreover cannot always be attributed to thematic aims.[12]

Also indicative of this evolution is that it is not only apparent in the language of the *History*. Karamzin also made significant changes in the *Letters of a Russian Traveler* when preparing it for republication in 1814. As Lotman and Uspenskii remark, "the publication of 1814 represents a stage [in Karamzin's development] reflecting the influence of the *History of the Russian State* on the style of the *Letters of a Russian Traveler*, i.e., supplementing the new style with subtle nuances by using Church Slavonic linguistic means" (Lotman and Uspenskii 1984, 523). In his investigation of this question V. V. Sipovskii shows that in the 1814 edition Karamzin "for the first time introduces the form of adjectives in *-ый* (instead of *-ой*) in huge quantities, for example, *желаемый, достойный, любезный*, etc.,

---

[12] No less indicative are changes in orthography, in particular, Karamzin's change to using normative bookish forms like *счастие, русский* where he earlier wrote *щастие, руской*; the choice of spelling was as an expression of his linguistic position (Lotman, Tolstoi, Uspenskii 1981, 315–6, 319–20).

and energetically removes barbarisms" (Sipovskii 1899, 229). This editing demonstrates with all clarity that the linguistic innovations of the *History* are not the specific stylistic peculiarities of this particular work but embody Karamzin's new linguistic and historical — cultural views that had been formed as the result of many years' work with monuments of the Russian past.

Therefore the relationship between Karamzin's and Shishkov's positions—their linguistic and cultural views, as well as their stylistic practices—are significantly more complex than the usual simple description of the archaists and innovators would suggest. In consequence, the dynamic of literary and linguistic processes involved is also more complex. Karamzin not only gives rise to Karamzinism, but is also the precursor of the synthesis of nationalism and Europeanism that Pushkin realized. Uspenskii rightly notes that Pushkin moved away from Karamzinism rather quickly and was open to the influence of Shishkov's linguistic and literary views (Uspenskii 1994, 171–3). Already in 1824 Pushkin sent his greetings to "grandpa Shishkov," acknowledging him "as a Rogue-Romantic" (Pushkin, XIII, 98), although in this avowal he was not so much switching from one literary camp to the other as completing the movement in Shishkov's direction that Karamzin himself had begun. A year later Pushkin started work on *Boris Godunov* in which his new views were to receive literary and linguistic embodiment. In it came together and organically merged lines of development both from Shishkov and from the *History of the Russian State,* to which it was also connected as a work of literature.

The starting stimulus for the conception of the "Slavenorossiiskii" literary language had been the aspiration to polyfunctionalism (§ III–1.1). By the end of the eighteenth century this was no longer felt, as the new literary language, however its content was interpreted, was already being used in all culturally significant spheres. At the same time particular differences in defining the scope of Russian letters (that which is subject to literary and linguistic norms) were significant for Shishkov's and Karamzin's followers. For the Karamzinists belles-lettres was paramount as the place where linguistic norms were to be worked out. For Shishkov and his group the circle of texts was significantly wider and was connected to their positive view of ancient literary monuments (thus Shishkov wrote a study of the rhetoric of the Bible, which the followers of Karamzin did not even consider literature, at least not in the early period). For all their differences, however, belles-lettres did remain at the center of attention. The conflict between cultures—Europeanized vs. traditional—was replaced by a conflict between literary movements. This literary conflict had its culturological parameters, but over time these were changeable in scope, even while their literary and linguistic programs remained relatively constant. Each of the opposing programs could be fitted into substantively different cultural paradigms, and this allowed such diverse figures as S. S. Uvarov, V. A. Zhukovski, and V. L. Pushkin to all be assigned to the camp of the innovators, and the even more dissimilar A. S. Shishkov, S. A. Shirinskii-Shikhmatov and K. F. Ryleev to the archaists.

Because of this it is not surprising that more important than cultural orientation turned out to be attitudes toward particular genres, that is, intraliterary problems. As we noted earlier, the decline of the cultural and linguistic synthesis of the second half of the eighteenth century brought the problems of individual consciousness and small genres to the fore. The small genres were the ones that the Karamzinists cultivated, and this was the main reason for their rejection of the Church Slavonic legacy (rather than anticlericalism, as had been the case in the early eighteenth century [§ I–2.1]). Indeed, a writer composing a madrigal for the salon or a sentimental tale about unhappy love who chose his words from the Menalogion or Prologue would have seemed like a caricature. "The style (slog) of church books," wrote Makarov, "has nothing in common with that which is demanded of writers in society... Our antique books cannot contribute the paints needed to depict the lush boudoirs of Aspasia, or for the paintings of the Villands, Meissners, or Dorats. A loud lyre may sometimes imitate David's harp, but a light-hearted, tender, romantic imagination fears the dark caves in which virtue hides itself away from the world's delights" (Makarov I, 2, 35). For Shishkov and his party the high genres kept their importance, although possibly not as types of "state" poetry but as "historical" lyrics (like Ryleev's "Dumy" [Meditations]). The significance of the Church Slavonic linguistic tradition was conditioned to a great extent by the use of its elements to create "a serious style" (vazhnost' sloga); Shishkov repeatedly emphasizes this function. It is indicative, however, that Church Slavonic was also acceptable to the Karamzinists to fulfill this same function, although not to the same extent (§ IV–1.1). Hence the question of genre precedes the question of linguistic and cultural tradition, demonstrating once again that the conflict was more a literary than a broader cultural one.

This situation created the basis on which the stabilization of linguistic norms could take place, a process that was primarily embodied in Pushkin's works, which very quickly took on the function of the texts on which in one way or another the whole further development of the literary language was modeled. In contrast to his predecessors, Pushkin did not occupy himself with normalizing the language. By his era the language was basically already normalized, and it was only particular issues within the

Chapter 4. The New Cultural Differentiation

generally accepted norm that divided the opposing literary trends. Pushkin was not concerned with working out new principles for the unification or separation of Russian and Church Slavonic, but with uniting diverse literary traditions whose adherents held various views on these principles. The issue of unity seemed to him an historical given about which it was pointless to argue. In the 1825 article "On Mr. Lemontey's Foreword to his Translation of Krylov's Fables," which evidently reflected his work on the language of *Boris Godunov*, Pushkin wrote:

> As material for literature the Slaviano-Russian (slaviano-russkii) language has an undeniable advantage over European ones; its fate was extremely lucky. In the eleventh century the ancient Greek language suddenly offered it its lexicon, a treasure house of harmony, presented it with the rules of its well-considered grammar, its beautiful expressions, its majestic flow of speech; in a word, it adopted it, in this way freeing it of the need for slow improvements over time. In itself already resonant and expressive, this is where it gets its flexibility and correctness. It was necessary that common speech be separated from the written, but subsequently they came together, and such is the elemental substance (stikhiia) which has been given us for the communication of our thoughts. (Pushkin, XI, 31)[13]

Thus the question of what is Russian and what is Slavonic, what is written and what spoken, ceases to interest Pushkin. Whatever the source of individual elements, they all make up "the material of literature." The criteria for selection, it follows, do not have the significance of general

---

[13] Pushkin is obviously repeating the well-known thesis about Russian's richness as a result of Greek's influence on Church Slavonic (§ II–2.1). Here Pushkin rejects the view, repeated by Lemont, concerning the influence of the Mongol invasion on the development of the Russian language. He writes: "Mr. Lemont unjustly thinks that Tatar rule left a residue of rust on the Russian language. A foreign language spreads [its influence] not by saber and fire, but by its own abundance and superiority. What kind of new ideas, demanding new words, could have come to us from a nomadic tribe of barbarians who had neither writing, nor trade, nor jurisprudence? Their invasion did not leave any traces on the language of educated Chinese, and our ancestors, groaning under the Tatar yoke during the course of two centuries, prayed to God, cursed their ferocious rulers, and shared their lamentations with one another all in their native language... Be that as it may, there are hardly fifty Tatar words that became part of Russian" (Pushkin, XI, 31). As we recall, the argument about Tatar influence had been voiced earlier by Dashkov (§ IV–1.1) and served as an argument in the polemics about (or simply — against) the unity of Russian and Church Slavonic. The presupposition of Dashkov's statements was the assertion that Russian, having been subject to Tatar influence, became separate from Slavonic, just as French had separated from Latin in its time. Pushkin, one must think, rejects this view, true, without mentioning the single nature of Russian and Church Slavonic (for him this kind of theoretical declaration was evidently empty scholasticism), but he does assert the organic union of Russian and Church Slavonic elements in the Russian language as the basic material of contemporary literature.

principles, as the realization of a single linguistic imperative, or for that matter a single cultural one. Selection becomes a matter of authorial taste and resourcefulness, and it is precisely here that the search for the correct path for the literary language culminates. Hunting for paths is replaced by the pursuit of the best linguistic means to embody the concrete goals of the author in the context of one particular text. This was achieved by the stabilization of the literary language, as general theoretical problems were now transformed into issues of literary stylistics.

And so in the conflict between archaists and innovators we see not a clash between Europeanized and traditional culture, but one of literary trends, a conflict that may be situated fully within the framework of Europeanized Russian culture. The very narrowing of the issue from a broad cultural to an intraliterary one testifies to the fact that the cultural antagonism that shook Russia during the Petrine and post-Petrine periods had taken a secondary place, if it still existed at all. Of course, on the larger Russian scale this antagonism was still there, and the lower levels of society continued to view the world in far different categories from those of the educated class. However, for the dominating culture those other categories no longer held any interest, and ceased to be a factor in its development. The dominating culture attained that level of self-sufficiency at which cultural oppositions merge with the battle between literary trends. This circumstance prepared the ground for the synthesizing stabilization of the Russian literary language which Pushkin was able to accomplish. But this development also brought the literary language into a new phase of development, beyond the parameters we set out to examine in this book—the history of the harmonization of European and traditional values in Russian culture and the literary language. The debates between archaists and innovators might have served as the epilogue to this investigation, were it not for one arena of literature in which the struggle between secular and religious traditions retained its importance: the religious literature of the first half of the nineteenth century.

2. Slavonicizing Purism and Its Reconceptualization in Religious Literature

The cultural and linguistic synthesis of the second half of the eighteenth century had two heirs: the traditions of secular and of religious literature. Brought together in synthesis by the force of state unity, they again separated after its disintegration. The social and cultural differences that contradicted the universalism of the literary language and that had only been hidden for a while by the Petersburg mirage again began to declare themselves, both in the properly cultural sphere as well as in that of language. As we have seen, each of these traditions had its own values and began to reconsider the legacy of the previous period in light of them. At first both traditions experienced some perplexity as to what direction to chose. In secular literature this manifested itself in the debates between the archaists and innovators. Religious literature did not experience such a polarization, although the problem of choosing a new path did lead to a series of collisions and controversies. The question arose first of all of defining the nature of religious education, that is, defining the kind of spirituality and cultural worldview of future members of the clergy.

In the eighteenth century education took on a professional and corporate character: people were trained for professions, and only those who were eligible by social position could choose a given profession. Education was designed to continually reproduce society's division into occupations that had been established by the state, creating a social structure which like any well-constructed mechanism required only the replacement of worn out parts (e.g., the son replaces the father) (see Vladimirskii-Budanov 1874). Religious education was designed for children of the clerical estate and was meant to prepare them for careers in the church. The estate-oriented character of education generated the prerequisites of a closed, caste culture (see Znameskii 1881; Freeze 1977, 210–15), although during the period of cultural synthesis the ideal of one single culture stood in the way of bringing this into being. A single unified culture had been part of absolutist state policy, and the entire educational system had been called to put it into practice.

Religious seminaries had acquired the character of classical colleges, where the study of the classics and classical rhetoric were central. This was precisely the case with the Trinity and Vifanskii seminaries which were under the supervision of Metropolitan Platon (Levshin) and served as models for other ecclesiastical educational institutions (cf. Smirnov 1867). There were specific differences from secular education and culture but they were not at all due to a conscious rejection or endorsement of their own spiritual values but rather to a degree of conservatism which perpetuated aspects of the Baroque educational model that had been formulated in seventeenth-century Europe and from there transplanted into Russia (cf. Lappo-Danilevskii 1990; Zhivov and Uspenskii 1984, 230–4). Moreover, there were attempts to introduce the teaching of modern European languages into seminaries and classes aimed at familiarizing students with the latest works of European literature (cf.

Titlinov 1916, 842–3).[14] Only toward the end of the eighteenth century did the tendency arise among a certain part of the clergy to praise their own learning, contrasting it to the often superficial knowledge of gentry society.

The partial liberation from the state's ideological monopoly made obvious the need to bring clerical education more into line with real social needs and to make it relevant to what the students would face upon graduating seminary. The current situation in which Latin and the Latin curriculum were to define the outlook and future activity of the seminarists was recognized as abnormal. "Today's curriculum (kurs) right through to philosophy is not a curriculum of the sciences, but only of Latin literature," wrote Evgenii Bolkhovitinov (Florovskii 1937, 113). And Filaret (Drozdov), evaluating the period retrospectively, wrote that "Before the reform of the church schools some of them considered their claim to fame in their superior teaching of the Latin language. The clergymen from there knew pagan writers better than holy and ecclesiastical ones, spoke and wrote Latin better than Russian, and were better able to shine within a circle of scholars by means of select phrases in a dead language than to illuminate the people with a living understanding of the truth" (Chistovich 1894, 272).[15] The time had come for a reform of religious education, and a special committee was formed for that purpose in 1807, and in 1809 the Commission on Church Schools. Projects were drawn up for a new type of school, and these projects revealed the diversity of opinion that had arisen as a result of the disintegration of the cultural synthesis of the preceding period.

---

[14] Characterizing the theological, philosophical and literary views of Platon Levshin, R. L. Nichols describes the direction religious education took in the second half of the eighteenth century: "Even this brief sketch of Platon's outlook, intellectual preoccupations, and contributions to the education of several generations of students makes clear that leading churchmen breathed much the same air as that making up the secular cultural and intellectual atmosphere of Catherine's reign. In fact, the problem was not the isolation of educated churchmen from the mainstream of Russia's westernization. Rather, as a consequence of the almost wholly western education which the clergy received, and in light of the ideals it inspired in the church's leading representatives, there was a real danger that the church might become simply a western institution or (in view of the state's use of the seminaries for its own benefit) an instrument of secularization" (Nichols 1978, 78).

[15] The biography of Avgustin Vinogradskii strikingly illustrates the importance of a Latin education in a cleric's career. As a student in the Moscow Academy, his poetry in Latin attracted the attention of Platon. He dedicated his first poem to the metropolitan in honor of his name day (Nov. 18, 1788) and was invited to dinner with him, an extraordinary honor for a student. Avgustin's next poems so impressed Platon that he ordered one to be printed and distributed to all religious educational institutions; one copy of these "golden" verses (Platon's word) was actually printed in gold, and Platon himself inscribed it to the author, also in gold (Avgustin Vinogradskii, 1856, v–viii). In 1804 Avgustin became Bishop of Dmitrovsk, Platon's assistant (vikarii), and after Platon's death, Archbishop of Moscow.

Chapter 4. The New Cultural Differentiation

There may have been consensus on the need to harmonize the school program with society's needs, but conceptions of just what that society was turned out to be quite diverse. On the one hand was educated secular society, and on the other, the entire remaining mass of the population. The majority of graduates would be working with the latter, but it was not accepted or customary to take this into consideration.[16] Religious education did not want to lag behind the secular; keeping pace with it had become customary during Catherine's reign. Furthermore, notions of culture continued to be associated with social position, and taking into consideration the needs of the "simple folk" might entail the loss of even those insignificant privileges that separated the clergy from the lower classes and brought them closer to the gentry.

Considerations of this sort clearly played a role for the influential Metropolitan Platon Levshin. In his instructions to the clergy he emphasized that clergymen should associate with the social elite instead of with just anyone, to instill respect for themselves (Platon Levshin 1775, 33). They clearly did not receive enough respect, and the gentry certainly did not endorse their rise in social status. The character of their education was to support their social pretensions, and this included, in particular, the knowledge of languages. The connection of foreign language learning with social privilege, the loss of which could mean that the clergy might finally merge with the lower classes, was a reason for Platon's opposition to have teaching in seminaries be in Russian. When this question was posed in the Synod in 1800, Platon wrote to Amvrosii Podobedov:

> I do not advise that lectures be given in Russian in our schools. Even so our clergymen are considered almost ignoramuses by foreigners because we don't know either French or German. But we maintain our honor by speaking and corresponding in Latin. If we will study Latin the way we do Greek, then we will lose this last bit of honor, insofar as we won't speak or correspond in any language at all. I ask you to forget this idea. In our tongue there are few even classical books. The perfect knowledge of Latin also greatly aids oratory in Russian. I am writing this on the collective advice of the rectors — of the academy, the Trinity [Seminary], and the prefects, and the Right Reverend Serafim. (Smirnov 1867, 340–1)[17]

---

[16] Of course it was inevitable that this was understood on some level. It is remarkable, for example, that in 1798 the Synod "recognized the need to have the Medical College compile a book for rural clergymen in which... would be described the number and character of sicknesses of the common people whose responsibility it is the clergy's to treat" (Chistovich 1857, 118). In the cultural sphere, however, Baroque — Enlightenment traditions continued to reign, and clerical students' future occupations were not reflected in their education.

[17] This desire not to lag behind secular learning was the reason for the spread of French language and culture among the clergy. Karamzin, describing his visit to the Trinity-Sergius Lavra

2. Slavonicizing Purism and Its Reconceptualization in Religious Literatures

This sort of consideration also lay at the basis of the projects for reform which one way or another tried to take into account the achievements of European secular culture. This may be especially seen in the selection of literary models which students learning oratory were supposed to follow. Differences of opinion on this point were extremely meaningful. In proposed regulations for spiritual academies drawn up [461] by Feofilakt Rusanov in 1809, the models for teaching the theory of aesthetics were listed as Cicero, Horace, Longinus, Quintilian, Dionysius of Halicarnassus, and as guides "from the moderns" were suggested "La Harpe, Gérard, with the addition of [excerpts from] Montesquieu, d'Alembert, Marmontel, Fénélon, Cardinal Mori, Chateaubriand, Burke, Batteux, Blair, Meissner, Eschenburg and L. de Lévizac" (Chistovich 1857, 206). This list makes clear both the desire not to lag behind secular education as well as a definite partiality for Enlightenment tastes that was the legacy of Catherine's reign. The same tendency is evident in the project that M. M. Speranskii proposed (before he became a government official, he taught a course in advanced oratory in the Alexander Nevskii seminary). Here "of the moderns" were named: "Fénélon, Rollin, Boileau, Sulzer, Baumgarten, Diderot, Buffon, and especially Beccaria" (Chistovich 1894, 122).

These proposals met resistance from the Academy directorate and Filaret Drozdov (at that time inspector of the Petersburg Spiritual Academy). In particular, Filaret wrote, "Who then are these preceptors in literature? They are Buffon, Du Marsais, Beccaria, naturalists—[all] advocates of Voltairean philosophy" (Chistovich 1894, 123). A document from the academy directorate argued that "In § 116 [of the proposed regulations] a student is required to recite, among other things, the opinion of Plato, Boileau, and Buffon concerning the fine arts (ob iziashchnom). Plato's dialogue called the Symposium (Simposion) is more enticing than edifying. Boileau did not add anything positive to Horace's epistle on poetry, except for information

---

in 1802, noted: "The Trinity seminary is one of the main religious schools in Russia. Apart from ancient languages, they also teach French and German here. This is admirable; in order to preach, one should know Bossuet and Massillion. Some of the monks here spoke with me in French, and the important teachers mix French phrases into their conversation. They showed me how gracious learning is; they walked with me and showed me everything with an air of sincere consideration. Education gives a person a kind of nobility, no matter what his condition" (Smirnov 1867, 483). Concerning the radical turnabout in attitude toward secular education among the clergy that took place in the 1810's-20's may testify the fact that in his "Staraia zapisnaia knizhka" [Old Notebook] Viazemskii describes as an oddity a priest from Moscow who "was rather educated and so knowledgeable in French that when he walked through the church past young ladies carrying the censer he would say 'pardon, mesdames'" (Viazemskii, VIII, 71).

about several French writers; his interpretation of Longinus does not deserve much attention; and the name of this writer should not be met in any good book, not to mention in the religious regulations. What discoveries Buffon made about the fine arts, nothing is known. For these reasons would it not be preferable instead of Plato to recommend Dionysius to students, instead of Boileau — Longinus, and instead of Buffon — Blair, who is known to every literary man for the merit of his rules?" (ibid).[18]

Thus without making their arguments explicit concerning the special nature of religious literature, the opponents of the "modernist" program raised objections to listing authors whose only reason for being on the list was as representatives of contemporary secular culture. In particular, Filaret proposed the following formulation for the regulation in question: "The professor of the class in literature should present the students with opinions about the beautiful (iziashchnoe) from the best writers who touched on the subject, who from the ancients are: Plato, Aristotle, Cicero, Horace, Quintilian, Longinus; and from the moderns—Fénélon, Rollin. Other modern authors must be used with care and perspicacity, because some of them have tried with brazen and destructive abstract reasoning to tear the beautiful away from the true and the good" (ibid, 123). In this way, even as they recognized the importance of European models, Filaret and those who agreed with him refused to accept the evaluations and opinions of secular culture (cf. Nichols 1978, 79–84). This was a significant moment, for with time Filaret's position won out; religious culture was heading for a conscious break with the secular. This gradually led to the creation of a religious educational curriculum that was directly opposed to the content and aims of a secular upbringing.

A similar process of cultural self-definition took place in language as well. The heritage of the period of cultural synthesis was the unity of the secular and religious literary language. The language of religion could now follow in the tracks of secular literature, and clergymen, addressing a secular audience, strove to write and speak in its tongue. This tendency received additional stimulus with the spread of mysticism and extra-confessional pietism. Due to the deep inner connection between mysticism and pietism, on the one hand, and Sentimentalism, on the other (cf. Florovskii 1937, 116–7), the language of mystical and pietistic literature was close to that of Sentimentalism, that is, precisely the language of Karamzin and his followers.

---

[18] It is curious to juxtapose this criticism of French writers with the fact that in 1772 Platon Levshin had purchased a library for the Trinity Seminary that included Boileau, Corneille, Montesquieu and Voltaire, and with money that was hard to come by (see Smirnov 1867, 378).

2. Slavonicizing Purism and Its Reconceptualization in Religious Literatures

In the late eighteenth century such a rapprochement presupposed a certain spiritual frame of mind on the part of the clergy which stressed religious "feeling" as a counterweight to "scholastic reason." This frame of mind was characteristic, for example, of M. M. Speranskii (see his psychological portrait in Florovskii 1937, 138–9); it was clearly reflected in his *Rules of Advanced Oratory* of 1792. As V. D. Levin notes, the language of this work "amazes one by its closeness to the language of Karamzin and his 'school'" (Levin 1964, 115). Linguistic similarity here was a natural consequence of the similarity of theoretical principles: Speranskii writes in the tradition of Vaugelas' purism, calling usage "a little tyrant" and asserting that "the god of good taste imposes" on the writer "the incontrovertible law of being clear" (Speranskii 1844, 161, 173).[19] At the start of the nineteenth century, mysticism and pietism became a kind of official ideology; correspondingly, using the "worldly" language (following the stylistic norms established by secular literature in literary practice) might not even have been dictated by convictions but by conformism. Texts of this kind have not been studied, and so it is hard to judge how well established this trend is in religious literature.[20]

---

[19] V. V. Vinogradov (1949, 206) puts this into the context of the Karamzinian struggle against high style and the book *Meditations on Oratory in General, and Especially on Preaching. From the Works of Mr. Abbot Trublet, Translated in the Voronezh Seminary...* (Trublet 1793), the translation of a French guide to oratory done by Evfimii Bolkhovitinov (the future Metropolitan Evgenii). Indeed the book contains a series of protests against the tradition of Baroque rhetoric. [...] However, there is no special connection with Karamzinian ideas here at all. In Evgenii's literary views (as shown, for example, by his correspondence with Derzhavin) he was a conservative Classicist. Hence his attacks on Baroque style sermons (and the general call for "naturalness") makes more sense in connection with Sumarokov's doctrines. That these doctrines were used by a religious writer and applied to religious literature indicates precisely the perception of religious and secular literature as a unity, guided by the one and same set of stylistic criteria (this is the position of the French abbot Bolkhovitivov translated [Trublet 1793, 78]). This perception was typical of the period of linguistic and cultural synthesis (and in this sense, Bolkhovitinov, as in many other respects, was an heir to the age of Catherine) but was by no means typical of the Karamzinists. One may also find analogous statements in Gedeon Krinovskii and Platon Levshin, whose theoretical linguistic views and practices also had nothing to do with Karamzin. Vinogradov does not distinguish between the commonplaces of European stylistic theory (which could appear both in Karamzinist writings as well as those of their predecessors and opponents) and original statements that relate to the Russian material, and this leads him to incorrect conclusions.

[20] It is evident that among clergy in the capitol who wanted success with their secularized congregations, the "worldly" trend was rather well established. Characteristic in this sense is Viazemskii's story about the priest with the predilection for French (see note 17). "He didn't like Metropolitan Filaret and criticized his language and style. Dmitriev... defended him. 'For goodness sake, your Excellency,' the priest once said to him, 'isn't it the languge in which your own "Fashionable Wife" is written?'" (Viazemskii, VIII, 71).

Whichever way it was, this was not the most important trend. At this same period, in the early years of the century, another tendency was developing based on the premise that it was not befitting the language of religious literature to emulate the secular. Parity with the norms of fashionable literature began to appear as a disregard for religious values and a vain chasing after worldly approval. As in education as a whole, a rift between secular and religious literature is revealed in its language. Refusing to follow the innovations of secular enlightenment, religious literature claims the Slavenorossiiskii language for itself, the language that sounded in Lomonosov's odes and of Platon's sermons alike. This language is now perceived as especially fitting for religious literature, combining as it does the "churchiness" of Slavonic and the comprehensibility of Russian. In this way, the literary principles advanced by Trediakovskii and Lomonosov were preserved and further developed in Russian religious literature. Of course, we are not speaking here of preserving all of the norms of the earlier language; insofar as grammatical norms had already been formulated by the start of the nineteenth century, the specifics of the language's stylistic variants ceased to be connected to grammatical elements, and were defined instead by vocabulary and phraseology. It was precisely in these areas that the language of religious literature preserved "Slavenorossiiskii" principles.

As said earlier (§ III–3.1), the development of Slavenorossiiskii turned Church Slavonic into an exclusively liturgical tongue, a language of cult. The natural result of such a view was to translate the Bible, as a book for reading, from Church Slavonic into Slavenorossiiskii, the Russian literary language, while preserving Church Slavonic in the liturgy. With the establishment of the Bible Society, work on such a translation began on a broad scale, moreover, as justification for it the same explanation of the obscurity of Church Slavonic was put forward as had at one time been expressed in the *Spiritual Regulation* (§ I–2.1), and then repeated by Platon Levshin and Gavriil Petrov as the reason for creating all religious literature in Slavenorossiiskii. Speaking of this translation, Alexander I asserted that "by itself it will remove the seal of an incomprehensible dialect which to this day bars many Russians from Jesus' Gospel, and it will open up this book even for the nation's children (dlia samykh mladentsev naroda), from whom it has been hidden not by design but by the darkness of time" (Florovskii 1937, 154; Chistovich 1899, 25, 34).

Those who took part in the translation included not only, and not principally, adherents of Alexandrine mysticism as much as zealots of religious enlightenment (Filaret Drozdov, Gerasim Pavskii, and others), for whom the translation seemed a necessary condition for educating the nation

2. Slavonicizing Purism and Its Reconceptualization in Religious Literatures

in Orthodoxy. The later rift between Filaret and Pavskii and reproaches against Pavskii for theological "neologism" (Batalden 1988) do not relate to this period; they have nothing to do with their common efforts on behalf of Bible translation, which by no means lay outside the Orthodox tradition. For Filaret and those who agreed with him this was just as essential a step as changing the language of religious education from Latin to Russian; both were aimed at making the clergy's pastoral work more effective. Filaret and his associates believed that the subordination of the Orthodox church to the state's ideological and cultural monopoly in the eighteenth century was one of the main reasons why the clergy had lost influence with a significant portion of the population (those who had joined the Schism or sects, or who had simply lost interest in religion). From Filaret's point of view, this process was explained not by the church's connection to the authoritarian structure of secular power but by insufficient religious enlightenment, subordination to secular models and lack of pastoral work (here as one cause the scholastic character of religious education was cited). Filaret wrote that "we need a kind of missionaries to the Orthodox people" (Filaret 1877, 186; cf. similar statements by Archbishop Evgenii Kazantsev in Malov 1876, 7). For the work of enlightenment a comprehensible text of the Bible was needed.

Slavenorossiiskii allowed for making the biblical text comprehensible without repudiating the beauty of the "Slavonic" model (at least, according to the project's defenders). Here the stylistic principles developed during the period of cultural synthesis retained full relevance. In the rules for the translation which Filaret Drozdov compiled in 1816 the orders were, in translating from Greek, to use "Slavonic words" "if they are closer to the Greek than the Russian, but without producing obscurity or clumsiness," or "if the corresponding Russian words do not belong to the pure bookish tongue" (that is, to the Russian literary language whose norms were established in the latter half of the eighteenth century). At the same time, the extremes of Slavonicizing purism were to be curbed. "The grandeur of holy writ," noted Filaret, "is in the power of the words and not in their external brilliance; it follows from this that one should not become too attached to Slavonic words and expressions for the sake of their apparent gravity" (Chistovich 1899, 27).

However, insofar as the translation was the project of the Bible Society it was carried out in the context of the religious and administrative reforms of Alexander I and A. N. Golitsyn, as one of various undertakings of the so-called "special ministry" of the Ministry of Religious Affairs and Popular Education created on October 14, 1817. It could be perceived therefore as an encroachment of the secular power, indifferent or even inimical to Orthodox traditions, on the church's independence (or whatever

Chapter 4. The New Cultural Differentiation

remained of it), and as interference in church doctrine. Because of this, the struggle to preserve Orthodox teaching and piety turned out to entail rejecting translation of the Bible into Russian. For the opponents of the translation, the linguistic position was identified with the cultural one (although, as has been suggested, in reality such a connection was lacking). For leaders of the church movement like Archimandrite Fotii or Metropolitan Serafim, Russian, when juxtaposed to Church Slavonic, seemed an emphatically worldly and secular language, while Church Slavonic was perceived as sacred (characteristically, Fotii wrote his own compositions in a language that should probably be characterized as hybrid Church Slavonic). Hence translating the Bible from Church Slavonic into Russian appeared as a kind of sacrilege. In 1824 the Bible Society ended its existence, and copies of the Russian translation of the Pentateuch which hadn't yet been sold were consigned to the flames.

Cultural and linguistic factors, of course, weren't the only things that came into play here. In particular, this touches Shishkov's position, as he played a significant role in the reversal of 1824, although linguistic considerations probably were not the least in importance. As he considered Church Slavonic and Russian as having a single nature, he thought that using Russian required special justification. This could have been worldly (civic) content or exhortatory address to the people in a sermon. Without sound basis translating from Church Slavonic into Russian represented a senseless profanation of the holy tongue. On the Bible translation Shishkov wrote that

> A language isolated from daily life is proper for the church. In the general opinion of pious people the Slavonic word of the Psalter somehow acts more strongly on the soul and inspires more reverence than the Russian Psalter. This is quite natural because the Slavonic language at the present time has not been defiled either by the expression of shameful passions, nor by idle verbiage, nor by explanations of vain actions. This all remained the lot of the language of daily life (iazyk obshchezhiltel'nyi). In the Slavonic tongue the simple folk hear only what is holy and edifying. The moderate obscurity of this language does not overshadow the truth, but serves it as a kind of elemental setting. Remove this veil, and then everyone will interpret the truths of writ according to his own notions. (Chistovich 1899, 302–3)

As this quote suggests, another reason for opposition to the Bible translation was the fear of free interpretation of the Bible. The concern was that independent study of the Biblical text could lead to deviation from Church doctrine[21] or that the people would derive "false ideas" about state power.[22]

---

[21] This argument had been used by Catholics who opposed unrestricted reading of the Bible and having the Bible translated into national languages (cf. § I–2.1).

[22] These opinions were also stated during arguments about teaching theological subjects in Russian. Metropolitan Filaret wrote to Filaret Gumilevskii: "On teaching theological lessons

2. Slavonicizing Purism and Its Reconceptualization in Religious Literatures

But be that as it may, for the linguistic program of religious literature the impact of the 1824 reversal was substantial. It emphasized the significance of Church Slavonic for religious literature; while religious literature was not to become Church Slavonic once again, Church Slavonic was held up as the obligatory model of correctness and purity. Notably, Filaret Drozdov's Orthodox catechism, which had been published in 1823 and written wholly in Russian, was removed from sale and when it was republished not only was Church Slavonic restored in biblical citations and prayers, but the entire text was Slavonicized (mostly its lexicon). The linguistic principle which was asserted in this way remained obligatory for religious literature throughout Nicholas I's entire reign, and defined—at least in terms of language—the opposition between religious and secular literature, which enjoyed a certain official support.

This differentiation of religious and secular traditions, underscored (rather than created) by the events of 1824, had still another aspect. As noted, religious education was estate-oriented, and the differentiation of religious and secular traditions now extended to secular and religious learning. In 1814, Filaret Drozdov gave his response "On the Synopsis of the Priestly Monk (hieromonakh) Feoktist Orlovskii, Teacher of Rhetoric at the Moscow Academy." Filaret commented that "the synopsis is written too much in the secular spirit," asserting that "The doctrine concerning the grace of truly natural objects does not belong to the category of literature, nor to the state of the writer" (Chistovich 1894, 138). What is curious here is not that the study of beauty in nature is being excluded from aesthetics, but that natural grace is defined as something with which the clerical estate is not to concern itself. In 1812 the senator Ivan Lopukhin complained about the ecclesiastical censorship: "Now look what they've latched onto today—not only not to permit what they find objectionable (according to their inadequate, perverted, or false idea of true spirituality), but this, they say, may be good, but is written by a lay person, and this we should have written this, so it dishonors us—so we won't let it through" (Dubrovin 1895: 76).

The perception of religious literature and education as belonging to a separate estate was characteristic of the whole first half of the nineteenth century.[23] In 1802, for example, the church censor did not want to accept the

---

in Russian for the convenience of explanation and about liberating Orthodox theology from the pagan and papist Latin language, I made a proposal in 1828 or 1829. Do you know who objected? Dibich. He had the idea that theological debates in the native language would spread divisive ideas among the people" (Filaret 1872, 50).

[23] This perception was not, it seems, characteristic of the eighteenth century, although one can't ignore various early signs of it. Thus in 1768 Kir'iak Kondratovich made an application

Mesiatseslov (church calendar) published by Glazunov and Kapustin "by reason of their status, that they are laypeople (svetskie)" (Kotovich 1909, 13). The same attitude may be seen in Metropolitan Filaret's letter to the Ober-Procuror of the Synod A. P. Akhmatov of May 1, 1862, in which the issue concerned permission for a lay person to publish saints lives in a supplement to a weekly magazine. Although Filaret departs from the hard line of the previous reign, the view that religious literature is the domain of authors who belong to the clergy emerges very clearly. "The reasoning is just," writes Filaret, "that members of the clerical rank are more dependable in compiling saints lives, as both their education and life prepares them for this. But the Most Holy Synod does not strictly hold to this argument" (Filaret, SMO, V, 257).[24]

Just as religious education and religious literature began to be perceived in terms of corporate values, so too the literary language. Church Slavonic words which were part of Slavenorossiiskii, could, in the appropriate semantic situation, be regarded as "religious" and hence as the exclusive possession of the clergy. When in 1808 Shishkov presented the Russian Academy with his *Attempt at a Slavonic Dictonary*, Amvrosii Podobedov and Feofilakt Rusanov remarked in their review that the word "*благодать*" [mercy] should never be used... in secular documents; but theologians, preachers, and in general all those who teach morality in the church may use it in their explanations when appropriate and needed" (Derzhavin, IV, 780). The ecclesiastical reviewers thus not only asserted the sacred character of

---

to Platon Levshin for support of his lexicographical work as a translator and requested remuneration for it. Complaining of the lack of such support, he wrote that: "One possible argument [against] my request might be that either your own subordinates can translate the books of the Holy Fathers, and that the clergy aren't interested in Cicero's speeches, and the same about printing Homer, or that they are satisfied with the lexicons that already exist" (Tikhonravov 1858, 232). Notably, Kondratovich is writing not about the clerical estate, but about Platon's "subordinates," and his exclamation about the non-religious character of Cicero and Homer is mostly for effect. In the first half of the nineteenth century a secular author's suitability to translate patristic literature would not even have been considered, whereas translations of Homer or Cicero were were regarded as obviously alien and unnecessary for clergymen.

[24] In the second half of the century, Filaret Gumilevskii wrote in the foreword to his *Survey of Russian Religious Writing (Obzor russkoi dukhovnoi literatury)*: "Today we do not dispute that works of sincere Christian piety, whoever their authors, should take their place in the history of religious literature. To whom would now occur the idea of insisting that a work on the Holy Gospel is not religious because it is the work of a Chebotarev?" (Filaret Gumilevskii, 1884, II, 277f; the reference is to Prof. L. A. Chebotarev's *Tetraevangelion or Union of the Four Evangelists* [*Chetveroevangelie, ili svod chetyrekh evangelistov*] of 1803). It follows from Filaret's words that in the first half of the century for many clerics lay status automatically prevented someone from authoring religious literature.

2. Slavonicizing Purism and Its Reconceptualization in Religious Literatures

the word, but also insisted that it be used exclusively by church people. The Slavonicized language was thus to function as the property of the clerical estate (cf. Zhivov 1981, 80; Zhivov 1984a, 369).

As secular literature broke with the "Slavenorossiiskii" heritage, so did this attitude spread to secular society. What was first asserted by the Kazamzinists later gained wide acceptance. When in 1811 Shishkov gave his "Speech on the Love for the Fatherland" at his literary society, the Colloquium, I. I. Dmiriev remarked: "If only for the metropolitan" (Khvostov 1938, 378). This appears to refer to the Slavonicizing language of the speech rather than its content, which was not specifically religious; Slavonicized language thus served as the distinguishing mark of belonging to the clergy. It should be noted that while this view might not provoke protest from the Karamzinists, who rejected the previous literary tradition, it was unacceptable to the Shishkovites. For them "Slavenorossiiskii" was the normal literary language, and the use of words taken from church books in secular literature was routine and fully justifiable. For this reason, Derzhavin, after learning of the clergymen's objections to Shishkov's dictionary (together with criticism of the improper use of the word *благодать,* they had also written that the epithet *неблазный* [foreign to temptation] "belongs exclusively to the Blessed Virgin" — Derzhavin, IV, 780), penned the line "Дом благодатныя, неблазныя Добрады" (Home of Dobrada, graceful and foreign alien to temptation) in his 1808 poem "Obitel' Dobrady" (Dobrada's Abode) that was addressed to Empress Mariia Fedorovna. (II, 693). In his explanatory notes to the poem he recounted the incident with Shishkov's dictionary and wrote that "Since the author considered their opinion unjust, he made bold to put these words into his composition. The censor let them though, the public accepted them, the Synod was silent; consequently they may be used anywhere, if the proper serious theme and those who are addressed are taken into consideration" (ibid).[25]

To the extent that the cultural and linguistic synthesis of the second half of the eighteenth century was becoming an alien and half forgotten tradition for the cultured elite, the "Slavenorossiiskii" literary language of the clergy began to be perceived as alien, artificial, and obscure. In 1838 the Ober-Procurator of the Synod Count Protasov told Nikodim Kazantsev, whom he had called to Petersburg in connection with new reforms in religious

---

[25] Derzhavin was basing himself here on the eighteenth-century literary tradition in which secularized use of the word *благодать* was very common (cf. Zhivov 1981, 81); the source of this usage was apparently the correlation between the Russian *благодать* and the French *grâce.*

education, that "Your theology is very high-flown. Your sermons are lofty. We don't understand you. You don't use the people's language... You've chosen for yourselves some kind of private language, like doctors, mathematicians, or sailors. You can't be understood without help. Talk to us in a language we understand, teach us God's Law so that the very last peasant will understand you right off" (Chistovich 1894, 322). He was clearly speaking about the clergy's literary language, which he was equating to a closed, professional, corporate jargon. This differentiation of the secular and religious linguistic traditions was also reflected in the view of the language that was current among the clergy, in their perception of particular linguistic phenomena, and in their literary practice. In the collisions that were played out here we may see the last reflection of the cultural-linguistic oppositions that had been created by the Petrine reforms.

2.1 The Understanding of Purist Rubrics

In this way the cultural and linguistic synthesis of the second half of the eighteenth century was preserved in the literary language of the clergy. Correspondingly the purist conception that lay at the heart of the idea of "Slavenorossiiskii" was also perpetuated. The scheme which Amvrosii Serebrennikov proposed at the end of the century (cited above, § III–3.2) in essence repeated itself in the 1840s in Ia. Amfiteatrov's course in homiletics, which faithfully reflected the clergy's purist views of the first half of the nineteenth century. Amfiteatrov likens Church Slavonic to "biblical" language, deeming the Bible to be its main model (Amfiteatrov, II, 132). On harmonizing this language with Russian he writes:

> Can the use of the Biblical language be brought into line with the spirit and purity of the modern national language? This may be done quite easily, because: a) The genius of the original languages of Writ is so natural, broad, and pliant that it may be conveniently applied to any language without violating either its own nature or that of the other language. b) It does not particularly contradict either the analogizing or idiomatic qualities of our national language, because of the mutual union of kinship that was effected in ancient times and strengthened over the ages. c) Our Biblical language is not a dead one, on the contrary, it is fully alive and has been operative in epochs that are most sacred for the people and [it is still used] for the liturgy in the church, in the sacraments, in domestic and everyday occasional offices. d) A great number of words from the Biblical language have already migrated into the people's speech (and continue to do so), without the consent of grammarians and philologists, and these words have

2. Slavonicizing Purism and Its Reconceptualization in Religious Literatures

earned the invincible right of citizenship. e) Assimilated by the people, the Biblical language imparts grandeur, naturalness, richness and newness to the national tongue. (ibid, 119–120)

These same ideas were the basis for Trediakovskii's and Lomonosov's Slavonicizing purism—the correspondence between the nature of Russian and that of the ancient tongues, with Greek as the source of this correspondence, and the language's special linguistic richness that results (§ III–2.1).

Amfiteatrov writes specifically on the relationship between Church Slavonic and the contemporary literary language:

> The main relation of this language to today's national tongue is the same as that noted of the Biblical language. Of their frequent contact one may add the following: however strong the calls of our modern writers for the purity of the Russian language, however just the demand that we write in a contemporary, living conversational language, we see that Slavonicisms, in spite of all contentions, triumphantly penetrate into our living contemporary speech. As soon as the subject of writing goes beyond the bounds of everyday objects, as soon as one's thought assumes a serious or elevated cast — the phrases and form of Church Slavonic speech immediately come to mind to express these things and ideas. To change this form would mean to deprive the word of its value; not to use it would be to deprive the thought of its value. It is for this reason that sometimes even the most ardent purists, esteeming the merit of their ideas, seemingly unconsciously give them Slavonic form and garb. What does this mean? It seems, nothing more than the most intimate and natural kinship of the Russian language with Slavonic and vice versa; the latter, one may say, intertwining not so much with our national language as with the spirit of the people itself. To completely ban all Slavonicisms would mean to impoverish the national tongue, to deny its richest and most vital element, to deprive many objects and ideas of perhaps their best or at least necessary development and expression. (Amfiteatrov, II, § 277, 132–3)

Accepting in principle a literary language oriented on conversational speech, Amfiteatrov immediately asserts that the Russian (spoken) language proper lacks the means to express abstract ideas or elevated stylistics. These of necessity Russian takes from Slavonic; it follows that purism that bases itself on ridding Russian of Slavonicisms is basically unsound, and is all the more inapplicable to religious literature.

It is significant that in his discussion of linguistic purity, Amvrosii Serebrennikov (like others at the time) had in mind the language of both religious and secular literature. Now the criterion for purity turns out to be different for each, and Amfiteatrov defines this divergence. He writes:

> Purity of style consists in using words and expressions a) which belong to

Chapter 4. The New Cultural Differentiation

the national language proper, [but] b) only those which the national language considers purified. Consequently, a) not everything is fit for writing that is in the national language; b) not everything in the entire popular language, used by various social classes, is fitting; c) but only what the best and most educated writers whose works are recognized as exemplary use... Insofar as the sermon accepts ecclesiastical-Biblical language, the purity of preaching style has far broader limits than the purity of other literary works. (ibid, II, § 300, 161–2)

This permissible mixing of language extends not only to lexicon but to grammatical elements as well, and produces a special understanding of grammatical correctness. Amfiteatrov writes: "Correctness of style consists in the proper observance of the language's legitimate forms, determined by etymology and syntax in particular, and by the genius of the language as a whole... Stylistic correctness in homilies, like purity, is manifested in a far broader way than in other styles, because the homily tolerates changes and combinations of Church Slavonic words" (Amfiteatrov II, § 300, 165).[26]

Such notions of purity also define the linguistic program of the clergy in the first half of the nineteenth century. The purist restrictions encompass the usual aggregate of rubrics. Thus the same Amfiteatrov, listing the words which impair "linguistic purity," lists "archaisms," "neologisms," "vulgarisms," and "peregrinisms"; the last term is defined as "the unnecessary use of foreign words and expressions which appear in great quantity in schools, in systems (v sistemakh), and in the conversation of people who like to make a show of their knowledge of languages" (ibid, 162–3; on still another of Amfiteatrov's original rubrics, see below). Various statements by other ecclesiastical figures on the style of religious literature also cite these rubrics. From the start of the nineteenth century purity of style acquired special semiotic significance for religious leaders (§ IV–2.2), and they were therefore constantly involved in editing in order to bring the language of religious works into line with their content; an ideal of religious language was being formulated, and everything in religious writing that didn't correspond to this ideal was felt as an offense to its sacred content. In this context, it is no surprise that at the start of the century the ecclesiastical censor was charged with safeguarding "purity and elegance of style" (PSZ, XXXII, no. 25673,

---

[26] Another view holds that the variation of grammatical forms represents unacceptable heterogeneity. Thus when editing the 1838 Slavonic translation of the Eastern patriarchs' documents concerning the establishment of the Synod, Metropolitan Filaret Drozdov noted the divergence of [infinitive] endings, sometimes ь, sometimes и"; although he thinks that "we should preserve this diversity as a feature of the time" (Filaret 1869, 53). We need to keep in mind that the variation of infinitive endings continued to exist (with certain limitations) in religious literature in the last third of the eighteenth century (§ III–3.2), so that Filaret's comments suggest the further development of purist views.

article 360, 943 [1814]; cf. PSZ XXV, no. 18888). Although the censorship code of 1828 prohibited the censors from "carping on individual words and expressions" and also from correcting style and "an author's mistakes in the literary regard" (2nd PSZ, III, no. 1979, §§ 7, 15, 461), in the "Regulations for Ecclesiastical Censorship" "purity of style" was indicated as a necessary quality of religious "writings intended for society's use" (ibid, no. 1981, § 44, 483), and stylistic correction based on ideological considerations continued to be the censors' usual practice. Taken together, surviving materials allow us to reconstruct the purist principles that guided religious writing.

One plank in the clergy's linguistic program was the elimination of all *borrowings*. In the first half of the eighteenth century borrowings had been a common element of the new religious literature, in sermons first of all, as an aspect of Baroque ornamentation (§ I–2.2; cf. Vinogradov 1938, 99); the Great Russian tradition was here based on the Kievan. During the second half of the eighteenth century, the use of borrowings significantly diminished (again, first of all in sermons); in assimilating the purist principles of the "Slavenorossiiskii" language, religious writers considered borrowings an element that detracted from stylistic purity. However, insofar as the use of borrowings at this time was not as a rule connected with any sort of ideological position, and were not perceived as an element of secular culture that was improper for religious works (purism was no less typical of secular than of religious literature of the time), some religious authors continued to make rather free use of borrowings (for example, Irinei Klement'evskii and Anastasii Romanenko-Bratanovskii).[27]

From the start of the nineteenth century the attitude toward borrowings changed. Thus in 1809 when a translation of Massillion's sermons was sent to the ecclesiastical censor, Archimandrite Vladimir Tret'iakov, he rejected the translation on the basis of its "literary deficiencies," even though he did

---

[27] Sukhomlinov notes such borrowings in Irinei Klement'evskii as *фамилия, лабиринт, компания, резон, критиковать*, and expressions like "Павел, сей атлет христианский" (Sukhomlinov, I, 240). He cites such words and expressions from Anastasii Bratanovskii's sermons as: *феномен, меланхолик, рецепт, пульс твоего сердца, театр просвещеннаго света* (ibid, 254–5). For both preachers the use of borrowings is noted as the distinguishing mark of their sermons. Concerning Anastasii, Sukhomlinov suggests that the given trait "is tied to the conversational language of society of that time and with Gallicisms which purists found in the *Letters of a Russian Traveler*" (ibid, 254). Connecting this to Karamzin's language may be justified to some extent, although in this case the use of borrowings was necessarily superimposed onto the earlier homiletic tradition and grew out of it. The borrowings found in the sermons of the future Petersburg Metropolitan Mikhail Desnitskii in the 1790's are of the same type, for example, "в натуральном положении, на горизонте, в видимой сей натуре, сообщенная от Бога натура, краскам натуры, весьма важны суть для человека сии два пункта: родиться и умереть," etc. (Mikhail Desnitskii, V, 17, 57, 70, 133, 152, 231, 235).

not find anything in it contrary to Orthodoxy. He indicated that, in particular, "words belonging to the church should be translated for the most part with Slavonic phrases, for the sake of the seriousness of the content and the value of the translation, but not only is this not observed, but words are used that are completely inappropriate to the church pulpit, like: *актер, роль, критика*..." (Kotovich 1909, 58). In the 1810's the censor Iakov Nikol'skii deleted the word *серьезно* from religious writings (ibid, 79; at this period the word could apparently be taken as a marker of secular speech—see Lotman and Uspenskii 1975, 286–7). At this same period such phrases as *организовать конституцию, характеристика иудея, религиозныя истины, революция мира* [*to organize a constitution, description of a Jew, religious truth, world revolution*] were deemed "intolerable in a religious book" (Kotovich 1909, 58). In exactly the same way at the end of the 1830's-start of the 40's the censor P. S. Delitsyn restricted the use of such words as *герой, идея, система, гармония, натурализм, патриотизм, контора* [*hero, idea, system, harmony, naturalism, patriotism, office*] (ibid, 451). In 1847 Filaret Drozdov proposed substituting the term *состав речи* [*composition of speech*] for the term *контекст* [*context*] (Filaret 1883, 19). Similar examples could be multiplied, likewise demonstrating that in the language of religious literature borrowings were clearly perceived as a proscribed element.

The struggle against **neologisms**, on the other hand, was hardly a discernible part of the clergy's linguistic program. In principle the very content of religious literature presented few possibilities for using neologisms; traditional themes called for using traditional linguistic material. Amfiteatrov defined neologism as "the pointless use of new-fashioned words and expressions" (Amfiteatrov, II, 162), that is, he did not forbid individual cases of word-creation, but deviation from traditional vocabulary. In essence the issue concerned the use of expressions that were typical of secular literature but unacceptable in religious works. He cited a series of such expressions whose use he condemned as contrary to homiletic style, and wrote that

> For young people writing sermons for practice, there is another lapse of taste: the desire to shine by using fashionable phrases. In the sermons of young preachers we have come across both *путеводную звезду* and *туманную даль* and *неземное наслаждение*; in these sermons *эта благодать навевает* and *эти духи напевают, отобразы вынаруживаются* and *перлы* often *горят*, and *идеи блещут высокия* , and *юныя силы цветут, как весна*, and *любовь застывает* and *надежда светлеется* and so on.[28] Of course, all these

---

[28] *guiding star; foggy distance; unearthly pleasure; this mercy is evoked; these spirits sing; reflections surface; pearls burn; loft ideas shine; young powers bloom, like spring; love grows cold; hope brightens.*

2. Slavonicizing Purism and Its Reconceptualization in Religious Literatures

words are innocent by themselves, but we must understand their worth and place. Because of this one meets the strangest jumble in sermons; holy truths are at variance with the spirit of the preacher, the spirit is at odds with the ideas, the ideas with the words, and completely lacking is the *homiletic style*. (Amfiteatrov, II, §264, 104)

At the start of the nineteenth century the protest against such innovations could also extend to calques from Western languages, so characteristic of secular literature of the time. Thus in 1807 the ecclesiastical censor protested against the phrase "*нравственный правитель мира*" (moral ruler of the world) (Kotovich 1909, 58), and Innokentii Smirnov wrote to Prince Golitsyn in 1817 concerning Father Sokolov's *A Confessor's Conversation with a Repentant Christian* that "the translator didn't heed the rules of linguistic purity and correctness, which is evident among other places in the first lines of the first page in the first question, where the one repenting asks for guidance in relation to the edification of his soul. In Russian one can't say 'guidance in relation to the edification' of the soul (наставление в отношении назидания)" (Zhemakin 1885, 76).

At the start of the century the purist struggle against *chancellery language* was not relevant. By this time, chancellery speech, the traditional language of bureaucracy which derived from the chancellery language of Muscovite Russia had long ceased to exist as a bona fide linguistic phenomenon, and even its remnants had practically disappeared (a major role here was played by the exams that Speranskii instituted for tsarist bureaucrats). The specifics of bureaucratic language, if it even played a role in this period, were reduced to a small group of expressions and constructions (what we now call "chancellarisms"). There was no need for them in religious writing, so protests against them were practically unheard of. Amfiteatrov does not include "juridical words" among his rubrics. However, we may cite Filaret Drozdov's apparently anecdotal criticism of a certain sermon: "I am not very comforted by the proliferation of titular, chancellery, and foreign words. It seems to me that they do not convey either religious quality or linguistic simplicity" (Filaret 1877, 137).

Much more pertinent were protests against *popular speech*. The limits here, however, were rather indefinite, and Slavonicizing purism could label elements that had nothing to do with the language of lower social orders as "popular" merely because they had Church Slavonic correlatives (cf. § III–1.3); this also became true for the purism of religious literature. Naturally, real vulgarisms were also seen as elements that detracted from linguistic purity. Thus in 1802 the ecclesiastical censor rejected a work "written in the style that is usually employed in Russian folktales which the common people have told one another from the most ancient unenlightened times" (Kotovich 1909, 57). At the end of the 1830's and start of the 40's the censor P. Delitsyn forbade as "low and coarse" such words as *жранье, цалую, ретко* (ibid, 451). In 1854 Metropolitan Filaret sent a religious work to the censor and specifically proposed "to ask the censor to clean up certain words and word combinations, for example, to replace *картошка* with *картофель*" (Filaret, III, 309). In other cases he could note that "the word *свечка* is petty for a serious and austere composition" (Filaret 1877, 184) or that the word *тятька* was "improper for print, especially in an article which aimed to argue on the basis of dogma and the canon" (SMO, I, 451; the word had been used in a child's directly quoted speech). In 1854 the ecclesiastical censor objected against such words and phrases as: *водить за нос, хлопать ушами, бабий народ, девки, плут, пьяница, мальчишка, (lead by the nose, fall on deaf ears, womanish people, gal, rogue, drunkard, urchin*), etc. (see Kotovich 1909, 418).

At the same time words that did not have especially low social overtones could also provoke objections. Indeed the category of popular speech stemmed from neutral literary usage, and notions of neutrality were different in religious and secular literature: Slavonicisms were a neutral element in religious writing but were marked as specifically bookish elements in secular literature. Still, in practice the secular literary language predominated and neither the linguistic ideas of religious writers nor the language of religious writing itself were fully immune to its influence. In the given case the correlation between linguistic views and practice is contradictory. On the one hand, the desire to revitalize traditional interaction with the Orthodox congregation prompted religious writers to use a language that was comprehensible to it; in cases when that congregation included members of the social elite—and these were the cases that set the general tone—this led the clergy to attend to the secular literary language. On the other hand, the hope of returning to traditional piety was connected to the Orthodox literary tradition and its forms of expression, and this tended toward isolating the language of religious literature from the secular. In linguistic practice both trends were active; in linguistic discussions the later isolationist tendency predominated.[29] This duality led to the fact that religious authors could make

---

[29] Amfiteatrov plainly took cognizance of both tendencies but tried to downplay the contradiction. He wrote: "Usage of the educated language. Whether this is the living language, used in live conversation by enlightened people from the upper classes, or the literary language that exists in well written books is all the same to us because we need an educated, refined language, wherever it exists. We need it because church discourse has the closest relation to it. Despite

use of varying viewpoints in characterizing this or that element as popular, and this conditioned a broad spectrum of applications of the given notion.

In particular, when this viewpoint was specifically religious usage, the rubric of popular speech could include practically any Russicism, juxtaposed to Slavonic equivalents. Thus for example Archimandrite Fotii Spasskii summoned Innokentii Borisov to reject the "bad and vulgar" words *этот, эти* and replace them with *сей, сии* (see Kotovich 1909, 166). In an analogous way, in his review of *Biblical History for Children* Filaret Drozdov wrote on January 9, 1838, that "the divine words that everyone knows and understands have been unnecessarily changed in favor of popular speech: *это тело мое; это кровь моя* (*This is my body; this is my blood*)" (Filaret, SMO, suppl.: 615; cf. Filaret 1891, 7). Hence elements that were neutral in secular literature could appear as vulgarisms in the context of religious writing, just as elements that were neutral in religious literature could appear to be archaicisms to a secular writer (e.g., Senkovskii's protests against *сей, оный* — Senkovskii, VIII, 205f and 235f). The dominating position held by the secular literary language prevented the full implementation of the religious purist program when it came into conflict with the principles of secular purism. Religious writers quite often, and apparently unintentionally, used the pronouns *этот, эти* as a neutral element, thus assimilating the predominant secular usage. Toward the end of the 1850's Metropolitan Filaret himself came to a certain compromise. Having received a Russian translation of the Gospel According to Mark, he wrote to Mmetropolitan Grigorii Postnikov on September 9, 1859, that "Just as you do not oppose the word *сей*, so I do not oppose the word *этот*. But it seems to me that it is better to use the former where you are indicating an object of importance, or where the tone of the speech itself approaches the Slavonic" (Filaret 1877, 181). Obviously, at this period *сей, сии* continued to be felt as neutral for religious literature but the "popular" nature of the Russicisms *этот, эти* ceased to be associated with elements of popular speech that were specific to lower social strata. Filaret's normalizing suggestion did not consist in getting rid of one of the variants but in their stylistic differentiation. In this way a three-

---

its separate situation, strictly limited by its special content and aim, homiletic literature, however, is not so isolated and self-contained that it is completely split off from the general human word. On the contrary, as a literary work, created according to the general laws of the educated — artificial word, it is a living branch of universal literature. [...] Hence the laws of the general word are also the laws of the homiletic word; the general characteristics of educated style are also the characteristics of church-homiletic style; and the particular features of this style, stemming from the use of Biblical, church and popular language, should be judged against the general law of stylistics, and find verification in it" (Amfiteatrov, II, § 296, 154–5).

part division of lexicon was established, into neutral elements (including Slavonicisms); "popular" ones, from the specifically religious point of view (but neutral for the secular language); and elements that were "popular" from any point of view. This three-way division is very clearly presented in Metropolitan Filaret's stylistic remarks on the Russian translation of the works of Basil the Great: "*Пока* is a pure word; *покуда* is more popular, if you will; *покудова* is a barbaric word, improperly used instead of the first two by people who do not understand linguistic analogy" (Filaret 1891, 8). If words of the last type are completely excluded, the choice between the first two lexical registers is determined by the stylistic context.

However, this compromise wasn't attained immediately and during the course of the entire first half of the nineteenth century protests could be sounded against the use of neutral Russian elements (from the secular point of view), and at times Russicisms were even replaced by Slavonicisms. Thus in the 1810's the censor Iakov Nikol'skii replaced *как* by *поелику, берлогу* with *логовище* (see Kotovich 1909, 79); similarly, he could replace relative subordinate clauses by participial phrases (ibid). In 1851 the ecclesiastical censor rejected the booklet *Conversations with a Sick Peasant*, arguing in particular that "the simplicity of the language of these conversations in many places goes beyond the bounds of propriety which the subjects of Christian edification demand because of their importance," and further, that "everywhere in the address to the sick man who is being admonished words of heartfelt tenderness are used for which lofty and holy Christian love has no need to express itself—words like *мой милый, мой сердечный, дружечек, голубчик* (*my dear, my heart, little friend, little dove*)" (ibid 419). In this context Metropolitan Filaret's philippic against popular elements, contained in a letter of Dec. 30, 1850, to Bishop Aleksei, is noteworthy. Filaret, reviewing the Russian translation of *Lestvitsa* (*Spiritual Ladder*), cited the expression *начинать с Бога* (to start from God) as inaccurate, suggesting *начинать от Бога* as the only correct way to say it. Generally speaking both expressions conformed to the norm of the secular language of the time, but Filaret insists that only the latter is acceptable (apparently based on actual Church Slavonic usage). Further, Filaret exclaims, "Why did the translator say it differently? There is no other apparent reason other than in his opinion this is the way the people speak, that is, the illiterate ones. Is it really necessary that this idolatry before the people, which is also destructive in other areas, make its way into religious literature?" (Filaret 1883, 77–8).

The interpretation of "popular language" that Amfiteatrov proposes is also quite characteristic. He insists that the preacher speak in a language his listeners understand, and this determines his positive view of popular speech

(Amfiteatrov, II, § 292, 149–50). His views also reflect a romanticizing of folk language which he believes has preserved the ancient original quality of the language and expresses the national spirit. He asserts that on the basis of the popular tongue "one may describe the genius of the language, frequently lost in books and in the modern living speech of educated society. In it are safeguarded the true features of the national character (narodnost'), while the language of the upper classes may be full of what is borrowed and alien" (II, 148). All the more striking is the set of elements that Amfiteatrov thinks may be taken from popular speech for use in sermons. He writes:

> The plebian has his own terminology, sometimes better than the learned man's; he has his own grammatical and rhetorical emphasis, his own aesthetic knowledge—but knowledge from nature. Thus he says *мир* rather than our conferences and gatherings; *общество, сходка* instead of parliaments; *свет* instead of our visible world and nature; *смута* instead of revolution; and so on. His *кровь моя, свет мой* are expressions of kinship and friendship; *время дорогое* and *времена плохия,* expressions of the difficulty of physical existence; *согрешить и прогневить Бога* — the reasons for all misfortunes, individual and collective ... For him *хлеб* is God's gift, a good day — *день Божий,* a coffin — *домовина,* domestic animals — *животы,* something's purpose its *наряд,* and so on. (Amfiteatrov, II, 151)

Elements that mostly have no particular popular coloring are presented here as specific examples of the "popular language." For most of them, their "narodnost'" boils down to an indefinite thematic primitivism and is not connected to any identification with dialect, whether local or social.[30] In relation to explicit popular elements, despite all of his declarations, Amfiteatrov holds to the purism that was typical of the clergy. He makes the special reservation that "while accepting that which in the popular language is good by itself and generally suitable, a church sermon should not fall into unrestrained vulgarism and sink to the tenor of the street; it shouldn't use low and coarse words; it shouldn't turn into village sayings... In a word, it should not clothe its serious ideas that demand a serious tone and speech in plebian witticisms (pribautki)..." (Amfiteatrov, II, § 294, 153).

Amfiteatrov's real attitude toward popular speech is revealed with particular clarity in his orthoepic recommendations. He writes that the laws of pronunciation "may be based a) on church etiquette (prilichie); b) on public taste; c) on the custom of the listeners being addressed" (ibid, 242). These

---

[30] Even the word *домвина* that Amfiteatrov cites in the meaning "coffin" (according to Dal', "regional" [Dal', I, 466], and *домовище,* "popular" in the SAR [II, col. 727]), could be used in the literary language of the eighteenth and early nineteenth century and not be seen as a popular form (see Sorokin 1949, 108–9).

correspond to bookish pronunciation, standard (Moscow) pronunciation, and dialectical pronunciation, and may be related, respectively, to the norm of religious literature, that of the secular literary language, and popular speech. This correlation reveals that the religious norm occupies the basic, neutral position, elements of secular literary pronunciation are allowed with significant restrictions, and dialectical speech is completely disallowed. It is indicative that from the perspective of religious literature secular pronunciation is not treated as neutral, but as popular, low, although permissible within certain limits. Indeed, concerning bookish (liturgical) pronunciation Amfiteatrov writes:

> Basing oneself on church etiquette one may pronounce every letter and word of a sermon as they are written and printed. On the one hand, such pronunciation conveys importance to a church sermon; on the other it is less dangerous for the preacher himself... A particularly bookish pronunciation is required in glorifications, prayers, the divine names and all expressions which enter the sermon from the ecclesiastic-Biblical language. This kind of pronunciation that we sometimes hear from young preachers is completely unsuitable: '*Ва имя-тца, Атца, и Сына и святова Духа, Гасподь Iсус — крястился; все упование мае; што ми подабаить тварити; изведём слезы из очесь*'— and a multitude of similar expressions. Only one drawback of bookish pronunciation, it distances the sermon from a simple friendly conversation, and thereby violates naturalness, and makes it very clear that the sermon is a [written] composition. Not a major drawback. (Amfiteatrov, II, 242; on the traditions of church pronunciation, see Uspenskii 1968; Uspenskii 1971).[31]

On Moscow pronunciation, Amfiteatrov writes: "Basing oneself on popular taste, one may use that dialect (vygovor) in a sermon that is recognized among other dialects as predominant and considered the best and most noble. Let us say, for ex., that for us the main and best pronunciation is the Muscovite and of the Moscow area, according to Grech's grammar... This is the pronunciation that the preacher should study; but even here ecclesiastical-Biblical words and phrases must be pronounced in the bookish way" (ibid, 242–3).[32] The non-neutral status of Muscovite vis à vis bookish pronunciation is clear from the fact that a sermon may be completely

---

[31] Note that the word for "sermon" here, *беседа*, itself also means "conversation." (Translator's note)

[32] Amfitreatrov adds: "Let us not defend Moscow pronunciation simply because it is Muscovite, if everywhere we will start, for example, to change the final *г* to *х* (*рох спасении, блах Бог наш, расторх узы, мох каяться*), unaccented *o* to *a* (*слава Писания* instead of *слова, пакайся*), *п* into *б* (*гроп, рап, слап*, instead of *гроб, раб, слаб*), *ч* before *н* into *ш* (*скушно, мрашно, тошно*), *г* into *к* (*друк, снек, порок* instead of *порог*, etc.)" (Amfitreatrov, II, 242–3).

read according to the bookish norm but not according to that of Moscow; everything that is explicitly connected to the church tradition requires the traditional church orthoepy. Lastly, dialectical pronunciation is considered incommensurate with the lofty content of the sermon (ibid, 243). Thus if in regard to vocabulary and phraseology Amfiteatrov could proceed from the perspectives of both the religious and secular literary languages, in regard to phonetics the religious norm clearly prevailed. For other representatives of religious literature this strict approach could naturally extend to all other linguistic levels.

Thus for religious literature Slavonicisms functioned as a neutral element. This also determined the clergy's attitude toward *archaisms*. Archaisms as a stylistic category that defined the norms of secular linguistic usage did not exist for the religious tradition. True, Amfiteatrov lists archaisms among those elements that mar the purity of the language, defining the category as "the unnecessary use of obsolete words which have gone out of use and which do not have any right to rehabilitation" (Amfiteatrov, II, 162). The examples he cites, however, demonstrate that archaicisms are not presented as objects for genuine purist protest but rather as examples of a traditional rubric of the accepted stylistic theory (as they had been earlier for Lomonosov and his followers, § III–1.3, § III–3.2). In fact, Amfiteatrov cites words like: *мща, краковат, клѣтуки, скута, имство, неоплазнство, смерд*—words which no one (with very rare exceptions) ever employed, so there was no need to warn against their use. Notably, among the numerous stylistic criticisms contained in the ecclesiastical censorship's records and in the correspondence of individual clergymen, attacks on the use of archaisms seem to be completely absent.[33]

---

[33] A seeming exception is Filaret's remark concerning the corrections he made in a translation of a certain patristic work. He writes: "I wanted to combine the Slavonic (slovenskii) aspect of the language with clarity, and therefore I sometimes changed the word order and used not very many new words instead of more ancient ones [that were] obscure or ambiguous to today's understanding" (Filaret, II, 273). The issue here is obviously not about archaisms in a Russian but a Slavonic text, and about words that had become completely incomprehensible (archaic), i.e., it had to do with modernizing Church Slavonic, which was a rather traditional task (§ I–2.1). In the same way, Slavonic translations from Greek done before the seventeenth century could be seen as archaic. Here the notion of archaism could extend to individual lexical elements as well as syntactic constructions which deviated from the usual and emulated the Greek original. In this context Metropolitan Filaret's response to a panegyric speech by Epifanii (Filaret, III, 164–5) and especially his juxtaposition of two chapters of Maksim Ispovednik's "On Love" that was submitted by Amfiteatrov (Amfiteatrov, II, § 282, 137f) is typical. This was the same understanding of archaisms in old Slavonic translations that resulted in the correction of liturgical texts in the second half of the nineteenth and early twentieth centuries (see Sove 1970; Pletneva 1994), which resulted in "the replacement of

Chapter 4. The New Cultural Differentiation

From the point of view of the secular language, the religious attitude toward archaisms was clearly positive. Amfiteatrov not only did not limit the use of usual Church Slavonic expressions and forms but even permitted the introduction (in Church Slavonic texts) of Slavonic elements that had gone out of use. Speaking about making use in sermons of "ancient translations" whose language "time has made not fully intelligible, and in some places completely obscure," Amfiteatrov foresaw "the selection of noteworthy words and expressions from old translations [and their] renewal and introduction into the modern living language" (ibid, II, § 281, 137). In general, the preacher could resort to "resurrecting forgotten words and expressions, renewal of worn out ones, [and] introducing into living speech those that have died out over time," although "the number of words that have an incontestable right to regeneration is in general very small" (ibid, II, § 285, 139). Clearly, this sort of recommendation turns prohibitions against using archaisms into empty declarations, a concession to traditional stylistic notions.

And so, even though the rubrics of religious purism coincided with those of secular literature, their content was quite different. That is how the matter stood with popular speech: if for secular literature popular speech comprised elements that were specific to the language of uneducated social groups, for religious purism this rubric could just as easily be applied to Russicisms which were neutral for the secular tradition. The rubric of archaisms was interpreted in similarly different ways: while for secular purism this rubric primarily consisted of Slavonicisms, for the religious tradition it had little practical importance. Hence the notion of linguistic purity for the religious tradition —as opposed to the secular— was directly dependent on the fact that religious literature assimilated both Russicisms and Slavonicisms as equally organic elements. Linguistic purity was gauged by two things: the measure of Russian and of Church Slavonic. In the place where "Russian" purism coincided with "Slavonic" purism, purist tendencies increased, and this made for a heightened sensitivity toward borrowings, neologisms, and elements of popular speech. On the other hand, where these two tendencies did not coincide, the very conception of purity changed, so that neutral Russicisms (from a socio-linguistic perspective, those in general use) could be defined as popular speech, while archaisms became exotic rarities that had no relation to actual usage.

---

antiquated Slavonic words [that were] incomprehensible at the present time or had [assumed] a different meaning" (in the formulation of the Bishop of Ekaterinoslav, Avgustin Gulianitskii — Sove 1970, 39).

Understandably, the purist tendencies of secular literature which restricted the use of Slavonicisms were unacceptable for religious literature, so that as a result religious purism became clearly opposed to the secular variant.[34]

2.2 The Attitude Toward the Linguistic Sign

The opposition between secular and religious purism is not reducible to their different interpretations of linguistic and stylistic rubrics. Their very conception of purism, its ideological foundation, was fundamentally dissimilar. Secular purism was primarily a stylistic notion, unquestionably connected to a certain aesthetic position, but only defining a norm of good taste and not a correct worldview. Religious purism was conceived primarily in religious terms, and deviation from the norm was understood not only as stylistic wrongdoing but as a manifestation of impiety. In a special note of 1862 Filaret Drozdov posed the question, "Would it not be beneficial if the leading member of the Most Holy Synod secretly reminded the diocesan authorities and through them their subordinates that church sermons should make pure teaching universally comprehensible, but in a *correct and pure* language, and not depicting shameful things in *ugly* language..."? (Filaret, SMO, V, 216 — my italics, V. Z.). Thus the issue of linguistic purity was directly tied to the purity of faith and the observation of piety. Introducing "impure" language brings profane elements into a sacred context, i.e., a kind of blasphemy. Religious purism becomes a doctrine of linguistic piety.

---

[34] It is notable that for Amfiteatrov purism was just as harmful for "linguistic purity" as was "excessive impurity" (Amfiteatrov, II, 162). Presumably he has the purist tendencies of secular literature in mind when he writes that "ruthless purity strips away the language and threatens it with extreme impoverishment; language always loses from it. Exiling old words from the language without rights, opposing the introduction of new ones, driving out the foreign, scorning its own — popular and regional, calling Slavonic un-Russian — what is left of the language? Undoubtedly, what is left is pure, but of such a character that you won't be able to clothe many ideas in it, and even so they will all seem stunted and forced into too narrow dress" (ibid, § 302, 163–4). These anti-purist sentiments closely recall Fénélon's letter to the French Academy which may even be the direct source of this passage. However, in contrast to the stylistic controversy within a single literature (between Fénélon and the French purists), here we have conflict between secular and religious literature. That Amfiteatrov is polemicizing precisely with the secular literary (aristocratic) tradition is suggested by his reference to those who call "Slavonic un-Russian." This was characteristic of the capital nobility in the eighteenth century (see Sumarokov 1748, 7; and § III–3.1 above), and Amfiteatrov may have this tradition in mind.

Chapter 4. The New Cultural Differentiation

From this point of view the language of secular literature is thought of as profane, opposed to the sacred tongue of religious literature, and this applies to the purity of the secular language as well. Insofar as this language assimilates as pure those linguistic elements that the religious language rejects (and rejects as impure and profaning sacred content — as we saw above in the case of borrowings, neologisms, and elements of popular speech), the secular language in its entirely begins to be perceived as impure, and consequently defiling the sacred content it may try to express. If some particular element, whatever its origin, is perceived as the specific property of the secular language, then on this basis it turns out to be impure from the point of view of religious purism.

This perception explains the fact that among the usual purist rubrics cited by Amfiteatrov, one appears that is not represented in any other stylistic classifications, and that is "romanticism" (романтизм). This is defined as "the senseless use of words and expressions borrowed from romance (romanicheskii)[35] and fairy-tale (skazochnyi) literature and the like" (Amfiteatrov, II, 162). A stylistic theory here acquires not stylistic but religious and social significance, as any use of language without religious sanction is declared to be contamination. The independence of religious literature's linguistic norm is thus elevated into a principle. The purity of the language of religious literature is sanctified by the purity of faith, while the stylistic principles of secular literature are based on criteria that are wholly profane; they are therefore inapplicable to religious literature and from its perspective lead to impure word-use.

In connection with this perception, Slavonicisms are credited with a sacred quality and Russicisms defined as correspondingly profane, and the substitution of profane for sacred elements in a sacred context appears as blasphemy. This view is explicitly formulated by Amfiteatrov:

> A church sermon is the reproduction of the Gospel; therefore not only must the main Biblical ideas be the primary basis for the sermon but Biblical words must also serve as the primary basis for the preacher's language. Such words are indeed met in any devout sermon; the homily assimilated them long ago, made them its substance. It has become used to employ these words constantly: *благодать, крест, искупление, грех* and *грехопадение, возрождение* or *пакибытие, самоотвержение, похоть плоти, душевный* and *внешний человек, внутренний* and *духовный, таинство, единение*,[36] in general, words

---

[35] Romanicheskii" may refer to Romanticism as well as to novels and romances (both "romany" in Russian). (Translator's note)

[36] *grace, cross, atonement, sin, the Fall, rebirth, renewal, self-abnegation, fleshly lust, person of the spirit* and *external person, sacrament, unity.*

of dogmatic and practical content. According to the demands of its pious taste, it says: *жезл, гортань, уста, мечь, благолепие, стопа* and *пята, риза* and *облачение, завеса* and *покров*,[37] — in general, words relating to religious aesthetics. These and similar words must by no means be translated or replaced by others, but be explained to people if they are unclear; for to replace them or translate them would mean distorting the language and committing sacrilege. What would result if we, for example, imitating the secular language, took it into our minds to replace the holy word *благодать* [grace] with secular graces, charities, charms? What kind of language would it be if instead of *Господь Иисус* [Lord Jesus] we began to say *господин* [master], instead of *владыка* [sovereign] we said *боярин* [boyar], instead of *ах братие* — *ах братцы*, instead of *самоумерщвление* – *самоубийство*, instead of *крещение* — *купание*, instead of *таинство* — *секрет*, instead *чудо* — *диковина*, instead of *песнь, песненный* — *песня, песенный*; if we replaced *гортань* with *горло* or *глотка*, *жезл* with *палица*, *мечь* with *шпага* and so on? (Amfiteatrov, II, § 270, 121–2; italics added)

The task of separating the secular and religious languages thus became central. At the same time as the struggle was taking place in secular literature for bringing the literary language closer to the spoken and for getting rid of Slavonicisms that had Russian correlatives, the opposite was going on in religious literature — an effort to minimize Russicisms and to assimilate Slavonicisms as an organic means of expressing holy content. Understood in religious terms, this effort was seen as separating the sacred from the profane, as a defense of confessional purity.

The special religiously motivated character of the religious language was felt as a literary fact, about which we have the testimony of not only church figures but of secular literary ones as well. Osip Senkovskii, insisting that we have "completely cut ourselves off from Slavonicizing (slavenshchizna)" (Senkovskii, VIII, 225), and, like the Karamzinists, seeing the model of literary speech "in conversation with decent, educated men in the presence of sweet, educated ladies" (ibid, 220), limits his program's demands to secular literature. Rejecting the existence of the "lofty style" (i.e., a special bookish language), at the same time he makes an exception for "the style of church oratory" whose special qualities are defined, in particular, by its connection to the Church Slavonic literary tradition. On religious oratory he writes: "This is another matter! There both the language and its forms are completely different from usual literature. Religious oratory is meant for other, higher goals, follows other rules, among which one of the most important is tradition (predanie)" (ibid, 246).

---

[37] *staff, larynx, lips, sword, splendor, foot; heel, chasuble,* and *vestments, screen, veil.*

Chapter 4. The New Cultural Differentiation

The separation of secular and religious literary languages is thus taken as a given, and it is indicative that Senkovskii can put his linguistic program into the mouth of a priest. In the "Letter of Landowners from Tver'" one voice is that of the enlightened parson, Father Paisii. When he is told that "Baron Brambeus [Senkovskii's pen-name]... wants to annul the friendship between the Russian and Slavonic word, to assert the independence of the Russian language and put a boundary between them, so that they will no longer be mixed," he responds:

> That should have been done long ago! *Ne misceantur sacra profanes*! Do not confuse the sacred and the profane! I have always been of the opinion that the Slavonic language must remain, like tradition, in our Orthodox church and serve the needs of the faith exclusively... I have always found it extremely inappropriate and incongruous when our gentlemen poets sometimes use the honored forms of this language for things completely [un]worthy of its grandeur, for singing the praises of *дев младых, волос златых* (young maidens, golden hair) and the like. I do not mention the incongruity of scattering words in another language and completely other form in a Russian story; this is pure macaronism, the height of bad taste, the absence of a feeling for the elegance of our native tongue (ibid, 222–3; cf. Zhivov 1984a, 375–6).

It is no less remarkable that Father Paisii places the blame for this mixing of Russian and Church Slavonic in the Russian literary language on Lomonosov. "If Lomonosov," he says, "had had the fortunate idea of clearly separating the two languages... by the present day the Russian language would already have been established on firm foundations... [and] would already be independent" (Senkovskii, III, 223–4).

This kind of formulation was precisely echoed by actual representatives of religious literature. Metropolitan Filaret Drozdov, for example, could compare mixing Slavonic and Russian to confusing "the pure and the dirty and the heavenly with the satanic" (Filaret 1891, 8). He gave the religious censor a harsh reprimand because he permitted the "poem *молитва при кресте* in which *арии* and *хоры* follow under this title..." "The censor's theological outlook and religious-ethical sense," wrote Filaret, "should have made him immediately feel the incongruity between the title *a prayer at the cross* and the *arias* and *choruses* that follow, that belong to the theater" (Filaret, SMO, III, 506–8). Filaret found the question of this incongruity so important that he wrote about it to the Ober-Procuror of the Synod Count Protasov (SMO, dop., 329), to the archimandrite of the Trinity-Sergius Lavra Antonii (Filaret, II, 206–7), and to the rector of the Moscow Spiritual Academy, Archimandrite Aleksii (Filaret 1883, 114; cf. Chistovich 1894, 357). The issue was very clearly about words; if, for example, in place of *арии и хоры* stood *единогласныя и многогласныя песнопения* there would have been no objections. The combining of "sacred" and "worldly" words was thus seen as blasphemy.

This type of understanding presumes a special perception of the linguistic sign that is not characteristic of the ordinary approach to language and that of representatives of secular literature. If in secular thought a linguistic sign is perceived as a convention, the given attitude to language is precisely based on non-conventional thinking (for a typology of perceptions, see Lotman and Uspenskii 1973). In European linguistic thought the perception of language as a convention became firmly established by the Cartesian tradition (see, for example, Lamy's formulation, § III–2.3). From here it was assimilated by eighteenth-century Russian writers, including religious ones. Thus in M. M. Speranskii's *Rules of Advanced Oratory* we read:

> And what are words? Arbitrary signs of thought. But signs, considering them in their entire scope, have only one merit, the merit of accurate expression; and therefore words, as types of signs, can only have this one excellence, to accurately arouse in our mind the ideas that they are meant to signify… Let us repeat again: words are arbitrary signs of thought. Consequently they cannot signify more than we command them to, only as much as the general agreement of minds that has formed the language allows. Once this agreement has been settled, no one can change it; only usage… may from time to time make little, gradual, and individual, hardly noticeable alterations. (Speranskii 1844, 160–1)

This attitude toward the sign became part of the nineteenth-century secular tradition, and in particular lay at the heart of the Karamzinist notion of the changeability of language as a necessary and legitimate process (cf. Uspenskii 1985, 21–2). Understandably, this kind of conception leaves not only no room for the notion of "holy" words, but none in general for any kind of "sacred" sign.

Such an approach, however, could not be consistently applied to the attempt to restore the Orthodox tradition, in whatever form it took. Indeed, in this tradition a whole series of signs were ascribed unconditional holiness, the opposite of the arbitrary (for example, crosses and icons). It was therefore natural that everything that concerned the sacred sphere in any way would be conceptualized in a similar way. The perception of the holiness of all objects and actions connected with Orthodox cult was known in old Russia (so-called "obriadoverie," "faith in rites"), and with certain modifications this was revived in the first half of the nineteenth century. Metropolitan Filaret Drozdov made the connection very clearly: "The law forbids depicting holy objects on household dishware. This particular rule has a more general one as its basis: do not confuse holy objects with worldly ones so as not to offend against piety and toward what is sacred (for example, at a current exhibit in Moscow there is an embossed [church] garment on an altar, on which they've put a samovar, while next to a [liturgical] chalice they have placed a sink with cupids on it)" (Filaret, SMO, V, 708). Over the course of his entire life Filaret insisted on the impermissibility of mixing the sacred and profane, as did a series of other church leaders. The clergy held that the state, which declared itself to be Orthodox and derived many benefits from this, should not allow objects of piety to become part of everyday cultural life, which generally speaking was typical of any secularizing culture. It is understandable that the state was not able to stop this process, so the clergy's insistent demands took on the nature of a hopeless struggle with external signs of secularization, at the same time as it lacked the means to engage with the process of inner secularization. On January 10, 1833, Filaret wrote to the Ober-procuror of the Synod S. D. Nechaev: "It must be ordered immediately that a procession of the cross not take place in a theater. But should we even speak about the vision of [the last] judgment, I don't know. What will happen to an age that doesn't understand how absurd it is *miscere sacra profanes*, and finds beauty where they put gold next to filth, and flowers beside dung? Say it's not so, they'll get angry and the absurdities will only multiply" (Filaret 1895, 96). Given this attitude, it was enough for some particular elements of the religious language to deviate from the secular usage for them to be perceived as sacred, and after this for the nonconventional view of signs to extend to them as well.

Nowhere perhaps was this approach to language as evident as in its attitude towards the alphabet. As we have seen (§ I–1.1), Peter's reform of the alphabet reflected all of the basic aspects of Petrine linguistic policy, signifying as it did the graphic opposition between secular and religious culture. Later, however, the contrast in alphabets was no longer correlated to a cultural opposition or to the juxtaposition of sacred and profane, and took on primarily socio-cultural significance. At least during the first two thirds of the eighteenth century elementary language learning preserved the traditional pattern, that is, it consisted in studying the Slavonic primer, prayer book and Psalter (see § 0–2), to which might be added Feofan Prokopovich's *Russian Catechism (Pervoe uchenie otrokom)* (on the significance of this text, see § I–2.1); attempts to introduce books in the civil script into primary education were not successful.[38] Because of this the ability to read civil script was

---

[38] On attempts to do this in the Ural mining schools under V. N. Tatishchev's supervision see Guzner 1980, 67–72; Nechaev 1956. As Gary Marker rightly notes (1994, 23), Max Okenfuss's suggestion (1980, 53–6) that this was due to the insufficient press run of *Iunosti chestnoe*

connected with intermediate and not primary education, or with the transition to it (Marker 1994, 14), and was therefore accessible only to the social elite. In the last third of the eighteenth century there were attempts to reorient primary education onto the civil alphabet. Thus in the general plan for the Foundling Hospital (Vospitatel'nyi dom) (1763 and 1767), I. I. Betskoi proposed beginning with printed primers "in the language used today... which we use naturally" (Zhitetskii 1903, 44),[39] but there were apparently no appreciable results until the early nineteenth century.

These socio-cultural considerations led to a situation in which the choice of script was tied not so much with content as with the audience for the edition. A series of publications intended for universal consumption could be issued in parallel, in both church and civil scripts. This was the case with two editions of Platon Levshin's *Orthodox Doctrine* that appeared in 1765 (Platon Levshin 1765), printed simultaneously in church and civil scripts. In the 1740's sermons were printed in civil script if they weren't sent to Moscow for publication in the Synodal typography; a series of them appeared in parallel editions. This was the case with Gedeon Krinovskii's sermons that came out at the end of Elizabeth's reign (§ III–3.1). Later theological works could also be published in civil script, apparently intended for the spiritual enlightenment of secular readers. In the post-Petrine period, however, secular literature was not published in the church script (cf. Marker 1985, 61–3). The Synodal typography was run by the church authorities and supported their activities, which naturally had little to do with publishing novels and the like. However, as late as 1817 Arakcheev could ask the Ober-Prokuror of the Synod Prince A. N. Golitsyn to have the *Statute on Military Settlements* printed in church type (see Kotovich 1909, 294).[40] The absence of a clear connection between publications' content and script did not create

---

    zertsalo (*Honest Mirror of Youth*), which was to serve as a textbook for the civil script, is groundless. The reason was devotion to traditional methods of teaching, and possibly also the insufficient readiness of teachers to deal with innovations.

[39]   Similarly, in Iankovich de Mirievo's *Rukovodstvo uchiteliam pervogo i vtorogo klassa* (*Guide to Teachers of First and Second Grade*), published in 1783, he wrote: "In Russian books they use two prints, church and civil. The knowledge of both of these is equally necessary to everyone, and therefore one should learn both together. But since when studying one should always start with what is easiest, and civil print has both the advantages of being easier for reading by syllable (v skladakh) and having a simpler and shorter alphabet, one should always start with the civil script" (Tolstoi 1886, 54; cf. Zhiteiskii 1903, 45).

[40]   The motive for this was evidently the desire to acquaint the largest number of people possible with this work, including peasants. Peasants usually received basic official information from rural clergymen who read official documents aloud. However, even at the end of the eighteenth century "the Synod had determined that most parish priests could not read the civil script and that they were consequently unable to perform their mandated duties" (Marker 1994, 12).

a predisposition to the semiotic opposition of scripts. In the context of the later eighteenth century cultural synthesis, both scripts were seen as part of a single culture, so that *kirillitsa* (the church alphabet) was not seen as the property of the clergy, and its use was not under its strict control. In particular, at the end of the eighteenth century, church script could be freely used in titles or for additional numeration in books of completely secular content (for example, M. Popov's translation of *Jerusalem Delivered* — Tass 1772).

With changes in the nature of primary education, secular society gradually grew unaccustomed to church type, and reading books printed in it became increasingly difficult. In time books in *kirillitsa* came to be perceived as meant for a religious rather than secular audience. Characteristically, in 1803, in the midst of a bitter struggle with the higher clergy, the Ober-Procurator of the Synod A. A. Iakovlev decided to reprint the *Spiritual Regulation*, and to reprint it in the civil script, so as to make it universally accessible and to make perfectly clear the limits which Peter I had put on the church's power. Iakovlev wrote: "I realized that the ignorance of our citizens concerning the precise limits of the clergy's power that are so clearly set forth in the *Spiritual Regulation* have contributed to no little injustice and to various abuses, and therefore, to spread knowledge of this book among the people, which was heretofore printed in Church Slavonic and in church letters... I proposed that the Synod order the *Spiritual Regulation* be reprinted in civil script—and anyone can easily imagine how little they liked this little idea" (Iakovlev 1915, 21; cf. Chistovich 1894, 7). The church script thus became limited to use in religious education and writing.[41] As a result the juxtaposition of typefaces again came to be correlated with the opposition between the sacred and profane and the clergy began to complain about violations of this relationship. In 1843, for example, the Synod forbade the printing of the church service commemorating St. Arsenii Konevskii in civil type, basing its decision on the argument that "all services to the holy saints have been printed, and are printed in church letters" (Kotovich 1909, 216; cf. Sove 1970, 36–7). And in 1830, when M. N. Zagoskin's novel *Iurii Miloslavskii*

---

[41] In the early nineteenth century the audience for books printed in church script (primers) could also clearly be seen as the lowest social strata whose education was limited to learning the catechism. In this period, teaching them the civic script, which gave entry to secular culture, could be seen as a sign of freethinking. Thus in the case of Staff-Captain Mit'kov, whose copy of Pushkin's "Gavriliada" was confiscated in 1828, the order he gave to his estate manager in which he "allowed him to teach peasant children to read, but in the civic rather than church script" drew special interest (Perepiska 1911, 200). For both Staff-Captain Mit'kov and his investigators the choice of primer was associated with the opposition of secular and religious culture.

2. Slavonicizing Purism and Its Reconceptualization in Religious Literatures

was being published, and had its section headings ("part one," "part two," etc.) set in church script, the Synod declared: "Have it known to the necessary parties that the Most Holy Synod considers it improper to use church type—which exists for liturgical books and those of religious content alone—in a novel or other secular books" (Kotovich 1909, 294; cf. Lotman, Tolstoi, Uspenskii 1981, 315). In this way the completely arbitrary signs of the civil and church alphabets were again semioticized and served to differentiate the two cultural spheres.

Thus the clergy returned to old views of the bookish language as one that was sacred by its very nature, as a language that was itself an image of orthodoxy, one that teaches the correct faith and which unconditionally (and untranslatably) conveys its content. It was just this way that in the seventeenth and early eighteenth century Russian bookmen could perceive Church Slavonic in its opposition to the non-bookish language (see Uspenskii 1984). Revived in the nineteenth century, this view was applicable both to Church Slavonic and to Slavonicized Russian (Slavenorossiiskii, which had become the literary language of the clergy); both were opposed to the profane tongue (both to the secular literary language and to the spoken language).[42] In these conditions the notion of the iconic, nonconventional nature of the sign, characteristic of pre-Petrine linguistic consciousness, was also revived. Of course, this new attitude toward the sign applied to the entire spectrum of semiotic behavior, and not only to language.

In ancient Russia the semiotization of all aspects of behavior that came into contact with the sacred sphere is usually associated with so-called "obriadoverie" ("faith in rites"), one of the characteristic features of Russian religious consciousness. In the nineteenth century externally similar phenomena have a completely different source; in any case, we should not apply the term to the majority of church leaders of the time (almost all of whom were to some degree influenced by Protestant theology, for which, understandably, the attitude toward religious rites was relativist). Emphasizing the semiotic significance of anything that came into contact with the sacral

---

[42] If in pre-Petrine Russia Church Slavonic was perceived as a kind of "icon of Orthodoxy" (Uspenskii 1984), foreign languages (Tatar, Turkish, Latin) could be seen as expressions of various kinds of non-Orthodox impiety (Islam, Catholicism). Curiously, this view finds an analogy in the cultural and linguistic views of proponents of religious purism. Thus talking about teaching in Latin, Metropolitan Filaret wrote to Filaret Gumilevskii: "I have written to you about theological lessons in Russian. And meanwhile, speaking about this here, I again met with vacillation. What can we do? People think that they are defending Orthodoxy, defending a non-Orthodox language" (Filaret 1872, 52 — letter of April 10, 1837). Latin thus turns out to be a "non-Orthodox" language; in another instance Filaret calls it "pagan and papist" (ibid, 50).

sphere became a way of fighting against the secularization of the Russian state and society (as noted above). This explains the pedantic insistence on the sacred status of objects of piety and the charge that confusing them with those of secular culture was blasphemy.

Concerns of this kind were constantly on the mind of Russian church leaders of this period. Thus, for example, Metropolitan Filaret gave a negative evaluation of N. V. Sushkov's "The Beginning of Moscow" that was written with the most virtuous of intentions. The drama depicts the hermit Bukal, man of prayer and missionary, surrounded by the pagan ways of ancient Rus'. This situation itself offends Metropolitan Filaret, who writes: "This mixing of the true and the false, plunging a saint into worldly impurity [would be] strange to see written in a book, and I think even stranger spoken in a theater. The writer, as I understand it, had the good idea of depicting the religious origins of Moscow. But when he dressed up this main idea in the various guises of life at that time, this clothing proved, in my opinion, too worldly for the spiritual idea" (Filaret 1905, 174 — review written on January 5, 1853). In 1866 Filaret protested against the proposal to send Russian historical treasures to Paris for a universal exhibition: "Icons, church vestments and objects for the altar, as consecrated objects, are protected from [being put in] places that are inappropriate for them and from being mixed with worldly objects" (Filaret 1905, 298). Similar ideas force Filaret to constantly protest against works with religious content being included in theatrical or concert programs (see Filaret, SMO, III, 504–5; SMO, V, dop., 328–9; Filaret IV, 426–7), and he even formulates this protest as a principle of Orthodox piety. In 1855 he writes concerning a concert: "Let art lovers get angry with me if they will, but I cannot hold back my opinion that lofty subjects, the creation of the world and the last judgment, that demand reverential meditation, are demeaned and slighted when they become a musician's plaything for the amusement of the listener. The impropriety is unavoidably compounded when words are added to the music" (Filaret, SMO, IV, 48–9).[43]

It is indicative that the person of an archdeacon could also be included among sacred objects, alongside religious artifacts and Biblical

---

[43] Similar protests could be made when the placement of sacred objects in a profane context was clearly unintentional; blasphemy was not seen as the result of a deliberate affront to something holy but as an objective fact due to an incorrect attitude to signs, revealing society's lack of spiritual feeling. Thus, for example, in 1858 Metropolitan Grigorii Postnikov wrote to the Petersburg governor-general protesting against pictures of fashionable Parisian dresses that appeared in the journal *Son of the Fatherland* that were decorated with crosses he found similar to those on sacerdotal robes [...] (Lemke 1904, 323–5), and Filaret took steps to prevent an iron factory from producing tiles with the image of a four-pointed cross (Filaret, III, 212–3).

2. Slavonicizing Purism and Its Reconceptualization in Religious Literatures

sayings. Thus in 1833 Filaret wrote a statement in the name of the Synod in which he criticized the improper nature of the celebrations taking place in Archangel in connection with the opening of a monument to Lomonosov. In it he described as blasphemous, in the first place, "the mixing of holy and secular, that was especially strange for the simple folk… in that the archdeacon who delivered a proclamation in church [also] read a speech at the monument," and secondly, that "in this speech the holy dictum 'This day which God created' was used inappropriately" (Filaret, SMO, dop., 581). Obviously, with such sensitivity to the mixing of sacred and profane any differences between the languages of secular and religious literature become semioticized and further motivate the desire to segregate the respective elements. Thus linguistic elements illustrate a particular case of a larger cultural and semiotic development.

2.3 The Secularization of Slavonicisms and the Juxtaposition of Religious and Secular Traditions

The religious conception of purism is manifested with special clarity in regard to those words which had entered the eighteenth-century literary language from Church Slavonic but had acquired new meanings, often precisely opposite from their older ones. This material demonstrates how the ideological understanding of linguistic facts leads to changes in language practices. In preserving the literary language of the late eighteenth century and making it their own, the clergy nonetheless transformed that language at those points which contradicted the idea that it represented a nonconventional expression of Orthodox culture.

The "secular" assimilation of Church Slavonic elements took place throughout the entire eighteenth century, and occurred in various ways. The process could be deliberate, as when Slavonic words with altered meanings were purposefully introduced into the literary language in order to enrich its vocabulary. The creation of this sort of semantic neologisms was acknowledged even by conflicting linguistic programs (§ IV–1.1). This process occurred with special intensity in translations, where Slavonic elements were used to express the corresponding meaning of the original. Insofar as translation was one of the main means of forming the literary language, the use of semantic calques had primary importance for the Russian literary language (on its scope one can judge by the evidence presented by G. Hüttl-Worth —

Hüttl-Worth 1956). Conversational speech could also clearly serve as another source of semantic calques, primarily the speech of the Europeanized gentry; here calques from French gradually lost their specifically conversational character and were perceived as neutral literary usage.

These processes significantly modified the use of Church Slavonic elements in the Russian literary language in comparison to Church Slavonic. Slavonic forms could be used in a syntactic function that was unusual for them (cf. in this connection participles in phrases like *блестящий оратор* — Isaatchenko 1974, 255). At the same time, Slavonic vocabulary could acquire meanings not only different from the original ones but directly opposite to them, and what is more the clash of meanings created could potentially be associated with the opposition between secular and religious. This makes it possible to define this development as a process of secularizing Church Slavonic vocabulary, or, from the later religious perspective, its profanation.[44]

Thus, for example, if in Church Slavonic usage *мечта, мечтание, мечтательный* (dream, dreaming, dreamy) signify false sensations which arise because of demonic delusion, in the process of secularization these words acquired a different meaning—of something desired, ideal, lofty; this new interpretation arose by the correlation of the Slavonic *мечта* with the French *rêve*. The lexemes *страсть, страстный, обаяние, обаятельный, соблазнительный* underwent the same kind of change under the influence of their French counterparts *passion, passioné, charme, charmant, séduisant* (see Vinogradov 1953, 208–9; Hüttl-Worth 1968, 14–5; Lotman 1970, 86–7). It is significant that to the extent that these innovations were assimilated by the conversational language they could become the arena in which social dialects of the nobility became differentiated from those groups of society that to one extent or another preserved traditional Orthodox culture. Hence

---

[44] G. Hüttl-Worth (1968, 10–12) makes a distinction between "secularized" Church Slavonicisms whose adaptation to the Russian literary language "primarily consists in the full or partial break with the religious sphere," with insignificant semantic changes, and Church Slavonicisms which "were subject to more significant changes in the Russian literary language" (words like *прелесть, восхищение*, etc.). The author, however, immediately notes that "precise division" of the two groups "is almost unrealizable in practical terms" (ibid, 13). It seems as if one should speak here only of various nuances in the framework of one single process of rethinking Church Slavonic lexicon for secular use. Therefore, in my opinion it is fair to speak of semantic secularization and secularized meanings. The degree of semantic difference can hardly be used as a differentiating parameter [...] The emergence of secularized meanings (in both groups Hüttl-Worth cites) is the result of a single cultural and linguistic process of adapting traditional symbolic forms to new conditions of secularized social consciousness and everyday life. It is revealing that from the retrospective view of the mid-nineteenth century, all aspects of this process were perceived as a single phenomenon — profanation of the holy.

2. Slavonicizing Purism and Its Reconceptualization in Religious Literatures

we have a typical dialogue in A. N. Ostrovskii and N. Ia. Solov'ev's comedy "The Shy Girl" (Dikarka). To the question of her nanny as to where she's been, Varia answers "I am dreaming," and this answer provokes Mavra Denisovna's quick response as she interprets the word *мечта* in the traditional sense: "What kind of dream are you having? Dreaming is sinful, people cross themselves to ward off dreams, while you, shameless, go off at night into the garden to cultivate them" (Ostrovskii and Solov;'ev 1915, 213; act III, scene 1). This is still another aspect of socio-cultural differentiation that contradicted the universality of the new literary language (cf. § 0–6).

A series of similar changes evidently originated in the conversational speech of the noble elite. It is most likely here that *прелесть* and *прелестный* began to be used in the meaning of *charme* and *charmant*, *очаровательный* in the meaning *séduisant*, *обожать* in the meaning of *idolâtrer*, *трогательный* in the meaning of *touchant*, *пленительный* in the meaning of *captivant* or the German *fesselnd*, and so on (see Hüttl-Worth 1956, 144–5; Hüttl-Worth 1963, 145; Hüttl-Worth 1968, 15; Lotman and Uspenskii 1975, 248–9, 296, 301–3, 307–8). From this also probably come the secularized use of such phrases as *Боже мой* (cf. *mon Dieu*) *мой ангел* (cf. *mon ange*), *о, небо* (cf. *o ciel*) (Lotman and Uspenskii 1975, 249, 290). These processes are by no means unique to eighteenth-century Russian; the same kind of semantic evolution was characteristic of sixteenth and seventeenth-century French; cf. in particular Bouhours complaints that "the caprice and tyranny of usage" are profaning words that formerly only had religious meanings (Bouhours 1671, 114; he is discussing use of the word *feste* [i.e, *fête*], in a secular context).

While religious and secular literature were thought of as one, using a single literary language, this new secularized usage could freely make its way into works by religious writers without triggering any objections. Thus for example M. M. Speranskii could demand of a sermon "that its virtue be *enchanting* (*прелестна*) but simple" (Speranskii 1844, 41). He further writes that "the main aim of church speaking… is to *touch* (*тронуть*) the heart" (ibid, 13), and he clearly also uses *мечтание* in the neutral, secularized meaning (ibid, 168). In translating Trublet's guide to homiletics Evfimii (Evgenii) Bolkhovitinov freely used such expressions as *очарование красноречия, трогать, пленять, чувствительныя и трогательныя сочинения (the charm of eloquence, to touch, to captivate, sensitive and touching compositions)* (Trublet 1793, 7, 11, 29, 38). Even Metropolitan Filaret Drozdov, who later strongly insisted on the purity of the religious language, in 1813 could write *о духе патриотического мечтания (about the spirit of patriotic dreaming)* and could exclaim: "Send me a salutary spirit… so that in a light dreaminess (*в легком мечтании*) it will also carry me above the interminable vistas of incredible events (*nad neobozrimym poprishchem neimovernykh sobytii*) " (Filaret, SMO, dop., 2, 12). Similarly, in his speech at the first celebratory session of the directorate (konferentsiia) of the Petersburg Spiritual Academy on August 13, 1814, he said that "this dwelling... is not so much *captivated* (*пленяется*) by solemnity as struck by the importance of the present event" (Chistovich 1857, 233). Examples like this could easily be multiplied.[45]

However, by the 1810's these semantic changes began to be seen as significant from a religious perspective,[46] so that any specifically secularized usage could potentially be perceived as blasphemous. At first the prohibition on such usage pertained equally to secular and religious literature, to which censorship activities at the end of the Alexandrine period testify. Surveying these activities, F. Bulgarin wrote: "What did the censor do under the influence of the mystics and their opponents? Disseminating books that were harmful for the pure faith, it only banished words and expressions that had become sanctified by time and usage. Here are a few little examples of expressions prohibited by our censorship as offending against the faith: *отечественное небо, небесный взгляд, ангельская улыбка, божественный Платон, ради Бога, ей Богу, Бог одарил его, он вечно занят был охотой* (*sky of the fatherland, heavenly glance, angelic smile, divine Plato, for God's sake, honest to God, God endowed him, he was eternally occupied by the hunt*), and the like. All of the marked words were forbidden by our censorship, and literature, especially poetry, was completely held back" (Lemke 1904: 380).

A large number of the expressions listed by Bulgarin had entered the Russian literary language in the eighteenth century (see for example such phrases in Lomonosov as *божественны науки* [divine sciences] or *небесныя очи* [heavenly eyes] — Lomonosov, I, 147; II, 282), and in many cases they were adapted under the influence of Western European languages (cf. the French *un regard céleste, un souris Angelique, le divin Virgile,*

---

[45] Examples from sermons by Feofilakt Rusanov may serve to characterize earlier practice, e.g.: "...двигнулся Сердобольный Монарх наш, *тронутый* воплем обиженных" (Feofilakt Rusanov 1807, 10); "Какое человеколюбивое сердце не *пленится* дружеским участием?" (Feofilakt Rusanov 1808, 12). This kind of word use is also characteristic of the Kievan preacher Archpriest Ioann Levanda: "...возвращает день, *пленяющий* мысли"; "Он тем сильнее *пленяет* очи и сердце твое"; "Как смешны пред небесным умом усилия и *мечты* его..." etc. (Levanda, II, 173, 215, 328). See also in Gavriil Petrov: "То, что ты рек, неоспоримо и тем *прелестнее*" (Barsov, I, 14).

[46] Characteristically, Metropolitan Filaret, when he later made use of this sort of word, might review their etymology, i.e., try and give them back their former, non-figurative meaning; cf. in his letter to A. N. Murav'ev of August 7, 1836: "The Christian philosophy of Abbot Beautain did not captivate (*пленила*) me, that is, did not force me to read to the end" (Filaret 1869, 40).

l'auteur le plus divin, pour Dieu, au nom de Dieu, etc.).

In the eighteenth century such word combinations seemed like natural rhetorical embellishments, making use of words in their figurative meanings that oratory could not do without. In his "Speech on Oratory" of 1745 Trediakovskii wrote that "when eloquence wants to depict a certain person, a certain mind, a certain purity which is so excellent that there is none superior, she articulates with solemnity: a *divine* man, *divine* reason, *angelic* purity; for there is nothing more perfect than divinity, or purer than the heavenly spirits" (Trediakovskii 1745, 89).[47] V. S. Podshivalov makes an analogous point: "one must however be careful not to search too far for a similarity between things if we want a metaphor to be good. One may for example call a beautiful person an angel, or gold the devil, but to call a flighty person a swallow… would be awkward" (Podshivalov 1796, 53–4); calling someone an *angel* is clearly not perceived as a religious issue. This norm constituted the contrasting background for early nineteenth century views.

In Bulgarin's statement cited above he connected the censors' actions with "the influence of the mystics and their opponents," that is, an actualization of the religious position unconnected with any particular ideological tendency—both the mystical and anti-mystical opinion of word use became subject to religious interpretation. As a result secularized word meanings ceased to be felt as neutral and were juxtaposed to "pious" ones and perceived as blasphemous. This process also links the consciousness of these defenders of linguistic piety to that of the seventeenth century, when metaphorical usage could be seen as unacceptable and sacrilegious in principle. In the late seventeenth and early eighteenth centuries the metaphorical tradition of the Baroque came into direct conflict with this traditional cultural-linguistic consciousness and required constant self-justification (see Uspenskii and Zhivov 1983, 25–30).

Together with this, once the religious perception of semantic relationships became established, as noted, it spread to all other linguistic

---

[47] Later Trediakovskii changed his opinion and protested against expressions like "heavenly beauty" and "eternity was revealed," basing himself precisely on religious grounds. His however was a lone voice of protest, which received no sympathy or official support. G. N. Teplov described his position as philological madness: "Not every writer finds the threat of atheism in trifling words… To his brain none of these adjectives may be used: *совершенный, безконечный, безпредельный, безчисленный, безмерный*, even if applied to such words as *хлеб, пища, народ, вкус*, etc. [...] And after such stupid sophistries he will exclaim like a madman, 'O declaration of atheism!'" (Teplov 1868, 76; for more detail see Uspenskii 1985, 166–7). In the eighteenth century Trediakovskii's position remained an individual eccentricity (in any case, from the perspective of the reigning culture), and the word usage he criticizes was seen as completely normal.

elements for which such categorization was possible, independent of the historical processes that may have led to a particular word having acquired both "secular" as well as "church" meanings. In particular, this was how Slavonicisms for which the given pairing was usual (that occurred within the framework of Church Slavonic) were perceived, but which in the Russian literary language acquired (Russian) synonyms that came to replace the corresponding Slavonicisms in secular word use. This mechanism of perception is clearly evident in the episode of the censors' ban on Zhukovskii's ballad "Ivan's Eve" in 1822 (later entitled "The Fortress of Smal'gol'm"), a translation of Sir Walter Scott's "The Eve of St. John." The censors rejected the work precisely because they thought it mixed the sacred with the profane, moreover they both demanded piety of a "general semiotic" sort[48] as well as linguistic piety; Zhukovskii was criticized for the secularized (and therefore sacrilegious) use of the word знаменье. Zhukovskii complained in a letter to A. N. Golitsyn of August 17, 1822, "I am not able to even imagine what Messrs the censors base their opinion on; but I have heard that among other things in the verse 'И ужасное знаменье в стол возжено!' (And a terrible sign was burned into the table!) the word знаменье scared them. Does one have to explain that the words знаменье and знак are the same thing, and that in neither is there anything blameworthy? If the censors think that the word знаменье belongs exclusively to holy objects and shouldn't express anything mundane, they are mistaken, and in order to agree with them in this case, one would have to deny one's knowledge of the Russian language" (Sukhomlinov 1865–1866, 38–9).

The history of the words знаменье and знак allow us to reconstruct the censors' reasoning. At first the two words indeed had a series of common meanings, but occurred in texts of different linguistic registers (see Sreznevskii, I, col. 988–9; SRIa, VI, 39, 42–3). In early eighteenth-century texts they could be used as synonyms (for example, in Prokopovich's works — see Kutina 1982, 33). In the *Dictionary of the Russian Academy* знак and знаменье are partial synonyms (SAR, III, col. 99, 105), more than that, the first meaning of the word знаменье is given precisely as "sign, signification, proof." In the eighteenth century, however, there was a differentiation in the use of these

---

[48] In justification for the ban it was argued, in particular, that "for many readers it will seem surprising and even improper that in a Scottish folksong, in a superstitious tale about the appearance of a dead man, in his unfaithful wife's seductive conversation with him, extremely inappropriate speech is directed to the Creator, the Cross, to the great Ivan's Day; and clergymen, monks, funeral rites and a chapel are presented" (Sukhomlinov 1865–1866, 45). Zhukovskii was also informed of the demand that he "replace the rites of the Greek church, supposedly depicted in Walter Scott's ballad, with *Scottish ones*" (ibid, 39).

words that corresponded to rethinking their genetic opposition (reflected in the examples cited in the Academy dictionary). The Slavonicism *знаменье* was primarily used to denote church phenomena, while the Russicism *знак* was applicable to the secular sphere; notably, the Academy dictionary of 1847 labels *знаменье* as "ecclesiastical" (STsRIa, II, 92). Correspondingly, applying the word *знаменье* to profane phenomena is perceived as using it in its secularized meaning and interpreted as blasphemous; references to past precedents were just as little convincing to linguistic consciousness of the early nineteenth century as the case of using the words "divine" and "heavenly" in the old way. This new perception forced Zhukovskii to change the disputed line, and in the final version we read "И печать роковая в столе возжжена" (And a fateful imprint was burned in the table).[49]

The situation changed when in 1824 A. S. Shishkov took A. N. Golitsyn's place as Minister of Education. In the new censorship code "caviling at words" was no longer to be a part of the censors' job. The new linguistic policy legitimized the use of words in their secularized meanings. In his "Second Epistle to the Censor" of 1824, Pushkin specially noted and welcomed this aspect of the new code:

> Когда ты разрешил по милости чудесной
> Заветные слова *божественный, небесный,*
> И ими назвалась (для рифмы) красота,
> Не оскорбляя тем уж Господа Христа!
>
> (Pushkin II: 367)

(When by miraculous grace you permitted the cherished words *divine* and *heavenly*, and they were used to designate beauty (for the sake of the rhyme), without insulting the Lord Christ!)

The innovations, however, only affected secular literature, although it was not left to its own devices right away and without a struggle, as the zealots of linguistic piety could make demands on secular literature of the type we have seen even after the new censorship code. Thus A. V. Nikitenko tells in his diary entry of March 16, 1834, how "Filaret [Drozdov] complained to Benkendorf about one line of Pushkin in *Onegin*, where in describing Moscow he has 'и стая галок на крестах' (and a flock of jackdaws on the crosses). Filaret found this to be an insult to the sacred. The censor, who was called to decide, said that 'jackdaws, as far as he knew, actually do sit on the crosses of Moscow churches, but in his opinion, the Moscow chief of

---

[49] This is actually even more accurate compared to the English original: "The sable score of fingers four,/Remains on that board impressed" (Scott 1831, 446).

police is more responsible for this than the poet or the censor.' Benkendorf politely answered Filaret that this matter was not worth the attention of such a respected spiritual figure" (Nikitenko, I, 139–40; cf. Lotman 1980, 328). Of course, Filaret's criticism was not about the jackdaws' behavior but the use of the word cross to depict an element of the landscape, i.e., in its profane, secular sense.

While the new code did not affect religious literature, secularized elements continued to be perceived as blameworthy. In this area the norm of the secular language diverged with that of the religious, as the secular was permitted word usage that in the religious context was considered blasphemous. Understandably, this intensified the clergy's view of the secular literary tongue (as opposed to the religious language) as emphatically profane and depraved. This was an additional argument for the conception of religious purism.

This norm of the religious language was explicitly articulated in Amfiteatrov's handbook. In it he demands "holiness" of the religious language and explains that this consists in

> the strict choice of words and expressions which are in the highest degree appropriate to the worthiness of the proposed subject, the worthiness of the holy place and time where and when the sermon is presented, that is, worthy of God's temple and the liturgy. This appropriateness is based in part on the meaning of the words themselves, and in part on their use. Hence: a) Words may be holy in and of themselves, if they designate holy objects; consequently only use holy words for expressing holy truths. b) Words may be holy of themselves, but their use may be impious; consequently do not use holy words to designate non-holy objects, for example, do not call a person a divinity as the secular language does or say "my angel" to someone who is by no means angelic, and so on. c) Words which are extremely solemn and holy in themselves are often distorted by worldly speech and the language of fashion; consequently, use words which have been profaned by the secular language with prudence and caution. Or, in the same vein, never use such words in the same tone and meaning as fashion does. (Amfiteatrov, II, § 274, 128–9).

Later, clarifying what he means by fashionable usage, Amfiteatrov directly addresses the process by which Slavonicisms become secularized, defining this process as immoral, and secularized usage as sacrilegious: "Immorality brought many words with it into human language which in general should not be there, and did even worse, applying holy words to dishonorable things and deeds. It is well known how the fashionable language uses the words: *божество, ангел, небесныя улыбки, святыня, святилище, завеса, заветный, провидение, промысл, храм, обожать, молиться, благоговеть, истаявать* (*divinity, angel, heavenly smiles, sacred object,*

2. Slavonicizing Purism and Its Reconceptualization in Religious Literatures

sanctuary, veil, cherished, providence, providence. temple, adore, pray, revere, melt away), and a host of other expressions. The language of the world and of the flesh stole these words from the holy tongue, and made idolatrous use of them" (ibid, 129). Correspondingly, Amfiteatrov formulates rules which prescribe the identity of Slavonicisms in religious literature with their original meaning in Church Slavonic: "a) use Biblical words in the precise sense in which they are used in the Bible; b) do not use one and the same words in various meanings" (ibid).

A series of comments by Filaret Drozdov suggest that such rules were not purely speculative but in fact prescribed religious practice (at least its public aspect). Filaret quickly responded to what he saw as violations of the given norm. Thus in 1844 he reproached the Moscow ecclesiastic censorship committee for permitting the phrase *малодушные и невежественные возгласы* in a translation of Basil the Great from *Works of the Church Fathers* (year 4, bk. 3). In a letter to F. Golubinskii he wrote: "*Возглас* is a Slavonic word, and for twenty years it has not been used anywhere but in the service-book, where it designates the doxology proclaimed by the priest after the sacramental prayer. Recently a penchant for mixing the pure and the dirty and the divine with the satanic has arisen, and the holy word has sacrilegiously been applied to ridiculous exclamations and proclamations. And Father Peter [Delitsyn, member of the censorship committee], a priest himself, emulates this!" (Filaret 1891, 8). That a new secular usage of the word *возглас* was indeed developing at the time may be judged by its appearance in I. S. Turgenev, cf. "First we called to one another ardently; then he began to respond to our cries [*возгласы*] more rarely" ("L'gov," from *Notes of a Hunter*). For the mid-nineteenth century this usage was common and neutral, and as such could penetrate into the speech of the clergy.[50] Thus Archbishop Filaret Gumilevskii wrote to Archbishop Innokentii Borisov on May 5, 1853: "Your Excellency wrote that one must not become discouraged listening to the yelling [*возгласы*] about our affairs" (Barsov, I, 143). One may conjecture that the secularized sense of the word in the meaning "exclamation" was the result of its correlation with the French *exclamation,* suggested in particular by the expressions *возгласы удивления, возгласы радости* which were calques of the French *exclamation de surprise, exclamation de joie.* If we suppose that the twenty-year period Filaret mentioned above was not accidental, it may be interpreted in the framework of the periodization set forth earlier, i.e., it was just at this time that secular literature was freed from

---

[50] However, the dictionary of 1847, like the *Dictionary of the Russian Academy*, gives the word only in its church meaning (see STsRIa, I, 144; SAR, II, col. 76).

Chapter 4. The New Cultural Differentiation

the censors' control over language, which allowed the unimpeded secularized use and reinterpretation of Slavonicisms. It was just this process that Filaret had in mind when he spoke of the developing taste for "mixing the pure and the dirty and the divine with the satanic."

In an analogous way Filaret objects to the use of the verb *гордиться* not to designate the sinful feeling of vanity but to signify a high opinion of something. Apropos of Alexander II's use of the phrase *горжусь вами* (I am proud of you) when addressing the troops, Filaret wrote a special confidential memorandum on December 8, 1855:

> I remember how before 1812 pious-thinking people complained that the tsar's acts used only the secular language, and God's name was absent. That year demonstrated where one must seek true support and unconquerable strength, and Emperor Alexander began to speak in Christian language. Emperor Nikolai Pavlovich spoke the same language, and with power and edification especially toward the end. This is also [true of] the most pious sovereign now reigning. But all the more glaring is the discrepancy when a too worldly word unintentionally slips in. Several pious-thinking people expressed dismay that they heard from the person of the late Sovereign resting in God's bosom, and also from the person of the present one, the following phrase in praise of the troops: *горжусь вами* (I am proud of you). Why, they ask, did this word, so alien to him, creep into the speech of the most pious of sovereigns? God's word does not condone pride, but says that *God resists the proud* [Proverbsa 3: 34]. Is there some means for the editor of the tsar's thoughts to suggest that when he puts together his expressions he consider the question, are they in harmony with the pious spirit of the tsar? (Filaret, SMO, IV, 54–5; cf. the report on this note in the letter to Archimandrite Antonii of December 15, 1855 — Filaret, III, 369–70).

It is indicative that in this memo Filaret directly juxtaposes the "worldly" and "Christian" languages and connects the use of the verb *гордиться* in its secular meaning with the influence of the "worldly tongue."[51]

---

[51] Filaret refers to 1812 as a turning point in the history of the language of state acts. As is well known, the war with Napoleon was perceived by contemporaries as a holy struggle between a righteous tsar and an apocalyptic beast. Russia appeared as the "new Israel," with Alexander I in the role of Moses and Napoleon as pharaoh. It was in this spirit that Alexander I's manifesto on the war was written, which Filaret may have in mind as the turning point. The manifesto was compiled by A. S. Shishkov, at that time state-secretary. It naturally reflected Shishkov's linguistic program, which was close to that of Filaret at least in the fact that Church Slavonic was considered the organic basis of the Russian literary language. Looking back retrospectively from the mid-nineteenth century, Shishkov's language could appear as "Christian," as opposed to the "secular" language of the Karamzinists. Characteristically, P. A. Viazemskii, who found the language of Shishkov's manifestos objectionable, was also ironic about their emphatic piety (Viazemskii, IX, 196). Thus for both Viazemskii and Filaret the notion of a "Christian" language was connected with Slavonicizing.

2. Slavonicizing Purism and Its Reconceptualization in Religious Literatures

Indeed in Church Slavonic *гордиться* only means "to laud oneself unjustly " (see Sreznevskii, I, col. 613; SRIa, IV, 82); the *Dictionary of the Russian Academy* also only lists this one meaning, interpreting *горжусь* to mean "I act haughtily, with disdain for others; I think a lot, highly of myself; I extol myself, act arrogantly" (SAR, II, col. 421). The dictionary of 1847 already includes another meaning as well — "to boast of" (*хвалиться*) giving as an example *Я горжусь именем Русскаго* (I boast [am proud] of the name Russian) (STsRIa, I, 278); it is significant that this secularized meaning has a shade of disapproval (*хвалиться* means to give something a high evaluation without sufficient basis). The given meaning evidently developed on the strength of the correlation between the Russian *гордый* and the French *fier,* so that *гордиться чем-то* enters the language as the equivalent of the French *être fier de quelque chose.*

In this way the expansion of secularized meanings served as one more basis for juxtaposing the secular and religious languages. Insofar as differences arose between traditional and new usage, where the traditional meaning was based on the language of church books, the differences were immediately seen in terms of an opposition between secular and religious. Given the iconic, non-conventional view of the sign, characteristic of the clergy's linguistic position in the first half of the nineteenth century, words in their traditional meaning were considered sacred, and in their secularized meaning profane, indeed the very process of secularizing word meanings was perceived as the sacrilegious desecration of sacred signs.

We should keep in mind, however, that the "secular" language was at the same time the "general" language, the language of the cultured elite, which the clergy could not help but to take into account. The dominating position of the secular literary language forced the writer or preacher to consider that the words he used in their "church" meaning might be understood by the audience according to accepted secular usage, and therefore the writer from the clergy had to continually try and avoid ambiguities. As Amfiteatrov cautioned in the passage cited above, "use words that have been profaned by worldly language carefully and with prudence" (Amfiteatrov, II,128–29). Filaret Drozdov, when editing the translation of some patristic writing, replaced a series of Slavonicisms "ambiguous (oboiudnykh) to contemporary understanding" with "somewhat new" words (Filaret, II, 273). The correction Filaret made to the akafist (akathistos hymn) to the Most Holy Virgin Mother may serve as an illustration of this. In a letter of March 17, 1860, to the Ober-Procuror of the Synod Count A. P. Tolstoi, Filaret suggested replacing "Оставиша Ирода, яко блядива" [they left Herod, as a babbler] with "Оставиша Ирода, яко празднослова" or "яко буесловяща," explaining that "this word now has a new, shameful meaning" (Filaret, SMO, IV, 510).[52] Filaret clearly was taking into account the irreverent associations that might have arisen for people unversed in Church Slavonic.

This fear of ambiguity was symptomatic. It demonstrates that the consistent separation of the secular and religious literary languages was more a desired goal than an actual fact. The clergy was fighting for the devout purity of its language and for its differentiation from the "contaminated" language of secular literature, but at the same time was conscious that this was an impossible battle. Given the church's subordination to the state and the clergy's isolated and inferior social position it was unable to impose its own language on its flock, and therefore had to accede to the language of its congregants. From the mid-nineteenth century the special, exclusive literary language of the clergy began to break down. This process was caused both by attempts on the part of the clergy to break out of its isolation (in this connection, attempts were made to make religious literature more comprehensible and accessible to society) and to close the gap between the secular and religious languages, which was connected to a new Slavonicizing of the secular literary language in the second half of the century under the influence of new writers from the "raznochintsy."

Thus the special religious literary language existed for somewhat more than half a century. With its demise disappeared the last arena in which the connection between the linguistic and cultural parameters that had arisen in connection with Petrine cultural politics was still operative. Linguistic behavior now ceased to be a direct factor in the secularization and Europeanization of Russian culture, and the character of the literary language was, in its main features, essentially independent of cultural positions. The opposition between Church Slavonic and Russian, the secular and religious, and between what was Europeanized or traditional, which the Petrine reforms had posed and which had defined the significance of language in the cultural conflicts of the eighteenth and early nineteenth centuries, ceased to have relevance and receded into the past. Their opposition no longer influenced theories of language or changes in linguistic practice. It might still be preserved in particular forms that were literary relics or serve as the basis for stylization in works of belles-lettres, but in the Russian cultural and linguistic consciousness it was overtaken by new conflicts generated by the changing structure of post-Emancipation Russian society and its new cultural concerns. The nature of these new paradigms could serve as the

---

[52] In Slavonic, the verb "блядити" meant "to err, deceive, prate, or lie" whereas the secularized meaning was unprintable (to whore). (Translator's note)

basis of a further special study, but they do not have a direct connection to the subject of the current one, which has attempted to trace the ways in which the cultural paradigms formed in the Petrine period were transformed, influencing the development of the language and taking on new meanings.

Abbrevations

БАН	— Библиотека Академии наук (Санкт-Петербург)
ГАРФ	— Государственный архив Российской Федерации (Москва)
ГИМ	— Государственный исторический музей (Москва)
ОРЯС	— Отделение русского языка и литературы
РГАДА	— Российский государственный архив древних актов (Москва)
РГБ	— Российская государственная библиотека (Москва)
РНБ	— Российская национальная библиотека (Санкт-Петербург)

Works Cited

Achinger 1970 — Achinger G. Der französische Anteil an der russischen Literaturkritik des 18. Jahrhunderts unter besonderer Berücksichtung der Zeitschriften (1730–1780). Berlin, 1970.

Adodurov 1731 — [Adodurov V.E.]. Anfangs-Gründe der Russischen Sprache, in Teutsch-Lateinisch- und Russischen Lexicon... SPb., 1731. (Cited from: Unbegaun 1969.)

Aesop 1700 — Притчи Эссоповы на латинском и Руском языке ихъже Авиении Стихами изобрази. Совокупноже Брань Жаб и Мышей Гомером древле описана. Со изрядными в Обоих Книгах Лицами, и с Толкованием. В Амстеродаме напечатася у Ивана Андреева Тесинга Лета 1700.

Afanasii Kholmogorskii 1682 — [Афанасий, архиепископ холмогорский]. Увет духовный. М., 1682.

Afiani, Zhivov, Kozlov 1989 — Афиани В. Ю., Живов В. М., Козлов В. П. Научные принципы издания. В кн.: Н. М. Карамзин. История государства российского, т. 1. М., 1989, 400–414.

AI, I–V — Акты исторические, собранные и изданные Археографическою комиссиею. Т. I–V. Спб., 1841–1842.

Alekseev 1977 — Алексеев А. А. Старое и новое в языке Радищева. XVIII век. Сб. 12. Л., 1977, с. 99–112.

Alekseev 1981 — Алексеев А. А. Эпический стиль «Тилемахиды». Язык русских писателей XVIII века. Л., 1981, с. 68–95.

Alekseev 1982 — Алексеев А. А. Эволюция языковой теории и языковая практика Тредиаковского. Литературный язык XVIII века. Проблемы стилистики. Л., 1982, 86–128.

Alekseev 1987a — Алексеев А. А. Пути стабилизации языковой нормы в России XI–XVI вв. Вопросы языкознания, 1987, №. 2, 34–46.

Alekseev and Likhacheva 1987 — Алексеев А. А., Лихачева О. П. Библия. Словарь книжников и книжности Древней Руси. Вып. I (XI — первая половина XIV в.). Л., 1987, 68–83.

Alekseev 1965 — Алексеев П. Т. "Статир" (Описание анонимной рукописи XVII века). Археографический ежегодник за 1964 год. М., 1965, 92–101.

Amvrosii Serebrennikov 1778 — [Московской Академии Префект Иеромонах Амвросий]. Краткое руководство к оратории российской, сочиненное в Лаврской семинарии, в пользу юношества, красноречию обучающегося. М., 1778.

Amvrosii Iushkevich 1741 — Слово в высочайший день рождения... Императрицы Елисаветы Петровны всея России декабря 18 дня, 1741 года проповеданное Амвросием Архиепископом Новгородским. СПб., 1741.

Amvrosii Iushkevich 1744 — Слово в день летняго воспоминания Богом дарованныя Коронации Ея Императорскаго Величества Елисаветы Первыя... проповеданное Синодальным членом Преосвященным Амвросием Архиепископом Новгородским. В придворной Ея Императорскаго Величества церкви в Санктпетербурге 1743 года, месяца априллия 25-го дня. М., 1744.

Amfiteatrov, I–II — Амфитеатров Я. Чтения о церковной словесности или гомилетика. Ч. I–II. Киев, 1846.

Anisimov 1982 — Анисимов Е. В. Податная реформа Петра I. Введение подушной подати в России. 1719 — 1728 гг. Л., 1982.

Apollodor 1725 — Аполлодора грамматика афинеискаго библиотеки или о богах. М., 1725.

Apollos Baibakov 1780 — [Аполлос Байбаков]. Правила пиитическия, в 1774 году изданныя в пользу юношества обучающагося в Московской славеногреколатинской Академии... Ныне с пополнением к познанию российскаго стихотворения напечатанныя вторым тиснением. М., 1780.

Apollos Baibakov 1794 — [Аполлос Байбаков]. Грамматика руководствующая к познанию Славенороссийскаго языка. Печатана в Типографии Киевопечерския лавры 1794 года.

Arnauld 1668 — [Arnault A.] La logiqve ou l'art de penser: contenant, outré les regles communes, plusieurs observations nouvelles, propres à former le jugement. 3-ème éd. Paris, 1668.

Arnauld 1996 — Arnauld, A. and Pierre Nicole, Logic or The Art of Thinking: Containing, Besides Common Rules, Several New Observations Appropriate for Forming Judgment. Translated and edited by J. L. Buroker. Cambridge Texts in the History of Philosophy. Cambridge [England], 1996.

Arnauld and Lancelot 1803 — Grammaire générale et raisonnée de Port-Royal. Par Arnauld et Lancelot. Précédée d'un Essai... par M. Petitot. Paris 1803.

Aver'ianova 1950 — Аверьянова А. П. В. Н. Татищев как филолог (К 200–летию со дня смерти). Вестник ЛГУ, 1950, 37, 45–57.

Aver'ianova 1957 — Аверьянова А. П. Рукописный лексикон Татищева. Учен. зап. Ленингр. ун-та, №.197, серия филол. наук, вып. 23, 1957, 25–83.

Aver'ianova 1964 — Рукописный лексикон первой половины XVIII века. Подготовка к печати и вступит. статья А. П. Аверьяновой. Л., 1964.

Avgustin Vinogradskii 1856 — Сочинения Августина, архиепископа Московского и Коломенского. СПб., 1856.

Avvakum 1960 — Житие протопопа Аввакума им самим написанное и другие его сочинения. Под ред. Н.К.Гудзия. М., 1960.

Babaeva 1989 — Бабаева Б. Э. История русской лингвистической мысли начала XVIII в. и языковая практика Петровской эпохи (лингвистическая и редакторская деятельность Ф.Поликарпова). Диссертация на соискние уч. Степени кандидата филолог. наук. М., МГУ, 1989.

Baklanova 1951 — Бакланова Н. А. "Тетради" старца Авраамия. Исторический архив, VI. М.-Л., 1951, 131–155.

Balzac 1658 — Guez de Balzac. Les oeuvres diverses. Leiden, Elzevier, 1658.

Barcchi 1990 — Barcchi Bavagnoli M. Le origini del poema epico russo. La Petrida di Antioch Kantemir. Milano, 1990.

Barsov 1775 — А. Б. [Барсов А. А.]. Ответ на письмо Англоманово. Опыт трудов Вольного Российского собрания при Московском университете, ч. II. М., 1776, 262–267.

Barsov 1981 — Российская грамматика Антона Антоновича Барсова. Под ред. Б. А. Успенского. М., 1981.

Barsov, I–II — Материалы для биографии Иннокентия Борисова, архиепископа херсонского и таврического. Собрал и издал... Н. Барсов. Вып. I–II. СПб. — Киев, 1884.

Batalden 1988 — Batalden S. K. Gerasim Pavskii's Clandestine Old Testament: The Politics of Nineteenth-Century Russian Biblical Translation. — Church History, vol. 57 (1988), № 4, 486–498.

Batiushkov, I–III — Батюшков К. Н. Сочинения. Т. I–III. СПб., 1885–1887.

Baumann 1969 — Baumann H. Die erste in deutscher Sprache gedrukte Grammatik des modernen Russischen und die Praxis der zeitgenössischen Literatursprache. Wissenschaftliche Zeitschrift der Friedrich-Schiller-Universitat Jena. Gesellschafts- und sprachwissenschaftliche Reihe, 18, № 5, 1969, 1–6.

Baumann 1980 — Baumann H. Groening und Adodurov. Sprache in Geschichte und Gegenwart. Jena, 1980.

Begichev 1898 — Послание Ивана Бегичева о видимом образе Божием. Подготовил А.И.Яцмирский. По рукописи XVII века собрания А.И.Яцмирского. — Чтения в Обществе истории и древностей российских, 1898, кн. 2, Отдел II, i–x, 1–13.

Belokurov i Zertsalov 1907 — Белокуров С. А. Зерцалов А. Н. О немецких школах в Москве в первой четверти XVIII века (1701–1715). Документы московских архивов. М., 1907 [Чтения в Обществе истории и древностей российских, т. 200, кн. 1, i–xli, 1–244].

Berezina 1980 — Березина О. Е. Два тематических лексикона начала XVIII в. (сравнительная характеристика). Словари и словарное дело в России XVIII в. Л., 1980, 6–22.

Berkov 1936 — Берков П. Н. Ломоносов и литературная полемика его времени. 1750 — 1765. М.-Л., 1936.

Berkov 1949 — Берков П. Н. О так называемых петровских повестях. Труды Отдела древне-русской литературы, VII (1949), 421–428.

Berkov 1950 — Берков П. Н. Начало русской журналистики. Очерки по истории русской журналистики и критики. Т. I: XVIII и первая половина XIX века. Л., 1950, 11–44.

Berkov 1951 — Сатирические журналы Н.И.Новикова. Под ред. П. Н.Беркова. М.-Л., 1951.

Berkov 1952 — Берков П. Н. История русской журналистики XVIII века. М.-Л., 1952.

Beron 1824 — Берон П. Букварь съ различны поученї. [Брашов], 1824.

Berkhgol'ts, I–IV — Дневник камер-юнкера Ф. В. Берхгольца, 1721–1725. Пер. с нем. И. Ф. Аммона. Ч. I–IV. М., 1902–1903.

Bircher i Ingen 1978 — Bircher M., van Ingen F. (Hrsg.). Sprachgesellschaften, Sozietäten, Dichtergruppen. Wolfenbüttler Arbeiten zur Barockforschung, 7. Hamburg 1978.

Birzhakova, Voinova, Kutina 1972 — Биржакова Е. Э., Войнова Л. А., Кутина Л. Л. Очерки по исторической лексикологии русского языка XVIII века. Языковые контакты и заимствования. Л., 1972.

Blume 1978 — Blume H. "Sprachgesellschaften und Sprache." Bircher M., van Ingen F. (Hrsg.). Sprachgesellschaften, Sozietäten, Dichtergruppen. Wolfenbüttler Arbeiten zur Barockforschung, 7. Hamburg 1978, 39–52.

Bobrik 1988 — Бобрик М. А. Книжная справа первой половины XVIII века и проблемы нормализации русского литературного языка. Автореферат диссертации на соискание уч. степени кандидата филолог. наук. М., МГУ, 1988.

Bobrik 1993 — Бобрик М. А. От рационализма к эпохе чувствительности: статья А. А. Ржевского 'О московском наречии' и языковые взгляды XVIII века. Russian Linguistics 17 (1993), 1, 37–55.

Bogoslovskii, I–V — Богословский М. М. Петр I: Материалы для биографии. Т. I–V. М., 1940–1948.

Boileau I–III — Boileau Despréaux N. Oeuvres complètes. 3 vols. Paris, 1832.

Bouhours 1671 — Bouhours D. Les Entretiens d'Ariste et d'Eugene. Derniere ed. Amsterdam, 1671.

Bragina 1985 — Сочинения итальянских гуманистов эпохи Возрождения (XV век). Под ред. Л. М. Брагиной. М., 1985.

Brailovskii 1894 — Браиловский С. Н. Федор Поликарпович Поликарпов-Орлов, директор Московской типографии. Журнал Министерства народного просвещения, 1894, № 9, 1–37, № 10, 242–286, № 11, 50–91.

Brey 1957 — Brey R. La formation de la doctrine classique en France. Paris, Libraire Nizet, 1957.

Brien 1983 — Brien N. Die Weißmannschen Worterbucher- ein kurzer Vergleich der Erst- und Zweitauflage. Weismanns Petersburger Lexikon von 1731, vol

3: Grammatischer Anhang. München, 1983, 23–37 [Specimina philologiae slavicae, Bd. 48].

Brunot, I–X — Brunot F. Histoire de la langue française des origines à nos jours. 10 vols. Paris, 1966–1969.

Brunot 1969 — Brunot F. La doctrine de Malherbe d'apres son commentaire sur Desportes. Paris, 1969.

Bubnov and Demkova 1981 — Бубнов Н. Ю., Демкова Н. С. Вновь найденное послание из Москвы в Пустозерск 'Возвещение от сына духовнаго ко отцу духовному' и ответ протопопа Аввакума (1676 г.). Труды Отдела древнерусской литературы, XXXVI (1981), 127–150.

Buck 1984 — Buck Ch. D. The Russian Language Question in the Imperial Academy of Sciences. Aspects of the Slavic Language Question. Ed. R. Picchio and H. Goldblatt. New Haven,1984. Vol. II, 187–233.

Budde 1908 — Будде Е. Очерк истории современного литературного русского языка (XVII–XIX в.). Энциклопедия славянской филологии, вып. 12. СПб., 1908.

Buffier 1741 — Buffier C. Grammaire françoise sur un plan nouveau. Nouv. ed. Paris, 1741.

Bulakhovskii 1958 — Булаховский Л. А. Исторический комментарий к русскому литературному языку. 5-е, доп. и перераб. изд. Киев, 1958.

Buslaev 1861 — Буслаев Ф. Историческая христоматия церковнославянского и древнерусского языков. М., 1861.

Bykova and Gurevich 1958 — Описание изданий напечатанных кириллицей, 1689 — январь 1725 г. Сост. Т. А. Быкова и М. М. Гуревич. М.-Л., 1958.

Caput, I–II — Caput J.-P. La langue française. Histoire d'une institution. T. I. 842–1715; T. II. 1715–1974. Paris, 1972–1975.

Chaikina 1991 — Чайкина Ю. И. Письменно-деловая и обиходно-разговорная речь старорусского города (По материалам писцовых и переписных книг Москвы, Ростова, Балахны, Устюга, Вятки, Вологды, Устюжны XVII — начала XVIII вв.). — Историко-культурный аспект лексикологического описания русского языка. Ч. 2. М., 1991, 14–33.

Chapelain, I–II — Chapelain J. Lettres. Vol. I–II. Paris, 1883.

Chapelain 1656 — La Pvcelle ov La France Delivree. Poëme Heroique. Par M. Chapelain. Paris, chez A. Covbre..., 1656.

Chernov 1977 — Чернов В. А. Русский язык XVII века. Свердловск, 1977.

Chernov 1984 — Чернов В. А. Русский глагол в XVII веке. Свердловск, 1984.

Chernykh 1953 — Черных П. Я. Язык Уложения 1649 года. Вопросы орфографии, фонетики и морфологии в связи с историей Уложенной книги. М., 1953.

Cherty iz istorii... 1868 — Черты из истории книжного просвещения при Петре Великом. Переписка директора Московской Синодальной типографии Федора Поликарпова с графом И.А.Мусиным-Пушкиным, начальником Монастырского приказа. 1715–1717 гг. — Русский архив, 1868, № 7–8.

Chistovich 1857 — Чистович И. А. История С.Петербургской духовной академии. СПб., 1857.

Chistovich 1868 — Чистович И. А. Феофан Прокопович и его время. СПб., 1868.

Chistovich 1894 — Чистович И. А. Руководящие деятели духовного просвещения в России в первой пол. текущего столетия. СПб., 1894.

Chistovich 1899 — Чистович И. А. История перевода Библии на русский язык. Изд. 2-е. СПб., 1899.

Christiani 1906 — Christiani W. Über das Eindringen von Fremdwörtern in die russische Schriftsprache des 17. und 18. Jahrhunderts. Berlin, 1906.

Cocron 1962 — Cocron F. La langue russe dans la seconde moitié du XVIIe siècle (morphologie). Bibiotheque russe de l'lnstitut d'etudes slaves, t. XXXIII. Paris, 1962.

Cooper 1972 — Cooper B. F. The History and Development of the Ode in Russia. A Dissertation submitted for the degree of Dr. of Philosophy in the Univ. of Cambridge. Cambridge, 1972.

Coulter 1976 — Coulter J. A. The Literary Microcosm. Theories of Interpretation of the Later Neoplatonists. Columbia Studies in the Classical Tradition, II. Leiden, 1976.

Cracraft 1971 — Cracraft J. The Church Reform of Peter the Great. London, 1971.

Cracraft 1978 — Сгасraft J. Feofan Prokopovich and the Kiev Academy. — Russian Orthodoxy under the 0ld Regime. Minneapolis, 1978, 44–64.

Cracraft 1982 — Cracraft J. (ed.). Рor God and Peter the Great. The Works of Thomas Consett, 1723–1729. East European Monographs, XCVI. New York, 1982.

Dal', I–1V — Даль В. Толковый словарь живого великорусского языка. Т. I–IV. Изд. 2-е. СП6.-М., 1880–1882.

Dan'ko 1940 — Данько Е. Я. Из неизданных материалов о Ломоносове. — XVIII век. Сб. 2. М.-Л., 1940, 248–275.

Dashkov 1810 — [Дашков Д. В.]. Рецензия на: Перевод двух статей из Лагарпа с примечаниями переводчика. — Цветник, 1810, ч. VIII, № 11, 256–303; № 12, 404–467.

Dashkov 1811 — Дашков Д. О легчайшем способе возражать на критики. СП6., 1811.

Dell'Agata 1984 — Dell'Agata G. The Bulgarian Language Question from the Sixteenth to the Nineteenth Century. — Aspects of the Slavic Language Question. Ed. by R. Picchio and H. GoldЫatt. New Haven, 1984. Vol. I, 157–188.

Dell'Agata 1986 — Dell'Agata G. Unità e diversità nello slavo ecclesiastico: il punto di vista del copista. — Studia slavica mediaevalia e humanistica Riccardo Picchio dicata. M. Colucci, G. Dell'Agata, H. Goldbatt curantibus. Roma, 1986, vol. 1, 175–191.

Demina, I–III — Демина Е. И. Тихонравовский дамаскин. Болгарский памятник XVII в. Исследование и текст. Т. I–III. София, 1968–1985.

Derrida 1967 — Derrida J. L'Ecriture et la difference. Paris, 1967.

Derrida 1968 — Derrida J. Sémiologie et grammatologie. — Information sur les sciences sociales, 7 (1968).

Derzhavin, I–1X — Державин Г. Р. Сочинения. С объяснительными примечаниями Я.Грога. Т. I–IX. СПб., 1864–1883.

Desmarets 1657 — [Desmarets J.]. Clovis ov la France Chrestienne. Poeme Heroique. Par I. Paris, Chez A. Covrbe..., 1657.

Dmitriev, I–II — Дмитриев И. И. Сочинения. Т. I–II. СПб., 1983.

Dmitriev, 1958 — Повести о житии Михаила Клопского. Подготовка текстов и статья Л. А. Дмитриева. М.-Л., 1958.

Dimitrii Rostovskii, I–VI — Св. Димитрий Ростовский. Собрание разных поучительных слов и других сочинений. Ч. I–VI. М., 1786.

Dimitrii Sechenov 1743 — Слово в день явления чудотворныя иконы пресвятыя богородицы во граде Казани, в Высочайшее присутствие Ея Священнейшаго Величества Благочестивейшия Самодержавнейшия Крестоносныя Императрицы Великия Государыни Нашея Елисаветы Петровны Всея России. Проповеданное Свияжским Архимандритом Димитрием Сеченовым, в Придворной Церкви в Москве. 1742 года, Иулиа 8 дня. М., 1743.

Druzhinin 1887 — Дружинин В. Г. Три неизвестные произведения князя Антиоха Кантемира. — Журнал Министерства народного просвещения, 1887, № 12, 194–204.

Dubrovin 1895 — Дубровин Н. Ф. Наши мистики-сектанты. А. Ф. Лабзин и его журнал «Сионский Вестник». — Русская Старина, 1895, год XXVI, январь.

Dukhovnyi Reglament 1904 — Духовный Регламент Всепресветлейшего, державнейшего государя Петра Первого, императора и самодержца всероссийского. М., 1904.

Durnovo 1931 — Дурново Н. Н. К вопросу о времени распадения общеславянского языка. — Sborník Prací I. Sjezdu slovanských filologů v Praze. Praha, 1929, 514–526.

Durnovo 1933 — Дурново Н. Н. Славянское правописание X–XII вв. Slavia, roč. 12 (1933), seš. 1–2, 45–82.

Ďurovič 1992 — Ďurovič L. Грамматика Академической гимназии. — Доломоносовский период русского литературного языка. The Pre-Lomonosov Period of the Russian Literary Language: (Материалы конференции на Фагеруде, 20–25 мая 1989 г.). Slavica Suecana, Series B, vol. 1. Stockholm, 1992, 171–211.

Ďurovič 1994 — Ďurovič Ĺ. Rudimenta Linguae Russicae by J. Chr. Stahl. — Russian Linguistics 18 (1994), n. 2, 185–195.

Ďurovič 1995 — Ďurovič Ĺ. Sources of Gorlickij's Grammaire francoise et russe. — Подобаєтъ память сътворнтн. Essays to the Memory of Anders Sjöberg. Ed. by P. Ambrosiani, B. Nilsson, L. Steensland. Acta Universitatis Stockholmiensis. Stockholm Slavic Studies, 24. Stockholm, 1995, 51–61.

Ďurovič and Sjöberg 1987 — Ďurovič Ĺ. and Sjöberg A. Древнейший источник парадигматики современного русского литературного языка. — Russian Linguistics, vol. 11 (1987), 255–278.

Dvukhsotletie… 1908 — Двухсотлетие русской гражданской азбуки 1708-1908 г. Издание Московской Синодальной Типографии. М., 1908.

Ebert, I–III — Ebert A. Allgemeine Geschichte der Literatur des Mittelalters im Abendlande bis zum Beginne des XI. Jahrhunderts. Bd. I–III. 2. Aufl. Leipzig, 1889.

Edelman 1946 — Edelman N. Attitudes of Seventeenth-Century France toward the Middle Ages. Moningside Heights, New York, 1946.

Edlichka 1974 — Едличка А. Проблематика нормы в кодификации литературного языка в отношении к типу литературного языка. — Проблемы нормы в славянских литературных языках в синхронном и диахронном аспектах: Доклады на IV заседании Международной комиссии по славянским литературным языкам. 22–25 октября 1974 г. М., 1976, 16–39.

Ekaterina 1770 — Наказ Ея Императорскаго Величества Екатерины Вторыя Самодержицы Всероссийския, данный Коммиссии о сочинении проекта новаго уложения. СПб., 1770 [edition with parallel texts in four languages].

Erazm 1716 – [Erasmus, Desiderius] Разговоры дружеския. Дезидерия Ерасма. С приложенными общими некиими разговоров образцами, и часто употребляемыми пословицами, от различных авторов избранными во употребление хотящим языка голанскаго учитися юношам. СПб., 1716.

Eremin 1966 — Еремин И. П. Литература древней Руси. М.-Л., 1966.

Esipov I–II — Есипов Г. В. Раскольничьи дела XVIII века. Т. I–I1. СПб., 1861–1862.

Evgenii Bolkhovitinov 1800 — [Евгений Болховитинов]. Разсуждение о надобности греческаго языка для богословии, и об особенной пользе его для российскаго языка. Изд. 2-ое пересмотр. Читано в Публичном Собрании 1793 года Июля 13 дня в Воронежской семинарии. Воронеж, 1800.

Fasmer, I–N — Фасмер М. Этимологический словарь русского языка. Пер. с нем. и дополнения О. Н. Трубачева. Т. I–IV. М., 1964–1973.

Fénélon, I–X — Fénélon Fr. de Salignac de la Motte. Oeuvres complètes. Vol. I–X. Paris, 1810.

Fenne, I–II — Tönnies Fenne's Low German Manual of Spoken Russian. Pskov, 1607. Ed. by L. L. Hammarich and Roman Jakobson. Vol. I–II. Copenhagen, 1970.

Feofan 1862 — Записки о. Феофана, архимандрита Кирилло-Новоезерского монастыря, бывшего келейника преосвященного Гавриила, митрополита Новгородского и С.Петербургского. — Странник, 1862, февраль, 533–558.

Feofan Prokopovich, I–IV — Феофан Прокопович. Слова и речи поучительные, похвальные и поздравительные. Ч. I–IV. СПб., 1760–1774.

Feofan Prokopovich 1721 — [Феофан Прокопович]. Розыскъ історіческій, коихъ ради вінъ, и въяковомъ разум были и наріцалися императоры рімстіи, какъ язычестіи, такъ и хрістіянстіи, понтіфексами или архіереами многобожнаго закона. А въ закон хрістіанстемъ, хрістіанстіи государи, могугь ли нарещіся епіскопи и архіереи, и въ какомъ разумѣ. СПб., 1721.

Feofan Prokopovich 1721a — [Феофан Прокопович]. О возношении имени патриаршаго в церковных молитвах, чего ради оное ныне в церквах российских оставлено. М., 1721.

Feofan Prokopovich 1725 — [Феофан Прокопович]. Слово на погребение

Всепресветлейшаго Державнейшаго Петра Великаго, Императора и Самодержца Всероссийскаго... СПб., 1725.

Feofan Prokopovich 1773 — [Феофан Прокопович]. История Петра Великого от Рождения Его до Полтавской баталии... сочиненная Феофаном Прокоповичем... Изданная с обретающегося в кабинетской архиве дел Его Императорского Величества Списка, правленного рукою самого сочинителя. СПб., 1773.

Feofan Prokopovich 1782 — Christianae orthodoxae theologiae in Academia Kiowiensi a Theophane Prokopowisz... adornatae e propositae volumen primum. Lipsiae, 1782.

Feofan Prokopovich 1790 — [Феофан Прокопович]. Первое учение отроком... М., 1790.

Feofan Prokopovich 1961 — Феофан Прокопович. Сочинения. Под ред. И. П. Еремина. М.-Л., 1961.

Feofilakt Rusanov 1807 — Слово по случаю торжественнаго объявления о мире России с Франциею, сочиненное Феофилактом, епископом Калужским и Боровским... СПб., 1807.

Feofilakt Rusanov 1808 — Слово на день Св. Пятьдесятницы, сочиненное... Феофилактом Епископом Калужским и Боровским... СПб., 1808.

Ferguson 1959 — Ferguson Ch. A. Diglossia. — Word 15 (1959), 325–340.

Filaret, I–IV — Письма митрополита Московского Филарета к наместнику Свято-Троицкия Сергиевы Лавры архимандриту Антонию. Т. I–IV. М., 1877–1881.

Filaret, СМО, I–V & доп. — Собрание мнений и отзывов Филарета, митрополита Московского и Коломенского по учебным и церковно- государственным вопросам. Т. I–V, дополнительный. М., 1885–1888.

Filaret 1869 — Письма митрополита Московского Филарета к А. Н. М[уравьеву]. 1832–1867. Киев, 1869.

Filaret 1872 — Письма Филарета Митрополита Московского к ректору М. Д. Академии архим. Филарету... — Чтения в обществе любителей духовного просвещения, 1872, ч. I–IV.

Filaret 1877 — Письма Филарета Митрополита Московского, к Григорию, митрополиту Новгородскому и Санктпетербургскому. — Чтения в обществе любителей духовного просвещения, 1877, ч. XI–XII.

Filaret 1883 — Письма Московского митрополита Филарета к покойному архиепископу тверскому Алексию. 1843–1867. М., 1883.

Filaret 1891 — Письма митрополита московского Филарета, хранящиеся в Собрании автографов имп. Публичной библиотеки. — Отчет имп. Публичной библиотеки за 1888 год. СПб., 1891, приложение.

Filaret 1895 — Переписка Филарета митрополита Московского с С. Д. Нечаевым. СПб., 1895.

Filaret 1905 — Мнения, отзывы и письма Филарета, митрополита Московского и Коломенского, по разным вопросам. М., 1905.

Filaret Gumilevskii 1884 — Филарет [Гумилевский]. Обзор русской духовной литературы. Кн. I–II. Изд. 3-е. СПб., 1884.

Filin 1949 — Филин Ф. П. Лексика русского литературного языка древне-киевской эпохи. (По материалам летописей). Ученые записки Ленинградского гос. пед. ин-та им. Герцена, т. 80. Л., 1949.

Filin 1981 — Филин Ф. П. Истоки и судьбы русского литературного языка. М., 1981.

Flashar 1959 — Флашар М. Sobria ebrietas. — Зборник филозофског факултета (Универзитет у Београду), књ. ИВ-2. Београд, 1959, 287–335.

Florovskii 1937 — Флоровский Г. Пути русского богословия. Париж, 1937.

Fontenelle, I–III — Fontenelle B. Oeuvres complètes. T. I–III. Paris, 1818.

Fonvizin, I–II — Фонвизин Д. И. Собрание сочинений. Т. I–II. М.-Л., 1959.

Fonvizin 1769 — Иосиф, в девяти песнях сочинение г. Битобе. [Перевод и предисл. Д. И. Фонвизина]. М., 1769, Ч. I.

Foucault 1984 — Foucault M. What Is Enlightenment? — In: P.Rabinow (ed.). The Foucault Reader. New York, 1984, 32–50.

Franko 1896 — Франко Ів. Апокріфи і легенди з українських рукописів. Т. I. Львів, 1896.

Freeze 1977 — Freeze G. L. The Russian Levites. Parish Clergy in the Eighteenth Century. Cambridge, Mass., 1977.

Freydank 1985 — Freydank D. Trediakovskij und de deutsche Literatur. — Die russische Literatur der Aufklärung (1650–1825). Hrsg. von H. Schmidt. Halle (Saale), 1985, 34–46.

Frick 1989 — Frick D. A. Polish Sacred Philology in the Reformation and the Counter-Reformation. Chapters in the History of the Controversies (1551–1632). University of California Publications in Modern Philology, vol. 123. Berkeley, 1989.

Garde 1986 — Garde P. Šiškov et Karamzin: deux enemis? — Studia slavica mediaevalia e humanistica Riccardo Picchio dicata. M. Colucci, G. Dell'Agata, H. Goldblatt curantibus. Roma, 1986, vol. 1, 279–285.

Gasparov 1984 — Гаспаров М. Л. Очерк истории русского стиха. Метрика, ритмика, рифма, строфика. М., 1984.

Gavriil 1777 — [Гавриил Петров]. Слово в день тезоименитства... имп. Екатерины Алексеевны всея России, проповеданное в придворной церкве, при высочайшем Ея Имп. Величества и их Имп. Высочеств присудствии, Святейшаго правительствующего синода членом Гавриилом архиепископом Новгородским и Санктпетербургским 24 ноября 1777 года. СПб., тип. Военной коллегии, 1777.

Gavriil and Platon, I–III — Собрание разных слов и поучений на все воскресные и праздничные дни. Ч. I–III. М., 1775 [составили Гавриил Петров и Платон Левшин].

Gedeon Krinovskii, I–IV — Собрание разных поучительных слов при высочайшем дворе Ея Имп. Величества сказанных... Гедеоном. Т. I–IV. СПб., 1755–1759.

Gezen 1884 — Гезен А. История славянского перевода символов веры. Критико-палеографические заметки. СПб., 1884.

Gippius 1992 — Гиппиус А. А. Новые данные о пономаре Тимофее — новгородском книжнике середины XIII века. — Международная ассоциация по изучению и распространению славянских культур. Информационный бюллетень, вып. 25. М., 1992, 59–86.

Gleason 1981 — Gleason W. J. Moral Idealists, Bureaucracy, and Catherine the Great. New Brunswick, New Jersey, 1981.

Glück 1994 — see Kaipert, Uspenskii, Zhivov 1994.

Goldblatt 1987 — Goldblatt H. Orthography and Orthodoxy. Constantine Kostenečki's Treatise on the Letters. Florence, 1987.

Goldblatt 1991 — Goldblatt H. On the Reception of Ivan Vyšens'kyj's Writings among the Old Believers. — Harvard Ukrainian Studies, XV (1991), n. 3/4, 354–382.

Golikov 1788 — Голиков И. И. Деяния Петра Великого. Ч. I. М., 1788. [Изд. 1-е]

Golubev 1971 — Голубев И. Ф. Встреча Симеона Полоцкого, Епифания Славинецкого и Паисия Лигарида с Николаем Спафарием и их беседа. — Труды отдела древнерусской литературы, XXVI. Л., 1971, 294–301.

Gordon, I–II — Гордон П. Дневник... Перевод с немецкого. Ч. I–II. М., 1892.

Gorodchaninov 1800 — [Городчанинов Г. Н.] Митрофанушка в отставке, комедия в пяти действиях, Российское сочинение Г. Г. М., 1800.

Gorskii and Nevostruev, I–III — Горский А. В., Невоструев К. И. Описание славянских рукописей Московской Синодальной библиотеки. Отд. I–III. М., 1855–1917.

Gottsched 1751 — Gottsched J. Ch. Versuch einer kritischen Dichtkunst... Leipzig, 1751. Цит. по репринту: Darmstadt, 1982.

Gottsched 1757 — Gottsched J. Ch. Vollständigere und Neuerläuterte Deutsche Sprachkunst, nach den Mustern der besten Schriftsteller des vorigen und itzigen Jahrhunderts abgefasset... 4. Aufl. Leipzig, 1757.

Gournay 1626 — Mlle de Gournay. L'Ombre. Paris, 1626.

Gournay 1962 — Uildriks A. Les idées littéraires de Mlle de Gournay. Reédition de ses Traités Philologiques des Advis et Presens, édition de 1641 avec les variantes des éditions de 1626 et de 634. Groningen, 1962.

Grasshoff 1961 — Grasshoff H. Lomonosov und Gottsched. Gottscheds «Ausführliche Redekunst» und Lomonosovs «Ritorika». — Zeitschrift für Slawistik, Bd. VI (1961), Hf. 4, 498–507.

Grasshoff 1966 — Grasshoff H. Antioch Dmitrievič Kantemir und Westeuropa. Berlin, 1966.

Grebeniuk 1979 — Панегирическая литература петровского времени. Изд. подготовил В. П. Гребенюк. М., 1979.

Grech, I–II — Греч Н. И. Чтения о русском языке. Ч. I–II. СПб., 1840.

Greshishcheva 1911 — Грешищева Е. Хвалебная ода в русской литературе XVIII в. — М. В. Ломоносов. Сборник статей под ред. В. В. Сиповского. СПб., 1911, 93–149.

Grimm 1987 — Grimm G. E. Muttersprache und Realienunterricht. Der pädagogische Realismus als Motor einer Verschiebung im Wissenschaftssystem (Ratke — Andreae — Comenius). — Res Publica Litteraria. Die Institutionen der Gelehrsamkeit in der frühen Neuzeit. Hrsg. von S. Neumeister und C. Wiedemann. Wolfenbüttler Arbeiten zur Barockforschung, Bd. 14. Wiesbaden, 1987, 299–324.

Grinberg and Uspenskii 1992 — Гринберг М.С., Успенский Б.А. Литературная война Тредиаковского и Сумарокова в 1740-х — начале 1750-х годов. — Russian Literature, XXXI (1992), 133–272.

Groening 1750 — Groening M. Российская грамматика. Thet är Grammatica Russica, eller Grundelig Handledning til Ryska Språket. Stockholm, 1750. Cited from: Unbegaun 1969.

Gröschel 1972 — Gröschel B. Die Sprache Ivan Vyšeńskyjs. Untersuchungen und Materialen zur historischen Grammatik des Ukrainischen. Slavistische Forschungen, Bd. 13. Köln — Wien, 1972.

Grot 1899 — Грот Я. Филологические разыскания. 4-е дополненное изд. СПб., 1899.

Gukovskaia 1957 — Гуковская З. В. «Заметки о французском языке» Вожля и проблема французского литературного языка XVII в. — Ученые записки Ленинградского пед. ин-та им. Покровского. Факультет иностранных языков, вып. 2. Т. XXVIII. Л., 1957, 207–242.

Gukovskii 1927 — Гуковский Г. А. Русская поэзия XVIII века. Л., 1927.

Gukovskii 1927а — Гуковский Г. А. Из истории русской оды XVIII века (Опыт истолкования пародии). — Поэтика, III. Л., 1927, 129–147.

Gukovskii 1936 — Гуковский Гр. Очерки по истории русской литературы XVIII века. Дворянская фронда в литературе 1750–1760-х годов. М.- Л., 1936.

Gukovskii 1941 — Гуковский Г. А. Сумароков и его окружение. — История русской литературы. Т. III. М.-Л., 1941.

Gurvich 1915 — Гурвич Г. «Правда воли монаршей» Феофана Прокоповича и ее западноевропейские источники. Юрьев, 1915.

Guzner 1980 — Гузнер И. А. Библиотека учебных заведений Сибири в первой половине XVIII века. — Книга в Сибири XVII — начала XX вв. Новосибирск, 1980.

Hatzfeld 1929 — Hatzfeld H. Der Barockstil der religiösen klassischen Lyrik in Frankreich. — Literaturwissenschaftliches Jahrbuch der Görres-Gesellschaft, 4, 1929, 30–60. Цит. по: Der literarische Barockbegriff. Hrsg. von W. Barner. Darmstadt, 1975, 143–182.

Hazard 1961 — Hazard P. La crise de la la conscience européene, 1680–1715. Paris: Fayard, 1961.

Hellie 1978 — Hellie R. The Stratification of Muscovite Society: The Townsmen. — Russian History, 2 (1978), 119–175.

Hellie 1982 — Hellie R. Slavery in Russia 1450–1725. Chicago, 1982.

Hepp 1968 — Hepp Noémi. Homère en France au XVIIIe siècle. Paris, 1968.

Horbatsch 1964 — Horbatsch O. Die vier Ausgaben der kirchenslavische Grammatik von M.Smotrickyj. Osteuropastudien der Hochschulen des Landes Hessen, Reihe III, Frankfurter Abhandlungen zur Slavistik, Bd. 7. Wiesbaden, 1964.

Hunold 1707 — Hunold Chr. Fr. Die allerneuste Art zur reinen und galanten Poesie zu gelangen. Hamburg, 1707.

Hüttl-Folter 1984–1985 — Hüttl-Folter G. Prinzipielles zur Untersuchung der neuren russischen Literatursprache. — Зборник Матице српске за филологију и лингвистику, XXVII–XXVIII. Нови Сад, 1984–1985, 895–898.

Hüttl-Folter 1987 — Hüttl-Folter G. Zur Sprache von Polikarpovs Übersetzung *Geografia generalnaja* (1718). — Dona slavica aenipontana in honorem Herbert Schelesniker. München, 1987, 57–64.

Hüttl-Worth 1956 — Hüttl-Worth G. Die Bereicherung des russischen Wortschatzes im XVIII. Jahrhundert. Wien, 1956.

Hüttl-Worth 1963 — Хютль-Ворт Г. Проблемы межславянских и славянско-неславянских лексических отношений. — American Contributions to the Fifth International Congress of Slavists. Sofia, 1963. The Hague, 1963, 133–152.

Hüttl-Worth 1968 — Хютль-Ворт Г. Роль церковнославянского языка в развитии русского литературного языка. К историческому анализу и классификации славянизмов. — American Contributions to the Sixth International Congress of Slavists. Prague, 1968, August 7–13. [The Hague, 1968. Preprint].

Hüttl-Worth 1978 — Hüttl-Worth G. Zum Primat der Syntax bei historischen Untersuchungen des Russischen. — Studia linguistica Alexandro Vasilii filio Issatschenko a collegis amicisque oblata. Lisse, 1978, 187–190.

Iagich 1896 — Ягич И. В. Рассуждения южнославянской и русской старины о церковнославянском языке. Исследования по русскому языку, I. СПб., 1885–1895. СПб. 1896.

Iakhontov 1883 — Яхонтов И. Иеродиакон Дамаскин, русский полемист XVII века. СПб., 1883.

Iakovlev 1915 — Записки А. А. Яковлева, бывшего в 1803 году обер-прокурором св. Синода. Изд. В. А. Андреев. М., 1915.

Ikonnikov 1915 — Иконников В. С. Максим Грек и его время. Киев, 1915.

Ioann Zlatoust, I–II — Святаго отца нашего Иоанна Златоустаго архиепископа Константинопольскаго беседы на первую моисееву книгу Бытия переведенныя с Греческаго на Российский язык. Ч. I–II. СПб., 1766.

Ioann Zlatoust 1792 — Слова избранныя из разных поучений святого Иоанна Златоустаго. Ч. I–II. М., 1792.

Isachenko 1974 — Issatschenko A. Vorgeschichte und Entstehung der modernen russischen Literatursprache. — Zeitschrift für slavische Philologie, Bd. 37 (1974), Hf. 2, 235–274.

Isachenko 1975 — Issatschenko A. Mythen und Tatsachen über die Entstehung der russischen Literatursprache. Osterreichische Akademie der Wissenschaften. Philosophisch-historische Klasse. Sitzungberichte, 298. Bd. 5. Abhandlung. Wien, 1975.

Isachenko 1975a — А.И[саченко]. (Рецензия на статью: З. М. Петрова. Страдательно-причастные формы в русском языке XVIII века /ВЯ, 1974, 2/). — Russian Linguistics, 2 (1975), № 1/2.
Isachenko 1976 — Isačenko A. V. Opera selecta. Forum slavicum, Bd. 46. München, 1976.
Isachenko 1980 — Issatschenko A. Geschichte der russischen Sprache. 1. Band. Von den Anfängen bis zum Ende des 17. Jahrhunderts. Heidelberg, 1980.
Isachenko 1983 — Issatschenko A. Geschichte der russischen Sprache. 2. Band. Das 17. und 18. Jahrhundert. Heidelberg, 1983.
Iunosti chestnoe zertsalo 1717 — Юности честное зерцало или показание к житейскому обхождению. Собранное от разных авторов. СПб., 1717.
Ivan Vishnevskii 1955 — Иван Вишенский. Сочинения. М.-Л., 1955.
Jakobson 1966 — Якобсон Р. О. Влияние народной словесности на Тредиаковского (1915). — Jakobson R. O. Selected Writings. Vol. IV. The Hague, 1966, 613–633.
Jaksche 1985 — Jaksche H. Arsenij Gluchoj — ein russischer «Philologe» des 17. Jahrhunderts. — Anzeiger für slavische Philologie, Bd. XV/XVI (1984/1985), 31–75.
Janik 1968 — Janik D. Geschichte der Ode und der «Stances» von Ronsard bis Boileau. Berlin, 1968.
Kaldor 1969–1970 — Kaldor I. The Genesis of the Russian Grazhdanskii Shrift of the Civil Type. — The Journal of Typographic Research, 1969, № 4; 1970, № 2.
Kamenskii 1992 — Каменский А. Б. «Под сению Екатерины»,.. Вторая половина XVIII века. СПб., 1992.
Kantemir, I–II — Кантемир А .Д. Сочинения, письма и избранные переводы. Под ред. П. А. Ефремова. Т. I–II. СПб., 1867–1868.
Kantemir 1744 — [А. Кантемир]. Квинта Горация Флакка десять писем первой книги. Переведены с латинских стихов на русские и с примечаниями изъяснены от знатнаго некотораго охотника до стихотворства с приобщенным при том письмом о сложении русских стихов. СПб., 1744.
Kapterev 1914 — Каптерев Н. Ф. Характер отношений России к Православному Востоку в XVI и XVII столетиях. Изд. 2-е. Сергиев Посад, 1914.
Karamzin, I–III — Карамзин Н. М. Сочинения. Т. I–III. СПб., 1848.
Karamzin, IGR, I–XIII — Карамзин Н. М. История государства Российского. Т. I–XII. М., 1989– (продолжающееся изд.).
Karamzin 1914 — Карамзин Н. М. Записка о древней и новой России. СПб., 1914.
Karamzin 1984 — Карамзин Н. М. Письма русского путешественника. Л., 1984.
Karin 1778 — Карин Ф .Г. Письмо к Николаю Петровичу Николеву о преобразователях российскаго языка на случай прествления Александра Петровича Сумарокова. М., 1778.
Karlinsky 1963 — Karlinsky S. Talleman and the Beginning of the Novel in Russia. — Comparative Literature, XV (1963), № 3, 226–233.
Karskii 1921 — Карский Е. Ф. Белорусы. Т. III. Очерк словесности белорусского племени. Ч. 2. Старая западнорусская письменность. Пг., 1921.

Katenin 1822 — Катенин П. Ответ на ответ. — Сын Отечества, 1822, ч. 77, № 18, 172–178.
Keil 1965 — Keil R. D. Ergänzungen zu russischen Dichterkommentaren 3. Trediakovskij. — Zeitschrift für slavische Philologie, XXXII (1965), 262–268.
Keipert 1981 — Keipert H. M. V. Lomonosov als Übersetzungs-theoretiker. — Wiener Slavistisches Jahrbuch, Bd. 27, 1981, 27–48.
Keipert 1983 — Keipert H. Die Petersburger «Teutsche Grammatica» und die Anfänge der Russistik in Rußland. — Studia slavica in honorem viri doctissimi Olexa Horbatsch. Bd. 3. München, 1983, 77–140.
Keipert 1984 — Keipert H. Die lateinisch-russische Terminologie der Petersburger «Teutsche Grammatica» von 1730. — Festschrift für Gerta Hüttl-Folter zum sechzigsten Geburtstag. Wiener Slavistischer Almanach, Bd. 13. Wien, 1984, 121–139.
Keipert 1986 — Keipert H. Adodurovs «Anfangs-Gründe der russischen Sprache» und der Petersburger Lateinunterricht um 1730. — Studia slavica mediaevalia e humanistica Riccardo Picchio dicata. M.Colucci, G. Dell'Agata, H. Goldbatt curantibus. Roma, 1986, vol. II, 393–408.
Keipert 1987 — Keipert H. Kirchenslavisch und Latein. Über die Vergleichbarkeit zweier mittelalterlicher Kultursprachen. — Sprache und Literatur Altrusslands. Aufzatzsammlung hrsg. Von G. Birkfellner. München, 1987, 81–109.
Keipert 1987a — Keipert H. Traditionsprobeme im grammatischen Fachwortschatz des Russischen bis zum Ende des 18. Jahrhunderts. — Die Welt der Slaven, 32, 2 (1987), 230–301.
Keipert 1988 — Keipert H. Einleitung. — In: F. Polikarpov. Leksikon trejazyčnyj. Dictionarium trilingue. Moskva 1704. Nachdruck und Einleitung von H. Keipert. Specimina philologiae Slavicae, Bd. 79. München, 1988
Keipert 1988a — Keipert H. The Sources of Michael Groening's Rossijskaja grammatika (Stockholm, 1750). — Oxford Slavonic Papers, XXI (1988), 89–104.
Keipert 1988б — Keipert H. Die Christianisierung Rußlands als Gegenstand der russischen Sprachgeschichte. — Tausend Jahre Christentum in Rußland. Zum Millennium der Taufe der Kiever Rus'. Göttingen, 1988, 313–346.
Keipert 1989 — Keipert H. Deutsches im russischen Donat. — Die Welt der Slaven, XXIX (1989), 2, 236–258.
Keipert 1989a — Keipert H. Groening und Schwanwitz. — «Прими собранье пестрых глав». Slavistische und slavenkundliche Beiträge für Peter Brang zum 65. Geburtstag. Slavica Helvetica, Bd. 33. Bern, 1989, 469–487.
Keipert 1991 — Keipert H. M. V. Lomonosovs Predislovie o pol'ze knig cerkovnych v rossijskom jazyke (1757–1758) als Entwurf eines linguistischen Modells für das Schrifttum Russlands im 18. Jahrhundert. — Studia z filologii polskiej i słowiańskiej, 1991, 81–95.
Keipert 1992 — Keipert H. Русская грамматика М. Шванвица 1731 г. (Предварительные замечания о рукописи БАН F. N. 250). — Доломоносовский период русского литературного языка. The Pre-Lomonosov Period of the

Russian Literary Language (Материалы конференции на Фагеруде, 20–25 мая 1989 г.). Slavica Suecana, Series B, vol. 1. Stockholm, 1992, 213–234.

Keipert 1994 — Keipert H. Die knigi cerkovnye in Lomonosovs «Predislovie o pol'ze knig cerkovnych v rossijskom jazyke». — Zeitschrift für slavische Philologie, LIV (1994), 1, 21–37.

Keipert, Uspenskii, Zhivov 1994 — Johann Ernst Glück. Grammatik der russischen Sprache (1704). Herausgegeben und mit einer Einleitung versehen von H. Keipert, B. Uspenskij und V. Živov. Bausteine zur slavischen Philologie und Kulturgeschichte. Reihe B, Editionen. Neue Folge, 5(20). Köln, 1994.

Khaburgaev 1991 — Хабургаев Г. А. Древнерусский и древнепольский глагол в сравнении со старославянским (К реконструкции праславянской системы претеритов). — Исследования по глаголу в славянских языках. История славянского глагола. Под ред. Г. А. Хабургаева и А. Бартошевича. М., 1991, 42–54.

Khaburgaev and Riumina 1971 — Хабургаев Г. А., Рюмина О. Л. Глагольные формы в языке художественной литературы Московской Руси XVII века (К вопросу о понятии литературности в предпетровскую эпоху). — Научные доклады высшей школы. Филологические науки, 1971, № 4, 65–76.

Kharlamovich 1914 — Харлампович К. В. Малороссийское влияние на великорусскую церковную жизнь. Т. I. Казань, 1914.

Khodasevich 1975 — Ходасевич В. Ф. Державин. Centrifuga, Russian Reprintings and Printings, Vol. 21, l. München, 1975.

Khrapovitskii 1874 — Храповицкий А. В. Дневник. СПб., 1874.

Khvostov 1938 — Из архива Хвостова. Публикация А. В. Западова. — Литературный архив. Материалы по истории литературы и общественного движения. Т. I. М.-Л., 1938, 359–407.

Kibal'nik 1981 — Кибальник С. А. Об одном французском источнике эстетических взглядов Тредиаковского. — XVIII век. Сб. 13. Л., 1981, 219–228.

Kibal'nik 1983 — Кибальник С. А. О «Риторике» Феофана Прокоповича. — XVIII век. Сб. 14. Л., 1983, 193–206.

Kirchner 1961 — Kirchner P. Lomonosov und Johann Christian Günther. — Zeitschrift für Slawistik, VI (1961), 4, 483–497.

Kirill Florinskii 1741 — Слово в высокоторжественный день рождения Ея Священнейшатго Имп. Величества... Елисаветы Первыя, Императрицы всея России проповеданное Архимандритом... Кириллом Флоринским. В Успенском Соборе в Москве 1741 года декабря 18 дня. СПб., б.г.

Kjellberg 1957 — Kjellberg L. La langue de Gedeon Krinovskij, predicateur russe du XVIIIe siècle. I. Acta Universitatis Upsaliensis 1957: 7. Uppsala, 1957.

Klein 1988 — Klein J. Die Schaferdichtung des russischen Klassizismus. Veröffentlichungen der Abteilung für slavische Sprachen und Literaturen des Osteuropa-Institut an der Freien Universität Berlin, Bd.. 67. Berlin, 1988.

Klein 1990 — Klein J. Sumarokov und Boileau. Die Epistel «Über die Verskunst» in ihrem Verhältnis zur «Art poëtique»: Kontextwechsel als Kategorie der

Vergleichenden Literaturwissenschaft. — Zeitschrift für slavische Philologie L (1990), Hf. 2, 254–304.

Klein 1993 — Клейн И. Русский Буало? (Эпистола Сумарокова «О стихотворстве» в восприятии современников). — XVIII век. Сб. 18. СПб., 1993, 40–58.

Klein 1995 — Клейн Й. Тредиаковский: Реформа русского стиха в культурно-историческом контексте. XVIII век. Сб. 19. СПб., 1995, 15–42.

Klein and Zhivov 1987 — Klein J., Živov, V. Zur Problematik und Spezifik des russischen Klassizismus: Die Oden des Vasilij Majkov. — Zeitschrift für slavische Philologie XLVII (1987), Hf. 2, 234–288.

Klenin 1993 — Klenin E. The Perfect Tense in the Laurentian Manuscript of 1377. — American Contributions to the Eleventh International Congress of Slavists. Bratislava, August-September 1993. Literature. Linguistics. Poetics. Ed. by R. A. Maguire and A. Timberlake. Columbus, 1993, 330–343.

Kliment Okhridskii, I–III — Климент Охридски. Събрани съчинения. Т. I–III. София, 1970–1973.

Kniaz'kova 1974 — Князькова Г. П. Русское просторечие второй половины XVIII в. Л., 1974.

Koblents 1958 — Кобленц И. Н. Андрей Иванович Богданов. 1682–1766. Из прошлого русской исторической науки и кииговедения. М., 1958.

Kochetkova 1974 — Кочеткова Н. Д. Ораторская проза Феофана Прокоповича и пути формирования литературы классицизма. — XVIII век. Сб. 9. Л., 1974, 50–80.

Kociuba 1975 — Kociuba O. The Grammatical Sources of Meletij Smotryckij's Church Slavonic Grammar of 1619. Ph.D. Dissertation. Columbia University, 1975.

Koporskii 1960 — Копорский С. А. Рецензия на кн.: Kjellberg 1957. — Вопросы языкознания, 1960, № 3, 125–130.

Koretskii 1968 — Корецкий В. И. Мазуринский летописец конца XVII в. и летописание Смутного времени. — Славяне и Русь. Сборник статей. М., 1968, 282–290.

Kosellek 1979 — Kosellek R. Vergangene Zukunft. Zur Semantik geschichtlicher Zeit. Frankfurt am Main, 1979.

Kotkov, Astakhina et al. 1984 — Памятники деловой письменности XVII века. Владимирский край. Изд. подготовили С. И. Котков, Л. Ю. Астахина и др. М., 1984.

Kotovich 1909 — Котович А. Духовная цензура в России (1799–1855 гг.). СПб., 1909.

Kovalevskaia 1958 — Ковалевская Е. Г. Славянизмы и русская архаическая лексика в произведениях Н. М. Карамзина. — Ученые записки Ленинградского пед. ин-та им. Герцена, 1958, т. 173.

Kovtun 1963 — Ковтун Л. С. Русская лексикография эпохи Средневековья. М.-Л., 1963.

Kovtun 1975 — Ковтун Л. С. Лексикография в Московской Руси XVI — начала XVII вв. Л., 1975.

Kovtun 1989 — Ковтун Л. С. Азбуковники XVI–XVII вв. (старшая разновидность). Л., 1989.

Kovtun et al. 1973 — Ковтун Л.С., Синицина Н. В., Фонкич Б Л. Максим Грек и славянская Псалтырь (сложение норм литературного языка в переводческой практике XVI в.). — Восточнославянские языки. Источники для их изучения. М., 1973, 99–127.

Kozlov 1988 — С. Л. Козлов. «Гений языка» и «гений нации» во французской культуре эпохи Людовика XIV. — Семиотика культуры. Тезисы докладов Всесоюзной школы-семинара по семиотике культуры 8–18 сентября 1988 года. Архангельск, 1988, 42–44.

Kratkoe opisanie 1728 — Краткое описание комментариев Академии наук. Часть первая на 1726 год. СПб., 1728.

Krivoshein 1962 — Krivochein B. Le theme de l'ivresse spirituelle dans la mystique de St. Syméon le Nouveau Théologien. — Studia Patristica, V, 1962, 368–376.

Krivoshein 1980 — Архиепископ Василий (Кривошеин). Преподобный Симеон Новый Богослов (949–1022). Париж, 1980.

Kuev 1967 — Куев К. М. Черноризец Храбър. София, 1967.

Kunik 1865 — Куник А. Сборник материалов для истории Императорской Академии наук. Ч. I–II. СПб., 1865.

Kutina 1964 — Кутина Л. Л. Формирование языка русской науки. М. Л., 1964.

Kutina 1966 — Кутина Л. Л. Формирование терминологии физики в России. Период предломоносовский: первая треть XVIII века. М.-Л., 1966.

Kutina 1981 — Кутина Л. Л. Феофан Прокопович. Слова и речи. Проблема языкового типа. — Язык русских писателей XVIII века. Л., 1981, 7–46.

Kutina 1982 — Кутина Л. Л. Феофан Прокопович. Слова и речи. Лексико-стилистическая характеристика. — Литературный язык XVIII века. Проблемы стилистики. Л., 1982, 5–51.

Kuz'mina 1964 — Кузьмина В. Д. Рыцарский роман на Руси. Бова, Петр златых ключей. М., 1964.

Lachmann 1981 — Lachmann R. Zur Frage der Wertung poetischer Verfahren (am Beispiel einer Lomonosov-Ode). — Colloquium Slavicum Basiliense. Gedankschrift für H. Schroeder. Hrsg. H. Riggenbach. Bern, 1981, 361–385.

Lachmann 1982 — Feofan Prokopovič. De arte rhetorica libri X. Hrsg. von R. Lachmann. Köln, 1982.

Lamy 1737 — Lamy B. La rhetorique, ou L'art de parler. 6-ème éd. La Haye, 1737.

Lappo-Danilevskii 1897 — Лаппо-Данилевский А. Собрание и свод законов Российской Империи, составленное в царствование императрицы Екатерины II. СПб., 1897 [Отд. оттиск из Журнала Министерства народного просвещения за 1897 г.].

Lappo-Danilevskii 1990 — Лаппо-Данилевский А. П. История русской общественной мысли и культуры XVII–XVIII вв. М., 1990.

Larin 1975 — Ларин Б. А. Лекции по истории русского литературного языка (X — середина XVIII в.). М., 1975.

Lavrov 1930 — Лавров П. А. Материалы по истории возникновения древнейшей славянской письменности. Труды Славянской комиссии, т. I. Л., 1930.

Lehfeldt 1992 — Lehfeldt W. О 'внутренних' связях между взглядами молодого и старшего Тредиаковского на литературный язык. — Доломоносовский период русского литературного языка. The Pre-Lomonosov Period of the Russian Literary Language: (Материалы конференции на Фагеруде, 20–25 мая 1989 г.). Slavica Suecana, Series B, vol. 1. Stockholm, 1992, 295–303.

Lemke 1904 — Лемке М. Очерки по истории русской цензуры и журналистики XIX столетия. СПб., 1904.

Lenhoff 1984 — Lenhoff G. Toward a Theory of Protogenres in Medieval Russian Letters. — The Russian Review, 43 (1984), 31–54.

Lentin 1996 — Lentin, Antony. Peter the Great: His Law on the Imperial Succession in Russia, 1722. The Official Commentary. Oxford: Headstart History, 1996.

Levanda, I–II — Слова и речи Иоанна Леванды, протоиерея Киево-Софийского Собора. Ч. I–II. СПб., 1821.

Levin 1964 — Левин В. Д. Очерк стилистики русского литературного языка конца XVIII — начала XIX в. (Лексика). М., 1964.

Levin 1972 — Левин В. Д. Петр I и русский язык (К 300-летию рождения Петра 1). — Известия АН СССР, Серия литературы и языка, т. XXXI (1972), вып. 3, 212–227.

Levin 1972 — Lewin P. Wykłady poetyki w uczelniach rossijskich, XVIII w. Wrocław, 1972.

Lewy 1929 — Lewy H. Sobria Ebrietas. Untersuchungen zur Geschichte der antiken Mystik. Giessen, 1929.

Likhachev 1958 — Лихачев Д. С. Некоторые задачи изучения второго южнославянского влияния в России. М., 1958.

Livet, I–II — Histoire de l'Académie françoise par Pellisson et d'olivet avec une introduction, des éclairissements et notes par M. Ch.-L. Livet. T. I–11. Paris, 1855.

Lomonosov, I–VIII — Ломоносов М. В. Сочинения. Т. I–VIII. СПб.-М.-Л., 1891–1948.

Lomonosov, I²–X² — Ломоносов М. В. Полное собрание сочинений. Т. I–X. М.-Л., 1950–1959.

Lomonosov 1778 — Покойнаго статскаго советника и профессора Михайлы Васильевича Ломоносова собрание разных сочинений в стихах и в прозе. [Изд. архимандритом Дамаскиным Семеновым-Рудневым.] Кн. I–II. М., 1778.

Lotman, I–III — Лотман Ю. М. Избранные статьи в трех томах. Т. I–III. Таллинн, 1992–1993.

Lotman 1970 — Лотман Ю. М. О соотношении поэтической лексики русского романтизма и церковно-славянской традиции. — Тезисы докладов

IV Летней школы по вторичным моделирующим системам. 17–24 августа 1970 г. Тарту, 1970, 85–87.

Lotman 1971 — Лотман Ю. Поэзия 1790–1810-х годов. — Поэты 1790–1810-х годов. Библиотека поэта. Большая серия. Л., 1971.

Lotman 1976 — Лотман Ю. М. Бытовое поведение и типология культуры в России XVIII в. — Культурное наследие Древней Руси. М., 1976, 292–297.

Lotman 1980 — Лотман Ю. М. Роман А. С. Пушкина «Евгений Онегин». Комментарий. Л., 1980.

Lotman 1983 — Лотман Ю. М. Об «Оде, выбранной из Иова» Ломоносова. — Известия АН СССР. Серия лит-ры и языка, т. 42 (1983), № 3, 253–262.

Lotman 1985 — Лотман Ю. М. «Езда в остров любви» Тредиаковского и функции переводной литературы в русской культуре первой половины XVIII в. — Проблемы изучения культурного наследия. М., 1985, 222–230.

Lotman, Tolstoi, Uspenskii 1981 — Лотман Ю. М., Толстой Н. И., Успенский Б. А. Некоторые вопросы текстологии и публикации русских литературных памятников XVIII века. — Известия АН СССР. Серия литературы и языка, т. 40 (1981), № 4, 312–323.

Lotman and Uspenskii 1973 — Лотман Ю. М., Успенский Б. А. Миф — имя — культура. — Ученые записки Тартуского университета, вып. 309. Труды по знаковым системам, VI. Тарту, 1973, 282–303.

Lotman and Uspenskii 1975 — Лотман Ю. М., Успенский Б. А. Споры о языке в начале XIX в. как факт русской культуры («Происшествие в царстве теней, или судьбина российского языка» – неизвестное сочинение Семена Боброва). – Ученые записки Тартуского ун-та, вып. 358. Труды по русской и славянской филологии, XXIV. Тарту, 1975, 168–322.

Lotman and Uspenskii 1977 — Лотман Ю. М., Успенский Б. А. Роль дуальных моделей в динамике русской культуры (до конца XVIII века). — Ученые записки Тартуского университета, вып. 414. Труды по русской и славянской филологии, XXVIII. Литературоведение. Тарту, 1977, 3–36.

Lotman and Uspenskii 1982 — Лотман Ю. М., Успенский Б. А. Отзвуки концепции «Москва — Третий Рим» в идеологии Петра Первого (К проблеме средневековой традиции в культуре барокко). — Художественный язык средневековья. М., 1982, 236–249.

Lotman and Uspenskii 1984 — Лотман Ю. М., Успенский Б. А. Текстологические принципы издания. — Н.М.Карамзин. Письма русского путешественника. Л. 1984, 516–524.

Ludolf 1696 — Ludolf H.-W. Grammatica Russica... Oxonii, 1696. Цит. по изд.: Oxford, 1959 (ed. B.O.Unbegaun).

Lukicheva 1974 — Лукичева Э. В. Федор Поликарпов — переводчик «Географии генеральной» Бернарда Варения. — Проблемы литературного развития в России первой трети XVIII века. XVIII век. Сб. 9. Л., 1974, 289–296.

Lunt 1950 — Lunt H. G. The Orthography of Eleventh Century Russian Manuscripts. University Microfilms, Ann Arbor, Michigan, 1950.

Lyzlov 1990 — Лызлов А. Скифская история. Подготовка текста, комментарий и аннотированный список имен А. П. Богданова. М., 1990.

Madariaga 1982 — Madariaga I. de. Russia in the Age of Catherine the Great. London, 1982.

Makagonenko 1987 — Макогоненко Г. П. Анакреонтика Державина и ее место в поэзии начала XIX в. — В кн.: Г. Р. Державин. Анакреонтические песни. Под ред. Г. П. Макогоненко. М., 1987, 251–205.

Makarov, I–II — Макаров П. И. Сочинения и переводы. Т. I (ч. 1–2) — II (ч. 1–2). Изд. 2-е. М., 1817.

Makeeva 1961 — Макеева В. Н. История создания «Российской грамматики» М. В. Ломоносова. М.-Л., 1961.

Maksim Grek, I–III — Сочинения Максима Грека. Ч. I–III. Казань, 1859–1862.

Malov 1876 — [Малов Е., Свящ.]. Материалы для истории Русской Церкви. Казань, 1876 [Приложение к "Православному Собеседнику"].

Marker 1985 — Marker G. Publishing, Printing, and the Origins of Intellectual Life in Russia, 1700 — 1800. Princeton, 1985.

Marker 1994 — Marker G. Faith and Secularity in Eighteenth-Century Russian Literacy, 1700–1775. — Christianity and the Eastern Slavs. Vol. 11. Russian Culture in Modern Times. Ed. by R. P. Hughes and I. Paperno. California Slavic Studies XVII. Berkeley 1994, 3–24.

Marmontel 1768 — Велизар, сочинения господина Мармонтеля, члена французской академии, переведен на Волге. М., 1768.

Martel 1933 — Martel A. Michel Lomonosov et la langue littéraire russe. Bibl. de l'Institut française de Leningrad, 13. Paris, 1933.

Marti 1989 — Marti, R. Handschrift, Text, Textgruppe, Literatur: Untersuchungen zur inneren Gliederung der frühen Literatur aus dem ostslavischen Sprachbereich in den Handschriften des 11. bis 14. Jahrhunderts. Veröffentlichungen der Abteilung für Slavische Sprachen und Literaturen des Osteuropa-Instituts (Slavisches Seminar) an der Freien Universität Berlin, Bd. 68. Wiesbaden, 1989.

Materialy, I–IX — Материалы для истории раскола за первое время его существования. Под ред. Н. И. Субботина. Т. I–IX. М., 1875–1890.

Materialy AN, I–X — Материалы для истории Императорской Академии наук. Под ред. М. И. Сухомлинова. Т. I–X. СПб., 1885–1900.

Mathiesen 1984 — Mathiesen R. The Church Slavonic Language Question: An Overview (IX–XX Centuries). — Aspects of the Slavic Language Question. Ed. by R. Picchio and H. Goldbatt. New Haven, 1984. Vol. I, 45–65.

Mauvillon 1751 — Mauvillon E. Traité général du stile avec un traité particulier du stile épistolaire. Amsterdam, 1751.

Mechkovskaia 1984 — Мечковская Н. Б. Ранние восточнославянские грамматики. Минск, 1984.

Meshcherskii 1962 — Мещерский Н. А. К изучению языка и стиля новгородских берестяных грамот. — Ученые записки Карельского пед. ин-та, т. 12 (1961). Петразаводск, 1962, 84–115.

Meshcherskii 1981 — Мещерский Н. А. История русского литературного языка. Л., 1981.

Mikhail Desnitskii, I–VII — Беседы, в разных местах и в разные времена говоренные... покойным Михаилом, Митрополитом Новгородским, Санктпетербургским... Т. I–VII. СПб., 1820–1824.

Mikhal'chi 1964 — Михальчи Д. Е. И. В. Паузе и его Славяно-русская грамматика. — Известия АН СССР. Серия литературы и языка, 23 (1964), вып. 1, 49–57.

Mikhal'chi 1968 — Михальчи Д. Е. Листы беловой рукописи "Славяно-русской грамматики" И. В. Паузе. — Вопросы грамматики и словообразования. Труды Университета дружбы народов им. П. Лумумбы, т. 41, вып. 4. М., 1968, 150–161.

Mikhal'chi 1969 — Михальчи Д. Е. Славяно-русская грамматика Иоганна Вернера Паузе. Автореферат диссертации на соискание уч. степени доктора филолог. наук. Л., 1969.

Mikhal'chi 1969a — Михальчи Д. Е. Славяно-русская грамматика Иоганна Вернера Паузе. Диссертация на соискание уч. степени доктора филолог. наук. Л., 1969.

Mladenovich 1982 — Младенович А. О неким питањима примања и измене рускословенског језика код Срба. — Зборник за филологију и лингвистику, XXV/2, 1982, 47–81.

Mladenovich 1989 — Младеновић А. Славеносрпски језик. Студије и чланци. Нови Сад, 1989.

Moisei Gumilevskii 1786 — [Моисей Гумилевский]. Разсуждение о вычищении, удобрении и обогащении Россійскаго языка. М., 1786.

Molière, I–II — Oeuvres complètes. Vol. I–II. Bibliothèque de la Pléiade. Paris, 1971.

Morev 1904 — Свящ. Иоанн Морев. «Камень веры» митрополита Стефана Яворского, его место среди отечественных противопротестантских сочинений... СПб., 1904.

Morozov 1965 — Морозов А. Ломоносов и барокко. — Русская литература, 1965, № 2, 70–96.

Morozov 1974 — Морозов А. Судьбы русского классицизма. — Русская литература, 1974, № 1, 13–27.

Morozov 1880 — Морозов П. Феофан Прокопович как писатель. СПб., 1880.

Mosheim 1765 — Mosheim I. L. Heilige Reden. Hamburg, 1765.

Murav'ev 1783 — [Муравьев М. Н.]. Разсуждение о различіи слогов высокаго, великолепнаго, величественнаго, громкаго, надутаго. — Опыт трудов Вольного Російского собрания при Московском Университете. Ч. VI. М., 1783, 1–24.

Naumov 1986 — Naumov A. Служба како жанр. — Научни састанак слависта у Вукове дане, 16 (1986), 5–18.

Nechaev 1956 — Нечаев Н. В. Горнозаводские школы Урала. М., 1956.

Neddermeyer 1988 — Neddermeyer U. Das Mittelalter in der deutschen Historiographie vom 15. bis zum 18. Jahrhundert. Geschichtsgliederung und Epochenverständnis in der frühen Neuzeit. Köln, 1988.

NGB, № 1–614 — Арциховский А. В., Тихомиров М. Н. Новгородские грамоты на бересте (из раскопок 1951 г.), М., 1953; Арциховский А. В. Новгородские грамоты на бересте (из раскопок 1952 г.), М., 1954; Арциховский А. В., Борковский В. И. Новгородские грамоты на бересте (из раскопок 1953–1954 гг.), М., 1958; Арциховский А. В., Борковский В. И. Новгородские грамоты на бересте (из раскопок 1955 г.), М., 1958; Арциховский А. В., Борковский В. И. Новгородские грамоты на бересге (из раскопок 1956–1957 гг.), М., 1963; Арциховский А.В. Новгородские грамоты на бересте (из раскопок 1958–1961 гг.), М., 1963; Арциховский А. В., Янин В. Л. Новгородские грамоты на бересте (из раскопок 1962–1976 гг.), М., 1978; Янин В. Л., Зализняк А. А. Новгородские грамоты на бересте (из раскопок 1977–1983 гг.), М., 1986; Янин В. Л., Зализняк А. А. Новгородские грамоты на бересте (из раскопок 1984–1989 гг.), М., 1993.

Neofit Rilski 1835 — Краткое и ιасное изложенїе за раздѣленїе то, начертанїе то, именованїе то, и произношенїе то на-писмена та, и правила за срицанїе то, просодїа та, и слогать, и за право то чтенїе на греческїа іазыкъ. отъ Неофита Іеромонаха П. П. Рылца. Въ Бѣлиградъ. 1835.

Nicole 1720 — Nicole P. Traité de la vraie et de la fausse beauté dans les oeuvres d'esprit. — Nouveau Recueil des épigrammatistes français, anciens et modernes. Ed. B. de La Martinière. Amsterdam, 1720, vol. II, 169–220.

Nichols and Timberlake 1991 — Nichols J., Timberlake A. Grammaticalization as Retextualization. — Approaches to Grammaticalization. Ed. by E. C.Traugott and B. Heine. Vol. I: Theoretical and Methodological Issues. Typological Studies in Language, vol. 19. Amsterdam, 1991, 129–146.

Nichols 1978 — Nichols R. L. Orthodoxy and Russia's Enlightenment, 1762–1825. — Russian Orthodoxy under the Old Regime. Minneapolis, 1978, 65–89.

Nikitenko, I–III — Никитенко А. В. Дневник. Т. 1–3. М., 1955–1956.

Nikol'skii 1892 — Никольский Н. О литературных трудах митрополита Климента Смолятича, писателя XII века. СПб., 1892.

Nouvelle Methode 1696 — Nouvelle Methode de Messieurs de Port Royal pour apprendre facilement la langue latine. 8-ème ed. Paris, 1696.

Novikov 1772 — Новиков Н. И. Опыт исторического словаря о российских писателях. СПб., 1772.

Obnorskii 1913 — Обнорский С. П. Формы склонения по сатирам Кантемира. — Русский филологический вестник, т. 69 (1913), 48–64.

Obnorskii and Bakhudarov, I–II — Обнорский С. П., Бархударов С. Г. Хрестоматия по истории русского языка. Ч. I–II. М.-Л., 1938–1949.

Obozrenie 1833 — Обозрение исторических сведений о своде законов. СПб., 1833.

ODDC, I–XLIX — Описание документов и дел, хранящихся в архиве Святейшего Правительствующего Синода. Т. I–XLIX. СПб., 1869–1914.

Okenfuss 1980 — Okenfuss M. The Discovery of Childhood in Russia: The Evidence of the Slavic Primer. Newtonville, Mass., 1980.

Orlov 1935 — Орлов А. С. «Тилемахида» В.К.Тредиаковского. — XVIII век. [Сб. 1]. М.-Л., 1935, 5–55.

Ostrovskii and Solov'ev 1915 — Островский А. Н., Соловьев Н. Н. Драматические сочинения. Пг., 1915.

Otten 1973 — Otten F. Die finiten Verbalformen und ihr Gebrauch in der Stepennaja kniga carskogo rodoslovija. Veröffentlichungen der Abteilung für Slavische Sprachen und Literaturen des Osteuropa-Instituts (Slavisches Seminar) an der Freien Univ. Berlin, Bd. 42. Berlin, 1973.

Otten 1985 — Otten F. Untersuchungen zu den Fremd- und Lehnwörtern bei Peter dem Grossen. Slavistische Forschungen, Bd. 50. Köln, 1985.

Panchenko 1973 — Панченко А. М. Русская стихотворная культура XVII века. Л., 1973.

Panchenko 1984 — Панченко А. М. Русская культура в канун петровских реформ. Л., 1984.

Pekarskii, IA, I–II — Пекарский П. П. История императорской Академии наук в Петербурге. Т. I–II. СПб., 1870–1873.

Pekarskii, NL, I–II — Пекарский П. П. Наука и литература при Петре Великом. Т. I–II. СПб., 1862.

Pekarskii 1865 — Пекарский П. Дополнительные известия для биографии Ломоносова. СПб., 1865 [Записки Академии наук, 1865, т. VIII, прилож. № 7].

Pekarskii 1867 — Пекарский П. П. Жизнь и литературная переписка Петра Ивановича Рычкова. СПб., 1867 [Сборник ОРЯС, т. II, № 1].

Pellisson, I–II — Histoire de l'Académie françoise. Par M. M. Pellisson, et d'Olivet. T. I–II. 3-ème ed. Paris, 1743.

Pennington 1980 — Kotošixin G. O Rossii v carstvovanije Alekseja Mixajloviča. Text and Commentary. Ed. by A. E. Pennington. Oxford, 1980.

Perepiska 1911 — Переписка по делу о развращении отставным шт. кап. Митьковым своих дворовых людей... — Старина и новизна, 1911, кн. XV, 184–213.

Perrault 1964 — Parallèle des anciens et des modernes en ce qui regarde les arts et les sciences. Par V. Perrault de l'Académie Française. Mit einer einleitenden Abhandlung von M. R. Jauss. München, 1964.

Peshtich, I–III — Пештич С. Л. Русская историография XVIII века. Ч. I–III. Л., 1961–1971.

Peskov 1989 — Песков А. М. Буало в русской литературе XVIII — первой трети XIX века. М., 1989.

Petr Mogila 1696 — [Петр Могила]. Православное исповедание веры соборныя и апостольския церкве восточныя. М., 1696.

Petrov 1921 — Петров А. Л. Материалы для истории Угорской Руси. Пг., 1921 [Сборник ОРЯС, т. 97, № 2].

Petrov, I–III — Петров В. Сочинения. Ч. I–III. Изд. 2-е. Спб., 1811.

Petrova 1966 — Петрова З. М. Сложные прилагательные в поэзии второй половины XVIII века. — Процессы формирования лексики русского литературного языка (От Кантемира до Карамзина). М.-Л., 1966, 146–204.

Petrukhin 1996 — Петрухин П. В. Нарративная стратегия и употребление глагольных времен в русской летописи XVII века. — Вопросы языкознания, 4 (1996), 62–84.

Petukhov 1916 — Петухов Е. В. Русская литература. Исторический обзор главнейших литературных явлений древнего и нового периода. Древний период. Пг., 1916.

PiB, I–XII — Письма и бумаги императора Петра Великого. Т. I–XII. СПб., М., 1887–1977.

Picchio 1973 — Picchio R. Models and Patterns in the Literary Tradition of Medieval Orthodox Slavdom. — American Contributions to the Seventh International Congress of Slavists. Vol. II. The Hague, 1973, 439–467.

Picchio 1975 — Picchio R. On Russian Humanism: The Philological Revival. — Slavia, XLIV (1975), 2, 161–171.

Picchio 1992 — Пиккио Р. Предисловие о пользе книг церковных М. В. Ломоносова как манифест русского конфессионального патриотизма. — Сборник статей к 70-летию проф. Ю. М. Лотмана. Тарту, 1992, 142–152.

Pis'ma rus. pisatelei 1980 — Письма русских писателей XVIII века. Под ред. Г. П. Макагоненко. Л., 1980.

Plato 1780 — Творений велемудраго Платона часть первая... СПб., 1780.

Platon Levshin 1765 — [Платон Левшин]. Православное Учение или сокращенная Христианская Богословия, для употребления Его Имп. Высочества... Павла Петровича, сочиненная Его Имп. Высочества учителем, Иеромонахом Платоном. М., 1765.

Platon Levshin 1775 — [Платон Левшин]. Инструкция благочинным иереям или протоиереям. М., 1775.

Platon Levshin 1782 — Житие преподобнаго и богоноснаго отца нашего Сергиа Радонежскаго, чудотворца, вкратце собранное, Синодальным членом, Преосвященным Платоном... М., 1782.

Platon Levshin 1891 — [Платон Левшин]. Записки о жизни Платона митрополита московского, им самим писанные, и оконченные Самуилом костромским епископом. — В кн.: Снегирев И. М. Жизнь московского митрополита Платона. Изд. 4-е. Ч. 2. М., 1891, 201–263.

Pleshcheev 1776 — [Плещеев М. И., под псевдонимом Англоман] Предложение о исправлении, распространении и установлении Аглинского языка, в письме к Лорду Оксфорду, Великобританскому главному Казначею. Примечания на предыдущую статью. — Опыт трудов Вольного Российского собрания при Московском университете, ч. III. М., 1776, 1–34, 35–38.

Pletneva 1987 — Плетнева А. А. Из истории формирования нормы русского литературного языка XVIII века. (На материале текстов В. К. Тредиаковского, М. В. Ломоносова, А. П. Сумарокова). Дипломная работа. Московский университет. М., 1987.

Pletneva 1994 — Плетнева А. А. Исправление богослужебных книг в начале XX века. — Славяноведение, 1994, № 2, 100–116.

Podshivalov 1796 — [Подшивалов В. С.]. Сокращенный курс российского слога, изданный Александром Скворцовым. М., 1796.

Podshivalov 1798 — [Подшивалов В. С.]. Краткая русская просодия, или правила, как писать русские стихи. Изданы для воспитанников Благородного Университетского Пансиона. М., 1798.

Poety XVIII veka, I–II — Поэты XVIII века. Сост. Г. П. Макагоненко и И. З. Серман. Библиотека поэта, Большая серия, 2-е изд. Т. I–II. Л., 1972.

Pogodin, I–II — М. П. Погодин. Историко-критические отрывки. Кн. 1–2. М., 1846–1867.

Pogodin 1860 — [М. П. Погодин]. Суд над царевичем Алексеем Петровичем. Эпизод из жизни Петра Великого. М., 1860.

Pokrovskii 1901 — Покровский И. Гавриил, митрополит Новгородский и С.-Петербургский, как церковно-общественный деятель (по поводу столетия с его кончины — 18 мая 1901 г.). — Христианское чтение, 1901, вып. 10 (октябрь), 482–510; вып. 11 (ноябрь), 687–718.

Pokrovskii 1971 — Покровский Н. Н. (изд.). Судные списки Максима Грека и Исака Собаки. М., 1971.

Polevoi, I–II — Полевой Н. А. Очерки русской литературы. Ч. I–II. СПб , 1839.

Polikarpov 1701 — [Поликарпов Ф .П.]. Книга букварь славенскими, греческими, римскими писмены, учитися хотящым, и любомудрие в ползу душеспасительную обрести тщащимся. М., 1701.

Polikarpov 1704 — [Поликарпов Ф. П.]. Лексикон треязычный, сиречь речений славенских, еллиногреческих и латинских сокровище... М., 1704.

Popov 1912 — Попов М. С. Арсений Мацеевич и его дело. СПб., 1912.

Popovskii 1755 — Поповский Н. Речь говоренная в начатии философических лекций... — Ежемесячные сочинения, 1755, т. II (август), 167–176.

Pozdneev 1961 — Позднеев А. В. Русская панегирическая песня в первой четверти XVIII века. — Исследования и материалы по древнерусской литературе. М., 1961, 338–358.

Preniia 1859 — Прения литовского протопопа Лаврентия Зизания с игуменом Ильею и справщиком Григорием по вопросу исправления составленном Лаврентием катехизиса. — Летописи русской литературы и древности. Изд. Н. Тихонравовым. Т. II. М., 1859, 80–100.

Primechaniia 1728–1741 — Месячные исторические, генеалогические и географические Примечания в ведомостях. СПб., 1728–1741 [титул по изданию 1728 г., в последующие годы частично меняется].

Proskurnin 1959 — Проскурнин Н. П. К 250-летию гражданского книгопечатания в России. — XVIII век. Сб. 4. М.-Л., 1959, 376–384.

PSRL, I–XXXIX — Полное собрание русских летописей, издаваемое Археографическою комиссиею. Т. I–XXXIX. СПб., М., 1841–1994.

PSZ, I–XLV — Полное собрание законов Российской империи [Собрание 1-е]. Т. 1–45. СПб., 1830.

PSZ 2, I–LV — Полное собрание законов Российской империи. Собрание 2-е. Т. 1 — 55. СПб., 1830–1884.

Pumpianskii 1937 — Пумпянский Л. В. Тредиаковский и немецкая школа разума. — Западный сборник, I, под ред. В. М. Жирмунского. М.-Л., 1937, 157–186.

Pumpianskii 1941а — Пумпянский Л. В. Кантемир. — История русской литературы. Т. III. М.-Л., 1941, 176–212.

Pumpianskii 1941б — Пумпянский Л. В. Тредиаковский. — История русской литературы. Т. III. М.-Л., 1941, 215–263.

Pumpianskii 1983 — Пумпянский Л. В. Ломоносов и немецкая школа разума. — XVIII век. Сб. 14. Л., 1983, 3–44.

Pumpianskii 1983а — Пумпянский Л. В. К истории русского классицизма (поэтика Ломоносова). — Контекст. 1982. Литературно-теоретические исследования. М., 1983, 303–331.

Pushkin I–XVI — Пушкин А. С. Полное собрание сочинений. Т. I–XVI. М.-Л., 1937–1949.

Pypin 1916 — Пыпин А. Н. Русское масонство XVIII и первая четверть XIX в. Ред. и примеч. Г. В. Вернадского. Пг., 1916.

Rak 1975 — Рак В. Д. Возможный источник стихотворения М. В. Ломоносова «случились вместе два астронома в пиру...» — XVIII век. Сб. 10. Л., 1975, 217–219.

Ransel 1975 — Ransel D. L. The Politics of Catherinian Russia. The Panin Party. New Haven, 1975.

Régnier-Demarais 1700 — Régnier-Demarais F. S. Le premier livre de l'Iliade en vers françois avec une dissertation sut quelques endroits d'Homere. Paris, 1700.

Riazanskaia 1988 — Рязанская Е. Л. Становление нормы русского литературного языка в первой половине XVIII в. и редакция «Немецкой грамматики» М.Шванвица. Дипломная работа. МГУ, 1988.

RIB, I–XXXIX — Русская историческая библиотека, изд. Археографического комиссиею. Т. I–XXXIX. СПб. (Пг., Л.), 1872–1927.

Riker 1995 — Рикер П. Конфликт интерпретаций. Очерки о герменевтике. М., 1995.

Rizhskii 1796 — Рижский И. И. Опыт риторики, сочиненный и преподаваемый в Санктпетербургском горном училище. СПб., 1796.

Rohde 1894 — Rohde E. Psyche. Seelencult und Unsterblichkeitsglaube der Griechen. Freiburg i.B.- Leipzig, 1894.

Rolli 1729 — Rolli P. A. Examen critique de l'essai de M. de Voltaire sur la poésie épique. Paris, 1729.

Rollin, I–II — Rollin Ch. De la manierè d'enseigner et d'étudier les belles lettres, par rapport à l'esprit et au coeur. Vol. I–II. 4-ème éd. Paris, 1732.

Ronsard, I–II — Ronsard P. Oeuvres complètes. Vol. I–II. Bibliotheque de la Pléiade. Paris, 1938.

Rotar 1901 — Ротар И. Епифаний Славинецкий, литературный деятель XVII в. Оттиск из журнала «Киевская старина». Киев, 1901.

Rothe 1984 — Rothe H. Religion und Kultur in den Regionen des russischen Reiches im 18. Jahrhundert. Erster Versuch einer Grundlegung. Rheinisch-Westfälische Akademie der Wissenschaften, Geisteswissen-schaften. Vorträge G267. Opladen,1984.

Rousseau 1823 — Rousseau J. B. Oeuvres poétiques. T. I–II. Paris, 1823.

Rubinshtein 1941 — Рубинштейн Н. Л. Русская историография. М., 1941.

Runkevich 1900 — Рункевич С. Г. Учреждение и первоначальное устройство Святейшего Правительствующего Синода (1721 — 1725). СПб., 1900.

RZ, I–IX — Российское законодательство X–XX веков. В девяти томах. Т. I–IX. М., 1984–1993.

Rzhevskii 1763 — [Ржевский А. А.]. О Московском наречии. — Свободные часы, 1763, февраль, 67–75.

SAR, I–VI — Словарь Академии Российской. Ч. I–VI. СПб., 1789–1794.

Sazonova 1987 — Сазонова Л. И. От русского панегирика XVII в. к оде М. В.Ломоносова. — Ломоносов и русская литература. М., 1987, 103–126.

Scott 1831 — The Poetical Works of Sir Walter Scott complete in one volume. Paris, 1831.

Scudery 1637 — Avtres Oevvres de M. de Scvdery. Paris, chez A. Covbre..., 1637.

Scudery 1654 — Alaric ov Rome Vaincuë. Poëme Heroïqve... Par M. de Scvdery... Paris, chez A. Covbre, 1654.

Semevskii 1885 — Семевский М. И. Слово и дело! 1700–1725. Изд. 3-е, вновь пересмотренное. СПб., 1885.

Senkovskii, I–IX — Сенковский О. И. (Барон Брамбеус). Собрание сочинений. Т. I–IX. СП6., 1858–1859.

Serman 1962 — Серман И. З. Тредиаковский и просветительство (1730-е годы). — XVIII век. С6. 5. М.-Л., 1962, 205–222.

Serman 1985 — Серман И. З. Бова и русская литература. — Slavica Hierosolymitana, VII (1985), 163–170.

Seznec 1961 — Seznec J. The Survival of the Pagan Gods. The Mythological Tradition and Its Place in Renaissance Humanism and Art. Trans. from the French by B. F.Sessions. New York, 1961.

SFA , I^2–II^2 — Nouveau dictionnaire de l'Académie françoise. 2nde éd. T. I–II. Paris, 1718.

SFA , I^3–II^3 — Dictionnaire de l'Académie françoise. 3ème éd. T. I–II. Paris, 1740.

Schenk 1972 — Schenk D. Studien zur anakreontischen Ode in der russischen Literatur des Klassizismus und der Empfindsamkeit. Osteuropastudien der Hochschulen des Landes Hessen, Reihe III, Frankfurter Abhandlunden zur Slavistik, Bd. 13. Frankfurt a. M., 1972.

Schottelius 1663 — Schottelius J.G. Ausführliche Arbeit von der Teutschen Haubt-Sprache. Braunschweig 1663 [Neudruk. Tübingen, 1967].

Seemann 1987 — Seemann K.-D. Zum Verhäl'stnis von Narration und Gattung im slavischen Mittelalter. — Gattung und Narration in den äl'steren slavischen Literaturen. Ed. K. — D. Seemann. Wiesbaden, 1987, 207–221.

Shevchenko 1981 — Ševčenko I. Levels of Style in Byzantine Prose. — XVI. Internationaler Byzantinistenkongress. Wien, 4.-9. Oktober 1981. Akten, I/1. Jahrbuch der Österreichischen Byzantinistik, 31/I. Wien, 1981, 289–312.

Shchapov 1976 — Древнерусские княжеские уставы XI–XV вв. Изд. подготовил Я. Н. Щапов. М., 1976.

Shcherbatov, I–II — Щербатов М. М. Сочинения. Под ред. И. П. Хрущева. СПб., 1896–1898.

Sheremetevskii 1914 — Шереметевский В. Гедеон Криновский. — Русский биографический словарь. Т. IV (Гааг — Гербель). М., 1914, 324–326.

Sheremetevskii 1914a — Шереметевский В. Гавриил Петров. — Русский биографический словарь. Т. IV (Гааг — Гербель). М., 1914, 43–47.

Shevelov 1951 — Šerech Y. [Shevelov G.]. Stefan Yavorsky and the Conflict of Ideologies in the Age of Peter the Great. — The Slavonic and East European Review, vol. XXX (1951), № 74, 40–62.

Shevyrev 1854 — Шевырев С. Отрывки оригинальные и переводные Н. М. Карамзина. — Москвитянин, 1854, № 3–4, 6–7, 9–12.

Shishkin 1989 — Шишкин А. Б. Судьбы «Псалтири» Тредиаковского. — В кн.: Тредиаковский 1989, 519–535.

Shishkov, I–XVI — Шишков А .С. Собрание сочинений и переводов. Ч. I–XVI. СПб., 1818–1834.

Shishkov 1813 — Шишков А. С. Опыт о российских писателях для чтения в «Беседе» (Феофан). — Чтение в Беседе любителей российского слова, 1813, № 8, 3–64.

Shishkov 1818 — Шишков А. С. Рассуждение о старом и новом слоге российского языка. Изд. 2-е. СПб., 1818.

Shitsgal 1959 — Шицгал А. Г. Русский гражданский шрифт. 1708–1958. М., 1959.

Shitsgal 1974 — Шицгал А. Г. Русский типографский шрифт. Вопросы истории и практика применения. М., 1974.

Shmurlo 1912 — Шмурло Е. Петр Великий в оценке современников и потомства. Вып. I (XVIII век). СПб., 1912.

Shvanvits 1730 — [Шванвиц М.] Немецкая грамматика из разных авторов собрана и российской юности в пользу издана от учителя немецкого языка при Санктпетербургской гимназии. СПб., 1730.

Shvanvits 1734 — [Шванвиц М.] Немецкая грамматика, собранная из разных авторов и в пользу Санктпетербургской гимназии вторым тиснением изданная. СПб., 1734.

Shvanvits 1745 — [Шванвиц М.] Немецкая грамматика собранная прежде из разных авторов, а ныне для употребления Санктпетербургской гимназии вновь пересмотренная. СПб., 1745.

Signorini 1988 — Signorini S. I concetti di «uso» e di «norma» nella teoria linguistica di M. Lomonosov. — Europa orientalis 7 (1988), 515–535.

Signorini 1991 — Signorini S. Lomonosov e la teoria della frase. — Probemi di morfosintassi delle lingue slave. 2. Atti del II° Seminario di Studi. Bologna 28, 29 e 30 settembre 1989. Bologna, 1991, 155–167.

Simeon Polotskii 1667 — [Симеон Полоцкий]. Жезл правления. М., 1667.

Simeon Polotskii 1681 — [Симеон Полоцкий]. Обед душевный. М., 1681.

Simon Todorskii 1743 — Слово в высочайшее присутствие ея священнейшаго имп. величества... Елисаветы Петровны императрицы всея России, в высокоторжественный день рождения его имп. Высочества государя наследника благовернаго великаго князя Петра Феодоровича... проповеданное Его Имп. Высочества придворным учителем Иеромонахом Симоном Тодорским в придворной церькве в Санктпетербурге Февраля 10 дня 1743 года. СПб., 1743.

Simon Todorskii 1745 — Божие особенное благословение имже всегда благословил бог и нане благословляет Всепресветлейший дом Петра Великаго перваго Императора всея России в день высочайшаго бракосочетания Его Имп. Высочества внука Петра Перваго благовернаго государя и великаго князя Петра Феодоровича наследника престола всероссийскаго и прочая с Ея Имп. Высочеством благоверною Государынею и великою княгинею Екатериною Алексеевною... проповеданное... Симоном Епископом Псковским и Нарвским 1745 года Августа 4 дня. СПб., 1745.

Sipovskii 1899 — Сиповский В. В. Н. М. Карамзин, автор «Писем русского путешественника». СПб., 1899.

Sipovskii 1905 — Сиповский В. В. Русские повести XVII–XVIII вв. СПб., 1905.

Skazaniia 1981 — Сказания о начале славянской письменности. Вступительная статья, перевод и комментарии Б. Н. Флори. М., 1981.

Skvortsov 1890 — Скворцов Д. Дионисий Зобниновский, Архимандрит Троицкого-Сергиева монастыря. Тверь, 1890.

Sobesednik, I–XVI — Собеседник любителей российского слова. Ч. I–XVI. СПб., 1783–1784.

Sobolevskii 1890 — Соболевский А. И. Когда начался у нас ложно-классицизм? — Библиограф, год 6-й (1890), № 1.

Sobolevskii 1903 — Соболевский А. И. Переводная литература Московской Руси XIV–XVII вв. СПИ., 1903 [Сб. ОРЯС, т. 74, № 1].

Sobolevskii 1908 — Соболевский А. И. Из переводной литературы петровской эпохи. Библиографические материалы. СПб., 1908. [Сборник ОРЯС, т. 84, № 3]

Sobolevskii 1980 — Соболевский А. И. История русского литературного языка. Л., 1980.

Sohier, I–II — Sohier Jean. Grammaire et Methode Russes et Françoises 1724. Факсимильное издание под ред. и с предисловием Б. А. Успенского. Bd. I–II. Specimina philologiae slavicae, Bd. 69–70. München, 1987.

Solosin 1913 — Солосин И. Отражение языка и образов Св. Писания и книг богослужебных в стихотворениях Ломоносова. — Известия ОРЯС, XVIII (1913), кн. 2, 238–293.

Solov'ev, I–XV — Соловьев С. М. История России. Кн. I–XV. М., 1962–1966.

Soluianova 1989 — Солуянова Е. Г. Язык русских исторических сочинений конца XVII — начала XVIII вв. Диссертация на соискание уч. степени кандидата филолог. наук. М. (МГУ), 1989.

Sorokin 1949 — Сорокин Ю. С. Разговорная и народная речь в «Словаре Академии Российской» (1789–1794). Материалы и исследования по истории русского литературного языка. Т. I. М.-Л., 1949, 95–160.

Sorokin 1976 — Сорокин Ю. С. Стилистическая теория и речевая практика молодого Тредиаковского (перевод романа П.Тальмана «Езда в остров любви»). — Венок Тредиаковскому. Волгоград, 1976, 45–54.

Sorokin 1982 — Сорокин Ю. С. У истоков литературного языка нового типа (Перевод «Разговоров о множестве миров» Фонтенеля). — Литературный язык XVIII века. Проблемы стилистики. Л., 1982, 52–85.

Sove 1970 — Сове Б. И. Проблема исправления богослужебных книг в России в XIX–XX веках. — Богословские труды, Сб. V. М., 1970, 25–68.

Smentsovskii 1899 — Сменцовский М. Братья Лихуды. Опыт исследования из истории церковного просвещения и церковной жизни конца XVII и начала XVIII веков. СПб., 1899.

Smirnov 1971 — Смирнов А. А. К проблеме соотношений русского предклассицизма и гуманистической теории поэзии. Ф. Прокопович и Ю. Ц. Скалигер. — Проблемы теории и истории литературы. Сборник статей, посвященных памяти проф. А.Н.Соколова. М., 1971, 67–73.

Smirnov 1910 — Смирнов Н. Западное влияние на русский язык в петровскую эпоху. СПб., 1910 [Сборник ОРЯС, т. 38, № 2].

Smirnov 1855 — Смирнов С. К. История Московской славяно-греколатинской академии. М., 1855.

Smirnov 1867 — Смирнов С. К. История Троицкой Лаврской семинарии. М., 1867.

Smolina 1981 — Смолина К. П. Развитие лексики русского литературного языка в Петровскую эпоху (конец XVII — начало XVIII в.). — История лексики русского литературного языка конца XVII — начала XVIII века. Под ред. Ф. П. Филина. М., 1981, 25–115.

Smotritskii 1619 — Грамматики славенския правилное синтагма. Потщанием... Мелетия Смотрицкого. В Еве, 1619. Цит. по изд.: М. Смотрицький. Граматика. Київ, 1979.

Smotritskii 1648 — [Мелетий Смотрицкий]. Грамматика. М., 1648.

Smotritskii 1721 — [Мелетий Смотрицкий]. Грамматика. М., 1721.

Stupperich 1940 — Stupperich R. Feofan Prokopovič und seine akademische Wirksamkeit in Kiev. — Zeitschrift für slavische Philologie, Bd. 17 (1940), 70–102.

Speranskii 1844 — Сперанский М. Правила высшего красноречия. СПб., 1844.

Sreznevskii, I–III — Срезневский И. И. Материалы для словаря древнерусского языка по письменным памятникам. Т. I–III. СПб., 1893–1912.

SRIa, I–XVII — Словарь русского языка XI–XVII веков. Т. I–XXI. М., 1975–1995 (продолжающееся издание).

SRIO, I–CXLVIII — Сборник Русского исторического общества. Т. I — CXLVIII. СПб. (Пг.), 1867–1916.

Stang 1952 — Stang Chr. S. La langue du livre Ученіе и хитрость ратнаго строенія пѣхотныхъ людей. 1647. Une monographie linguistique. Skrifter utgitt av Det Norske Videnskaps-Akademii i Oslo. II. Hist.- Filos. KIasse. 1952, № 1. Oslo, 1952.

Strahlenberg 1730 — Strahlenberg Ph. J. von. Das Nord- und Ostliche Theil von Europa und Asia, In so weit solches Das gantze Rußische Reich mit Sibirien und der grossen Tatarey in sich begreiffet, In einer Historisch-Geographischen Beschreibung der alten und neuern Zeiten, und vielen andern unbekannten Nachrichten vorgestellet... Stockholm, 1730.

Strakhova 1986 — Страхова О. Б. К вопросу о греческой филологической традиции в восточнославянской книжной среде. (Страничка из истории церковнославянского языка конца XVII — начала XVIII века). — Советское славяноведение, 1986, № 4, 66–75.

Strakhova 1988 — Страхова О. Б. Из истории церковнославянской окказиональной лексики конца XVII в. — Этимология 1985. М., 1988, 57–62.

Strakhova 1990 — Strakhov O. B. Attitudes to Greek Language and Culture in Seventeenth-Century Muscovy. — Modern Greek Studies Yearbook, University of Minnesota. Vol. 6 (1990), 123–155.

Stefan Iavorskii 1841–1842 — [Стефан Яворский]. Камень Веры Православным Церкве святыя сыном на утверждение и духовное созидание... Т. I–III. М., 1841–1842.

Strycek 1976 — Strycek A. La Russie de lumières. Denis Fonvizine. Paris, 1976.

STsRIa, I–IV — Словарь церковно-славянского и русского языка, составленный Вторым отделением Имп. Академии наук. Т. I–IV. СПб., 1847.

Sukhomlinov, I–VIII — Сухомлинов М. И. История Российской Академии. Вып. I–VIII. СПб., 1874–1888.

Sukhomlinov 1865–1866 — Сухомлинов М. И. Материалы для истории просвещения в России в царствование императора Александра I. б. м., б. г. [отд. оттиск из Журнала Министерства народного просвещения, 1865–1866].

Sukhomlinov 1908 — Сухомлинов М. И. Исследования по древней русской литературе. СПб., 1908 [Сб. ОРЯС, т. 85, № 1].

Sumarokov 1748 — Две Епистолы, Александра Сумарокова. В перьвой предлагается о Руском языке, а во второй о Стихотворстве. СПб., 1748.

Sumarokov 1769 — Сумароков А. П. Разные стихотворения. СПб., 1769.

Sumarokov 1773–1774 — Сумароков А. П. Стихотворения духовные. Ч. I. Стихотворения духовные. Ч. II. Некоторые духовные сочинения. Ч. III. Дополнение к Духовным стихотворениям. СПб., 1773–1774.

Sumarokov 1774 — Сумароков А. П. Эклоги. СПб., 1774.

Sumarokov 1774а — [Сумароков А. П.] Наставление хотящим быти писателями от Александра Сумарокова. СПб., 1774.

Sumarokov, I–X — Сумароков А. П. Полное собрание всех сочинений. Ч. I–X. Изд. 2-е. М., 1787.

Sumarokov 1957 — Сумароков А. П. Избранные произведения. Библиотека поэта, Большая серия. Изд. 2-е. Л., 1957.

Sumkina 1981 — Памятники московской деловой письменности XVIII века. Издание подготовила А. И. Сумкина. М., 1981.

Svetov 1779 — В. С. [Светов В.]. Некоторыя общая примечания о языке российском. — Академические известия на 1779 г. Ч. III, сентябрь, 77–91.

Talev 1973 — Talev I. Some Problems of the Second South Slavic Influence in Russia. München, 1973.

Talmoudi 1984 — Talmoudi F. The Diglossia Situation in North Africa: A Study of Classical Arabic... Orientalia gothoburgensia, vol. 8. Göteborg, 1984.

Tass 1772 — Тасс Т. Освобожденный Иерусалим, прозаическая поэма. Ч. 1–2. Перев. с франц. М. Попова. СПб., 1772.

Tatishchev, I–VII — Татищев В. Н. История Российская. Т. I–VII. Изд. 2-е. М.-Л., 1962–1968.

Tatishchev 1979 — Татищев В. Н. Избранные произведения. Под общей ред. С. Н. Валка. Л., 1979.

Tatishchev 1990 — Татищев Василий Никитич. Записки. Письма 1717–1750 гг. Научное наследство, т. 14. М., 1990.

Teplov 1868 — [Теплов Г. Н.]. Записка о Тредиаковском [1755 г.]. — Записки Имп. Академии наук, т. XIV (1868), кн. 1, 71–80.

Terlaich 1801 — Нума или процветающий Рим. С российскаго преобличений Григорием Терлаичем. В Будине Граде, 1801.

Ternovskii 1864 — Терновский Ф. М. Стефан Яворский (Биографический очерк). — Труды Киевской духовной академии, 1864, т. I, 36–70, 237–290.

Ternovskii 1879 — Терновский Ф. Очерки из истории русской иерархии в XVIII в. Стефан Яворский. — Древняя и новая Россия, год 5 (1879), т. II, № 8, 305–326.

Tetzner 1958 — Tetzner J. Theophan Prokopovič und die russische Frühaufklärung. — Zeitschrift für Slawistik, 1958, n. 3, 351–368.

Tikhonravov, I–III — Тихонравов Н. С. Сочинения. Т. I–III. М., 1898.

Tikhonravov 1858 — Тихонравов Н. С. Кирьяк Кондратович. Переводчик прошлого столетия. — Библиографические записки, 1858, № 8, 225–236.

Tikhonravov 1874, I–II — Тихонравов Н. Русские драматические произведения 1672–1725 годов. Т. I–II. СПб., 1874.

Timberlake 1995 — Timberlake A. Avvakum's Aorists. — Russian Linguistics 19 (1995), 25–43.

Timberlake 1996 — Timberlake A. «Чему кси слѣпилъ бра͡т свои»: Templates and the Development of Animacy. — Russian Linguistics 20 (1996).

Titlinov 1913 — Титлинов Б. Феофан Прокопович. — Русский биографический словарь, т. XXV (Яблоновский — ѳомин). СПб., 1913, 399–448.

Titlinov 1916 — Титлинов Б. В. Гавриил Петров, митрополит новгородский и санктпетербургский. Пг., 1916.

Titov 1907 — Титов Ф. К биографии Гедеона Криновского. Казань, 1907.

Tolstoi 1886 — Толстой Д. А. Городские училища в царствование Императрицы Екатерины II. СПб., 1886.

Tolstoi 1963 — Толстой Н. И. Взаимоотношение локальных типов древнеславянского литературного языка позднего периода (вторая половина XVI–XVII вв.). — Славянское языкознание. Доклады советской делегации. V Международный съезд славистов... М., 1963, 230–272.

Tolstoi 1976 — Толстой Н. И. Старинные представления о народно-языковой базе древнеславянского литературного языка (XVI–XVII вв.). — Вопросы русского языкознания, вып. 1. М., 1976, 177–204.

Tolstoi 1978 — Толстой Н. И. Однос старог српског књишког језика према старом словенском језику. — Научни састанак слависта у Вукове дане, VIII (1978), 15–25.

Tomashevskii 1959 — Томашевский Б. В. Стилистика и стихосложение. Курс лекций. Л., 1959.

Torzhestvennaia vrata... 1703 — Торжественная врата, Вводящая в храм безсмертныя славы... Поставленая Лета господня 1703-го месяца ноемвриа в 9 день. М., 1703.

Trediakovskii, I–III — Тредиаковский В. К. Сочинения. Т. I–III. СПб., 1849.

Trediakovskii, DI, I–X — Древняя история об египтянах и карфагенянах об ассирианах и вавилонянах о мидянах, персах о македонянах и о греках. Соч. чрез г. Ролленя... А ныне с фр. перев. чрез Василья Тредиаковского. Т. I–X. СПб., 1749–1762.

Trediakovskii, RI, I–XVI — Римская история... сочиненная г. Ролленем... а с Французского переведенная тщанием и трудами В.Тредиаковского... Т. I–XVI. СПб., 1761–1767.

Trediakovskii 1730 — [Тальман П. (Paul Tallement)]. Езда в остров любви. Переведена с французскаго на руской чрез студента Василья Тредиаковскаго. СПб., 1730.

Trediakoivskii 1734 — Тредиаковский В. Ода торжественная о здаче города Гданска. СПб., 1734.

Trediakovskii 1735 — Тредиаковский В. К. Новый и краткий способ к сложению российских стихов с определениями до сего надлежащих званий. СПб., 1735.

Trediakovskii 1735a — Тредиаковский В. К. Речь... в Санктпитерфургской имп. Академии наук к членам Российского собрания, во время первого оных заседания, марта 14 дня 1735 года. СПб., 1735.

Trediakovskii 1737 — Военное состояние Отгоманския империи. Сочинено чрез графа де Марсильи... [Перевод и примечания В. К.Тредиаковского]. Ч. I. СПб., 1737.

Trediakovskii 1745 — Тредиаковский В. Слово о богатом, различном, искусном и несхотсвенном витийстве. СПб., 1745.

Trediakovskii 1748 — Тредиаковский В. К. Разговор между чужестранным человеком и российским об ортографии старинной и новой и о всем что принадлежит к сей материи. СПб., 1748.

Trediakovskii 1751 — Аргенида повесть героическая сочиненная Иоанном Барклаем и с латинскаго на славено-российский переведенная от В. Тредиаковскаго. Т. I–II. СПб., 1751.

Trediakovskii 1752 — Тредиаковский В. Сочинения и переводы как стихами так и прозою... Т. I–II. СПб., 1752.

Trediakovskii 1766 — Тилемахида или Странствование Тилемаха сына Одисеева описанное в составе ироическия пиимы Василием Тредиаковским... Т. I–II. СПб., 1766.

Trediakovskii 1773 — Тредиаковский В. Три разсуждения о трех главнейших древностях российских. СПб., 1773.

Trediakovskii 1849 — Тредиаковский В. К. Избранные произведения. М., 1849.

Trediakovskii 1851 — Просьба Тредиаковского в Сенат. — Москвитянин, 1851, № 11, 227–236 [Июнь, кн. 1].

Trediakovskii 1935 — Тредиаковский В. К. Стихотворения. Библиотека поэта, Большая серия, 1-е изд. Л., 1935.

Trediakovskii 1963 — Тредиаковский В. К. Избранные произведения. Библиотека поэта, Большая серия, 2-е изд. М.-Л., 1963.

Trediakovskii 1989 — Vasilij Kirillovič Trediakovskij Psalter 1753. Erstausgabe. Besorgt und kommentiert von A.Levitsky. Hrsg. von R. Olesch und H. Rothe. Russische Psalmenübertragungen, 2; Biblia Slavica. Serie III. Ostslavische Bibeln, Bd. 4b. Paderborn, 1989.

Trésor 1988 — Trésor de la langue française. T. XIII. Paris, 1988.

Trubetzkoy 1973 — Trubetzkoy N. S. Vorlesungen über die altnassische Literatur. Studia historica et philologica. Sectio slavica, 1. Firenze, 1973.

Trublet 1793 — [Trublet, Nicolas-Charles-Joseph, Abbé.] Размышления о красноречии вообще, и особенно о проповедническом красноречии. Из сочинений Г. Аббата Трюблета, переведенныя в Воронежской Семинарии, для пользы юношества, воспитывающегося в той же Семинарии. М., 1793.

Tschižewskij 1940 — Čyževskyj D. Literarische Lesefrüchte VIII. 69. Zu den Komposita in der Sprache Tredjakovskijs. — Zeitschrift für slavische Philologie, XVII (1940), 114–120.

Tschižewskij 1960 — Tschižewskij D. History of Russian Literature from the Eleventh Century to the End of the Baroque. s' Gravenhage, 1960.

Tschižewskij 1970 — Tschižewskij D. Das Baroque in der russischen Literatur. — Slavische Baroqueliteratur. Bd. 1. Hrsg. D. Tschižewskij. München, 1970.

Tschižewskij 1970a — Tschižewskij D. Zu Lomonovs Theorie der drei Stilarten. — Die Welt der Slaven, XV (1970), 3, 286–288.

Tselunova 1985 — Целунова Е. А. Псалтырь 1683 года в переводе Авраамия Фирсова (филологическое исследование памятника). Автореферат диссертации на соискание уч. степени кандидата филолог. наук. М., 1985.

Tselunova 1988 — Целунова Е. А. Псалтырь 1683 г. на «простом словенском» языке. — Ученые записки вузов Литовской ССР. Языкознание, 39 (2). Вильнюс, 1988, 112–118.

Tselunova 1989 — Псалтырь 1683 года в переводе Авраамия Фирсова. Подготовка текста, составление словоуказателя и предисловие Е. А. Целуновой. Slavistische Beiträge, Bd. 243. München, 1989.

Tsoinska 1988 — Цойнска Р. Съпоставително разглеждане на някои едици в граматичните трудове на Неофит Рилски. — Славистичен сборник. По случай X Международен конгрес на славистите — София, 1988, 73–84.

Uhlenbruch 1985 — Fedor Kvetnickij. Clavis poetica. Eine Handschrift der Leninbiblothek Moskau aus dem Jahre 1732 mit einer Einleitung hrsg. von B. Uhlenbruch. Slavistische Forschungen, Bd.27. Rhetorica slavica, Bd. III. Köln, 1985.

Unbegaun 1935 — Unbegaun B. Les débuts de la langue littéraire chez les Serbes. Travaux publiés par l'Institut d'études slaves, XV. Paris, 1935.

Unbegaun 1935a — Unbegaun B. La langue russe au XVIe siécle (1500–1550). I. La flexion des noms. Bibiothèque de L'Institut français de Leningrad, t. XVI. Paris, 1935.

Unbegaun 1958 — Unbegaun B. O. Russian Grammars before Lomonosov. — Oxford Slavonic Papers, VIII (1958), 98–116.

Unbegaun 1965 — Unbegaun B. O. Le russe littéraire est-il d'origine russe? — Revue des études slaves, 44 (1965), 19–28.

Unbegaun 1965a — Унбегаун Б. О. Язык русского права. — На темы русские и общие. Сборник статей и материалов в честь проф. Н. С.Тимашева. Нью Йорк, 1965, 178–184.

Unbegaun 1969 — Drei russische Grammatiken des 18. Jahrhunderts. Nachdruck der Ausgaben von 1706, 1731 und 1750 mit einer Einleitung von B. O. Unbegaun. Slavische Propyläen, Bd. 55. München, 1969.

Unbegaun 1970 — Унбегаун Б. О. Происхождение русского литературного языка. — Новый журнал [Нью Йорк], кн. 100, 1970, 306–319.

Unbegaun 1971 — Унбегаун Б. О. Русский литературный язык: проблемы и задача его изучения. — Поэтика и стилистика русской литературы. Памяти академика В. В. Виноградова. Л., 1971.

Upotreblenie knigi Psaltyr' 1857 — [Неизв. автор] Употребление книги Псалтырь в древнем быту русского народа. — Православный собеседник, 1857, 814–856.

Uspenskii 1968 — Успенский Б. А. Архаическая система церковнославянского произношения (Из истории литургического произношения в России). М., 1968.

Uspenskii 1970 — Успенский Б. А. Старинная система чтения по складам (Глава из истории русской грамоты). — Вопросы языкознания, 1970, но. 5, 80–100.

Uspenskii 1971 — Успенский Б. А. Книжное произношение в России. Опыт исторического исследования. Автореферат диссертации на соискание уч. степени доктора филолог. наук. М., 1971.

Uspenskii 1975 — Успенский Б. А. Первая русская грамматика на родном языке. Доломоносовский период отечественной русистики. М., 1975.

Uspenskii 1976 — Успенский Б. А. Historia sub specie semioticae. — Культурное наследие Древней Руси: Истоки, становление, традиция. М., 1976.

Uspenskii 1982 — Успенский Б. А. Царь и самозванец: самозванчество в России как культурно-исторический феномен. — Художественный язык средневековья. М., 1982, 201–235.

Uspenskii 1983 — Успенский Б. А. Языковая ситуация Киевской Руси и ее значение для истории русского литературного языка. М., 1983.

Uspenskii 1984 — Uspensky B. A. The Language Situation and Linguistic Consciousness in Muscovite Rus': the Perception of Church Slavic and Russian. — Medieval Russian Culture. Ed. by H. Birnbaum and M. S. Flier. Berkeley, 1984, 365–385.

Uspenskii 1984a — Успенский Б. А. К истории одной эпиграммы Тредиаковского (Эпизод языковой полемики середины XVIII в.). — Russian Linguistics, vol. VIII (1984), № 2, 75–127.

Uspenskii 1985 — Успенский Б. А. Из истории русского литературного языка XVIII — начала XIX века. Языковая программа Карамзина и ее исторические корни. М., 1985.

Uspenskii 1987 — Успенский Б. А. История русского литературного языка (XI–XVII вв.). München, 1987.

Uspenskii 1992 — Успенский Б. А. Доломоносовские грамматики русского языка (итоги и перспективы). — Доломоносовский период русского литературного языка. The Pre-Lomonosov Period of the Russian Literary Language (Материалы конференции на Фагеруде, 20–25 мая 1989 г.). Slavica Suecana, Series B, vol. 1. Stockholm, 1992, 63–169.

Uspenskii 1994 — Успенский Б. А. Краткий очерк истории русского литературного языка (XI–XIX вв.). М., 1994.

Uspenskii and Zhivov 1983 — Uspenskij B. A., Živov V.M. Zur Spezifik des Barock in Rußland. Das Verfahren der Åquivokation in der russischen Poesie des 18. Jahrhunderts. — Slavische Barockliteratur II. Gedenkschrift für Dmitrij Tschižewskij (1894–1977). Hrsg. R. Lachmann. Forum Slavicum, Bd. 54. München, 1983, 25–56.

Uspenskii and Shishkin 1990 — Успенский Б .А., Шишкин А. Б. Тредиаковский и янсенисты. — Символ, вып. 23. Париж, 1990, 105–264.

Ustrialov, I–VI — Устрялов Н. Г. История царствования Петра Великого. Т. I–IV, VI. СПб., 1858–1859.

Vachek 1964 — Vachek J. (ed.). A Prague School Reader in Linguistics. Bloomington, 1964.

Varenii 1718 — [Варений Б.]. Географиа генералная... Преведена с латинска языка на российски... М., 1718.

Vasilevskaia 1967 — Василевская И. К методологии изучения заимствований (Русская лексикографическая практика XVIII в.). — Известия АН СССР. Серия литературы и языка, т. XXVI (1967), № 2, 165–171.

Vaugelas, I–II — [Vaugelas C. F. de] Remarques sur la langue françoise par Vaugelas. Nouvelle éd. ... par A. Chassang. Vol. I–II. Versailles, 1880.

Vaugelas 1647 — Vaugelas C. F. de. Remarques sur la langue françoise vtiles a cevx qvi veviant bien parler e bien escrire. Paris, 1647. Цит. по изд.: Vaugelas C.F. de. Remarques sur la langue françoise. Facsimile de l'éd. originale. Introduction bibiographique, index par J. Streicher. Paris, 1934.

Verkhovskoi, 1–I1 — Верховской П. В. Учреждение Духовной Коллегии и Духовный Регламент. Т. 1–II. Ростов-на-Дону, 1916.

Veselitskii 1972 — Веселитский В. В. Отвлеченная лексика в русском литературном языке XVIII — начала XIX в. М., 1972.

Veselitskii 1974 — Веселитский В. В. Антиох Кантемир и развитие русского литературного языка. М., 1974.

Vesti-kuranty 1983 — Вести-куранты. 1648–1650 гг. Под ред. С. И. Коткова. М., 1983.

Viau, I–II — Théophile [de Viau]. Oeuvres complètes. T. I–II. Paris, 1855–1856.

Viazemskii, I–XII — Вяземский П. А. Полное собрание сочинений. Т. I–XII. СПб., 1878–1896.

Viëtor 1923 — K. Viëtor. Geschichte der deutschen Ode. München, 1923.

Vinogradov 1935 — Виноградов В. В. Язык Пушкина. Пушкин и история русского литературного языка. М.-Л., 1935.

Vinogradov 1938 — Виноградов В. В. Очерки по истории русского литературного языка XVII–XIX вв. Изд. 2-е. М., 1938.

Vinogradov 1949 — Виноградов В. В. Из наблюдений над языком и стилем И. И. Дмитриева. — Материалы и исследования по истории русского литературного языка. Т. 1. М.-Л., 1949, 160–278.

Vinogradov 1953 — Виноградов В. В. О некоторых вопросах русской исторической лексикологии. — Известия АН СССР. Отделение литературы и языка, т. XII (1953), вып. 3, 185–210.

Vinogradov 1958 — Виноградов В. В. Основные проблемы изучения образования и развития древнерусского литературного языка. М., 1958 [IV Международный съезд славистов. Доклады].

Vinogradov 1969 — Виноградов В. В. О новых исследованиях по истории русского литературного языка. — Вопросы языкознания, 1969, №. 2, 3–18.

Vinogradov 1978 — Виноградов В. В. Избранные труды. История русского литературного языка. М., 1978.

Vinokur 1948 — Винокур Г. О. Орфографическая теория Тредиаковского. — Известия АН СССР. Отделение литературы и языка, т. VII (1948), вып. 2, 141–158.

Vinokur 1959 — Винокур Г. О. Избранные работы по русскому языку. М., 1959.

Vinokur 1983 — Винокур Г. О. Язык литературы и литературный язык. — Контекст. 1982. М., 1983, 255–282.

Vladimirskii-Budanov 1874 — Владимирский-Буданов М. Государство и народное образование в России XVIII-го века. Ч. I. Система профессионального образования (от Петра I до Екатерины II). Ярославль, 1874.

Vladykin 1774 — Владыкин И. Ода Е. И. В. великой монархине Екатерине Алексеевне... на вожделенный и всерадостный мир между Империею Российскою и Портою Отоманскою заключенный... СПб., 1774.

Vnutrennii byt, I–II — Внутренний быт Русского государства с 17-го декабря 1740 года по 25-е ноября 1741 года, по документам, хранящимся в Московском архиве Министерства юстиции. Кн. I–II. М., 1880–1886.

Voltaire, I — Voltaire F. M. A. Oeuvres complètes, avec des notes et une notice historique sur la vie de Voltaire. Vol. I–XII. Paris, 1835–1837.

Vomperskii 1968 — Вомперский В. П. Ненапечатанная статья В.К.Тредиаковского «О множественном прилагательных целых имен окончении». — Филологические науки, 1968, No. 5, 81–90.

Vomperskii 1970 — Вомперский В. П. Стилистическое учение М.В.Ломоносова и теория трех стилей. М., 1970.

Vomperskii 1988 — Вомперский В. П. Риторики в России XVII–XVIII вв. М., 1988.

Vostokov 1842 — Востоков А. Описание русских и словенских рукописей Румянцевского музеума. СПб., 1842.

Winter 1958 — Winter E. Ein Bericht von Johann Werner Paus aus dem Jahre 1732 über seine Tätigkeit auf dem Gebiete der russischen Sprache, Literatur und der Geschichte Russlands. — Zeitschrift für Slawistik, 1958, n. 3, 744–770.

Winter 1966 — Винтер Е. Феофан Прокопович и начало русского просвещения. — XVIII век. С6. VII. Л., 1966, 43–46.

Wittram, 1–11 — Wittram R. Peter I. Czar und Keiser. Zur Geschichte Peters des Grossen in seiner Zeit. Bd. I–II. Göttingen, 1964.

Worth 1983a — Worth D. S. The Origins of Russian Gratmar. Notes on the State of Russian Philology Before the Advent of Printed Grammars. Columbus, 1983.

Worth 1983б — Worth D. S. The "Second South Slavic Influence" in the History of the Russian Literary Language. — American Contribution to the Ninth International Congress of Slavists. Vol.I. Linguistics. Ed. by M. Flier. Columbus, 1983, 349–372.

Wortman 1995 — Wortman R. S. Scenarios of Power. Myth and Ceremony in Russian Monarchy. Vol. I. From Peter the Great to the Death of Nicholas I. Princeton, 1995.

Yalamas 1988 — Yalamas D. The Students of the Leikhudis Brothers at the Slavo-graeco-latin Academy of Moscow. — Cyrillomethodianum. n. XII. Thessalonili, 1992.

Yalamas 1992 — Яламас Д. А. Филологическая деятельность братьев Лихудов в России. Автореферат на соискание уч. степени кандидата филолог. наук. М. [МГУ], 1992.

Yates 1975 — Yates F. A. The Rosicrucian Enlightenment. London — Reading — Fakenham, 1975.

Yates 1977 — Yates F. A. Astrae. The Imperial Theme in the Sixteenth Century. Harmondsworth, 1977.

Zalizniak 1986 — Зализняк А. А. Новгородские берестяные грамоты с лингвистической точки зрения. — Янин В. Л., Зализняк А. А. Новгородские грамоты на бересте (из раскопок 1977–1983 гг.). М., 1986, 89–219.

Zalizniak 1995 — Зализняк А. А. Древненовгородский диалект. М., 1995.

Zamkova 1975 — Замкова В. В. Славянизм как стилистическая категория в русском литературном языке XVIII в. Л., 1975.

Zapiski OR GBL, I–XLIX — Государственная библиотека СССР им. В.И.Ленина. Записки отдела рукописей. Т. I–XLIX. М., 1934–1990.

Zapol'skaia 1985 — Запольская Н. Н. «Усеченные» причастия в русском литературном языке XVIII в. — Вестник Московского университета. Серия филология, 1985, № 3, 34–45.

Zapol'skaia 1999 — Запольская Н. Н. «История Российская» Татищева: грамматическая дистанция между «древним наречием» и «новым наречием». — Эволюция грамматической мысли славян XIV–XVIII вв. М.: Институт славяноведения РАН, 1999, 131–139.

Zakhar'in 1991 — Захарьин Д. Б. О немецком влиянии на русскую грамматическую мысль. — Russian Linguistics, vol. 15 (1991),1–29.

Zen'kovskii 1970 — Зеньковский С. Русское старообрядчество. Духовные движения семнадцатого века. Forum Slavicurn, Bd. 21. München 1970.

Zhivov 1981 — Живов В. М. Кощунственная поэзия в системе русской культуры конца XVIII — начала XIX века. — Семиотика культуры. Труды по знаковым системам, вып. 13. Ученые записки Тартуского гос. университета, вып. 546. Тарту, 1981, 56–91.

Zhivov 1984 — Живов В. М. Правила и произношение в русском церковнославянском правописании XI–XIII века. — Russian Linguistics, vol. 8 (1984), n. 3, 251–293.

Zhivov 1984a — Живов В. М. Лингвистическое благочестие в первой половине XIX века. Из истории размножения литературных языков в послепетровскую эпоху. — Wiener Slavistisches Almanach. Bd. 13. Festschrift für Gerta Hüttl-Folter zum sechzigsten Geburtstag. Wien, 1984, 363–395.

Zhivov 1985 — Живов В. М. Язык Феофана Прокоповича и роль гибридных вариантов церковнославянского в истории славянских литературных языков. — Советское славяноведение, 1985, № 3, 70–85.

Zhivov 1985a — Живов В. М. Рецензия на книгу: Feofan Prokopovič. De arte rhetorica libri X. Hrsg. von R. Lachmann. Köln — Wien, 1982. — Известия АН СССР. Серия литературы и языка, т. 44 (1985), № 3, 274–278.

Zhivov 1986 — Живов В. М. Славянские грамматические сочинения как лингвистический источник. О книге: D. S. Worth. The Origins of Russian Grammar... Columbus, 1983. — Russian Linguistics, 1986, vol. 10, 73–113.

Zhivov 1986a — Живов В. М. Еще раз о правописании ц и ч в древних новгородских рукописях. — Russian Linguistics, vol. 10 (1986), 291–306.

Zhivov 1986b — Живов В. М. Новые материалы для истории перевода «Географии генеральной» Бернарда Варения. — Известия АН СССР. Серия литературы и языка, 1986, № 3, 246–260.

Zhivov 1986b — Живов В. М. Азбучная реформа Петра I как семиотическое преобразование. — Труды по знаковым системам, вып. 19. Ученые записки Тартуского гос. университета, вып. 720. Тарту, 1986, 54–67.

Zhivov 1987a — Живов В. М. Неизвестное сочинение митрополита Стефана Яворского как памятник церковной мысли эпохи петровских преобразований. — Вторая Международная научная церковная Конференция, посвященная 1000-летию Крещения Руси «Богословие и духовность Русской Православной Церкви». Москва, 11–19 мая 1987 года [препринт].

Zhivov 1988 — Живов В. М. Роль русского церковнославянского в истории славянских литературных языков. — Актуальные проблемы славянского языкознания. М., 1988, 49–98.

Zhivov 1988a — Живов В. М. Смена норм в истории русского литературного языка XVIII века. — Russian Linguistics, 12 (1988), 3–47.

Zhivov 1988b — Живов В. М. История русского права как лингвосемиотическая проблема. — Semiotics and the History of Culture. In Honor of Jurij Lotman. Columbus, Ohio, 1988, 46–128.

Zhivov 1988c — Живов В. М. Актуальные проблемы истории русской риторической традиции (По поводу издания поэтики Ф. Кветницкого). — Советское славяноведение, 1988, № 4 2, 94–99.

Zhivov 1989 — Живов В. М. Государственный миф в эпоху Просвещения и его разрушение в России конца XVIII века. — Век Просвещения. Россия и Франция. Le siècle des lumières. Russie. France. Материалы научной конференции «Випперовские чтения — 1987», вып. XX. М., 1989, 141–165.

Zhivov 1991 — Живов В. М. «Простота» языка и ее реализации: о языке книги «Статир» (1683–1684 гг.). — Зборник Матице српске за филологију и лингвистику, XXXIII (1990). Посвећено професору др. Александру Младеновићу поводом 60-годишњице живота. Нови Сад, 1990, 141–154.

Zhivov 1992 — Живов В. М. Slavic Christiana и историко-культурный контекст Сказания о русской грамоте. — Русская духовная культура. Под ред. Л. Магаротто и Д.Риции. Dipartimento di storia della civiltà europea. Testi e ricerche, n. 11. Тренто, 1992, 71–125.

Zhivov 1992a — Живов В. М. Из истории русской грамматики: итеративы и имперфективы в структуре глагольной парадигмы. — Доломоносовский период русского литературного языка. The Pre-Lomonosov Period of the Russian Literary Language (Материалы конференции на Фагеруде, 20–25 мая 1989 г.). Slavica Suecana, Series B, vol. 1. Stockholm, 1992, 247–270.

Zhivov 1993 — Живов В. М. Унификация склонения существительных в косвенных падежах мн. числа в памятниках XVII века: характер вариативности и обусловливающие ее факторы. — Исследования по славянскому историческому языкознанию. Памяти профессора Г. А. Хабургаева. М., 1993, 93–110.

Zhivov 1993a — Живов В. М. Гуманистическая традиция в развитии грамматического подхода к славянским литературным языкам в XVI–XVII вв. —

Славянское языкознание. XI Международный съезд славистов. Братислава, сентябрь 1993 г. Доклады российской делегации. М., 1993, 106–121.

Zhivov 1995 — Живов В. М. Светский и духовный литературный язык в России XVIII века: взаимодействие и взаимоотталкивание. — Russica Romana, vol. II (1995), 65–81.

Zhivov 1995a — Живов В. М. Usus scribendi. Простые претериты у летописца-самоучки. — Russian Linguistics, vol. 19 (1995), n. 1, 45–75.

Zhivov 1996 — Живов В. М. Историческая морфология русского литературного языка XVIII века: узус, нормализация и норма. — A Window on Russia. Papers from the V International Conference of the Study Group on Eighteenth-Century Russia Gargano, 1994. Ed. M. Di Salvo and L. Hughes. Rome, 1996, 285–92.

Zhivov 2004 — Очерки исторической морфологии русского языка XVII–XVIII веков. М.: Языки славянской культуры, 2004.

Zhivov and Keipert 1996 — Живов В., Кайперт Г. О месте грамматики И.-В. Пауса в развитии русской грамматической традиции: интерпретация отношений русского и церковнославянского. — Вопросы языкознания, 1996, № 3, 3–30.

Zhivov and Uspenskii 1983 — Живов В. М., Успенский Б. А. Выдающийся вклад в изучение русского языка XVII века. О книге: G. Kotošixin. O Rossii v carstvovanije Alekseja Mixajloviča. Ed. by A. E. Pennington. Oxford, 1980. — International Journal of Slavic Linguistics and Poetics, vol. 28 (1983), 149–180.

Zhivov and Uspenskii 1984 — Живов В. М., Успенский Б. А. Метаморфозы античного язычества в истории русской культуры XVII–XVIII вв. — В кн.: Античность и культура в искусстве последующих веков. Гос. музей изобразительных искусств, Материалы научной конференции 1982. М., 1984, 204–285.

Zhivov and Uspenskii 1986 — Живов В. М., Успенский Б. А. Grammatica sub specie theologiae. Претеритные формы глагола быти в русском языковом сознании XVI–XVIII веков. — Russian Linguistics, vol. 10 (1986), 259–279.

Zhivov and Uspenskii 1987 — Живов В. М., Успенский Б . А. Царь и Бог. Семиотические спекты сакрализации монарха в России. — Языки культуры и проблема переводимости. М., 1987, 47–153.

Zhitetskii 1903 — Житецкий П. И. К истории литературной русской речи в XVIII в. — Известия ОРЯС, т. VIII (1903), кн. 2, 1–51.

Zhmakin 1885 — Жмакин В. Иннокентий, епископ пензенский и саратовский. Биографический очерк. СПб., 1885.

Zinovii Otenskii 1863 — Зиновий [Отенский]. Истины показание к вопросившим о новом учении. Казань, 1863.

Znamenskii 1875 — Знаменский П. В. Чтения из истории русской церкви за время царствования Екатерины II. — Православный собеседник, 1875, № 2, 99–143, № 4, 392–418, № 5, 3–44, № 8, 327–347.

Znamenskii 1881 — Знаменский П. Духовные школы в России до реформы 1808 года. Казань, 1881.

Zoltan 1984 — Золтан А. Западнорусско-великорусские языковые контакты в области лексики в XV в. (К вопросу о западной традиции в деловой письменности Московской Руси). Автореферат диссертации на соискание уч. степени кандидата филолог. наук. М. [МГУ], 1984.

Zoltan 1987 — Золтан А. Се азъ... (К вопросу о происхождении начальной формулы древнерусских грамот. — Russian Linguistics, vol. 11 (1987), 179–186.

Zoltan 1987a — Золтан А. Из истории русской лексики. На правах рукописи. Будапешт, 1987.

Zol'nikova 1981 — Зольникова Н.Д. Сословные проблемы во взаимоотношениях церкви и государства в Сибири (XVIII в.). Новосибирск, 1991.

Index

Absolutism:
    and the monarch's rights 49–50, 61, 95–96, 102, 105
    and the model of classical empire 59–61, 65
    and the cult (sacralization) of the monarch 61, 213, 350–351, 355
    and court culture 44, 192, 303
    and the church 72, 95–96, 102, 105–106, 304, 352–354, 414, 425–426
    and Enlightenment 349–354
    and the function of literature 192, 208
    see also: Cultural synthesis of absolutism.
Academy of Sciences:
    as center of language activities 121, 122, 127, 134, 157, 215, 220, 231, 284
    mentioned 214, 332, 337
Achinger, G., 133, 196, 197, 252
Adaptation:
    of Church Slavonic by the Eastern Slavs 12–13, 24
    in connection with the development of the living language 16
Adjectival endings:
    variatity that is not relevant for opposing registers of the written language 79–81, 312–314, 316, 317
    editing in manuscripts of the Petrine period 74–75, 79–81
    normalization within the framework of the Academy grammatical tradition 122–124, 128–130, 226
    conceptualized in genetic categories 154–165, 226
    interpreted as poetic license 163–164, 175–176, 180–182
    nom.–ac. sg. masc. 4–6, 79–80, 120–121, 123, 128–129, 159–160, 161–162, 164–165, 176, 180–181, 229–230, 242, 276–279, 317, 325–326, 377
    gen sg. fem. 78–80, 82–83, 89, 120–121, 128–129, 154, 159–160, 178–179, 240–241, 266–267, 277–278, 316, 317, 325–326
    gen.-acc. sg. masc. and neut. 15–16, 79–80, 121, 123, 128–129, 159–162, 277–279, 317, 325–326
    nom.-acc. pl. 79–80, 128–129, 159–160, 164, 226, 229, 299–300, 325–326
    short adjectives 175, 181–182
Adodurov, V. E.:
    linguistic program of the 1730's 126–129, 138, 140, 142, 144, 160–161, 176, 219–220
    and the "learned guard" 114, 122
    grammatical essay of 1731 122, 126–129, 156–157, 160–162, 163–164, 177, 181, 219–220, 227–228, 277
    and linguistic normalization 121–122, 127–129, 153–154
    relationship to Paus' grammar 160, 220–221
    relationship to Ludolf's grammar 154, 155 161
    orthographic treatise of 1738–40 121–122, 220
    editing of Shvanvits' *German Grammar* 128, 129, 165
    on the spelling of Grecicisms 114–115
    mentioned 121, 206, 239, 359
Adrian, Patriarch of Moscow, 97, 106, 147
Adverbs:
    in -ѣ/-о 74, 77, 159–160
Aesop 62
Afanasii, Bishop of Kholmogory 31, 38, 57

Index

Afiani, V. Iu., 377
Akhmatov, A. P., Ober–Procuror of the Synod 392
Alekseev, A. A., 22, 24, 92, 121, 140, 142, 179, 213, 229, 231, 238, 240, 245, 249, 256, 272
Alekseev, P. T. 37, 311
Aleksei Mikhailovich, Tsar 45, 93
Aleksei, Tsarevich 51, 52, 107, 111, 114
Aleksii, Bishop of Tver 402, 410
Aleksii, Metropolitan of Moscow 147
Alexander I:
    his religious policy 354, 388, 389
    on the translation of the Gospels into Russian 388
    mentioned 426
Alexander II 426
Alexander Nevskii Lavra 107, 306, 308
Alexander Nevskii Seminary 385
All-Jesting and All-Drunken Council 51, 95
Alternation of velars and sibilants in noun declensions 78–81, 154, 158–160, 164, 230
Alvar, author of a Latin grammar 122
Amfiteatrov, Ia. K.:
    on the relationship between Russian and Church Slavonic 394
    conception of religious purism 394–396, 398–401, 406–409, 424–427
    on "Biblical" language 394
    on "popular" language 402, 403
    on "secular" language 406–407
    orthographic recommendations 403–405
Amvrosii (Iushkevich), Archbishop of Novgorod 316, 317, 318, 320, 324
Amvrosii (Podobedov), Metropolitan of Novgorod and St. Petersburg 384, 392
Amvrosii (Serebrennikov):
    and the unity of secular and religious literature 332, 334, 395
    on the sources of the linguistic norm 341–343
    on the mixture of Russian and Church Slavonic in Slavenorossiiskii 343–344, 394
    on the purist rubrics 344–345
    on linguistic heterogeneity 344
Anastasii (Romanenko-Bratanovskii), Archbishop of Astrakhan 397
Ancient languages 249–255, 257–259, 260–261, 262–263, 360–362, 368–369, 394–395
    the "Quarrel between Ancients and Moderns" 135–136, 174–175, 195–197, 250–251
Andrella, M. 38
Anisimov, E. V. 2
Anna Ioannovna, empress 177, 178, 316
Antiquity (of language, of national traditions)
    and the spirit of the language 222, 227–228, 369–371, 374
    and the Slavenorossiiskii language 230, 369–371
    see also: Language.
Antonii (Medvedev), Archimandrite of the Trinity-Sergius Lavra 410, 426
Aorist, see Preterits.
Apollodorus' *Library*:
    translation into Russian 71–72
    corrections in the translation 75–77, 79, 81
    linguistic variability in the translation 79, 81, 119, 121
    use of mythological material 71–72
    Feofan Prokopovich's foreword 50, 72, 73
Apraksin, P. M. 55
Arabic (language) 16, 360
Arakcheev, A. A. 413
Archaisms:
    in Church Slavonic (outdated words, unused phrases) 100, 101, 206, 235–236, 273, 405–406
    as a rubric of French Purism 139
    in poetry 171, 173–174
    reconceptualization of this rubric in Russia 140, 235–236, 343, 359
    status in religious Purism 396, 405–406
Archaists (followers of A. S. Shishkov):
    linguistic program 366, 367, 368–373
    cultural position 370–372, 374–376, 378, 379
    reception of Lomonosov 372
Ariosto, L. 297
Aristotle 257, 386
Arnauld, A. 130, 131, 252, 287
Arsenii Glukhoi 36
Arsenii Konevskii, Saint 414
Arsenii (Matseevich), Metropolitan of

Index

Rostov 303
Aspasia, Pericles' lover 379
Astakhina, L. Iu. 90
Augustus 52
Auxiliary words:
    as markers of bookishness 86–87, 120, 205–206, 234, 236–237, 313–314, 317, 319–320
    differences in Russian and Church Slavonic 223–225
    their editing in the change to the "simple" language 74–77, 245
    in Slavenorossiiskii 240–242, 245–246, 270–271, 363
    archaic Eastern Slavic auxiliary words 235–236
Aver'ianova, A. P. 116, 150–152
Avgustin (Gulianitskii), Bishop of Ekaterinoslav 406
Avgustin (Vinogradskii), Archbishop of Moscow 383
Avramii, elder 39
Avvakum (Petrov), Archpriest 33, 35, 39, 45, 312

Babaeva, E. E. 58, 78
Bak, Ch. D. 134
Baklanova, N. A. 39
Balzac, Guez de 133, 138
Barkhudarov, S. G. 112, 113, 239
Baronius (Cesare Baronio) 43
Baroque:
    Poetics 60, 173–175, 193–194
    linguistic doctrine 109, 137–138, 171–172
    reception by Russian writers 174, 421
    remnants in panegyric literature 193, 194, 198–203
    in religious literature and culture 312–313, 323, 336, 382, 387
Barsov, A. A.:
    linguistic position 259, 260, 294, 359
    Russian grammar 339
Barsov, A. K. 72, 75, 76, 77, 121
Barsov, N. 420, 425
Basil the Great, Saint 330, 402, 425
Batalden, S. K. 389
Batiushkov, K. N. 359
Batteux, Charles 373, 385
Baumann, G. 122, 128, 129, 161

Baumgarten, A. G. 385
Bayle, P. 216
Beautain, Abbé Louis-Eugène-Marie 420
Beccaria, Cesare 350, 385
Begichev, Ivan 43
Belokurov, S. A. 122
Benkendorf, A. Kh. 423, 424
Berezina, O. E. 149
Berkhgol'ts, F. B. (F. W. von Bergholz), kamer-junker 49, 117
Berkov, P. N. 48, 121, 178, 182, 191, 192, 205, 206, 246, 249
Berynda, P. 149
Betskoi, I. I. 413
Bible Society in Russia 331, 388, 390
Bible translations:
    correction of the Church Slavonic translation 69, 98–99, 101–102
    problem of translation into living languages 107–108
    cultural status of translations 205–206, 374, 378
    significance for the literary language 211–212, 218, 232, 259–262, 376
    Russian translations 156–157, 331, 388–391, 401
Bible, see: Church books.
Bielfeld, Jacob Friedrich 333
Bircher, M. 133
Birzhakova, E. E. 110, 111, 112
Blair, Hugh 385, 386
Blok, G. P. 316
Blume, H. 133, 223, 246, 247
Bobrik, M. A. 70, 101, 243
Bobrov, S. S. 370
Bogdanov, A. I. 59, 60
Bogdanovich, I. F. 333
Bogoslovskii, M. M. 96
Boileau-Despréaux, Nicholas:
    leading role in literature 133, 198
    and the "Quarrel Between Ancients and Moderns" 136, 174, 196–197
    view of the poetic language 172, 174–175, 201–202
    on stability of usage 263–264
    on naturalness in language 297
    Ode on the Taking of Namur and Discourse on the Ode 136–137, 174–175, 196–203, 206–207, 262
    L'art poétique 190, 193–194, 201–202

Réflections on Longinus and translation of Pseudo–Longinus' treatise 196–198, 199, 252
  mentioned 136–138, 167, 172, 189–191, 193, 263–265, 297, 300, 349, 362, 385, 386
Bookish language:
  as the basis for Slavenorossiiskii 264–265
  see also: Church Slavonic; Written language of medieval Rus'.
Borrowings:
  in the language of the Petrine era 65–67, 337–338
  their role in Peter's linguistic policies 110–114
  their spelling 81–82
  glossed in the *General Regulation or Charter* of 1720 111
  as a rubric of French purism 139, 170
  in the language of poetry 171
  and genius of the language 222–223
  the purist rejection of borrowings in Russia 136–137, 140–141, 237–240, 246, 293–294, 337–338, 343–345, 377
  this rubric in religious purism 396–398, 406–407
  in the language of the social elite 169–170
  Slavonicisms as a "pure" correlative to borrowings 237–238, 344–345, 367–368
  as a factor conditioning the change of "Slavonic" into Russian 152, 358, 371–372, 380
  borrowings in religious literature 397–398
  Slavonicisms as borrowings 85, 359
Bossuet, Jacques–Bénigne 211, 335, 336, 385
Bouhours, Dominique:
  linguistic doctrine 256, 257, 286, 419
  on the character of various languages 201, 216, 223, 256, 297
  attitude toward the poetic language 172, 201
  on linguistic richness 360
  on the a language's geographical spread 217

  on the role of the monarch in establishing linguistic norms 52, 220
  attitude toward Italian 187, 202
  mentioned 138
Bouillon, de 297
Bourdaloue, Louis 328, 335, 337
Bragina, L. M. 251
Brailovskii, S. N. 53, 101
Brey, R. 173, 200
Brunot, F. 133, 138, 171, 172, 175, 205, 211, 212, 216, 242, 246, 269, 368
Bubnov, N. Iu. 45
Budde E. 91, 314
Buffier, Claude 138, 286
Buffon, Georges-Louis Leclerc, Comte de 385
Bulgarian (language) 18, 35,
Bulgarin, F. B. 420, 421
Bureaucratic language (prikaznoi iazyk):
  as a register of the written language of medieval Rus' 3, 246
  its decline 3–4, 91–93, 141, 245
  in connection with the formation of the literary language of the new type 82–83, 89–93, 141, 170, 245
Bureaucratic words (prikaznye slova), chancellarisms:
  as a linguistic category 90
  as a rubric of French purism 139, 170, 243, 245
  the connection of the new literary language with the bureaucratic language 91, 93, 170
  the reconceptualization of this rubric in Russia 141, 243–246, 368–369
  place in religious purism 398–400
  the conjunction *понеже* 90, 245
Burke, Edmund 385
Buslaev, F. I. 8
Buturlin, I. I. 96
Buturlin, P. I. 96
Bykova, T. A. 54

Caesar, Julius 60
Calques 113, 227, 238–239, 368–369, 398–399, 417–419, 425–427
  вкус as a calque of *goût* 112–113, 168–169
Campredon, Jacques de 50
Canitz, Friedrich Rudolf Ludwig
  Investigation of Good Taste in Poetry and Prose 134

Index

Caput, Jean-Paul 134, 139, 212, 264, 287, 288
Cartesianism 247, 253, 287, 411
Catherine I 319–320
Catherine II:
    and the ideology of Enlightenment 303–304, 308, 350–352, 371
    and autocracy 347–348, 353–354
    the *Nakaz* (*Instruction*) 113–114, 351
    Odds and Ends 353
    Notes Regarding Russian History 371
    mentioned 305–307, 319–321, 326, 332–334, 348, 355–358, 374, 383–385, 387
Catullus 242
Caussinus, Nico 44, 188
Censorship:
    and state cultural politics 352–354
    cultural position 391–394
    linguistic editing as part of its activity 396–400, 410–411, 420–426
Chaikina, Iu. I. 91
Chancellarisms, see Bureaucratic words.
Chapelain, Jean 134, 138, 168, 172–174, 249, 250, 268
Charles V, Holy Roman Emperor 216
Charpentier, F. 242
Chateaubriand, François–René de 385
Chebotarev, L. A. 392
Chernov, V. A. 39
Chernykh, P. Ia. 89
Chinese (language) 255, 380
Chistovich, I. A. 103, 106, 383, 384, 385, 388, 389, 390, 391, 394, 410, 414, 420
Chivalric novels in Russia 43
Christiani, W. 110
Chronicles:
    in connection with the hybrid register of the written language of medieval Rus' 12, 19–21
    and linguistic continuity 22–23
    and changes as the result of the bookish language's rejection of the living language 145
    in relation to the opposition of religious and secular literature 24–25, 41–43
    their interpretation as historiographical works 43
    and lexical archaisms 236–237
    the *Laurentian Chronicle* 20
    the *Primary Chronicle* 20, 236–237, 376–377
    the *Book of Degrees* (Stepennaia kniga) 21, 43
    the *Rogozhskii Chronicle* 25
    mentioned 152, 341
Chrysostom, John, see Ioann Zlatoust.
Church books:
    as the basis of Orthodox culture 10–11, 23–24, 26–27, 32–33, 37, 42–43, 54
    as the corpus that defines the norm of the written language 16–17, 23–24, 26–27, 30–31, 42–43, 158, 223–224, 308–310
    as source of the richness of the Russian literary language 233, 236–237, 249, 251–253, 259–263, 290, 294–295, 334, 394–395
    as source of the norm of the Russian literary language 291, 299–302, 333–335, 3436 356–357, 359–360, 371–372, 379
    and Church Slavonic vocabulary 235–238
    and neologisms 247–248, 300–301, 344–345, 365
    the "Biblical" language as basis of the church language 394–395
    the Bible of 1633 101
    the Elizabethan Bible (1751) 101
    see also: Psalter.
Church Slavic as "hard" and "harsh" 126, 137–138
    the nature of its differences from "Slavenorossiiskii" 308–309
    alternation with Russian within one text 318
Church Slavonic (language) (the traditional written language):
    its culturological significance 3–4, 23–24, 31–33, 40–41, 72, 96–97, 115–117, 165–167
    as the literary language of old Rus' 2–3, 65–66
    how it was taught 7–10, 19–20, 311, 412
    the standard and hybrid registers 3, 11–12, 16–25, 29–32, 39, 66–67, 109–110, 145, 231–232, 313–314
    the consolidation of registers

Index

22–24

    the basic corpus of texts (Holy Writ and liturgy) 16–17, 23–24, 26–27, 30–31

    development of the grammatical approach to it 26–30, 69–70

    as a "learned" language 29–31, 97–98, 311

    its lack of polyfunctionalism 2–3, 69–70

    the broadening of its polyfunctionalism in the seventeenth century 30

    perfecting Church Slavonic 31–33, 69–70, 99–100

    the Church Slavonic literary tradition and the literary language of the new type 142, 143, 170–171, 192–193, 198–200, 204–209, 356–357

    its displacement by the new literary language 52–53, 65–69, 71–73, 93–94

    its parodic use by Peter I 95–97

    its natural unity with Russian 218, 220–232, 261–262, 297, 358, 367, 380, 394–395

    as a component of Slavenorossiiskii 228–229, 233–234, 248–249, 254, 264–266, 308–310

    as source of Russian's richness 249, 253–254, 259–263, 340, 344–345, 359–360, 394–396

    as source of the norms for the Russian literary language 264–266, 297, 299–302

    its relationship to Greek 30–32, 69–70, 98–99, 228, 253, 259–262, 376–377

    analogy with Latin 7, 69–70, 126–127, 143–145, 148–149, 211, 224–225, 228, 231–232, 358, 380

    as a holy language 31–33, 390, 414–115

    its obscurity 39–40, 96–99, 108, 117, 125–126, 326–328, 329–331, 359, 388

    its conceptualization as a church (clerical) language 40–41, 52, 54, 72–74, 94–95, 99, 103–104, 108, 109, 117, 126–127, 218, 220

    as a cult language 231, 232, 310, 331, 342, 356–357, 388

    its South Slavic nature 143–144, 358–359

    as the language of Slavic antiquity 227, 369–370, 374–375

    as one of the "ancient" (Classical) languages 252–254, 394–395

    individual interpretations of the markers that separate it from Russian 180–185

Cicero 133, 216, 263, 264, 334, 335, 337, 338, 362, 385, 386, 392

Ciceronianism 142

Civil script (alphabet):

    its creation 52, 53–65

    cultural significance 53, 63–65, 93–94, 412–415

    first instances of its use 55–56

    relationship to the Latin script 57–61

    relationship to *skoropis'* 63–64

    relationship to the church script in various periods 53–56, 71, 412–415

    its use in education 11, 412–413

Classical culture:

    its reception in Classicism 250–251, 262

    its methods of linguistic modeling 178–179, 184

Classicism:

    ideological basis 208

    attitude the literary past 166–168, 188–193, 228–229

    attitude toward the Classical period 250–251

    linguistic doctrine (purism) in France 132–134, 137–139, 195–196, 210–211, 233, 251, 262, 267–269, 274, 285–290, 295–296

    linguistic doctrine in Germany 133–134, 286–287, 295–296

    conception of the poetic language 171–175, 187–189

    principle of naturalness 173–174, 297–299, 336, 367

    system of genres 191–193, 208–209, 267–268

    the reconceptualization of its linguistic doctrine in Russia 132–135, 137–143, 160–162, 165–167, 169–171, 212–213, 234, 235–248, 264–266, 272–274, 292, 297–299, 337–338, 365–369, 372–373, 406–407

rejection of France's hegemony 187–189, 254, 256–258, 262
see also: Purism, religious; Purism, rationalist; Purism, Slavonicizing.
Clergy:
political and cultural position 47–48, 302–304, 308–309, 346, 351–354, 382–387, 390–394, 411–412, 417–418, 427–429
social status 303–304, 308–309, 320–321, 382–385, 414, 427
Clericalism and anticlericalism:
nature of the conflict in Russia 105–106, 212–213, 301–304
reflection in linguistic and cultural politics 101–108, 117, 146–147, 310, 319–321, 343, 379
in connection with linguistic polyfunctionalism 212–213, 310
Cocron, F. 39, 90
Coeffeteau, Nicholas 286
Colloquium of Lovers of the Russian Word 393
Commission on Church Schools 383
Commission to Compose a New Law Code 305, 306, 308
Comparative degree:
as marker of bookishness 18, 77–78
editing in changing to the simple tongue 73–74, 77
as object of grammatical normalization 158–159, 277–279
Compound words:
as specifically bookish lexicon 147
as a characteristic of "ancient" (classical) languages 173, 251–252, 255–257, 361
in connection with the question of the richness and antiquity of a language 251–252, 255–257, 260–261, 361
as a trait of poetic language 188, 256–257
Conjugation:
forms of athematic conjugation as a trait of Church Slavonic and their replacement with analogical forms in changing to the simple language 73–74, 77, 177–178, 228–229, 318–319
forms of the 2nd pers. sg. present in -*ши* and -*шь* 73, 74, 77, 160, 162–164, 175–177, 325–326
compound future 160
forms of the type *глядь*, *бряк* 240
see also: Infinitives.
Connotations of traditional lexicon 130–132
Consett, Thomas 94
Constantine the Great, Saint, Roman emperor 61
Continuity in language:
as a characteristic of the written usage (the written tradition) 19–20, 311
the factor of genre 22–23, 41–43
the relation of the Russian literary language of the new type to previous linguistic traditions 82–94, 170, 188–189, 210, 233, 235–237, 253, 259–260
continuity in the language of the sermon 311
Conversational language;
and the written language 19, 54
in connection with the bookish language 25–27, 153–154
as point of reference for the French literary language 137–139, 167–170
as point of reference for the Russian literary language of the new type 5–7, 123, 126–127, 138–139, 165, 168–171, 210–211, 213–214, 233, 262–263, 285–288, 291–301, 395–396
the lack of a normalized conversational language 139, 168–169, 365–366
the significance of women's speech 293–294
as "natural" from the perspective of Neogrammarians and Structuralists 19
Cooper, B. F. 206, 207, 231
Corneille, Pierre 386
Corneille, Thomas 138
Costar, Pierre 133
Coulter, J. A. 199
Cracraft, James 95, 103, 105, 106
Cultural conflicts:
grammatical education and the traditional approach to texts 29, 32–33
Old Believers and Nikonians 30–31, 39
Grecophiles and Latinophiles 69–70
traditional culture and religious reformation 312

secularized and religious culture 39–41, 43–46, 57–58, 65, 94–95, 210, 212–213, 302–304, 355–356, 380–381, 398–399, 401, 408–412, 414–417, 421–429
    the transformation of this conflict into one between literary trends 378–379, 381
        as an element of state politics 45–47, 50–53
Cultural synthesis of absolutism:
        as a mythological phenomenon 301–304, 307–309, 349–352
    and Catherine II's politics 307–309, 352–353, 382
    and the unity of literature 303–304, 310, 331–337, 338–341, 343, 345, 387, 419
        significance for the literary language 308–310
        its decline 346–349, 351–357, 369–371, 382
    and the emergence of the cult of poetry 355–356
Cyril (Constantine), "the Philosopher," Saint 30, 108, 376

D'Alembert, Jean le Rond 385
Dal', V. I. 403
Damascene, see John of Damascus.
Damaskin (Semenov-Rudnev), Bishop of the Nizhegorodskii district 334, 335
Damaskin Studite 35
Damaskin, hierodeacon 105
Dan'ko, E. Ia. 207
Dashkov, D. V. 357, 358, 361, 364, 380
David, king and prophet 97, 318, 379
Deimier, Pierre de 175
Delitsyn, P. S., priest 398, 400, 425
Dell'Agata, G. 35, 144, 221
Demetrius Phalereus 257
Demina, E. I. 35
Demkova, N. S. 45
Demosthenes 334
Derrida, Jacques 19
Derzhavin, G. R.:
    and the tradition of the ode 348–349, 354
        "Dobrada's Abode" 393
        mentioned 208, 333, 347, 366, 387, 392, 393
Descartes, René 211

Desmarets, Jean, Sieur de Saint–Sorlin 138, 173
Dialectical elements (dialecticisms):
        as a rubric of French purism 139
        reconceptualization of this rubric in Russia 140, 142, 243, 338, 368–369
        dialectical pronunciation 403–405
Dibich, I. I. 391
Dictionaries:
        their need in order to create a literary language of the new type 132, 134
        translation dictionaries as opposed to those whose purpose is to establish norms 145, 148–149
Dictionary of the Russian Academy 294, 333, 357, 422, 425, 427
Diderot, Denis 385
Differentiation, social and cultural 47–48, 51–53, 112–113, 141, 168–170, 212–213, 292, 302–303, 308–309, 346, 351–353, 355–356, 380–386, 417–419
Diglossia:
        the question of its applicability to the linguistic situation of old Rus' 16, 32
Dimitrii (Sechenov), Metropolitan of Novgorod 315, 316
Dimitrii Rostovskii (Tuptalo), Saint 312, 333
Dionisii Zobninovskii 35, 36
Dionysius of Halicarnassus 385
Dmitriev, I. I. 333, 365, 370, 372, 387
Dmitriev, L. A. 23
Dobrotoliubie 308
Dokukin, Larion, clerk 52
Dolgorukii, Ia. F. 114
Dometskii, Gavriil 105
Dorat, Claude Joseph 379
Dositheos, Patriarch of Jerusalem 106
Dostoevskii, F. M. 52
Druzhinin, V. G. 140, 259
Du Bellay, Joachim 171, 362
Du Marsais, César Chesneau 385
Dual number:
        as marker of bookishness (a specific Church Slavonic form) 15, 18, 78, 162, 225–229, 313
        as an archaism 100
        replaced by plural forms in the change to the "simple" language 74, 76
        interpretation in the Academic grammatical tradition 154, 156, 158
        the opinion of its derivation from

Index

Greek 227–228
Dubrovin, N. F. 391
Durnovo, N. N. 13, 15
Ďurovič, L. 123, 127, 156, 157
Dutch (language) 54, 66, 71, 215, 368

Ebert, A. 60
Ecstasy, poetic (vostorg), or enthusiasm:
    its linguistic manifestation 130,
    137, 198–204, 283, 329, 339
    see also: Prophetic gifts.
Edelman, N. 250
"Edinoglasie" and "mnogoglasie"
    (sequential and non-sequential singing)
    34
Editing, book 27–28, 81, 100–101, 405–406
Edlichka, A. 24
Efrem Sirin, Saint 328
Efremov, M., type-maker 55, 58
Elagin, I. P. 213, 356
Elizabeth I 196, 213, 214, 219, 316, 317,
    318, 320, 374, 413
Elizaveta Alekseevna, Grand Princess 191
English (language):
    its lack of correlation to purist
    criteria 187, 368, 371–372
        as a model for Russian 187, 215,
    218, 368
Enlightenment:
    in Western Europe 349–350,
    352–353
        as a utopia 346–347, 352–353
        and the emancipation of culture
    349–350, 352–356
        and the religious life of Russian
    society 72, 302–309, 327–329, 351–354
        in Peter I's cultural policy 102–
    103
Enrichment of the language:
    in French linguo-stylistic theories
    171–172, 360
        Russian authors' view of 131–132,
    136–137, 184, 215–216, 406–407
Epic poetry:
    and the special poetic language
    173–175
        place in the Classicist generic
    hierarchy 209
Epifanii (Premudryi) 405
Epifanii Slavinetskii 8, 30, 101, 102, 147
Erasmus, Desiderius, of Rotterdam 26, 71
Eschenburg, Johann Joachim 385

Esipov, G. V. 52
Eugene, Prince of Savoy 207
Europeanization of Russian culture:
    and the different linguistic
    situation in Russia 43–44, 45–47, 93–
    95, 135, 148–149, 167–171, 188–192
    and the cultural differentiation of
    society 47–48, 112–113, 213, 355–356,
    380–381
    and the development of national
    self-consciousness 125, 212–214, 369–
    371, 373–377
    and Russian Enlightenment 349–
    352
    and the reception of Western
    European literary and linguistic
    conceptions 121–122, 132–144
    and Freemasonry 353–354
    and mysticism 353–354, 387
    and the clergy 382–386, 411–412,
    417–418
Eusebius of Caesarea 199
Evdokim, elder, author of *Prostoslovie* 29
Evfimii, Chudov monk 30, 69, 70, 101, 102,
    147
Evgenii (Bolkhovitinov), Metropolitan of
    Kiev 252, 257, 257, 261, 261, 383, 387,
    419
Evgenii (Kazantsev), Archbishop of
    Iaroslavl' 389

False Dmitri (I) 43
Faret, Nicholas 139, 268
Fasmer, M. 243
Fedor Alekseevich, Tsar 58
Fénélon, F. S. de la Motte 131, 173, 178,
    223, 247, 256, 258, 264, 294, 385, 386,
    407
Fenne, Tönnies 64
Feodosii Ianovskii 107
Feofan Prokopovich:
    cultural and historical position 49,
    50, 102–109, 113–114
    attitude toward Catholicism and
    Protestantism 103–108
    his defense of Peter I's policies
    50, 115–117
    attitude toward Church Slavonic
    96–99, 101–106, 126, 326–327
    attitude toward functional
    linguistic registers 72–73, 108–110,
    313–314, 322–323

and the "learned guard" 113–114, 116, 121–122
    the language of his sermons 109–110, 183–184, 312–315, 323, 339–340
    The Right of a Monarch's Will 49, 111
    Investigation of the Pontifex 61
    foreword to Apollodorus' *Library* 50, 72
    his *Rhetoric* and rhetorical teaching 104, 109, 188, 323
    Poetics 104
    Insupportable Yoke 304
    History of Peter the Great and corrections in this manuscript 75–77, 79, 110, 119–120, 313
    Spiritual Regulation (Dukhovnyi Reglament) 97, 102, 104, 105, 323, 327, 388, 414
    First Lesson to Youth 97, 103, 412
    opinion on Bible translation 98–99, 126
    influence on the later homiletic tradition 314, 319–320
    evaluations of his language 335–338
    mentioned 44, 48, 190–191, 208, 303, 321–322, 330, 335–336, 350, 365, 422
Feofan, Gavriil Petrov's cell-mate 308
Feofilakt (Rusanov), Bishop 385, 392, 420
Feofilakt Bolgarskii 97, 327
Feoktist Orlovskii, Hieromonk 391
Ferguson, C. A. 16
Filaret (Drozdov), Saint:
    views on religious education 382–383, 385–387, 391, 414–115
    relationship to secular authority 389
    relationship to religious culture 391–392, 408–412, 415–417, 423–424
    opinion on the Bible translation 389
    editing of the catechism 391
    views on language 396–402, 405–406, 408–409, 414–115, 424–428
    language usage 397–398, 419–420
    mentioned 387
Filaret (Gumilevskii) 323, 390, 392, 415, 425
Filin, F. P. 84, 145
Firsov, Avraamii 23, 38, 39

Flashar, M. 199
Fléchier, Esprit 321, 335, 336
Florentine Academy 133
Florovskii, G. V. 308, 352, 354, 383, 386, 387, 388
Folk usage:
    as model for linguistic usage 170, 181–182
Foma, priest, addressee of Kliment Smoliatich's epistle 33
Fontenelle, Bernard le Bovier de 120, 183, 250, 258, 259
Fonvizin, D. I.:
    on absolute rule 347
    translation of Bitaubé's *Joseph* 339, 357, 363
    P. A. Viazemskii's criticism of his language 356–357, 363
    Brigadier 91–92, 246
    mentioned 351, 353, 356, 358, 366
Fops (petimetry) 169, 213, 233, 266
    see also: Usage, foppish speech.
Fotii (Spaskii), Archimandrite 390, 401
Foucault, Michel 349, 350
Franko, I. 108
Freeze, Gregory 382
French (language):
    as object of purist normalization 137–139
    its polyfunctionalism 127–129, 217–218
    in relation to Latin 126–127, 143–144, 211, 214, 222–225, 228, 254, 380
    as one of the "new" (modern) languages 249–252, 262–263
    clarity and simplicity as its attributes 187–188, 221–222, 251, 297–298
    its poverty (narrowness) and dryness 172, 173, 188, 251–252, 254, 257–258, 263–264
    before the purist normalization 137–138, 173, 359
    as a model for Russian 126–127, 132–134, 136–143, 148–149, 167–168, 211, 214–216, 218, 359
    as the conversational language in Russia 219, 365–366, 369–371, 384–385
    mentioned 238–239, 254, 261–262, 265–266, 297–298, 305, 344–345, 368–369, 384–385

French Academy 133, 134, 263, 407
French Academy Dictionary 263
Freydank, D. 137, 258
Frick, David 107
Functional characteristic of linguistic elements:
    as opposed to genetic elements 6–7, 15–16, 65–68, 123–124

Gagarin, M. P. 53, 56, 64
Gallomania 370
Garde, P. 369, 370
Gasparov, M. L. 283, 361
Gavriil (Buzhinskii) 71, 94, 114, 319
Gavriil (Petrov), Metropolitan of Petersburg
    his career 305–306
    his views 304–305
    the dedication of the translation of Marmontel's Belisarius to him 304
    relations with Gedeon Krinovskii 306, 321, 326, 327
    attitude toward monasticism 308
    Collection of Sermons for All Sundays and Holidays 306–307, 327–330, 331, 339–340
    mentioned 335, 358, 388, 420
Gedeon (Krinovskii):
    his career 320
    the orientation on "simplicity" in his sermons 320–322
    using Russian in sermons 324–325
    normalization of the language 325–326
    patronage of Gavriil (Petrov) and Platon (Levshin) 305, 320, 327
    mentioned 328–330, 333–336, 338, 340, 387, 413
Gedeon (Slonimskii) 101
Gedeon (Vishnevskii) 106
Genetic characteristics of linguistic elements:
    as opposed to functional elements 6–7, 15, 65–68, 84–86, 88–89, 145–146
    their functional reconceptualization 12–16, 25–26, 67–68, 123–124
    the actualization of genetic parameters 78–79, 126, 144–154, 153–154, 163–166, 188–189, 210–211
    and their stylistic characteristics 270–271, 272–273, 275–280, 364
Genius of the language 188, 222, 223, 396, 403

Gennadii (Gonzov), Archbishop of Novgorod 9
Gennadii, Patriarch of Constantinople 62
Genres:
    the problem of using the concept in regard to old Russian writing 24–25
    and generic continuity 22–24, 41–43
    the generic differentiation of languages 108–110
    new and old genres in Russian Classicism 190–193
    hierarchy of genres 267–268, 270–272, 354–356
    religious literature in the system of genres 207, 332
    and linguistic programs 207–209
    the transformation of the genre system in post–Classicist literature 354–356, 379
Gerard, Alexander 385
Gerasimov, Dmitrii 27, 28
German (language):
    its polyfunctionalism 211, 218
    its similarity to Greek 256
    and the spirit of the language 222
    as a model for Russian 189, 215, 216, 218, 368–369
    mentioned 66, 218–219, 226, 238, 254, 256–258, 260, 261, 266, 287, 298, 305, 373–375, 384–385, 419
Gesner, J. M. 328
Gesta Romanorum, Acts of the Romans (Rimskie deianiia) 67
Gezen, A. 147
Gippius, A. A. 23
Glazunov, I. P., bookseller 392
Gleason, Walter J. 347
Glück (Gliuk), Johann Ernst, Pastor:
    the juxtaposition of Russian and Church Slavonic elements in his grammar 155–158
    influence on the subsequent grammatical tradition 122–123, 153, 161
    use of his work by Paus 122, 155, 157, 159, 160
    his school in Moscow 122–123
Gnedich, N. I. 359, 362
Goldblatt, Harvey 27, 33
Golikov, I. I. 52
Golitsyn, A. N. 389, 399, 413, 422, 423
Golovin, F. A. 45

Index

Golubev, I. F. 30
Golubinskii, F. A. 425
Gorbach, O. 100, 102
Gordon, Patrick 95
Gorlitskii, I. S. 156, 157, 157, 214
Gorodchaninov, G. N. 112
Gorskii, A. V. 70, 108, 115, 147
Gothic, as a period of linguistic decline 250, 254, 255, 258, 358, 372–373, 374
Gottsched, Johann Christoph:
 his linguistic doctrine 248, 256, 287, 295
 influence on Lomonosov 207, 252, 287
 opinion of Günther's poetry 207
 mentioned 134, 258
Gournay M. de 171, 172, 205, 246, 250
Grammar:
 development of the grammatical approach to the bookish language 26–30, 57, 88, 100–102, 145
 role in education 29, 39, 98–99, 311
 as source of Church Slavonic's norm 27, 68–69
 connected to other humanistic disciplines 31–33
 protests against it 32–33
 the task of creating a grammar for the literary language of the new type 132–134
 descriptive and synthetic grammars of Russian 155–158, 163, 229–231, 276
 as source of the norm (purity) of the literary language 288–290, 293–294, 342
 as source of the norm for the literary language of the new type 79–80, 233–234, 290–296, 342
 and the grammatical tradition 5–6, 122–123, 129, 153–154, 163–166
 as the basic object of attention for a functional approach 86, 88
 Lateinischen Grammatica Marchica 122
 Institutio Grammatica 122
 Teutsche Grammatica 122
Gramoty, birchbark documents 8
Grasshoff, Helmut 187, 253
Great Menalogions for Reading 145
Grebeniuk, V. P. 60, 60, 61

Grech, N. I. 362, 404
Grecianisms (Grecianized constructions):
 Feofan Prokopovich's criticism of them 101, 114, 316
Grecophilism:
 as related to Latinophilism 63, 69–70, 104–106, 114–115
 and Church Slavonic erudition 32–33, 56, 57–58, 69–70, 101–103, 146–147
Greek (language):
 its richness 172, 249–252
 and the existence of a special poetic language 172, 202, 250
 as a profane language 31–32
 as the language of religious literature 62–63, 103
 as one of the "ancient" languages 249–253, 256–257, 394–395
 as source of the richness of Latin and other languages 253, 260–262, 362
 as source of the richness of Russian and Church Slavonic 253–254, 259–262, 334, 360–361, 376–377, 380
 and Modern Greek 254
 as model for the traditional bookish language in Russia 30–32, 69–70
 its closeness to Church Slavonic 32–33, 101
 differences from Church Slavonic 100–102
 as model for the Russian literary language of the new type 188–189, 215–217, 254–259, 360–361
 "simple" Greek and its equivalence to Russian 70, 97–98
 Greek writing and orthography as model for Russian and Church Slavonic 56–57, 102, 114–115, 255–256, 284
 and the formation of the dual number in Church Slavonic 227–228
 mentioned 259, 334, 344–345
Gregory of Nyssa, Saint 199
Gregory the Theologian, Saint 101, 328
Greshishcheva, E. 206
Grigorii (Postnikov), Metropolitan of Petersburg 401, 416
Grimarest, Jean–Léonor le Gallois 287
Grimm, G. E. 211
Grinberg, M. S. 234, 235, 283, 292, 337
Groening, M.:

484

relation of his grammar to
Adodurov's essay on grammar 161
mentioned 163
Gröschel, B. 38
Guanini, Alexander 43
Gukovskaia, Z. V. 133, 175, 286
Gukovskii, G. A. 6, 192, 192, 195, 200, 209, 346
Gundulić, Ivan 182
Günther, Johann Christian:
his influence on Lomonosov 207
Gurevich M. M. 54
Gurvich G. 50
Guzner, I. A. 412

Hagiography:
and the registers of the language of medieval Rus' 25
Russian in hagiographic texts 331
Hammer on the Rock of Faith 304
Hatzfeld, H. 174
Hazard, Paul, 135
Heinsius, Daniel 138
Hellie, R. 1
Hepp, N. 223, 250
Herder, Johann Gottfried 370
Heterogeneity, linguistic:
in hybrid texts 19–21
seen as macaronism and something to be eliminated 266–267, 269–274, 276, 277–280, 343, 410
Hexameter:
and linguistic richness 258–259, 361–362
in the German literary tradition 258
History of Korolevich Arkhilabon 48
History of the Swedish War 83, 119
Hobbes, Thomas 50
Holy Writ, see: Church books.
Homer:
in the context of the "Quarrel Between Ancients and Moderns" 138, 174, 196, 222, 250, 258
as model for Russian writers 256, 258–259
mentioned 293, 334, 335, 392
Homiletics:
in early modern Western European culture 211–212, 218, 310
in seventeenth-century Russian culture 39, 310–313

its place in eighteenth-century Russian culture 192–193, 303–304
its addressees 312, 312–314, 319–320
influence on panegyric poetry 192–193, 206–207
the peculiarities of its language 109–110, 183–184
standard Church Slavonic in sermons 38, 311–313
hybrid Church Slavonic in sermons 39, 109–110, 312–320, 337–338
Russian (Slavenorossiiskii) in sermons 212, 323–330, 338–341, 395–396, 398–399
Quotations from Holy Writ in sermons 324, 328–329, 342
Homonymy, the desire to eliminate it as a factor of linguistic change and grammatical normalization 27, 78
Honest Mirror of Youth 58, 80, 81, 83, 413
Horace 136, 177, 184, 197, 295, 297, 338, 385, 386
Hosius, Stanisław, Cardinal 107
Huet, Pierre–Daniel 222
Humanism:
Humanist attitude toward texts 26
relation to Greek and Latin 251
Humboldt, Wilhelm von 223
Hunold, Christian Friedrich 182
Hüttl-Worth, G. 417, 418, 419
Hybrid language (the hybrid register of the bookish language):
its genesis 11–12, 17–18
continuity of linguistic evolution 19–22
its consolidation as a special register 22–24
as "semi–literate" 27, 31
its reduction 3
its reconceptualization as a "simple" language 23–24, 35, 37–39, 313
significance for linguistic consciousness 78
relationship to the literary language of the new type 77–80, 82–84, 88–89, 93–94, 120, 124, 162, 170, 181
the view of it as the same language as Slavenorossiiskii 232
the view of it as "impure" 232, 338
in sermons 312–319
use by Archimandrite Fotii

(Spasskii) 390
Hyperbole, as a feature of Baroque poetics 174, 196, 200, 203

Iagich, I. V. 27–32
Iakhontov, I. 105
Iakov (Nikol'skii), censor 398, 402
Iakovlev, A. A., Ober-Procuror of the Synod 414
Iankovich de Mirievo, F. I. 413
Ignat'ev, S., General-Lieutenant 214
Ikonnikov, V. S. 31
Il'ia Miniat (Elias Miniates):
    The Stumbling Block 328
Il'ia, Hegumen 28
Il'inskii, Prefect of the Trinity Lavra seminary 330
Ilarion, Metropolitan:
    Sermon on Law and Grace 12
Ilarion, Rector of the Trinity Lavra seminary 330
Imperfect (tense), see: Preterites.
Inadequate translation, see: Translation.
Infinitives:
    as marker of bookishness 120
    forms of the infinitive as variants that are not relevant for contrasting Russian and Church Slavonic 315–319, 325–326
    forms in *-mu* as "Slavonic" 149–151, 155, 178–179, 205–207, 223–224, 226, 229, 363, 369–370
    changing forms in *-mu* to *-mь* to switch to the "simple" language 73–76, 176
    normalization of forms 129, 325–326
    forms defined in grammars 155–156, 159–164, 276
    as poetic license 175–177, 205, 229, 242, 364
    in Slaveno-rossiiskii 240–242, 396
    in Sumarokov's works 282, 283, 338–339
    stylistic use of 283, 338–340
    see also: Stylistic constructions.
Ingen, F. van 133
Innokentii (Borisov), Archbishop 401, 425
Innokentii (Smirnov), Bishop 399
Inversions:
    eliminating them from the Russian literary language of the new type 73–75
    as a feature of poetic language 173–174, 257–258, 365
Ioakim, Patriarch 38, 69, 102
Ioann Alekseevich, Tsar 76
Ioann Lestvichnik, Saint 308
Ioann Zlatoust, Saint (John Chrysostom) 97, 311, 327, 328, 329, 330, 331, 333
Ioannikii Galiatovskii 310
Irinei (Klement'evskii), Archbishop of Pskov 397
Isaac the Syrian 308
Isachenko, A. V. 2, 66, 84, 141, 227, 270, 316, 418
Isaiah, prophet 206
Isocrates 334
Italian (language):
    its lack of correspondence to purist criteria 187–188;
    as object of purist criticism 172, 187–188
    its special poetic language 172, 188, 202
    as a model for Russian writers 187, 215–216
    relationship to Latin 126–127, 143–144, 223–225, 256–257
    mentioned 363
Iusupov, B., Prince 214
Ivanov, Ivan, priest 330, 331

Jakobson, Roman 182
Janik, D. 196
Jansenism 130, 212
Jodelle, Étienne, 362
John of Damascus, Saint 253, 328
Juncker, Gottlob Friedrich Wilhelm 133, 134
Junius, Melchior 44
Jurisprudence:
    socio-cultural significance 49–50, 141
    its language 93, 113–114
    borrowings in monuments of law 111, 113
Justinian I, Byzantine emperor 105

Kachenovskii, M. T. 359
Kakailovich, Faddei 101
Kal'dor, I. 58
Kamenskii, A. T. 371
Kant, Immanuel 349
Kantemir, A. D.:
    his linguistic position 140, 142, 162–164

Index

attitude toward borrowings 140, 240
attitude toward the poetic
language 186–189, 257
view of poetic license 162–163,
174–178, 181–186, 205
principles of translation 184
orientation on Italian 187–189
attitude toward the previous
literary tradition 114, 189–190
early works in hybrid Church
Slavonic 177
Description of Paris 177–178
Petrida 186
translation of *Justinian's History*
140, 240, 259
translation of Fontenelle's
*Conversations About the Plurality of
Worlds* 120
satires 142, 169–170, 177–178,
180, 183, 184, 240
"Speech to the Most Pious
Sovereign Anna Ioannovna" 178
Psalm paraphrases 178
Anacreontic songs 178
translation of Horace's epistles
177–178, 184
"Letter of Khariton Makentin"
164, 175–176, 180, 187
connection with Feofan
Prokopovich 114, 187–189
attitude toward Fedor Polikarpov
114, 190
Trediakovskii's references to him
170–171, 184
mentioned 190–191, 196, 245,
303, 337, 350, 356
Kantemir, D. K.:
the "simple" language in his
translations 72
criticism of Feofan Prokopovich
103–104
Kapterev, N. F. 106
Kapustin, bookseller 392
Karamzin, N. M.:
his linguistic program 356, 359–
360, 361–366, 367–368
his cultural position 355, 372–
374, 376, 378
linguistic practice 370, 376–377
*Memoir on Ancient and Modern
Russia* 50
History of the Russian State 375–378

Letters of a Russian Traveler 373, 376
on Feofan Prokopovich's language
336–337
mentioned 245, 371, 384, 386, 397
Karamzinists ("innovators"):
condemnation of the previous
literary-linguistic tradition 356–358, 367
continuity with the previous
literary-linguistic tradition 363–366,
409–411
linguistic program 356–371,
374–375, 378–379, 411–412
reception of Lomonosov 371–374
the genres they cultivated 379–380
mentioned 387, 393
Karin, F. G. 335, 336
Karlinsky, Simon 130
Karskii, E. F. 35
Katenin, P. A. 372
Keil, R. D. 134
Keipert, H. 3, 7, 27, 63, 122, 127, 160, 161,
216, 218, 223, 247, 263
Khaburgaev, G. A. 21, 86
Kharlampovich, K. V. 310
Kheraskov, M. M. 48, 208, 332, 333
Khodasevich, V. F. 348
Khovanskii, I. I. 51
Khrabr, monk 32
Khrapovitskii, A. V. 347, 353
Khvostov, D. I. 393
Kibal'nik, S. A. 44, 252
Kingdom of the World (Tsarstvo mira) 255
Kirchner, A. 69
Kirchner, P. 207
Kirill (Florinskii), Archimandrite 101, 316
Kirill Trankvillion-Stavrovetskii 312
Kirillov-Novoezerskii Monastery 308
Klein, Joachim 44, 137, 182, 191, 192, 193,
196, 235, 243, 258, 292, 350
Klenin, Emily 20
Kliment Okhridskii, Saint 108
Kliment Smoliatich 33
Kniaz'kova, G. P. 142
Kniazhnin, Ia. B. 333, 348
Koblents, I. N. 59
Kochetkova, N. D. 323, 337
Kociuba, O. 30
Kondratovich, K. A. 391, 392
Kopievskii (Kopievich) Il'ia:
Nomenklator 149
mentioned 156, 157
Koporskii, S. A. 326

487

Koretskii, V. I. 23
Korf, I. A., President of the Academy of Sciences 134
Kosellek, R. 208
Kostechenskii, Konstantin 27
Kostrov, E. I. 358
Kotkov, S. I. 90
Kotoshikhin, G. 3, 92
Kotovich, A. 392, 398, 399, 400, 401, 402, 413, 414, 415
Kovalevskaia, E. G. 356
Kovtun, L. S. 28, 145, 146
Kozlov, S. L. 222
Kozlov, V. P. 377
Krechetovskii, I., corrector (spravshchik) 75, 77
Krivoshein, Vasilii, Archbishop 199
Kromer, Martin 43
Krylov, I. A. 380
Kuev, K. 32
Kunik, A. 6, 191, 193, 194, 200, 202, 241, 242, 243, 247, 249, 267, 271, 272, 281, 300
Kutina, L. L. 87, 109, 110, 111, 112, 184, 246, 313, 314, 422
Kuz'mina, V. D. 141

La Fontaine, Jean de 297
La Harpe, Jean–François de 361, 373, 385
La Suze, Henrietta de Coligny, Comtesse de 135
Lachmann, R. 44, 104, 109, 142, 188, 195
Lamy, Bernard:
    view of the "genius of the language" 222, 297
    and the synthesis of the traditions of Vaugelas and Port-Royal 247, 248, 287–288
    on the significance of grammar 264, 289, 295
        linguo-stylistic doctrine 268, 274
        Lomonosov's familiarity with his ideas 253
        mentioned 258, 297, 411
Lancelot, D. K. 252, 287
Language (spirit, nature, genius, root or natural qualities) 182, 221–227, 296, 358–360, 362, 367–370, 374–375, 394–396
Lappo–Danilevskii, A. S. 191, 351, 382
Larin, B. A. 65
Latin:
    the teaching of Latin 7, 251, 263–264
    as an "impious" language 391, 414–115
    as an ancient language 249–252, 254–257, 262–263
    its relation to Greek 251, 253
    and European national literary languages 36, 41–42, 126–127, 143–145, 211–212, 214, 217–218, 222–225, 228, 236–237, 249–252, 358, 380
    as a language of secular culture 62–63
    and a special poetic language 202
    and "learned" Church Slavonic 30, 68–69
    as analogue to Church Slavonic 7, 69–70, 126–127, 143–145, 148–149, 211, 231–232, 358
    role in religious education 63, 382–385
    the Latin alphabet as model for the Russian civil script 57–61
    mentioned 188–189, 194, 255, 259, 262, 284, 334
Lavrov, P. A. 199
Law Code (Ulozhenie) of 1649 156
Learned words:
    as a purist rubric 139, 169–170, 234–235
    the rubric's reconceptualization in Russia 144–145, 169–170, 234–235, 368–369
Lebedev, V. 127
Lecoutz de Lévizac, Jean-Pons-Victor 385
Lehfeldt, W. 168, 182
Leipzig Association 133
Lemke, M. K. 416, 420
Lemontey, Pierre-Edouard 380
Lenhoff, Gail 22
Levanda, I., Archpriest 420
Levin, P. 104
Levin, V. D. 66, 110, 119, 245, 343, 356, 366, 387
Lewy, H. 199
Lexical oppositions:
    their role in opposing standard bookish and the "simple" language 73–75
    their absence in texts of the hybrid register 12, 17–18, 79–80
    their irrelevance for early texts in the "simple" language 79–80, 144–145
    the opposition of specifically

bookish and neutral lexicon 145–148
    lexical correction in texts in the "simple" language 74–75, 147–148, 150–151
    rethinking lexicon in genetic terms 148–152
    its attestation in grammars 154–155, 158
    their irrelevance for poetic texts 178–181
    correlative pairs of genetic Russicisms and Slavonicisms 149–152, 241–242, 365–366

Lexical–morphological correspondences:
    pleophony (pleophonic forms) 12, 14–15, 79–81, 82–85, 120–121, 149–151, 154, 184–186, 205–206, 223–224, 228, 240–241, 315–316, 318, 377
    *or, *ol reflexes 14
    the prefix раз-/роз- 79, 82, 86, 121, 150, 241
    e/o at the start of a word 82, 154
    ж/жд in place of *dj 120, 150, 179
    ч/щ in place of *tj, *kt 150
    the alternation of velars and sibilants 80–81
    the prefix вы-/из- 150
    the prefix в-/во- 150
    nouns in -ий/-ей 159

Lexicon:
    bookish and non-bookish 79–80, 87–88, 145–148
    lexical correction in texts of the Petrine period 87–88
    the problem of lexical selectivity in French purism and its reconceptualization in Russia 139–143, 169–170, 235–248
    the problem of generic-stylistic classification 141–143, 242, 267–275
    specifically bookish lexicon 88, 101–102, 115–116, 145–148
    specifically non-bookish lexicon 145
    neutral lexicon 145–148
    genetic Russicisms and Slavonicisms 84–85, 87, 88, 144–146, 148–152, 165–166, 211, 270–271, 272–274
    the common lexical fund of Russian and Church Slavonic 273–274
    Church Slavonic lexicon as stylistically neutral 273–275, 343
    Church Slavonic lexicon as stylistically elevated 233, 273–275, 363–367
    as the main object of interest in the genetic approach 85–86

Ligarid, Paisii, Metropolitan of Gaza 30
Likhachev, D. S. 26
Likhacheva, O. P. 40
Likhud Sofronii:
    his cultural and linguistic position 69–70, 73, 77–78
    his corrections to Varenius' *General Geography* 92–96, 73–75, 77, 80–82, 88–90, 99, 121–122, 147–151, 181, 245, 255, 325
    participation in Bible translation editing 69–70
    and the "simple" Greek language 70
    relations with Fedor Polikarpov 69–70

Linguistic practice:
    and the realization of linguistic directives 4–7, 66–68, 165–166, 178–179, 245
    and the lack of correspondence to linguistic programs 167–171, 188–189, 210–211, 277–278, 280, 400
    the justification of individual practices 185–186, 292

Linguistic programs:
    their significance in the formation of the literary language 4–7, 124, 125
    and linguistic practice 66–68, 139–143, 165–171, 188–189, 210–211, 214, 245, 277–278, 280, 292

Linguistic signs:
    conventional and non–conventional perception 287, 410–411, 414–416, 426–428

Literary tradition:
    its significance in France 189–191
    its significance in Russia 189–193
    its significance in the development of the bookish language 21–24, 37
    continuity as a factor of literary development 21–23, 47–48, 135, 185, 188–189, 191–193, 205–207, 209, 210
    rejecting tradition as characteristic of the new Russian literature 166–169, 170–171, 189–191, 210, 235–236

the problem of its legitimization 193, 195–196, 201–202, 204–207, 228–229
formation of new literary tradition in Russia 213–214, 363–364
as source for the linguistic norm 286–287, 290–295, 298–302, 342, 363–366, 380, 400
as a means for fixing usage 262–266
its relation to the richness of a language 233, 236–237

Liturgy:
the liturgical basis of Orthodox culture 24, 212
place in Enlightenment culture 306
and new national languages 211–212, 218, 301–302
and the knowledge of Church Slavonic 299–300

Livet, Charles–Louis 134, 168, 268

Livy 334

Lomonosov, M. B.:
linguistic program and practice in his early period 164–165, 170, 177–178, 188–189, 205–207
linguistic program 216–218, 229–230, 231–234, 236–238, 240–244, 246, 249, 252, 290–291
stylistic theory 142–143, 233, 271–280, 405
principles of grammatical normalization 276–280
on the sources of the linguistic norm 205–206, 233–234, 243, 249, 290–291, 301–302
genetic parameters in grammar and lexicon 164, 229–230, 272–280
attitude toward the previous literary tradition 170, 189–192, 206–207
the poetics of his odes 194–196, 200, 202–204, 206–207
the relation of Russian and Church Slavonic to Greek 228, 253, 259–260
the differences between Church Slavonic and Russian 164, 228, 230
the merits of the Russian literary language 215–217, 237–238, 262–263
on its richness 253, 262–263
on Muscovite dialect as the model 243
on polyfunctionalism 217–218, 221
on a language's geographical spread 216–217
on the natural unity of Russian and Church Slavonic 228–230
relationship to French literary–linguistic theories and to French 188–189, 217
familiarity with Western literary and linguistic theories 216, 252, 268–269
on Feofan Prokopovich's language 231–232, 337
familiarity with Paus' grammar 160, 164–165
polemics with Sumarokov 194–195, 200, 202–203, 234–235, 242–243, 284, 291–294
translation of Fénélon's ode 131, 178
marginal notes on Trediakovskii's *New and Short Guide* 178, 180, 183, 205
"Letter on the Rules of Russian Versification" 182, 188, 190, 206
"Ode on the Taking of Khotin" 178, 206–207
Rhetoric (1744) 206–207, 233, 290, 337
"On the Plural Ending of Long-form Adjectives" 164, 229–231
translation of *Wolff's Experimental Physics* 246
Short Manual of Oratory 202, 216–217, 284
comments on I. Shishkin's translation 263
Russian Grammar 123, 128, 164–165, 230, 231, 240, 275–279, 290–291, 293
"Materials for the Grammar" 230, 235, 238, 244, 279
"On the Current State of the Verbal Arts in Russia" 217, 274
"Foreword on the Use of Church Books" 217, 232, 238, 240, 249, 253, 275, 301
Odes 178, 196, 200, 203, 231
"Philological Research and Evidence" 217, 236, 262
"On Translations" 223, 262
"Hymn to the Beard" 316
reception of his literary and linguistic activity 259–260, 262, 333–335, 342–343, 356–359, 362, 371–374
mentioned 67, 238–239, 242–246, 282–287, 292, 318, 329, 333–337, 339, 340, 342–343, 345, 356–359, 366, 369,

388, 395, 410, 417, 420
Lopatinskii, Feofilakt 71, 99, 106, 114, 304
Lopukhin, I. V. 391
Lotman, Iu. M. 44, 52, 59, 61, 63, 117, 130, 135, 190, 208, 344, 356, 364, 370, 371, 377, 398, 411, 415, 418, 419, 424
Louis XIV 52, 208, 220
Louis XVI 352
Ludolf, G. V. (Heinrich-Wilhelm):
    his linguistic doctrine 156
    juxtaposition of the functions of Russian and Church Slavonic 55, 156
    juxtaposition of Russian and Church Slavonic elements in his grammar 154–155
    influence of his grammar on the later grammatical tradition 153
    use of his material by Paus 158, 159, 160
    use of his material in Adodurov's essay on grammar 161
Lukicheva, E. V. 68, 88
Lunt, H. G. 13
Lyzlov, A. 43

Macaronism:
    as a mark of Baroque texts and pedants' usage 266–267, 269–270
    in lexicon 267–268, 274, 280
    in grammar 266–268, 276
    seen as characteristic of Slavenorossiiskii by the Karamzinists 358, 410–411
Madariaga, Isabel de 47, 351
Maikov, V. I. 231, 333
Makarov, P. I. 359–362, 366, 370, 374, 379
Makeeva, V. N. 340
Makogonenko, G. P. 349
Maksim Grek, Saint 27, 28, 29, 30, 31, 36, 147
Maksim Ispovednik, Saint 405
Maksimov, Fedor 69, 70
Maksimovich, I., corrector (spravshchik) 75, 77
Malherbe, F. 136, 137, 138, 171, 172, 173, 175, 208, 286, 335, 359, 362
    and Malherbistes 171, 173, 205
Malov, E. B., priest, 389
Marfa, Posadnitsa (governess) of Novgorod 236
Mariia Fedorovna, Empress 393
Markel Rodyshevskii 304
Marker, Gary 353, 412, 413

Markers of bookishness:
    their establishment in the process of learning the bookish language 9–11
    their role in constituting the registers of the written language of medieval Rus' 12, 14, 16–18, 35, 39–40, 82–83, 91, 119, 144–145, 181, 231–232
    dependence on the character of the conversational tongue 12, 18
    their elimination from the literary language of the new type 73–84, 87–91, 94, 119–120, 153–155, 162, 164–165, 176
    the view of them as elements of Slavonic antiquity 227
    their reconceptualization as indicators of style 231, 323, 328–331
    their use in the language of religious literature 312–320, 324–325, 327–328
Marmontel, Jean-François 304, 352, 385
Martel, A. 139, 230, 231, 245, 273, 280, 340
Marti, P. 22
Martial 242
Massillion, Jean-Baptiste 336, 385, 397
Mathiesen, R. 19
Mauvillon, E. 269
Maxentius, Roman emperor 61
Mechkovskaia, N. B. 27, 30
Medvedev, Sil'vestr 114, 190
Mefodii (Smirnov), Bishop of Voronezh 331
Meissner, August Gottlieb 379, 385
Mela, Pomponius 184
Melchior Junius 44
Merilo Pravednoe (Scale of Righteousness) 34
Meshcherskii, N. A. 8, 65, 66
Metaphor:
    permissibility from the point of view of purism 173–174, 187, 204–205
    in Russian panegyric poetry 194–196
    and the non–conventional linguistic sign 420–422
Methodius (Mefodii), Saint, Enlightener of the Slavs 30, 376
Mikhail (Desnitskii), Metropolitan of Petersburg 397
Mikhail Klopskii, Saint 23
Mikhal'chi, D. E. 157
Miller G.-F. (Gerhard Friedrich Müller), 300
Minich, Count von (Burkhard Christoph von Münnich) 200
Miraculous:
    as an attribute of Baroque poetics

173–174, 200, 202–203
Mit'kov, V. F., Staff-Captain 414
Młodzianowski, T. 104
Moisei (Gumilevskii), Bishop of Theodosia 257, 260, 262
Moisei (Putilov), Archimandrite of Optina Pustyn' 352
Molière 169
Monin, J. E. du 138
Montaigne, M. 359, 362
Montesquieu, C. L. 350, 385, 386
Morev, I. 107
Mori, J. S., Cardinal 385
Morozov, A. 194
Morozov, P. 105, 111, 193
Moscow dialect:
    as model for the literary language 243, 294, 404–405
Moses, prophet 426
Mosheim, J. L. von 328, 337
Murav'ev, A. N. 420
Murav'ev, M. N. 191, 260, 274
Musin-Pushkin, I. A. 53, 55, 56, 57, 68, 69, 71

Nakoval'nin, S. F. 338, 339
Napoleon I 352–353
Nasedka, Ivan 28, 35, 36
Nationality (narodnost'):
    as a category of national self-consciousness 50, 369–370, 373–377, 378
    in language 166–167, 369–372, 402–403
Nechaev, N. V. 412
Nechaev, S. D., Ober-Procuror of the Synod 412
Necker, Madame (Suzanne Curchod) 269
Nectarius, Patriarch of Jerusalem 97
Neddermeyer, U. 250
Negation:
    single and double 74, 325, 369
Neologisms:
    as a rubric of French and German purism 139, 170, 246, 248
    in poetry 171
    reconceptualization of this rubric in Russia 137, 239, 246–248, 344, 368–369
    reconceptualization in religious purism 396, 398, 406
    Fedor Polikarpov's neologisms 115, 146, 147
    Trediakovskii's neologisms 115, 248
    and the reclamation of words from Church books 300–301, 344, 368, 406
Neronov, Ioann, priest 39, 312
Nestor, Saint, chronicler 236, 376
Nevostruev, K. I. 70, 108, 115, 147
Nicholas I 346, 353, 391, 426
Nichols, J. 22
Nichols, R. L. 352, 383, 386
Nicole, P. 138, 264, 288
Nikitenko, A. V. 423, 424
Nikodim (Kazantsev), Bishop of Krasnoiarsk 393
Nikol'skii, N. 33
Nikon, Patriarch 33, 38, 102, 105
Normalization:
    in texts of the Petrine era 78–82, 121–122, 181
    as a principle of perfecting Church Slavonic 99–101
    as the main process in forming the Russian literary language of the new type in the post-Petrine period 119–124, 127–130, 142–143, 212–214
    the completion of normalization and the change in focus onto the problem of style 367, 369–370, 380–381, 388
    in the language of religious literature 324–326, 327–328
    in morphology 153–167, 226, 271–272
    working out its principles 123, 130, 138–139
    on the basis of style 123, 275–280
Notes to the Gazette (Primechaniia k vedomostiam) 121, 141, 177, 248
Noun endings:
    variatitvity that is not relevant for opposing registers of the written language 78–83, 312–314, 315–317
    editing in manuscripts of the Petrine period 80–81
    normalization within the framework of the Academy grammatical tradition 155, 158–165
    conceptualized in genetic categories 154–165
    interpreted as poetic license 175–176, 182–184, 186
    syncretism of animate masc. and gen. 158–159
    second genitive 78–79, 120, 154, 277, 279–280, 324–325

second prepositional 277, 279–280, 324–325
    gen.-prep. sg and gen sg.
i-declensions 158–159
    dat. sg. *ja*-declensions 158–161
    instr. sg. 176
    nom. pl. *o*-declensions 325–326
    nom. pl. *i*-declensions 158–159
    nom.-acc. pl. neut. 324–326
    gen. pl. *o*-declensions 175
    dat. pl. 78–80, 89, 120–121, 155, 158–159, 164, 230, 311, 313–314, 316, 318–319, 325–326
    instr. pl. 79–80, 89, 120–121, 155, 176, 182–184, 186, 229, 231, 311, 315–319, 325–326, 339–340
    prep. pl. 79–81, 89, 120–121, 155, 158–159, 311, 315, 318–319, 325–326
    the paradigm *господин – господь* 159
    the paradigm *мать, дочь* 159
    declension of neuter nouns with stem ending in a consonant 163–165
    the paradigm *дитя* 164–165
Novgorod dialect 224, 225
Novikov, N. I. 246, 353, 354, 357

Obnorskii, S. P. 112, 113, 183, 239
Ode, see: Panegyric poetry.
Okenfuss, Max 412
Olga, Princess and Saint 142
Olivet, Abbé Pierre-Joseph Thoulier 263
Onfim, author of writings on birch bark 8
Opitz, Martin 182
Ordinal numerals:
    normalization in Lomonosov's grammar 277–280
Orientation on texts:
    as a mechanism of learning the bookish language 9–11, 17, 21–22
Origen 199
Orlov, A. S. 256
Orthography:
    as an object of normalization 13, 81, 82, 127–129, 154, 255–256, 284–285, 377
Ostrovskii, A. N. 419
Otten, F. 21, 110
"Overblown" language 170, 274, 297
Ovid 302, 216, 334, 335
Oxymoron, as a feature of Baroque poetics 198, 203

Paisii Velichkovskii, Saint 308
Pakhomov, M. 345
Panchenko, A. M. 52, 192, 193
Panegyrical poetry, ode:
    as a special literary tradition 136–137, 191–209, 270–271
    place in early modern culture 208, 303–304
    functioning 191–193
    Baroque elements 198–204
    decline of the tradition 347–349
    linguistic characteristics 192–193, 231, 270–272
Panin, N. I. 347
Participles:
    as markers of bookishness 12, 16, 18, 86, 120
    correction in the changeover to the "simple" language 74, 76, 77
    in the literary language of the new type 227, 277–280, 363–364
    present passive participles 277–279
    past passive participles 299–230
    truncated participles 230
    participles in *-ай/-яй* as marked Slavonicisms 231, 313, 315, 324–325
    their normalization in Lomonosov's grammar 277–280
Participles:
    in *-ще* as marker of bookishness 38
    their normalization in Lomonosov's grammar 277–279
Patriarchate:
    and the symphonic relation of clergy and kingdom 65, 96, 101–102, 105–106
Patru, Olivier 133
Paul I 309
Paus, I. V. (Johann Werner Paus[e]):
    on the correlation of Church Slavonic and Russian 157–160, 162, 220, 225–227, 229
    on polyfunctionalism 156, 220
    orientation on written usage 157
    Grammatica Slavono-Russica 122, 157–162, 164–165, 181, 225–226, 273
    Observations 157, 160, 226
    use of Glück's grammar 122, 160
    use of Ludolf's grammar 159–161
    use of Smotritskii's grammar 159
    influence on the later grammatical tradition 153, 160–162

influence on Adodurov 160–162, 220
influence on Trediakovskii 160, 220, 225–227, 229
influence on Lomonosov 160, 164–165
mentioned 221, 277
Pavskii, G. P. 388, 389
Pedantry, pedants:
as a cultural and linguistic concern 234, 235, 269–270
Pekarskii, P. P. 59, 63, 71, 72, 112, 116, 122, 126, 128, 149, 169, 214, 215, 221, 232, 235, 239, 240, 242, 248, 255, 256, 263, 265, 271, 296, 298–300, 332
Pellisson-Fontanier, Paul 134
Pennington, A. E. 3, 89, 90
Peplier, Ropert Jean de 216
Perfect tense, see: Preterites.
Perrault, Charles:
on the significance of a national language 2
and the "Quarrel Between Ancients and Moderns" 136–138, 196, 222, 250
Peshtich, S. L. 76, 83
Peskov, A. M. 136
Peter I:
his cultural policy 45–47, 58–59, 72–73, 95–96, 113–114
church policy 72, 95–96, 414
his historical conception 117
and the process of secularization 44–46, 49–53, 94
language policy 52–53, 65–69, 71–74, 91, 94, 117, 126, 148, 160, 165–166, 211–213
attitude toward Church Slavonic 95–97, 144–145, 160, 371–372
the introduction of the civil script 53–56, 94
Triumph (his entry into Moscow in 1703) 59–62
poteshnyi ("amusing") regiments 95–96
election and ordination of a prince–pope 96
Father of the Fatherland 117
mentioned 90, 99, 109–111, 145, 147, 168, 169, 213, 268–269, 284–285, 313–314, 318–319, 339–341, 350, 353–354, 370–371, 373–376

Peter Mohyla (Petr Mogila):
Catechesis or Confession of the Orthodox Faith 97, 98
Petersburg culture:
and new national self-consciousness 125, 167–167, 212–214, 303–304, 369–377
and achieving self-sufficiency 380–381
as court culture 192–193, 303–304
as aristocratic culture 346–347, 375–376
and the clergy 307–309, 346, 351–353, 414
and linguistic programs 125, 132–135
Petit-maîtres, see: Fops.
Petersburg Spiritual Academy 385, 420
Petrov, A. L. 38
Petrov, V. P. 230, 358
Petrova, Z. M. 256
Petrukhin, P. V. 19
Petukhov, E. V. 45
Philo of Alexandria 199
Picchio, Ricardo 24, 26, 42, 218, 259
Pietism 354, 386–387
and Sentimentalism 386
Pindar 136, 174, 196–198, 200, 201, 204, 206, 207, 252, 334, 335
Pisanus, Alphonsus (Al'phons Pizan)147
Plato 345, 385, 386, 420
Platon (Levshin), Metropolitan of Moscow:
teaching literacy 9
view of religious education 382–384
relations with Gedeon Krinovskii 321, 326
Collection of Sermons for All Sundays and Holidays 306, 327–330, 331, 339
Orthodox Doctrine 329, 413
translation of John Chrysostom's sermons 331
his *Life of St. Sergius of Radonezh* 331
mentioned 331, 335, 354–355, 386–388, 392
Pléiade, poets of the Pléiade 171, 197, 362
Pleophony, see: Lexical–morphological correspondences.
Pleshcheev, M. I. (under the pseudonym "Anglomane") 368
Pletneva, A. A. 283, 405

Pliny (the Elder) 43
Podshivalov, V. S. 333, 334, 364, 365, 421
Poetic language:
    its correlation to the language of prose in various linguistic traditions 171–175, 186–189, 256–258
    its relation to the conversational language 136–137, 171–173, 184–185
    its relation to the traditional bookish language in Russia 186
    as a manifestation of poetic ecstasy 136
Poetic license (or liberties):
    its interpretation in Classicist poetics 172, 174–175, 250–251
    as a way of legitimizing the Church Slavonic linguistic legacy 149–150, 162–164, 174–186, 188–189, 205–206, 265–266, 363–365
    change in attitude to it in the development of Slavonicizing purism 229
    Russicisms as poetic license 242, 344
Pogodin, M. P. 51, 52, 118
Pokrovskii, I. 308
Pokrovskii, N. N. 28
Polemical versus practical position in literary issues 193–196, 198–200, 203–205, 234–235, 240–241, 247, 271–272, 291
Polevoi, N. A. 372
Polikarpov, Fedor:
    his cultural and linguistic position 61–64, 78, 99–102, 106–107
    on educational methods 9, 100
    justification of the grammatical approach to the written language 68, 99–102
    defense of Grecified orthography 54, 56–58, 114–116, 147, 255
    his Grecophilism 63, 101, 147
    his participation in Bible translation 99
    his use of Church Slavonic 30
    on the dual number 100, 228
    Trilingual Primer 57, 61–62, 114, 147–148, 149
    Trilingual Lexicon 63–64, 100, 103, 115, 116, 248
    as translator of Varenius' General Geography 68–71, 77, 80, 87, 90, 94, 115, 148
    Chin tekhnologii (1721) 228
    grammatical treatise (1724) 56, 58, 64
    Tekhnologiia (1725) 57–58, 78, 147, 154, 161, 277
    diary entries 30
    his relations with Sofronii Likhud 68–70
    Kantemir's view of him 114, 190
    Trediakovskii's view of him 114–115, 259
    mentioned 54, 255
Polish (language):
    its lack of correspondence to purist criteria 372
Polonisms 90, 91
Polyfunctionalism of the new literary language:
    as a general requirement 2–3
    its absence in the written language of medieval Rus' 2–3, 69–70
    the contradictory nature of Peter I's language program 94–95, 108–110, 211–214
    its establishment in the Russian literary language of the new type 46–48, 83–84, 92–93, 126–127, 214–221, 228–229, 331, 378
Polyglossia, and the problem of linguistic misunderstanding as a result of social differentiation 112–113, 355–356, 418–419
Pomey, François Antoine 252
Popov, M. S. 303
Popov, M. V. 231, 339, 344, 414
Popovskii, N. N. 254
"Popular" speech, vulgarisms:
    as a rubric of French purism 139, 169–170, 234–235
    the reconceptualization of this rubric in Russia 141–142, 169–170, 234–235, 239–242, 272–273, 315, 367–368
    the rejection of "popular speech" in Platon Levshin's translations 329–330
    the reconceptualization of this rubric in religious purism 399–405
    as a category of linguistic description 123–124, 141–142, 315
Port-Royal grammar and grammatical tradition 251, 253, 287
Potemkin, G. A. 347
Pozdneev, A. V. 193
Pozharskii, D. M., Prince 376
Preterites:

simple preterits as marker of bookishness (as specifically Church Slavonic forms) 10–11, 14, 16–18, 38, 77–78, 86, 96–97, 120, 165, 224–227, 229–230, 312–319

    attested in grammars as distinguishing feature of Church Slavonic 77–78, 154, 159–160, 164, 230, 255

    the functioning of simple preterits in various registers of the bookish language 14, 19–21

    their semantic reinterpretation in chronicles 19–21

    and book editing 27–28

    artificial normalization 30

    correction in the changeover to the "simple" language 73–77, 328–330

    their occasional use in texts in the new literary language 231

    simple preterits as an element of elevated style 283, 328–330, 331, 338–339

    simple preterits in religious literature 312–320, 324–325, 328–330, 331, 339

    the aorist in -*тъ* as an archaism 100

    aorist in emulation of classical themes 183–185

    the aorist *бысть* in the incohative meaning 231

    the perfect with linking verb in changeover to the simple language 73–74, 77, 120

    the perfect with linking verb as an archaism 100

    the perfect with linking verb as an element of elevated style 283

    the perfect with linking verb in religious literature 314–320, 324–325

Prévost, A. F. d'Exiles 334

Pronouns:

    personal 164, 230, 317, 325–326

    personal first pers. sg. 90, 159–160, 324

    personal second pers. *ты* and *вы* (as the polite form) 168–170

    enclitic pronouns as a specific trait of Church Slavonic 77, 155, 159–160, 177–178, 317

    enclitic pronouns as poetic license 175–179, 205–206

    enclitic pronouns as a way of creating a classical feeling 177–179, 184–185

    possessive pronouns 155

    relative pronouns (*иже*, *еже*, *юже*, *яже*) 77, 159, 234, 316, *который* 279

    interrogative pronouns 159–162, indicative pronouns 100, 159–160

    the indicatives *сей*, *оный*, *этот* 241, 271, 364, 401

Pronunciation, bookish:

    as basis for local adaptation and unification of the bookish language 13

    in sermons 403–405

Prophetic gifts (prophetic speech):

    in poetry 136, 198–199, 201–204, 283

    see also: Ecstasy, poetic.

Proskurnin, N. P. 54

Protasov, N. A., Ober-Procuror of the Synod 393, 410

Psalter:

    its use in teaching the bookish language 9–11, 29, 102–103, 412

    and book editing 28

    Avraamii Firsov's translation 23, 38, 39

    and the poetics of French literature 196–197, 204–206

    and the poetics of Russian literature 194, 197, 204–207

    and the language of panegyric poetry 170, 192–193, 197, 204–207, 379

    and the lexicon of Church Slavonic 235–237

    Psalm paraphrases 177–178, 183, 194, 228–229, 231, 283, 338–339

    mentioned 390

Pseudo-Longinus:

    "On the Sublime" 199

    mentioned 196, 252, 385, 386

Pufendorf, Samuel von 50

Pugachev, E. I. 346

Pumpianskii, L. V. 114, 125, 133, 134, 135, 137, 186, 192, 208, 252

Purism, see: Classicism, linguistic doctrine; Purism, religious; Purism, rationalist; Purism, Slavonicizing.

Purism, rationalist:

    and the sources of the norm of the literary language 5–7, 138–139, 287–289, 290–302

and Vaugelas' ideas 287–289
Purism, religious:
    interpretation of the purist rubrics 394–407
    contrasted to secular purism 388, 390–391, 394–397, 398–408
    as a doctrine of linguistic piety 406–411, 414–115, 420–421, 423–428
Purism, Slavonicizing:
    relationship to French purism 235–248, 264–265, 290, 293–294, 297–299, 399–400
    as basis for the Slavenorossiiskii language 228–234, 259–260, 264–266, 297–302, 345, 394–395
    its interpretation in religious literature 389, 394–407
Pushkin, A. S.:
    linguistic position 364, 379–381
    relationship to the archaists and innovators 378
    and the problem of nationality 378
    and literary traditions 378, 380–381
    "Notes on the Uprising" 346
    Boris Godunov 378, 380
    "On Mr. Lemontey's Foreword to his Translation of Krylov's Fables" 380
    "On the Insignificance of Russian Literature" 362
    Gavriliada 414
    "Second Epistle to the Censor" 423
    mentioned 352, 366, 423
Pushkin, V. L. 379
Pypin, A. N. 354
Pythagorus 202, 203, 243

Quintilian 264, 289, 295, 373, 385, 386

Rabelais, François 359
Racan, Honorat de Bueil, seigneur de 138
Racine, Jean 172, 191, 213, 300, 335
Radishchev, A. N. 231, 353
Rak, V. D. 216
Ransel, David L. 347
Reflexive verbs:
    changing -ся to -сь as part of the "simple" language 77
Régnier-Demarais, F. S. 223
Religious literature:
    the emergence of the opposition between religious and secular literatures 41–43
    debates over the character of its language in the Petrine period 96–99
    as source for secular literature 192–193, 198–200
    and the juxtaposition between the civil and church language 212, 218–220, 331, 390–391
    choice between Church Slavonic and "Slavenorossiiskii" 310, 320–321, 323–324, 326–327, 328–331, 391
    its unity with secular literature 303–304, 310, 331–337, 338–341, 343, 345, 383–384, 387, 419
    its assimilation of the "secular" literary language 308–309, 323, 325–326, 329–330, 338–340, 386–387, 400, 419–420
    the search for a tradition 351–352, 411
    the break from traditions of secular literature 351–353, 380–381, 383, 386, 388, 390–391, 408–417
    as the property of the clerical estate 391–393
Retabulation, the mechanism of markers of bookishness 9–11, 13, 17, 21–22, 92
Rhetoric:
    as part of grammatical education 30–33
    function as social regulator (Dekorum-Rhetorik) 44
    the rhetorical classification of styles 141–143, 267–271, 274
    rhetorical manuals' view of poetic inspiration 199
Rhymed and unrhymed verse:
    in connection with linguistic richness 184–185, 256–258
    masculine and feminine rhyme 170, 190–191
    infinitive rhymes 177–178, 189–190
Riazanskaia, E. L. 128, 129, 165
Richelieu, Armand-Jean Plessis de, cardinal 351
Richness (abundance) of a literary language 171, 172, 211, 233, 236–239, 249–263, 334, 340, 359–362, 376, 394–395
    and the rejection of borrowings 238–239, 344–345, 368
Riker, P. 4
Riumina, O. L. 86
Rizhskii, I. S. 267, 280, 294, 343

Rohde, E. 199
Rolli, P. A. 187, 188, 256
Rollin, Charles:
    view of "genius of the language" 222
    view of the difference between "ancient" and "modern" languages 251–253
    attitude toward poetic language 174–175, 197
    on Roman teaching of Latin 264
    Trediakovskii's view of him 174–175, 252
    mentioned 174, 248, 253, 256, 257, 258, 286, 385, 386
Roman empire:
    as model for Russian absolutism 59–63, 65
Romanticism:
    and the problem of the national spirit 191, 369–370
"Romantizm":
    as a purist rubric in Ia. K. Amfiteatrov 408–409
Romodanovskii, F. Iu. 96
Ronsard, Pierre de 138, 167, 171, 173, 197, 201, 362
Root characteristics of language, see: Language, spirit.
Rotar, I. 101
Rothe, H. 47, 193, 195, 335, 354
Rousseau, Jean-Baptiste 196, 205, 335
Rubinshtein, N. L. 52
Rules:
    as the source of Church Slavonic's norms 68–69
    as the basis for pure language 173–174, 288–293, 294–296, 342
Runkevich S. G. 106
Russian Academy 134, 247, 260, 294, 306, 331, 333, 341, 351, 369, 392, 422, 425, 427
Russian Assembly (Rossiiskoe sobranie) 128, 132
Russian literary language of the new type:
    its formation in contrast to Church Slavonic 46–47, 54, 65–79, 82–85, 94, 142–143, 210–211
        polyfunctionalism 2–4, 46, 48, 83–84, 91–95, 108–110, 156, 212–213, 218–221, 228–229, 331, 378
        universality 2–4, 47–48, 94–95, 112, 119, 298–299, 308–310, 335, 340, 355–356, 382
    codification 2–4, 48, 119–124
    stylistic differentiation 2–4, 48, 86, 88, 123, 231, 269–280
    method of learning it 121–123, 127–128, 153, 155, 212–214
    its connection with the previous literary and linguistic tradition 142–143, 210–211, 228–229, 236–237, 245, 249, 264–266, 298–302
    relation to the simple language of the Petrine era 121, 123, 170
    its grammatical normalization 4–7, 78–82, 121–124, 128–130, 138–139, 142–143, 153–167
    application of purist criteria to it 4–7, 138–143, 165–167, 169–171, 233–248
    its place among European literary languages 126–128, 132–134, 187–189, 213–218, 237–238, 253–254, 257–258, 259–262
    its evaluation in the context of Petrine cultural policies 46–47, 61–62, 68–70, 71–73, 94–95, 115–117
    its connection with secularization 47–48, 94–95, 210–212
    as a special "civil" tongue 68–69, 71, 94–95, 108, 157, 212, 218, 220–222, 331
    as an instrument of power 1, 3–4, 10–11, 46–48, 52–53, 119
    its evaluation in aesthetic terms 126–127, 137–138
    change from the mechanism of registers to that of styles 231–232
    place of lexical Slavonicisms in it 65–66, 83–88, 143–152, 165–166, 176, 188–189, 207, 211, 224–225, 231–235, 270–275, 363–367
    individual approaches to markers that differentiate it from Church Slavonic 180–185
    the unity of its nature with Church Slavonic 218, 220–232, 261–262, 297, 357–358, 367, 380, 390, 394–395
    its connection with Greek through Church Slavonic 253–254, 259–262, 360–361, 376–377, 380
    as "Slavenorossiiskii" 228–229, 231–235, 264–266, 308–310, 356–361, 388
    its richness 233, 236–239, 249, 253–263, 334, 340, 344–345, 359–363,

367–368, 394–396
    its use in religious literature 212, 308–309, 323–331, 338–341
    in religious education 384–385, 391
    the rejection of "Slavenorossiiskii" 356–361
    its Slavonicized variant as the language of the clerical caste 388
    the purity of its Slavonicized variant as an ideological category 396–397, 406–411, 414–115
    the opposition of secular and religious literary languages 388, 390–396, 399–411, 421–428
    the problem of its derivation 83–87
Russkaia Pravda 376
Rychkov, P. I. 116, 239, 240
Ryleev, K. F. 379
Rzhevskii, A. A. 243, 294

Saint-Amant, Antoine Girard de 167
Saint-Gellais, Mellin de 201
Sappho 135
Saul, king of Israel 318
Saurin, Jacques 328
Sazonova, L. I. 193
Schenk, D. 348
Schottelius, J. G. 223
Schumacher, J.-D. (I.-D. Shumakher) 214
Scipio 376
Scott, Walter 422, 423
Scudery, Georges de 173, 174, 274, 281
Scudery, Madeleine de 135
Second South Slavic Influence 25–27, 56, 57, 88, 145, 146
Secular literature:
    as a missing category of East Slavic medieval culture 41–43
    in Church Slavonic 68–69
    as opposed to religious literature 212, 218, 220, 378–379, 388, 390–391, 408–415
    connections with religious literature in the framework of the panegyric tradition 192–193, 337, 379
    its unification with religious literature into one single literature 303–304, 310, 331–337, 338–341, 343, 345, 387, 419
    and the opposition between civil and church languages 211–213, 217–220, 308–309, 390–391
    and the opposition between civil and church scripts 412–415
    the perception of its language as profane 390, 408–411, 415–416, 421–425
    see also: Religious literature.
Secularization of culture:
    in Western Europe 40–42
    in Russia 41–45, 130–131, 334, 411–412, 415–416, 418
    as a phenomenon of court culture 44–45
    secular culture as a means of educating society 45–46
    its influence on language 46–48, 94–95, 130–131, 210–211, 418
Seemann, K.-D., 22
Semantic innovation 130–131
Semantic reinterpretation:
    in the transmission of texts 19–20
Semenov, N., pupil of the Likhudis 69
Semiotization of behavior:
    in the Petrine period 51–52, 93, 111
    and religious purism 355–356, 415–417
Senate 111, 215, 332, 350, 351
Seneca 322
Senkovskii, O. I. (Baron Brambeus) 401, 409, 410
Serafim (Glagolevskii), Metropolitan of St. Petersburg 384, 390
Serbian (language) 359, 376
Sergii (Sergius) Radonezhskii, Saint 331
Serman, I. Z. 252
Sermons, see: Homiletics.
Seznec, J. 41
Shchapov, Ia. N. 145
Shcherbatov, M. M.:
    on the language of jurisprudence 113
    on Feofan Prokopovich's language 338–339
    and the publication of Feofan Prokopovich's *History of Peter the Great* 75–76, 338–339
Sheremetevskii, V. 308
Shevchenko, I. I. 42, 43
Shevelov, G. 105
Shevyrev, S. P. 360
Shirinskii-Shikhmatov, S. A. 379
Shishkin, A. B. 131, 333
Shishkin, I. V. 263
Shishkov, A. S.:

Index

cultural position 369–372, 374–376, 378–379
    attitude toward Slavic antiquity 369–371, 374–376
    on compound words 361
    his linguistic conception 367–369, 372–373, 390
    attitude toward Feofan Prokopovich's language 337–338
    on the translation of the Bible into Russian 390–391
    mentioned 393, 423, 426
Shitsgal, A. G. 74, 53, 55, 58, 59, 64
Shmurlo, E. 76
Short Description of the Commentaries of the Academy of Sciences 214
Shtelin, Ia. Ia. (Jakob von Stählin) 128
Shuvalov, A. P. 304
Shuvalov, I. I. 321
Shvanvits, M. (Martin Schwanwitz) 121, 122, 127, 128, 155, 160, 161, 165, 220
Sidorovskii, I. I., priest 331, 345
Signorini, S. 138, 253, 291
Simeon Polotskii 30, 37, 38, 192, 197, 310, 311, 322, 383, 340
Simon (Todorskii), Bishop of Kostroma 318–320
Simonov Monastery, Moscow 308
Simple language:
    the possibility of various linguistic realizations 37–40, 97–98
    the hybrid register in this function 23–24, 36–37, 312–314
    defined negatively, in relation to the traditional bookish language in the Petrine era 74–76, 77–79, 150–151
    unclear principles of normalization 78–81, 92–93, 118–122
    as the language of the new culture 71–73, 108–109
    see also: Simplicity in language.
Simplicity in language:
    and religious conflict 34–35
    in connection with the development of the grammatical approach 36, 97–98
    and the registers of the bookish language 36–37, 97–98
    the contradiction between traditionalism and comprehensibility 37, 39–41
    declarations and their realization in language 37–38, 97–99, 322–323
    standard Church Slavonic as the "simple" language 37–38, 97–98, 311–313
    hybrid Church Slavonic as the "simple" language 23–24, 35, 38–40, 312–314
    in Petrine linguistic policy 68–69, 71–73, 88, 96–99
    contradiction with the semiotic functions of the civil tongue 46–47, 110–111
    as characteristic of "new" literary languages 297–299
Simvol Very (the Orthodox creed) 147
Sipovskii, V. V. 48, 377, 378
Sisyphus 132
Sjöberg, A. 123, 156, 157
Skazkin, Isidor, compiler of the Mazurinskii chronicle 23
Skorina, Fransiscus 36
Slavenorossiiskii (language):
    as synthesis of Church Slavonic and Russian 228–233, 235–239, 248–249, 264–266, 272–274, 299–302, 308–309, 331
    as a language embodying a synthesis of secular and religious culture 310, 325–326, 331, 333, 340–345
    the mutual interaction of the language of secular and religious literature in the framework of this synthesis 338–340, 419–420
    Trediakovskii's understanding of it 228–229, 264–266, 299–302
    as the object of criticism by Karamzinists 356–358, 409–411
    its survival in religious literature 388
    as the property of the clerical estate 392–394
Slaviano-Greco-Latino Academy (Spasskii schools, Moscow Spiritual Academy) 59, 63, 65, 71, 104, 166–167, 190–192, 199, 305–306, 320–321, 383–384, 410–411
Slavonicisms (grammatical):
    as a category of linguistic description 86–88, 123–124
    the task of eliminating them from the literary language of the new type 152–153, 160–161, 165, 170–171, 211, 228
    attested in Russian grammars

Index

153–156, 158–165
    as object of stylistic differentiation 144–145, 275–280
    the problem of their legitimization in the new literary language 171, 176, 178–179, 181, 205–207
    their culturological reconceptualization 165–167
    grammatical and lexical Slavonicisms 163–166, 178–179, 369–370
Slavonicisms (lexical):
    as a category of linguistic description 65–67, 84–85, 87, 88
    the task of eliminating them from the literary language of the new type 148–150, 152, 170–171, 179–180, 188–189, 211, 365–367
    Slavonicisms as borrowings 85, 359
    Slavonicisms as archaisms 359, 405–406
    the appearance of this lexical category 144–145, 148–152, 165–167
    as the analogue of Latinisms in French 144–145, 148–149, 211
    as learned words 144–145, 169–170, 224–225, 234
    as poetic license 175, 178–181, 188–189, 205–206, 265–266, 270–271, 363–365
    as object of stylistic differentiation 144–145, 266–275, 279–281, 343, 363–367, 377, 379
    the problem of their legitimization in the new literary language 176, 188–189, 207, 365, 368–369
    in Slavenorossiiskii 233–235, 240–242, 246, 266–275, 368–369
    as a "pure" correlative of borrowings 237–238, 344–345, 367–368
    their culturological reconceptualization 148–149, 408–409
    in the poetic language 149–150, 175–176, 178–181, 205–207, 242, 363–366
    in the language of religious literature 329–330, 399–401, 405–407
    their secularization 393–394, 417–428
Smentsovskii, M. 69
Smirnov, A. A. 104
Smirnov, N. 110
Smirnov, S. K. 65, 330, 382, 384, 385, 386

Smolina, K. P. 91
Smotritskii, Meletii:
    interpretation of the system of past tenses 29, 30
    the differences between Church Slavonic and Greek 101–102
    the publication of 1721 9, 79, 99–100, 181
    the influence of his grammar on the later grammatical tradition 99–101, 123, 153–155, 159
Sobolevskii, A. I. 27, 30, 58, 66, 70, 115, 193
Social contract, the theory of 50, 346
Social stratification 1–2, 42–43, 47–48, 332, 382
Sofiia Alekseevna, Tsarevna 58
Sofronii Mladenovich, Hieromonk 330
Sohier, J. 123, 155, 156
Sokolov, priest 399
Solosin, I. 206
Solov'ev, N. Ia. 419
Solov'ev, S. M. 51
Soluianova, E. G. 178, 181
Song of Igor's Campaign 42, 360, 376
Sorokin, Iu. S. 120, 121, 140, 179, 183, 403
Sove, B. I. 405, 406, 414
Spafarii, Nikolai 30
Spanish (language):
    its lack of correspondence to purist criteria 187–188, 202
    relationship to Latin 223–224, 254
    mentioned 215–216
Speranskii, M. M. 385–387, 399, 411, 419
Spiritual Regulation, see Feofan Prokopovich.
Sreznevskii, I. I. 243, 316, 422, 427
Stahl, J. C. 156, 157
Stang, C. S. 3
State:
    as a philosophical and cultural category 208, 302–303, 349, 351–352, 354–355
    the period of its leading role in cultural history 45–46, 49–52, 192–193, 303–304, 349–355
Statir, book of sermons by an anonymous priest from Perm 37, 311
Stefan Iavorskii 99, 105–107, 114, 303
Strahlenberg, P. J. von 52
Strakhova, O. B. 70, 101, 147
Streshnev, S. 38
Strycek, A. 92

Stupperich, R. 103
Stylistic differentiation 2–4, 48, 86, 88, 123, 136–137
Sukhomlinov, M. I. 11, 216, 305, 307, 311, 328, 331, 333, 340, 341, 369, 397, 422
Sulzer, Johann Gaspar 385
Sumarokov, A. P.:
    linguistic program 4–7, 234–237, 242–244, 280–286
    as advocate of Classicism 198, 202–205, 234–235, 269–270
    attitude toward the previous literary tradition 190–192
    on the sources of the linguistic norm 5–7, 234–237, 243–244, 291–294
    the criterion of taste 280–281
    on the merits of the Russian literary language 215–216, 255
    on the richness of Russian 236–237, 255, 259–260
    on generic-stylistic differentiation 270–271, 281
    on pedantry and pedantic normalization 269–270, 281, 283–286
    on the Moscow dialect 243
    on the reform of the alphabet 58–59
    struggle against the language of clerks 244–245
    polemics with Trediakovskii 4–7, 58–59, 191–192, 193–194, 200, 202, 234, 235, 242–243, 247, 249, 265–267, 270–272, 281, 284–286, 291, 299–301
    polemics with Lomonosov 194–196, 200, 202–204, 234–235, 242–243, 284, 291–294, 336
    on Feofan Prokopovich's language 231–232, 335–338
    on religious literature and its language 307, 321–322, 335–338
    Periphrastic ode of Psalm 143 194
    Epistle on Poetry 137, 191, 270, 282, 292
    Epistle on the Russian Language 215, 235, 292, 337, 407
    Khorev 236, 247
    Hamlet (Gamlet) 247, 271
    Tresotinius 193, 234, 269, 283
    Monsters (Chuovishchi) 239, 283
    "Answer to Criticism" 193, 198, 281
    "On Ridding Russian of Foreign Words" 238
    "On Root Words in Russian" 238
    "To Typographical Typesetters" 285, 292
    "Several Articles on Virtue" 282
    "To Senseless Rhymesters" 291
    Nonsense odes 195, 203–204
    "On Spelling" 59, 284, 291, 292
    Spiritual Verse 283
    "The Monkey Poet" 204
    triumphal odes 195–196, 200, 202
    eclogues 282
    mentioned 48, 191, 213, 320–321, 340, 342–343, 351, 387
Sumkina, A. I. 169
Sushkov, N. V. 416
Svetov, V. 340, 341
Syllabic poetry 140, 170, 189–193, 197
Syllables (sklady), reading by 7–8
Symeon the New Theologian, Saint 199
Synod, Holy Governing 71, 72, 101, 106, 306, 308, 331, 332, 384, 392, 393, 396, 407, 410, 412, 413, 414, 415, 417
Syntactic constructions (specifically bookish):
    dative absolute 18, 73–74, 76–77, 86, 228–229, 231, 312–313, 315
    еже + infinitive 74, 75, 77, 86, 102
    яко + infinitive 316
    да + present 74, 77
    inversion 74, 75
    конструкции с иже 234, 315–317
    genitive of possession 74, 76 102
    accusativus cum infinitivo 77
    genitive of exclamation 315–317
    adverb of time + infinitive 102
    short adjectives in their attributive function 74–75, 181–182
    (specifically non-bookish):
    passive participle made from a reflexive verb 141
    gerundial constructions 228–229, 312–313
Syntax:
    its defining importance for the bookish language 16–17
    the stylistic reevaluation of syntactic constructions 142–143, 365

Tale of Bova Korolevich 43, 47, 48, 244
Tale of Frol Skobeev 43
Tale of Peter of the Golden Keys 47, 67, 141, 244
Tale of Russian Letters (*Skazanie o russkoi gramote*) 32

Index

Tale of Savva Grudtsyn 43
Tale of the Novgorodians' Betrayal 145
Talev, I. 56
Talmoudi, F. 16
Tasso, Torquato 188, 231, 339, 344, 414
Taste (aesthetic choice):
    as a criteria of linguistic usage
234–235, 281–282, 366, 381
Tatishchev, V. N.:
    his cultural and linguistic program
139–141, 150–152, 239
    on the legal language 113
    attitude toward borrowings 139–141, 239–240
    his dictionaries 150–152, 163
    changeover to the simple language in his *Russian History* 76–77
    mentioned 112–114, 116, 120, 340, 412
Taubert, I. I. 127, 129, 300
Tautology 193–194
Teplov, G. N. 421
Terence 297
Ternovskii, F. 105
Tessing (Thessing), Jan 54, 62
Tetzner, J. 103
Theater:
    its beginnings under Aleksei Mikhailovich 45
    under Peter I 45–46
    and religious values 410, 412, 416
Themistocles 376
Thomas, Antoine Léonard 287
Three styles, the theory:
    Western European models 268–270, 275
    its Russian transformation 143, 270–275
    mentioned 104
Tikhonravov, N. 107, 169, 392
Timberlake, Alan 22, 39
Timofei, sexton 23
Titlinov, B. V. 106, 305, 383
Titov, F. 321
Tiutchev, F. I. 355
Tolstoi, A. N., Ober-Procuror of the Synod 427
Tolstoi, D. A. 413
Tolstoi, N. I. 20, 38, 53, 184, 452, 4947, 22, 35, 144, 377, 413, 415
Tomashevskii, B. V. 138, 363
Tragedy:
    linguistic characteristics of the genre 209, 270–272, 281
Translation:
    mechanism of inadequate translation 43–44, 46–47, 63, 349–350
Translations:
    from Greek as the basis of the Church Slavonic language 16–17, 30–33, 260–262, 334
    their incomprehensibility 96–99, 101, 326–327, 405–406
    and the richness (or poverty) of Russian 132, 184–185, 213–214, 248–249, 253, 259–263, 334, 360–361, 376–377, 380
    and the formation of the literary language 215–216, 334, 417–418
Trediakovskii, V. K.:
    his linguistic program of the 1730's 125–135, 138–145, 149–150, 170–171, 188–189, 214, 220, 224–225
    the later development of his linguistic views 4–7, 214–229, 231–238, 240–244, 247–249, 252, 254–260, 264–266, 294–302
    on the ways to perfect the Russian language 132–134, 138–139, 215–217
    on the merits of Russian 126–127, 254
    on its polyfunctionalism 218–220
    on its universality 298–299
    on the natural unity of Russian and Church Slavonic 218, 220–229
    on the sources of the linguistic norm 4–7, 126, 138–139, 170–171, 226, 233, 243–244, 249, 264–266, 294–302
    attitude toward the previous literary tradition 170–171, 189–190, 191–192, 198–199, 228–229, 264–266
    stylistic classification of lexicon 141–143, 207, 270–272
    on poetic license 149–150, 163, 174–186, 228–229, 242
    on the poetic language 186, 200–202, 256–259
    attitude toward the "Quarrel of Ancients and Moderns" 135–137, 195–196, 258–259
    synthesizing approach to Western European culture 134–138
    his Grecophilism 255–259
    difference between theory and

practice in the 1730's 168–171
   influence of theory on practice in his mature period 338–229
   attitude toward Grecianized orthography 57–59, 114–115, 255–256
   attitude toward specifically bookish lexicon 115–116
   on the pronouns ты and вы 168–170
   on the Moscow dialect 243
   the use of complex words 256–257
   on linguistic heterogeneity 266–267, 270–272
   on sacred words 420–421
   and the "learned guard" 114–116
   and the Russian Assembly 128–129, 132–134, 138–139, 214, 297
   collaboration with Adodurov 114–115, 126, 128–129, 138–144, 163–164, 177, 220
   connection with Paus 160, 220–221, 225–227
   his polemic with Sumarokov 4–7, 58–59, 191–194, 200, 202, 234–235, 242–243, 247, 249, 265–267, 270–272, 281, 284–286, 291, 299–301
   attitude toward Fedor Polikarpov 114–116, 259
   attitude toward Charles Rollin 174–175, 252
   promotion to professor 332
   Voyage to the Island of Love 115, 121, 125, 128, 131, 138, 140, 141, 142, 177, 179, 181–182, 220, 309
   "Ode on the Taking of Gdansk" 136, 177, 179, 183, 206, 238
   "Discourse on the Ode in General" 128, 136, 142, 183, 196, 270
   New and Short Guide 128, 136, 163, 177, 178, 180, 183, 192, 205
   "Epistle of Russian Poetry to Apollo" 136, 191
   Letter of a Certain Russian 138
   on the translation of *The Military State of the Ottoman Empire* 143
   translation of Fontenelle's *Speech on Patience* 259
   "Speech on Oratory" 215, 218, 221, 421
   "On the Spelling of Adjectives" (1746) 221, 226, 295, 299
   translation of *Short and Powerful Speech* 169
   translation of Rollin 248, 256
   Conversation About Orthography 115, 128, 129, 223, 227, 232, 240, 244, 296
   verse transposition of the Psalter 183, 229, 332
   "Letter from a Friend to a Friend" 191, 193, 194, 242–243, 247, 266, 271, 299–301
   Argenida 236, 237, 357
   Feoptiia 332
   "Speech on Wisdom, Prudence and Virtue" 247, 300
   epigram, "I don't know who of the singers…" 232, 241, 265
   "On the Spelling of Adjectives" (1755) 222, 232, 236, 241–242, 255–256, 265, 297–299
   "On Ancient, Middle and New Russian Verse" 258
   Tilemakhida 183, 229, 231, 254, 256–258, 272, 297–298
   "Three Discourses" 237, 241, 254, 301
   mentioned 104, 155, 237, 239, 244–245, 281, 282, 287, 290–293, 318, 329, 340, 341, 344, 345, 359, 361, 363–366, 369, 388, 395

Trinity-Sergius Lavra 308, 321, 410
Trissino, Gian Giorgio 188, 256
Trubetskoi, N. S. 41
Trublet, Abbé Nicolas-Charles-Joseph 387, 419
Tschižhewskii, D. 194, 256, 270
Tselunova, E. A. 38
Tuchkov, Vasilii 23
Turgenev, I. S. 425
Turoboiskii, Iosif 60
Tveritinov, Dmitrii 105, 107

Uhlenbruch, B. 104
Ukraine:
   Church Slavonic in Ukraine 30, 148–149
   protests against the view of Church Slavonic as a learned language 32–33
   spread of the "simple" language 33, 37
   tradition of homiletics 311
Unbegaun, B. O. 84, 86, 87, 89, 90, 91, 126, 161
Usage:

Index

conversational 126–127, 137–139, 154, 165, 167–169, 188–189, 205–207, 210–211, 213–214, 233, 262–263, 285–288, 291–292, 293–301, 363, 400
 usage as the basis for purist criteria 134, 136–137, 167–168, 171, 233, 285–301
 usage as the "tyrant" of language 285–286, 288, 294–295, 419
 fictitious references to it 167–169, 171, 185, 188–189, 234–235, 286–287, 292, 365–366
 foppish speech 168–170
 "popular" usage (low, base, common, folk, gutter, pancakemonger's, peasant, etc.) 141–142, 169–170, 240–242, 258, 264–266, 270–271, 291–292, 295–298, 363
 stable usage 263–266, 298–300
 "rational" usage 287–290, 294–297
Uspenskii, B. A. 2, 8, 28, 30, 32, 33, 35, 37, 41, 50, 56, 59–61, 63, 64, 68, 70, 78, 88, 90, 96, 100, 102, 109, 114–117, 122, 126, 128, 130, 131, 136, 138, 140, 141, 143–145, 154, 157, 161, 163, 165, 168–170, 190, 193, 206, 219, 229, 233–235, 241–243, 248, 255, 259, 265, 274, 277, 278, 283, 292, 294, 297, 299, 310, 311, 317, 331, 337, 344, 356, 359, 361, 363–366, 368, 370, 371, 377, 378, 382, 398, 404, 411, 415, 419, 421
Ustav (Charter) of Prince Vladimir 145
Ustrialov, N. G. 50, 51, 111
Uvarov, S. S. 361, 379

Valaam Monastery 308
Valla, Lorenzo 251
Varenius, Bernhard:
 Fedor Polikarpov's translation of his *General Geography* 68–71, 77, 80, 87, 90, 94, 115, 148
 Sofronii Likhud's corrections to his *General Geography* 92–96, 73–75, 77, 80–82, 88–90, 99, 121–122, 147–151, 181, 245, 255, 325
 mentioned 184
Variability:
 as result of the functional reconceptualizing of genetic heterogeneity 13–15, 85
 in various registers of the written language of Medieval Rus' 18, 145

 as characteristic of the hybrid register 78–79, 313
 as legacy of the hybrid register in the literary language of the new type 78–82, 120, 124, 151–152, 154
 the attempt to exclude it from the literary language of the new type 118–124, 128–130, 163, 226–227, 275–276, 282, 328
 reconceptualizing it in genetic terms 79–80, 159–160, 162–166, 180, 229–230
 in the language of religious literature 313, 315–318, 325–326, 328, 396
Varlaam Liashchevskii 101
Vasilevskaia, I. 111
Vaugelas, Claude Favre de:
 linguistic doctrine 133, 134, 137–138, 168, 189, 286–290, 366
 attitude toward the poetic language 172, 174–175, 187
 influence on Russian writers 133, 134, 138, 187, 362
 and the tradition of Port–Royal 287–288
 mentioned 167, 246, 292, 295 341, 342, 387
Vauquelin, Jean, de la Fresnaye 171
Venetian Academy 142
Verkhovskoi, P. B. 97, 102, 104, 105
Versification reform in Russia 170, 182, 188–191
Veselitskii, V. V. 140, 240, 246
Vesti-kuranty 90
Viau, Théophile de 138
Viazemskii, P. A.:
 as Karamzinist 357–358, 360, 364–365, 368, 372–373, 426
 on the hexameter 361–362
 his criticism of Fonvizin 356–357, 363
 understanding of national self-consciousness 375–376
 Old Notebook 385, 387
Viëtor, K. 205, 207
Vifanskii Seminary 382
Villeroi, François de Neufville, duc de 177
Vinogradov, V. V. 2, 18, 65, 66, 84, 142, 146, 245, 270, 356, 361, 372, 387, 397, 418
Vinokur, G.O. 40, 82, 86, 90, 128, 179
Virgil 69, 138, 173, 216, 264, 297, 334, 335, 420

Vishenskii, Ivan 33, 38
Vladimir (Tret'iakov), Archimandrite 397
Vladimir, Saint, Grand Prince 260, 376
Vladimirskii-Budanov, M. F. 382
Vladykin, I. A. 231
Vocative:
    as marker of bookishness 78
    its fixation in grammars 78, 154, 158
    as poetic license 175, 184–186
    as means of creating classical coloration 178, 183–185
    in homiletic language 183, 317
Voinova, L. A. 110, 111, 112
Voltaire:
    his view of the "genius" of a language 187, 188, 217
    on Boileau 196
    mentioned 196, 304, 349, 352, 385
Vomperskii, V. P. 142, 221, 270, 295, 298
Voronezh Religious Seminary 387
Vostokov, A. Kh. 311, 361
Vulgarisms ("low words"):
    as a rubric of French purism 139, 241–242
    reconceptualization of this rubric in Russia 179–180, 239–242, 343
    reconceptualization in religious literature 396, 399–403
    see also: "Popular" speech.
Vymeni, Prince of the Samoyeds, Peter I's jester 55, 169

War of Syllables (la guerre aux syllables) 242
Weismann's lexicon (*Weismanns Petersburger Lexikon*, 1731) 129, 165, 166
Wieland, Christoph Martin 379
Winter, E. 154, 157, 160, 226
Wittram, R. 96
Word order:
    free word order and linguistic "richness" (or "antiquity") 251–252, 256–258, 260–262, 362
Worth, D. S. 26, 27, 56
Wortman, R. S. 61
Written language of medieval Rus':
    its registers (fragmentariness) 3, 6–7, 15–16
    bookish and non-bookish languages 3–4, 10–12, 15–17, 126–127, 144–145, 169–170
    see also: Church Slavonic (language).

Yalamas, D. 69, 70
Yates, F. A. 208

Zagoskin, M. N. 414
Zaikonospasskii Monastery, Moscow 305
Zakhar'in, D. B. 27
Zalizniak, A. A. 22, 8, 15
Zamkova, V. V. 152
Zapol'skaia, N. N. 72, 230
Zen'kovskii, S. A. 34, 35, 310
Zertsalov, A. N. 122
Zhitetskii, P. I. 413
Zhivov, V. M. 3, 6, 12, 13–15, 19, 23, 27, 28, 32, 37, 39, 41, 44, 50, 53, 57, 60, 61, 63, 68, 73, 74, 76, 80, 82, 89–91, 93, 96, 102, 104, 106, 109, 111, 113, 122, 137, 141, 142, 160, 161, 167, 177, 181, 184, 188, 192, 193, 196, 208, 232, 235, 243, 245, 311, 313, 318, 325, 355, 365, 377, 382, 393, 410, 421
Zhmakin, V. 399
Zhukovskii, V. A. 191, 361, 375, 422, 423
Zinovii Otenskii 36, 145, 147
Zizanii Lavrentii 28, 149
Znamenskii, P. V. 98, 306, 321, 382
Zol'nikova, N. D. 303
Zoltan, A. 90
Zotov, N. 51

www.ingramcontent.com/pod-product-compliance
Ingram Content Group UK Ltd.
Pitfield, Milton Keynes, MK11 3LW, UK
UKHW020857160426
5217IPUK00036B/1629